Collector's Guide To

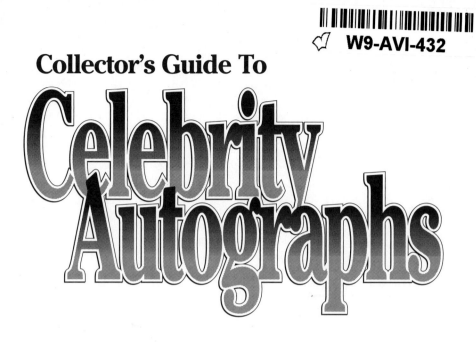

Celebrity Autographs

Mark Allen Baker

Published by

krause
publications

700 E. State Street • Iola, WI 54990-0001
Telephone: 715/445-2214

Library of Congress Catalog Number: 96-76692
ISBN: 0-87341-464-0
Printed in the United States of America

To Jeffrey Ford Baker

My brother,
although time and distance
have stolen much from our relationship,
remember that I love you.

Contents

Acknowledgments

First and foremost I would like to thank everyone at Krause Publications for their continued confidence in my work, especially Deborah Faupel, Mark K. Larson, Pat Klug, Bob Lemke, Hugh McAloon, Chris Williams and Marge Larson. Few authors are fortunate enough to have a publisher who is not only insightful but dedicated to the education and concerns of the collector.

Also, to a group of wonderful individuals who came to my assistance when a considerable amount of this manuscript was lost, thank you very much: Debbie Krol, Justin Krol, Kelly Scutt, and Alison Long.

Thanks to all those celebrities who still believe that their fans are an important part of their career, and that an autograph request is a privilege to answer, not an inconvenience.

To the staff of the United States Postal Service - Bayberry Branch, Liverpool, NY 13089 - who handle thousands of pieces of mail a year for me, thank you so very much for all your assistance.

To the Liverpool Public Library, Liverpool, New York, thank you for allowing me to take some photographs inside your wonderful facility and for allowing me access to your research material.

A special thank you to The Gallery of Stars, Syracuse, New York, for allowing me to photograph some of the wonderful autographed pieces available to customers. Thank you, Tom and Steve!

To my parents, Mr. and Mrs. Ford W. Baker, for their love and support.

To Tracey and Haysam Rachid, Matthew and Jennifer Baker, and to Katie Rachid and Bradford Baker. I miss you all dearly.

To Aaron A. Baker, my son, who was so helpful with suggestions for this book, especially regarding Magic card illustrators.

To Elizabeth M. Baker, my oldest daughter, who was so helpful with suggestions for this book, especially regarding children television stars and of course JTT!

To Rebecca J. Baker, my youngest daughter, who provides me so much inspiration every day.

To Alison M. Long, for always being there for me, I love you!

Introduction

Celebrity autograph collecting for me is not a hobby, nor a job, nor a way to spend some idle time, but an obsession. It has haunted me for over three decades. What started as a small school project in the fifth grade has grown beyond my wildest imaginings. Having published seven books, all somehow related to this obsession, I can even say it has helped pay a few bills along the way.

This simple interest has allowed me to meet many celebrities I otherwise never would have met, provided me with an excellent base of research materials that allowed me to achieve much higher grades in college, and given me an opportunity to share my knowledge through another passion, writing.

Because I am not, and never have been, an autograph dealer, I have always managed to derive a tremendous amount of satisfaction from my hobby. This is not to say that autograph dealers don't derive satisfaction from the hobby: they do, but from their monetary gain and not from the autograph itself. Since I never possessed any monetary expectations, I have seldom been disappointed with even the simplest responses to my autograph requests.

During the last five years I have concentrated on teaching others about the hobby and sharing what I have learned in books, magazine articles and on numerous radio shows. Over 3,000,000 people now collect autographs and manuscripts, and an additional 25,000 join the hobby each year. Many consider it the fastest growing hobby of this decade.

Autographs have a thrill and a magic about them that offer a far greater experience than many other hobbies. It is a thrill to meet a celebrity, but an autograph is a guarantee that the memory of that meeting will never fade. In recent years the increased interest in autograph collecting has fueled a rise in prices for many celebrity signatures. This rise is driven not only by the growing demand, but by an increased awareness that there is big money in buying and selling autographs.

Many collectors have limited access to in-person celebrity signatures and thus have to rely upon two primary alternative acquisitions methods. The first and most popular form is requesting a signature via mail, while the other is purchasing a signature from an autograph dealer. While the latter is often considered to be the least cost-effective, requesting signatures by mail can also be an expensive proposition. Many requests are unanswered or sent back due to an incorrect address, and some fail to make it into the hands of the celebrity. An accurate celebrity address, with proven successful results, can prevent an autograph collector from spending a significant amount of money on an easy-to-acquire signature.

Most collectors agree that accurate celebrity addresses are not always easy to find because of their dynamic nature. Constant changes are difficult and time-consuming to monitor. Collectors could save a significant amount of money on postage and material if they knew the probable result of an autograph request. If the collector knows his/her request will probably be answered with a facsimile signature, s/he may decide to pursue a different subject.

Collector's Guide to Celebrity Autographs is the first resource available to autograph collectors that not only provides accurate celebrity addresses, but estimates the type of response collectors can expect. This allows collectors to take a more cost-effective approach to acquisitions, saving both time and money.

Section I of this book will identify the various ways of acquiring celebrity autographs. Readers will be able to choose a cost-effective approach that best fits their collecting needs. Also included are instructions on using other sources to locate celebrities.

Section II contains thousands of celebrity addresses for hobbyists who are looking for just the right addition to their collection. Already proven successful through previous mailings, these addresses can be used with confidence that the time and money spent generating a request will be well worth the effort. By using the evaluations given with each address, the collector can anticipate the response (or lack thereof) to each request. In many cases we have even included photographs of previous celebrity responses.

Although an up-to-date list of celebrity addresses is difficult to maintain, assistance from the reader can ease this burden. I would like to ask each of you who use or purchase this book to pass along any forwarding addresses you may receive. Collectors who assist us will receive periodic updates to the addresses included in this book. Send forwarding addresses to me c/o Krause Publications, 700 E. State Street, Iola, WI, 54990-0001.

Section I

Collecting Celebrity Autographs

Chapter 1

Celebrity Status

A "celebrity" is defined by Webster's as a celebrated person, one who is "widely known and often referred to." Being celebrated is synonymous with being famous, but famous implies little more than the fact of being, sometimes briefly, widely and popularly known. As a celebrity you can be famous, renowned, celebrated, noted, notorious, distinguished, eminent and illustrious. Celebrities come in all shapes and sizes, and from all walks of life. Although it's not always difficult becoming a celebrity, it is difficult staying one. For many celebrities, glory is only fleeting.

Since celebrities come and go so fast, we like to review our own individual celebrity list at the end of each year and decide who deserves to stay and who has simply faded into mediocrity. Where better to start than with the events of the past year? Let's see what some of our celebrities have been doing.

Turning Back the Clock to 1995

The year 1995 proved that being famous isn't always as great as people imagine: just ask Hugh Grant. His L.A.P.D. mug shot # BK445481306-27-95 received more attention than his movie *Nine Months*. Hillary Clinton's shifting hairstyles garnered more media attention than anything important she did. It's a sad commentary on this society that such small things can become of paramount interest to the public. Shannon Faulkner gained our respect as we followed her attempts to breach the all-male Citadel. We watched in awe as daytime television desperately tried to retain viewers against the melodrama of the O. J. Simpson trial. And we nearly ran out of fingers trying to keep up with all the movie releases that featured Antonio Banderas. How could anyone keep up such a rigorous schedule and still maintain a high maintenance catch like Melanie Griffith?

These notables proved that being a celebrity is not for the faint of heart. It's certainly not all it's cracked up to be, unless of course you're Antonio Banderas! It's much easier to press your nose against the celebrity aquarium and just watch what happens.

A keepsake year indeed, 1995 was rocked by four major events:

Roseanne's form letter sent to autograph seekers states that "the coolest part of being a celebrity is being able to read the letters that people send."

the trial of O. J. Simpson, the turmoils of the Windsors on that big island across the ocean, the fall from grace of David Letterman (ignited by the Oscars); and a warm night in Baltimore when Cal Ripken Jr. took the field for the 2131st consecutive time without a day off!

That doesn't mean there weren't other important people and events keeping the media busy all year long. Read on.

On Center Stage

General Colin Powell was briefly considered a possible presidential candidate and produced the book *My American Journey*. John F. Kennedy, Jr., drew attention as editor-in-chief of the politics and pop culture magazine *George*. *Friends* was a television breakthrough hit with cast members David Schwimmer, Matthew Perry, Matt Le Blanc, Lisa Kudrow, Courtney Cox and Jennifer Aniston.

Kenneth "Babyface" Edmonds penned two number one hits: "I'll Make Love to You" by BoyZ II Men and Madonna's "Take A Bow." Alicia Silverstone was far from *Clueless* in 1996 and still hasn't completed her second decade of life. Robert McNamara admitted *In Retrospect* that the Vietnam War was unwinnable. Now he tells us. Greg Louganis came out with *Breaking Through the Surface* about AIDS. Ellen DeGeneres proved her point with a successful sitcom, *Ellen*. Michael Crichton, who could play Bill Bradley if there was a movie, was executive producer of *ER* and gave us a sequel to *Jurassic Park*: *The Lost World*.

Keith Lockhart gave Bean Town its third conductor of the Boston Pops orchestra in the last 65 years. Randy and Robyn Miller put us on a deserted island with their CD-ROM adventure MYST. Gillian Anderson and David Duchovny told Fox "the truth is out there" and gave the television net-

Gillian Anderson and David Duchovny told Fox "The Truth Is Out There" and gave the television network its highest rated television show -- The X-Files.

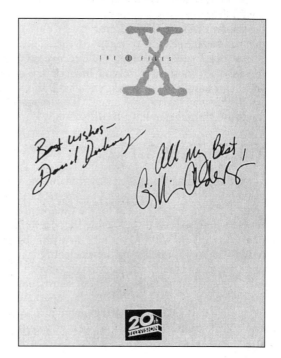

9

work its highest rated show, *The X-Files*. Hootie & The Blowfish gave us their debut album, *Cracked Rear View*, showed up in an ESPN commercial, and made a few friends along the way. *Babe* brought home the bacon, while *Pocahontas* proved Mel Gibson can't sing. Antonio Banderas reinforced why you *Never Talk to Strangers*.

Sandra Bullock woke to the limelight after *While You Were Sleeping*. Shania Twain showed us if it ain't broke, don't fix it, or was it "Whose Bed Have Your Boots Been Under?". Macaulay Culkin, now 15, was home alone as his parents fought court custody battles. Anna Nicole Smith, who at the age of 27 married Houston oil tycoon J. Howard Marshall II, fought with Marshall's family following her husband's death of pneumonia.

Guess Who's Back

Mario Lemieux returned to the Pittsburgh Penguins after taking the previous year off because

Macauley Culkin was "Home Alone" as his parents fought court custody battles.

of a bad back. Speaking of backs, Monica Seles returned to the tennis courts after more than two years, during which she'd recovered from a stab wound inflicted by a crazed fan. Mike Tyson finished serving time for rape and was back to boxing with an old King and a new castle. Violin prodigy Rachel Barton lost her leg in a freak train accident but fought her way back to the stage. His Airness Michael Jordan returned to Chicago as things in Birmingham looked partly cloudy.

Trials and Tribulations

The entire country was mesmerized during what many called the trial of the century, as the life of O. J. Simpson was traced, retraced, outlined and highlighted in front of a court and a camera. So much for the Lindbergh kidnapping case!

O. J. Simpson, who spent more than $6 million dollars on his defense, was cleared of all charges, but will forever face the Lizzie Borden syndrome: many still believe he's guilty. The trial created many new celebrities, some cushy publishing deals, and even a few villains. Lost in all the post-trial hoopla, in typical American fashion, were the victims, most of whom will fade into obscurity until they resurface as characters in made-for-television movies.

In June it was no mystery Hughdunnit. Hugh Grant, who shot to stardom as the bumbling bachelor in *Four Weddings and a Funeral*, was in Los Angeles to promote *Nine*

Months, when suddenly he found himself exchanging words (I think it was words) with Divine Marie Brown, a prostitute. He was later arrested by two policemen and pleaded no contest to a charge of lewd conduct in a public place. Within hours, the media world was having a field day.

Shannon Faulkner attempted to become the first female cadet at The Citadel, a military college in Charleston, South Carolina. Her battles were waged both in the courtrooms and on the campus, before the rigorous antics of the school's Hell Week orientation finally ended her dreams.

Other notable trials included that of Susan Smith, accused of drowning her children Michael and Alex Smith. Smith eventually confessed to the horrendous crime.

Actor Christopher Reeve suffered a near-fatal accident while riding his 7-year-old thoroughbred horse during a spring show. Reeve fell forward during a failed jump and suffered multiple fractures to his spinal column. Five days after the accident Reeve had only a 50-50 chance of living, but he made a miraculous recovery and has become an inspiration to the many people who suffer from similar injuries.

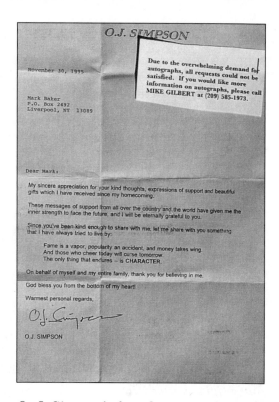

O. J. Simpson's form letter sent from jail to autograph seekers states, "Since you've been kind enough to share with me, let me share with you something that I have always tried to live by: Fame is a vapor, popularity an accident, and money takes wing. And those who cheer today will curse tomorrow. The only thing that endures -- is **CHARACTER.**

Rep. Enid Waldholtz of Salt Lake City, a newly elected fast-track Republican, found out just how quickly you can fall from grace when her husband Joe was arrested for financial improprieties. An FBI investigation uncovered a suspected $1.6 million check-cashing scheme. If investigators discover that Enid knew about the financial irregularities, she too could face charges.

Winners and Losers

Tom Hanks became the first actor since Spencer Tracy to win back-to-back Oscars. Hanks starred in the box office smash *Apollo 13* and even managed to do a voice in Disney's *Toy Story*. Alan Jackson took the 29th Annual Country Music Award for Entertainer of the Year: not bad for someone with 16 number one singles over the past few years. Alison Krauss became the first bluegrass artist to be inducted into the Grand Ole Opry since Jim & Jesse three decades ago. Just 24 years old, Alison has years to fiddle with in the future. Speaking of young winners, Jeff Gordon edged out Dale Earnhardt in

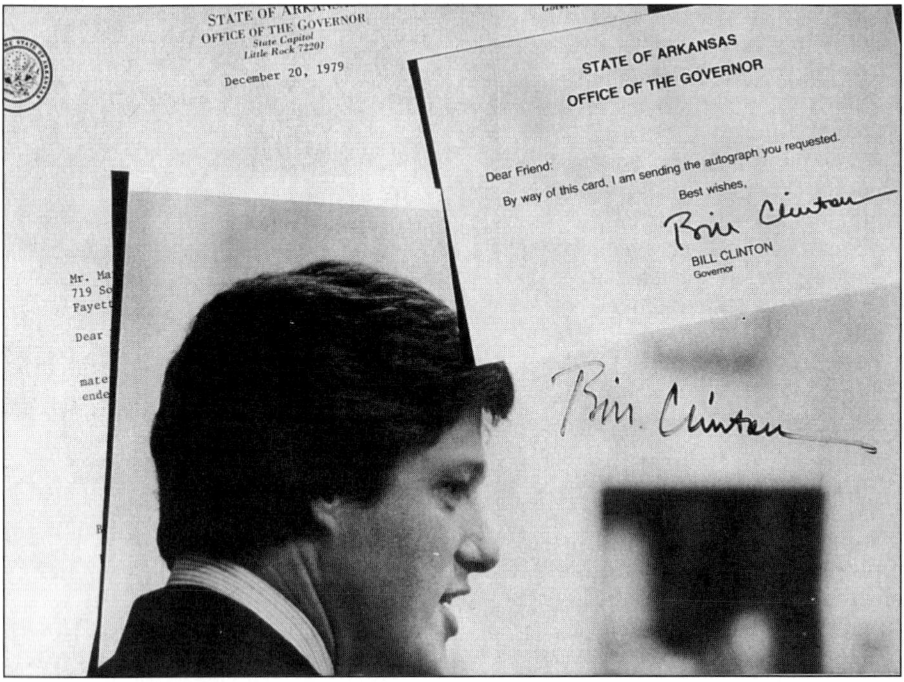

STATE OF ARKANSAS
OFFICE OF THE GOVERNOR
State Capitol
Little Rock 72201

December 20, 1979

STATE OF ARKANSAS
OFFICE OF THE GOVERNOR

Dear Friend:

By way of this card, I am sending the autograph you requested.

Best wishes,

Bill Clinton

BILL CLINTON
Governor

Mr. Ma
719 So
Fayett

Dear

mate
ende

*Autographs received from then-Governor William Clinton and First Lady
Hillary Rodham Clinton.*

THE WHITE HOUSE
WASHINGTON

Enclosed is the material you requested.
Please do not hesitate to contact our office
if we can be of any further assistance.

Thank you for writing.

The Office of the First Lady

Hillary Rodham Clinton

points to win his first NASCAR Winston Cup Championship.

In addition to Tom Hanks, other 1995 Oscar Award Winners included: Jessica Lange, *Blue Sky*; Martin Landau, *Ed Wood*; Dianne Wiest, *Bullets Over Broadway*; Robert Zemeckis, *Forrest Gump*; Quentin Tarantino and Roger Avary, *Pulp Fiction*; and Eric Roth, *Forrest Gump*.

Daytime Emmy winners in 1995 included Oprah Winfrey, talk show host; Jerry ver Dorn, *Guiding Light*; Rena Sofer, *General Hospital*; Justin Deas, *Guiding Light*; and Erika Slezak, *One Life to Live*.

The 47th Annual Prime-Time Emmy Award winners included Mandy Pantinkin, *Chicago Hope*; Kathy Baker, *Picket Fences*;

Jeff Gordon, 1995 NASCAR Winston Cup Champion.

Kelsey Grammer, *Frasier*; Candice Bergen, *Murphy Brown*; Glenn Close, *Serving in Silence*; Ray Walston, *Picket Fences*; Julianna Marguilies, *ER*; David Hyde Pierce, *Frasier*; Christine Baranski, *Cybill*; Donald Sutherland, *Citizen X*; Judy Davis, *Serving in Silence*, Shirley Knight, *Indictment: The McMartin Trial*; and Barbra Streisand, *Barbra Streisand The Concert*.

The 49th Annual Tony Awards winners included: Ralph Fiennes, *Hamlet*; Cherry Jones, *The Heiress*; Matthew Broderick, *How to Succeed in Business*; Glenn Close, *Sunset Boulevard*; John Glover, *Love! Valor! Compassion!*; Frances Sternhagen, *The Heiress*; George Hearn, *Sunset Boulevard*; and Gretha Boston, *Show Boat*.

The 37th Annual Grammy Award winners included: "All I Wanna Do," Sheryl Crow; "Streets of Philadelphia," Bruce Springsteen; "MTV Unplugged," Tony Bennett; "Can You Feel the Love Tonight," Elton John; "I Swear," All 4 One, and "Come to My Window," Melissa Etheridge; "Crazy," Aerosmith; "I'll Make Love to You," Babyface; "Breathe Again," Toni Braxton; "I'll Make Love to You," BoyZ II Men; "U.N.I.T.Y.," Queen Latifah; "None of Your Business," Salt 'N' Pepa; "Black Hole Sun," Soundgarden; and "Dookie," Green Day.

The 1995 MTV Music Awards included: "Waterfalls," TLC; "You Don't Know How It Feels," Tom Petty; "Take A Bow," Madonna; "Keep Their Heads Ringin'," Dr. Dre; "Scream," Michael Jackson and Janet Jackson; "More Human Than Human," White Zombie; "Buddy Holly," Weezer; and "Hold My Hand," Hootie & The Blowfish.

Female phenoms in 1995 included Rebecca Marier, the first woman to graduate at the top of the West Point cadet class; Nicole Bobek , U.S. figure skating champion; Rebecca Lobo, who led the University of Connecticut's Huskies to a perfect season; and Tiffany Roberts, youngest of the defending world champion U.S. women's soccer team, who helped grab the bronze.

Losers in 1995 included Tonya Harding's Golden Blades music group; Susan Powter, who despite a number of successes filed for personal bankruptcy; and Nick Leeson, Britain's Baring Bank lone assassin who needed only two months to send the company into bankruptcy.

Going Separate Ways

When one celebrity marries a non-celebrity, the latter takes on immediate celebrity status. However, when the couple decides a divorce is in order, as was the case with Liz Taylor and Larry Fortensky, the newest celeb must learn to defend his or her status alone.

In some instances celebrities may marry other celebrities, such as Lyle Lovett marrying Julia Roberts. In such a case, if and when they decide to split (which these two did in 1995), both are still celebrities. That is, of course, if they have maintained that status throughout the marriage. Gotta Lovett!

Notable celebrity partings in 1995 included Michael & Diandra Douglas, Val Kilmer & Joanne Whalley, Jim & Melissa Carrey, Matt Lattanzi & Olivia Newton-John, Melanie Griffith & Don Johnson, Kevin & Cindy Costner, Jimmie Page & Patricia Ecker, Patricia Richardson & Ray Baker, Will & Sheree Smith, Mariette Hartley & Patrick Boyriven, James & Ingrid Caan, Ray & Ruth Walston, Barbara Rush & Warren Cowan, Cheryl Tiegs & Anthony Peck, Robert Duvall & Shannon Brophy, Kenneth Branagh & Emma Thompson, Lee Iacocca & Darrien Earle, Dorothy Hamill & Kenneth Forsythe, Danielle Steele and John Traina, Beverly D'Angelo & Lorenzo Salviati, James Brolin & Jan Smithers, Christian Slater & Nina Huang, Ralph Fiennes & Alex Kingston, John Hurt & Jo Dalton, Roger & Luisa Moore,Tommie Lee & Kimberlea Jones, Christie Brinkley & Guy Ricky Taubman, Anthony & Iolanda Quinn, Phil & Jill Collins, Richard Gere & Cindy Crawford, Shirley Jones & Marty Ingels, Tracy & Frances Lawrence, Whoopi Goldberg & Lyle Trachtenberg, Frank & Ruth Langella, David Carradine & Gail Jensen, Nicholas & Jami Turturro, Natalie Cole & Andre Fischer, Jason Hervey & Kelley Patricia O'Neill, Johnny & Laura Bench, Bob Packwood & the U.S. Senate, Aleksandr Solzhenitsyn & Russian television, Connie Chung & CBS, Winnie Mandela & the South African cabinet, Joe Montana & the NFL, Hubert de Givenchy & fashion design, Robert MacNeil & The MacNeil/Lehrer News-Hour, Bonnie Blair & skating competitions, Dorothy Hamill & The Ice Capades, and Bill Bradley, Sam Nunn, Patricia Schroeder & the U.S. Senate.

Tying The Knot

Remember, in celebrity matrimonial philosophy when one celebrity marries a non-celebrity, such as Andrew Shue marrying his former agent Jennifer Hageney, the latter immediately takes on celebrity status. Fortunately for celebrity autograph seekers, the rate of matrimony seldom exceeds the rate of separation, making it a bit easier to keep up with. In addition, celebri-

Cindy Crawford is a solo act after her divorce from Richard Gere.

ties typically marry other celebrities, making names easier to remember and even occasionally saving a stamp.

Notable celebrity pairings in 1995 included William Baldwin & Chynna Phillips, Melissa Gilbert & Bruce Boxleitner, Stephen Hawking & Elaine Mason, Al Roker & Deborah Roberts, Pamela Anderson & Tommy Lee, Lisa Kudrow & Michel Stern, John Daly & Paulette Dean, John Ehrlichman & Karen Hilliard, Suzanne Vega & Mitchell Froom, Nicolas Cage & Patricia Arquette, LL Cool J (James Smith) & Simone Johnson, Roseanne & Ben Thomas, Nancy Kerrigan & Jerry Solomon, Shaun Cassidy & Susan Diol, Julie Warner & Jonathan Prince, Stephanie Seymour & Peter Brant, Ike Turner & Jeanette Bazzell, Tom Arnold & Julie Champnella, Christie Hefner & Bill Marovitz, Richard Holbrooke & Kati Marton, Martin Lawrence & Patricia Southall, Brian Wilson & Melinda Ledbetter, Tristan Rogers & Teresa Parkinson, Meg Tilly & John Calley, Amy Brenneman & Brad Silberling, Gladys Knight & Les Brown, Natasha Henstridge & Damian Chapa, Gail O'Grady & Steven Fenton, Steven Weber & Juliette Hohnen, Don Henley & Sharon Summerall, Arthel Neville & Derrick Lassic, Holly Robinson & Rodney Peete, Dennis Franz & Joanie Zeck, Ted Danson & Mary Steenburgen, Sammie Hagar & Kari Karte, Ivana Trump & Riccardo Mazzucchelli, and Anthony Smith & Denise Matthews (Vanity).

Celebrity Temperatures

Who's hot and who's not changes like the weather, so as a celebrity autograph collector you must also become a celebrity weather forecaster. Those celebrities who are hot are highly sought by autograph collectors and a far more difficult target to reach than those who are not. Getting an authentic signature from Brad Pitt, Jim Carrey or George Clooney in 1996 is a greater challenge than you may think, but had you had the foresight to get a signature from them earlier in their careers you may have found greater success. Fortunately for collectors most celebrities who are hot today are often cold tomorrow, making them a bit more accessible. If you don't think celebrity temperatures can change, just ask John Travolta!

Those celebrities who were hot in 1995 include Brad Pitt, Princess Diana, Christopher Reeve, Elizabeth Hurley, Colin Powell, Nicole Kidman, O.J. Simpson, Marcia Clark, Susan Smith, Jay Leno, C. Delores Tucker, Shania Twain, Babe, Louis Farrakhan, Ted Turner, Jeff Gordon, Hootie & The Blowfish, The Unabomber, Jennifer Aniston, John F. Kennedy, Jr., Monica

A self-drawn caricature with autograph by talk show host Jay Leno.

Seles, R.L. Stine, Selena, Cal Ripken, Jr., Mr. & Mrs. William J. Clinton, Scott O'Grady, Timothy McVeigh, Mark Fuhrman, George Clooney, Sandra Bullock, Michael Jordan, The Atlanta Braves, The Dallas Cowboys, Hideo Nomo, Mike Tyson, Jim Carrey, Tim Allen, Jeffrey Katzenberg, the cast of *Sunset Boulevard*, the cast of *Friends*, Alan Jackson, Tom Hanks, Grant Hill, and John Grisham.

Those celebrities who were only warm in 1995 include Daniel Benzali, Gwyneth Paltrow, Irina, Live, Mekhi Phifer, Stephanie Miller, Mother Angelica, Kristin Herold, Toni Collette, Ed Burns, Alanis Morissette, Linda Davies, Minnie Driver, Andrew Lawrence, Cheri Oteri, Newt Gingrich and Tea Leoni. This is the group you will want to keep your eye on, as most are only a spotlight away from stardom!

Keeping up with celebrity temperatures will require a regular visit to the library to read some of the many newspapers and periodicals that cover worldwide news. If you can afford to invest in subscriptions there are numerous periodicals and newspapers worth reading.

Keeping Up with Celebrity Temperatures

Periodicals and Newspapers Worth Consulting

Africa Report
American Artist
American Film
America Journalism and Review
American Record Guide
American Scholar
Art & Artists
Artforum
Art In America
ARTnews
Arts
Arts & Architecture
Atlantic Monthly
Audubon
Autograph Collector
Autograph Times
Barron's
Book World
Broadcasting
Business Week
Cable Guide
Catholic World
Chicago Sun-Times
Chicago Tribune
Christian Science Monitor
Classic CD
Columbia Journalism Review
Commonweal
Congressional Digest
Congressional Quarterly Weekly Review
Current History
Dance & Dancers
Dancemagazine

Details
Discover
Down Beat
Ebony
Economist
Elle
Encounter
Entertainment Weekly
Esquire
Essence
Films & Filming
Financial Times
Foreign Affairs
Foreign Policy Bulletin
Forbes
Fortune
GQ
German Tribune
Goldmine
Good Housekeeping
Gramaphone
Guardian
Harper's
Hi/Fi Stereo Review
Inside Sports
International Wildlife
Interview
Ladies Home Journal
Lear's
Le monde
Library Journal
Life
London Observer

London Review of Books
Los Angeles Times
Maclean's
Manchester Guardian Weekly
McCall's
Mirabella
Modern Maturity
Mother Jones
Ms
NY Daily News
NY Newsday
NY Observer
NY Post
New York Review of Books
NY Times
New York Times Book Review
New York Times Magazine
National Geographic Magazine
National Review
Nation
Nation's Business
Natural History
Nature
New Leader
New Republic
New Scientist
New Statesman & Society
New York
New Yorker
Newsweek
Omni
Opera News
Ovation
Parade
People
Philadelphia Inquirer
Playbill
Plays & Players

Premiere
Publishers Weekly
Reader's Digest
Rolling Stone
Scala
Scientific American
Scientific Monthly
Scientific News Letter
Science
Sight & Sound
Smithsonian
Spectator
Spiegel
Spin
Sport
Sporting News
Sports Collectors Digest
Sports Illustrated
Stereo Review
London Sunday Times
Time
Times - London Times
Toronto Globe and Mail
TV Guide
USA Today
U.S. News & World Report
Vanity Fair
Variety
Village Voice
Vogue
Wall Street Journal
Washington Monthly
Washington Post
Wilson Library Bulletin
Women's Wear Daily
Working Woman
World Monitor
World Press Review

As a celebrity autograph collector, if you dedicate yourself to the task, it won't take long to build a very impressive collection. The key will be your ability to single out potential celebrities before they become stars. From comedy clubs to minor league baseball, tomorrow's stars are already out there. Your mission is to find them!

"...and hence we came forth to see again the stars."

- Dante, *The Inferno*

Chapter 2

Why Do We Collect Autographs?

What's the very first question someone asks you after you tell them you met a celebrity? Nine times out of ten I bet it's: Did you get an autograph? Now ask yourself why this is such a common response to your question, and you will know why we collect autographs. An autograph not only functions as a reinforcement to our claim, but it is a simple way to preserve an often very special moment. I think of it as a relic, although by definition a relic is an object esteemed and venerated because of its association with a saint or martyr. Replace the words "saint" and "martyr" with "celebrity" and "notable" and you'll see what I mean.

Individuals seek this simple pleasure of possessing someone's signature not just because they don't have a camera or are reluctant to ask for a lock of hair, but it is something unique to each person.

Some believe simple pleasures such as collecting an autograph evoke childhood memories. These are memories not only of a specific game, television show or movie, but of an era when we had little responsibility and when we still thought anything could

Here is an autograph collector's "Wall of Fame."

happen. Celebrities intrigue us, maybe because we want to know why their dreams came true and ours, well, didn't. Certainly we all, at one time or another, have wondered what it would be like to stand in the shoes of Meryl Streep, Michael Jordan, Arnold Schwarzenegger or Aretha Franklin. We want to know what it feels like to be the best, and by following a celebrity's life we can experience that feeling vicariously. Maybe it helps us feel that our childhood dreams are still alive.

We also collect celebrity autographs to preserve a moment, and to remind us of the human spirit that succeeds despite all adversity. Artifacts speak without

NASCAR racing driver Ken Shrader meeting with fans at an autograph signing session.

words: they represent the undefinable. After all, who can accurately describe the challenges faced by Mother Teresa, Jackie Robinson, or Anne Frank?

Each artifact becomes a reflection of its time. We cannot stop its deterioration, but we can try to preserve its relevance. Through it we share an association with the subject. As we stare at our autographed Gale Sayers football, we remember gathering around our black and white television set and watching the Sunday afternoon broadcast live from Soldier Field. After so many years it is still unbelievable that anyone could run with the style

and grace exhibited by Sayers on those frigid winter days in Chicago. That vivid memory is evoked by a glance to the shelf where an autographed football rests.

By collecting celebrity autographs we share the triumphs of our subjects: we feel success through association. Everyone wants to be associated with a winner and to share the happiness of others. Because the details of celebrities' lives are so accessible to the public it is easy to imagine a connection with them.

It is the wise collector, however, who remains mindful that the celebrity is quite human and should be accorded the same level of respect as friends and family. It is an even wiser collector who understands that although one's own accomplishments might go unrecognized, they are at least as significant as any celebrity's.

Hockey Hall of Famer Daryl Sittler signing autographs.

Chapter 3

Tools and Terms of the Trade

A basic understanding of writing instruments and materials can enhance a collector's knowledge of authenticity, because writing instruments can be dated. Choosing the correct writing instrument to use on a particular material can also help in the preservation of the piece. Both are critical elements of collecting and of paramount concern to the autograph collector. By understanding the evolution of writing instruments, you can determine what type could have been used by Charlie Chaplin, Ernest Hemingway, Harry Houdini, and even Vincent van Gogh.

Although references to the existence of ink are found in literature as early as the Old Testament, modern celebrity autograph collectors will generally only need to be concerned with iron gall inks.

Writing Instruments

Historians typically divide writing instruments into four categories: quills, durable pens, reservoir pens, and pencils. Since quills were replaced by metal pens in the nineteenth century, a discussion of their development would be impertinent to the majority of the collectors of modern celebrity autographs. Pencil, although a popular writing device since its "lead strip" discovery in 1564, has decreased in popularity and is not often used by today's collectors. Limited adherence qualities and easy erasability has limited pencil use to informal, non-permanent applications. Although ink was a bit more troublesome during its evolution, it was the favored medium.

The writing instruments of greatest interest to the collectors of celebrity autographs are durable pens, reservoir pens, and pencils. An understanding of these writing instruments and their ability to adhere to a variety of surfaces can allow the collector to avoid many preservation problems.

Durable Pens

Steel, gold, and glass pens were used in the late 1700s and the 1800s. They provided more

Parker became the leading American fountain pen manufacturer by the end of the 1930s.

durability than the quill, but still required an independent ink reservoir. Later they gave way to the still more practical reservoir pens, which carried the ink in an interior cartridge.

Steel Pens

Only isolated references to metallic pens were made before the end of the eighteenth century. Conflicting reports leave the steel pen's date of origin unknown, but it was successfully reintroduced in England in 1780. Constructed of a sheet of steel rolled to form a cylinder, one end of the pen was cut and trimmed to a point (similar to the quill). The seam, where both edges met, formed the slit of the pen. The first patent in England for metal pens was awarded in 1808 to Bryan Donkin. Machine-made pens were introduced about 1822. A U.S. patent for a "metallic writing pen" was issued to Peregrine Williamson in 1809. Although the steel pen was commonplace by the mid 1840s, it wasn't until 1858, the year after Henry Chadwick invented the box score, that the first steel pen company was established in the United States by Richard Esterbrook Jr., a former pen salesman.

Use of a steel pen can be readily confirmed by examining strokes under magnification. In contrast to its predecessor, the quill, a steel pen leaves "nib tracks," which are the result of the pen's point or nib, a metal slit, separating under pressure on the downstroke and digging into the writing material. Nib choices affect the line quality of writing in a predictable manner. Special types of steel pens produced distinctive line quality, due to the flow of the ink into the nib. For example, the "stub pen" produced a slightly outlined yet uniform stroke that became lighter as the ink neared its end inside the nib. The stub pen, although of limited use in the 1870s, grew in popularity and represented about one third of the total pen consumption by the early 1930s.

Gold Pens

The "gold pen" was created by dipping quills into a solution of nitromuriate of gold, in an effort to increase their durability. This method was patented in 1818 by Charles Watt. Although the gold was useful in resisting the corrosive tendencies of acidic ink, the points still lacked sufficient hardness and quickly broke.

Glass Pens

Pen makers experimented with glass as early as 1850. A U.S. patent of 1890 describes a glass pen as "a pen formed of a piece of round glass drawn out to a point and having grooves running spirally down the sloping sides and meeting at the point." Many early glass pens were sold as "marking pens" for writing on fabric. They used indelible inks and their permanence made them a favored tool for many applications, but the pen was never very plentiful or widely used.

The demise of the durable pen is attributed, ironically, to its lack of extended durability. The frequent need to replenish the pen's ink source required repeated dipping into the inkwell.

Reservoir Pens

Dip pen writing, produced by durable pens, is identified by regular changes in the ink's intensity: from dark to light, to dark again. This "ink failure" was one of the motivations for developing reservoir pens. Fountain, ballpoint, and porous tip pens are examples of writing instruments that use a reservoir ink system. These instruments, most still popular today, are the writing instruments of greatest concern to the collector of celebrity autographs.

Fountain Pens

Attempts to solve ink failure included a "solid ink" fountain pen, circa 1870s, which held a stick of concentrated ink that was dipped into water for writing. Fountain pen patents were regularly advertised in periodicals by the late 1870s. During this time stylographic pens also became popular. These pens had a plunger that was pushed back while writing, allowing ink to flow out, and interchangeable pen points that allowed the user to vary the diameter of the strokes. Stylographic pen writing is characterized by thin strokes of uniform diameter.

In 1864 Lewis E. Waterman marketed the first truly successful fountain pen. Perhaps motivated by Waterman's achievement, George S. Parker established in 1888 the pen company that would become a household name. Developer of several patents for improving ink feed design, Parker became the leading U.S. fountain pen manufacturer by the end of the 1930s.

Ballpoint Pens

The popular fountain pen, with its numerous variations in style, was displaced in the late 1940s by the ballpoint pen. Although ballpoint pen patents can be traced as far back as 1888, it wasn't until 1935 that two Czechoslovakians, Frank Klimes and Paul Eisner, began producing a modern-style ballpoint. Two Hungarian brothers, Ladislao and George Biro, also developed a rotatable ball pen in 1938. The Eberhard Faber Company eventually obtained rights to it, but when the U. S. Army expressed interest in purchasing large quantities of the pen, Scheaffer outbid its competitors to share the U.S. rights with Faber. The Biro pen became so popular that one U.S. businessman marketed and sold almost 25,000 pens through Gimbel's department store in New York City.

Early ballpoint pen writing is easily recognizable by its blotting and skipping. These characteristics were attributed to the ink, which was a dye solution in a base of oil, that, although smooth flowing, dried very slowly. Also worth noting is the fading of the ink when exposed to light. This characteristic is most noticeable with those pens produced before 1954.

Most of the deficiencies in the ballpoint pen design were remedied by Parker's introduction of the Jotter in 1954. The Jotter, made entirely of stainless steel, wrote five times as long as its competitors and also offered a variety of point sizes.

Parker also introduced the Liquid Lead Pencil in 1955. This pen contained a liquid graphite solution that was erasable. Failing to gain acceptance, this pen was phased out of production in the 1960s. Ironically, the Paper Mate division of the Gillette Company introduced the Eraser Mate pen in April, 1979, capturing what was thought to be a nonexistent portion of the market.

Porous Tip Pens

The ballpoint pen began to face competition in the early 1940s when a "porous point" pen began to be marketed. It was composed of fibrous materials that acted like a nib, while storing ink in a spongy material. By the early 1950s these pens began to be known as markers and included airtight leakproof stems that fed ink into a wedge-shaped wick. After some Japanese enhancements, the pen was reintroduced and popularized around 1964. Additional varieties of colored inks were subsequently introduced, but many of the inks were not permanent and became badly faded after a few days' exposure to sunlight.

Sanford's Sharpie, a highly water-resistant, permanent, large fiber tip marker that writes on virtually every surface, found a home in the collectibles market in the mid

1970s. Although the marker was available in 1963 (black) and 1964 (blue), it did not gain popularity until nearly a decade later. This writing device soon became a hobby standard due to its surface adherence qualities and ease of use. Over the years concerns about its deterioration characteristics surfaced among many collectors, particularly in the area of autographed sports equipment. On official league-autographed baseballs many Sharpie signatures began to bleed into the surface. Collectors migrated away from the Sharpie for use on highly porous surfaces, but continued to use it for most other occasions. A good quality fine-tipped ink pen remains the best choice among celebrity autograph collectors. Many collectors also began avoiding the marker because of its large strokes, which impair character definition. For all nonporous surfaces, however, and when the item presented for autographing is ideal for a large signature, the Sharpie remains a practical solution.

Several types of pens and ink were introduced during the last

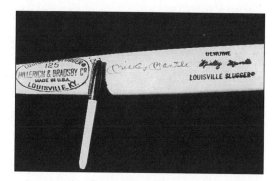

Sanford's Sharpie writes on virtually every surface, including baseball bats.

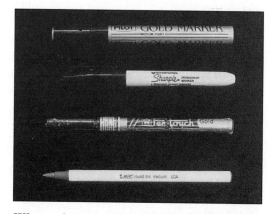

When obtaining autographs, always be prepared with a handy arsenal of pens.

fifteen years, from gold and silver markers to hot colored pens and metallic inks. For many of these materials it is far too early to determine what deterioration characteristics they will exhibit. For collectors who are serious about preservation and safety, material safety data sheets (MSDSs) are available from every manufacturer. Each sheet describes the ink's ingredients and any potential safety hazards.

Pen and Ink Identification

Pen and ink are just a few of the elements that collectors have at their disposal to help identify or authenticate an autographed item. Although more complex than simple dating methods, pen and ink identification can provide collectors with additional information.

Because writing instruments can be identified by period, knowledge of their evolution is an obvious aid to dating an autograph. From steel and fountain pens to ballpoint and felt tip pens, each instrument produces distinctive stylographic characteristics. Using many common and inexpensive tools, collectors can carefully analyze signatures. Under magnification and with a good light source, beginning and ending strokes can immediately be associated with a particular writing instrument. A pen identification chart has been provided here to help simplify the task.

Pen Identification Chart

Origin date	Writing device	Characteristics/Comments
Early 1950s	Porous tip pens	Porous material tips, in a variety of shapes and sizes. Relatively uniform line width, lack "nib tracks" or roller marks. Ending strokes often appear dry. "Sharpie" popular in mid-1970s, although available in late 1960s. Some permanent markers will evidence bleeding. Early felt-tip markers badly fade.
Mid-1940s	Ballpoint pen	Distinctive line appearance due to ink and ball combination. Produces line of even width. Early samples will exhibit blotting, skipping and fading. Recent pen varieties produce more free-flowing ink.
1884*	Fountain pen	Continuous ink flow. Contrast between upstrokes and heavier downstrokes.
1870s	Stylographic pen	Continuous ink flow. Uniform width on upstrokes and downstrokes.
1858**	Steel pen	Nib tracks evident, indentation may be possible. Dip pen writing characteristics. Stub pen; more shaded strokes, distinguishable on tops of rounded letters. Dip pen writing characteristics. Double line pen; dual line effect. Dip pen writing characteristics.

* Waterman manufactured
** Esterbrook, U.S. manufactured

Ink also has a value in determining the age of a writing sample. From iron gall ink varieties to nigrosine inks, each has specific properties that can be identified by a sample's reaction to chemical reagents. To determine if a document was prepared with different pens, an authenticator can study the chemical composition of the ink. A typical nondestructive approach for ink comparisons uses a device called a microspectrophotometer. This device studies the amount of certain lights absorbed by the ink. Additionally, a method called thin-layer chromatography separates dyes that make up certain inks such as those used in a ballpoint pen.

Many advanced methods of analysis exist that utilize a small amount of ink removed from the writing surface. Many federal agencies have a complete library of commercial inks and the unique dye patterns, or ink fingerprints, they exhibit. From these patterns a specific writing instrument can be identified and the ink dated to the year it was used.

Considerable attention arose last year from the development of a DNA pen by a manufacturer. The pen's ink combines basic ingredients with human hair and saliva. The result is an ink stroke unique to each person. It has been endorsed in the animation trade by industry giant Joseph Barbara, who uses his DNA pen to sign cartoon cels. Cost, availability, detection, and training are just a few of the issues still surrounding the device. Only time will tell if this is the proper direction for the hobby to turn to solve its authentication problems.

Perhaps one day these advanced methods will be so simple and cost effective that the risk of acquiring a forged signature will be dramatically reduced.

Terms

Like any hobby, autograph collecting has terms unique to its trade. Fortunately for collectors they are uncomplicated and easy to learn. The table below contains both hobby terms and handwriting terms that dealers may use to describe signatures to collectors.

Hobby Terms

ALS	autograph letter signed: a letter written entirely in the hand of the celebrity
AMQS	autograph musical quotation signed: a musical quotation handwritten by celebrity or a bar of music signed by celebrity
ANS	autograph note signed: a short note handwritten by celebrity and also signed
AQS	autograph quotation signed: a quote handwritten and signed by celebrity
C	color
Cachet	a special design, in honor of a person or event, printed or drawn on an envelope
CS	card signed: the celebrity's signature on a card, often a 3" x 5" index card
DS	document signed: often a legal agreement, land grant, etc., signed by the celebrity

SP (signed photograph), autographed cachet and endorsed check -- all items signed by HOF (Hall of Fame) boxer Max Schmeling.

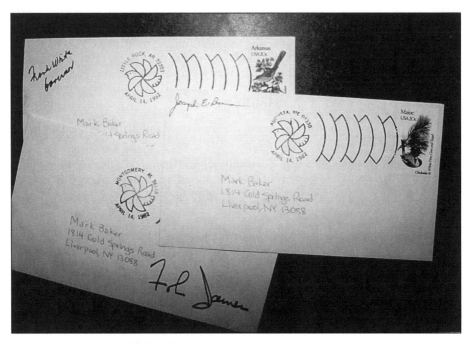

An example of an F.D.C. (First Day Cover) series signed by state governors.

Facsimile	an exact reproduction of a person's signature, often photographed, printed, stamped, or autopenned on an item; a forgery can also be considered a facsimile
FDC	first day cover, or an envelope, often a cachet with a stamp affixed and canceled on the first day it was available for public sale
HOF	Hall of Fame
Holograph	a writing sample in the hand of the subject
I	inscribed or personalized, such as "To Mark, Best Wishes"
IP	in person: an autograph obtained personally
ISP/SPI/IPS	inscribed signed photograph
Legal size	8.5" x 14" standard paper size (U.S. Government 8" x 12.5")
Letter size	8.5" x 11" standard paper size (U.S. Government 8" x 10.5")
Lot	a group of materials sold at one time
LS	letter signed: a letter written by someone other than celebrity, but signed by celebrity
MOC	member of Congress
MOH	medal of honor
Provenance	the record of ownership of an item or collection
SASE	self-addressed stamped envelope: often included with autograph requests

SIG/sig	signature: this usually refers to the actual signature on a card or album page, or possibly cut from a letter or document
SP	signed photograph: color or black & white
TCS	trading card signed: signature on a baseball or basketball card, etc.
TLS	typed letter signed
UV coated	a high-gloss finish applied to an item that protects it from environmental damage; the coating has limited adherence qualities, making it difficult to sign

Handwriting Terms

Ascender	the segment of a letter that extends above the main body or lower case letter height
Arm	the part of a letter that extends perpendicular to or upwards from its stem
Baseline	an often invisible line that a subject's signature seems to rest upon
Character formation	the way in which the writer typically forms a letter; character formations often include loops which may be closed (touching strokes) or open
Descender	the segment of a letter that extends below the baseline of a signature
Height	refers to the distance above the signature's baseline; height varies according to the writer's style and whether lower case or upper case script is used
Leg	the part of a letter that extends downward from its stem
Signature break	a common characteristic of most signatures, it refers to the space between where one stroke ends and another stroke begins
Slant	the direction and degree to which signatures vary from a perpendicular or 90 degree angle
Stroke	the main ingredient of every signature, it begins at the point where ink or a similar substance is applied to a surface, and ends where the application is discontinued

An autograph from Senator Edward Kennedy is an example of a MOC (Member of Congress). Here are various photos signed and sent out by Senator Kennedy during his career.

Chapter 4

Acquiring Autographs

As a celebrity autograph collector it is useful to have a goal. Remember, if you don't know where you're going, any road will take you there! Your particular goal is the framework that determines how you go about acquiring items. Collectors who have chosen to specialize in autographed entertainment contracts realize that their acquisition channels will be limited and probably costly. Those who collect the autographs of living actors on index cards benefit from choosing a more accessible and probably less expensive goal. Whatever method you choose to acquire signatures, it should be compatible with your collecting goal.

For many collectors, acquiring celebrity autographs will require a combination of indirect and direct methods.

There are seven primary ways to acquire celebrity autographs:

Direct method: In-person request

Indirect methods: Correspondence with the individual, usually by mail
                    Acquiring item through a friend, relative or associated personnel
                    Purchasing items from dealers, promoters, memorabilia outlets, catalogs, shopping networks, etc.
                    Purchasing item at an auction
                    Trading
                    Autographed trading card inserts (primarily limited to sports celebrities)

In-Person Request

The preferred and most enjoyable form of acquiring celebrity autographs is in person. Not only does the collector have the opportunity to meet a celebrity, he or she has absolute confirmation of the signature's authenticity. Timing is usually the critical factor for success acquiring signatures in person. Being at the right place at the right time is a great formula for success, but most collectors don't know where that place is and when to get there.

Each year I make it a point to track down the celebrity entertainment that appears at the New York State Fair in Syracuse, New York. Syracuse, with a population of just over 160,000, is very accessible and it's easy to get around there. I have found that celebrities are easy to track down in cities with a population under 200,000 because there is usually only a handful of quality hotels, restaurants, limousine services, theaters and auditoriums. Additionally, cities of this size have small airports and limited charter jet service.

The first two questions to answer are: How is the celebrity traveling? and Where are they staying? Typically I answer both of these questions in less than two hours. Smaller musical acts, such as Bon Jovi or Dolly Parton, charter custom tour buses that are very dif-

Members of the musical group Cheap Trick departing motel via taxi.

ficult to hide, so look for them outside the hotels. The group typically stays where the road crew stays, unless it's a high-caliber band such as The Rolling Stones. Always start first by visiting the five best hotels in town, looking for charter deluxe tour buses, active limousine services outside, and road crew, unusual security, and blocked floor access inside.

Here are just a few of the celebrities I have met and received autographs from using this method and simply waiting patiently in a hotel lobby: President Ford, Linda Ronstadt, Mrs. Ronald Reagan, Wayne Newton, Genesis, Waylon Jennings, The Beach Boys, Bon Jovi, Cheap Trick, Amy Grant, Adam Ant, The Doobie Brothers, Bob Dylan, Kris Kristofferson, Mikhail Baryshnikov, Heart, Boston, Van Halen, The Rolling Stones, Peabo Bryson, Sting, REO Speedwagon, Greg Lake, The Who, Charlie Daniels, and Jefferson Starship.

A common mistake among novice celebrity autograph collectors is thinking that the only chance to obtain a signature is at the very beginning or end of an event. This in fact is probably the worst approach to take. Most successful celebrity autograph collectors never even buy a ticket. They opt instead to become totally familiar with daily routines of their subjects, and choose specific times and places for all their autograph requests. This may mean standing around in a hotel lobby for an hour before the event, or after the event stopping by a premier gourmet restaurant known to be frequented by certain celebrities. It's ridiculous to wait for hours, pushing and shoving, outside an arena, when you'll have far greater success at an airport, hotel, or restaurant.

If you are a serious sports celebrity autograph collector, you should spend an afternoon scouting the major sports facilities in your town or city of choice, especially when there is a home game scheduled for that evening. The first two areas you should locate are the player entrances and player parking lot. Public access to both of these areas, especially if they are unguarded, allows for direct player contact. Familiarize yourself with the players' cars and the time they usually arrive at the facility. The visiting team generally arrives by bus, van or taxi, about three hours before the game. Since most of the visiting players stay at the same hotel, they usually arrive at the arena or stadium in groups, making it hectic to stop each player individually. The best approach in this situation is to team up with three other collectors and predetermine which collector is go-

Chartered tour buses used by the musical group Bon Jovi.

ing to stop which player. A group of four collectors, each stopping a different player, is particularly useful for players arriving in vans or cabs.

Inside the sports facility, familiarize yourself with areas that offer the greatest opportunity for direct player contact. Accessible areas between the clubhouse or locker room exit and the area of play usually provide the best autograph opportunities. Monitor the accessibility to team bench or dugout areas. Often these areas are guarded or have ushers that keep autograph seekers at a distance. Many times, however, a player will begin signing near one area of the bench, causing autograph seekers to flood the aisles nearest that point. That type of distraction usually leaves other aisles near the bench unguarded, allowing you the perfect opportunity to walk unnoticed to the front row of that section. It is the patient and subtle celebrity autograph seeker who is the most successful.

When you finally find the right autographing position inside the facility, act like you belong. Don't be conspicuous. Adapt to the crowd around you. If you look like an autograph seeker, with your six hockey sticks under your arm and three pairs of skates wrapped around your neck, then you'll probably be treated like one. If you are bringing any items into the facility to be autographed they should not be directly visible. Don't walk around the ballpark with a binder filled with trading cards and four pens in your hand.

It is not unusual for a celebrity to make numerous appearances at local vendors or sponsors. If you know Colin Powell is appearing at a local bookstore, make every effort to get there and take advantage of a free autograph. Depending on building access, you may even have better luck catching the celebrity at the door rather than inside the store. If you are unaware of any local celebrity appearances, consult your local newspaper. Usually the advertisements in the sports or entertainment sections are a great place to start. Book signings are common among authors, and typically happen on a weekly basis. I know of many outstanding celebrity autograph collections built strictly by attending book signings.

The most often overlooked in-person source for acquiring celebrity autographs is at local businesses, especially restaurants, nightclubs, and shopping malls. Following a performance, most celebrities will join their crew, family, friends, or teammates for dinner, generally at one of the finest local establishments.

In my experience celebrities are more than happy to autograph items for their fans, especially away from the chaos of an event. Make your requests congenially and not while the celebrity is in the middle of a meal. Nothing upsets celebrities more than autograph collectors who completely disrespect their right to privacy.

Correspondence with the Individual, Usually by Mail

ESPN's Chris Berman and Peter Gammons awaiting a live broadcast.

Most collectors choose to add to their collections by autograph requests sent to the celebrity through the U.S. Postal Service or other international postal services. This method of obtaining a signature has a success rate of 25% to 35%. Not only do many requests go unanswered, but often they are lost. Because of the increased popularity of collecting celebrity autographs, many entertainers and professional athletes are inundated with mail requesting their signature. Because autograph collecting has become a business to many, some celebrities are skeptical of the sincerity associated with a mail request. Add to that the many invitations professional athletes receive to attend sports trading card shows as autograph guests, and you can understand why many of these requests are not answered. The lowest return rates are from professional baseball players, most of whom ignore mailed autograph requests.

Certain individuals do respond to autograph requests, particularly if they are perceived as sincere and are brief in length and include a self-addressed stamped envelope. A comprehensive listing of those celebrities who have good response rates is included in Section II of this book. This is not to say that they are the only ones who respond, or that their response is guaranteed, it is only to point out their better-than-average tendency to respond.

Putting together a direct mailing of autograph requests can be a costly undertaking for collectors. To help explain the hidden expenses of such a project, I have included a cost breakdown for mailing one hundred baseball autograph requests through the U. S. Postal Service. Of course the variables included in this cost breakdown may change, but the collector should be prepared to invest the initial expense, with no guarantee for success.

Acquiring Through a Friend, Relative, or Associated Personnel

As might be expected, this method of adding signatures to your collection is usually very successful. The greater your access to the subject, the higher your chance of adding another autograph to your collection. As a collector you should make a sincere effort to get to know anyone affiliated with major hotels, local professional sports teams, limousine services, charter airlines, event promotions and restaurant owners. From ushers to waitresses, people who may have access to a celebrity will only serve to increase your

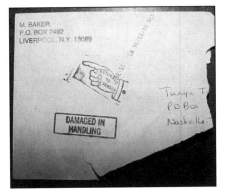

UNITED STATES POSTAL SERVICE

DEAR POSTAL CUSTOMER:

Please accept our apologies for the enclosed damaged article of mail. We sincerely regret any inconvenience you may experience.

The Postal Services realizes that your mail is important to you, and that you have every right to expect it to be delivered in good condition.

Please be assured that corrective steps are continuously being taken to minimize such damage. We are constantly striving to improve our processing procedures so that these rare occurrences of damage are eliminated.

If you have any questions or comments you can contact me at (212) 330-2300 or the Senior Manager, Distribution Operations at (212) 330-2667.

Plant Manager
Morgan GMF
341 Ninth Avenue
New York, NY 10199-9701

Here are three good reasons not to send valuable materials through the mail.

R.E.M. ▲ Box 8032 ▲ Athens, GA 30603

$10 U.S. ▲ $12 Foreign

R.E.M. Fan Club ▲

Dear Mark,

I'm very sorry but there are no autographs available. The guys are not in the office enough to start on the dozens of requests our office receives everyday.

Again, sorry.

REM/Athens, LTD

An R.E.M. autograph rejection notice.

autograph success rate. Additionally, don't forget about the media, especially newspaper reporters. They have tremendous access to celebrities and are usually very willing to discuss the subject of their current story. If you see a reporter in a restricted area at a sports facility or an auditorium, watch closely, because he or she is usually waiting to interview a celebrity. Reporters are typically working under strict deadlines and waste little time in pursuing their subject.

Getting to know a celebrity's family or friends can be a bit more difficult. This can be accomplished, however, if your approach is gradual and sincere. At professional sports facilities, theaters, and auditoriums, celebrities participating in a particular event are allowed complimentary tickets and guest passes. These tickets or passes are most often assigned to a specific designated area, usually in close proximity to a team bench or stage. Obviously this depends on the facility, and also whether the celebrity or athlete is visiting or local. An astute collector will recognize this area by the concentration of women and small children or by the presence of the passes worn by the guests. I will admit that this task is easier to do at a small minor league ballpark than at Madison Square Garden, but it still can be accomplished. Arriving early will help you find this area and identify celebrity friends or family. Often athletes or celebrities will talk with friends and relatives before an event begins, during practice or a soundcheck. Watch who the celebrity approaches and where that individual sits after the conversation.

Following the event or game, monitor who walks in and out of the player/artist entrance at the facility. Believe me, it won't take long to recognize family members, even by name. It will also help to have a media guide or program. Alongside the celebrity's photograph you can write the names of their friends and family.

Always remember to respect an individual's right to privacy. Use discretion when approaching with an autograph request. A celebrity who has had a bad show is not going to be thrilled about being deluged with autograph requests and will not be very accommodating.

Purchasing from Dealers, Promoters, Catalogs, and Shopping Networks

The advice I could give in this category could fill a book, but it boils down to this: let the buyer beware. Purchasing items from an established dealer with a good reputation for quality, service, price and availability is paramount. An established dealer will often offer a wide variety of autographed material at a fair market price. When you are purchasing autographed celebrity memorabilia of any kind, each item should carry an unconditional guarantee of authenticity. This type of guarantee is not based solely on a printed certificate of authenticity, but also upon the dealer's willingness to accept a returned item due to authenticity concerns.

An established dealer should provide a reasonable return policy. Typically this is fourteen days from time of purchase. If you are unsatisfied with an item you have purchased from a dealer, you should promptly return it in the same condition. If the item you are purchasing for your collection is extremely unique or costly, don't hesitate to ask the dealer about its origin, or provenance. This method is used often among collectors of rare historical documents.

Another benefit of working with established dealers is having access to their knowledge base, useful not only in authenticating a specific item, but in acquiring certain autographed collectibles. Developing a good relationship with a variety of established dealers will only add to your collecting satisfaction. Once a dealer learns of your commitment to a particular collecting goal, she or he may help by providing you access to purchasing sources. As a serious collector, you should always maintain a comprehensive "want list" of items desired for your collection. That list should indicate desired price range, condition, and time to acquisition. Many quality autographed celebrity items never reach dealer advertisements, but are instead acquired by known collectors who specialize in a certain field.

Always request to be added to a dealer's mailing list for future catalogs or sale notifications. Most dealers will comply, but since catalogs can be very expensive to produce and distribute, staying on a dealer's mailing list will probably require either a purchase or a catalog fee. On average, a good collector receives between three and five catalogs a week. They are an excellent source of comparison shopping and provide collectors with hobby insights, knowledge of recent acquisitions, and an understanding of each dealer's specialties. Periodic contact with established dealers is necessary to avoid missing key acquisitions, because a catalog represents only a small amount of available inventory.

It won't take long for a collector to realize that dealer prices for identical items can vary significantly. Dealers base their prices primarily on local appeal and demand, and on the availability of the item. If you choose to buy autographed baseball memorabilia in Cooperstown, New York, or autographed rock 'n' roll items from a store in Cleveland, Ohio, you will pay more than usual, as both of these regions have an established clientele based on location alone.

To illustrate the concept of market variability, I have included a chart that compares prices of the same single-signature autographed baseballs as advertised by four different dealers. Assuming the dealers are of equal integrity, offer the same return policy, and an identical product, you can see that by purchasing a Joe DiMaggio autographed single-signature baseball from dealer C you can save yourself $111. It's easy to see that comparison shopping can save you money, but also keep in mind the importance of dealer integrity. If the deal sounds too good to be true, it probably is.

Purchasing from satellite shopping networks and gift catalogs is an interesting dichotomy. Although they offer collectors instant access to a wide variety of autographed celebrity memorabilia, they do so at what most collectors consider to be extravagant prices. These companies claim that there are substantial costs associated with marketing products this way, and that is the justification for the pricing. Certainly there are significant costs involved in printing catalogs and renting satellite time, but I do not believe most items are worth such large price tags. I am not implying that all products offered through these sources are high priced: they are not. Nor am I implying that you can't find an outstanding limited edition celebrity collectible at a great price: you can. Just be realistic in your purchases and keep your collecting goal in mind. I think this method of acquiring autographed celebrity collectibles will eventually prove to be very worthwhile to collectors.

Another source for celebrity autographs is major collectibles shows, where professional athletes or entertainers are often signing for a fee. Athletes or celebrities attending these shows are guaranteed a certain amount of money for their services, so in essence you are purchasing your autographs from the promoter. The advantage to this method is clear: you are guaranteed an authentic signature on the item of your choice and a brief encounter with a celebrity. The disadvantages are the long waiting lines and other inconveniences associated with attending a public event, and the cost. Included in this chapter is a chart entitled "Attending a Major Collectibles Show," which I hope will put into perspective the associated costs of attending this type of event. The cost will vary depending upon the show's location, the guests and the show's promoter. Keep in mind that the more autographs you acquire at a show like this, the lower the average cost of each.

Purchasing at an Auction

As the hobby of collecting autographs has matured, many major auction houses have increased their level of participation. These auctions have become a platform for the sale of some of the hobby's finest examples. From record contracts signed by John Lennon to a rarely seen autographed 8" x 10" photograph of "Shoeless" Joe Jackson, these major auction houses are unearthing some of the finest pieces available in the market and attracting some very prominent buyers. In addition to discovering key collectibles, these auction houses are also gauging market demand and keeping collectors current on what is attracting buyers.

Although shrewd buyers may find bargains, the excitement of the event usually lends itself to overpriced acquisitions. Many agree that the greatest advantage these auction houses offer the average collector is their catalogs, most of which provide detailed descriptions and photographs and are generally available for public purchase weeks before the event. Serious collectors who for some reason cannot attend the auctions should still purchase these catalogs for their research value and consider submitting mail bid forms on items that interest them most. Before participating in this method of acquisition, however, collectors should be aware of all the terms and conditions of sale.

Trading

Trading with fellow collectors is another option available to the collector of sports autographs. Many veteran collectors have built a wonderful network across the country. This method of acquiring celebrity autographs is particularly gratifying because you can receive items to fill your needs while helping a fellow collector toward his or her hobby goals. Choose your trading partners in the same manner you choose a local dealer. Try to find a dealer who specializes in the same type of material that you collect. Before you make or approve any trade be sure that all items involved in the transaction are clearly identified, especially with regard to condition. Should you receive any material in a trade that does not meet your level of satisfaction, immediately return it. Collectors vary in their interpretation of the condition of an item, often referred to as grading, as well as their knowledge of signature variations. Do not be surprised if a collector rejects a trade item because of either factor. Don't take it personally: a return reflects the judgement of only that one collector.

Finding someone to trade with is simply a matter of contacting those individuals whose names appear in advertisements in trade periodicals such as *Autograph Collector*, *Autograph Times*, *Goldmine*, *Today's Collector*, *Collecting*, *Sports Collector Digest*, *Sports Cards*, and the *Sports Card Price Guide*. Also many collectors own personal computers with the ability to access networks. These computer networks have the ability to submit and receive electronic mail, and many offer autographed celebrity memorabilia for sale.

Autographed Trading Card Inserts

Although not usually cost effective and certainly not predictable, this method of acquiring celebrity autographs is another option, especially for those who collect sports autographs. Many collectors relish the excitement of searching through packs of sports trading cards hoping to find an autographed insert. As an area of specialization, however, it is restricted to those few who have less concern for cost and greater interest in production or availability.

This marketing strategy has lured many trading card collectors into the field of autographs. What card manufacturers intended as a buying incentive for collectors has turned into a whole new hobby niche. While many trading card dealers continue to complain about new card issues, they praise the increased use of autographed inserts. Most collectors welcome the change and say that it has increased their interest in the hobby.

Below is a collection of charts that I thought would be helpful.

Attending a Major Collectibles Show

Cost Breakdown

Travel Costs

400 miles (round trip) x $.24 per mile* = $96.00

Show Costs

Parking = $5.00*
Show Admission = $5.00* (Note: A weekend pass was available for $8.00)

Autograph Costs

Guest: Willie Mays (Baseball)

	Cost of materials:**	
	12 Official League Baseballs	$70.20
	Shipping & handling	$5.00
		$75.20
	Autograph fee: $35.00 per baseball	$420.00
	Subtotal	$495.20

Guest: Emmitt Smith (Football)

	Cost of materials:**	
	10 Unofficial League Footballs	$500.00
		$500.00
	Autograph fee: $75.00 per football	$750.00
	Subtotal	$1250.00

Guest: Mike Bossy (Hockey)

	Cost of materials:**	
	10 Official Logo Pucks	$80.50
	Shipping & handling	$5.00
		$85.50
	Autograph fee: $12.00 per puck	$120.00
	Subtotal	$205.50

* Figure based on average corporate expense allowance
** Purchased prior to show

Summary

Travel Costs	$96.00
Show Costs	$10.00
Autograph Costs	$1,950.70
Total	$2,056.70

Note: This cost summary does not include food or beverage costs and assumes no free parking is available. The number of materials to be signed was predetermined by the collector.

Analysis

Total pieces signed = 32

Cost per item, prior to travel and show costs:

A single-signed Willie Mays baseball	$41.26
A single-signed Emmitt Smith football	$125.00
A single-signed Mike Bossy puck	$20.55

Cost per item, after adding travel and show costs ($106.00):

A single-signed Willie Mays baseball	$44.57
A single-signed Emmitt Smith football	$128.31
A single-signed Mike Bossy puck	$23.86

Note: Travel and show costs divided between 32 items comes to $3.31 per item. The more pieces you have signed, the lower the average cost of each signing.

Direct Mailing

Cost Breakdown for Mailing 100 Baseball Autograph Requests

Item	Cost	Comments
200 4-1/8" x 9-1/2" envelopes	$6.00	For S.A.S.E.
1 ballpoint pen	$.59	
200 .32 postage stamps	$64.00	2 for each letter*
1996 World Almanac	$10.95	For address reference
15 packs of Topps (current release year) Baseball Cards ($1.50 per pack)	$22.50	Needed 15 packs to get 100 different players
Total	$104.04	

Cost per single baseball autograph request: $1.04**

* 1 stamp for request, 1 for S.A.S.E. This assumes no international mailing.
** Assumes only 1 baseball card included per request

Autographed Single-Signature Baseballs

Dealer Pricing Variances

Player Name	A	B	C	D
Joe DiMaggio	$350	$275	$239	$295
Ted Williams	125	99	99	145
Willie Mays	45	40	29	35
Hank Aaron	45	35	-	-
Stan Musial	50	40	-	35
Johnny Bench	35	35	-	-
Steve Carlton	30	28	-	25
Brooks Robinson	25	20	-	-
Lou Brock	30	25	-	-

- = not available

Prices do not include postage and handling. All prices quoted from advertisements in the March 18, 1994 issue of *Sports Collectors Digest*.

Acquiring In-Person Autographs
Autograph Collector Hints

Be Prepared
Often you will only have ONE autograph opportunity, so be prepared. Have both a new Sharpie and ballpoint pen immediately accessible. Know what you're going to have signed by each celebrity and have it at your fingertips.

Be Timely with Your Request
Timing is the element that will determine the success of an autograph request. Try to put yourself in the celebrity's position. For example, you're at the Golden Globe awards. Who is more likely to oblige an autograph request following the ceremony: the celebrity who won an award or the celebrity who lost?

Don't Be Conspicuous
Blend into your surroundings as much as possible. Act like you belong in your environment. Always look and act professional.

Conceal the Material to Be Autographed
Keep all of the material you are going to have signed concealed until the last possible minute.

Stop the Subject
Try to prevent the celebrity from moving while the autograph is signed. As the celebrity walks he or she decreases the available signing arena, causing other collectors to lose their autograph opportunity. Additionally, when walking the celebrity is not usually concentrating on the item to be signed, resulting in a very poor autograph. Always approach directly and allow the subject as little space as possible to move around you. Placing your shoulder bag (which contains the material to be signed) directly in front of the celebrity will help the task.

Block the Path Between Subject and Destination
Working with other collectors, you can strategically place yourselves so that there is no clear path between the subject and his or her destination. The celebrity will always choose the path of least resistance: in this case, the direction that holds the least number of autograph seekers. Your placement along an autograph path is also critical. If you recognize a celebrity's friend, spouse or relative, who is also waiting for the celebrity, stand nearby. Standing near an attractive member of the opposite sex will also increase your chances of being recognized.

Place Flat Items on a Clipboard
Flat items are cumbersome to sign if a similar surface area is not available. Clipping the items gently to a clipboard allows for the necessary support. Additionally, index card collectors can place more than a single item underneath the clip, side by side, allowing for a quick additional signature.

Free Subject's Hands
It is not unusual for your subject to be carrying a suitcase, umbrella, locker room bag, etc. If you see that a subject has both hands occupied, you are going to have to find a way to free one of them so that the celebrity can autograph your items. The easiest way is to offer to hold the item while he or she signs your material.

Learn a Few Words in Another Language
Not everyone who is a celebrity in this country is fluent in English. Learning some basic phrases in Spanish, French and even Russian will prove to be particularly helpful in many instances.

Be Courteous Yet Firm

Always be courteous to your subject. For instance, say "May I please have your auto-graph Mr. Baldwin?" and "Thank you very much, I really appreciate it." Respect your subject, but do not be timid with an autograph request. You must be assertive, but not overbearing. A celebrity is not required to comply with an autograph request, but the more appealing you make the situation, the better likelihood of a positive response.

Exercise Perseverance

Not everyone will comply with your request. Some celebrities will ignore your solicitations. These situations can be difficult: some may require a different approach, or just repeated solicitations. Whatever your plan of action, be patient and don't give up!

Know Your Subject

Doing a little biographical research on a subject can be helpful. Knowing a celebrity's hometown, hobbies or even alma mater can lead to conversation that ends with an autograph request fulfilled.

Top Ten Best and Worst Autograph Signers (In Person)

The Best

1. Val Kilmer: still hasn't let fame go to his head. "It must be the car, chicks dig the car!"
2. Johnny Depp: party down, a good signer
3. Jack Nicholson: must be Magic, still good after all these years
4. Charlie Sheen: not smart with his baseball memorabilia purchases, but has that animal magic
5. Patricia Arquette: a doll, still congenial
6. Tom Hanks: horrible by mail, runs hot and cold, like a box of chocolates
7. Jean Claude Van Damme: facsimile by mail, not bad by night
8. Brad Pitt: slowing down a bit!
9. Kelsey Grammer: Cheers in person, we're closed by mail
10. Jodie Foster: moody, have to be a bit delicate

Honorable Mentions: Faye Dunaway, Pierce Brosnan, Martin Landau, Steven Spielberg, Sharon Stone, Sally Field, John Travolta, Jamie Lee Curtis, Brooks Robinson, Tony Curtis, and Willie Pep

The Worst

1. The Artist Formerly Known as Prince: a king without a kingdom
2. Mel Gibson: rude, crude and in a mood
3. Kevin Costner: K-line -- thinks the alphabet has only one letter
4. Anna Paquin: daughter dearest
5. Bruce Willis: should change his name to Bruce Willnot
6. Macauley Culkin: who knows what's going on here; Culkin vs. Culkin
7. Jerry Seinfeld: stinks by mail, I went to school with him and couldn't stand him
8. Richard Gere: Richard "Can't find first" Gere
9. Angela Bassett: should change name to Angela Forgetit
10. Bette Midler: just woke up on the wrong side of the broomstick

Honorable Mentions: Julia Roberts, Christian Slater, Kevin Bacon, Roseanne, Frank Sinatra, Jack Palance, Nicole Kidman, Tom Cruise, Mike Tyson, Troy Aikman, John Malkovich, and Joe DiMaggio.

My Top Ten Worst Autograph Experiences of All Time

1. Being informed by the U.S. Secret Service, "If you don't leave that spot in three seconds I'll let this German shepherd attack dog go, and he hasn't eaten in three days."

2. Watching a very intoxicated Dennis Wilson of The Beach Boys try to pick a fight with someone three times his size

3. Standing next to Bob Dylan, about to ask for an autograph, when someone in the crowd decides to punch him in the face

4. Trying to block The Rolling Stones motorcade with my GEO Tracker

5. Walking past Robert Plant in the Syracuse airport with my mother, and neither she nor I have a pen

6. A phone call from The White House while I was working at General Electric: some of my correspondence had gotten too far and I knew too much. Sorry, guys!

7. Carrying the family diapers up an elevator for Tony Banks of Genesis, because he couldn't get anyone to help him

8. Watching Johnny Mize, a member of the Baseball Hall of Fame and former teammate of Joe DiMaggio, ask the "Yankee Clipper" for an autograph, and getting turned down flat

9. Receiving an autographed baseball from The Marshall Tucker Band less than 24 hours before band member Tommy Caldwell was killed in an accident. I had two signed and gave one to Charlie Daniels. (Charlie signed my baseball and I signed Charlie's!)

10. Watching my brother pick a fight with Bill Wyman's (The Rolling Stones) son, because he felt The Who were a much better rock band than the band Wyman got involved with

Chapter 5

Organizing Your Celebrity Search

It will probably surprise you to learn just how easy it is to find someone: not just a celebrity, but anyone. This chapter is included not only to help you find celebrities not listed in Section II, but also to assist you in finding celebrities whose addresses have changed. To find someone you don't have to have the skills of a detective, just a bit of common sense and self-discipline.

Nearly everyone exists on record somewhere. To find that record in the shortest amount of time and with the least amount of cost is a common task among serious celebrity autograph collectors. The process itself can be frustrating but also exciting and gratifying. Logic, persistence and dedication to a solid research plan will typically lead to success.

The First Step

Using yourself as an example, think of all the different ways you can be contacted -- home address, work address, organizations -- and the medium used for that contact -- phone, mail, e-mail. Once you write them down on a piece of paper, it will probably surprise you to find out just how accessible you really are. Now add to this the constant media exposure that is associated with being a celebrity and you begin to realize why celebrities can run, but they can never hide.

Assuming you have no research tools at home -- no phone or computer, or even phone book -- we will begin our search in the public library. Since you are looking for someone who has already reached celebrity status, you can be almost guaranteed of the existence of biographical references. In other words, someone else has already found out how

Begin your search in the public library.

and where to contact this person. A partial list of biographical references has been provided here for your use. Although it is lengthy, it is in no way intended to be comprehensive.

Biographical References

Almanac of American Politics
American Art Directory
American Catholic Who's Who
American Medical Directory
American Men and Women of
    Science
Bakers Biographical Dictionary
    of Musicians
Biographical Directory of the
    United States Congress
Biographical Encyclopedia &
    Who's Who of the American Theatre
Biographical Encyclopedia of
    Scientists
Canadian Almanac & Directory
Canadian Who's Who
Celebrity Register
China Yearbook

The reference section of the public library contains volumes of biographical reference books.

Columbia Dictionary of Political Biography
Concise Oxford Dictionary of Ballet
Congressional Directory
Congressional Quarterly Almanac
Contemporary (individual directories):
    Authors, Composers, Dramatists, Foreign Language Writers, Literary Criticism,
    Musicians, Novelists, Poets, Poets of the English Language, Theatre, Film and
    Television, Women Dramatists and World Writers
Country Music Encyclopedia
The Dictionary of Composers and Their Music
Directory of American Scholars
Directory of British Scientists
Dictionary of Contemporary American Artists
Dictionary of Film
Dictionary of International Biography
Dictionary of Literary Biography
Directory of Medical Specialists
Dictionary of National Biography
Dictionary of Twentieth-Century Composers
Encyclopedia of Pop, Rock & Soul
Film Encyclopedia
Filmgoer's Companion
Football Register
Grove's Dictionary of Music and Musicians

International Authors and Writers Who's Who
International Encyclopedia of Music and Musicians
International Dictionary of Architects and Architecture
International Dictionary of Films and Filmmakers
International Dictionary of Opera
International Dictionary of Theatre
International Motion Pictures Almanac
International Television Almanac
International Who's Who
International Who's Who in (individual directories):
    Art and Antiques, Education, Medicine, Music and Musicians Directory, Poet and
    Poet's Encyclopedia, (of) the Arab World, and (of) Women
International Year Book and Statesmen's Who's Who
Martindale-Hubbell Law Dictionary
McGraw-Hill Encyclopedia of World Biography
McGraw-Hill Encyclopedia of World Drama
McGraw-Hill Modern Scientists and Engineers
Medical Science International Who's Who
New Grove Dictionary of (individual directories):
    American Music, Jazz, Music and Musicians
New Grove Gospel, Blues and Jazz
Nobel Prize Winners
Notable Names in American Theatre
Notable Women in the American Theatre: A Biographical Dictionary
Official Catholic Directory
Oxford Companion to (individual directories):
    American Theatre, Film, Theatre, and Twentieth-Century Art
Oxford Guide to British Women Writers
Poor's Register of Corporations, Directors and Executives
Prominent Personalities in the USSR
Something About the Author
Twentieth-Century (individual directories):
    Authors, Children's Writers, Crime and Mystery Writers, Romance and Historical
    Writers, Science Fiction Writers, and Western Writers
Webster's New Biographical Dictionary
Who's Who
Who's Who (individual directories):
    Among Asian Americans, Among Black Americans, and Among Hispanic Amer-
    icans
Who's Who in (individual directories):
    Advertising, Africa, America, American Art, American Education, American
    Film Now, American Law, American Music: Classical, American Politics, Art,
    Australia and the Far East, Canada, Congress, Economics, Engineering, Entertain-
    ment, Finance and Industry, France, Germany, International Affairs, International
    Organizations, Israel, Italy, Japan, Labor, Malaysia and Singapore, Mexico Today,
    Music, Opera, Philosophy, Poetry, Rock Music, Saudi Arabia, Science in Europe,
    Space, Spain, Switzerland, Arab World, East, Midwest, the Motion Picture Indus-
    try, the People's Republic of China, the South and Southwest, the Soviet Union,
    the Theatre, TV and Cable, the United States, West, U.S. Executives, Western Eu-
    rope, the World, World Jewry, and Writers, Editors & Poets
Who's Who of (individual directories):
    American Women, British Engineers, British Scientists, Jazz, and Southern Africa

Who's Who on Television
World (individual directories):
    Artists, Authors, and Film Directors
World's Who's Who (individual directories):
    Science and Women
Writers Directory

Note: Directories vary publication dates: many are annual. Some of these biographical references may be out of publication but still provide useful information. Not all publications include addresses.

By the time you have exhausted this list, you will have either found an address for the celebrity, or determined that the task will require significantly more research than you anticipated.

Most celebrities reach their status because they are accomplished in their field. For example, Garth Brooks is a celebrity because of his outstanding contribution to the field of country music. Sending an autograph request to him in care of his record company, music publisher, fan club, or talent agency might find its way into his hands. As a fan of his you probably own a CD, so pick it up and read the information included inside. You may find not only an address for one of these sources, but also the name of his tour manager, booking agent or record producer.

The information you find in the fine print of a CD can be useful even for in-person autograph seeking. A typical trick I use for sniffing out a music group's presence in a hotel involves using the name of the band's manager. A good source for this information is the small print inside a CD or even a tour program. A quick phone call to the hotel usually provides great results: I ask if this individual is staying there or simply ask for him or her by name. A first-class hotel will never acknowledge that a celebrity is their guest, so don't even bother asking. If the celebrity's manager is at the hotel, then it's extremely likely that the celebrity is also there. Most celebrities will ask that their phone calls be held, while a manager would never even consider it.

Directories vary publication dates; many are annual. Some of these biographical references may be out of publication, but still provide useful information.

Typically, the bigger the celebrity, the bigger the name of the booking agent, manager, record company, professional team, agent, producer, etc. If you're going to collect celebrity autographs, it will be worth your time to memorize the following addresses. Keeping updated client lists from all these agencies will

prove very useful for your autograph collecting. All of these agencies are good about forwarding fan mail to their clients.

Selected Celebrity Talent Agencies

Entertainers

William Morris Agency, 151 El Camino Drive, Beverly Hills, CA 90212

Creative Artists Agency, 9830 Wilshire Boulevard, Beverly Hills, CA 90212

International Creative Management (ICM), 8942 Wilshire Boulevard, Beverly Hills, CA 90211

United Talent Agency, 9560 Wilshire Boulevard, Suite 500, Beverly Hills, CA 90212

Models

Elite Modeling Agency, 111 E. 22nd Street, New York, NY 10010

Ford Models Inc. 334 E. 59th Street, New York, NY 10022

Autograph collector groups and organizations and hobby periodicals are also useful sources of addresses. Not all areas of the country have local autograph collecting groups, but national groups such as the Universal Autograph Collectors Club (UACC) are excellent sources for hobby information. The UACC, with 2000 members in thirty countries, is the largest autograph organization in the world. The club's journal, *The Pen and Quill*, is published six times a year and features articles in all fields of collecting. The publication also includes addresses and is sent to all members. Additionally, the organization sponsors autograph shows all over the world and periodically publishes low-cost reference works that are available to its members. Annual membership fees are as follows: United States $22, Canada/Mexico $25, all other countries $36. A lifetime individual membership is available for $600. The organization can be contacted at P.O. Box 6181, Washington, DC 20044.

Hobby publications such as *Autograph Collector, Autograph Times, Sports Collectors Digest, Today's Collector, Goldmine, The Autograph Review, Boxing Collectors' News, Collecting,* and *Kovels Sports Collectibles* are just a few of the many publications useful to the celebrity autograph collector. In addition to informative articles, some of these periodicals include addresses. Many of these publications also include advertisements from individuals who sell address lists. These lists typically vary in quality and there are no guarantees for accuracy.

Some address books are very useful to collectors: *The Celebrity Directory*, published by Axiom Information Resources; *The Sports Americana Baseball Address List*, published by Edgewater Book Co.; and *The Address Book: How to Reach Anyone Who's Anyone*, published by HarperPerennial. Be sure you purchase the most current edition, as

Hobby publications such as Autograph Collector, Autograph Times, Sports Collectors Digest, Today's Collector, Goldmine, The Autograph Review, Collecting, *and* Kovel's Sports Collectibles *are just a few of the many useful publications available to the celebrity autograph collector.*

these types of books require periodic updates to guarantee the accuracy of their addresses. Books such as the annual *People Entertainment Almanac*, published by Little Brown and Company, and *The All Sport Autograph Guide* and *The Complete Guide to Boxing Collectibles*, published by Krause Publications, also include some celebrity addresses.

Computer software and computer networks are another option. The PhoneDisc, created by Digital Directory Assistance, Inc., has been extremely useful to me. I purchased both their two Residential CD-ROMs and their single Business CD-ROM for use on my Apple Macintosh Performa 550. Since many celebrities choose to have unlisted phone numbers, phone disks are not always useful for discovering their addresses, but the disks are good for finding obscure "overnight" celebrities or misplaced entertainers of the past. Access to addresses on the Net or through other networks depends on the source. My advise here is U.R.ON.YOUROWN.COM.

The final step, should all these methods fail, is to begin a very comprehensive search similar to that investigators use to find a missing person. It begins by creating a missing person profile.

Missing Person Profile

1. A photograph(s) of the individual you are looking for: photos from various angles are helpful
2. Full Name: include nicknames
3. Gender: male or female
4. Vital statistics: date of birth and social security number
5. Physical description: height, weight, eye color, etc.
6. Descent: white, black, Latin, etc.
7. Last three addresses, if known
8. Education level: grammar, high, college, etc.
9. Occupation or profession
10. Organizations: business, labor, etc.
11. Religion: denomination and frequency of attendance
12. Military record, if applicable
13. Licenses: driver, pilot, etc.
14. Hobbies
15. Reasons for search: health crisis, financial crisis, etc.
16. Friends and relatives
17. Possible locations

In your search you will use the postal service, the telephone and public records. For this reason access to a missing person's profile is extremely useful. The two most essential items on your profile are the subject's complete name, spelled correctly, and date of birth, followed by the subject's place of birth and social security number. Because entire books have been written about the process of finding missing people, and because it is unlikely that you will need to go this far to find a celebrity address, I will just briefly outline some of the services available to you.

Missing Person Search Outline

Or How to Find an Elusive Address

Library/Public Records

1. Contact via U.S. Mail a public or private agency that might have access to the missing person's address
2. Contact former friends and neighbors

3. Search telephone directories or telephone directory software
4. Utilize crisscross directories, such as Haines and similar software, to find out the names, addresses and phone numbers of every former occupant of a particular address

City Records

5. Reference all services available to you at public, university and law libraries
6. Reference all services available to you at area law enforcement agencies
7. Research city/county permits and licenses, typically at city hall

County Records

8. Try your local sheriff office for information (usually difficult to obtain)
9. Research birth, death and marriage records
10. Research real and unsecured property records
11. Research former business names
12. Research all court records, family, civil, criminal, etc.
13. Check voter registration records
14. Consult public welfare information
15. Review worker's compensation records
16. Check all miscellaneous permits and licenses

State Records

17. Consult driver/vehicle records
18. Consult corporate records
19. Consult state police and highway patrol records
20. Consult state permits and licenses
21. Consult the state sales tax board

Federal Records

22. Utilize the Freedom of Information Act and the Privacy Act where applicable
23. Consult the Social Security Administration
24. Utilize U.S. Postal Service. If you send $1 and the last known address to the attention of that specific postmaster, a forwarding address will be provided to you. This is only the case if it has been less than six months since the person has left the address.
25. Consult U.S. District Court records
26. Consult bankruptcy court records
27. Take advantage of Military Locator Services
28. Don't forget about the National Cartographic Information Center, Internal Revenue Service, Interstate Commerce Commission, Bureau of Alcohol, Tobacco and Firearms, Government Printing Office, Federal Aviation Administration and other government agencies, where applicable

Alternative Channels

29. Catalogs and mailing lists, unions and associations, insurance records, all maintain addresses

Note: These channels vary in the levels of information they can provide. Many will also vary significantly in their level of cooperation. Some channels may require you to provide specific information, fill out forms, or possibly pay a fee. Detailed information regarding the proper procedure may be obtained at the specific agency or possibly a public library.

Your final option is to hire a private investigator or nationwide search service to do your work for you. At this point you may have to ask yourself if the celebrity address is really worth the cost associated with these services.

Chapter 6

Celebrity Autograph Values

Finding out how much your autographed Arnold Schwarzenegger photograph is worth usually means turning to a certain page in a price guide, but understanding just how that value was determined requires a greater understanding of the hobby. The key factors that influence the value of autographed celebrity memorabilia are condition, supply, demand, form, and source. For those individuals in the business of buying and selling autographed celebrity memorabilia, understanding these factors is essential to success. To a novice or casual collector they are important, but far less significant than pure enjoyment of the hobby.

A Brief History of Celebrity Autograph Values

There is a demand for celebrity autographs and there are individuals willing to sell them: therefore a market exists. Where there is a market, there is a need to understand value, by both the buyer and seller. Most of us started collecting because of an interest in a particular area, occupation or individual. Collecting autographs gave us an opportunity to share in the achievements of the celebrities we cherished, and of course it was proof that we really did have contact with the person or persons we admired.

During the 1950s most autograph collectors weren't interested in values, because many of their autographs were obtained in person and the value was in the moment, not on the paper. Television brought many of our heroes to life and allowed collectors to finally see for themselves, from a different perspective, the faces of Joe DiMaggio, Bob Hope, Judy Garland, and Groucho Marx. Television became a maternity ward for Hollywood's next biggest and brightest stars.

The mark of a great television show can be found in the depth of its impact on our culture and in its uncanny ability to portray a particular era. Characters such as Archie Bunker and Hawkeye Pierce take on bigger-than-life importance and the actors who play them are catapulted into almost instant celebrity status, guaranteeing a steep value for their autographs.

Fifty Unforgettable Television Shows

Show	Autograph Comments
The Adventures of Superman	A George Reeves signature can command $900
All in the Family	All cast members good signers except O'Connor
All My Children	Limited market
The Andy Griffith Show	Griffith, Knotts and Howard are not great signers
The Beverly Hillbillies	Donna Douglas is the best signer
Bonanza	Authentic Green, Blocker and Landon photo is worth $475
Burns & Allen	Burns was always a great signer, a Grace autograph can run $35

Show	Autograph Comments
Candid Camera	Funt doesn't sign much anymore
Charlie's Angels	Kate Jackson is the best signer from Charlie's team
Cheers	Danson is a notorious non-signer: good luck
The Cosby Show	Good shot at an entire cast photo here, all are good
Dallas	Some evasive signers here: Hagman is the key
The Dick Van Dyke Show	Moore is the key
Dragnet	Webb is the key, but he was never real responsive
Dynasty	Some evasive signers here
The Ed Sullivan Show	Sullivan was always good for an autographed photo
Gunsmoke	Arness has always been a great signer
Hill Street Blues	Some elusive signers here
The Honeymooners	A classic cast photo can command $300 to $350
Jeopardy	Make your request in the form of an answer
Leave It to Beaver	The Beaver still signs: you can get about $60 for The Cleavers
Mary Hartman, Mary Hartman	Louise Lasser is excellent
The Mary Tyler Moore Show	MTM has never been an easy signature, worth only $10
M*A*S*H	Stiers is a notorious non-signer, all others good for 1
Miami Vice	Both Johnson and Thomas are often unresponsive
Mission: Impossible	Graves signs in person only, rest of cast good
The Monkees	Nesmith is the key signature here: you can buy the others
Nightline	Koppel is the man, often unresponsive by mail
N.Y.P.D. Blue	A good chance at getting everyone here
The Odd Couple	Klugman is key; Randall is great
The Rockford Files	Garner is an excellent signer
Roseanne	Not a chance here, save your stamps
Rowan & Martin's Laugh-In	Authentic signature on photo by both, about $80
St. Elsewhere	Some elusive signers here
Saturday Night Live	Belushi and Radner deceased, Aykroyd tough
Seinfeld	Seinfeld responds with facsimile-signed photos
Sesame Street	We all miss Jim Henson
77 Sunset Strip	Edd Byrnes requests $19.95 per photo. Fat chance!
The Simpsons	Groenig tough, responds with information only
60 Minutes	Original cast-autographed photo tough to get
Star Trek	Shatner and Nimoy good for facsimiles only
thirtysomething	Some elusive signers here
TODAY	Tough to get existing cast to respond
The Tonight Show	Leno almost as bad as Carson was at responding
The Twilight Zone	Rod Serling will cost you about $100
Walt Disney Presents	One of the most sought after signatures, worth about $1,000
The X-Files	Anderson and Duchovny supply facsimiles and ghosts only
You Bet Your Life	Groucho on a photo about $250
Your Show of Shows	Sid Caesar often unresponsive

Although the attendance of some sports waned during the 1960s, it began to flourish again in the 1970s. The word "athlete" was slowly being replaced by the term "sports personality" or "sports celebrity." The growing interest in professional athletics prompted an increased interest in collectibles, especially sports trading cards and autographs. Companies began to wonder what new products they could sell into this market and became more interested in the appeal of the sports celebrity to sell products. We knew "Broadway Joe" Namath could throw a football, but could he convince those men watching television to buy a brand of shaving cream?

The competitive cable market, new and affordable satellite equipment, and a seemingly insatiable appetite for this visual medium were the motivation for the birth of many new networks, including FOX, ESPN and numerous others. Increased competition meant higher fees for the rights to broadcast certain events, especially professional sports. And of course there were the celebrities, who felt that they too were entitled to a share of the revenues. Multimillion dollar contracts soon became necessary to ensure a team's "sports celebrities" would remain in town for another season or a particular character wouldn't disappear from an actor's repertoire.

Professional athletes turned celebrities were turning up in magazine advertisements, syndicated television shows, commercials, shopping networks and even movies. The growth in sports trading cards, specifically baseball, led to the increased number of sports trading card shows. These shows soon found themselves expanding to include autograph guests to boost revenues and attendance. The additional cost of a sports celebrity's attendance meant that a promoter was often forced to charge a fee for each autograph. For many celebrities, the greater exposure was accompanied by an increase in autograph requests. Many collectors of sports autographs branched out into other fields such as entertainment, politics and music.

Major league baseball was the first of the four major sports to combine all the necessary ingredients to entice autograph collectors. For a market to be viable collectors need access to their subjects, at the ballpark or at home (*Baseball Address List, No.1*); a cost-effective acquisition method, through dealers, in person or mail; a price guide to validate an autograph's value (numerous sources); a way to confirm a signature's authenticity (*The Baseball Autograph Handbook, No.2*); and a vehicle for monitoring the market (*Sports Collectors Digest*).

As the market has matured, in-person access to many major players has been reduced, while indirect sources such as satellite shopping networks and product catalogs have expanded. You may not be able to obtain a free Cal Ripken signature at the ballpark, but at least you still have the opportunity to obtain an autograph, despite the purchase price. Although the cost of sending an autograph request through the mail has doubled since 1980, many celebrities still respond, making it a cost-effective method of acquiring signatures. Also fortunate for collectors is that autograph values, for the most part,

Autographed baseballs have led the sports memorabilia market in price increases.

have kept pace with the market (see chart below). At least this way you know that all the time and effort you put into acquiring a signature will probably prove to be worthwhile. Another refreshing factor is that the issue of authenticity is constantly being addressed in the market. Never before have so many facsimile signatures been available to collectors for comparison purposes to confirm an item's authenticity.

Baseball Autograph Value Comparison

Player	1983			1993		
	Cut	Photo	Ball	Cut	Photo	Ball
Ted Williams	3.50	12.00	27.00	20.00	65.00	145.00
Mickey Mantle	6.00	13.00	40.00	20.00	60.00	90.00
Whitey Ford	1.00	3.00	11.00	4.00	15.00	25.00
Al Kaline	.75	3.50	10.00	3.00	14.00	20.00
Stan Musial	.75	3.50	11.00	8.00	25.00	50.00

Note: All prices courtesy of *Sports Collectors Digest*. Prices were averaged from randomly selected advertisements appearing in issues from the time period noted.

The Definition of Value

Value itself has two different meanings to collectors. Many collectors perceive the word value to mean whatever makes a thing more or less desirable or worthwhile. These celebrity autograph collectors can't put a monetary value on their collection, because there is no monetary equivalent to the satisfaction they have derived from building it. It is this definition that I hear most from satisfied collectors and hobbyists who still have fun.

The other definition some collectors use can be called "estimated worth." These collectors, or more accurately, business people, can readily estimate the fair market value for every item in their collection. If you view your collection with very little emotional attachment, if there is little or no remorse attached to the sale of your Hugh Grant autographed photograph, then your definition of value is indeed "estimated worth." In either case, your definition of value is going to affect how you collect autographed celebrity memorabilia.

Collectors who are concerned with an item's estimated value can't wait for next month's or year's price guide to come out, to track the level of appreciation in their collections. They are interested in their subjects' face value: not the human emotion involved in an athletic triumph or a beautiful performance, but the dollar level attached to the achievement. This is the collector who turns the stomach of many professional athletes and some celebrities, for it is this opportunist who is the first to run to the nearest autograph store to dispose of recently acquired celebrity autographs. A friend of mine recently told me why Pittsburgh Penguins star Mario Lemieux has been so reluctant to sign trading cards. Apparently Lemieux gave his autograph to a young child at rink side, only to watch the boy immediately turn to his friend and ask $10 for the autographed hockey card. Unfortunately this type of collector has become an unavoidable part of the hobby.

The collector seldom reviews a price guide who defines value as having inherent worth. This hobbyist may in fact not even own a price guide, or if so, only to aid in the reluctant task of determining the collection's price level as required by the insurance policy. For this collector there is no price that can be put on an autographed copy of *The Rainmaker* by John Grisham, and it's worth it to drive four hours just to attend one of his book signings. This collector owns every single Grisham novel, considering

Grisham to be the best author of his time, and waits in line for two hours before having the opportunity to ask Grisham for his signature. When the author complies, the hobbyist responds with an unforgettable smile. For this collector no monetary value can be attached to this autograph, because there is no replacement for the moment.

Unfortunately celebrities are unable, in most cases, to identify which type of collector is approaching them. As a group we need to put more emphasis on the person, rather than the money.

The Factors That Influence Value

Not all collectors are fortunate enough to have a professional team, major concert hall or museum located in the city where they live. These collectors are forced to acquire most celebrity autographs indirectly, sometimes from dealers. In order to efficiently purchase celebrity autographs from dealers it is necessary to have an understanding of value. Understanding the key factors that influence value will help prevent you from spending too much for an item.

There are five key factors that determine the value of a celebrity autograph: condition; scarcity, or supply; demand; form, or what you have signed; and source, or from whom you purchase.

Condition

The condition of an autographed celebrity collectible is considered by most dealers to be the paramount factor affecting an item's value. When assessing the value of an autographed celebrity collectible, both the condition of the signature and the condition of the material that was signed are thoroughly examined. The signature should be bold, clear and unobstructed by any portion of the material that was signed or any other signatures that appear with it. The material that was signed should reflect, as much as possible, the original state of that object. The only exception would be some costumes and game/event equipment, which naturally would show some indications of wear. For those collectors of autographed game-worn equipment or costumes, it is important to understand that severe damage to the item, such as uniform tears or large pieces missing from certain items, can detract from the value of the autographed item.

It is not unusual for some autographed items to reflect certain aging characteristics. The aging characteristics of paper-based collectibles are probably the most familiar to collectors: they include light stains, discoloration due to fading, and inconsistent wear due to folding. Sports equipment, such as hockey sticks and baseball bats, will typically exhibit discoloration due to the aging of the finish applied during final stages of production. Jerseys will exhibit loose threads and some fading. Certain aging characteristics are anticipated by collectors and thus have little to no effect on value. Any flaw that is not part of the normal aging process will have a negative impact on the value of the piece. For example, excessive wear due to mishandling of autographed baseballs, costumes or playbills will detract from the value of those pieces.

The type of ink and the writing device used for an autograph can effect an item's condition and thus its value. All material has a level of porosity: this is the degree to which fluids, air or light can pass through or into them. The higher the level of porosity the greater the chance of deterioration in the item. Unfinished wood and certain fabrics are very porous, so that when certain inks are applied to them the fluid spreads into the surface. This is why so many collectors of autographed baseballs prefer ballpoint pen signatures over those produced by porous tip markers. Many inks react negatively to the surfaces they are in contact with, causing dramatic discoloration over a short period of time.

Scarcity or Supply

The scarcity or supply of a form of autographed celebrity memorabilia will typically have a reciprocal effect on the demand for the piece. This is particularly true of the signatures of deceased individuals and many of the pioneers in certain fields. In the sport of baseball, the autograph of Babe Ruth has always been in great demand. Even though he signed frequently, the supply continues to be insufficient to meet the demand of the collector. Although "Shoeless" Joe Jackson is not a member of the Baseball Hall of Fame, his signature is highly sought, not only because of the mystique created by recent movies depicting him, but because he was considered an illiterate for many years and didn't learn to sign his name until the later part of his life.

The Jacksons owned a liquor store in Greenville, South Carolina. When accompanied by his wife, Joe would never sign anything. If forced he signed an X. On the occasions when he was left alone, his wife would leave a piece of paper with his name written on it, just in case he needed to sign for merchandise or possibly an autograph. Jackson would essentially draw his autograph, sometimes taking close to a minute to complete it. Today the autograph of "Shoeless" Joe Jackson is considered the most valuable sports autograph in history. The first Jackson clipped signature that entered the market was sold for $23,000. A few years ago an 8" x 10" photograph of "Shoeless" Joe sold for $28,000 at a sale held by Odyssey Auctions of Corona, California.

Scarcity can often be difficult to determine. Many times the market will move based on a rumor and a celebrity's signature will immediately skyrocket in value, even if there has been no confirmation of the information. A few years ago a collector I knew began buying Stan Musial autographed baseballs at twice the current market price because he heard a rumor that Musial wasn't going to sign baseballs anymore. The rumor was incorrect and the collector ended up spending an awful lot of money foolishly.

Fluctuations in supply are often temporary, as is the case with most celebrities who are actively involved in their field. The demand for the signatures of the field's biggest stars or contributors builds during certain seasons, and is typically met during the off season when many celebrities are more accessible. Many entertainers sign during tours, but less frequently. There are also occasions where a dealer has purchased a large number of autographed checks or documents from an estate and offered them for resale. This flooding of material will fill current demand and drive values down for that type of autographed item. In this case it may take many years for the market to replenish the demand and drive values upward.

In the sport of baseball, the autograph of Babe Ruth has always been in great demand. Even though he signed frequently, the supply continues to be insufficient to meet the demand of the collector. Babe Ruth signatures run from $725 - $900.

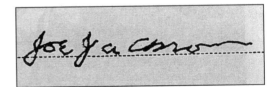

Would you pay $23,000 for this signature? Today the autograph of "Shoeless" Joe Jackson is considered the most valuable sports autograph in history.

Demand

The current demand for many celebrity autographs has been so strong that athletes, entertainers

This ALS (Autograph Letter Signed) by author Ernest Hemingway sold for $5,000. An ALS is probably the most desirable form for collectors of historical autographs.

and musicians have had to resort to facsimile (stamped), secretarial, or machine-signed (autopen) autographs. The massive number of requests sent to celebrities like Michael Jordan, Tim Allen, Jay Leno, and Roseanne, if answered personally, would leave little time for their own everyday needs. To reduce the response time to signature requests made by mail, some celebrities will only sign one item per person. This technique is used by many celebrities, including Alan Alda, Shirley Temple-Black, and Norman Mailer. In this way they help meet current market demand without frustrating collectors or resorting to unauthentic responses. The casts of some television shows, such as *Beverly Hills 90210*, will respond to requests for autographs with 4" x 6" color postcards that bear facsimile signatures on the back. Although collectors are grateful that their requests are acknowledged, this method only serves to increase demand for authentic signatures.

Significant achievements such as reaching a career milestone or winning an Emmy, Oscar or Golden Globe can immediately affect demand. An example of this is certainly Tom Hanks, who was accessible to collectors for many years both through the mail and in person. It wasn't until he won an Oscar for best actor in *Philadelphia* (1993) that anyone saw a noticeable increase in the demand for his signature. This level of interest will remain constant until all public demand has been met.

Changes in a celebrity's popularity, for whatever reason, affect demand. Usually such changes are triggered by a poor performance, poor judgment or career-threatening injuries, but they can also be brought about by an event that the public considers distasteful. For example, Tonya Harding, Paul Reubens, Mike Tyson, and Hugh Grant have all seen the demand for their signature reduced because they have not met the public's expectations. For the contrarian in the autographed celebrity memorabilia market this is the best time to buy these celebrities' signatures, because they are probably at the lowest possible price. Because these demand changes are often cyclical, many of these celebrities still have the potential for a tremendous year.

Immediately after a celebrity's death, the autographs he or she left behind increase in value, often commanding two or three times their former price. When an unpredictable circumstance claims a celebrity's life, demand can be enormous, as exemplified by the reaction of collectors following the deaths of Natalie Wood, River Phoenix and Brandon Lee.

Form

An item's value is determined in part by the type of material the celebrity signs and its relevance to the celebrity. This is why a Sylvester Stallone-autographed boxing glove is worth more than Sly's signature on a photograph. This is not to say that you can't be creative, and have a baseball signed by Kevin Costner, Charlie Sheen and Michael Jordan, for instance, but try to prevent yourself from having foolish or unrelated items autographed. How many times have we all seen unprepared fans flock to request the signature of a celebrity on a napkin? I have never in all my years of collecting ever met a collector of napkins, either the dinner or cocktail variety. If you're going to collect autographed celebrity memorabilia, try to choose a form that is appealing and accepted by the majority of others already participating in the hobby. While popular forms of collecting may be less creative, they offer a greater range of acquisition possibilities.

Baseball collectors generally ly use Official League base-'s for autographs, primarily

This SP (Signed Photograph) of aviator Charles A. Lindbergh went for $1,500. The SP is probably the most popular form for autographs in the entertainment field.

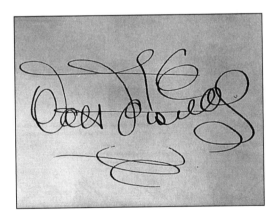

Walt Disney's signature is one of the most sought after at $1,000.

56

because they are datable and subject to less authentication scrutiny. Additionally, Official League baseballs are identical to those used by the professionals. Because this has become an accepted form of collecting, Official League autographed baseballs have greater value than other varieties. When an autographed sports collectible can be dated the collector's concern for authenticity is reduced, and the value of that item increases. Collectors of autographed baseballs also prefer single-signature baseballs, or balls with only one autograph on the "sweet spot" or side opposite the name of the league's president, over multiple signature

This DS (Document Signed) by Davy Crockett is worth $7,000.

This signature belonging to inventor Thomas A. Edison sold for $500.

balls. This is why a single-signature baseball from Lou Gehrig is worth more than a baseball with the equivalent Gehrig signature accompanied by the names of Johnny Allen, Frank Crosetti, Bill Dickey and Doc Farrell. In this case, less is more.

Autographed letters containing relevant or even controversial content are highly sought by collectors. A letter from Bob Hope discussing his style of golf is far more intriguing than a simple note thanking someone for an autograph request. Admittedly, most celebrities are not known for their letter-writing prowess, but if you choose to collect these items remember that value is a function of content.

Source

Until recently I have been reluctant to acknowledge that the source of an item could have an impact on its value. Increasing market concerns for authenticity have forced me to reconsider. However, I continue to maintain that the source of a signature has less impact on an autograph's value than any of the factors listed previously. Recently, advertisements in many autograph-collecting periodicals have placed an increased value on in-person signatures. Whether this trend continues or not, it is certainly worth noticing.

When collectors focus more on source, they are willing to pay more to receive proof of authenticity. This kind of collector is not afraid to spend the extra money to purchase an autographed Roger Staubach football directly from the Dallas Cowboys-recognized source for $129.99. Yes, the same item may have cost $40 less from an alternative source, but the collector's level of confidence would have been reduced. In this case, lack of expertise in authentication determined the purchasing source.

One unsavory effect of the increased focus on source is the practice, followed by many larger companies, of intimidating collectors with "forgery fear." Using this marketing tactic these companies hope to convince collectors to purchase their products. Let me state clearly to all collectors that the signature you receive in person, be it at a show or an arena, is of equal if not greater value than a purchase you make from a major autograph memorabilia supplier. Letter of Authenticity or not, if a major company or dealer files for bankruptcy, how much time and money do you think it's going to take to redeem your $79.95 autographed Reggie Jackson baseball because you have authenticity concerns?

A Final Word on Value

Remember, it is not the dealer, celebrity, or promoter who determines value: it is the collector. Your willingness, justifiable or not, to pay a certain price for an autographed celebrity item has an impact on value. While there is little doubt in my mind that an autographed photograph of Bob Hope will eventually increase in value, there is a point at which the collector refuses to purchase an item. You, the collector, make that decision. These major dealers and companies are in business to make money. If they can not get the price they are asking for an autographed item, they have only one alternative: lower it. Stagnant inventory doesn't pay bills or impress investors, but sales do. As my father once told me, "An item is only worth what someone is willing to pay for it."

Autograph Values

Assorted Selected Celebrities and Fields

Celebrity	Signature	LS/DS*	ALS*	SP	Comments
Leonardo Da Vinci	5,750	14,000	35,000	—	Artist
Rembrandt van Rijn	2,750	13,500	38,000	—	Artist
Andrew Wyeth	140	250	—	450	Artist
Roger Chafee	300	—	—	600	Astronaut
Edward White	300	—	—	400	Astronaut
James Lovell, Jr.	20	—	—	35	Astronaut
Samuel L. Clemens (Mark Twain)	725	1,725	4,500	3,750	Author
Ernest M. Hemingway	1,000	2,500	5,000	3,000	Author
Kurt Vonnegut	12	100	125	40	Author
Charles A. Lindbergh	650	1,225	1,425	1,500	Aviator
anfred von Richthofen	700	2,650	5,600	2,800	Aviator

Celebrity	Signature	LS/DS*	ALS*	SP	Comments
Chuck Yeager	15	40	45	30	Aviator
George H. Ruth	725	—	—	3,000	Baseball Player
Lou Gehrig	720	—	—	2,500	Baseball Player
Hank Aaron	10	—	—	40	Baseball Player
Jack Johnson	425	—	—	1,200	Boxer
Jack Dempsey	55	—	—	145	Boxer (heavywt)
Muhammad Ali	15	—	—	50	Boxer
Walt Disney	1,000	2,450	3,500	4,000	Businessman
Henry Ford	1,200	1,700	4,450	2,350	Businessman
Lee Iacocca	6	22	38	30	Businessman
Aaron Burr	340	850	850	—	Vice President
Alexander Hamilton	500	2,100	2,500	—	Cabinet Member
Edmund Muskie	5	15	40	10	Cabinet Member
James Thurber	100	—	—	**500	Cartoonist
Thomas Nast	125	—	—	750	Cartoonist

Celebrity	Signature	LS/DS*	ALS*	SP	Comments
Cathy Guisewhite	5	—	—	20	Cartoonist
Al Capone	1,200	6,000	—	—	Celebrity
Davey Crockett	2,000	7,000	10,300	—	Celebrity
Charles Kuralt	8	20	40	13	Celebrity
Brigham Young	600	1,900	5,000	—	Clergy
Saint Vincent De Paul	475	1,350	4,000	—	Clergy
Billy Graham	12	20	65	50	Clergy
Johann S. Bach	2,800	25,000	38,000	—	Composer
Stephen Foster	1,100	3,500	10,000	—	Composer
John Williams	10	25	50	25	Composer
Hank Williams	450	—	—	900	Country Musician
Patsy Cline	300	—	—	600	Country Musician
Dolly Parton	5	—	—	15	Country Musician
Enrico Caruso	215	450	650	1,200	Entertainer
Gary Cooper	150	250	475	400	Entertainer

Celebrity	Signature	LS/DS*	ALS*	SP	Comments
Tom Hanks	15	17	50	45	Entertainer
Jim Thorpe	2,000	—	—	***6,500	Football Player
Sammy Baugh	65	—	—	300	Football Player
Johnny Unitas	15	—	—	115	Football Player
Walter Hagen	200	—	—	400	Golfer
Bobby Jones	500	—	—	1,600	Golfer
Jack Nicklaus	12	—	—	40	Golfer
Catherine I (Russia)	600	2,150	5,000	—	World Leader
Charles De Gaulle	300	—	1,225	—	World Leader
King Hussein (Jordan)	45	100	400	70	World Leader
Terry Sawchuk	—	—	—	40	Hockey Player
Jacques Plante	—	—	—	30	Hockey Player
Wayne Gretzky	—	—	—	45	Hockey Player
Douglas MacArthur	160	420	850	650	Military
Erwin Rommel	750	1,800	3,300	1,700	Military
William Westmoreland	14	25	70	45	Military

Celebrity	Signature	LS/DS*	ALS*	SP	Comments
Alex. Graham Bell	440	875	2,300	1,300	Science
Thomas A. Edison	500	1,200	2,400	1,300	Science
Carl Sagan	15	35	55	35	Science
Abraham Lincoln	3,000	5,000	10,000	—	U.S. President
John F. Kennedy	850	1,200	2,400	—	U.S. President
Gerald R. Ford	35	200	1,000	125	U.S. President

* = content dependent, ** = sketch, *** = football
LS/DS = letter signed/document signed
ALS = autograph letter signed
SP = signed photograph

Chapter 7

What to Collect?

Oscar Wilde once said, "Consistency is the last refuge of the unimaginative." The creativity in autograph collecting begins with the question, What to collect? As a celebrity autograph collector anything that can be signed is available for your use. Most collectors choose to build their collection around a specific individual, team, field, or type of item that is to be autographed. For example, one collector I know chooses only to collect items autographed by Mario Lemieux, from *Sports Illustrated* covers to golf balls: if it can be signed by the Pittsburgh Penguins Captain, he wants it. Another person I know collects only autographed bats, but doesn't limit himself to a specific occupational field. His collection includes such notables as Wayne Gretzky (hockey), President Clinton (politician), Stephen King (writer), John Glenn (astronaut), and Kevin Costner (actor). Most celebrity autograph collectors, however, tend to concentrate in one field and specialize in one particular type of collectible, such as equipment, 8" x 10" color photographs, or trading cards.

Set a Goal for Yourself

If you are collecting celebrity autographs just to have fun, then don't worry about what to collect. Just enjoy yourself. The fact that you are reading this book, however, indicates that in addition to having fun, you also want to learn more about the hobby. The first step in becoming a serious collector of celebrity autographs is to set a realistic goal for yourself. The key word here is realistic. I've provided two very different examples of collectors' goals.

Collector A collects only handwritten letters from the great writer Edgar Allen Poe. His collection includes:

* A short note responding to information. Cost: $18,500. Purchased from a dealer.
* An envelope addressed in Poe's hand and initialed E.A.P. Cost: $4,500. Purchased from a dealer.

Collector B collects only 8" x 10" autographed color photos of current celebrities. His collection includes:

* Arnold Schwarzenegger. Acquired in person while Arnold was getting out of a car at the gym. The cost of the photo was $3.00. Schwarzenegger did not charge for his signature.
* Steven Seagal. Acquired from a dealer. Cost: $40.00.
* Jim Brown. Wearing his Syracuse University uniform, acquired in person at a local bookstore while Brown was promoting his book *Out Of Bounds*. The cost of the photo was $3.00. Brown did not charge for his signature.

These celebrity autograph collectors have both set goals. Each of them knows that meeting their goal will require dealing with particular standards of availability, cost, acquisition or purchasing time, acquisition or purchasing method, and storage requirements. Both are dedicated collectors, both are having fun, and both are concerned about their collections. Using this example it is very easy to see the advantages and disadvantages each collector faces while trying to meet his or her collecting goal.

Collector A is vice-president of a bank, where he spends over forty hours a week. Because he chooses to collect only documents signed by Edgar Allen Poe, he has restricted purchasing avenues and significant authenticity concerns. Additionally, since he has budgeted only $1,000 a month for collecting, he seldom adds more than two pieces a year to his collection, if he's fortunate enough to find them. As he cannot afford to spend a lot of time on collecting, he buys all of his items through very reputable and experienced dealers. He loves literature, enjoys collecting and believes that he is preserving and building a very valuable collection. His collection is stored in a large safe deposit box at his place of employment at a cost of $65.00 a year.

Collector B is a junior in high school. Because he chooses to collect 8" x 10" autographed color photographs he is not restricted in supply or availability. He purchases about four photographs a week at a cost of $3.00 each. He then mails the photographs to a celebrity, along with an autograph request and a self-addressed stamped envelope. He has been fairly successful at acquiring celebrity signatures this way, but also takes advantage of every opportunity to have a photograph autographed in person. Because he has a part-time job his finances are limited. He does, however, have plenty of free time and doesn't mind waiting in line for an hour for a free signature. Meeting a celebrity is the part of the hobby he enjoys most, and an autographed photograph is a way for him to preserve that moment. He keeps all of his photographs preserved in individual polypropylene sheets in a binder on a shelf in his room. Each sheet cost him $.10 and he paid $6.00 for the binder.

By setting an autograph collecting goal you determine the parameters by which you will collect. The best goal has definable limits, making it easier for you to track your progress, yet is exciting enough to pursue. Below is a list of collecting goals given to me by a group of celebrity autograph collectors.

Collecting Goals

* A single-signed Official League baseball from every living member of the National Baseball Hall of Fame
* An autographed color photo of every living Academy Award Winner
* Autographed vintage cast photos from television's greatest shows
* A complete set of autographs from every astronaut who has walked on the moon

Availability

Building a collection of single-signed Official League baseballs from every living member of the National Baseball Hall of Fame is a realistic pursuit. Official League baseballs manufactured by the Rawlings Sporting Goods Company are in plentiful supply and available to the average collector at a cost of about $8.00 each. Another factor in favor of this goal is that most of the inductees still attend and sign autographs at sports trading card shows. Signing fees are usually in the $10 to $20 range. Trying to find a single-signed baseball from the more reclusive inductees, such as Joe DiMaggio or Sandy Koufax, will prove a greater challenge. Limited availability or supply often means an increased demand, and thus a higher price tag. This is the case with an autographed single-signature baseball from Joe DiMaggio, which now can command around $250. Despite the price of certain autographed baseballs, the goal remains realistic since the supply is still considered plentiful.

This would not be the case with a collector who wished to acquire a single-signature baseball from every member (living and dead) of the National Baseball Hall of Fame.

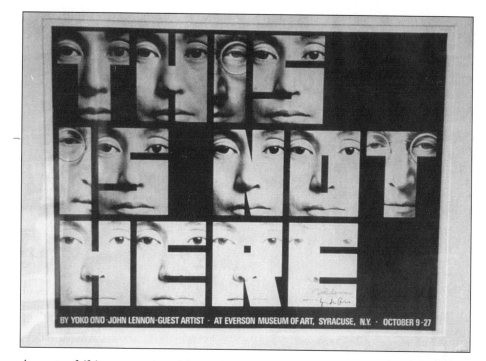

An art exhibit poster signed by John Lennon and Yoko Ono.

Supply is limited for some of the items. The signatures of some members, particularly the pioneers of the sport, are rarely offered for sale on the market in any form. The best examples of this are the signatures of Mickey Welch, Charles Radbourn, Sam Thompson, Tom McCarthy, Addie Joss, Pud Galvin, Buck Ewing and Ed Delahanty. To restrict your goal to this type of item, in this case a single-signature baseball from particular players, would make this task nearly impossible, even for the advanced collector.

Cost

Cost is one factor in determining whether or not a collector's goal is realistic. Before you start collecting, it is extremely important to decide how much money you can afford to spend on the hobby. In addition to signatures,

A guitar signed by the rock group Van Halen.

65

the money you allocate to the hobby will be used for postage, telephone calls, traveling expenses and purchasing everything from storage supplies to reference materials.

The type of object you choose to have autographed may have the greatest impact on the cost of your collection. If you can't afford to collect autographed hockey jerseys, try sticks, and if you can't afford sticks, try photographs.

ITEMS AUTOGRAPHED BY MARIO LEMIEUX

Item	Purchase Price
Signature on piece of paper	$9.00 *
Action Packed postcard	$34.95
Penguins logo golf ball	$34.95
8" x 10" color photo	$39.95
All-Star ticket	$39.95
Official baseball	$49.95
Baseball cap	$49.95
Framed crest and ticket	$99.95
Sports Illustrated issue	$109.95
Sporting News cover	$109.95
Authentic hockey stick	$169.95
Authentic helmet	$229.95
Authentic hockey glove	$314.95
Lithograph stick	$349.95
Authentic jersey	$369.95
Official skates	$895.95

Source: Penguins Authentic Memorabilia - Collector's edition
* Not available in catalog

Acquisition Time

Your collecting goal determines how quickly you can add items to your collection. Remember Collector A, who seeks only handwritten documents from Edgar Allen Poe and is fully aware of the rarity of such items. He understands that few if any items will appear on the market during a given year. Due to the limited availability of such items, Collector A does not have the option of just picking up the phone and purchasing from a major dealer, even though he may have the money. Instead he may have to wait years for such an item to surface in an advertisement or auction. During that same time period Collector B may have added one hundred new color 8"x 10" photographs to his collection.

Cost also has a major impact on acquisition time. Do you purchase an 8" x 10" autographed color photograph of Julia Roberts from a major dealer for $75.00, or do you wait outside a major movie studio, where you know she's shooting a motion picture, in hopes of having her sign something of yours? If you don't have $75.00 to spend and you do have hours to wait outside the studio, the alternative is clear.

If money is not a factor, however, and you have chosen a common type of item to be autographed, such as a photograph or index card, your acquisition is usually just a phone call away.

Acquisition Method

Hobbyists can add to their collections directly, by in-person autograph requests, or indirectly, through mail requests, trading or purchasing from dealers. Lack of proximity is usually the factor that limits in-person requests. If you do not live in a town or city that is frequented by the type of celebrities whose signatures you collect, then indirect acquisition modes are a logical route.

Most collectors choose indirect methods. Depending upon the type of material you collect, certain methods may not be cost effective and may involve a high degree of risk. For example, if you collect authentic NFL football helmets, manufactured by Riddell, you may not want to take the risk of mailing your helmet to a player to have it autographed, for fear of having it lost or damaged. An alternative would be to purchase the helmet already autographed, or wait for an opportunity to have it signed in person. The other type of risk associated with indirect sources is forgery. Unless a collector actually sees an item being signed, he or she can never really be sure of its authenticity.

Expertise may also restrict collectors from purchasing various items. If you collect only vintage Hollywood actor and actress autographs, then you may want to use an expert to purchase some of the key autographs for you.

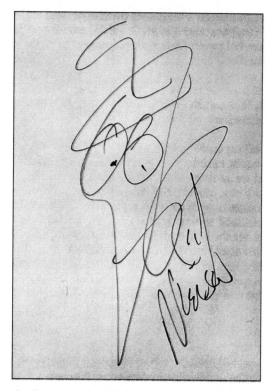

A drawing by Rick Nielson of the rock group Cheap Trick.

Storage Requirements

Collectors often overlook storage requirements when they decide on their goals. Certain collectibles, such as paper-based products, must be stored properly to avoid environmental damage. This may require collectors to purchase certain types of expensive storage materials. Other collectibles, such as football helmets and hockey sticks, are very cumbersome and difficult to store. Living in an apartment or home with restricted space can quickly alter a collector's goal.

A collector I know once said, "If it doesn't fit in a safe deposit box, I don't collect it." This collector's concern was obviously safety. The more valuable the item, the greater concern for its protection. Protection also comes at a cost: safe deposit box fees range from $50 to $200 annually, depending upon size and availability.

Enjoyment

Choosing a realistic goal for collecting celebrity autographs will prolong your enjoyment of the hobby. Meeting your goal can give you a tremendous feeling of satisfaction and sense of completeness. You will also find that those collectors who have realistic goals also have very cost-effective collections. These collectors have remained focused on the task at hand and have wasted little time and money on unrelated material. Those collectors without goals often accumulate haphazard, overpriced and unrelated collections.

Enjoy what you collect and remember: Try to find gratification in the pursuit of collecting celebrity autographs, not just in the monetary rewards that may come your way.

Autographs can be obtained from the following sources:

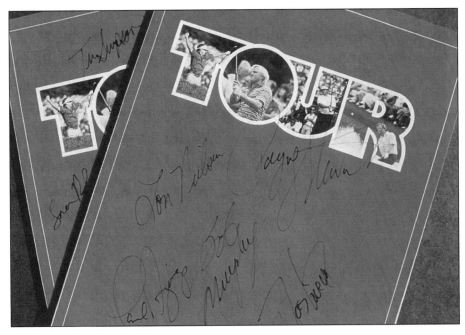

Contracts. These contracts came from entertainment booking agencies.

Official programs. This one depicts a golf tour.

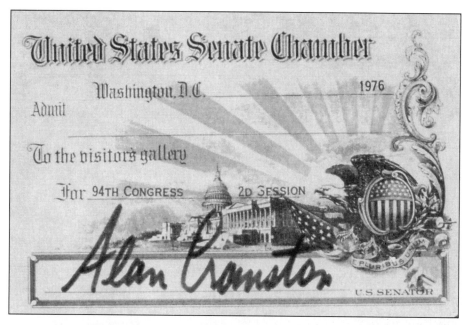

Official passes. These are examples of U.S. Senate and Supreme Court chamber cards.

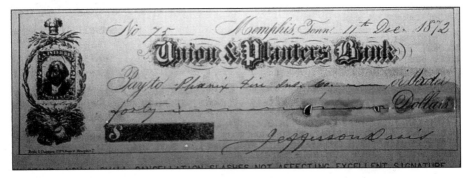

BERLIN, 20. August 1941

ADOLF HITLER

Mein lieber Mölders,

möchte Ihnen, sowie Ihrer werten Frau Gemahlin auf diesem
Wege, nochmals meinen besten Dank, für die mir erwiesene
Gastfreundschaft bekunden.

mit deutschem Gruss

Documents and correspondence. Here is a letter dated 8/20/41 signed by Adolf Hitler.

No. 75   Memphis, Tenn. 11th Dec. 1872

Union & Planters Bank

Pay to Phœnix Fire Ins. Co.   or Order

forty   Dollars

Jefferson Davis

Bank checks. This one is signed by Jefferson Davis, who was President of the Confederacy. The check is dated December 11, 1872.

A leather jacket auto-graphed by the members of The Rolling Stones.

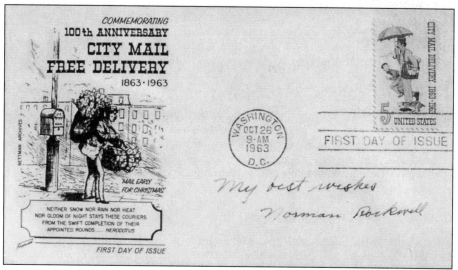

Artist Norman Rockwell.

What to Collect?

ARTISTS AND PHOTOGRAPHERS

Clipped signatures, index cards, autograph album pages, postcards, business cards, canceled checks, contracts and documents, typed letters, handwritten letters, photographs, books, cachets and commemorative envelopes, posters (specifically acknowledging exhibits, signed reproductions, and signed original work)

ASTRONAUTS

Clipped signatures, index cards, autograph album pages, postcards, business cards, canceled checks, contracts and documents, typed letters, handwritten letters, NASA-issued photographs (both individual and crew), books, cachets and commemorative envelopes, and posters

AUTHORS

Clipped signatures, index cards, autograph album pages, postcards, business cards, canceled checks, contracts and documents, typed letters, handwritten letters, photographs, books, cachets and commemorative envelopes, signed editions (sought after are first editions), uncorrected proofs, limited editions, book plates, and first page type scripts (the very first page of a classic, typed)

AVIATORS

Clipped signatures, index cards, autograph album pages, postcards (especially with their plane), business cards, canceled checks, contracts and documents, typed letters, handwritten letters, photographs, books, and cachets and commemorative envelopes

BASEBALL NOTABLES

Baseballs, bats, game jerseys, practice jerseys, pants, socks, cleats, T-shirts, caps, jackets, gloves (batting and fielding), sweatbands, helmets, home plates, pitching rubbers, bases, lineup cards, catcher's equipment, index cards, tickets, schedules, programs, yearbooks, media guides, trading cards, postcards (especially HOF), magazines, photographs, artwork, posters, newspapers, books, advertisements, cachets and commemorative envelopes, pennants, dolls and figurines, clipped signatures, autograph album pages, contracts and documents, typed letters, handwritten letters and assorted souvenirs

BOXERS

Clipped signatures, index cards, autograph album pages, postcards (especially early exhibits), business cards, canceled checks, contracts and documents, typed letters, handwritten letters, photographs, books, cachets and commemorative envelopes, fight posters, trading cards, *The Ring* or *LIFE* magazine covers, bag gloves, fight gloves, commemorative gloves, fight press kits, jump rope, speed bag, ring corner posts, robe, trunks, head gear, and shoes

BUSINESS LEADERS AND FINANCIERS

Clipped signatures, index cards, autograph album pages, postcards (especially with products), business cards (very popular), canceled checks, contracts and documents, typed letters, handwritten letters, photographs, books, stock certificates, currency (although it's illegal), related products and cachets and commemorative envelopes

CERNAN SALUTES FLAG AT APOLLO 17 LANDING SITE

Astronaut Gus Cernan signed this photograph commemorating Apollo 17's landing.

Author Charles Dickens.

A photo of the crew, and autographs of two of the crew members of the B-29 bomber Enola Gay, which dropped the bomb on Hiroshima.

Signed by the First Pilot and the First Passenger

Chas. W. Furnas. First passenger flown in a plane.

VIA AIR MAIL

Capt. Charles Jelleff Wood,

C/o Miss Ellen A. Wood,

RIDGEVILLE,

Ind.

Aviator Orville Wright's signature.

An autograph collector's wall of signed photographs from baseball notables.

A collector's display of autographed baseball bats. (Can we explain why some of these are signed by non-baseball personalities like Fran Tarkenton and Mario Andretti?)

Boxer George Foreman.

Popcorn entrepreneur Orville Redenbacher, with other noted businessmen.

An autographed photo of President Franklin D. Roosevelt and Cabinet members.

A signed drawing by illustrator James Montgomery Flagg, famous for his rendition of the "Uncle Sam Wants You" poster.

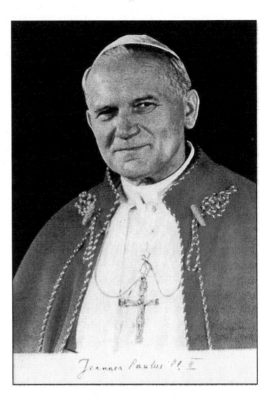

Signed photographs of Pope John Paul II (facsimile) and Bishop Desmond Tutu.

FROM THE ANGLICAN ARCHBISHOP OF CAPE TOWN
The Most Reverend Desmond M. Tutu, D.D. F.K.C. — ☎PHONE: (021) 761-2531
4193

BISHOPSCOURT CLAREMONT ⬡

17.03.93

Mark Baker
P.O. Box 2492
Liverpool, NY 13089
USA

Dear Mark Baker

The Archbishop th
has asked me to
and his good wis

Yours sincerely

Lavinia Browne
Secretary

Thanks Mark — God
Bless
Desmon
back 93

Autographs from composers Leonard Bernstein and Henry Mancini.

An autograph from country music performer/musician Charlie Daniels.

An autograph of magician and escape artist Harry Houdini.

A signed photograph reading "Thanks for the Memory" from entertainer Bob Hope (facsimile).

An autograph from Dallas Cowboys running back Emmitt Smith.

A favorite of mine, King Hussein I of Jordan.

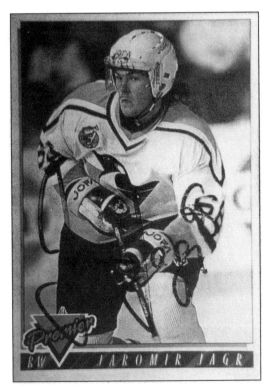

Hockey player Jaromir Jagr, always responsive to autograph requests.

A signed photo from the "Wizard of Menlo Park" inventor Thomas A. Edison.

IEEE TRANSACTIONS ON   R-153

ELECTRON DEVICES

The Path to the Conception of the Junction Transistor

WILLIAM SHOCKLEY, FELLOW, IEEE

JULY 1976   VOLUME ED-23   NUMBER 7   pp. 597-620

A PUBLICATION OF THE IEEE ELECTRON DEVICES SOCIETY

A signed cover page of a scientific research article written by scientist William Shockley.

83

Autographs of U.S. military leaders.

Autographs from pro golfers Arnold Palmer, Jack Nicklaus and Sam Snead.

A collection of autographs received from state governors.

Signatures of former U.S. Presidents Richard Nixon, Gerald Ford, Lyndon B. Johnson, Jimmy Carter and First Lady "Lady Bird" Johnson.

CABINET MEMBERS AND U.S. VICE PRESIDENTS

Clipped signatures, index cards, autograph album pages, postcards, business cards, canceled checks, contracts and documents, typed letters (official stationery), handwritten letters (official stationery), photographs (especially signed cabinet shots), books, cachets and commemorative envelopes, campaign posters, campaign flyers, bumper stickers, buttons, and hats

CARTOONISTS AND ILLUSTRATORS

Clipped signatures, index cards, autograph album pages, postcards, business cards, canceled checks, contracts and documents, typed letters, handwritten letters, photographs, books, cachets and commemorative envelopes, posters, signed reproductions, animation art (original production cels), and signed original work, especially of key characters and original strip art

CLERGY

Clipped signatures, index cards, autograph album pages, postcards, canceled checks, contracts and documents, typed letters, handwritten letters, photographs, books (especially religious works like the Bible), cachets and commemorative envelopes, posters (religious), flyers, and prayer cards

COMPOSERS

Clipped signatures, index cards, autograph album pages, postcards, business cards, canceled checks, contracts and documents, typed letters, handwritten music and letters, photographs, books, cachets and commemorative envelopes, posters (musical), albums, compact discs, sheet music and instruments

COUNTRY MUSIC

Clipped signatures, index cards, autograph album pages, postcards, business cards, canceled checks, contracts and documents, typed letters, handwritten music and letters, photographs, books, cachets and commemorative envelopes, posters (musical), albums, compact discs, sheet music, boots, hats, fan club items, instruments and song related items

ENTERTAINERS

Clipped signatures, index cards, autograph album pages, postcards, business cards, canceled checks, contracts and documents, typed letters, handwritten music and letters, photographs (especially cast photos), programs, playbills, tickets, books, cachets and commemorative envelopes, posters (movie posters and music-related), albums, compact discs, sheet music, costumes, artwork, fan club items, instruments, movie related items, song related items, and scripts

FAMOUS PEOPLE (miscellaneous occupations)

Clipped signatures, index cards, autograph album pages, postcards, business cards, canceled checks, contracts and documents, typed letters, handwritten letters, photographs, books, cachets and commemorative envelopes, posters, any common or unusual item related to that specific individual

FOOTBALL PLAYERS

Footballs, game jerseys, practice jerseys, pants, socks, cleats, T-shirts, hats, helmets, jackets, gloves, sweatbands, headbands, down markers, goal posts, replica uniforms, clipped signatures, index cards, autograph album pages, postcards, canceled checks, contracts and documents, typed letters, handwritten letters, photographs, books, cachets and commemorative envelopes, posters, tickets, schedules, programs, yearbooks, media guides, trading cards, magazines, artwork, newspapers, advertisements, pennants, dolls and figurines, and assorted souvenirs

HEADS OF STATE

Clipped signatures, index cards, autograph album pages, postcards, business cards, canceled checks, contracts and documents, typed letters (official stationery), handwritten letters (official stationery), photographs (especially signed cabinet shots), books, cachets and commemorative envelopes, campaign posters, campaign flyers, bumper stickers, buttons, flags, banners, and hats

HOCKEY PLAYERS

Hockey pucks, hockey sticks, game jerseys, practice jerseys, pants, socks, skates, T-shirts, hats, helmets, jackets, gloves, sweatbands, headbands, goalie masks, goalie sticks, goal posts, replica uniforms, clipped signatures, index cards, autograph album pages, postcards, canceled checks, contracts and documents, typed letters, handwritten letters, photographs, books, cachets and commemorative envelopes, posters, tickets, schedules, programs, yearbooks, media guides, trading cards, magazines, artwork, newspapers, advertisements, pennants, dolls and figurines, Zamboni, and assorted souvenirs

MILITARY LEADERS

Clipped signatures, index cards, autograph album pages, postcards, business cards, canceled checks, contracts and documents, typed letters (official stationery), handwritten letters (official stationery), photographs (especially signed war photos), books, cachets and commemorative envelopes, posters, flyers, bumper stickers, buttons, flags, banners, weapons, maps, hats, facsimile historical documents, postage stamps, and assorted military-issue items

SCIENTISTS AND TECHNOLOGISTS

Clipped signatures, index cards, autograph album pages, postcards, business cards, canceled checks, contracts and documents, typed letters (official stationery), handwritten letters (official stationery), photographs (especially at work in lab), books, cachets and commemorative envelopes, posters, documents, patent information, scientific notes, science related lab equipment, drawings, products and equipment related to a particular individual

SPORTS (tennis, golf, auto racing, bowling, etc.)

Clipped signatures, index cards, autograph album pages, postcards, business cards, canceled checks, contracts and documents, typed letters, handwritten letters, photographs, books, cachets and commemorative envelopes, posters, tennis balls, tennis rackets, tennis apparel, tennis shoes, programs, tickets, press passes, press kits, golf balls, golf clubs, golf hats, golf bags, spikes, tees, ball markers, towels, scorecards, racing helmets, racing gloves, tires, steering wheels, car hoods, car parts (damaged and undamaged), die-cast cars, models, racing suits, hats, sunglasses, bowling balls, bowling shoes, bowling pins, basketballs, backboards, uniforms, sneakers, pool balls (especially cue and 8 balls), skates, skis, goggles, ski poles, ski boots, jockey suits, whips, swim trunks, gym suits, cricket sticks, racing numbers, weights, weight belts, and anything common or unusual associated with the sport

STATE GOVERNORS, SENATORS AND REPRESENTATIVES

Clipped signatures, index cards, autograph album pages, postcards, business cards, canceled checks, contracts and documents, typed letters (official stationery), handwritten letters (official stationery), photographs (especially with presidents), books, cachets and commemorative envelopes, campaign posters, campaign flyers, bumper stickers, buttons, chamber passes, flags, banners and hats

UNITED STATES PRESIDENTS

Clipped signatures, index cards, autograph album pages, postcards, free franks, business cards, canceled checks, contracts and documents (for instance, land grants), typed letters (official stationery), handwritten letters (official stationery), photographs, books, cachets and commemorative envelopes, campaign posters, campaign flyers, bumper stickers, buttons, flags, banners, hats, baseballs, golf balls, photocopies of speeches (state of the union and inaugural addresses) , and any item that includes a presidential seal

Section II

Celebrity Autographs and Addresses

The accuracy of the celebrity addresses included in this section cannot be guaranteed. The dynamic nature of this book's subject matter prohibits it from being totally accurate. Every celebrity received the same letter (1/2 page), 4 blank index cards and an S.A.S.E.

Celebrity Rating Chart

Response Time:

A = Quick, usually within two weeks
B = Good, usually within four weeks
C = Slow, well over a month
U = Undetermined

Response Quality:

A+ = Celebrity signed all four cards, included an autographed photograph (not requested), and may have thrown in some other items, such as fan club information, etc. (GENEROUS)
A = Celebrity signed all four cards and included an unrequested autographed photograph (OUTSTANDING)
B+ = Celebrity signed all four cards and included an unrequested note or letter
B = Celebrity signed all four cards (EXCELLENT)
C = Celebrity signed three cards (VERY GOOD)
D = Celebrity signed only one or possibly two cards (GOOD)
F = Responded with a facsimile, requested a fee, or failed to respond at all (WHY BOTHER?)
U = Undetermined, unpredictable or illegible penmanship (YOU'RE ON YOUR OWN)

Remember, responses of any nature are no guarantee of an item's authenticity. Responses may be from a secretary, from autopens, stamped signatures, or even photographic reproductions of an original. A majority of the quality ratings are based only on the material received during the fall and winter of 1995, when a celebrity's work schedule, illness, travel or other circumstances may have impacted the rating. Please note that these ratings may vary dramatically over time.

If you think about it, any response above a D is a good response. Remember, the response was based on a form letter. Although I am not an advocate of sending form letters to celebrities, I had to do so in this case to guarantee consistency. I would like to apologize to every celebrity for the impersonal nature, or, as Garth Brooks stated "BS form letter," of my request. As expected, this project was never mentioned in the letter.

Country music, golf and auto racing are clearly good areas to begin an autograph collection. Big stars and baseball players are not. Since Jim Carrey reportedly receives 50, 000 letters a month, it's not a surprise that he hasn't gotten to my form letter yet.

Worth noting is the sincere and honest affection many celebrities feel for their fans. Maybe the time it takes me to write Shaq, Barry Bonds or Ted Danson would be better spent writing to someone like that, who is more likely to respond to my autograph request.

Name	Address	City	State	Zip Code	Resp. Time	Resp. Qual.	Comments
AADLAND, BEVERLY	P.O. BOX 1115	CANYON COUNTRY	CA	91350	A	B	ACTRESS
AARON, HENRY	1611 ADAMS DR. S.W.	ATLANTA	GA	30311	U	U	BASEBALL HALL OF FAME
ABBOTT, DIHANNE	460 W. AVE. 46	LOS ANGELES	CA	90056	U	U	ACTRESS
ABBOTT, GREGORY	P.O. BOX 68	BERGENFIELD	NJ	07621	A	B	SINGER
ABBOTT, JOHN	6424 IVARENE AVE.	LOS ANGELES	CA	90068	A	B	ACTOR
ABBOTT, PHILIP	5400 SHIRLEY AVE.	TARZANA	CA	91356	U	U	ACTOR/DIRECTOR
ABDUL, PAULA	14046 AUBREY RD.	BEVERLY HILLS	CA	90210	C	F	SINGER - "STRAIGHT UP" - FAN CLUB INFO ONLY!
ABDUL-JABBAR, KAREEM	1170 STONE CANYON RD.	LOS ANGELES	CA	90077	U	U	MEMBER OF BASKETBALL HALL OF FAME
ABDULLAH, AL-AMIN JANIL	THE COM. STORE, 1128 OAK ST. S.W.	ATLANTA	GA	30310	U	U	ACTIVIST
ABERCROMBIE, IAN	1040 N. GARDNER	LOS ANGELES	CA	90046	U	U	ACTOR
ABRAHAM, F. MURRAY	40 FIFTH AVE. #2C	NEW YORK	NY	10011	U	U	ACTOR - AMADEUS
ABRUZZO, RAY	20334 PACIFIC COAST HWY.	MALIBU	CA	90265	U	U	ACTOR
ABZUG, BELLA	2 FIFTH AVE.	NEW YORK	NY	10011	U	U	POLITICIAN
ACE OF BASE	C/O ARISTA REC., 6 W. 57TH ST.	NEW YORK	NY	10019	U	U	MUSIC GROUP
ACKERMAN, BETTYE	302 N. ALPINE DR.	BEVERLY HILLS	CA	90210	U	U	ACTRESS
ACKERMAN, FORREST	2495 GLENDOWER	LOS ANGELES	CA	90027	U	U	AUTHOR
ACKERMAN, LESLIE	950 - 2ND ST. #201	SANTA MONICA	CA	90403	U	U	ACTRESS
ACKROYD, DAVID	12425 OTSEGO ST.	NORTH HOLLYWOOD	CA	91607	C	B	ACTOR
ACOVONE, JAY	3811 MULTIVIEW DR.	LOS ANGELES	CA	90068	A	B	ACTOR
ADAIR, DEBORAH	9826 WARDER PK.	BEVERLY HILLS	CA	90210	U	U	ACTRESS
ADAMS, BRYAN	406-68 WATER ST.	VANCOUVER, BC	CAN.	V6B 1A4	C	F	SINGER - "EVERYTHING I DO" - FAN CLUB INFO ONLY!
ADAMS, CINDY	1050 FIFTH AVE.	NEW YORK	NY	10028	U	U	ACTRESS
ADAMS, DON	2160 CENTURY PARK E.	LOS ANGELES	CA	90067	U	U	ACTOR/DIRECTOR - GET SMART
ADAMS, EDIE	8040 OKEAN TERR.	LOS ANGELES	CA	90046	B	B	ACTRESS/SINGER - THE ERNIE KOVACS SHOW
ADAMS, JOEY	1050 FIFTH AVE.	NEW YORK	NY	10028	U	U	ACTOR/WRITER/DIRECTOR
ADAMS, JULIE	5915 CORBIN AVE.	TARZANA	CA	91356	A	B	ACTRESS
ADAMS, MASON	900 FIFTH AVE.	NEW YORK	NY	10021	A	B	ACTOR
ADAMS, MAUD (WILKSTROM)	1 CENTURY PARK W. #403	LOS ANGELES	CA	90067	U	U	ACTRESS/MODEL - OCTOPUSSY
ADC BAND	17397 SANTA BARBARA	DETROIT	MI	48221	U	U	ROCK BAND
ADDY, WESLEY	88 CENTRAL PARK W.	NEW YORK	NY	10023	A	D	ACTOR
ADELSON, MERV	600 SARBONNE RD.	LOS ANGELES	CA	90077	U	U	TELEVISION PRODUCER
ADLER, LOU	3969 VILLA COSTERA	MALIBU	CA	90265	A	B	DIRECTOR/PRODUCER
ADOLFO	36 E. 57TH ST.	NEW YORK	NY	10022	U	U	FASHION DESIGNER

John Aprea

Paul Anka

Name	Address	City	State	Zip Code	Resp. Time	Resp. Qual.	Comments
ADRIAN, IRIS	355 S. GRAND AVE. #2600	LOS ANGELES	CA	90071	U	U	ACTRESS
AGAR, JOHN	639 N. HOLLYWOOD WAY	BURBANK	CA	91505	A	A+	ACTOR - *THE SANDS OF IWO JIMA*
AGASSI, ANDRE	ATP TOUR NORTH AMER., 200 ATP BLVD.	PONTE VEDRA BEACH	FL	32082	U	U	TENNIS STAR - **AUTHOR'S CHOICE!**
AGRONSKY, MARTIN	4001 BRANDYWINE ST.	WASHINGTON	DC	20016	U	U	TELEVISION PRODUCER
AGUTTER, JENNY	6882 CAMROSE DR.	LOS ANGELES	CA	90068	U	U	ACTRESS - *LOGAN'S RUN*
AIELLO, DANNY	4 THORNHILL DR.	RAMSEY	NH	07446	U	U	ACTOR - *MOONSTRUCK*
AIKMAN, TROY	C/O DALLAS COWBOYS, 1 COWBOY PKWY.	IRVING	TX	75063	F	F	FOOTBALL STAR - **AUTHOR'S CHOICE!** ATTENDS SHOWS-$70/PHOTO
AILES, ROGER	440 PARK AVE. S.	NEW YORK	NY	10016	U	U	PRODUCER/DIRECTOR
AIR SUPPLY	P.O. BOX 25909	LOS ANGELES	CA	90025	A	D	ROCK BAND
AJAYE, FRANKLIN	1312 S. ORANGE DR.	LOS ANGELES	CA	90019	B	B	COMIC/ACTOR - *CAR WASH*
ALABAMA	P.O. BOX 529	FT. PAYNE	AL	35967	C	B	COUNTRY WESTERN GROUP - VERY RESPONSIVE TO FANS!
ALAN, BUDDY	600 E. GILBERT	TEMPE	AZ	85281	U	U	SINGER
ALBANO, CAPT. LOU	P.O. BOX 3859	STAMFORD	CT	06905	U	U	WRESTLER/MANAGER
ALBEE, EDWARD	226 LAFAYETTE ST.	NEW YORK	NY	10021	U	U	WRITER/PRODUCER
ALBERGHETTI, ANNA MARIA	10333 CHRYSANTHEMUM LN.	LOS ANGELES	CA	90077	U	U	ACTRESS/SINGER
ALBERT, EDDIE	719 AMALFI DR.	PACIFIC PALISADES	CA	90272	U	U	ACTOR - *GREEN ACRES*
ALBERT, MARV	C/O NBC SPORTS, 30 ROCKEFELLER PLAZA	NEW YORK	NY	10012	U	U	SPORTSCASTER - BLOOPER VIDEOTAPE EXPERT!
ALBRIGHT, DR. TENLEY	2 COMMONWEALTH AVE.	BOSTON	MA	02117	U	U	SKATER
ALBRIGHT, LOLA	P.O. BOX 250070	GLENDALE	CA	91225	U	U	ACTRESS
ALBRIGHT, MADELEINE	799 UNITED NATION PLAZA	NEW YORK	NY	10017	B	B	U.S. AMBASSADOR TO THE U.N.
ALDA, ALAN	641 LEXINGTON AVE. #1400	NEW YORK	NY	10022	C	D	ACTOR/DIRECTOR - *M*A*S*H*
ALDA, ANTONY	15 SEAVIEW DR. N.	ROLLING HILLS	CA	90274	U	U	ACTOR
ALDEN, GINGER	4152 ROYAL CREST PL.	MEMPHIS	TN	38138	U	U	MODEL
ALDEN, NORMAN	106 N. CROFT AVE.	LOS ANGELES	CA	90048	U	U	ACTOR
ALDRIN, DR. ED "BUZZ", JR.	233 EMERALD BAY	LAGUNA BEACH	CA	92651	B	F	ASTRONAUT - NOT SIGNING ANYMORE
ALETTER, FRANK	5430 CORBIN AVE.	TARZANA	CA	91356	A	B	ACTOR
ALEXANDER, JASON	NBC TELEVISION, 3000 W. ALAMEDA AVE.	BURBANK	CA	91523	U	U	ACTOR - *SEINFELD* - **AUTHOR'S CHOICE!**
ALEXIS, KIM	345 N. MAPLE DR. #185	BEVERLY HILLS	CA	90210	U	U	MODEL
ALI, MUHAMMAD	ALI FARM, P.O. BOX 187	BERRIEN SPRING	MI	49103	U	U	BOXER - MEMBER INTER. BOXING HALL OF FAME
ALICIA, ANA	9744 WILSHIRE BLVD. #308	BEVERLY HILLS	CA	90212	A	B	ACTRESS - *FALCON CREST* - SENDS BIBLE SCRIPTURE LISTING
ALL-4-ONE	ATLANTIC REC., 75 ROCKEFELLER PL.	NEW YORK	NY	10019	U	U	MUSIC GROUP
ALLAN, JED	10320 MISSISSIPPI AVE.	LOS ANGELES	CA	90025	U	U	ACTOR

Marty Allen

John Agar

Name	Address	City	State	Zip Code	Resp. Time	Resp. Qual.	Comments
ALLEN, BETTY	645 ST. NICHOLAS AVE.	NEW YORK	NY	10030	U	U	MEZZO-SOPRANO
ALLEN, CHAD	12049 SMOKEY LN.	CERRITOS	CA	90701	U	U	ACTOR
ALLEN, DEBBIE	607 MARGUERITA AVE.	SANTA MONICA	CA	90402	U	U	ACTRESS/SINGER - FAME
ALLEN, JONELLE	8730 SUNSET BLVD. #480	LOS ANGELES	CA	90069	U	U	ACTRESS/SINGER
ALLEN, MARCUS	C/O K.C. CHIEFS, 1 ARROWHEAD DR.	KANSAS CITY	MO	64129	F	F	FOOTBALL STAR
ALLEN, MARTY	5750 WILSHIRE BLVD. #580	LOS ANGELES	CA	90036	A	B	ACTOR/COMEDIAN
ALLEN, REX	P.O. BOX 430	SONOITA	AZ	85637	C	D	SINGER
ALLEN, REX JR.	128 PINE OAK DR.	HENDERSONVILLE	TN	37075	U	U	SINGER
ALLEN, SEAN BARBARA	1622 SIERRA BONITA AVE.	LOS ANGELES	CA	90046	U	U	ACTRESS/WRITER
ALLEN, STEVE	16185 WOODVALE	ENCINO	CA	91316	A	D	ACTOR/WRITER - THE STEVE ALLEN SHOW
ALLEN, TIM	200 N. ROBERTSON BLVD. #223	BEVERLY HILLS	CA	90212	B	F	ACTOR/COMEDIAN - HOME IMPROVEMENT - SAVE YOUR STAMPS
ALLEN, WOODY	930 FIFTH AVE.	NEW YORK	NY	10018	A	D	ACTOR/DIRECTOR - RESPONSIVE TO FAN MAIL - AUTHOR'S CHOICE!
ALLINSON, MICHAEL	11 KNOLLWOOD DR.	LARCHMONT	NY	10538	A	B	ACTOR
ALLISON, BOBBY	140 CHURCH ST.	HUEYTOWN	AL	35020	A	B	AUTO RACER
ALLISON, MOSE	34 DOGWOOD ST.	SMITHTOWN	NY	11787	U	U	PIANIST/COMPOSER
ALLPORT, CHRISTOPHER	121 N. SAN VICENTE BLVD.	BEVERLY HILLS	CA	90211	U	U	ACTOR
ALLRED, GLORIA	6380 WILSHIRE BLVD. #1404	LOS ANGELES	CA	90048	A	B	LAWYER/FEMINIST
ALLYSON, JUNE	1651 FOOTHILL RD.	OJAI	CA	93020	A	D	ACTRESS - THE GLENN MILLER STORY
ALOMAR, ROBERTO	C/O BALT. ORIOLES, 333 W. CAMDEN ST.	BALTIMORE	MD	21201	U	U	BASEBALL STAR - AUTHOR'S CHOICE!
ALONSO, MARIA CONCHITA	P.O. BOX 537	BEVERLY HILLS	CA	90213	B	B+	ACTRESS
ALTMAN, JEFF	5065 CALVIN AVE.	TARZANA	CA	91356	A	C	COMEDIAN/ACTOR
ALTMAN, ROBERT	502 PARK AVE. #15G	NEW YORK	NY	10022	U	U	WRITER/DIRECTOR/PROD - THE PLAYER
ALTMAN, ROBERT	9200 HARRINGTON DR.	POTOMAC	MD	20854	U	U	FINANCIER
AMATEAU, RODNEY	133 1/2 S. LINDEN DR.	BEVERLY HILLS	CA	90212	A	D	FILM WRITER/PRODUCER
AMES, ED	1457 CLARIDGE	BEVERLY HILLS	CA	90210	U	U	SINGER
AMES, RACHEL	303 S. CRESCENT HEIGHTS	LOS ANGELES	CA	90048	C	B+	AUTHOR
AMORY, CLEVELAND	200 W. 57TH ST.	NEW YORK	NY	10019	U	U	WRITER
AMOS, FAMOUS (WALLY)	215 LANIPO DR.	KAILUA	HI	96734	A	D	COOKIE MAKER
AMOS, TORI	ATLANTIC RECORDS, 75 ROCKEFELLER PL.	NEW YORK	NY	10019	U	U	SINGER - "CRUCIFY" - AUTHOR'S CHOICE!
ANDERSON, BARBARA	P.O. BOX 10118	SANTA FE	NM	87504	U	U	ACTRESS
ANDERSON, BILL	P.O. BOX 888	HERMITAGE	TN	37076	A	B+	SINGER
ANDERSON, DARYL	5923 WILBUR AVE.	TARZANA	CA	91356	U	U	ACTOR

95

Aerosmith signed guitar

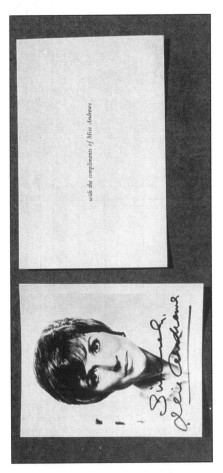

Julie Andrews

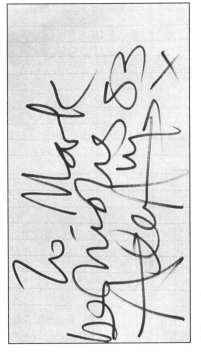

Adam Ant

Name	Address	City	State	Zip Code	Resp. Time	Resp. Qual.	Comments
ANDERSON, ERNIE	4141 KNOBHILL DR.	SHERMAN OAKS	CA	91403	U	U	ACTOR
ANDERSON, HARRY	2305 ASHLAND ST. #C	ASHLAND	OR	97520	U	U	ACTOR/COMEDIAN - *NIGHT COURT*
ANDERSON, JACK	1200 ETON COURT	WASHINGTON	DC	20007	U	U	NEWS CORRESPONDENT
ANDERSON, JOHN	NOVA UNIVERSITY CENTER FOR LAW	FT. LAUDERDALE	FL	33314	A	B	POLITICIAN
ANDERSON, LONI	20652 LASSEN ST.	CHATSWORTH	CA	91311	B	F	ACTRESS - *WKRP IN CINCINNATI*
ANDERSON, LOUIE	109 N. SYCAMORE AVE.	LOS ANGELES	CA	90036	U	U	COMEDIAN
ANDERSON, LYNN	4925 TYNE VALLEY BLVD.	NASHVILLE	TN	37220	C	B	SINGER - OFTEN ADDS TRADING CARD!
ANDERSON, MARY	1127 NORMAN PL.	LOS ANGELES	CA	90049	U	U	ACTRESS
ANDERSON, MELISSA SUE	20722 PACIFIC COAST HWY.	MALIBU	CA	90265	U	U	ACTRESS - *LITTLE HOUSE ON THE PRAIRIE*
ANDERSON, RICHARD	10120 CIELO DR.	BEVERLY HILLS	CA	90210	A	C	ACTOR - *THE SIX MILLION DOLLAR MAN*
ANDERSON, SAM	2611 N. BEACHWOOD DR.	LOS ANGELES	CA	90068	U	U	ACTOR
ANDERSON, SPARKY	P.O. BOX 6415	THOUSAND OAKS	CA	91360	U	U	FUTURE MEMBER OF BASEBALL HALL OF FAME
ANDRETTI, MARIO	53 VICTORY LN.	NAZARETH	PA	18064	A	D	RACE DRIVER
ANDREWS, JULIE	P.O. BOX 666	BEVERLY HILLS	CA	90213	A	F	ACTRESS/SINGER - *THE SOUND OF MUSIC*
ANDREWS, PATTY	9823 ALDEA AVE.	NORTHRIDGE	CA	91354	A	C	SINGER
ANGELO, MICHAEL	4914 ENCINO TERR.	ENCINO	CA	91316	A	D	ACTOR/WRITER - *THE MOD SQUAD*
ANGELOU, MAYA	80 HILLTOP BLVD.	EAST BRUNSWICK	NJ	08816	U	U	AUTHOR
ANGLE, JIM	3240 VALLEY RD.	WINSTON-SALEM	NC	27106	U	U	POET/WRITER - **AUTHOR'S CHOICE!**
ANGLIM, PHILIP	C/O NPR, 2025 "M" ST. N.W.	WASHINGTON	DC	20036	U	U	NEWS CORRESPONDENT
ANHALT, EDWARD	2404 GRAND CANAL	VENICE	CA	90291	A	D	ACTOR
ANKA, PAUL	500 AMALFI DR.	PACIFIC PALISADES	CA	90272	A	B	WRITER/PRODUCER
ANNENBERG, WALLIS	10573 W. PICO BLVD. #159	LOS ANGELES	CA	90064	B	B	SINGER - "DIANA" - SIGNED PHOTO IN SILVER INK
ANNENBERG, WALTER	10273 CENTURY WOODS PL.	LOS ANGELES	CA	90067	U	U	MAGAZINE EXECUTIVE
ANSARA, MICHAEL	P.O. BOX 98	RANCHO MIRAGE	CA	92270	U	U	PHILANTHROPIST
ANSPACH, SUSAN	4624 PARK MIRASOL	CALABASAS	CA	91302	A	B	ACTOR
ANTHONY, RAY	473 - 16TH ST.	SANTA MONICA	CA	90402	U	U	ACTRESS - *FIVE EASY PIECES*
ANTONIO, LOU	9288 KINGLET DR.	LOS ANGELES	CA	90069	U	U	ORCHESTRA LEADER
AOKI, ROCKY	530 GAYLORD DR.	BURBANK	CA	91505	U	U	ACTOR/WRITER/DIRECTOR
APPLEGATE, CHRISTINA	8685 N.W. 53RD TERR.	MIAMI	FL	33155	B	B	BENIHANA CREATOR
APPOLLONIA	20411 CHAPTER DR.	WOODLAND HILLS	CA	91364	U	U	ACTRESS - *MARRIED....WITH CHILDREN*
APREA, JOHN	9000 SUNSET BLVD. #1200	LOS ANGELES	CA	90069	U	U	SINGER
APTED, MICHAEL	727 N. MARTEL AVE.	LOS ANGELES	CA	90046	A+	A+	ACTOR
ARBUS, LOREEN	19 LATIMER RD.	SANTA MONICA	CA	90402	A	U	FILM DIRECTOR
	8841 APPIAN WAY	LOS ANGELES	CA	90046	U	U	WRITER

97

Hoyt Axton

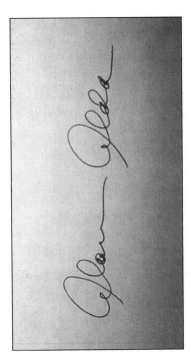

Alan Alda

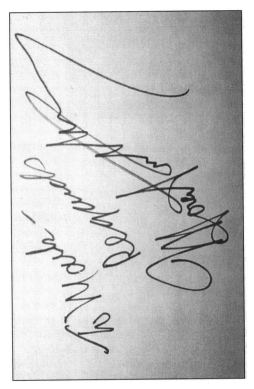

Morey Amsterdam (deceased)

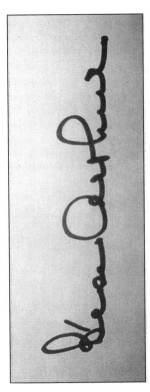

Bea Arthur

Name	Address	City	State	Zip Code	Resp. Time	Resp. Qual.	Comments
ARCARO, EDDIE	11111 BISCAYNE BLVD.	MIAMI	FL	33161	A	D	JOCKEY
ARCHER, ANNE	13201 OLD OAK LN.	LOS ANGELES	CA	90049	U	U	ACTRESS - *FATAL ATTRACTION*
ARCHERD, JEFFREY	93 ALBERT EMBANKMENT	LONDON	ENG.	SE1	A	B+	AUTHOR
ARCHERD, ARMY	442 HILGARD AVE.	LOS ANGELES	CA	90024	A	D	COLUMNIST
ARDEN, TONI	34-34 75TH ST.	JACKSON HEIGHTS	NY	11372	U	U	SINGER
ARKIN, ALAN	1350 AVE. OF THE AMERICAS	NEW YORK	NY	10019	U	U	ACTOR - *THE IN-LAWS*
ARKOFF, SAMUEL Z.	500 S. BUENA VISTA	BURBANK	CA	91521	A	B	FILM PRODUCER
ARLEDGE, ROONE	ABC, 47 W. 66TH ST., 5TH FL.	NEW YORK	NY	10023	U	U	TELEVISION EXECUTIVE
ARMANI, GIORGIO	650 FIFTH AVE.	NEW YORK	NY	10019	U	U	FASHION DESIGNER - **AUTHOR'S CHOICE!**
ARMS, RUSSELL	2918 DAVIS WAY	PALM SPRINGS	CA	92262	A	B	ACTOR/SINGER
ARMSTRONG, ANNE	ARMSTRONG RANCH	ARMSTRONG	TX	78838	A	D	POLITICIAN
ARMSTRONG, BESS	151 EL CAMINO DR.	BEVERLY HILLS	CA	90212	C	F	ACTRESS - *ON OUR OWN* - FACSIMILE SIGNED PHOTO
ARMSTRONG, BILLIE JOE	WARNER BROS. REC., 300 WARNER BLVD.	BURBANK	CA	91505	U	U	SINGER - GREEN DAY - **AUTHOR'S CHOICE!**
ARMSTRONG, GARNER TED	P.O. BOX 2525	TYLER	TX	75710	C	B	EVANGELIST
ARMSTRONG, NEIL	1739 N. STATE, RT. 123	LEBANON	OH	45036	F	F	ASTRONAUT - SAVE YOUR STAMPS
ARNESS, JAMES	P.O. BOX 49599	LOS ANGELES	CA	90049	A	D	ACTOR - *GUNSMOKE*
ARNETT, PETER	111 MASSACHUSETTS N.W.	WASHINGTON	DC	20001	U	U	NEWS CORRESPONDENT
ARNETTE, JEANETTA	9024 DORRINGTON AVE.	LOS ANGELES	CA	90048	U	U	ACTRESS
ARNGRIM, ALISON	1340 N. POINSETTIA #422	LOS ANGELES	CA	90046	U	U	ACTRESS
ARNOLD, EDDY	P.O. BOX 97	BRENTWOOD	TN	37027	U	U	SINGER
ARNOLD, ROSEANNE	C/O WILLIAM MORRIS AGCY., 151 EL CAMINO BLVD.	BEVERLY HILLS	CA	90212	A	F	ACTRESS - *ROSEANNE*
ARNOLD, TOM	14755 VENTURA BLVD. #1-710	SHERMAN OAKS	CA	91403	U	U	ACTOR - *ROSEANNE*
ARNSTEN, STEFAN	1017 LAUREL WAY	BEVERLY HILLS	CA	90210	U	U	ACTOR
ARQUETTE, DAVID	616 N. GOWER ST.	LOS ANGELES	CA	90004	U	U	ACTOR
ARQUETTE, PATRICIA	616 N. GOWER ST.	LOS ANGELES	CA	90004	U	U	ACTRESS - *TRUE ROMANCE*
ARRANTS, ROD	4441 RADFORD AVE.	VALLEY VILLAGE	CA	91607	U	U	ACTOR
ARRESTED DEVELOPMENT	151 EL CAMINO DR.	BEVERLY HILLS	CA	90212	U	U	ROCK GROUP
ARRIOLA, GUS	P.O. BOX 3275	CARMEL	CA	93921	A	C	CARTOONIST - ADDS RECIPE CARD
ARTHUR, BEATRICE	2000 OLD RANCH RD.	LOS ANGELES	CA	90049	A	B	ACTRESS - *THE GOLDEN GIRLS*
ARTHUR, ROBERT	1711 KINGS WAY	LOS ANGELES	CA	90069	A	D	PRODUCER
ARTIST FORMERLY KNOWN AS PRINCE	CREATIVE ART. AGCY., 9830 WILSHIRE BLVD.	BEVERLY HILLS	CA	90212	C	F	SINGER - "PURPLE RAIN" - **AUTHOR'S CHOICE!** - SENDS OLD BACKSTAGE PASSES
ASH, MARY KAY	8787 N. STEMMONS FREEWAY	DALLAS	TX	75247	A	A+	COSMETIC EXECUTIVE - A FIRST CLASS LADY

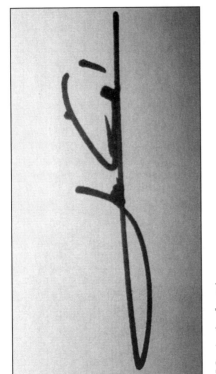

Mario Andretti

Woody Allen

Steve Allen

Red Aeurbach

Name	Address	City	State	Zip Code	Resp. Time	Resp. Qual.	Comments
ASHBROOK, DANA	7019 MELROSE AVE. #332	LOS ANGELES	CA	90038	U	U	ACTRESS
ASHBROOK, DAPHNE	3355 N. MAPLE DR. #250	BEVERLY HILLS	CA	90210	U	U	ACTRESS
ASHER, JANE	644 N. DOHENY DR.	LOS ANGELES	CA	90069	U	U	ACTRESS
ASHER, PETER	644 N. DOHENY DR.	LOS ANGELES	CA	90069	A	C	RECORD PRODUCER
ASHFORD & SIMPSON	254 W. 72ND ST. #1A	NEW YORK	NY	10023	U	U	SINGERS
ASHFORD, EVELYN	818 PLANTATION LN.	WALNUT	CA	91789	C	A	ATHLETE
ASHLEY, EDWARD	4054 PYLON WAY	OCEANSIDE	CA	92056	U	U	ACTOR
ASHLEY, ELIZABETH	9010 DORRINGTON AVE.	LOS ANGELES	CA	90048	U	U	ACTRESS - *EVENING SHADE*
ASHLEY, JOHN	18067 LAKE ENCINO DR.	ENCINO	CA	91316	A	B	ACTOR/PRODUCER
ASLEEP AT THE WHEEL	606 N. CENTRAL EXPRESSWAY #428	DALLAS	TX	75205	U	U	ROCK BAND
ASNER, EDWARD	P.O. BOX 7407	STUDIO CITY	CA	91604	A	B	ACTOR - *LOU GRANT* - ALWAYS RESPONSIVE TO FAN MAIL!
ASSANTE, ARMAND	RD #1, BOX 561	CAMPBELL HALL	NY	10916	C	B	ACTOR
AST, PAT	12456 VENTURA BLVD. #1	STUDIO CITY	CA	91604	U	U	ACTRESS
ASTAIRE, ROBYN	1155 SAN YSIDRO DR.	BEVERLY HILLS	CA	90210	A	D	WIDOW OF FRED ASTAIRE
ASTIN, JOHN	P.O. BOX 49698	LOS ANGELES	CA	90049	U	U	ACTOR/DIRECTOR/WRITER - *THE ADDAMS FAMILY*
ASTIN, SEAN	4354 LAUREL CANYON BLVD. #301	STUDIO CITY	CA	91604	U	U	ACTOR - *ENCINO MAN*
ASTLEY, RICK	4-7 THE VINEYARD SANCTUARY	LONDON	ENG.	SE1 1QL	U	U	SINGER - "NEVER GONNA GIVE YOU UP"
ATHERTON, WILLIAM	5102 SAN FELICIANO DR.	WOODLAND HILLS	CA	91364	A	B	ACTOR
ATKINS, CHET	1096 LYNWOOD BLVD.	NASHVILLE	TN	37215	A	D	GUITARIST
ATKINS, CHRISTOPHER	7072 PARK MANOR AVE.	NORTH HOLLYWOOD	CA	91605	A	C	ACTOR - *THE BLUE LAGOON*
ATKINS, TOM	10100 SANTA MONICA BLVD. #2500	LOS ANGELES	CA	90067	U	U	ACTOR
ATTENBOROUGH, DAVID	5 PARK RD., RICHMOND GREEN	SURREY	ENG.		U	U	TELEVISION PRODUCER/ADVENTURING NATURIST
ATTENBOROUGH, SIR RICHARD	OLD FRIARS, RICHMOND GREEN	SURREY	ENG.		U	U	WRITER/PRODUCER - *GANDHI*
ATWOOD, MARGARET	OXFORD UNIV. PRESS, 70 WYNFORD DR.	DON MILLS, ONTARIO	CAN.	M3C1J9	U	U	AUTHOR
AUBERJONOIS, RENE	5555 MELROSE PL.	LOS ANGELES	CA	90069	U	U	ACTOR - *DEEP SPACE NINE*
AUBREY, JAMES	16161 VENTURA BLVD. #402	ENCINO	CA	91436	U	U	ACTOR
AUBUCHON, JACQUES	20978 RIOS ST.	WOODLAND HILLS	CA	91364	U	U	ACTOR
AUCHINCLOSS, LOUIS	1111 PARK AVE.	NEW YORK	NY	10028	A	D	AUTHOR/CRITIC
AUERBACH, RED	151 MERRIMAC ST.	BOSTON	MA	02114	A	D	BASKETBALL EXECUTIVE
AUERMANN, NADJA	ELITE MODELING AGCY., 111 E. 22ND ST.	NEW YORK	NY	10010	U	U	SUPERMODEL - **AUTHOR'S CHOICE!**
AUGUSTAIN, IRA	3900 RAMBOZ DR.	LOS ANGELES	CA	90063	U	U	ACTOR
AUSTIN, KAREN	3356 ROWENA AVE.	LOS ANGELES	CA	90027	U	U	ACTRESS
AUSTIN, PATTI	9000 SUNSET BLVD. #1200	LOS ANGELES	CA	90069	U	U	SINGER

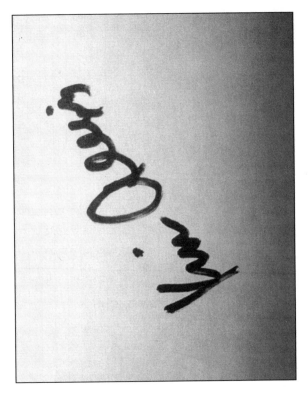

Kim Alexis

Mary Kay Ash

Name	Address	City	State	Zip Code	Resp. Time	Resp. Qual.	Comments
AUSTIN, TERI	4245 LAUREL GROVE	STUDIO CITY	CA	91604	U	U	ACTRESS
AUSTIN, TRACY	26406 DUNWOOD RD.	ROLLING HILLS ESTATES	CA	90274	C	D	TENNIS PLAYER
AUTRY, GENE	P.O. BOX 710	LOS ANGELES	CA	90078	A	F	SINGER/ACTOR/EXECUTIVE - THIS WILL COST YOU SOME MONEY
AVALON, FRANKIE	6311 DE SOTO ST. #1	WOODLAND HILLS	CA	91367	U	U	SINGER - "BEACH BLANKET BINGO"
AVEDON, RICHARD	407 E. 75TH ST.	NEW YORK	NY	10021	A	B	PHOTOGRAPHER
AVERY, MARGARET	P.O. BOX 3493	HOLLYWOOD	CA	90078	A	B	ACTRESS
AVERY, STEVE	C/O ATLANTA BRAVES, P.O. BOX 4064	ATLANTA	GA	30302	U	U	BASEBALL STAR!
AXTON, HOYT	642 FRED BURR RD.	VICTOR	MT	59875	A	B	SINGER/SONGWRITER - "JOY TO THE WORLD"
AYKROYD, DAN	CREATIVE ART. AGCY., 9830 WILSHIRE BLVD.	BEVERLY HILLS	CA	90212	C	D	ACTOR - GHOSTBUSTERS
AYRES, LEAH	9300 WILSHIRE BLVD. #410	BEVERLY HILLS	CA	90210	U	U	ACTRESS
AYRES, LEW	675 WALTHER WAY	LOS ANGELES	CA	90049	A	B	ACTOR - OFTEN ADDS AGE UNDER SIGNATURE
AZZARA, CANDY	1155 N. LA CIENEGA BLVD. #307	LOS ANGELES	CA	90069	A	A+	ACTRESS - VERY RESPONSIVE TO FAN MAIL
BABASHOFF, SHIRLEY	17254 SANTA CLARA ST.	SANTA ANA	CA	92708	U	U	SWIMMER
BABBITT, HARRY	7 RUE ST. CLOUD	NEWPORT BEACH	CA	91660	A	B	CONDUCTOR
BABBITT, SEC. BRUCE	DEPT. OF INTERIOR, "C" ST. BETWEEN 18TH & 19TH N.W.	WASHINGTON	DC	20240	U	U	SECRETARY OF INTERIOR
BABILONIA, TAI	933 - 21ST ST. #6	SANTA MONICA	CA	90402	U	U	SKATER
BACALL, LAUREN	1 W. 72ND ST. #43	NEW YORK	NY	10023	A	B	ACTRESS - KEY LARGO
BACH, CATHERINE	14000 DAVANA TERR.	SHERMAN OAKS	CA	91403	U	U	ACTRESS
BACHARACH, BURT	658 NIMES RD.	LOS ANGELES	CA	90077	U	U	COMPOSER - "RAIN DROPS KEEP FALLING ON MY HEAD"
BACHARDY, DON	145 ADELAIDE DR.	SANTA MONICA	CA	90402	A	B	WRITER
BACKSTREET BOYS	C/O JIVE RECORDS, 137-139 W. 25TH ST.	NEW YORK	NY	10001	U	U	MUSIC GROUP!
BACKUS, HENNY	10914 BELLAGIO RD.	LOS ANGELES	CA	90077	A	B	ACTRESS - ADDS HEART WITH ARROW TO SIGNATURE
BACON, JAMES	10982 TOPEKA DR.	NORTHRIDGE	CA	91324	A	C	ACTOR
BACON, KEVIN	9830 WILSHIRE BLVD.	BEVERLY HILLS	CA	90212	C	F	ACTOR - FOOTLOOSE - FACSIMILE SIGNED PHOTO
BADLER, JANE	11620 WILSHIRE BLVD. #1100	LOS ANGELES	CA	90025	U	U	ACTRESS
BAER, MAX JR.	10433 WILSHIRE BLVD. #103	LOS ANGELES	CA	90024	U	U	FILM DIRECTOR
BAER, PARLEY	4967 BILMOOR AVE.	TARZANA	CA	91356	U	U	ACTOR
BAEZ, JOAN	P.O. BOX 1026	MENLO PARK	CA	94025	A	B+	SINGER - HER MOTHER OFTEN ADDS NICE NOTE!
BAILEY, F. LEE	1400 CENTRE PARK BLVD. #909	WEST PALM BEACH	FL	33401	A	B	LAWYER - MEMBER OF O. J. SIMPSON "DREAM TEAM"
BAILEY, G.W.	4972 CALVIN	TARZANA	CA	91356	U	U	ACTOR

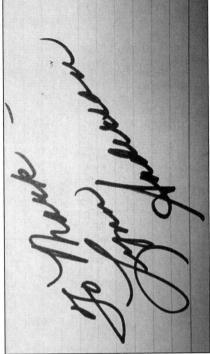

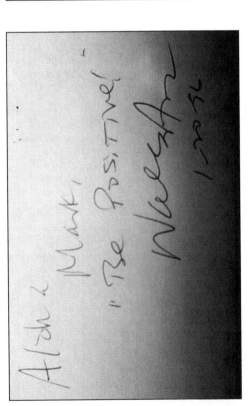

Wally Amos

Lynn Anderson

Chet Atkins

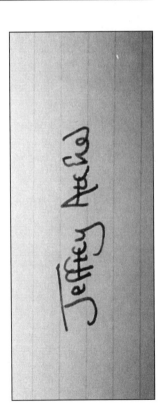

Jeffrey Archer

Name	Address	City	State	Zip Code	Resp. Time	Resp. Qual.	Comments
BAILEY, JIM	5909 W. COLGATE AVE.	LOS ANGELES	CA	90036	U	U	ACTOR
BAILEY, JOEL	6550 MURIETTA RD.	VAN NUYS	CA	91401	A	B	ACTOR
BAIN, BARBARA	1501 SKYLARK LN.	WEST HOLLYWOOD	CA	90069	U	U	ACTRESS - *MISSION IMPOSSIBLE*
BAIN, CONRAD	1230 CHICKORY LN.	LOS ANGELES	CA	90049	A	B	ACTOR
BAIO, SCOTT	4333 FORMAN AVE.	TOLUCA LAKE	CA	91602	U	U	ACTOR - *CHARLES IN CHARGE*
BAKER, ANITA	804 N. CRESCENT DR.	BEVERLY HILLS	CA	90210	U	U	SINGER
BAKER, BLANCHE	70 FLOWER AVE.	HASTINGS-ON-HUDSON	NY	10706	U	U	ACTRESS
BAKER, CARROLL	630 MASSELIN AVE. #221	LOS ANGELES	CA	90036	U	U	ACTRESS - *KINDERGARTEN COP* - SEND $20 FOR PHOTO!
BAKER, HOWARD	P.O. BOX 8	HUNTSVILLE	TN	37756	C	B+	FORMER SENATOR
BAKER, JAMES III	1001 PENNSYLVANIA AVE.	WASHINGTON	DC	20004	U	U	FORMER SECRETARY OF STATE
BAKER, JOE DON	23339 HATTERAS	WOODLAND HILLS	CA	91364	U	U	ACTOR - *WALKING TALL*
BAKER, RAYMOND	151 EL CAMINO DR.	BEVERLY HILLS	CA	90212	U	U	ACTOR
BAKER, RICK	C/O IATSE LOCAL 706, 11519 CHANDLER BLVD.	NORTH HOLLYWOOD	CA	91601	U	U	MAKE-UP GURU!
BAKKER, TAMMY FAYE	P.O. BOX 94	LARGO	FL	34649	U	U	TELEVISION EVANGELIST
BAKULA, SCOTT	9560 WILSHIRE BLVD. #500	BEVERLY HILLS	CA	90212	A	F	ACTOR - *QUANTUM LEAP* - SAVE YOUR STAMPS!
BALABAN, BOB	390 W. END AVE.	NEW YORK	NY	10024	U	U	ACTOR - *MIDNIGHT COWBOY*
BALASKI, BELINDA	280 S. BEVERLY DR. #400	BEVERLY HILLS	CA	90212	C	B	ACTRESS
BALDWIN, ADAM	8882 LOOKOUT MOUNTAIN RD.	LOS ANGELES	CA	90046	U	U	ACTOR - *MY BODYGUARD*
BALDWIN, ALEC	C/O CREATIVE ARTISTS AGCY., 9830 WILSHIRE BLVD.	BEVERLY HILLS	CA	90212	U	U	ACTOR - *THE HUNT FOR RED OCTOBER* - **AUTHOR'S CHOICE!**
BALDWIN, STEPHEN	P.O. BOX 447	CAMILLUS	NY	13031	U	U	ACTOR - **AUTHOR'S CHOICE!**
BALDWIN, WILLIAM	955 S. CARRILLO DR. #200	LOS ANGELES	CA	90048	U	U	ACTOR - **AUTHOR'S CHOICE!**
BALE, CHRISTIAN	151 EL CAMINO DR.	BEVERLY HILLS	CA	90212	U	U	ACTOR
BALENDA, CARLA	15848 WOODVALE	ENCINO	CA	91316	A	B	ACTRESS
BALIN, MARTY	436 BELVEDERE ST.	SAN FRANCISCO	CA	94117	A	B+	SINGER/SONGWRITER - JEFFERSON AIRPLANE
BALLANTINE, CARL	6767 FOREST LAWN DR. #115	LOS ANGELES	CA	90068	A	B	ACTOR/COMEDIAN
BALLARD, CHRISTINE	11501 CHANDLER BLVD.	NORTH HOLLYWOOD	CA	91601	U	U	TELEVISION WRITER/DIRECTOR
BALLARD, HANK	11457 HARRISBURG RD.	LOS ALAMITOS	CA	90720	U	U	SINGER
BALLARD, KAYE	1204 - 3RD AVE. #152	NEW YORK	NY	10121	U	U	ACTRESS/SINGER
BALLARD, ROBERT	WOODS HOLE OCEANOGRAPHIC, WATER ST.	WOODS HOLE	MA	02543	A	A	FOUND THE TITANIC
BALLESTEROS, SEVERIANO	FAIRWAY SSA, PASJE DE PENA 2-4	39008 SANTANDER		SPAIN	U	U	GOLFER
BALLOU, MARK	40 ENCLOSURE	NUTLEY	NJ	07110	A	B	ACTOR

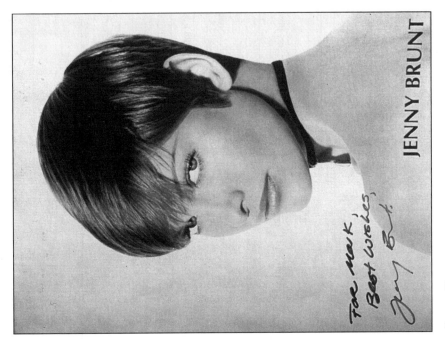

Jenny Brunt

Marty Balin

Name	Address	City	State	Zip Code	Resp. Time	Resp. Qual.	Comments
BALSAM, TALIA	1999 AVE. OF THE STARS #2850	LOS ANGELES	CA	90067	C	B	ACTRESS
BANCROFT, ANNE	2301 LA MESA DR.	SANTA MONICA	CA	90405	A	B	ACTRESS/WRITER/DIRECTOR - THE GRADUATE
BANDERAS, ANTONIO	C/O CREATIVE ARTISTS AGCY., 9830 WILSHIRE BLVD.	BEVERLY HILLS	CA	90212	U	U	ACTOR - ASSASSINS - AUTHOR'S CHOICE! - "THE VALENTINO OF THE DECADE!"
BANDY, MOE	P.O. BOX 748	ADKINS	TX	78101	U	U	SINGER
BANKS, JONATHAN	909 EUCLID ST. #8	SANTA MONICA	CA	90403	U	U	ACTOR
BANKS, TYRA	C/O CREATIVE ARTIST AGCY., 9830 WILSHIRE BLVD.	BEVERLY HILLS	CA	90212	U	U	ACTRESS/MODEL - AUTHOR'S CHOICE!
BANNEN, IAN	1999 AVE. OF THE STARS #2850	LOS ANGELES	CA	90067	U	U	ACTOR
BANNER, BOB	2409 BRIARCREST DR.	BEVERLY HILLS	CA	90210	A	B	DIRECTOR/PRODUCER
BANNON, JACK	5832 NAGLE AVE.	VAN NUYS	CA	91401	A	B	ACTOR
BARBEAU, ADRIENNE	P.O. BOX 1334	NORTH HOLLYWOOD	CA	91604	A	B	ACTRESS - MAUDE
BARBERA, JOSEPH	3617 ALOMAR DR.	SHERMAN OAKS	CA	91403	U	U	FILM PRODUCER
BARBOUR, JOHN	4254 FORMAN AVE.	TOLUCA LAKE	CA	91602	U	U	WRITER/COMEDIAN
BARDOT, BRIGITTE	LA MADRIGUE 83990	ST. TROPEZ VAR	FRA.		U	U	ACTRESS - AND GOD CREATED WOMEN
BARE, BOBBY	1210 W. MAIN ST.	HENDERSONVILLE	TN	37075	U	U	SINGER/SONGWRITER
BARKER, BOB	1851 OUTPOST DR.	LOS ANGELES	CA	90068	A	B	TELEVISION HOST - THE PRICE IS RIGHT
BARKIN, ELLEN	3100 N. DAMON WAY	BURBANK	CA	91505	U	U	ACTRESS - SEA OF LOVE - AUTHOR'S CHOICE!
BARKLEY, CHARLES	2910 N. CENTRAL AVE.	PHOENIX	AZ	85002	U	U	BASKETBALL PLAYER
BARLOW, RANDY	5514 KELLY RD.	BRENTWOOD	TN	37027	U	U	SINGER
BARNES, BINNIE	838 N. DOHENY DR. #B	LOS ANGELES	CA	90069	A	D	ACTRESS
BARNES, JOANNA	267 MIDDLE RD.	SANTA BARBARA	CA	93108	C	D	TELEVISION WRITER
BARR, DOUG	515 S. IRVING BLVD.	LOS ANGELES	CA	90020	U	U	ACTOR
BARR, JULIA	420 MADISON AVE. #1400	NEW YORK	NY	10017	A	B	ACTRESS
BARRAULT, MARIE-CHRISTINE	2429 BEVERLY AVE.	SANTA MONICA	CA	90406	U	U	ACTRESS
BARRETT, MAJEL	10615 BELLAGIO RD.	LOS ANGELES	CA	90077	A	C	ACTRESS
BARRIS, CHUCK	17 E. 76TH ST.	NEW YORK	NY	10021	U	U	TELEVISION HOST/PRODUCER
BARROW, JOE LOUIS JR.	10790 W. 50TH AVE.	WHEAT RIDGE	CO	80033	U	U	SON OF JOE LOUIS
BARROWS, SIDNEY BIDDLE	210 W. 70TH ST.	NEW YORK	NY	10023	A	B	"THE MAYFLOWER MADAM," SOCIALITE
BARRY, DAVE	614 N. PALM DR.	BEVERLY HILLS	CA	90210	U	U	COLUMNIST/COMEDIAN
BARRY, GENE	622 N. MAPLE DR.	BEVERLY HILLS	CA	90210	U	U	ACTOR
BARRY, JOHN	540 CENTRE ISLAND RD.	OYSTER BAY	NY	11771	U	U	COMPOSER
BARRY, PHILIP JR.	12742 HIGHWOOD ST.	LOS ANGELES	CA	90049	U	U	WRITER/PRODUCER
BARRY, RAYMOND	435 S. LAFAYETTE PARK PL. #316	LOS ANGELES	CA	90057	U	U	FORMER FOOTBALL PLAYER

Drew Barrymore

Lisa Hartman Black

Name	Address	City	State	Zip Code	Resp. Time	Resp. Qual.	Comments
BARRY, SY	34 SARATOGA DR.	JERICHO	NY	11753	U	U	CARTOONIST
BARRYMORE, DREW	3960 LAUREL CANYON BLVD. #159	STUDIO CITY	CA	91604	C	F	ACTRESS - BATMAN FOREVER - SAVE YOUR STAMPS!
BARRYMORE, JOHN BLYTH	144 S. PECK DR.	BEVERLY HILLS	CA	90212	U	U	ACTOR
BARRYMORE, JOHN III	7551 SUNSET BLVD. #203	LOS ANGELES	CA	90046	U	U	ACTOR
BARTEL, JEAN	229 BRONWOOD AVE.	LOS ANGELES	CA	90049	A	B	ACTRESS
BARTEL, PAUL	7860 FAREHOLM DR.	LOS ANGELES	CA	90046	A	B	ACTOR/DIRECTOR - EATING RAOUL
BARTLETT, BONNIE	3500 W. OLIVE #1400	BURBANK	CA	91505	U	U	ACTRESS
BARTON, PETER	2265 WESTWOOD BLVD. #2619	LOS ANGELES	CA	90064	U	U	ACTOR
BARTY, BILLY	4502 FARMDALE AVE.	NORTH HOLLYWOOD	CA	91602	U	U	ACTOR
BASILIO, CARMEN	67 BOXWOOD DR.	ROCHESTER	NY	14617	A	A	MEMBER OF INT'L BOXING HALL OF FAME!
BASINGER, KIM	C/O CREATIVE ARTISTS AGCY., 9830 WILSHIRE BLVD.	BEVERLY HILLS	CA	90212	U	U	ACTRESS - 9 1/2 WEEKS - AUTHOR'S CHOICE!
BASS, SAUL	337 S. LAS PALMAS AVE.	LOS ANGELES	CA	90020	U	U	DIRECTOR/PRODUCER
BASSETT, ANGELA	AMBROSIO/MORTIMER & ASSOC., 9150 WILSHIRE BLVD. SUITE 175	BEVERLY HILLS	CA	90212	U	U	ACTRESS - WHAT'S LOVE GOT... - AUTHOR'S CHOICE!
BAST, WILLIAM	6691 WHITLEY TERR.	LOS ANGELES	CA	90068	U	U	SCREENWRITER
BATEMAN, CHARLES	303 S. CRESCENT HEIGHTS	LOS ANGELES	CA	90048	U	U	ACTOR
BATEMAN, JASON	2628 - 2ND ST.	SANTA MONICA	CA	90405	U	U	ACTOR - THE HOGAN FAMILY
BATES, DAISY	1510 IZARD ST.	LITTLE ROCK	AR	72202	U	U	ACTIVIST
BATES, KATHY	121 N. SAN VICENTE BLVD.	BEVERLY HILLS	CA	90211	B	B	ACTRESS
BATINKOFF, RANDALL	P.O. BOX 555	FERNDALE	NY	12734	U	U	ACTOR
BAUER, BRUCE	12456 VENTURA BLVD. #1	STUDIO CITY	CA	91604	U	U	ACTOR
BAUER, JAMIE LYN	3500 W. OLIVE AVE. #1400	BURBANK	CA	91505	B	B+	ACTRESS
BAUGH, SAMMY	C/O GENERAL DELIVERY	ROTAN	TX	79546	U	U	FORMER FOOTBALL PLAYER
BAUMAN, JON 'BOWZER'	3168 OAKSHIRE DR.	LOS ANGELES	CA	90068	U	U	ACTOR/SINGER
BAXTER, MEREDITH	10100 SANTA MONICA BLVD. #700	LOS ANGELES	CA	90067	U	U	ACTRESS - FAMILY TIES
BAYLOR, DON	56325 RIVIERA	LA QUINTA	CA	92253	U	U	COACH & BASEBALL PLAYER
BAYLOR, ELGIN	3939 S. FIGUEROA ST.	LOS ANGELES	CA	90037	B	D	BASKETBALL PLAYER
BEACHAM, STEPHANIE	31538 BROAD BEACH RD.	MALIBU	CA	90264	A	B+	ACTRESS - THE COLBYS
BEAL, JOHN	205 W. 54TH ST.	NEW YORK	NY	10019	U	U	ACTOR
BEAME, ABE	1111 - 20TH ST. N.W.	WASHINGTON	DC	20575	A	B	FORMER POLITICIAN
BEAN, ALAN	26 SUGARBERRY CIRCLE	HOUSTON	TX	77024	F	F	ASTRONAUT/PAINTER - SENDS PRICE LIST!
BEAN, ORSEN	444 CAROL CANAL	VENICE	CA	90291	C	D	ACTOR/COMEDIAN
BEARSE, AMANDA	4177 KLUMP AVE.	NORTH HOLLYWOOD	CA	91602	U	U	ACTRESS

Letter from Joan Baez, Sr.

Best Wishes
Hillary Brooks

Hillary Brooks

Name	Address	City	State	Zip Code	Resp. Time	Resp. Qual.	Comments
BEASLEY, ALLYCE	2415 CASTILIAN DR.	LOS ANGELES	CA	90068	U	U	ACTRESS - MOONLIGHTING
BEASTIE BOYS	298 ELIZABETH ST.	NEW YORK	NY	10012	U	U	RAP GROUP
BEATTY, NED	2706 N. BEACHWOOD DR.	LOS ANGELES	CA	90027	U	U	ACTOR - DELIVERANCE
BEATTY, WARREN	2029 CENTURY PARK E. #300	LOS ANGELES	CA	90067	U	U	ACTOR/DIRECTOR/WRITER - BUGSY
BECK, JEFF	11 OLD S. LINCOLNS INN	LONDON	ENG.	WC2	U	U	GUITARIST/SINGER
BECK, MARILYN	P.O. BOX 11079	BEVERLY HILLS	CA	90213	A	B	COLUMNIST/CRITIC
BECKER, BORIS	NUSSLOCHER STR. 51	6906 LEIMAN	GER.		U	U	TENNIS PLAYER
BEDELIA, BONNIE	8942 WILSHIRE BLVD.	BEVERLY HILLS	CA	90211	U	U	ACTRESS - PRESUMED INNOCENT
BEE GEES	1801 BAY RD.	MIAMI BEACH	FL	33139	B	F	ROCK GROUP - SENDS FACSIMILE SIGNED PHOTO!
BECROFT, DAVID	4558 LONGRIDGE AVE.	SHERMAN OAKS	CA	91423	A	C	ACTOR
BEENE, GEOFFREY	550 - 7TH AVE.	NEW YORK	NY	10018	U	U	FASHION DESIGNER
BEERY, NOAH JR.	P.O. BOX 108	KEENE	CA	93531	U	U	ACTOR
BEGLEY, ED JR.	3850 MOUNDVIEW AVE.	STUDIO CITY	CA	91604	U	U	ACTOR - ST. ELSEWHERE
BEILINA, NINA	400 W. 43RD ST. #7D	NEW YORK	NY	10036	U	U	VIOLINIST
BEL GEDDES, BARBARA	15 MILL ST.	PUTNAM VALLEY	NY	10579	C	B	ACTRESS - DALLAS
BELAFONTE, HARRY	300 W. END AVE.	NEW YORK	NY	10023	U	U	SINGER/ACTOR - THE BANANA BOAT SONG
BELAFONTE-HARPER, SHARI	10345 W. OLYMPIC BLVD. #200	LOS ANGELES	CA	90064	U	U	ACTRESS/MODEL - HOTEL
BELFORD, CHRISTINE	12747 RIVERSIDE DR. #208	NORTH HOLLYWOOD	CA	91607	U	U	ACTRESS
BELFOUR, ED	C/O CHICAGO BLACKHAWKS, 1800 W. MADISON ST.	CHICAGO	IL	60612	U	U	HOCKEY GOALIE
BELITA	ROSE COTTAGE, 44 CRABTRESS LN.	LONDON	ENG.	SW6 6LW	U	U	BALLERINA/ACTRESS
BELL, GREG	110 - 12TH ST.	LOGANSPORT	IN	46947	U	U	TRACK ATHLETE
BELL, GRIFFIN	206 TOWNSEND PL. N.W.	ATLANTA	GA	30327	A	B	FORMER GOVERNMENT OFFICIAL
BELL, LAURA LEE	7800 BEVERLY BLVD. #3305	LOS ANGELES	CA	90036	C	A	ACTRESS
BELL, SAVED BY THE	NBC-TV 3000 W. ALAMEDA AVE.	BURBANK	CA	91523	U	U	CAST: JONATHAN ANGEL, SAMANTHA BECKER, NATALIA CIGLIUTI, SALIM GRANT, RICHARD JACKSON, AND SARAH LANCASTER.
BELLER, KATHLEEN	2018 N. WHITLEY	LOS ANGELES	CA	90068	U	U	ACTRESS
BELLOW, SAUL	C/O UNIV. OF CHICAGO, 1126 E. 59TH ST.	CHICAGO	IL	60637	U	U	AUTHOR
BELLSON, LOUIE	P.O. BOX 2608	LAKE HAVASU CITY	AZ	86405	U	U	DRUMMER
BELLWOOD, PAMELA	7444 WOODROW WILSON DR.	LOS ANGELES	CA	90046	U	U	ACTRESS/PHOTOGRAPHER - DALLAS
BELMONDO, JEAN-PAUL	77 AVE. DONFERT ROCHEREAUX	PARIS	FRA	16E	U	U	ACTOR
BELUSHI, JAMES	8033 SUNSET BLVD. #88	LOS ANGELES	CA	90046	U	U	ACTOR - K-9
BELZER, RICHARD	813 HUNTLEY DR.	WEST HOLLYWOOD	CA	90069	U	U	ACTOR

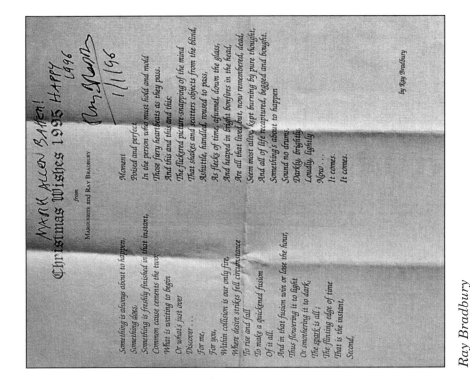

Something is always about to happen,
Something does.
Something is freshly finished in that instant,
Common cause cements the two:
What is waiting to begin
Or what is just over
Discover . . .
For me,
For you,
Within collision is our only fire,
Where desire strikes fell circumstance
To rise and fall
To make a quickened fusion
Of it all
And in that fusion win or lose the hour,
Thus flowering it to light
Or smothering it to dark.
The spark is all;
The flinting edge of time
That is the instant,
Second,

Moment.
Poised and perfect
In the person who must field and mold
Those fiery heart beats as they pass.
And this and this and this:
The flickered picture-snapping of the mind
That shakes and scatters objects from the blind,
As flecks of time affirmed, down the glass,
And heaped in bright bonfires in the head,
Are all that lived but, now remembered, dead,
Seem most alive, kept burning by pure thought,
And all of life recaptured, begged and bought.
Something's about to happen
Sound no drums.
Darkly, brightly,
Loudly, lightly
Now . . .
It comes.
It comes.

by Ray Bradbury

Ray Bradbury

---

the believer magazine
"A Country Music Magazine featuring Garth Brooks"

Thank you so much for your letter and interest in Garth! I am sorry to inform you that we are no longer able to obtain personally autographed photos. Garth is away from the office through March of 1996 working on his new stage show, lighting system and next album project. At that time his '96 tour will begin.

If you are interested in purchasing a photo with Garth's reproduced signature you may Call 1-800-94-Garth.

Thanks for believing!

Tami Rose

from: Tami Rose, Editor
(615) 859-5336
P.O. Box 507 / Goodlettsville, TN 37070-0507

One type of Garth Brooks response

Name	Address	City	State	Zip Code	Resp. Time	Resp. Qual.	Comments
BEN & JERRY'S ICE CREAM	P.O. BOX 240	WATERBURY	VT	05676	U	U	BEN COHN AND JERRY GREENFIELD - OWNERS
BENATAR, PAT	5721 BONSALL RD.	MALIBU	CA	90265	U	U	SINGER - "HEARTBREAKER"
BENCH, JOHNNY	661 REISLING KNOLL	CINCINNATI	OH	45226	F	F	BASEBALL PLAYER - SENDS BACK UNSIGNED!
BENCHLEY, PETER	35 BOUDINOT ST.	PRINCETON	NJ	08540	A	A	AUTHOR - *JAWS* - ADDS SHARK DRAWING!
BENDETTI, MICHAEL	3151 CAHUENGA BLVD. W. # 310	LOS ANGELES	CA	90068	U	U	ACTOR
BENEDICT, BILLY	1347 N. ORANGE GROVE AVE.	LOS ANGELES	CA	90046	A	B	ACTOR
BENEDICT, PAUL	P.O. BOX 451	CHILMARK	MA	02535	U	U	ACTOR
BENEKE, TEX	2275 FAUST AVE.	LONG BEACH	CA	90815	A	B	ORCHESTRA LEADER
BENING, ANNETTE	C/O CREATIVE ARTISTS AGCY., 9830 WILSHIRE BLVD.	BEVERLY HILLS,	CA	90212	U	U	ACTRESS - *BUGSY* - MRS. WARREN BEATTY!
BENJAMIN, RICHARD	719 N. FOOTHILL RD.	BEVERLY HILLS	CA	90210	U	U	ACTOR - *GOODBYE, COLUMBUS*
BENNETT, BRUCE	2702 FORESTER RD.	LOS ANGELES	CA	90064	A	C	ACTOR
BENNETT, TONY	101 W. 55TH ST. #9A	NEW YORK	NY	10019	B	F	SINGER - "'I LEFT MY HEART IN SAN FRANCISCO"
BENNETT, WILLIAM	1776 'I' ST. N.W. #800	WASHINGTON	DC	20006	U	U	FORMER GOVERNMENT OFFICIAL
BENNY, JOAN	1131 COLDWATER CANYON	BEVERLY HILLS	CA	90210	U	U	WIFE OF JACK BENNY
BENOIT, JOAN	R.R. #1, BOX 145AA	FREEPORT	ME	04302	A	A+	MARATHON RUNNER
BENSON, GEORGE	519 NEXT DAY HILL DR.	ENGLEWOOD	NJ	07631	A	F	JAZZ SINGER/GUITARIST - "ON BROADWAY"
BENSON, MELISSA	C/O WIZARDS OF THE COAST, INC. P.O. BOX 707	RENTON	WA	98057	U	U	ILLUSTRATOR - "MAGIC" CARDS!
BENTON, BARBI	40 N. 4TH ST.	CARBONDALE	CO	81623	U	U	ACTRESS/MODEL
BERENGER, TOM	P.O. BOX 1842	BEAUFORT	SC	29901	U	U	ACTOR - *PLATOON*
BERENSON, BERRY	2840 SEATTLE DR.	LOS ANGELES	CA	90046	U	U	MRS. ANTHONY PERKINS
BERENSON, MARISA	80 AVE. CHARLES DE GAULLE	F92200 NEUILLY	FRA		U	U	ACTRESS - *BARRY LYNDON*
BERG, PATTY	P.O. BOX 9227	FT. MEYERS	FL	33902	C	B	GOLFER - TOUGH TO CADDY FOR!
BERGEN, CANDICE	955 S. CARRILLO DR. #200	LOS ANGELES	CA	90048	C	F	ACTRESS - *MURPHY BROWN* - **AUTHOR'S CHOICE!**
BERGEN, MRS. EDGAR	1485 CARLA RIDGE	BEVERLY HILLS	CA	90210	U	U	ACTRESS
BERGERE, LEE	2385 CENTURY HILL	LOS ANGELES	CA	90067	U	U	ACTOR
BERGMAN, ALAN	714 N. MAPLE DR.	BEVERLY HILLS	CA	90210	A	D	LYRICIST - TYPICALLY SIGNS ONLY ONE!
BERGMAN, INGMAR	P.O. BOX 27127	S-10252 STOCKHOLM	SWE.		U	U	FILM DIRECTOR - *THE SILENCE*
BERGMAN, MARILYN	714 N. MAPLE DR.	BEVERLY HILLS	CA	90210	A	D	LYRICIST - TYPICALLY SIGNS ONLY ONE!
BERGMAN, PETER	4799 WHITE OAK AVE.	ENCINO	CA	91316	U	U	ACTOR
BERGMAN, SANDAHL	9903 SANTA MONICA BLVD. #274	BEVERLY HILLS	CA	90212	U	U	ACTRESS/MODEL
BERKHOFF, STEVEN	9255 SUNSET BLVD. #155	LOS ANGELES	CA	90069	U	U	ACTOR
BERLE, MILTON	10750 WILSHIRE BLVD. #1003	LOS ANGELES	CA	90024	A	C	ACTOR/COMEDIAN - *THE MILTON BERLE SHOW*

113

Edd Byrnes

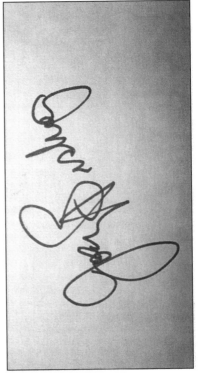

Shirley Temple

Joey Bishop

114

Name	Address	City	State	Zip Code	Resp. Time	Resp. Qual.	Comments
BERLINGER, WARREN	10642 ARNEL PL.	CHATSWORTH	CA	91311	U	U	ACTOR
BERMAN, CHRIS	C/O ESPN, ESPN PLAZA	BRISTOL	CT	06010	U	U	SPORTSCASTER - HE COULD "GO ALL THE WAY" OR MAIL YOUR REQUEST "BACK, BACK, BACK..."
BERMAN, SHELLEY	268 BELL CANYON RD.	BELL CANYON	CA	91307	U	U	COMEDIENNE
BERNARD, CRYSTAL	151 EL CAMINO DR.	BEVERLY HILLS	CA	90212	U	U	ACTRESS - WINGS
BERNARD, ED	18851 BRAEMORE RD.	NORTHRIDGE	CA	91326	U	U	ACTOR
BERNHARD, SANDRA	11233 BLIX ST.	NORTH HOLLYWOOD	CA	91602	A	D	ACTRESS - ROSEANNE
BERNHARDT, KEVIN	9300 WILSHIRE BLVD. #410	BEVERLY HILLS	CA	90212	U	U	ACTOR
BERNSEN, CORBIN	3500 W. OLIVE #920	BURBANK	CA	91505	U	U	ACTOR - L.A. LAW
BERNSTEIN, JAY	9360 BEVERLY CREST DR.	BEVERLY HILLS	CA	90210	A	D	TALENT AGENT
BERNSTEIN, KENNY	1105 SEMINOLE	RICHARDSON	TX	75080	A	B	DRAG RACER
BERRA, YOGI	19 HIGHLAND AVE.	MONTCLAIR	NJ	07042	U	U	MEMBER OF THE BASEBALL HALL OF FAME
BERRY, CHUCK	BUCKNER RD.	WENTZVILLE	MO	63386	U	U	SINGER/SONGWRITER - "JOHNNY B. GOODE"
BERRY, HALLE	40 POINT RIDGE	ATLANTA	GA	30328	U	U	ACTRESS - LOSING ISIAH - AUTHOR'S CHOICE!
BERRY, KEN	4704 CAHUENGA BLVD.	NORTH HOLLYWOOD	CA	91602	U	U	ACTOR/DANCER
BERTINELLI, VALERIE	12700 VENTURA BLVD. #100	STUDIO CITY	CA	91604	A	D	ACTRESS - ONE DAY AT A TIME - MRS. EDDIE VAN HALEN!
BESSEL, TED	1415 STONE CANYON RD.	LOS ANGELES	CA	90077	U	U	ACTOR - THAT GIRL
BEST, KEVIN	P.O. BOX 1164	HESPERIA	CA	92345	U	U	ACTOR
BESTWICKE, MARTINE	131 S. SYCAMORE AVE.	LOS ANGELES	CA	90036	U	U	ACTRESS
BETHUNE, IVY	3096 LAKE HOLLYWOOD DR.	LOS ANGELES	CA	90068	A	B	ACTRESS
BETHUNE, ZINA	3096 LAKE HOLLYWOOD DR.	LOS ANGELES	CA	90068	A	B	ACTRESS
BETTENHAUSEN, GARY	109 GASOLINE ALLEY	SPEEDWAY	IN	46222	C	B	AUTO RACER
BETTENHAUSEN, TONY	5234 WILTON WOOD COURT	INDIANAPOLIS	IN	46254	A	B	AUTO RACER
BETTGER, LYLE	P.O. BOX 1076	PAI	HI	96779	U	U	ACTOR
BEVERLY HILLS 90210	C/O FOX BROADCASTING CO., 10201 W. PICO BLVD.	LOS ANGELES	CA	90035	U	U	SEE INDEPENDENT ENTRIES FOR CAST!
BEYER, TROY	151 EL CAMINO DR.	BEVERLY HILLS	CA	90212	U	U	ACTRESS
BEYMER, RICHARD	1818 N. FULLER AVE.	LOS ANGELES	CA	90046	U	U	ACTOR
BIALIK, MAYIM	1419 PEERLESS PL. #120	LOS ANGELES	CA	90035	U	U	ACTRESS - BLOSSOM
BIEHN, MICHAEL	3737 DEERVALE DR.	SHERMAN OAKS	CA	91403	U	U	ACTOR - THE TERMINATOR
BIERDZ, THOM	1435 N. STANLEY	LOS ANGELES	CA	90046	U	U	ACTOR
BIERI, RAMON	19963 ARCE ST.	NORTHRIDGE	CA	91324	A	C+	ACTOR
BIKEL, THEODORE	1131 ALTA LOMA RD. #523	LOS ANGELES	CA	90069	A	B+	ACTOR/SINGER
BILGE, MARY J.	8942 WILSHIRE BLVD.	BEVERLY HILLS	CA	90211	U	U	SINGER

115

April 21, 1980

Dear Mark:

Remember the letter you sent to Erma Bombeck?

Well, she finally received it.

Since you have such a terrific imagination and a great sense of humor, try to imagine this pot is filled with $60 a dozen roses.

I knew it wouldn't work.

You'll just have to accept my thanks and know how appreciative I am of your thoughtfulness in writing. I hope a future column or appearance on Good Morning America will prompt you to write again.

Regards,

Erma Bombeck

Erma Bombeck

EB:ak
encl.

Erma Bombeck

Erma Bombeck (deceased)

Bruce Boxleitner

Billy Wilder

116

Name	Address	City	State	Zip Code	Resp. Time	Resp. Qual.	Comments
BILL, TONY	73 MARKET ST.	VENICE	CA	90291	A	B	ACTOR/DIRECTOR
BILLINGSLEY, BARBARA	P.O. BOX 1320	SANTA MONICA	CA	90403	U	U	ACTRESS - *LEAVE IT TO BEAVER*
BILLINGSLEY, PETER	118 E. COUNTRY CLUB DR.	PHOENIX	AZ	85014	U	U	CHILD ACTOR - *A CHRISTMAS STORY*
BIONDI, MATT	1404 RIMER DR.	MORAGA	CA	94556	A	D	SWIMMER - WRITES SMALL!
BIRD, BILLIE	9255 SUNSET BLVD. #515	LOS ANGELES	CA	90069	U	U	ACTRESS
BIRD, LARRY	501 HIBISCUS DR.	HALLENDALE	FL	33009	U	U	BASKETBALL PLAYER
BIRNEY, DAVID	20 OCEAN PARK BLVD. #11	SANTA MONICA	CA	90405	A	C	ACTOR - *ST. ELSEWHERE*
BISHOP, JOEY	534 VIA LIDO NORD	NEWPORT BEACH	CA	92650	A	B	COMEDIAN - THE JOEY BISHOP SHOW
BISHOP, KRISTEN	C/O WIZARDS OF THE COAST, INC. P.O. BOX 707	RENTON	WA	98057	U	U	ILLUSTRATOR - MAGIC CARDS!
BISSET, JACQUELINE	1815 BENEDICT CANYON DR.	BEVERLY HILLS	CA	90210	A	B	ACTRESS - *THE DEEP*
BISSETT, JOSIE	C/O ICM, 8942 WILSHIRE BLVD.	BEVERLY HILLS	CA	90211	U	U	ACTRESS - *MELROSE PLACE* - **AUTHOR'S CHOICE!**
BLACK OAK ARKANSAS	1487 RED FOX RUN	LILBURN	GA	30247	U	U	COUNTRY ROCK GROUP
BLACK, CLINT	P.O. BOX 299386	HOUSTON	TX	77299	A	D	SINGER - **AUTHOR'S CHOICE!**
BLACKWOOD, NINA	22968 VICTORY BLVD. #158	WOODLAND HILLS	CA	91367	U	U	MUSIC CORRESPONDENT
BLACQUE, TAUREAN	4207 DON ORTEGA PL.	LOS ANGELES	CA	90008	U	U	ACTOR
BLADES, RUBEN	521 - 12TH ST.	SANTA MONICA	CA	90402	U	U	ACTOR/SINGER - *THE MILAGRO BEANFIELD WAR*
BLAINE, NEIL WALDEN	3 LEDGE RD.	GLOUCESTER	MA	01930	A	D	PAINTER
BLAIR, BONNIE	1907 W. SPRINGFIELD	CHAMPAIGN	IL	61820	A	B	SPEED SKATER - **AUTHOR'S CHOICE!**
BLAKE, J.W.	P.O. BOX 146	DAMARISCOTTA	ME	04543	A	D	CARTOONIST - *TIGER*
BLAKE, ROBERT	11604 DILLING ST.	NORTH HOLLYWOOD	CA	91608	U	U	ACTOR - *BARETTA*
BLAKE, STEPHANIE	14322 DICKENS ST. #8	SHERMAN OAKS	CA	91423	U	U	ACTRESS
BLAKE, WHITNEY	P.O. BOX 6088	MALIBU	CA	90265	U	U	ACTRESS
BLAKELEY, ART	C/O BRIDGE, 106 FORT GREEN PL.	BROOKLYN	NY	11217	U	U	JAZZ MUSICIAN!
BLAKLEY, RONEE	8033 SUNSET BLVD. #693	LOS ANGELES	CA	90046	A	B	SINGER/ACTRESS
BLANC, NOEL	702 N. RODEO DR.	BEVERLY HILLS	CA	90210	A	B	WRITER, VOICE HEIR!
BLANCHARD, NINA	957 N. COLE AVE.	LOS ANGELES	CA	90028	A	D	TALENT AGENT
BLANDA, GEORGE	P.O. BOX 1153	LA QUINTA	CA	92253	A	D	MEMBER OF FOOTBALL HALL OF FAME!
BLANE, SALLY	1114 S. ROXBURY DR.	LOS ANGELES	CA	90035	A	D	ACTRESS
BLANKFIELD, MARK	141 S. EL CAMINO DR. #205	BEVERLY HILLS	CA	90212	U	U	ACTOR
BLASS, BILL	550 -7TH AVE.	NEW YORK	NY	10019	A	B	FASHION DESIGNER
BLASSIE, FREDDIE	P.O. BOX 3859	STAMFORD	CT	06905	A	B	WRESTLER/MANAGER
BLATNICK, JEFF	848 WHITNEY DR.	SCHENECTADY	NY	12309	A	D	WRESTLER - **AUTHOR'S CHOICE!**

Pat Boone

Valerie Bertinelli

Anne Bancroft

George Burns (deceased)

Gary Busey

Name	Address	City	State	Zip Code	Resp. Time	Resp. Qual.	Comments
BLEDSOE, DREW	C/O NEW ENGLAND PATRIOTS, RT. ONE	FOXBORO	MA	02035	B	D	FOOTBALL PLAYER - ONE OF THE SPORT'S BETTER SIGNERS!
BLEIER, ROCKY	580 SQUAL RUN RD. E.	PITTSBURGH	PA	15238	A	B	FOOTBALL PLAYER - **AUTHOR'S CHOICE!**
BLOCK, HERB	1150 - 15TH ST. N.W.	WASHINGTON	DC	20071	U	U	CARTOONIST
BLOCKER, DIRK	924 WESTWOOD BLVD. #900	LOS ANGELES	CA	90024	U	U	ACTOR
BLODGETT, MICHAEL	10485 NATIONAL BLVD. #22	LOS ANGELES	CA	90034	U	U	ACTOR
BLOODWORTH-THOMASON, LINDA	9220 SUNSET BLVD. #311	LOS ANGELES	CA	90069	U	U	TELEVISION PRODUCER - *DESIGNING WOMEN*
BLOOM, BRIAN	11 CROYDON COURT	DIX HILLS	NY	11746	U	U	ACTOR
BLOOM, CLAIRE	109 JERMYN ST.	LONDON	ENG.	W1	U	U	ACTRESS - *RICHARD III*
BLOOM, VERA	327 E. 82ND ST.	NEW YORK	NY	10028	U	U	ACTRESS
BLOOMINGDALE, BETSY	131 DELFERN DR.	LOS ANGELES	CA	90024	U	U	BUSINESSWOMAN
BLOSSOM	WITT/THOMAS PROD., 1438 N. GOWER ST.	HOLLYWOOD	CA	90028	U	U	TELEVISION SERIES
BLOUNT, LISA	151 EL CAMINO DR.	BEVERLY HILLS	CA	90212	U	U	ACTRESS
BLOUNT, MEL	R.D. 1, BOX 91	CLAYSVILLE	PA	15323	U	U	FOOTBALL PLAYER
BLUME, JUDY	54 RIVERSIDE DR.	NEW YORK	NY	10023	U	U	WRITER - *ARE YOU THERE GOD? IT'S ME, MARGARET*
BLYTH, ANN	P.O. BOX 9754	RANCHO SANTA FE	CA	92067	A	B	ACTRESS
BOARDMAN, TRUE	2951 PAISANO RD.	PEBBLE BEACH	CA	93593	A	B+	ACTOR
BOATMAN, MICHAEL	1571 S. KIOWA CREST DR.	DIAMOND BAR	CA	91765	U	U	ACTOR
BOCHCO, STEVEN	FOX STUDIOS, 10201 W. PICO BLVD.	LOS ANGELES	CA	90064	U	U	PRODUCER - *NYPD BLUE* - **AUTHOR'S CHOICE!**
BOCHNER, HART	223 OCEAN DR.	OXNARD	CA	93035	U	U	ACTOR
BOCHNER, LLOYD	42 HALDEMAN RD.	SANTA MONICA	CA	90402	A	D	ACTOR
BOETTICHER, BUDD	23969 GREEN HAVEN LN.	RAMONA	CA	92065	B	B	FILM DIRECTOR
BOGGS, WADE	6006 WINDHAM PL.	TAMPA	FL	33647	U	U	BASEBALL PLAYER - **AUTHOR'S CHOICE!**
BOGGUSS, SUZY	4155 E. JEWELL AVE. #412	DENVER	CO	80222	A	D	SINGER - ALSO INCLUDES FAN CLUB INFO!
BOTANO, BRIAN	109 PANORAMIC WAY	BERKELEY	CA	94704	C	B	ICE SKATER
BOLLING, TIFFANY	12483 BRADDOCK DR.	LOS ANGELES	CA	90066	U	U	ACTRESS
BOLOGNA, JOSEPH	613 N. ARDEN DR.	BEVERLY HILLS	CA	90210	U	U	ACTOR - *CHAPTER TWO*
BOLTON, MICHAEL	130 W. 57TH ST. #10B	NEW YORK	NY	10019	U	U	SINGER - **AUTHOR'S CHOICE!** CATCH HIM PLAYING SOFTBALL!
BON JOVI, JON	P.O. BOX 326	FORDS	NJ	08863	U	U	ROCK GROUP - **AUTHOR'S CHOICE!** - GOOD IN PERSON!
BONADUCE, DANNY	3 BALA PLAZA E. #580	BALA CYNWYD	PA	19004	A	D	ACTOR - *THE PARTRIDGE FAMILY*
BOND, JULIAN	361 W. VIEW DR.	ATLANTA	GA	30310	A	B	POLITICIAN
BOND, TOMMY "BUTCH"	14704 RD. 36	MADERA	CA	93638	A	D	ACTOR

119

All the best

Jacqueline Bisset

F. Lee Bailey

To Mark Allen ~
Sincerely,
Tex Beneke

Tex Beneke

Clint Black (facsimile)

Name	Address	City	State	Zip Code	Resp. Time	Resp. Qual.	Comments
BONDS, BARRY	C/O S.F. GIANTS, CANDLESTICK PARK	SAN FRANCISCO	CA	94124	F	F	BASEBALL PLAYER! HORRIBLE SIGNER!
BONDS, GARY U.S.	141 DUNBAR AVE.	FORDS	NJ	08863	B	B	SINGER
BONERZ, PETER	3637 LOWRY RD.	LOS ANGELES	CA	90027	U	U	ACTOR/DIRECTOR
BONET, LISA	6435 BALCOM	RESEDA	CA	91335	A	D	ACTRESS - THE COSBY SHOW
BONNER, FRANK	10100 SANTA MONICA BLVD. #700	LOS ANGELES	CA	90067	U	U	ACTOR/DIRECTOR
BONO	ISLAND RECORDS, 14 E. 4TH ST.	NEW YORK	NY	10003	U	U	SINGER - U2 - "THE JOSHUA TREE" - AUTHOR'S CHOICE!
BONO, SONNY	1700 N. INDIAN AVE.	PALM SPRINGS	CA	92262	U	U	SINGER/POLITICIAN
BONSALL, BRIAN	11712 MOORPARK ST. #204	STUDIO CITY	CA	91604	U	U	ACTOR
BOONE, DEBBY	4334 KESTER AVE.	SHERMAN OAKS	CA	91403	U	U	SINGER
BOONE, PAT	904 N. BEVERLY DR.	BEVERLY HILLS	CA	90210	A	B	ACTOR/SINGER - ALSO ADDS FAN CLUB INFO!
BOONE, RANDY	14250 CALIFA ST.	VAN NUYS	CA	91401	U	U	ACTOR
BOOSLER, ELAYNE	11061 WRIGHTWOOD LN.	NORTH HOLLYWOOD	CA	91604	A	B+	COMEDIENNE
BOOTH, BRIAN	3922 GLENRIDGE DR.	SHERMAN OAKS	CA	91423	A	B	ACTRESS
BOOTHE, POWERS	23629 LONG VALLEY RD.	HIDDEN HILLS	CA	91302	U	U	ACTOR
BORG, BJORN	8 RUE BELLEVUE	MONTE CARLO	MON.		U	U	TENNIS PLAYER
BORGE, VICTOR	FIELDPOINT PARK	GREENWICH	CT	06830	A	D	PIANIST/COMEDIAN
BORGNINE, ERNEST	3055 LAKE GLEN DR.	BEVERLY HILLS	CA	90210	A	F	ACTOR - THE POSEIDON ADVENTURE
BORGNINE, TOVA	3055 LAKE GLEN DR.	BEVERLY HILLS	CA	90210	A	C	ACTRESS/COSMETICS
BORK, ROBERT	1150 - 17TH ST. N.W.	WASHINGTON	DC	20036	U	U	JUDGE
BORMAN, MAJOR FRANK	6628 VISTA HERMOSA	LAS CRUCES	NM	88005	A	F	ASTRONAUT - $10 PER SIGNATURE!
BORN, ROSCOE	8444 WILSHIRE BLVD. #800	BEVERLY HILLS	CA	90211	U	U	ACTOR
BOROS, JULIUS	2900 N.E. 40TH ST.	FT. LAUDERDALE	FL	33308	U	U	GOLFER
BOSCO, PHILIP	337 W. 43RD ST. #1B	NEW YORK	NY	10036	U	U	ACTOR
BOSLEY, TOM	2822 ROYSTON PL.	BEVERLY HILLS	CA	90210	U	U	ACTOR
BOSSON, BARBARA	694 AMALFI DR.	PACIFIC PALISADES	CA	90272	U	U	ACTRESS
BOSTON, RALPH	3301 WOODBINE AVE.	KNOXVILLE	TN	37914	A	B	TRACK ATHLETE
BOSTWICK, BARRY	2770 HUTTON DR.	BEVERLY HILLS	CA	90210	U	U	ACTOR
BOSWORTH, BRIAN	230 PARK AVE. #230	NEW YORK	NY	10169	U	U	ACTOR/FOOTBALL PLAYER
BOTTOMS, JOE	1015 GAYLEY AVE. #300	LOS ANGELES	CA	90024	U	U	ACTOR
BOTTOMS, SAM	4719 WILLOWCREST AVE.	TOLUCA LAKE	CA	91602	U	U	ACTOR
BOTTOMS, TIMOTHY	532 HOT SPRINGS RD.	SANTA BARBARA	CA	93108	A	C	ACTOR
BOUDREAU, LOU	15600 ELLIS AVE.	DOLTON	IL	60419	A	C	MEMBER OF BASEBALL HALL OF FAME!
BOUTON, JIM	P.O. BOX 188	NORTH EGREMONT	MA	01252	U	U	BASEBALL PLAYER

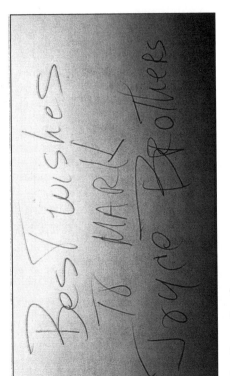

Danny Bonaduce

Dr. Joyce Brothers

Barbara Taylor Bradford

Rocky Blier

Name	Address	City	State	Zip Code	Resp. Time	Resp. Qual.	Comments
BOWE, RIDDICK	40 CHANNING ST. N.W.	WASHINGTON	DC	20001	U	U	WORLD BOXING CHAMPION
BOWMAN, CHRISTOPHER	5653 KESTER AVE.	VAN NUYS	CA	91405	U	U	SKATER
BOXCAR WILLIE	1300 DIVISION ST. #103	NASHVILLE	TN	37203	U	U	SINGER
BOXLEITNER, BRUCE	24500 JOHN COLTER RD.	HIDDEN HILLS	CA	91302	A	B	ACTOR
BOY MEETS WORLD	ABC-TV, 2040 AVE. OF THE STARS	LOS ANGELES	CA	90067	U	U	TELEVISION SHOW
BOYLE, LARA FLYNN	606 N. LARCHMONT BLVD. #309	LOS ANGELES	CA	90004	U	U	ACTRESS
BOYLE, PETER	130 E. END AVE.	NEW YORK	NY	10028	U	U	ACTOR
BOYS II MEN	6255 SUNSET BLVD. #1700	LOS ANGELES	CA	90028	U	U	R&B GROUP
BRACKEN, EDDIE	69 DOUGLAS RD.	GLEN RIDGE	NJ	07028	A	A	ACTOR
BRADBURY, RAY	10265 CHEVIOT DR.	LOS ANGELES	CA	90064	A	C	AUTHOR
BRADFORD, BARBARA TAYLOR	450 PARK AVE.	NEW YORK	NY	10022	A	B	AUTHOR - A WOMAN OF SUBSTANCE
BRADFORD, RICHARD	6605 HOLLYWOOD BLVD. #220	LOS ANGELES	CA	90028	U	U	ACTOR
BRADLEE, BENJAMIN	1150 - 15TH ST. N.W.	WASHINGTON	DC	20071	A	D	JOURNALIST
BRADLEY, ED	285 CENTRAL PARK W.	NEW YORK	NY	10024	U	U	NEWSCASTER - 60 MINUTES
BRADLEY, OWEN	P.O. BOX 120838	NASHVILLE	TN	37212	U	U	PIANIST
BRADLEY, SEN. BILL	731 HART OFFICE BLDG.	WASHINGTON	DC	20510	U	U	POLITICIAN - WATCH FOR AUTOPEN!
BRADSHAW, TERRY	8911 SHADY LANE DR.	SHREVEPORT	LA	71118	A	D	MEMBER OF FOOTBALL HALL OF FAME!
BRADY, JAMES	1255 "I" ST. #1100	WASHINGTON	DC	20005	U	U	FORMER WHITE HOUSE PRESS SEC.
BRAEDEN, ERIC	13723 ROMANY DR.	PACIFIC PALISADES	CA	90272	U	U	ACTOR
BRAGA, SONIA	295 GREENWICH ST. #11B	NEW YORK	NY	10007	U	U	ACTRESS - THE MILAGRO BEANFIELD WAR
BRAGG, DON	P.O. BOX 171	NEW GRETNA	NJ	08224	U	U	TRACK ATHLETE
BRANAGH, KENNETH	83 BERWICK ST.	LONDON	ENG.	W1V 3PJ	U	U	ACTOR/DIRECTOR -HENRY V - AUTHOR'S CHOICE!
BRAND X	17171 ROSCOE BLVD. #104	NORTHRIDGE	CA	91325	A	B	ACTOR
BRANDIS, JONATHAN	C/O SEAQUEST 2032, NBC-TV, 3000 W. ALAMEDA AVE.	BURBANK	CA	91523	U	U	ACTOR!
BRANDO, MARLON	13828 WEDDINGTON	VAN NUYS	CA	91401	U	U	ACTOR - THE GODFATHER - EXTREMELY TOUGH!
BRANDON, CLARK	9000 SUNSET BLVD. #1200	LOS ANGELES	CA	90069	U	U	ACTOR
BRANDY	C/O ATLANTIC RECORDS, 75 ROCKEFELLER PLAZA	NEW YORK	NY	10019	U	U	SINGER!
BRAVERMAN, BART	524 N. LAUREL AVE.	LOS ANGELES	CA	90048	A	B	ACTOR - ADDS COMMENTS ABOUT FORM LETTER!
BRAXTON, TONI	LAFACE RECORDS, 3350 PEACHTREE RD., #1500	ATLANTA	GA	30326	U	U	SINGER - "BREATHE AGAIN" - AUTHOR'S CHOICE!
BREGMAN, BUDDY	11288 VENTURA BLVD. #700	STUDIO CITY	CA	91604	U	U	DIRECTOR/PRODUCER
BREMER-RECHT, TRACEY	7800 BEVERLY BLVD. #3305	LOS ANGELES	CA	90036	U	U	ACTRESS
BRENNAN, MELISSA	23635 EMELITA ST.	WOODLAND HILLS	CA	91367	U	U	ACTRESS

123

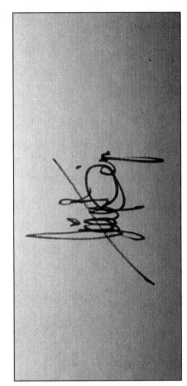

Lauren Bacall

Victor Borge

George Benson (facsimile)

Jim Bunning

Name	Address	City	State	Zip Code	Resp. Time	Resp. Qual.	Comments
BRENNER, DAVID	813 BONITA DR.	ASPEN	CO	81611	U	U	COMEDIAN/TALK SHOW HOST
BRENNER, DORI	2106 CANYON DR.	LOS ANGELES	CA	90068	U	U	ACTRESS
BRESLIN, JIMMY	75 CENTRAL PARK W.	NEW YORK	NY	10023	U	U	AUTHOR/COLUMNIST
BREST, MARTIN	831 PASEO MIRAMAR	PACIFIC PALISADES	CA	90272	U	U	FILM WRITER/DIRECTOR
BRETT, GEORGE	P.O. BOX 419969	KANSAS CITY	MO	64141	A	F	BASEBALL PLAYER - ALWAYS BEEN TOUGH!
BREWER, TERESA	384 PINEBROOK BLVD.	NEW ROCHELLE	NY	10803	C	B	SINGER
BRIAN, MARY	4107 TROOST AVE.	NORTH HOLLYWOOD	CA	90212	U	U	ACTRESS
BRICKELL, BETH	9933 ROBBINS DR. #2	BEVERLY HILLS	CA	90212	A	A+	WRITER/DIRECTOR
BRIDGES, BEAU	5525 N. JED SMITH RD.	HIDDEN HILLS	CA	91302	C	B	ACTOR/DIRECTOR - THE FABULOUS BAKER BOYS
BRIDGES, JEFF	C/O CREATIVE ARTISTS AGCY., 9830 WILSHIRE BLVD.	BEVERLY HILLS	CA	90212	U	U	ACTOR - THE FABULOUS BAKER BOYS - AUTHOR'S CHOICE!
BRIDGES, LLOYD	225 LORINA AVE.	LOS ANGELES	CA	90077	A	B	ACTOR - AIRPLANE
BRILL, CHARLIE	3635 WRIGHTWOOD DR.	STUDIO CITY	CA	91604	A	B	ACTOR
BRIMLEY, WILFRED	10000 SANTA MONICA BLVD. #305	LOS ANGELES	CA	90067	U	U	ACTOR
BRINKLEY, CHRISTIE	2124 BROADWAY # 104	NEW YORK	NY	10023	U	U	MODEL
BRINKLEY, DAVID	1717 DESALES ST. N.W.	WASHINGTON	DC	20036	U	U	BROADCAST JOURNALIST
BRITT, MAY	P.O. BOX 525	ZEPHYR COVE	NV	89448	A	B	ACTRESS
BRITTANY, MORGAN	3434 CORNELL RD.	AGOURA HILLS	CA	91301	U	U	ACTRESS/MODEL
BROCCOLI, ALBERT "CUBBY"	809 N. HILLCREST RD.	BEVERLY HILLS	CA	90210	U	U	FILM PRODUCER - JAMES BOND FILMS
BROCK, ALICE MAY	69 COMMERCIAL ST.	PROVINCETOWN	MA	02657	U	U	ALICE OF ALICE'S RESTAURANT FAME!
BROCK, LOU	P.O. BOX 28398	ST. LOUIS	MO	63146	U	U	MEMBER OF THE BASEBALL HALL OF FAME
BRODERICK, MATTHEW	C/O CREATIVE ARTISTS AGCY., 9830 WILSHIRE BLVD.	BEVERLY HILLS	CA	90212	U	U	ACTOR - FERRIS BUELLER'S DAY OFF - AUTHOR'S CHOICE!
BRODIE, KEVIN	4292 ELMER AVE.	NORTH HOLLYWOOD	CA	91602	U	U	ACTOR
BRODY, LANE	P.O. BOX 24775	NASHVILLE	TN	37202	A	A+	SINGER - SENDS EVERYTHING BUT THE KITCHEN SINK BACK TO YOU!
BROKAW, NORMAN	530 VICK PL.	BEVERLY HILLS	CA	90210	U	U	TALENT AGENT
BROKAW, TOM	941 PARK AVE. #14C	NEW YORK	NY	10025	U	U	TELEVISION NEWS ANCHOR - AUTHOR'S CHOICE!
BROMFIELD, JOHN	1750 WHITTIER AVE.	COSTA MESA	CA	92627	U	U	ACTOR
BRONFMAN, EDGAR M.	375 PARK AVE.	NEW YORK	NY	10022	U	U	LIQUOR EXECUTIVE
BRONSON, CHARLES	P.O. BOX 2644	MALIBU	CA	90265	A	B	ACTOR
BRONSON, LILLIAN	32591 SEVEN SEAS DR.	LAGUNA NIGUEL	CA	92677	U	U	ACTRESS
BROOKE KLUNE, HILARY	40 VIA CASITAS	BONSALL	CA	92003	A	B	ACTRESS
BROOKS, AVERY	20 LAYNE RD.	SUMMERSET	NJ	08873	C	B	ACTOR
BROOKS, FOSTER	315 S. BEVERLY DR. #216	BEVERLY HILLS	CA	90212	U	U	COMEDIAN

Bob Barker

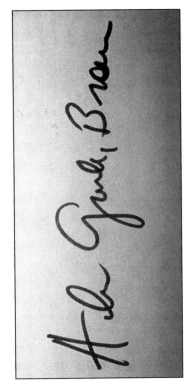

Helen Gurley Brown

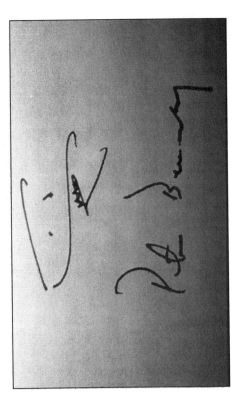

Peter Benchley

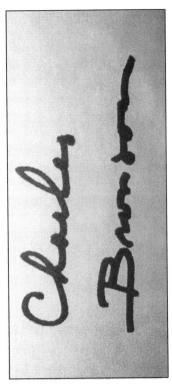

Charles Bronson

Name	Address	City	State	Zip Code	Resp. Time	Resp. Qual.	Comments
BROOKS, GARTH	3322 W. END AVE. #1100	NASHVILLE	TN	37203	A	D	SINGER - **AUTHOR'S CHOICE!** - SENT CARD BACK WITH QUOTE - "NICE (BS) FORM LETTER" - SORRY GARTH!
BROOKS, GWENDOLYN	THE CONT. FORUM, 2528A W. JEROME ST. CHICAGO		IL	60640	U	U	POET/AUTHOR - **AUTHOR'S CHOICE!**
BROOKS, JAMES L.	C/O ICM, 8942 WILSHIRE BLVD.	BEVERLY HILLS	CA	90211	U	U	PRODUCER - *MARY TYLER MOORE SHOW* - **AUTHOR'S CHOICE!**
BROOKS, MEL	2301 LA MESA DR.	SANTA MONICA	CA	90405	U	U	ACTOR/WRITER/DIRECTOR - *BLAZING SADDLES* - **AUTHOR'S CHOICE!**
BROOKS, PHYLLIS	P.O. BOX 14	CAPE NEDDICK	ME	03902	U	U	ACTRESS
BROOKS, RAND	1701 CAPISTRANO CIRCLE	GLENDALE	CA	91207	A	D	ACTRESS
BROPHY, KEVIN	15010 HAMLIN ST.	VAN NUYS	CA	91411	C	B	ACTOR
BROSNAN, PIERCE	1538-D E. WILSON AVE.	GLENDALE	CA	91206	A	F	ACTOR - *GOLDENEYE* - SENDS ALONG FAN CLUB INFO! - **AUTHOR'S CHOICE!**
BROTHERLY LOVE	NBC-TV, 3000 W. ALAMEDA AVE.	BURBANK	CA	91523	U	U	CAST: ANDREW, JOEY, AND MATTHEW LAWRENCE!
BROTHERS, DR. JOYCE	1530 PALISADES AVE.	FORT LEE	NJ	07024	A	D	PSYCHOLOGIST
BROUGH, LOUISE	1808 VOLUNTARY RD.	VISTA	CA	92083	U	U	TENNIS PLAYER
BROUN, HAYWOOD HALE	189 PLOCHMAN	WOODSTOCK	NY	12498	A	D	SPORTSWRITER/SPORTSCASTER
BROUSSARD, REBECCA	9911 W. PICO BLVD. PH A	LOS ANGELES	CA	90035	U	U	ACTRESS
BROWN, BLAIR	10 E. 44TH ST. #500	NEW YORK	NY	10017	U	U	ACTRESS
BROWN, BOBBY	3350 PEACHTREE RD. N.E.	ATLANTA	GA	30326	U	U	SINGER - "PREROGATIVE" **AUTHOR'S CHOICE!**
BROWN, BRYAN	11620 WILSHIRE BLVD. #1000	LOS ANGELES	CA	90025	U	U	ACTOR
BROWN, DWIER	248 SAN JUAN AVE. #B	VENICE	CA	90291	U	U	ACTOR
BROWN, EDMUND "JERRY"	3022 WASHINGTON	SAN FRANCISCO	CA	94115	A	B+	FORMER GOVERNOR
BROWN, HELEN GURLEY	1 W. 81ST ST. #22D	NEW YORK	NY	10024	A	B+	AUTHOR/MAGAZINE EDITOR - A FIRST CLASS LADY!
BROWN, JAMES	1217 W. MEDICAL PARK RD.	AUGUSTA	GA	30909	A	C+	SINGER - "I FEEL GOOD...."
BROWN, JIM	1851 SUNSET PLAZA DR.	LOS ANGELES	CA	90069	U	U	FOOTBALL PLAYER/ACTOR - NICE IN PERSON!
BROWN, JIM ED	P.O. BOX 121089	NASHVILLE	TN	37212	A	B	SINGER
BROWN, LES	1787 FERMALD PT. LN. #PELICAN	MONTECITO	CA	93108	A	D	ORCHESTRA LEADER
BROWN, NACIO HERB JR.	1739 DECAMP DR.	BEVERLY HILLS	CA	90210	U	U	ACTOR
BROWN, PETER	854 CYPRESS AVE.	HERMAN BEACH	CA	90254	U	U	ACTOR
BROWN, REB	5454 LAS VIRGINES RD.	CALABASAS	CA	91302	U	U	ACTOR
BROWN, RUTH	600 W. 165TH ST. #4-H	NEW YORK	NY	10032	U	U	SINGER
BROWN, SUSAN	11931 ADDISON ST.	NORTH HOLLYWOOD	CA	91607	B	B	ACTRESS
BROWN, T. GRAHAM	1516 - 16 AVE. S.	NASHVILLE	TN	37212	C	B	SINGER - ADDS FAN CLUB INFO!
BROWN, THOMAS WILSON	5918 VAN NUYS BLVD.	VAN NUYS	CA	91401	U	U	ACTOR
BROWN, VANESSA	14340 MULHOLLAND DR.	LOS ANGELES	CA	90024	U	U	ACTRESS

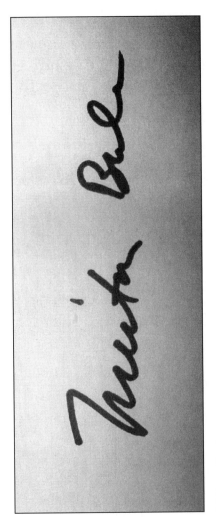

Milton Berle

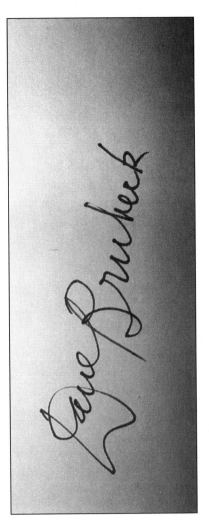

Dave Brubeck

Name	Address	City	State	Zip Code	Resp. Time	Resp. Qual.	Comments
BROWN, WILLIE L. JR.	1388 SUTTER ST. #1002	SAN FRANCISCO	CA	94109	U	U	MAYOR
BROWN, WOODY	6548 COLBATH AVE.	VAN NUYS	CA	91604	U	U	ACTOR
BROWNE, JACKSON	C/O CREATIVE ARTISTS AGCY., 9830 WILSHIRE BLVD.	BEVERLY HILLS	CA	90212	U	U	SINGER - "TENDER IS THE NIGHT" - **AUTHOR'S CHOICE!**
BROWNE, KATHY	P.O. BOX 2939	BEVERLY HILLS	CA	90213	U	U	ACTRESS
BROWNE, ROSCOE LEE	3531 WONDERVIEW DR.	LOS ANGELES	CA	90068	U	U	ACTOR/WRITER/DIRECTOR
BROWNING, KURT	11160 RIVER VALLEY RD. #3180	EDMONTON, ALBERTA	CAN.	T5J 2G7	U	U	SKATER
BRUBECK, DAVE	221 MILLSTONE RD.	WILTON	CT	06897	C	D	PIANIST
BRUCE, CAROL	1361 N. LAUREL APT. 20	LOS ANGELES	CA	90046	A	B	ACTRESS
BRUNT, JENNY	C/O ELITE MGMT., 111 E. 22ND ST.	NEW YORK	NY	10010	U	U	MODEL
BRY, ELLEN	2800 NEILSON WAY #1113	SANTA MONICA	CA	90405	C	B	ACTRESS
BRYAN, JANE	P.O. BOX 1033	PEBBLE BEACH	CA	93953	U	U	ACTRESS
BRYSON, PEABO	999 PEACHTREE ST. #2680	ATLANTA	GA	30309	U	U	SINGER - **AUTHOR'S CHOICE!** - NICE IN PERSON!
BREZINSKI, ZBIGNIEW	SCHOOL OF GOVT., COLUMBIA UNIV.	NEW YORK	NY	10027	A	D	POLITICIAN - OFTEN SENDS SIGNED BUSINESS CARD!
BUCHANAN, PATRICK	1017 SAVILE LN. N.	MC LEAN	VA	22101	C	F	POLITICIAN/COLUMNIST - AUTOPEN RESPONSE
BUCHWALD, ART	2000 PENNSYLVANIA AVE. N.W.	WASHINGTON	DC	20006	U	U	COLUMNIST
BUCKINGHAM, LINDSAY	900 AIROLE WAY	LOS ANGELES	CA	90077	U	U	SINGER/SONGWRITER - FLEETWOOD MAC
BUCKLEY, BETTY	420 MADISON AVE. #1400	NEW YORK	NY	10017	C	B	ACTRESS - *EIGHT IS ENOUGH*
BUCKLEY, WILLIAM F. JR.	150 E. 35TH ST.	NEW YORK	NY	10016	A	C	AUTHOR/EDITOR
BUDD, JULIE	156 W. 68TH	NEW YORK	NY	10024	U	U	ACTRESS
BUDGE, DON	P.O. BOX 789	DINGMAN'S FERRY	PA	18328	A	D	TENNIS PLAYER - TYPICALLY SIGNS ONLY ONE!
BUFFET, JIMMY	500 DUVAL ST. #B	KEY WEST	FL	33040	A	F	SINGER/SONGWRITER - "MARGUERITAVILLE" - SENDS FACSIMILE SIGNED PHOTO!
BUGLIOSI, VINCENT T.	8530 WILSHIRE BLVD. #404	BEVERLY HILLS	CA	90210	A	D	LAWYER/AUTHOR - MANSON PROSECUTOR - NICE IN PERSON!
BUJOLD, GENEVIEVE	27258 PACIFIC COAST HWY.	MALIBU	CA	90265	B	B	ACTRESS
BULLOCK, JIM J.	6210 TEMPLE HILL DR.	LOS ANGELES	CA	90069	U	U	ACTOR
BULLOCK, SANDRA	9560 WILSHIRE BLVD. #500	BEVERLY HILLS	CA	90212	U	U	ACTRESS - *SPEED* - **AUTHOR'S CHOICE!**
BUMBRY, GRACE	165 W. 57TH ST.	NEW YORK	NY	10019	U	U	OPERA SINGER
BUMPERS, DALE	P.O. BOX 98	CHARLESTON	AR	72933	A	B	FORMER GOVERNOR
BURDETTE, LOU	2019 BEVEVA RD.	SARASOTA	FL	34232	A	D	FORMER BASEBALL PLAYER
BURE, PAVEL	C/O VANCOUVER CANNUCKS, 100 N. REMFREW ST.	VANCOUVER, BC	CAN.	V5K 3N7	B	C	HOCKEY PLAYER!
BURGE, GREGG	420 MADISON AVE. #1400	NEW YORK	NY	10017	U	U	SINGER
BURKE, DELTA	427 N. CANON DR. #215	BEVERLY HILLS	CA	90210	C	B	ACTRESS - *DESIGNING WOMEN*

129

Name	Address	City	State	Zip Code	Resp. Time	Resp. Qual.	Comments
BURKE, PAUL	2217 AVENIDA CABALLEROS	PALM SPRINGS	CA	92262	A	B	ACTOR
BURKE, ROBERT	151 EL CAMINO DR.	BEVERLY HILLS	CA	90212	U	U	ACTOR
BURKLEY, DENNIS	5145 COSTELLO AVE.	SHERMAN OAKS	CA	91423	U	U	ACTOR
BURLESON, TOM	C/O GENERAL DELIVERY	NEWLAND	NC	28657	U	U	ATHLETE
BURNETT, CAROL	P.O. BOX 1298	PASADENA	CA	91031	A	D	ACTRESS/COMIC - THE CAROL BURNETT SHOW
BURNETT, T-BONE	211 - 20TH ST.	SANTA MONICA	CA	90402	U	U	SINGER
BURNS, EILEEN	400 W. 43RD ST.	NEW YORK	NY	10036	U	U	ACTRESS
BURNS, JAMES MACGREGOR	BEE HILL RD.	WILLIAMSTOWN	MA	01267	U	U	POLITICAL SCIENTIST/HISTORIAN
BURNS, JERE	5513 OAKEN COURT	AGOURA HILLS	CA	91301	U	U	ACTOR
BURNS, KEN	MAPLE GROVE RD.	WALPOLE	NH	03608	C	B	DOCUMENTARY PRODUCER - BASEBALL
BURRELL, LEROY	1801 OCEAN PARK BLVD. #112	SANTA MONICA	CA	90405	C	B	TRACK ATHLETE
BURROWS, JAMES	5555 MELROSE AVE. #D-208	LOS ANGELES	CA	90038	U	U	WRITER/PRODUCER
BURSTYN, ELLEN	FERRY HOUSE, BOX 217, WASHINGTON SPRING RD.	SNEDENS LANDING, PALISADES	NY	10964	C	A+	ACTRESS - RESPONSIVE TO FAN MAIL
BURTON, LEVAR	13601 VENTURA BLVD. #209	SHERMAN OAKS	CA	91423	U	U	ACTOR - STAR TREK: THE NEXT GENERATION
BURTON, TIM	1041 N. FORMOSA AVE. #10	LOS ANGELES	CA	90046	U	U	ACTOR
BURTON, WARREN	280 S. BEVERLY DR. #400	BEVERLY HILLS	CA	90212	U	U	ACTOR
BURTON, WENDELL	6526 COSTELLO DR.	VAN NUYS	CA	91401	U	U	ACTOR
BUSCAGLIA, LEO	BOX 599	GLENBROOK	NV	89413	U	U	AUTHOR - LIVING, LOVING & LEARNING
BUSEY, GARY	18424 COASTLINE DR.	MALIBU	CA	90265	B	C	ACTOR - THE BUDDY HOLLY STORY
BUSFIELD, TIM	C/O WM. MORRIS AGCY., 151 EL CAMINO DR.	BEVERLY HILLS	CA	90212	U	U	ACTOR - THIRTYSOMETHING - AUTHOR'S CHOICE!
BUSH, BARBARA	10000 MEMORIAL DR.	HOUSTON	TX	77024	A	B	FORMER FIRST LADY - SENDS AUTOGRAPHED BOOKMARK! A FIRST CLASS LADY!
BUSH, BILLY GREEN	3500 W. OLIVE #1400	BURBANK	CA	91505	U	U	ACTOR
BUSH, GEORGE	10000 MEMORIAL DR.	HOUSTON	TX	77024	F	F	FORMER PRESIDENT OF THE U.S.
BUSHKIN, JOE	435 E. 52ND ST.	NEW YORK	NY	10022	U	U	PIANIST/COMPOSER
BUSS, DR. JERRY	P.O. BOX 10	INGLEWOOD	CA	90306	A	B	BASKETBALL TEAM OWNER
BUTKUS, DICK	3500 W. OLIVE #1400	BURBANK	CA	91505	A	D	MEMBER OF FOOTBALL HALL OF FAME!
BUTLER, BRETT	C/O ICM, 8942 WILSHIRE BLVD.	BEVERLY HILLS	CA	90211	U	U	ACTOR - GRACE UNDER FIRE - AUTHOR'S CHOICE!
BUTLER, DEAN	6220 ROGERTON DR.	LOS ANGELES	CA	90068	A	D	ACTOR
BUTROS GHALI, BUTROS	1 U.N. PLAZA	NEW YORK	NY	10017	U	U	U.N. SECRETARY GENERAL
BUTTAFUOCO, JOEY	1025 MERRICK RD.	BALDWIN	NY	10107	C	C	MECHANIC
BUTTAFUOCO, MARY JO	1025 MERRICK RD.	BALDWIN	NY	10107	A	C	WIFE - SENDS NICE NOTE!
BUTTON, DICK	250 W. 57TH ST. #1818	NEW YORK	NY	10017	U	U	TELEVISION PRODUCER/FORMER ICE SKATER

130

Name	Address	City	State	Zip Code	Resp. Time	Resp. Qual.	Comments
BUTTONS, RED	778 TORTUOSO WAY	LOS ANGELES	CA	90024	A	C	ACTOR
BUZZI, RUTH	2309 MALAGA RD.	LOS ANGELES	CA	90068	A	B	ACTRESS - *LAUGH-IN*
BYNER, JOHN	P.O. BOX 232	WOODLAND HILLS	CA	91365	U	U	COMEDIAN/WRITER
BYRD, TOM	121 N. SAN VICENTE BLVD.	BEVERLY HILLS	CA	90211	A	B	ACTOR
BYRNE, DAVID	7964 WILLOW GLEN RD.	LOS ANGELES	CA	90046	U	U	SINGER/SONGWRITER - **AUTHOR'S CHOICE!**
BYRNES, EDD	P.O. BOX 1623	BEVERLY HILLS	CA	90213	C	F	ACTOR - CHARGES $19.95 PER PHOTO - GET REAL!
CAAN, JAMES	1435 STONE CANYON RD.	LOS ANGELES	CA	90024	B	C	ACTOR - *THE GODFATHER*
CAEN, HERB	901 MISSION ST.	SAN FRANCISCO	CA	94119	C	D	COLUMNIST
CAESAR, SID	1910 LOMA VISTA	BEVERLY HILLS	CA	90210	U	U	ACTOR/COMEDIAN
CAGE, NICHOLAS	5647 TRYON	LOS ANGELES	CA	90068	C	D	ACTOR - *RAISING ARIZONA* - **AUTHOR'S CHOICE!**
CAGNEY, MRS. JAMES	P.O. BOX 281, VERNEY FARM	STANFORDVILLE	NY	12581	U	U	WIDOW OF JAMES CAGNEY
CAIN, DEAN	C/O LOIS & CLARK, ABC-TV, 2040 AVE. OF THE STARS	LOS ANGELES	CA	90067	U	U	ACTOR - *LOIS & CLARK*
CAINE, MICHAEL	315 TROUSDALE PL.	BEVERLY HILLS	CA	90210	U	U	ACTOR - *BLAME IT ON RIO* - **AUTHOR'S CHOICE!**
CALABRO, TOM	C/O MELROSE PLACE, FOX BROADCASTING CO., 10201 W. PICO BLVD.	LOS ANGELES	CA	90035	U	U	ACTOR - *MELROSE PLACE*
CALHOUN, RORY	10637 BURBANK BLVD.	NORTH HOLLYWOOD	CA	91601	U	U	ACTOR
CALL, JOSEPH	247 S. BEVERLY DR. #102	BEVERLY HILLS	CA	90212	U	U	ACTOR
CALIFANO, JOSEPH	1775 PENNSYLVANIA AVE. N.W.	WASHINGTON	DC	20006	U	U	POLITICIAN
CALIFORNIA DREAMS	NBC-TV, 3000 W. ALAMEDA BLVD.	BURBANK	CA	91523	U	U	TELEVISION SERIES
CALL, ANTHONY	305 MADISON AVE. #4419	NEW YORK	NY	10165	U	U	ACTOR
CALL, BRANDON	5918 VAN NUYS BLVD.	VAN NUYS	CA	91401	U	U	ACTOR
CALLAHAN, JOHN	342 N. ALFRED ST.	LOS ANGELES	CA	90048	U	U	ACTOR
CALLAN, K.	4957 MATILIJA AVE.	SHERMAN OAKS	CA	91423	A	B	ACTRESS
CALLAN, MICHAEL (MICKEY)	1730 CAMDEN AVE. #201	LOS ANGELES	CA	90025	A	B	ACTOR
CALLAS, CHARLIE	P.O. BOX 67B69	LOS ANGELES	CA	90067	U	U	COMEDIAN/ACTOR
CALLAWAY, THOMAS	10000 SANTA MONICA BLVD. #305	LOS ANGELES	CA	90067	U	U	ACTOR
CALLEY, LT. WILLIAM	V.V. VICKS JEWELRY, CROSS COUNTRY PLAZA	COLUMBUS	GA	31906	U	U	FORMER MILITARY OFFICER
CALVET, CORINNE	1431 OCEAN AVE. #109	SANTA MONICA	CA	90401	A	B	ACTRESS - SENDS FLYER WITH PHOTOS - $5 EACH
CAMERON, CANDACE	C/O FULL HOUSE, 4000 WARNER BLVD.	BURBANK	CA	91522	U	U	ACTRESS - *FULL HOUSE*
CAMERON, JAMES	2233 N. 4TH ST.	MILWAUKEE	WI	53212	U	U	ACTIVIST
CAMERON, JOANNA	P.O. BOX 1400	PEBBLE BEACH	CA	93953	U	U	ACTRESS/DIRECTOR
CAMP, COLLEEN	760 N. LA CIENEGA BLVD.	LOS ANGELES	CA	90069	A	B	ACTRESS - *DALLAS*
CAMPANELLA, JOSEPH	4647 ARCOLA AVE.	NORTH HOLLYWOOD	CA	91602	U	U	ACTOR

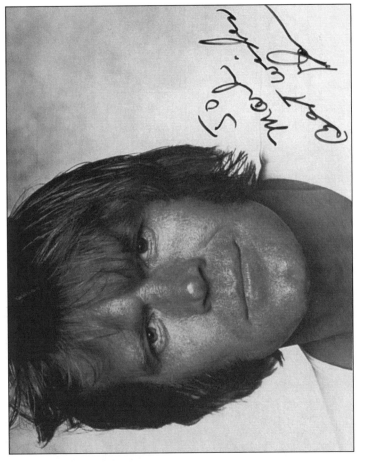

Glen Campbell

Phil Collins

132

Name	Address	City	State	Zip Code	Resp. Time	Resp. Qual.	Comments
CAMPBELL, BILL	8942 WILSHIRE BLVD.	BEVERLY HILLS	CA	90211	U	U	ACTOR - *THE ROCKETEER*
CAMPBELL, BRUCE	13323 WASHINGTON BLVD. #301	LOS ANGELES	CA	90066	B	B	ACTOR - *THE ADV. OF BRISCOE COUNTY JR.*
CAMPBELL, EARL	UNIV. OF TEXAS, P.O. BOX 7399	AUSTIN	TX	78713	A	B	MEMBER OF FOOTBALL HALL OF FAME
CAMPBELL, GLEN	5290 EXETER BLVD.	PHOENIX	AZ	85018	C	C	SINGER/ACTOR - *THE GLEN CAMPBELL GOODTIME HOUR*
CAMPBELL, LUTHER	8400 N.E. 2ND AVE.	MIAMI	FL	33138	U	U	RAP SINGER
CAMPBELL, NAOMI	C/O FORD MODELS INC., 334 E. 59TH ST.	NEW YORK	NY	10022	U	U	MODEL - **AUTHOR'S CHOICE!**
CAMPBELL, WILLIAM	21502 VELICATA ST.	WOODLAND HILLS	CA	91364	U	U	ACTOR
CANARY, DAVID	903 S. MANSFIELD AVE.	LOS ANGELES	CA	90036	A	B	ACTOR
CANBY, VINCENT	215 W. 88TH ST.	NEW YORK	NY	10024	U	U	FILM CRITIC
CANNELL, STEPHEN	7083 HOLLYWOOD BLVD.	LOS ANGELES	CA	90028	U	U	TELEVISION WRITER/PRODUCER
CANNON, BILLY	1640 SHERWOOD FOREST BLVD.	BATON ROUGE	LA	70815	U	U	FOOTBALL PLAYER
CANNON, DYAN	8033 SUNSET BLVD. #254	LOS ANGELES	CA	90046	U	U	ACTRESS/WRITER - *BOB & CAROL & TED & ALICE*
CANNON, FREDDIE	18641 CASSANDRA ST.	TARZANA	CA	91356	A	B	SINGER/SONGWRITER
CANNON, J.D.	9255 SUNSET BLVD. #515	LOS ANGELES	CA	90069	U	U	ACTOR
CANNON, KATHERINE	10100 SANTA MONICA BLVD. #700	LOS ANGELES	CA	90067	U	U	ACTRESS
CANSECO, JOSE	4525 SHERIDAN AVE.	MIAMI BEACH	FL	33140	U	U	BASEBALL PLAYER - SAVE YOUR STAMPS!
CANTRELL, LANA	300 E. 71ST ST.	NEW YORK	NY	10021	A	B	ACTRESS/SINGER
CAPPELLETTI, JOHN	28791 BRANT LN.	LAGUNA NIGUEL	CA	92677	A	B	FOOTBALL PLAYER
CAPRI, AHNA	8227 FOUNTAIN AVE.	LOS ANGELES	CA	90046	A	C+	ACTRESS - INCLUDES LIP PRINTS!
CAPRIATI, JENNIFER	5700 SADDLE BROOK WAY	WESLEY CHAPEL	FL	33543	C	B	TENNIS PLAYER - **AUTHOR'S CHOICE!**
CAPSHAW, KATE (SPIELBERG)	P.O. BOX 869	PACIFIC PALISADES	CA	90272	U	U	ACTRESS - *INDIANA JONES & THE TEMPLE OF DOOM*
CAPTAIN & TENNILLE	3612 LAKE VIEW RD.	CARSON CITY	NV	89703	C	D	MUSIC DUO
CARA, IRENE	8033 SUNSET BLVD. #735	LOS ANGELES	CA	90046	U	U	ACTRESS/SINGER - *FAME*
CARAS, ROGER	22108 SLAB BRIDGE RD.	FREELAND	MD	21053	A	B	NEWS CORRESPONDENT - AN AUTOGRAPH COLLECTOR!
CARAY, HARRY JR.	P.O. BOX 3256	DURANGO	CO	81302	A	B	BASEBALL EXECUTIVE
CARAY, HARRY SR.	C/O CUBS, WRIGLEY FIELD,1060 W. ADDISON	CHICAGO	IL	60613	U	U	HOF BASEBALL ANNOUNCER - 7TH INNING SINGER!
CAREW, ROD	5144 E. CRESCENT DR.	ANAHEIM	CA	92807	A	B	MEMBER OF THE BASEBALL HALL OF FAME - **AUTHOR'S CHOICE!** - AN INSPIRATION!
CAREY, MAC DONALD	1543 BENEDICT CANYON DR.	BEVERLY HILLS	CA	90210	U	U	ACTOR
CAREY, MARIAH	130 W. 57TH ST. #12B	NEW YORK	NY	10019	U	U	SINGER - "FANTASY" - **AUTHOR'S CHOICE!**
CAREY, RICK	119 ROCKLAND AVE.	LARCHMONT	NY	10538	U	U	SWIMMER
CAREY, TIMOTHY	P.O. BOX 1254	TEMPLE CITY	CA	91780	U	U	ACTOR

133

Walter Cronkite

Sec. Henry Cisneros (autopen)

Name	Address	City	State	Zip Code	Resp. Time	Resp. Qual.	Comments
CARIOU, LEN	100 W. 57TH ST. #149	NEW YORK	NY	10019	A	D	ACTOR
CARLE, FRANKIE	P.O. BOX 7415	MESA	AZ	85216	A	B	BAND LEADER
CARLIN, GEORGE	901 BRINGHAM AVE.	LOS ANGELES	CA	90049	U	U	COMEDIAN - "THE 7 WORDS YOU CAN'T SAY ON TELEVISION"
CARLIN, LYNN	15301 VENTURA BLVD. #345	SHERMAN OAKS	CA	91403	A	C	ACTRESS
CARLISLE, BELINDA	3375 CAHUENGA BLVD. W. #470	LOS ANGELES	CA	90068	U	U	SINGER/SONGWRITER
CARLISLE, MARY	517 N. RODEO DR.	BEVERLY HILLS	CA	90210	A	B	ACTRESS
CARLISLE-HART, KITTY	32 E. 64TH ST.	NEW YORK	NY	10021	U	U	ACTRESS
CARLTON, STEVE	P.O. BOX 736	DURANGO	CO	81302	U	U	MEMBER OF THE BASEBALL HALL OF FAME
CARNEY, ART	RR 20. BOX 911	WESTBROOK	CT	06498	A	B	ACTOR - *THE HONEYMOONERS*
CAROTHERS, A.J.	2210 THE TERRACE	LOS ANGELES	CA	90049	U	U	SCREENWRITER
CARPENTER, CARLETON	R.D. #2 CHARDAVOYNE RD.	WARWICK	NY	10990	U	U	ACTOR
CARPENTER, JOHN	8532 HOLLYWOOD BLVD.	LOS ANGELES	CA	90046	U	U	ACTOR - *HALLOWEEN*
CARPENTER, MARY-CHAPIN	7003 CARROLL AVE.	SILVER SPRING	MD	20912	U	U	SINGER - **AUTHOR'S CHOICE!** - "HE THINKS HE'LL ..."
CARPENTER, RICHARD	P.O. BOX 1084	DOWNEY	CA	90240	A	B	PIANIST/COMPOSER - RESPONSIVE TO FAN MAIL!
CARR, ALLAN	P.O. BOX 691670	LOS ANGELES	CA	90069	U	U	FILM WRITER/PRODUCER
CARR, DARLENE	1604 N. VISTA AVE.	LOS ANGELES	CA	90046	U	U	ACTRESS
CARR, VIKKI	BOX 5126	BEVERLY HILLS	CA	90210	U	U	SINGER/SONGWRITER
CARRADINE, DAVID	9753 LA TUNA CANYON RD.	SUN VALLEY	CA	91352	U	U	ACTOR - *KUNG FU*
CARRADINE, KEITH	P.O. BOX 2669	TELLURIDE	CO	81435	U	U	SINGER/ACTOR - *THE WILL ROGERS FOLLIES*
CARRERE, TIA	8638 FRANKLIN AVE.	LOS ANGELES	CA	90069	U	U	ACTRESS
CARREY, JIM	C/O UNITED TALENT AGCY., 9560 WILSHIRE BLVD. SUITE 500	BEVERLY HILLS	CA	90212	U	U	ACTOR - *ACE VENTURA* - **AUTHOR'S CHOICE!**
CARROLL, DIAHANN	P.O. BOX 2999	BEVERLY HILLS	CA	90213	U	U	ACTRESS/SINGER - *DYNASTY*
CARROLL, PAT	6523 W. OLYMPIC BLVD.	LOS ANGELES	CA	90048	U	U	ACTRESS
CARRUTHERS, KITTY	22 E. 71ST. ST.	NEW YORK	NY	10021	U	U	ICE SKATER - NICE IN PERSON!
CARRUTHERS, PETER	22 E. 71ST. ST.	NEW YORK	NY	10021	C	D	ICE SKATER - NICE IN PERSON!
CARSON, JOANNA	400 ST. CLOUD RD.	LOS ANGELES	CA	90024	U	U	EX-WIFE OF JOHNNY CARSON
CARSON, JOHNNY	6962 WILDLIFE	MALIBU	CA	90265	C	F	TELEVISION HOST/COMEDIAN - **AUTHOR'S CHOICE!**
CARTER FAMILY	P.O. BOX 508	HENDERSONVILLE	TN	37075	U	U	COUNTRY WESTERN GROUP
CARTER, AMY	1 WOODLAND DR.	PLAINS	GA	31780	U	U	EX-PRESIDENT'S DAUGHTER/ILLUSTRATOR
CARTER, BENNY	8321 SKYLINE DR.	LOS ANGELES	CA	90046	A	B	SAXOPHONIST
CARTER, CARLENE	1114 - 17TH AVE. #101	NASHVILLE	TN	37212	U	U	SINGER
CARTER, DIXIE	100 UNIVERSAL CITY PLAZA #490A	UNIVERSAL CITY	CA	91608	U	U	ACTRESS - *DESIGNING WOMEN*

Jack Carter

David Copperfield

Jeff Corey

Name	Address	City	State	Zip Code	Resp. Time	Resp. Qual.	Comments
CARTER, HELENA	1655 GILCREST	BEVERLY HILLS	CA	90210	A	D	ACTRESS
CARTER, HODDING III	211 S. ST. ASAPH	ALEXANDRIA	VA	22314	A	C	NEWS CORRESPONDENT
CARTER, JACK	1023 CHEVY CHASE DR.	BEVERLY HILLS	CA	90210	A	A	COMEDIAN/ACTOR
CARTER, JIMMY	1 WOODLAND DR.	PLAINS	GA	31780	U	U	39TH U.S. PRESIDENT/AUTHOR - **AUTHOR'S CHOICE!**
CARTER, LYNDA	9200 HARRINGTON DR.	POTOMAC	MD	20854	U	U	ACTRESS/SINGER - *WONDER WOMAN*
CARTER, RALPH	104-60 QUEENS BLVD. #1D	FOREST HILLS	NY	11375	U	U	ACTOR
CARTER, ROSALYN	1 WOODLAND DR.	PLAINS	GA	31780	U	U	FORMER FIRST LADY/AUTHOR - **AUTHOR'S CHOICE!**
CARTER, RUBIN "HURRICANE"	1313 BROOKEDGE DR.	HAMLIN	NY	14464	U	U	BOXER/EX-CONVICT
CARTER, TERRY	447 - 9TH ST.	SANTA MONICA	CA	90402	U	U	ACTOR
CARTER, THOMAS	10958 STRATHMORE DR.	LOS ANGELES	CA	90024	U	U	ACTOR/DIRECTOR
CARTLAND, BARBARA	CAMFIELD PL., HATFIELD	HERTFORDSHIRE	ENG.		U	U	ROMANCE NOVELIST
CARTWRIGHT, ANGELA	10112 RIVERSIDE DR.	TOLUCA LAKE	CA	91602	U	U	ACTRESS
CARTWRIGHT, VERON CA	5915 TUXEDO TERR.	LOS ANGELES	CA	90068	A	B	ACTRESS - *ALIEN*
CARUSO, ANTHONY	1706 MANDEVILLE LN.	LOS ANGELES	CA	90049	A	D	ACTOR
CARUSO, DAVID	C/O UNITED TALENT AGCY., 9560 WILSHIRE BLVD. SUITE 500	BEVERLY HILLS	CA	90212	U	U	ACTOR - *NYPD BLUE* - **AUTHOR'S CHOICE!**
CARVEY, DANA	1733 RANCHO ST.	ENCINO	CA	91316	U	U	COMEDIAN/ACTOR - **AUTHOR'S CHOICE!** - SEE IF YOU'RE WORTHY!
CARVILLE, JAMES	17TH & PENNSYLVANIA AVE. N.W. #160	WASHINGTON	DC	20503	U	U	POLITICAL CONSULTANT - "WAR ROOM" STAR!
CASELOTTI, ADRIANA	201 N. LARCHMONT BLVD.	LOS ANGELES	CA	90004	U	U	ENTERTAINER - $38 FOR 3 SIGNATURES - VOICE OF SNOW WHITE!
CASEY, BERNIE	6145 FLIGHT AVE.	LOS ANGELES	CA	90056	U	U	ACTOR/FOOTBALL PLAYER
CASEY, LAWRENCE	4139 VANETTA PL.	NORTH HOLLYWOOD	CA	91604	U	U	ACTOR
CASH, JOHNNY	711 SUMMERFIELD DR.	HENDERSONVILLE	TN	37075	U	U	SINGER - "I WALK THE LINE" - **AUTHOR'S CHOICE!**
CASH, JUNE CARTER	711 SUMMERFIELD DR.	HENDERSONVILLE	TN	37075	U	U	SINGER
CASH, ROSANNE	CAPITOL RECORDS, 1750 N. VINE ST.	HOLLYWOOD	CA	90028	U	U	SINGER - "I DON'T KNOW WHY..." - **AUTHOR'S CHOICE!**
CASPER, BILLY	P.O. BOX 1088	CHULA VISTA	CA	91912	A	B	GOLFER
CASS, PEGGY	200 E. 62ND ST.	NEW YORK	NY	10021	U	U	ACTRESS - *TO TELL THE TRUTH*
CASSAVETES, NICK	22223 BUENA VENTURA ST.	WOODLAND HILLS	CA	91364	U	U	ACTOR
CASSELL, SEYMOUR	2800 NEILSON WAY #1610	SANTA MONICA	CA	90405	A	B	ACTOR
CASSIDY, DAVID	701 N. OAKHURST DR.	BEVERLY HILLS	CA	90210	U	U	ACTOR/SINGER - *THE PARTRIDGE FAMILY*
CASSIDY, JOANNA	2530 OUTPOST DR.	LOS ANGELES	CA	90068	C	C	ACTRESS
CASSIDY, PATRICK	10433 WILSHIRE BLVD. #605	LOS ANGELES	CA	90024	U	U	ACTOR
CASSIDY, RYAN	701 N. OAKHURST DR.	BEVERLY HILLS	CA	90210	A	D	ACTOR
CASSINI, OLEG	135 E. 19TH ST.	NEW YORK	NY	10003	A	C	FASHION DESIGNER

Glenn Close (possible ghost signature)

Susan Clark

Name	Address	City	State	Zip Code	Resp. Time	Resp. Qual.	Comments
CATES, PHOEBE	9560 WILSHIRE BLVD. #500	BEVERLY HILLS	CA	90212	U	U	ACTRESS - FAST TIMES AT RIDGEMONT HIGH
CATHCART, DICK	6414 LUBAO AVE.	WOODLAND HILLS	CA	91364	U	U	COMPOSER
CATLETT, MARY JO	4375 FARMDALE AVE.	STUDIO CITY	CA	91604	A	C	ACTRESS
CAUTHEN, STEVE	RFD BOONE COUNTY	WALTON	KY	41094	A	D	JOCKEY
CAVETT, DICK	2200 FLETCHER AVE.	FT. LEE	NJ	07024	U	U	TELEVISION HOST - THE DICK CAVETT SHOW
CAZENOVE, CHRISTOPHER	9169 SUNSET BLVD.	LOS ANGELES	CA	90069	A	B	ACTOR
CERNAN, EUGENE	900 TOWN & COUNTRY LN. #210	HOUSTON	TX	77024	C	F	ASTRONAUT - DOES NOT SIGN CARDS
CETERA, PETER	1880 CENTURY PARK E. #900	LOS ANGELES	CA	90067	U	U	SINGER/MUSICIAN - CHICAGO
CHADWICK, FLORENCE	814 ARMADA TERR.	SAN DIEGO	CA	92106	U	U	SWIMMER
CHAKIRIS, GEORGE	7266 CLINTON ST.	LOS ANGELES	CA	90036	A	B	ACTOR
CHAMBERLAIN, RICHARD	11755 WILSHIRE BLVD. #2270	LOS ANGELES	CA	90025	U	U	ACTOR/PRODUCER - DR. KILDARE
CHAMBERLAIN, WILT	15216 ANTELO PL.	LOS ANGELES	CA	90024	U	U	MEMBER OF THE BASKETBALL HALL OF FAME
CHAMBERS, JULIE	99 HUDSON ST., 16TH FL.	NEW YORK	NY	10013	U	U	ACTIVIST
CHAMBERS, MARILYN	4528 W. CHARLESTON BLVD.	LAS VEGAS	NV	89102	U	U	ACTRESS
CHAMPION, MARGE	484 W. 43RD ST.	NEW YORK	NY	10036	U	U	ACTRESS/DANCER
CHAMPLIN, CHARLES	2169 LINDA FLORA DR.	LOS ANGELES	CA	90024	A	C	FILM CRITIC
CHANDLER, OTIS	1421 EMERSON	OXNARD	CA	93033	A	C	PUBLISHER
CHANEL, PATRICE	19216 ANDMARK AVE.	CARSON	CA	90746	U	U	ACTRESS
CHANG, MICHAEL	1025 N. HOLT DR.	PLACENTIA	CA	92670	U	U	TENNIS PLAYER
CHANNING, CAROL	9301 FLICKER WAY	LOS ANGELES	CA	90069	U	U	ACTRESS - HELLO, DOLLY
CHANNING, STOCKARD	10390 SANTA MONICA BLVD. #300	LOS ANGELES	CA	90025	U	U	ACTRESS - GREASE
CHAO, ROSALIND	924 WESTWOOD BLVD. #900	LOS ANGELES	CA	90024	U	U	ACTRESS - M*A*S*H
CHAPIN, LAUREN	P.O. BOX 922	KILLEEN	TX	76541	U	U	ACTRESS
CHAPIN, TOM	57 PIERMONT PL.	PIERMONT	NY	10968	U	U	SINGER - HARRY'S BROTHER
CHAPLIN, GERALDINE	6 RUE ASSELINE	75015 PARIS	FRA.		U	U	ACTRESS - DR. ZHIVAGO
CHAPLIN, LITA GREY	8440 FOUNTAIN AVE. #302	LOS ANGELES	CA	90069	U	U	ACTRESS
CHAPLIN, SYDNEY	69950 FRANK SINATRA DR.	RANCHO MIRAGE	CA	92270	U	U	SON OF CHARLIE CHAPLIN
CHAPMAN, LONNY	3973 GOODLAND AVE.	STUDIO CITY	CA	91604	U	U	ACTOR
CHAPMAN, MARGUERITE	11558 RIVERSIDE DR. #304	HOLLYWOOD	CA	91602	A	C	ACTRESS
CHAPMAN, MARK DAVID	ATTICA STATE PRISON, BOX 149	ATTICA	NY	14011	U	U	JOHN LENNON'S KILLER
CHARBONNEAU, PATRICIA	10100 SANTA MONICA BLVD. #700	LOS ANGELES	CA	90067	U	U	ACTRESS
CHARISSE, CYD	10724 WILSHIRE BLVD. #1406	LOS ANGELES	CA	90024	U	U	ACTRESS/DANCER - BRIGADOON
CHARLES, RAY	2107 W. WASHINGTON BLVD.	LOS ANGELES	CA	90018	A	B	SINGER/PIANIST
CHARLESON, LESLIE	2314 LIVE OAK DR. E.	LOS ANGELES	CA	90068	A	B	ACTRESS - GENERAL HOSPITAL

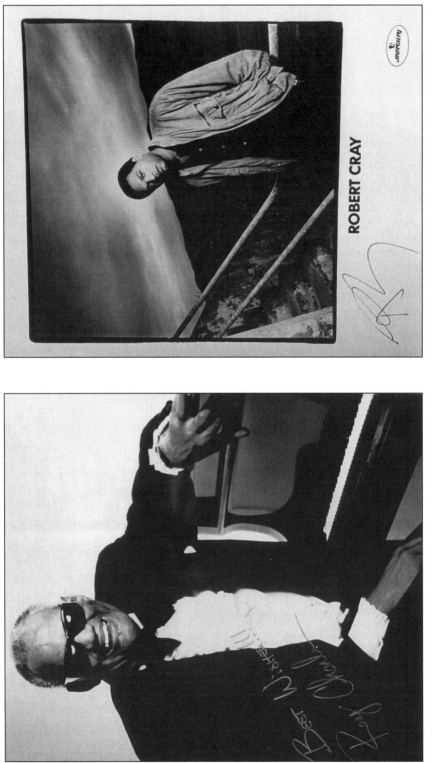

Robert Cray

Ray Charles

Name	Address	City	State	Zip Code	Resp. Time	Resp. Qual.	Comments
CHARMOLI, TONY	1271 SUNSET PLAZA DR.	LOS ANGELES	CA	90069	U	U	DIRECTOR/CHOREOGRAPHER
CHARO	P.O. BOX 1007	HANALEI, KAUI	HI	96714	B	C	SINGER/ACTRESS - *THE LOVE BOAT*
CHARTOFF, MELANIE	8075 W. THIRD ST. #303	LOS ANGELES	CA	90048	U	U	ACTRESS
CHASE, BARRY	3750 BEVERLY RIDGE DR.	SHERMAN OAKS	CA	91423	U	U	ACTOR/DANCER
CHASE, CHEVY	17492 CAMINO DE YATASTO	PACIFIC PALISADES	CA	90272	A	C	ACTOR/WRITER - **AUTHOR'S CHOICE!** - ILLEGIBLE SIGNATURE!
CHAVIS, BEN	4805 MT. HOPE DR.	BALTIMORE	MD	21215	U	U	ACTIVIST
CHEATHAM, MAREE	9169 SUNSET BLVD.	LOS ANGELES	CA	90069	U	U	ACTRESS
CHEEK, MOLLY	15038 LANDALE	STUDIO CITY	CA	91604	U	U	ACTRESS
CHELIOS, CHRIS	C/O CHICAGO BLACKHAWKS, CHICAGO STADIUM, 1800 W. MADISON ST.	CHICAGO	IL	60612	C	D	HOCKEY PLAYER - I WAITED 1 YEAR FOR 1 CARD!
CHEN, JOAN	2601 FILBERT ST.	SAN FRANCISCO	CA	94123	U	U	ACTRESS
CHENAULT, MRS. ANNA	2510 VIRGINIA AVE. N.W. #1404	WASHINGTON	DC	20005	A	B	AUTHOR/JOURNALIST
CHENEY, DICK	1150 - 17TH ST. N.W.	WASHINGTON	DC	20036	C	B	FORMER SEC. OF DEFENSE
CHER	P.O. BOX 960	BEVERLY HILLS	CA	90213	C	F	ACTRESS/SINGER - *MOONSTRUCK*
CHESTNUT, MORRIS	10351 SANTA MONICA BLVD. #211	LOS ANGELES	CA	90025	U	U	ACTOR
CHEW, SAM JR.	8075 W. 3RD ST. #303	LOS ANGELES	CA	90048	U	U	ACTOR
CHICAGO	345 N. MAPLE DR. #235	BEVERLY HILLS	CA	90210	U	U	ROCK GROUP
CHILD, JULIA	103 IRVING ST.	CAMBRIDGE	MA	02138	A	F	CHEF - "MASTERING THE ART OF FRENCH COOKING"
CHILDS, TONI	1350 AVE. OF THE AMERICAS	NEW YORK	NY	10019	U	U	SINGER/SONGWRITER
CHILES, LINDEN	2521 TOPANGA SKYLINE	TOPANGA	CA	90290	A	B	ACTOR
CHILES, LOIS	644 SAN LORENZO	SANTA MONICA	CA	90402	C	B	ACTRESS - *THE WAY WE WERE*
CHLUMSKY, ANNA	70 HUBBARD #200	CHICAGO	IL	60610	A	B	ACTRESS
CHOCOLATE MILK	P.O. BOX 82	GREAT NECK	NY	11021	U	U	R&B GROUP
CHONG, TOMMY	11661 SAN VICENTE #1010	LOS ANGELES	CA	90049	A	D	ACTOR/COMEDIAN - *CHEECH & CHONG*
CHOPRA, DEEPAK	SHARP INST., 973B LOMAS SANTA FE	SOLANA BEACH	CA	92075	U	U	AUTHOR - **AUTHOR'S CHOICE!**
CHRISTENSEN, TODD	991 SUNBURST LN.	ALPINE	UT	84004	A	A	FOOTBALL PLAYER
CHRISTIE, JULIE	23 LINDEN GARDENS	LONDON	ENG.	W2	U	U	ACTRESS - *DR. ZHIVAGO*
CHRISTIE, LOU	1645 E. 50TH ST. #10H	CHICAGO	IL	60615	U	U	SINGER - "LIGHTNIN' STRIKES"
CHRISTOPHER, SEC. WARREN	2201 "C" ST. N.W.	WASHINGTON	DC	20520	A	D	SECRETARY OF STATE
CHRISTOPHER, WILLIAM	P.O. BOX 50698	PASADENA	CA	91105	A	C	ACTOR - *M*A*S*H*
CHUNG, CONNIE	C/O GELLER MEDIA MGMT., 250 W. 57TH ST. SUITE 213	NEW YORK	NY	10019	A	C	TELEVISION JOURNALIST - **AUTHOR'S CHOICE!**
CIMINO, MICHAEL	9015 ALTA CEDRO	BEVERLY HILLS	CA	90210	U	U	WRITER/PRODUCER
CINDERELLA	P.O. BOX 543	DREXEL HILL	PA	19026	U	U	ROCK GROUP

Leslie Charleson

John Conte

Name	Address	City	State	Zip Code	Resp. Time	Resp. Qual.	Comments
CIOFFI, CHARLES	GLOVER AVE.	NORWALK	CT	06850	U	U	ACTOR
CISNEROS, SEC. HENRY	451 - 7TH ST. S.W.	WASHINGTON	DC	20401	A	F	SECRETARY OF H.U.D. - AUTOPEN RESPONSE!
CLAIBORNE, LIZ	300 E. 56TH ST.	NEW YORK	NY	10022	A	C	FASHION DESIGNER
CLAPTON, ERIC	C/O CREATIVE ARTISTS AGCY., 9830 WILSHIRE BLVD.	BEVERLY HILLS	CA	90212	U	U	SINGER - "LAYLA" - **AUTHOR'S CHOICE!**
CLARK, CANDY	5 BRIARHILL RD.	MONTCLAIR	NJ	07042	A	D	ACTRESS
CLARK, CHRISTIE	16342 ROCKAWAY	PLACENTIA	CA	92670	U	U	ACTRESS
CLARK, DANE	1680 OLD OAK RD.	LOS ANGELES	CA	90049	A	B	ACTOR/DIRECTOR
CLARK, DICK	3003 W. OLIVE AVE.	BURBANK	CA	91505	B	D	TELEVISION HOST/PRODUCER - *AMERICAN BANDSTAND*
CLARK, DORAN	10100 SANTA MONICA BLVD. #2500	LOS ANGELES	CA	90067	U	U	ACTRESS
CLARK, JOE	366 S. RIDGEWOOD RD.	SOUTH ORANGE	NJ	07079	U	U	HIGH SCHOOL PRINCIPAL, MOVIE SUBJECT
CLARK, LYNN	247 S. BEVERLY DR. #102	BEVERLY HILLS	CA	90212	U	U	ACTRESS
CLARK, MARCIA	C/O OFFICE OF THE D.A., CRIMINAL COURTS BLDG., 210 W. TEMPLE ST.	LOS ANGELES	CA	90012	U	U	PROSECUTOR - "PEOPLE VS. O. J. SIMPSON"
CLARK, MARY HIGGINS	210 CENTRAL PARK S.	NEW YORK	NY	10019	B	B	WRITER
CLARK, PETULA	15 CHEMIN RIEU COLIGNY	GENEVA	SWI.		U	U	SINGER/ACTRESS - "DOWNTOWN"
CLARK, RAMSEY	36 E. 12TH ST.	NEW YORK	NY	10003	U	U	POLITICIAN/LAWYER
CLARK, ROY	1800 FORREST BLVD.	TULSA	OK	74114	A	B	SINGER/GUITARIST - *HEE HAW*
CLARK, SUSAN	7943 WOODROW WILSON DR.	LOS ANGELES	CA	90046	A	B	ACTRESS
CLARK, ANGELA	7557 MULHOLLAND DR.	LOS ANGELES	CA	90046	U	U	ACTRESS
CLARKE, BRIAN PATRICK	333-D KENWOOD	BURBANK	CA	91505	A	D	ACTOR
CLARKE, STANLEY	1807 BENEDICT CANYON	BEVERLY HILLS	CA	90210	U	U	GUITARIST/COMPOSER
CLARY, ROBERT	10001 SUN DIAL LN.	BEVERLY HILLS	CA	90210	A	B	ACTOR
CLASH, THE	268 CAMDEN RD.	LONDON	ENG	NW1	U	U	ROCK GROUP
CLAY, ANDREW DICE	1340 LONDONDERRY PL.	LOS ANGELES	CA	90069	U	U	COMEDIAN/ACTOR - *THE ADV. OF FORD FAIRLANE*
CLEAVER, EDRIDGE	C/O RANDOM HOUSE, 201 E. 50TH ST.	NEW YORK	NY	10022	U	U	ACTIVIST
CLEESE, JOHN	82 LADBROKE RD.	LONDON	ENG	W11 3NU	U	U	ACTOR/WRITER - *MONTY PYTHON'S FLYING CIRCUS*
CLEMENS, ROGER	10131 BECKMAN PL.	HOUSTON	TX	77043	U	U	BASEBALL PLAYER
CLENNON, DAVID	954 - 20TH ST. #B	SANTA MONICA	CA	90403	U	U	ACTOR
CLIBURN, VAN	455 WILDER PL.	SHREVEPORT	LA	71104	U	U	PIANIST
CLIFFORD, CLARK	9421 ROCKVILLE PIKE	BETHESDA	MD	20814	A	F	LAWYER - FACSIMILE USER!
CLIFT, ELEANOR	1750 PENNSYLVANIA AVE. N.W. SUITE #1220	WASHINGTON	DC	20001	A	C	NEWS CORRESPONDENT

143

to Mark
"Rocky"

[musical notation]

Bill Conti

Bill Conti

Art Carney

MART CROWLEY

4, January '96

Dear Mark Allen Baker,

Thank you and
Happy New Year.
Sincerely,
Mart Crowley

Mart Crowley

Billy Crystal

Name	Address	City	State	Zip Code	Resp. Time	Resp. Qual.	Comments
CLINTON, CHELSEA	1600 PENNSYLVANIA AVE.	WASHINGTON	DC	20500	U	U	DAUGHTER OF THE PRESIDENT OF THE U.S.
CLINTON, HILLARY RODHAM	1600 PENNSYLVANIA AVE.	WASHINGTON	DC	20500	B	F	FIRST LADY/LAWYER - FACSIMILE PHOTO!
CLINTON, PRESIDENT BILL	1600 PENNSYLVANIA AVE.	WASHINGTON	DC	20500	U	U	42ND PRESIDENT OF THE UNITED STATES
CLOHESSY, ROGER	9000 SUNSET BLVD. #1200	LOS ANGELES	CA	90069	U	U	MUSICIAN/PRESIDENT'S BROTHER
CLOONEY, ROBERT	9000 SUNSET BLVD. #1200	LOS ANGELES	CA	90069	U	U	ACTOR
CLOONEY, GEORGE	11655 LAURELCREST DR.	STUDIO CITY	CA	91604	U	U	ACTOR - ER - **AUTHOR'S CHOICE!**
CLOONEY, ROSEMARY	1019 N. ROXBURY DR.	BEVERLY HILLS	CA	90210	A	C	SINGER
CLOSE, CHUCK	C/O PACE PRINTS, 32 E. 57TH ST., 3RD. FL.	NEW YORK	NY	10022	U	U	ARTIST - **AUTHOR'S CHOICE!**
CLOSE, GLENN	9830 WILSHIRE BLVD.	BEVERLY HILLS	CA	90212	A	B	ACTRESS - FATAL ATTRACTION - **AUTHOR'S CHOICE!**
CLOWER, JERRY	P.O. BOX 121089	NASHVILLE	TN	37212	A	D	COMEDIAN
COBB, JOE	3746 1/2 CLARINGTON	CULVER CITY	CA	90230	U	U	ACTOR
COBB, JULIE	9744 WILSHIRE BLVD. #308	BEVERLY HILLS	CA	90212	U	U	ACTRESS
COBURN, JAMES	3550 WILSHIRE BLVD. #840	LOS ANGELES	CA	90010	U	U	ACTOR/DIRECTOR - THE MAGNIFICENT 7
COCA, IMOGENE	200 E. 66TH ST. #1803D	NEW YORK	NY	10021	U	U	ACTRESS - YOUR SHOW OF SHOWS
COCHRAN, JOHNNY L.	4929 WILSHIRE BLVD. SUITE 1010	LOS ANGELES	CA	90010	U	U	LEAD MEMBER OF O. J. SIMPSON "DREAM TEAM" - ATTORNEY - **AUTHOR'S CHOICE!**
CODY, IRON EYES	2017 GRIFFITH PARK BLVD.	LOS ANGELES	CA	90039	A	F	ACTOR - SENDS 4 MANGLED OLD FLYERS - NO AUTOGRAPH! - WHAT?
COELHO, SUSIE	2814 HUTTON	BEVERLY HILLS	CA	90210	U	U	ACTRESS/MODEL
COGHLAN, FRANK "JUNIOR"	12522 ARGYLE AVE.	LOS ALAMITOS	CA	90720	A	A	ACTOR - RESPONSIVE TO FAN MAIL!
COHEN, ALEXANDER	25 W. 54TH ST. #5-F	NEW YORK	NY	10019	A	B	TELEVISION/THEATER PRODUCER
COLBERT, ROBERT	10000 RIVERSIDE DR. #6	TOLUCA LAKE	CA	91602	A	B	ACTOR
COLE, DENNIS	2160 CENTURY PARK E. #1712	LOS ANGELES	CA	90067	U	U	ACTOR
COLE, GARY	1122 S. ROBERTSON BLVD.	LOS ANGELES	CA	90035	U	U	ACTOR
COLE, MICHAEL	6332 COSTELLO AVE.	VAN NUYS	CA	91401	A	C	ACTOR - THE MOD SQUAD
COLE, MRS. MARIE	SOUTH HOUSE	TYRINGHAM	MA	01264	U	U	WIDOW OF NAT KING COLE
COLE, NATALIE	1801 AVE. OF THE STARS #1105	LOS ANGELES	CA	90067	U	U	SINGER - "UNFORGETTABLE" - **AUTHOR'S CHOICE!**
COLE, OLIVIA	9744 WILSHIRE BLVD. #308	BEVERLY HILLS	CA	90212	U	U	ACTRESS
COLEMAN, DABNEY	360 N. KENTER	LOS ANGELES	CA	90049	A	C	ACTOR - NINE TO FIVE
COLEMAN, DURELL	800 S. ROBERTSON BLVD. #5	LOS ANGELES	CA	90033	U	U	ACTOR
COLEMAN, GARY	4710 DON MIGUEL DR.	LOS ANGELES	CA	90008	C	F	ACTOR - DIFFERENT STROKES - FACSIMILE SIGNED PHOTO
COLEMAN, JACK	7358 WOODROW WILSON DR.	LOS ANGELES	CA	90046	U	U	ACTOR
COLEMAN, NANCY	484 W. 43RD ST. #42-G	NEW YORK	NY	10036	A	B	ACTRESS
COLIN, MARGARET	366 W. 11TH ST. PH C	NEW YORK	NY	10014	U	U	ACTRESS

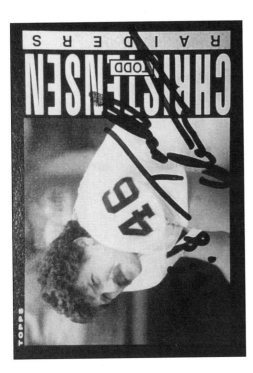

Todd Christensen

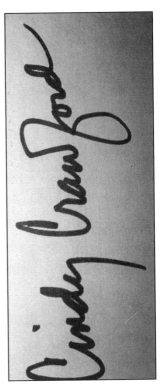

Cindy Crawford

Lynda Carter

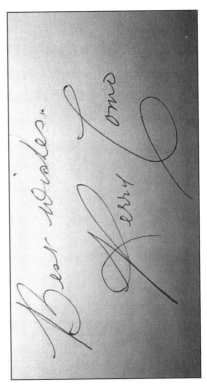

Perry Como

Name	Address	City	State	Zip Code	Resp. Time	Resp. Qual.	Comments
COLLINS, GARY	2751 HUTTON DR.	BEVERLY HILLS	CA	90210	A	B	TELEVISION HOST/ACTOR - HOME
COLLINS, JACKIE	13701 RIVERSIDE DR. #608	SHERMAN OAKS	CA	91423	A	A+	AUTHOR - A FIRST CLASS LADY!
COLLINS, JOAN	19 EATON PL. #2	LONDON	ENG	SW1	U	U	ACTRESS/AUTHOR - DYNASTY
COLLINS, JUDY	845 W. END AVE.	NEW YORK	NY	10024	U	U	SINGER/SONGWRITER - "SEND IN THE CLOWNS"
COLLINS, KATE	1410 YORK AVE. #4-D	NEW YORK	NY	10021	U	U	ACTRESS
COLLINS, MARVA	4146 W. CHICAGO AVE.	CHICAGO	IL	60651	A	F	EDUCATOR - FACSIMILE SIGNED PHOTO!
COLLINS, PHIL	9401 SUNSET BLVD.	BEVERLY HILLS	CA	90210	U	U	SINGER/DRUMMER - GREAT IN PERSON!
COLLINS, STEPHEN	15 E. 91ST ST. APT. 11A	NEW YORK	NY	10128	U	U	ACTOR - TALES OF THE GOLD MONKEY
COLOMBY, SCOTT	12424 WILSHIRE BLVD. #840	LOS ANGELES	CA	90025	U	U	ACTOR
COLSON, CHARLES	P.O. BOX 40562	WASHINGTON	DC	20016	A	D	AUTHOR
COLT, MARSHALL	151 S. EL CAMINO DR.	BEVERLY HILLS	CA	90212	A	D	ACTOR
COLTER, JESSE	1117 - 17TH AVE. S.	NASHVILLE	TN	37212	U	U	SINGER
COLTRANE, CHI	5955 TUXEDO TERR.	LOS ANGELES	CA	90068	U	U	SINGER
COLUMBU, FRANCO	2947 S. SEPULVEDA BLVD.	LOS ANGELES	CA	90064	A	C	ACTOR/BODYBUILDER
COLUMBUS, CHRIS	290 W. END AVE.	NEW YORK	NY	10023	U	U	DIRECTOR - HOME ALONE
COLVIN, JACK	9744 WILSHIRE BLVD. #308	BEVERLY HILLS	CA	90212	U	U	ACTOR/DIRECTOR
COMANECI, NADIA	2325 WESTWOOD DR.	NORMAN	OK	73069	A	B	GYMNAST
COMI, PAUL	1665 OAK KNOLL AVE.	SAN MARINO	CA	91108	A	B	ACTOR
COMO, PERRY	305 NORTHERN BLVD. #3-A	GREAT NECK	NY	11021	A	C	SINGER
COMPTON, JOYCE	23388 MULHOLLAND DR.	WOODLAND HILLS	CA	91364	U	U	ACTRESS
CONFORTI, GINO	1427 - 3RD ST. #205	SANTA MONICA	CA	90401	U	U	ACTOR
CONIFF, RAY	P.O. BOX 46395	LOS ANGELES	CA	90046	B	B	COMPOSER
CONLEE, JOHN	38 MUSIC SQUARE E. #117	NASHVILLE	TN	37203	U	U	SINGER/SONGWRITER
CONLEY, DARLENE	4455 LOS FELIZ BLVD. #902	LOS ANGELES	CA	90027	C	B+	ACTRESS
CONLEY, EARL THOMAS	1222 - 16 AVE. S.	NASHVILLE	TN	37203	U	U	SINGER/SONGWRITER
CONN, DIDI	14820 VALLEY VISTA BLVD.	SHERMAN OAKS	CA	91403	U	U	ACTRESS
CONNELLY, JENNIFER	50 BETHEL ST.	CRANSTON	RI	02920	U	U	ACTRESS - THE ROCKETEER
CONNER, BART	2325 WESTWOOD DR.	NORMAN	OK	73069	U	U	GYMNAST
CONNER, DENNIS	720 GATEWAY CENTER DR.	LOS ANGELES	CA	92102	U	U	YACHTSMAN
CONNERY, SEAN	22 GRAFTON ST.	LONDON	ENG	W1	U	U	ACTOR - THE UNTOUCHABLES - AUTHOR'S CHOICE!
CONNICK, HARRY JR.	260 BROOKLINE ST.	CAMBRIDGE	MA	02139	C	F	SINGER/PIANIST - AUTHOR'S CHOICE!
CONNIFF, RAY	P.O. BOX 46395	W. HOLLYWOOD	CA	90046	A	B	CONDUCTOR, COMPOSER, ARRANGER
CONNORS, CAROL	1709 FERRARI DR.	BEVERLY HILLS	CA	90210	U	U	SONGWRITER
CONNORS, JIMMY	200 S. REFUGIO RD.	SANTA YNEZ	CA	93460	U	U	TENNIS PLAYER

147

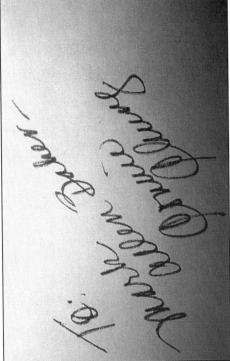

Connie Chung

Nicolas Cage

Jackie Collins

James Caan

Name	Address	City	State	Zip Code	Resp. Time	Resp. Qual.	Comments
CONNORS, MIKE	4810 LOUISE AVE.	ENCINO	CA	91316	A	D	ACTOR - *MANNIX*
CONRAD, BARNABY	3530 PINE VALLEY DR.	SARASOTA	FL	34239	U	U	AUTHOR/PAINTER
CONRAD, CHARLES JR.	5301 BOLSA AVE.	HUNTINGTON BEACH	CA	92647	A	F	ASTRONAUT - AGENCY FLYER WITH PRICES!
CONRAD, CHRISTIAN	15301 VENTURA BLVD. #345	SHERMAN OAKS	CA	91403	U	U	ACTOR
CONRAD, KIMBERLY	10236 CHARING CROSS RD.	LOS ANGELES	CA	90024	A	D	MRS. HUGH HEFNER
CONRAD, PAUL	28649 CRESTRIDGE RD.	PALOS VERDES	CA	90274	U	U	CARTOONIST
CONRAD, ROBERT	21355 PACIFIC COAST HWY.	MALIBU	CA	90265	U	U	ACTOR/WRITER - *WILD, WILD WEST*
CONROY, KEVIN	10100 SANTA MONICA BLVD. #2500	LOS ANGELES	CA	90067	A	B	ACTOR - VOICE OF *BATMAN ANIMATED SERIES*
CONSIDINE, JOHN	1930 CENTURY PARK W. #403	LOS ANGELES	CA	90067	A	C	ACTOR/WRITER
CONSTANTINE, MICHAEL	10351 SANTA MONICA BLVD. #211	LOS ANGELES	CA	90025	U	U	ACTOR
CONTE, JOHN	75600 BERYL DR.	INDIAN WELLS	CA	92260	A	A	ACTOR
CONTI, BILL	117 FREMONT PL.	LOS ANGELES	CA	90005	A	B+	COMPOSER/ARRANGER - *ROCKY*
CONVERSE, PEGGY	2525 BRIARCREST DR.	BEVERLY HILLS	CA	90210	U	U	ACTRESS
CONWAY, GARY	2035 MANDEVILLE CANYON	LOS ANGELES	CA	90049	A	D	ACTOR
CONWAY, TIM	P.O. BOX 17047	ENCINO	CA	91416	A	C	ACTOR/DIRECTOR - *THE CAROL BURNETT SHOW*
COODER, RY	326 ENTRADA DR.	SANTA MONICA	CA	90402	U	U	GUITARIST/SONGWRITER
COOGAN, KEITH	3500 W. OLIVE AVE. #1400	BURBANK	CA	91505	U	U	ACTOR
COOK, CAROLE	8829 ASHCROFT	LOS ANGELES	CA	90048	U	U	ACTRESS
COOKE, ALISTAIR	NASSAU POINT	CUTCHOGUE	NY	11935	A	B	JOURNALIST/TELEVISION ANNOUNCER - ADDED A CARICATURE OF HIMSELF!
COOKE, JACK KENT	KENT FARMS	MIDDLEBURG	VA	22117	A	B	LAWYER/FOOTBALL TEAM OWNER
COOKSON, PETER	30 NORFOLK RD.	SOUTHFIELD	MA	01259	U	U	ACTOR
COOLEY, DR. DENTON	3014 DEL MONTE DR.	HOUSTON	TX	77019	A	B	HEART SURGEON
COOLIDGE, RITA	1330 N. WETHERLY DR.	LOS ANGELES	CA	90069	C	B	SINGER/ACTRESS
COOPER, ALICE	4135 E. KEIM DR.	PARADISE VALLEY	AZ	85253	U	U	SINGER/SONGWRITER
COOPER, BEN	20838 EXHIBIT COURT	WOODLAND HILLS	CA	91367	U	U	ACTOR
COOPER, HENRY	36 BRAMPTON GROVE	LONDON	ENG	NW4	U	U	TELEVISION PERSONALITY
COOPER, JACKIE	9621 ROYALTON	BEVERLY HILLS	CA	90210	U	U	ACTOR/DIRECTOR - *SUPERMAN*
COOPER, JEANNE	8401 EDWIN DR.	LOS ANGELES	CA	90046	U	U	ACTRESS
COOPER, L. GORDON	5011 WOODLEY AVE.	ENCINO	CA	91436	U	U	ASTRONAUT
COPAGE, MARK	P.O. BOX 461677	LOS ANGELES	CA	90046	U	U	ACTOR
COPELAND, JOAN	88 CENTRAL PARK W.	NEW YORK	NY	10023	U	U	ACTRESS
COPLEY, TERI	18019 SAN FERNANDO MISSION	GRANADA HILLS	CA	91344	U	U	ACTRESS
COPPERFIELD, DAVID	515 POST OAK BLVD. #300	HOUSTON	TX	77027	A	B	MAGICIAN - **AUTHOR'S CHOICE!**

149

Jennifer Caprioti

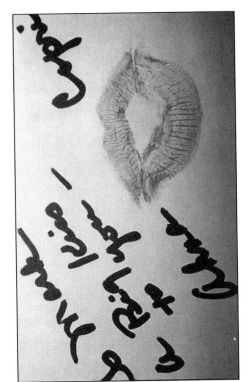

Ahna Capri

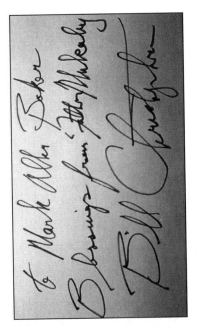

William Christopher

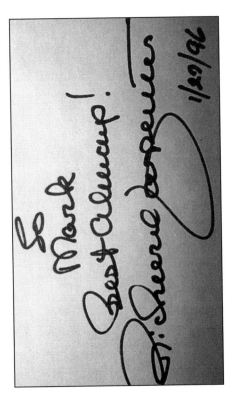

Richard Carpenter

150

Name	Address	City	State	Zip Code	Resp. Time	Resp. Qual.	Comments
COPPOLA, FRANCIS	916 KEARNY ST.	SAN FRANCISCO	CA	94133	U	U	WRITER/PRODUCER/DIRECTOR
COPPOLA, SOPHIA	781 - 5TH AVE.	NEW YORK	NY	10022	U	U	ACTRESS
CORBETT, MICHAEL	1434 N. SPAULDING #A	LOS ANGELES	CA	90046	A	B	ACTOR
CORBIN, BARRY	4529 TYRONE AVE.	SHERMAN OAKS	CA	91423	A	B	ACTOR - *NORTHERN EXPOSURE*
CORBY, ELLEN	9026 HARRATT	LOS ANGELES	CA	90069	U	U	ACTRESS
CORCORAN, KEVIN	8617 BALCOM	NORTHRIDGE	CA	91325	C	D	ACTOR
CORCORAN, NOREEN	5926 JAMIESON AVE.	ENCINO	CA	91316	U	U	ACTRESS
CORD, ALEX	10100 SANTA MONICA BLVD. #700	LOS ANGELES	CA	90067	U	U	ACTOR
CORDAY, BARBARA	532 S. WINDSOR BLVD.	LOS ANGELES	CA	90020	U	U	SOAP OPERA WRITER/PRODUCER
CORDAY, MARA	P.O. BOX 800393	VALENCIA	CA	91355	A	D	ACTRESS
CORDERO, ANGEL	P.O. BOX 90	JAMAICA	NY	11411	U	U	JOCKEY
COREA, CHICK	2635 GRIFFITH PARK BLVD.	LOS ANGELES	CA	90039	A	D	MUSICIAN - SIGNED LETTER, FACSIMILE SIGNED PHOTO! TRADITIONALLY RESPONSIVE!
COREY, JEFF	29445 BLUEWATER RD.	MALIBU	CA	90265	U	U	ACTOR/DIRECTOR
COREY, PROF. IRWIN	58 NASSAU DR.	GREAT NECK	NY	11022	A	B	COMEDIAN
CORIO, ANN	1706 MANDEVILLE LN.	LOS ANGELES	CA	90049	U	U	BURLESQUE
CORMAN, ROGER	11611 SAN VICENTE BLVD.	LOS ANGELES	CA	90049	U	U	WRITER/PRODUCER
CORNELL, CHRIS	A&M RECORDS, 1416 N. LA BREA AVE.	LOS ANGELES	CA	90028	U	U	SINGER - SOUNDGARDEN - **AUTHOR'S CHOICE!**
CORNELL, DON	P.O. BOX C	RIVER EDGE	NJ	07661	U	U	SINGER
CORNELL, LYDIA	142 S. BEDFORD DR.	BEVERLY HILLS	CA	90212	U	U	MODEL/ACTRESS
CORTESE, JOE	2065 COLDWATER CANYON DR.	BEVERLY HILLS	CA	90210	A	B	ACTOR
CORWIN, NORMAN	1840 FAIRBURN AVE. #302	LOS ANGELES	CA	90025	A	D	WRITER/PRODUCER
COSBY, BILL	P.O. BOX 4049	SANTA MONICA	CA	90411	A	C	COMEDIAN/ACTOR - *THE COSBY SHOW* - **AUTHOR'S CHOICE!**
COSSETTE, PIERRE	8899 BEVERLY BLVD. #100	LOS ANGELES	CA	90048	U	U	FILM PRODUCER
COSTANZA, MIDGE	11811 W. OLYMPIC BLVD.	BEVERLY HILLS	CA	90210	U	U	EX-PRESIDENTIAL AID
COSTELLO, ELVIS	9028 GREAT WEST RD.	MIDDLESEX	ENG	TW8 9EW	C	B	SINGER - **AUTHOR'S CHOICE!**
COSTELLO, MARICLARE	8271 MELROSE AVE. #110	LOS ANGELES	CA	90046	U	U	ACTRESS
COSTER, NICHOLAS	1624 N. GARDNER	LOS ANGELES	CA	90046	U	U	ACTOR
COSTNER, KEVIN	P.O. BOX 275	MONTROSE	CA	91021	F	F	ACTOR - *DANCES WITH WOLVES* - SAVE YOUR STAMPS!
COUPLES, FRED	8251 GREENSBORO DR. #530	MCLEAN	VA	22102	U	U	GOLFER
COURIC, KATIE	C/O NBC, 30 ROCKEFELLER PLAZA	NEW YORK	NY	10122	F	F	BROADCAST JOURNALIST - *TODAY*
COURT, HAZEL	1111 SAN VICENTE BLVD.	SANTA MONICA	CA	90402	C	B	ACTRESS

Name	Address	City	State	Zip Code	Resp. Time	Resp. Qual.	Comments
COURTLAND, JEROME	27354 LANDON PL.	VALENCIA	CA	91354	U	U	FILM DIRECTOR
COUSINS, ROBIN	9229 W. SUNSET BLVD. SUITE 303	LOS ANGELES	CA	90069	U	U	ICE SKATER
COUSY, BOB	459 SALISBURY ST.	WORCHESTER	MA	01609	A	D	BASKETBALL PLAYER - NBA LOGO MODEL!
COVER, FRANKLIN	1422 N. SWEETZER #402	LOS ANGELES	CA	90069	A	B+	ACTOR
COX, ARCHIBALD	GLESEN LN.	WAYLAND	MA	01778	A	C	POLITICIAN
COX, COURTNEY	9830 WILSHIRE BLVD. #500	BEVERLY HILLS	CA	90211	U	U	ACTRESS - FRIENDS - **AUTHOR'S CHOICE!**
COX, RONNY	13948 MAGNOLIA BLVD.	SHERMAN OAKS	CA	91423	U	U	ACTOR/FILM PRODUCER - BEVERLY HILLS COP
COYOTE, PETER	9 ROSE AVE.	MILL VALLEY	CA	94941	U	U	ACTOR - JAGGED EDGE
CRABBE, CUFFY	11216 N. 74TH ST.	SCOTTSDALE	AZ	85260	U	U	ACTOR
CRADDOCK, BILLY "CRASH"	P.O. BOX 16426	GREENSBORO	NC	27416	U	U	SONGWRITER/SINGER
CRAFT, CHRISTINE	500 MEDIA PL.	SACRAMENTO	CA	95815	U	U	TELEVISION PERSONALITY
CRAIG, JENNY	445 MARINE VIEW DR. #300	DEL MAR	CA	92014	A	A+	DIET/PHYSICAL DIRECTOR
CRAIG, JIM	36 N. MAIN ST.	NORTH EASTON	MA	02156	A	C	HOCKEY PLAYER - OLYMPIC GOALIE!
CRAIN, JEANNE	354 HILGARD AVE.	LOS ANGELES	CA	90024	U	U	ACTRESS
CRAMER, DOUGLAS	738 SARBONNE RD.	LOS ANGELES	CA	90077	U	U	TELEVISION WRITER/PRODUCER
CRANE, CHERYL	1271 OZETA TERR.	LOS ANGELES	CA	90069	U	U	LANA TURNER'S DAUGHTER
CRAVEN, WES	1000 W. WASHINGTON BLVD. #3011	CULVER CITY	CA	90232	U	U	WRITER/PRODUCER - NIGHTMARE ON ELM STREET
CRAWFORD, CHRISTINA	3530 PINE VALLEY DR.	SARASOTA	FL	34239	U	U	AUTHOR - MOMMIE DEAREST
CRAWFORD, CINDY	111 E. 22ND ST. , 2ND FL.	NEW YORK	NY	10010	A	C	MODEL - **AUTHOR'S CHOICE!**
CRAWFORD, JOHNNY	2240 EL CONTENTO DR.	LOS ANGELES	CA	90068	U	U	ACTOR
CRAWFORD, RANDY	911 PARK ST. S.W.	GRAND RAPIDS	MI	49504	A	A	CARTOONIST
CRAY, ROBERT	P.O. BOX 170429	SAN FRANCISCO	CA	94117	C	B	BAND LEADER - "SMOKING GUN"
CRENNA, RICHARD	3951 VALLEY MEADOW RD.	ENCINO	CA	91316	A	D	ACTOR/DIRECTOR - RAMBO: FIRST BLOOD PT. II
CRENSHAW, BEN	1811 W. 35TH ST.	AUSTIN	TX	78703	U	U	GOLFER
CRICHTON, MICHAEL	2210 WILSHIRE BLVD. #433	SANTA MONICA	CA	90403	A	C	WRITER/DIRECTOR - **AUTHOR'S CHOICE!**
CRICKETS, THE	RT.1, BOX 222	LYLES	TN	37098	U	U	ROCK GROUP
CRISP, QUENTIN	46 E. 3RD ST.	NEW YORK	NY	10003	A	B	ACTOR
CRIST, JUDITH	180 RIVERSIDE DR.	NEW YORK	NY	10024	A	B	FILM CRITIC
CRISTAL, LINDA	9129 HAZEN DR.	BEVERLY HILLS	CA	90210	A	B	ACTRESS
CROFT, MARY JANE	2160 CENTURY PARK E. #812	LOS ANGELES	CA	90068	U	U	ACTOR
CRONKITE, WALTER	519 E. 84TH ST.	NEW YORK	NY	10028	A	B	BROADCAST JOURNALIST - CBS EVENING NEWS
CRONYN, HUME	63-23 CARLTON ST.	REGO PARK	NY	11374	U	U	ACTOR - THE POSTMAN ALWAYS RINGS TWICE
CROSBY, CATHY LEE	1223 WILSHIRE BLVD. #404	SANTA MONICA	CA	90403	U	U	ACTRESS - THAT'S INCREDIBLE
CROSBY, MRS. KATHRYN	P.O. BOX 85	GENDA	NV	89411	A	D	WIDOW OF BING CROSBY

Name	Address	City	State	Zip Code	Resp. Time	Resp. Qual.	Comments
CROSBY, NORM	1400 LONDONDERRY PL.	LOS ANGELES	CA	90069	A	B	COMEDIAN/ACTOR
CROSBY, PHILIP	21801 PROVIDENCIA	WOODLAND HILLS	CA	91364	U	U	ACTOR
CROUSE, LINDSAY	8428 MELROSE PL. #C	LOS ANGELES	CA	90069	U	U	ACTRESS - THE VERDICT
CROW, SHERYL	C/O WILLIAM MORRIS AGCY., 151 EL CAMINO DR.	BEVERLY HILLS	CA	90212	U	U	SINGER - "ALL I WANNA DO" - AUTHOR'S CHOICE!
CROWELL, RODNEY	P.O. BOX 120576	NASHVILLE	TN	37212	U	U	SINGER/SONGWRITER
CROWLEY, MART	8955 BEVERLY BLVD.	LOS ANGELES	CA	90048	A	B+	WRITER
CROWLEY, PATRICIA	2672 HUTTON DR.	BEVERLY HILLS	CA	90210	U	U	ACTRESS
CRUISE, TOM	505 S. BEVERLY DR. SUITE #20	BEVERLY HILLS	CA	90212	U	U	ACTOR - TOP GUN - AUTHOR'S CHOICE!
CRUMM, DENNY	23015 THIRD ST.	LOUISVILLE	KY	40292	A	B	COLLEGE BASKETBALL COACH
CRYSTAL, BILLY	860 CHAUTAUQUA BLVD.	PACIFIC PALISADES	CA	90272	C	D	ACTOR/COMEDIAN - CITY SLICKERS - AUTHOR'S CHOICE!
CULEA, MELINDA	5504 CALHOUN AVE.	VAN NUYS	CA	91401	U	U	ACTRESS
CULKIN, MACAULAY	C/O WILLIAM MORRIS AGCY., 151 EL CAMINO DR.	BEVERLY HILLS	CA	90212	A	F	ACTOR - HOME ALONE - AUTHOR'S CHOICE!
CULP, ROBERT	357 CROWN DR.	LOS ANGELES	CA	90049	U	U	ACTOR/WRITER/DIRECTOR - I SPY
CUMMINGS, QUINN	121 N. SAN VICENTE BLVD.	BEVERLY HILLS	CA	90211	U	U	ACTRESS
CUOMO, MARIO	2 WORLD TRADE CTR., 57TH FL.	NEW YORK	NY	10047	U	U	FORMER GOVERNOR/LAWYER
CURREN, KEVIN	5808 BACK COURT	AUSTIN	TX	78764	U	U	TENNIS PLAYER
CURTIN, VALERIE	15622 MEADOWGATE RD.	ENCINO	CA	91316	A	C	ACTRESS/WRITER
CURTIS, DAN	10000 W. WASHINGTON BLVD. #3014	CULVER CITY	CA	90232	U	U	ACTOR
CURTIS, JAMIE LEE	P.O. BOX 2235	RUNNING SPRINGS	CA	92382	U	U	ACTRESS - TRUE LIES - AUTHOR'S CHOICE!
CURTIS, KEENE	6363 IVARENE AVE.	LOS ANGELES	CA	90068	A	B	ACTOR
CURTIS, TONY	11831 FOLKSTONE LN.	LOS ANGELES	CA	90077	U	U	ACTOR/DIRECTOR - SOME LIKE IT HOT
CUSACK, JOHN	151 EL CAMINO DR.	BEVERLY HILLS	CA	90212	U	U	ACTOR - THE GRIFTERS
CYRUS, BILLY RAY	818 - 18TH AVE. S.	NASHVILLE	TN	37203	A	B	SINGER - "ACHY BREAKY HEART"
D'ABO, OLIVIA	7495 MULHOLLAND DR.	LOS ANGELES	CA	90046	U	U	ACTRESS
D'AMBOISE, JACQUES	244 W. 71ST ST.	NEW YORK	NY	10023	A	B+	CHOREOGRAPHER
D'ANGELO, BEVERLY	8033 SUNSET BLVD. #247	LOS ANGELES	CA	90046	U	U	ACTRESS
D'ARBY, TERENCE TRENT	CHURCHWORKS NO. VILLAS	LONDON	ENG	NW1 9AY	U	U	SINGER
DABNEY, AUGUSTA	N. MOUNTAIN RD.	DOBBS FERRY	NY	10522	A	B	ACTRESS
DAFOE, WILLEM	33 WOOSTER ST.	NEW YORK	NY	10013	U	U	ACTOR - MISSISSIPPI BURNING
DAGGETT, TIM	53 HARMON ST.	LONG BEACH	NY	11561	U	U	GYMNAST
DAHL, ARLENE	P.O. BOX 116	SPARKILL	NY	10976	C	B	ACTRESS

153

Thanks for Caring

DORIS DAY PET FOUNDATION
P.O. Box 8509
Universal City, California 91618

Dedicated To Improving
The Lives of Our Best Friends

A Doris Day response

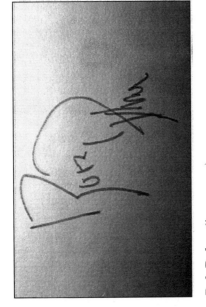

Bob Dylan (in-person)

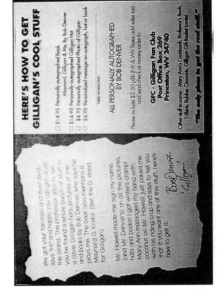

**HERE'S HOW TO GET
GILLIGAN'S COOL STUFF**

☐ $14.95 Personally autographed Book
   Maynard, Gilligan & Me By Bob Denver
☐ $14.95 Personally autographed Gilligan Hat
☐ $4.95 Personally autographed Photo of Gilligan
☐ $4.95 Personalized message on autograph, hat or book

ALL PERSONALLY AUTOGRAPHED
BY BOB DENVER

GFC- Gilligan Fan Club
Post Office Box 269
Princeton, WV 24740

A Bob Denver response

154

Name	Address	City	State	Zip Code	Resp. Time	Resp. Qual.	Comments
DAILEY, BILL	5245 E. COLDWATER CANYON	VAN NUYS	CA	91401	U	U	ACTOR
DAILEY, JANET	STAR RT. 4, BOX 2197	BRANSON	MO	65616	U	U	AUTHOR
DALANCIE, JOHN	1313 BRUNSWICK AVE.	S. PASADENA	CA	91030	U	U	ACTOR
DALEY, RICHARD M.	121 N. MAIN ST.	CHICAGO	IL	60602	A	D	MAYOR OF CHICAGO
DALEY, ROSIE	C/O HARPO PRODUCTIONS, 110 N. CARPENTER ST.	CHICAGO	IL	60607	U	U	CHEF - "OPRAH WINFREY'S PERSONAL CHEF!" - **AUTHOR'S CHOICE!**
DALLAS COWBOY CHEERLEADERS	1 COWBOY PKWY.	IRVING	TX	75063	U	U	CHEERLEADING TEAM
DALTON, AUDREY	15227 DEL GADO DR.	SHERMAN OAKS	CA	91403	U	U	ACTRESS
DALTON, TIMOTHY	15 GOLDEN SQUARE #315	LONDON	ENG	W1	U	U	ACTOR - *THE LIVING DAYLIGHTS*
DALTRY, ROGER	48 HARLEY HOUSE, MARYLEBONE RD.	LONDON	ENG	NW1 5HL	U	U	SINGER/ACTOR
DALY, JOHN	P.O. BOX 109601	PALM BEACH GARDENS	FL	33418	A	B	GOLFER
DALY, TIMOTHY	5555 MELROSE AVE.	LOS ANGELES	CA	90038	A	B	ACTOR - *WINGS*
DALY, TYNE	700 N. WESTKNOLL DR. #302	LOS ANGELES	CA	90069	U	U	ACTRESS - *CAGNEY & LACEY* - **AUTHOR'S CHOICE!**
DAMIAN, LEO	25366 MALIBU RD.	MALIBU	CA	90265	U	U	CONDUCTOR
DAMIAN, MICHAEL	P.O. BOX 25573	LOS ANGELES	CA	90025	U	U	ACTOR
DAMON, MARK	2781 BENEDICT CANYON	BEVERLY HILLS	CA	90210	U	U	ACTOR
DAMON, STUART	367 N. VAN NESS AVE.	LOS ANGELES	CA	90004	U	U	ACTOR
DAMONE, VIC	P.O. BOX 2999	BEVERLY HILLS	CA	90213	C	C	SINGER - *THE VIC DAMONE SHOW*
DANA, BILL	5965 PEACOCK RIDGE RD. #563	RANCHO PALOS VERDES	CA	90274	U	U	ACTOR/COMEDIAN
DANA, JUSTIN	16830 VENTURA BLVD. #300	ENCINO	CA	91436	A	B	ACTOR
DANCE, CHARLES	1311 N. CALIFORNIA ST.	BURBANK	CA	91505	U	U	ACTOR - *THE JEWEL IN THE CROWN*
DANDRIDGE, RUBY	3737 DON FELIPE DR.	LOS ANGELES	CA	90008	U	U	ACTRESS
DANES, CLAIRE	C/O ABC, 77 W. 66TH ST.	NEW YORK	NY	10023	U	U	ACTRESS - *MY SO-CALLED LIFE* - **AUTHOR'S CHOICE!**
DANFORTH, LIZ	C/O WIZARDS OF THE COAST, INC., P.O. BOX 707	RENTON	WA	98057	U	U	ILLUSTRATOR - "MAGIC" CARDS
DANGERFIELD, RODNEY	530 E. 76TH ST.	NEW YORK	NY	10021	A	B	COMEDIAN/ACTOR - *BACK TO SCHOOL*
DANIEL, CLIFTON	830 PARK AVE.	NEW YORK	NY	10028	A	B	JOURNALIST
DANIELS, JEFF	C/O ICM, 8942 WILSHIRE BLVD.	BEVERLY HILLS	CA	90211	U	U	ACTOR - *DUMB AND DUMBER* - **AUTHOR'S CHOICE!**
DANIELS, WILLIAM	10000 SANTA MONICA BLVD. #305	LOS ANGELES	CA	90067	A	B	ACTOR - *ST. ELSEWHERE*
DANILOFF, NICHOLAS	2400 "N" ST. N.W.	WASHINGTON	DC	20037	U	U	NEWS CORRESPONDENT
DANILOV, ALEXANDRA	100 W. 57TH ST.	NEW YORK	NY	10019	U	U	BALLERINA
DANNER, BLYTHE	8942 WILSHIRE BLVD.	BEVERLY HILLS	CA	90211	A	B	ACTRESS - *THE PRINCE OF TIDES*
DANNING, SYBIL	3575 CAHUENGA BLVD. W. #200	LOS ANGELES	CA	90068	U	U	ACTRESS

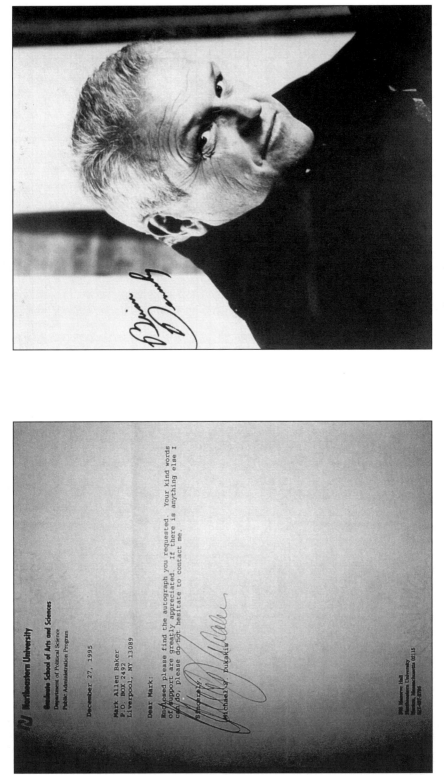

Brian Dennehy

Michael Dukakis

Name	Address	City	State	Zip Code	Resp. Time	Resp. Qual.	Comments
DANNY & THE JUNIORS	P.O. BOX 1987	STUDIO CITY	CA	91604	A	B+	VOCAL GROUP
DANSON, TED	9830 WILSHIRE BLVD.	BEVERLY HILLS	CA	90212	U	U	ACTOR - *CHEERS* - A VERY TOUGH SIGNATURE! - **AUTHOR'S CHOICE!**
DANZA, TONY	19722 TRULL BROOK DR.	TARZANA	CA	91356	A	C	ACTOR - *WHO'S THE BOSS?*
DARBY, KIM	4255 LAUREL GROVE	STUDIO CITY	CA	91604	U	U	ACTRESS
DARDEN, CHRISTOPHER	C/O OFFICE OF THE D.A., CRIMINAL COURTS BLDG., 210 W. TEMPLE ST.	LOS ANGELES	CA	90012	U	U	ATTORNEY - "THE PEOPLE VS. O. J. SIMPSON"
DARK, JOHNNY	1100 N. ALTA LOMA #707	LOS ANGELES	CA	90069	A	B	COMEDIAN
DARLING, JOAN	P.O. BOX 6700	TESUQUE	NM	87574	U	U	WRITER/DIRECTOR
DARREN, JAMES	P.O. BOX 1088	BEVERLY HILLS	CA	90213	A	D	ACTOR/SINGER
DARROW, HENRY	9169 SUNSET BLVD.	LOS ANGELES	CA	90069	A	D	ACTOR
DASH, SAM	1100 NEWLANDS	CHEVY CHASE	MD	20015	A	B	WATERGATE CO-CONSPIRATOR
DAUGHTRY, HERBERT	415 ATLANTIC AVE.	BROOKLYN	NY	11217	U	U	ACTIVIST
DAVALOS, ELYSSA	9229 SUNSET BLVD. #607	LOS ANGELES	CA	90069	U	U	ACTRESS
DAVALOS, RICHARD	1958 VESTAL AVE.	LOS ANGELES	CA	90026	U	U	ACTOR/DIRECTOR
DAVI, ROBERT	6568 BEACHVIEW DR. #209	RANCHO PALOS VERDES	CA	90274	U	U	ACTOR
DAVICH, MARTY	1044 ARMADA DR.	PASADENA	CA	91103	U	U	ACTOR
DAVIDOVICH, LOLITA	8942 WILSHIRE BLVD.	BEVERLY HILLS	CA	90211	U	U	ACTRESS
DAVIDSON, DOUG	3641 E. CHEVY CHASE DR.	GLENDALE	CA	91206	U	U	ACTOR
DAVIDSON, EILEEN	13340 GALEWOOD DR.	SHERMAN OAKS	CA	91423	U	U	ACTRESS
DAVIDSON, GORDON	165 MABERY RD.	SANTA MONICA	CA	90406	U	U	FILM DIRECTOR
DAVIDSON, JAYE	C/O ICM, 8942 WILSHIRE BLVD.	BEVERLY HILLS	CA	90-211	U	U	ACTOR - *THE CRYING GAME* - **AUTHOR'S CHOICE!**
DAVIDSON, JOHN	6051 SPRING VALLEY RD.	HIDDEN HILLS	CA	91302	A	B	SINGER/ACTOR - *HOLLYWOOD SQUARES*
DAVIDTZ, EMBETH	151 EL CAMINO DR.	BEVERLY HILLS	CA	90212	U	U	ACTOR
DAVIES, LANE	9200 SUNSET BLVD. #625	LOS ANGELES	CA	90069	U	U	ACTOR
DAVIS, AL	332 CENTER ST.	EL SEGUNDO	CA	90245	U	U	FOOTBALL TEAM OWNER
DAVIS, ANGELA	C/O ETHNIC STUDIES DEPT.	SAN FRANCISCO	CA	94132	U	U	ACTIVIST
DAVIS, ANN B.	1427 BEAVER RD.	AMBRIDGE	PA	15003	A	B	ACTRESS - *THE BRADY BUNCH*
DAVIS, BENJAMIN	1001 WILSON BLVD. # 906	ARLINGTON	VA	22209	A	B	MILITARY GENERAL
DAVIS, GEENA	C/O CREATIVE ARTISTS AGCY., 9830 WILSHIRE BLVD.	BEVERLY HILLS	CA	90212	U	U	ACTRESS - *THELMA AND LOUISE* - **AUTHOR'S CHOICE!**
DAVIS, GLENN	47-650 EISENHOWER DR.	LA QUINTA	CA	92253	A	B	ACTOR
DAVIS, JIM	200 PARK AVE.	NEW YORK	NY	10166	A	B+	CARTOONIST - *GARFIELD* - OUTSTANDING!
DAVIS, JIMMIE	P.O. BOX 15826	BATON ROUGE	LA	70895	A	B	SINGER
DAVIS, MAC	759 NIMES RD.	LOS ANGELES	CA	90024	U	U	SINGER/ACTOR - *THE MAC DAVIS SHOW*

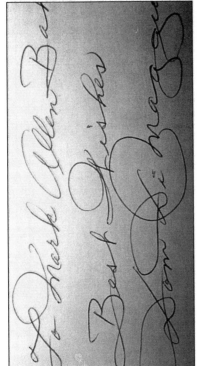

Dom DiMaggio

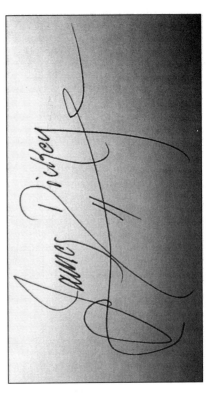

James Dickey

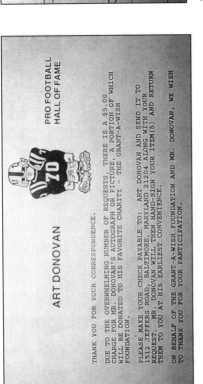

ART DONOVAN

PRO FOOTBALL
HALL OF FAME

THANK YOU FOR YOUR CORRESPONDENCE.

DUE TO THE OVERWHELMING NUMBER OF REQUESTS, THERE IS A $5.00
CHARGE FOR MR. DONOVAN'S AUTOGRAPH OR PICTURE, A PORTION OF WHICH
WILL BE DONATED TO HIS FAVORITE CHARITY - THE GRANT-A-WISH
FOUNDATION.

PLEASE MAKE YOUR CHECK PAYABLE TO: ART DONOVAN AND SEND IT TO
1512 JEFFERS ROAD, BALTIMORE, MARYLAND 21204 ALONG WITH YOUR
REQUEST. MR. DONOVAN WILL THEN HAND-SIGN YOUR ITEM(S) AND RETURN
THEM TO YOU AT HIS EARLIEST CONVENIENCE.

ON BEHALF OF THE GRANT-A-WISH FOUNDATION AND MR. DONOVAN, WE WISH
TO THANK YOU FOR YOUR PARTICIPATION.

An Art Donovan response

Fats Domino

Name	Address	City	State	Zip Code	Resp. Time	Resp. Qual.	Comments
DAVIS, MARTHA	10513 CUSHDON AVE.	LOS ANGELES	CA	90064	U	U	SINGER
DAVIS, MARVIN	1120 SCHUYLER RD.	BEVERLY HILLS	CA	90210	U	U	FILM EXECUTIVE
DAVIS, OSSIE	44 CORTLAND AVE.	NEW ROCHELLE	NY	10801	U	U	ACTOR/DIRECTOR/WRITER - *EVENING SHADE*
DAVIS, SKEETER	508 SEWARD RD.	BRENTWOOD	TN	37027	U	U	SINGER
DAVISON, BRUCE	P.O. BOX 57593	SHERMAN OAKS	CA	91403	C	B	ACTOR
DAWBER, PAM	2236-A ENCINITAS BLVD.	ENCINITAS	CA	92024	U	U	ACTRESS - *MORK AND MINDY*
DAWKINS, PETE	178 RUMSON RD.	RUMSON	NJ	07760	U	U	FORMER POLITICIAN
DAWSON, RICHARD	1117 ANGELO DR.	BEVERLY HILLS	CA	90210	C	B	ACTOR - *FAMILY FEUD*
DAY, DORIS	P.O. BOX 223163	CARMEL	CA	93922	A	F	ACTRESS - *THE DORIS DAY SHOW* - SENDS FACSIMILE PHOTO THEN ASKS FOR DONATION!
DAY, LARAINE	10313 LAURISTON AVE.	LOS ANGELES	CA	90025	A	C	ACTRESS
DAY, LINDA	3335 COY DR.	SHERMAN OAKS	CA	91423	A	B+	ACTRESS
DAY-LEWIS, DANIEL	C/O WM. MORRIS AGGY., 151 EL CAMINO DR.	BEVERLY HILLS	CA	90212	U	F	ACTOR - *MY LEFT FOOT* - **AUTHOR'S CHOICE!**
DE BAKEY, DR. MICHAEL	BAYLOR COLLEGE OF MEDICINE , 1200 MOURSUND AVE.	HOUSTON	TX	77030	U	U	HEART SURGEON
DE BENNING, BURR	4235 KINGFISHER RD.	CALABASAS	CA	91302	U	U	ACTOR
DE BURGH, CHRIS	BARGY CASTLE, TONHAGGARD	WESXORD	IRE		U	U	SINGER/GUITARIST - "LADY IN RED"
DE CAMP, ROSEMARY	317 CAMINO DE LAS COLINAS	REDONDO BEACH	CA	90277	A	B	ACTRESS
DE CORDOVA, FRED	1875 CARLA RIDGE DR.	BEVERLY HILLS	CA	90210	A	B	FILM/TELEVISION DIRECTOR
DE LA RENTA, OSCAR	BROOK HILL FARM, SKIFF MOUNTAIN RD.	KENT	CT	06757	U	U	FASHION DESIGNER
DE LA SOUL	1700 BROADWAY #500	NEW YORK	NY	10019	U	U	MUSIC GROUP
DE LAURENTIS, DINO	VIA POUTINA KU 23270	ROME	ITA		U	U	FILM PRODUCER - *KING KONG*
DE LUGG, MILTON	2740 CLARAY DR.	LOS ANGELES	CA	90024	U	U	COMPOSER/CONDUCTOR
DE MORNAY, REBECCA	760 N. LOS ANGELES CIENEGA BLVD.	LOS ANGELES	CA	90069	U	U	ACTRESS - *THE HAND THAT ROCKS THE CRADLE*
DE NIRO, ROBERT	375 GREENWICH ST.	NEW YORK	NY	10013	A	B	ACTOR - **AUTHOR'S CHOICE!**
DE PALMA, BRIAN	270 N. CANYON DR. #1195	BEVERLY HILLS	CA	90210	U	U	WRITER/PRODUCER
DE PASSE, SUZANNE	1100 N. ALTA LOMA #805	LOS ANGELES	CA	90069	U	U	TELEVISION WRITER
DE VREES, WILLIAM	HUMAN HEART INSTITUTE, ONE AUDOBON PLAZA DR.	LOUISVILLE	KY	40202	A	B	HEART SURGEON
DE WITT, JOYCE	11940 SAN VICENTE BLVD.	LOS ANGELES	CA	90049	C	F	ACTRESS - *THREE'S COMPANY* - STAMPED SIGNATURE
DE YOUNG, CLIFF	766 KINGMAN AVE.	SANTA MONICA	CA	90402	U	U	ACTOR - *THE HUNGER*
DEAN, BILLY	1207 - 16TH AVE. S.	NASHVILLE	TN	37212	A	B	SINGER
DEAN, EDDIE	32161 SAILVIEW LN.	WESTLAKE VILLAGE	CA	91360	A	D	ACTOR/SINGER

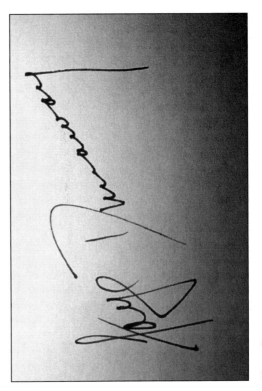

Faye Dunaway

Richard Dreyfuss

Name	Address	City	State	Zip Code	Resp. Time	Resp. Qual.	Comments
DEAN, JIMMY	28035 DOROTHY DR. #210-A	AGOURA	CA	91301	U	U	SINGER - *THE JIMMY DEAN SHOW*
DEAN, JOHN	9496 REMBERT LN.	BEVERLY HILLS	CA	90210	U	U	AUTHOR
DEARIE, BLOSSOM	P.O. BOX 21	EAST DURHAM	NY	12423	A	B	SINGER
DEBORBA, DOROTHY	1810 MONTECITO AVE.	LIVERMORE	CA	94550	U	U	ACTRESS
DECKER SLANEY, MARY	2923 FLINTLOCK ST.	EUGENE	OR	97401	U	U	TRACK ATHLETE
DEE, FRANCES	RT. 1	CAMARILLO	CA	93010	U	U	ACTRESS
DEE, JOEY	141 DUNBAR AVE.	FORDS	NJ	08863	U	U	SINGER - "JOEY DEE & THE STARLIGHTS"
DEE, RUBY	44 CORTLAND AVE.	NEW ROCHELLE	NY	10801	A	B	ACTRESS - *DO THE RIGHT THING*
DEE, SANDRA	10351 SANTA MONICA BLVD. #211	LOS ANGELES	CA	90025	U	U	ACTRESS - *GIDGET*
DEEMS, MICKEY	13114 WEDDINGTON ST.	VAN NUYS	CA	90401	U	U	ACTOR/DIRECTOR
DEES, MORRIS	ROLLING HILLS RANCH, RT. 1	MATHEWS	AL	36052	A	D	LAWYER
DEES, RICK	KIIS FM, 6255 SUNSET BLVD.	LOS ANGELES	CA	90069	A	B	RADIO PERSONALITY
DEEZEN, EDDIE	1570 N. EDGEMONT #602	LOS ANGELES	CA	90027	A	B	ACTOR
DEGENERES, ELLEN	C/O UNITED TALENT AGCY., 9560 WILSHIRE BLVD., 5TH FL.	BEVERLY HILLS	CA	90212	U	U	ACTRESS - ELLEN - **AUTHOR'S CHOICE!**
DEHAVEN, GLORIA	73 DEVONSHIRE RD.	CEDAR GROVE	NJ	07009	U	U	ACTRESS
DEHAVEN, PENNY	P.O. BOX 83	BRENTWOOD	TN	37027	U	U	SINGER
DEHAVILLAND, OLIVIA	BOITE POSTAL 156-16	PARIS CEDEX	FRA	75764	U	U	ACTRESS - *GONE WITH THE WIND*
DEL VIKINGS, THE	P.O. BOX 70218	FT. LAUDERDALE	FL	33307	U	U	MUSIC GROUP
DELANCIE, JOHN	1313 BRUNSWICK AVE.	S. PASADENA	CA	91030	U	U	ACTOR
DELANEY, KIM	4724 POE AVE.	WOODLAND HILLS	CA	91364	U	U	ACTRESS
DELANY, DANA	C/O ICM, 8942 WILSHIRE BLVD.	BEVERLY HILLS	CA	90211	A	B	ACTRESS - *CHINA BEACH* - **AUTHOR'S CHOICE!**
DELL, MYRNA	1295 VALLEY HEART DR.	STUDIO CITY	CA	91604	C	F	ACTRESS - $20 PER PHOTO
DELO, KEN	844 S. MASSELIN	LOS ANGELES	CA	90048	A	B	SINGER
DELON, ALAN	4 CHAMBIGES, TROIS ETAGE	PARIS	FRA	75008	U	U	ACTOR - *IS PARIS BURNING?*
DELOY, GEORGE	11460 AMANDA DR.	STUDIO CITY	CA	91604	U	U	ACTOR
DELUISE, DOM	1186 CORSICA DR.	PACIFIC PALISADES	CA	90272	A	A+	ACTOR
DELUISE, MICHAEL	1186 CORSICA DR.	PACIFIC PALISADES	CA	90272	U	U	ACTOR
DELUISE, PETER	5632 VAN NUYS BLVD. #286	VAN NUYS	CA	91401	U	U	ACTOR - *21 JUMP STREET*
DEMME, JONATHAN	9830 WILSHIRE BLVD.	BEVERLY HILLS	CA	90212	U	U	DIRECTOR - *THE SILENCE OF THE LAMBS*
DEMPSEY, PATRICK	431 LINCOLN BLVD.	SANTA MONICA	CA	90402	C	B	ACTOR - *LOVERBOY*
DENEUVE, CATHERINE	76 RUE BONAPARTE	PARIS	FRA	6	U	U	ACTRESS - *THE LAST METRO*
DENIER, LYDIE	8485-E MELROSE PL.	LOS ANGELES	CA	90069	U	U	ACTRESS
DENNEHY, BRIAN	121 N. SAN VICENTE BLVD.	BEVERLY HILLS	CA	90211	A	B	ACTOR - *COCOON*

Name	Address	City	State	Zip Code	Resp. Time	Resp. Qual.	Comments
DENSMORE, JOHN	49 HALDERMAN RD.	SANTA MONICA	CA	90402	U	U	MUSICIAN
DENVER, BOB	GENERAL DELIVERY	PRINCETON	WV	24740	U	U	ACTOR - *GILLIGAN'S ISLAND* - SENDS CARD WITH PRICES!
DENVER, JOHN	P.O. BOX 1587	ASPEN	CO	81612	C	F	SINGER/SONGWRITER - "ANNIE'S SONG"
DEPARDIEU, GERARD	4 PLACE DE LOS ANGELES CHAPELLE	BOUGIVAL	FRA		U	U	ACTOR - *GREEN CARD*
DEPP, JOHNNY	8942 WILSHIRE BLVD.	BEVERLY HILLS	CA	90211	U	U	ACTOR - *21 JUMP STREET* - **AUTHOR'S CHOICE!**
DEREK, BO	3625 ROBLAR	SANTA YNEZ	CA	93460	F	F	ACTRESS/MODEL - *10* - SAVE YOUR STAMPS!
DEREK, JOHN	3625 ROBLAR	SANTA YNEZ	CA	93460	F	F	ACTOR/WRITER/DIRECTOR - *THE TEN COMMANDMENTS* - SAVE MORE STAMPS!
DERN, LAURA	760 N. LOS ANGELES CIENEGA BLVD.	LOS ANGELES	CA	90069	B	B	ACTRESS - *JURASSIC PARK*
DERSHOWITZ, ALAN	2 TUDOR CITY PL.	NEW YORK	NY	10017	C	D	LAWYER
DESHANNON, JACKIE	7526 SUNNYWOOD LN.	LOS ANGELES	CA	90069	U	U	SINGER
DEVERS, GAIL	20214 LEADWELL	CANOGA PARK	CA	91304	U	U	TRACK ATHLETE
DEVITO, DANNY	31020 BROAD BEACH RD.	MALIBU	CA	90265	U	U	ACTOR - *TAXI* - **AUTHOR'S CHOICE!**
DEVO	P.O. BOX 6868	BURBANK	CA	91510	U	U	ROCK GROUP
DEWIT, JACQUELINE	436 S. ALANDELE AVE.	LOS ANGELES	CA	90036	U	U	ACTRESS
DEY, SUSAN	10390 SANTA MONICA BLVD. #300	LOS ANGELES	CA	90025	U	U	ACTRESS - *L.A. LAW*
DI BONA, VINCENT	1912 THAYER AVE.	LOS ANGELES	CA	90025	U	U	DIRECTOR/PRODUCER
DI CENZO, GEORGE	RD 1, BOX 728, STONE HOLLOW FARM	PIPERSVILLE	PA	18947	A	B	ACTOR
DI MUCCI, DION	3099 N.W. 63RD ST.	BOCA RATON	FL	33434	U	U	SINGER - DION & THE BELMONTS
DIAMOND, BOBBY	633 CALLE ARROYO	THOUSAND OAKS	CA	91360	U	U	ACTOR
DIAMOND, NEIL	161 S. MAPLETON DR.	LOS ANGELES	CA	90024	C	F	SINGER/SONGWRITER - *THE JAZZ SINGER* - SENDS FACSIMILE SIGNED PHOTO!
DIAMONT, DON	5757 WILSHIRE BLVD.	LOS ANGELES	CA	90036	U	U	ACTOR
DICAPRIO, LEONARDO	9830 WILSHIRE BLVD.	BEVERLY HILLS	CA	90212	U	U	ACTOR - *THIS BOY'S LIFE* - **AUTHOR'S CHOICE!**
DICK, DOUGLAS	604 GRETNA GREEN WAY	LOS ANGELES	CA	90049	A	C	ACTOR
DICKENS, JIMMY	510 W. CONCORD	BRENTWOOD	TN	37027	A	B	SINGER
DICKEY, JAMES	4620 LELIAS COURT, LAKE KATHERINE	COLUMBIA	SC	29206	A	B	POET/NOVELIST - BEAUTIFUL SIGNATURE!
DICKINSON, ANGIE	9580 LIME ORCHARD RD.	BEVERLY HILLS	CA	90210	A	B	ACTRESS - *POLICE WOMAN*
DIERDORF, DAN	C/O ABC SPORTS, 1330 AVE. OF THE AMERICAS	NEW YORK	NY	10019	U	U	SPORTSCASTER - MEMBER OF THE PRO FOOTBALL HALL OF FAME
DIERKOP, CHARLES	10637 BURBANK BLVD.	NORTH HOLLYWOOD	CA	91601	U	U	ACTOR
DIETRICH, DENA	1155 N. LOS ANGELES CIENEGA BLVD. #302	LOS ANGELES	CA	90069	U	U	ACTRESS
DIFFER, JOE	P.O. BOX 125	NASHVILLE	TN	37202	U	U	SINGER

Name	Address	City	State	Zip Code	Resp. Time	Resp. Qual.	Comments
DILLER, BARRY	1365 ENTERPRISE DR.	WEST CHESTER	PA	19280	U	U	BUSINESS EXECUTIVE
DILLER, PHYLLIS	163 S. ROCKINGHAM AVE.	LOS ANGELES	CA	90049	A	B+	COMEDIENNE - *THE PHYLLIS DILLER SHOW*
DILLMAN, BRADFORD	770 HOT SPRINGS RD.	SANTA BARBARA	CA	93103	A	D	ACTOR
DILLON, KEVIN	49 W. 9TH ST. #5B	NEW YORK	NY	10010	U	U	ACTOR - *THE DOORS*
DILLON, MATT	235 W. 46TH ST.	NEW YORK	NY	10036	U	U	ACTOR - *THE OUTSIDERS*
DIMAGGIO, DOM	162 POINT RD.	MARION	MA	02738	A	D	BASEBALL PLAYER - ASKS FOR DONATIONS, MAYBE HE SHOULD START WITH HIS BROTHER!
DIMAGGIO, JOE	C/O MORRIS ENGELBERG, 4000 SHERIDAN ST	HOLLYWOOD	FL	33021	U	U	MEMBER OF THE BASEBALL HALL OF FAME - EVASIVE, WILL COST YOU SOME CASH!
DION, CELINE	C.P. 65, REPENTIGUY	QUEBEC	CAN	J6A 5H7	U	U	SINGER - **AUTHOR'S CHOICE!**
DIRE STRAITS	16 LAMBTON PL.	LONDON	ENG	W11 2SH	U	U	ROCK GROUP
DIRT BAND, THE	P.O. BOX 1915	ASPEN	CO	81611	U	U	MUSIC GROUP
DISHY, BOB	20 E. 9TH ST.	NEW YORK	NY	10003	U	U	ACTOR/WRITER
DISNEY, MRS. LILLIAN	355 CAROLWOOD DR.	LOS ANGELES	CA	90024	A	F	MRS. WALT DISNEY - DOESN'T RESPOND TO AUTOGRAPH REQUESTS ANYMORE!
DISNEY, ROY	500 S. BUENA VISTA ST.	BURBANK	CA	91521	U	U	WRITER/PRODUCER
DIVAC, VALDE	P.O. BOX 10	INGLEWOOD	CA	90306	A	D	BASKETBALL PLAYER
DIVOFF, ANDREW	10637 BURBANK BLVD.	NORTH HOLLYWOOD	CA	91601	U	U	ACTOR
DIXON, DONNA	8955 NORMA PL.	LOS ANGELES	CA	90069	U	U	ACTRESS - *BOSOM BUDDIES*
DIXON, JEANNE	1225 CONNECTICUT AVE. N.W. SUITE #411	WASHINGTON	DC	20036	A	F	ASTROLOGER - HAS SENT OUT THE SAME FACSIMILE PRAYER CARD FOR DECADES!
DIZON, JESSE	6427 GLORIA AVE.	VAN NUYS	CA	91406	U	U	ACTOR/WRITER
DMYTRYK, EDWARD	3945 WESTFALL DR.	ENCINO	CA	91436	U	U	DIRECTOR
DOBKIN, LAWRENCE	1787 OLD RANCH RD.	LOS ANGELES	CA	90049	U	U	ACTOR/WRITER/DIRECTOR
DOBSON, KEVIN	11930 IREDELL ST.	STUDIO CITY	CA	91604	U	U	ACTOR - *KNOTS LANDING*
DOBSON, PETER	1351 N. CRESCENT HEIGHTS #318	LOS ANGELES	CA	90046	U	U	ACTOR
DOBY, LARRY	NISHUANA RD. #45	MONTCLAIR	NJ	07042	A	F	BASEBALL PLAYER - SENDS OUT PRICE LIST!
DODA, CAROL	P.O. BOX 387	FREMONT	CA	94537	U	U	DANCER
DOER, BOBBY	33705 ILLAMO AGNES RD.	AGNESS	OR	97406	U	U	MEMBER OF THE BASEBALL HALL OF FAME - GREAT IN PERSON!
DOHERTY, SHANNON	151 EL CAMINO DR.	BEVERLY HILLS	CA	90212	U	U	ACTRESS - *BEVERLY HILLS 90210* - **AUTHOR'S CHOICE!**
DOLAN, DON	708 FOURTH AVE.	ASHLAND	OR	97520	A	B	ACTOR
DOLE, SEN. ROBERT J.	141 HART OFFICE BLDG.	WASHINGTON	DC	20510	U	U	SENATOR/PRESIDENTIAL HOPEFUL
DOLENZ, AMI	6058 ST. CLAIR AVE.	NORTH HOLLYWOOD	CA	91607	U	U	ACTRESS

163

Name	Address	City	State	Zip Code	Resp. Time	Resp. Qual.	Comments
DOLENZ, MICKEY	8369A SAUSALITO AVE.	WEST HILLS	CA	91304	U	U	MUSICIAN/ACTOR - *THE MONKEES*
DOMINGO, PLACIDO	150 CENTRAL PARK S.	NEW YORK	NY	10019	U	U	TENOR
DOMINO, FATS	5515 MARAIS ST.	NEW ORLEANS	LA	70117	A	B	SINGER/PIANIST - "BLUEBERRY HILL"
DONAHUE, ELINOR	4525 LEMP AVE.	NORTH HOLLYWOOD	CA	91602	U	U	ACTRESS
DONAHUE, PHIL	420 E. 54TH ST. #22-F	NEW YORK	NY	10022	F	F	TALK SHOW HOST - UNRESPONSIVE TO FAN MAIL! - **AUTHOR'S CHOICE!**
DONAHUE, TROY	1022 EUCLID AVE. #1	SANTA MONICA	CA	90403	A	B	ACTOR - *HAWAIIAN EYE*
DONALDSON, SAM	1717 DESALES N.W.	WASHINGTON	DC	20007	U	U	BROADCAST JOURNALIST - *PRIME TIME LIVE*
DONAT, PETER	1030 BRODERICK ST.	SAN FRANCISCO	CA	94115	U	U	ACTOR
DONFELD	2900 HUTTON DR.	BEVERLY HILLS	CA	90210	U	U	COSTUME DESIGNER
DONNER, CLIVE	1466 N. KINGS RD.	LOS ANGELES	CA	90069	U	U	FILM DIRECTOR
DONNER, RICHARD	4000 WARNER BLVD. BLDG. #102	BURBANK	CA	91522	U	U	ACTOR
DONNER, ROBERT	3828 GLENRIDGE DR.	SHERMAN OAKS	CA	91423	A	B	ACTOR
DONOGHUE, MARY AGNES	427 ALTA AVE.	SANTA MONICA	CA	91423	U	U	WRITER
DONOHUE, AMANDA	10100 SANTA MONICA BLVD. #700	LOS ANGELES	CA	90067	U	U	ACTRESS - *L.A. LAW*
DONOHUE, TERRY	11918 LAURELWOOD	STUDIO CITY	CA	91604	U	U	FOOTBALL COACH
DONOVAN	P.O. BOX 472	LONDON	ENG	SW1 2QB	U	U	SINGER/SONGWRITER - "MELLO YELLOW"
DONOVAN, ART	1512 JEFFERS RD.	BALTIMORE	MD	21204	A	F	FOOTBALL PLAYER, ESPN COMMERCIAL STAR - SENDS OUT FLYER - $5 PER AUTOGRAPH!
DOOBIE BROTHERS	15140 SONOMA HWY.	GLEN ELLEN	CA	95442	U	U	ROCK GROUP, GREAT IN PERSON!
DOOHAN, JAMES	5533 MATILIJI AVE.	VAN NUYS	CA	91401	U	U	ACTOR
DORAN, ANN	3939 WALNUT AVE.	CARMICHAEL	CA	95608	A	D	ACTRESS
DORN, DOLORES	7461 BEVERLY BLVD. #400	LOS ANGELES	CA	90036	U	U	ACTRESS
DORN, MICHAEL	3751 MULTIVIEW DR.	LOS ANGELES	CA	90068	U	U	ACTOR
DORSETT, TONY	1 COWBOY PKWY.	IRVING	TX	75063	U	U	MEMBER OF THE FOOTBALL HALL OF FAME!
DORTORT, DAVID	133 UDINE WAY	LOS ANGELES	CA	90024	A	D	WRITER/PRODUCER
DOUCETTE, JOHN	P.O. BOX 252	CABAZON	CA	92230	U	U	ACTOR
DOUGLAS, CARL	4929 WILSHIRE BLVD. SUITE 100	LOS ANGELES	CA	90010	U	U	LAWYER - MEMBER OF O. J. SIMPSON "DREAM TEAM"
DOUGLAS, DONNA	P.O. BOX 49455	LOS ANGELES	CA	90049	A	B	ACTRESS/SINGER - *THE BEVERLY HILLBILLIES*
DOUGLAS, ERIC	9000 SUNSET BLVD. #405	LOS ANGELES	CA	90069	A	B+	ACTOR
DOUGLAS, JERRY	8600 HILLSIDE AVE.	LOS ANGELES	CA	90069	U	U	ACTOR
DOUGLAS, KIRK	805 N. REXFORD DR.	BEVERLY HILLS	CA	90210	A	B	ACTOR - *SPARTACUS*
DOUGLAS, MICHAEL	P.O. BOX 49054	LOS ANGELES	CA	90049	U	U	ACTOR/PRODUCER - *FATAL ATTRACTION* - **AUTHOR'S CHOICE!**

Name	Address	City	State	Zip Code	Resp. Time	Resp. Qual.	Comments
DOUGLAS, MIKE	602 N. ARDEN DR.	BEVERLY HILLS	CA	90210	U	U	TELEVISION HOST/SINGER
DOULAS, ROBERT	1810 PARLIAMENT RD.	LEUCADIA	CA	92024	A	B+	ACTOR/DIRECTOR
DOURIF, BRAD	213 1/2 S. ARNAZ DR.	BEVERLY HILLS	CA	90211	U	U	ACTOR
DOVE, BILLIE	P.O. BOX 5005	RANCHO MIRAGE	CA	92270	A	D	ACTRESS
DOW, PEGGY	2121 S. YORKSTOWN AVE.	TULSA	OK	74114	U	U	ACTRESS
DOWNEY, ROBERT JR.	29169 HEATHERCLIFF RD.	MALIBU	CA	90265	U	U	ACTOR - *CHAPLIN* - **AUTHOR'S CHOICE!**
DOWNS, HUGH	P.O. BOX 1132	CAREFREE	AZ	85331	A	C	BROADCAST JOURNALIST - *20/20*
DOWNS, JOHNNY	812 SAN LUIS REY	CORONADO	CA	92118	U	U	ACTOR/DANCER
DOYLE, DAVID	4731 NOELINE AVE.	ENCINO	CA	91316	A	D	ACTOR/DIRECTOR - *CHARLIE'S ANGELS*
DRAGOTI, STAN	WELLS, RICH, GREEN, BDDP INC., 9 W. 57TH ST. 12TH FL.	NEW YORK	NY	10019	U	U	WRITER/PRODUCER
DRAI, VICTOR	1201 DES RESTO DR.	BEVERLY HILLS	CA	90210	U	U	FILM PRODUCER
DRAKE, BETSY	2223 VETERAN AVE.	LOS ANGELES	CA	90064	U	U	ACTRESS
DRAKE, FRANCES	1511 SUMMIT RIDGE DR.	BEVERLY HILLS	CA	90210	U	U	ACTRESS
DRAKE, LARRY	1901 AVE. OF THE STARS #620	LOS ANGELES	CA	90067	U	U	ACTOR
DRAPER, POLLY	1324 N. ORANGE GROVE	LOS ANGELES	CA	90046	U	U	ACTRESS
DRAVECKY, DAVE	P.O. BOX 3505	BOARDMAN	OH	44513	A	B	BASEBALL PLAYER - AN INSPIRATION - **AUTHOR'S CHOICE!**
DRE, DR.	C/O INTERSCOPE RECORDS, 10900 WILSHIRE BLVD. SUITE 1230	LOS ANGELES	CA	90024	U	U	RAP ARTIST - "THE CHRONIC" - **AUTHOR'S CHOICE!**
DREESEN, TOM	14570 BENEFIT ST. #201	SHERMAN OAKS	CA	91403	A	B+	COMEDIAN
DREXLER, CLYD	C/O HOUSTON ROCKETS, 10 GREENWAY RIVER PL., P.O. BOX 272349	HOUSTON	TX	77277	U	U	BASKETBALL PLAYER - "THE GLIDE"
DREYFUSS, RICHARD	2809 NICHOLS CANYON	LOS ANGELES	CA	90046	A	D	ACTOR - *MR. HOLLAND'S OPUS* - **AUTHOR'S CHOICE!**
DRIER, MOOSIE	11350 VENTURA BLVD. #206	STUDIO CITY	CA	91604	U	U	ACTOR
DRIFTERS, THE	10 CHELSEA COURT	NEPTUNE	NJ	07753	U	U	VOCAL GROUP
DRURY, ALLEN	P.O. BOX 674	TIBURON	CA	94920	A	B	AUTHOR - VERY SMALL SIGNATURE!
DRURY, JAMES	12755 MILL RIDGE #622	CYPRUS	TX	77429	A	F	ACTOR - SENDS PRICE LIST - SAVE YOUR STAMPS!
DRUSKY, ROY	131 TRIVETT DR.	PORTLAND	TN	37148	A	B	SINGER/SONGWRITER
DRYER, FRED	4117 RADFORD AVE.	STUDIO CITY	CA	91604	C	F	ACTOR/FOOTBALL PLAYER - FACSIMILE SIGNATURE
DU PONT, PIERRE	PATTERNS	ROCKLAND	DE	19732	A	B	FORMER GOVERNOR
DUCHIN, PETER	305 MADISON AVE. #956	NEW YORK	NY	10165	U	U	PIANIST
DUCHOVNY, DAVID	C/O ICM, 8942 WILSHIRE BLVD.	BEVERLY HILLS	CA	90211	A	F	ACTOR - *THE X-FILES* - **AUTHOR'S CHOICE!** - RESPONDS WITH FACSIMILE SIGNED PHOTO - "THE TRUTH'S OUT THERE"

Name	Address	City	State	Zip Code	Resp. Time	Resp. Qual.	Comments
DUCOMMUN, RICK	7967 WOODROW WILSON DR.	LOS ANGELES	CA	90046	U	U	COMEDIAN
DUDIKOFF, MICHAEL	8485 MELROSE PL. #E	LOS ANGELES	CA	90069	A	B+	ACTOR - AMERICAN NINJA
DUFFY, JULIA	10100 SANTA MONICA BLVD. #700	LOS ANGELES	CA	90067	U	U	ACTRESS - NEWHART
DUFFY, PATRICK	P.O. BOX D	TARZANA	CA	91356	U	U	ACTOR - DALLAS
DUKAKIS, MICHAEL	85 PERRY ST.	BROOKLINE	MA	02146	A	C	FORMER GOV./PRESIDENTIAL CANDIDATE - ILLEGIBLE SIGNATURE!
DUKAKIS, OLYMPIA	222 UPPER MOUNTAIN RD.	MONTCLAIR	NJ	07043	U	U	ACTRESS - MOONSTRUCK
DUKE, ANGIER BIDDLE	435 E. 52ND ST.	NEW YORK	NY	10022	U	U	DIPLOMAT/EXECUTIVE
DUKE, BILL	8306 WILSHIRE BLVD. #438	BEVERLY HILLS	CA	0211	U	U	ACTOR
DUKE, DAVID	500 N. ARNOULT	METAIRIE	LA	70001	U	U	POLITICIAN
DUKE, PATTY	326 N. FOREST DR.	COEUR D'ALENE	ID	83814	U	U	ACTRESS - THE PATTY DUKE SHOW
DUKES, DAVID	255 S. LORRAINE BLVD.	LOS ANGELES	CA	90004	U	U	ACTOR - SISTERS
DUKES, HAZEL	1501 BROADWAY	NEW YORK	NY	10036	U	U	ACTIVIST
DULLEA, KEIR	320 FLEMING LN.	FAIRFIELD	CT	06430	U	U	ACTOR - 2001: A SPACE ODYSSEY
DUMMAR, MELVIN	DUMMAR'S RESTAURANT	GABBS	NV	89409	U	U	ALLEDGED HOWARD HUGHES HEIR
DUNCAN, SANDY	10390 SANTA MONICA BLVD. #300	LOS ANGELES	CA	90025	U	U	ACTRESS - FUNNY FACE
DUNDEE, ANGELO	1700 WASHINGTON AVE.	MIAMI BEACH	FL	33142	U	U	BOXING TRAINER
DUNNE, DOMINICK	155 E. 49TH ST.	NEW YORK	NY	10017	U	U	AUTHOR/PRODUCER
DUNNE, GRIFFIN	40 W. 12TH ST.	NEW YORK	NY	10011	U	U	ACTOR - AFTER HOURS
DURAN DURAN	P.O. BOX 21	LONDON	ENG	W10 GXA	U	U	ROCK GROUP
DURAN, ROBERTO	P.O. BOX 157, ARENA COLON	PANAMA CITY	PAN.		U	U	BOXER
DURANTE, MARGIE	511 N. BEVERLY DR.	BEVERLY HILLS	CA	90210	A	D	WIDOW OF JIMMY DURANTE
DURBIN, DEANNA	B.P. 7677	75123 PARIS CEDEX 03	FRA		U	U	ACTRESS - ONE HUNDRED MEN & A GIRL
DURNING, CHARLES	10590 WILSHIRE BLVD. #506	LOS ANGELES	CA	90024	U	U	ACTOR - EVENING SHADE
DUSAY, MARJ	1930 CENTURY PARK W. #303	LOS ANGELES	CA	90067	U	U	ACTRESS
DUSSAULT, NANCY	12211 IREDELL ST.	STUDIO CITY	CA	91604	A	B	ACTRESS
DYLAN, BOB	P.O. BOX 870, COOPER STATION	NEW YORK	NY	10276	F	F	SINGER/SONGWRITER - A VERY TOUGH SIGNATURE - AUTHOR'S CHOICE!
DYSART, RICHARD	654 COPELAND COURT	SANTA MONICA	CA	90405	A	C	ACTOR - L.A. LAW
DZUNDZA, GEORGE	151 S. EL CAMINO DR.	BEVERLY HILLS	CA	90212	U	U	ACTOR
EAGLEBURGER, LAWRENCE	350 PARK AVE. #2600	NEW YORK	NY	10022	U	U	FORMER GOVERNMENT OFFICIAL
EAGLETON, THOMAS F.	1 MERCANTILE CTR.	ST. LOUIS	MO	63101	U	U	FORMER SENATOR
EARNHARDT, DALE	RDE, INC., 1675 CODDLE CREEK HWY.	MOORESVILLE	NC	28115	A	D	RACING LEGEND - AUTHOR'S CHOICE! - GREAT IN PERSON!

166

Name	Address	City	State	Zip Code	Resp. Time	Resp. Qual.	Comments
EASON, TONY	1000 FULTON RD.	HEMPSTEAD	NY	11550	U	U	FOOTBALL PLAYER
EAST, JEFF	5521 RAINBOW CREST DR.	AGOURA	CA	91301	U	U	ACTOR
EASTERBROOK, LESLIE	17352 SUNSET BLVD. # 401-D	PACIFIC PALISADES	CA	90272	U	U	ACTRESS
EASTHAM, RICHARD	1529 ORIOLE LN.	LOS ANGELES	CA	90069	U	U	ACTOR
EASTON, ROBERT	C/O PAUL KOHNER INC., 9300 WILSHIRE BLVD. SUITE 555	BEVERLY HILLS	CA	90212	U	U	ACTOR
EASTON, SHEENA	151 EL CAMINO DR.	BEVERLY HILLS	CA	90212	U	U	SINGER/SONGWRITER - "MORNING TRAIN"
EASTWOOD, CLINT	P.O. BOX 4366	CARMEL	CA	93921	U	U	ACTOR - *DIRTY HARRY* - **AUTHOR'S CHOICE!**
EASTWOOD, KYLE	2628 LARMAR RD.	LOS ANGELES	CA	90068	U	U	ACTOR
EBB, FRED	146 CENTRAL PARK W. #14D	NEW YORK	NY	10020	A	C	LYRICIST
EBERSOLE, CHRISTINE	1244 - A 11TH ST.	SANTA MONICA	CA	90401	A	D	ACTRESS
EBERT, ROGER	C/O DONALD EPHRAIM, 108 W. GRAND	CHICAGO	IL	60610	U	U	FILM CRITIC/WRITER - SISKEL & EBERT
EBSEN, BONNIE	P.O. BOX 356	AGOURA	CA	91301	U	U	ACTRESS
ECKERSLEY, DENNIS	263 MORSE RD.	SUDBURY	MA	01776	A	B	BASEBALL PLAYER
EDBERG, STEFAN	SPINNAREGATEN 6	VASTERVIK	SWE	S-59300	U	U	TENNIS PLAYER
EDEN, BARBARA	9816 DENBIGH	BEVERLY HILLS	CA	90210	C	F	ACTRESS - *I DREAM OF JEANNIE* - SENDS FACSIMILE SIGNED PHOTO PLUS FAN CLUB INFO!
EDERLE, GERTRUDE	4465 S.W. 37TH AVE.	FL. LAUDERDALE	FL	33312	U	U	SWIMMER
EDLER, LEE	1725 "K" ST. N.W. #1201	WASHINGTON	DC	20006	U	U	GOLFER
EDMONDS, KENNETH "BABYFACE"	C/O EPIC RECORDS, 2100 COLORADO AVE.	SANTA MONICA	CA	90404	U	U	SINGER/SONGWRITER/PRODUCER - "WHEN CAN I SEE YOU" - **AUTHOR'S CHOICE!**
EDWARDS, ANTHONY	8820 LOOKOUT MOUNTAIN	LOS ANGELES	CA	90046	U	U	ACTOR - *ER* - **AUTHOR'S CHOICE!**
EDWARDS, BLAKE	P.O. BOX 666	BEVERLY HILLS	CA	90213	U	U	WRITER/PRODUCER/DIRECTOR - *THE PINK PANTHER SHOW*
EDWARDS, RALPH	610 ARKELL DR.	BEVERLY HILLS	CA	90210	U	U	TELEVISION HOST/PRODUCER
EDWARDS, STEPHANIE	533 - 18TH ST.	SANTA MONICA	CA	90402	U	U	ACTRESS
EDWARDS, STEVE	3980 ROYAL OAKS PL.	ENCINO	CA	91436	U	U	TELEVISION HOST
EGGAR, SAMANTHA	15430 MULHOLLAND DR.	LOS ANGELES	CA	90024	U	U	ACTRESS - *THE COLLECTOR*
EGGERT, NICOLE	20591 QUEENS PARK	HUNTINGTON BEACH	CA	92646	U	U	ACTRESS/SINGER
EGGERTH KIEPURA, MARTA	PARK DR. N.	RYE	NY	10508	A	B	ACTRESS/SINGER
EICHORN, LISA	19 W. 44TH ST. #1100	NEW YORK	NY	10036	U	U	ACTRESS
EIKENBERRY, JILL	2183 MANDEVILLE CANYON	LOS ANGELES	CA	90049	U	U	ACTRESS - *L.A. LAW*
EILBACHER, CYNTHIA	11051 OPHIR DR.	LOS ANGELES	CA	90024	U	U	ACTRESS
EILBACHER, LISA	2949 DEEP CANYON DR.	BEVERLY HILLS	CA	90210	U	U	ACTRESS
EISNER, MICHAEL	500 S. BUENA VISTA	BURBANK	CA	91521	A	B	DISNEY EXECUTIVE

Linda Evans

A Roy Rogers / Dale Evans response

Dale Earnhardt

Janet Evans

Name	Address	City	State	Zip Code	Resp. Time	Resp. Qual.	Comments
ELAM, JACK	P.O. BOX 5718	SANTA BARBARA	CA	93108	A	D	ACTOR
ELENIAK, ERIKA	9200 SUNSET BLVD. # 625	LOS ANGELES	CA	90069	U	U	ACTRESS
ELFMAN, DANNY	6525 SUNSET BLVD. #402	LOS ANGELES	CA	90028	U	U	COMPOSER/SINGER
ELIAS, ROSALIND	C/O R. LOMBARDO, 61 W. 62ND ST. #65	NEW YORK	NY	10023	A	B	MEZZO-SOPRANO
ELIZANDO, HECTOR	5040 NOBEL AVE.	SHERMAN OAKS	CA	91403	A	B	ACTOR
ELLENSTEIN, ROBERT	5215 SEPULVEDA BLVD. #23-F	CULVER CITY	CA	90230	A	D	ACTOR/DIRECTOR
ELLERBEE, LINDA	17 ST. LUKES PL.	NEW YORK	NY	10014	U	U	JOURNALIST - OUR WORLD
ELLIOT, JANE	606 N. LARCHMONT BLVD. #309	LOS ANGELES	CA	90004	U	U	ACTRESS
ELLIOT, ROSS	5702 GRAVES AVE.	ENCINO	CA	91316	U	U	ACTOR
ELLIOTT, SAM	33050 PACIFIC COAST HWY.	MALIBU	CA	90265	U	U	ACTOR - TOMBSTONE
ELLIOTT, STEPHEN	3948 WOODFIELD DR.	SHERMAN OAKS	CA	91403	U	U	ACTOR
ELLSBERG, DANIEL	90 NORWOOD AVE.	KENSINGTON	CA	94707	A	B	AUTHOR
ELVIRA	P.O. BOX 38246	LOS ANGELES	CA	90038	U	U	ACTRESS
ELWAY, JOHN	C/O DENVER BRONCOS, 13655 E. DOVE VALLEY PKWY.	ENGLEWOOD	CO	80112	F	F	FOOTBALL PLAYER
ELWES, CARY	22611 VOST ST.	WEST HILLS	CA	91307	U	U	ACTOR - THE PRINCESS BRIDE
ELY, RON	4141 MARIPOSA DR.	SANTA BARBARA	CA	93110	U	U	ACTOR
EMBERG, KELLY	1608 N. POINSETTIA	MANHATTAN BEACH	CA	90266	A	C	MODEL
EMERSON, DOUGLAS	1450 BELFAST DR.	LOS ANGELES	CA	90069	U	U	ACTOR
EMHARDT, ROBERT	P.O. BOX 303	OJAI	CA	93023	U	U	ACTOR
EN VOGUE	151 EL CAMINO DR.	BEVERLY HILLS	CA	90212	U	U	HIP/HOP GROUP
ENGEL, GEORGIA	350 W. 57TH ST. #10E	NEW YORK	NY	10019	U	U	ACTRESS
ENGLAND DAN	P.O. BOX 82	GREAT NECK	NY	11021	U	U	SINGER/SONGWRITER
ENTWHISTLE, JOHN	1705 QUEEN COURT	LOS ANGELES	CA	90069	U	U	MUSICIAN/SINGER
EPHRON, NORA	390 W. END AVE.	NEW YORK	NY	10024	U	U	SCREENWRITER - WHEN HARRY MET SALLY... - **AUTHOR'S CHOICE!**
ERDMAN, RICHARD	5655 GREENBUSH AVE.	VAN NUYS	CA	91401	A	C	ACTOR/DIRECTOR
ERSKINE, CARL	6214 S. MADISON AVE.	ANDERSON	IN	46013	A	B	BASEBALL PLAYER
ERVING, JULIUS	1420 LOCUST ST. #12K	PHILADELPHIA	PA	19102	U	U	MEMBER OF THE BASKETBALL HALL OF FAME - **AUTHOR'S CHOICE!** - "DR. J"
ERWIN, BILL	12324 MOORPARK ST.	STUDIO CITY	CA	91604	A	B	ACTOR
ESIASON, "BOOMER"	1000 FULTON AVE.	HEMPSTEAD	NY	11550	A	D	FOOTBALL PLAYER
ESMOND, CARL	576 TIGERTAIL RD.	LOS ANGELES	CA	90049	A	B	ACTOR
ESPY, WILLIAM GREY	205 W. 54TH ST. #3D	NEW YORK	NY	10019	U	U	ACTOR
ESTEFAN, GLORIA	6205 BIRD RD.	MIAMI	FL	33155	A	F	SINGER - SENDS FAN CLUB INFO - $18 A YEAR!

Name	Address	City	State	Zip Code	Resp. Time	Resp. Qual.	Comments
ESTES, BILLIE SOL	C/O GENERAL DELIVERY	BRADY	TX	76825	A	B	FINANCIER/EX-CONVICT
ESTES, SIMON	165 W. 57TH ST.	NEW YORK	NY	10019	U	U	OPERA SINGER
ESTES, WILL	KIRK, WB NETWORK, 3701 W. OAK ST., BLDG. 34R, RM., 124A	BURBANK	CA	91523	U	U	ACTOR
ESTEVEZ, EMILIO	31725 SEA LEVEL DR.	MALIBU	CA	90265	U	U	ACTOR - *REPO MAN*
ESTEVEZ, RAMON	837 OCEAN AVE. #101	SANTA MONICA	CA	90402	U	U	ACTOR
ESTRADA, ERIK	3768 EUREKA DR.	STUDIO CITY	CA	91604	U	U	ACTOR - *CHIPS*
ESTRICH, SUSAN	124 S. LAS PALMAS	LOS ANGELES	CA	90004	U	U	ACTRESS
ETHRIDGE, MELISSA	C/O ISLAND RECORDS, 14 E. 4TH ST.	NEW YORK	NY	10012	U	U	SINGER - "COME TO MY WINDOW" - **AUTHOR'S CHOICE!**
EUBANKS, BOB	5900 HIGHRIDGE RD.	HIDDEN HILLS	CA	91302	A	B	TELEVISION HOST - *THE NEWLYWEDS*
EURE, WESLEY	P.O. BOX 69405	LOS ANGELES	CA	90069	U	U	ACTOR
EVANGELISTA, LINDA	121 RUE LEGENDRE	F-75017 PARIS	FRA		U	U	MODEL
EVANS ROGERS, DALE	15650 SENECA RD.	VICTORVILLE	CA	92392	A	F	ACTRESS - *THE YELLOW ROSE OF TEXAS*
EVANS, EVANS	3114 ABINGTON DR.	BEVERLY HILLS	CA	90210	A	B+	ACTRESS
EVANS, GENE	P.O. BOX 93	MEDON	TN	38356	A	D	ACTOR
EVANS, JANET	424 BROWER	PLACENTIA	CA	92670	A	B	SWIMMER
EVANS, LINDA	6714 VILLA MADERA DR.	TACOMA	WA	98499	A	B	ACTRESS - *DYNASTY*
EVANS, MIKE	12530 COLLINS ST.	NORTH HOLLYWOOD	CA	91605	U	U	ACTOR - *THE JEFFERSONS*
EVANS, ROBERT	10033 WOODLAWN DR.	BEVERLY HILLS	CA	90210	U	U	ACTOR/PRODUCER
EVANS, ROLAND	1750 PENNSYLVANIA AVE. N.W., SUITE 1312	WASHINGTON	DC	20006	A	D	COLUMNIST
EVERLY, DON	P.O. BOX 120725	NASHVILLE	TN	37212	C	F	SINGER - THE EVERLY BROTHERS
EVERLY, PHIL	P.O. BOX 120725	NASHVILLE	TN	37212	C	F	SINGER - THE EVERLY BROTHERS
EVERS, CHARLES	1072 LYNCH ST.	JACKSON	MS	39203	U	U	CIVIL RIGHTS ACTIVIST
EVERS, JASON	232 N. CRESCENT DR. #101	BEVERLY HILLS	CA	90210	A	B	ACTOR
EVERT, CHRIS (MILLS)	500 N.E. 25TH ST.	WILTON MANORS	FL	33305	A	F	TENNIS PLAYER - SENDS FACSIMILE SIGNED PHOTO!
EVERTS, KELLIE	P.O. BOX 45	OUAQUAGA	NY	13826	A	B	AUTHOR/PREACHER
EVIGAN, GREG	5472 WINNETKA AVE.	WOODLAND HILLS	CA	91364	C	B	ACTOR/SINGER - *B. J. AND THE BEAR*
EWBANK, WEEB	7 PATRICK DR.	OXFORD	OH	45056	A	C	MEMBER OF THE FOOTBALL HALL OF FAME
EWING, PATRICK	4 PENNSYLVANIA PLAZA	NEW YORK	NY	10001	A	F	BASKETBALL PLAYER - A TOUGH SIGNATURE
EYER, RICHARD	2739 UNDERWOOD LN.	BISHOP	CA	93514	A	D	ACTOR
FABARES, SHELLEY	P.O. BOX 6010 #85	SHERMAN OAKS	CA	91413	A	A+	ACTRESS
FABIO	C/O ROGER RICHMAN AGCY., 9777 WILSHIRE BLVD. SUITE 915	BEVERLY HILLS	CA	90212	U	U	MODEL FOR ROMANCE NOVELS - **AUTHOR'S CHOICE!**

170

Name	Address	City	State	Zip Code	Resp. Time	Resp. Qual.	Comments
FABRAY, NANETTE	14360 SUNSET BLVD.	PACIFIC PALISADES	CA	90272	A	D	ACTRESS - ONE DAY AT A TIME
FAHEY, JEFF	250 N. ROBERTSON BLVD. #518	BEVERLY HILLS	CA	90211	A	B	ACTOR
FAIRBAIRN, BRUCE	9744 WILSHIRE BLVD. #308	BEVERLY HILLS	CA	90212	U	U	ACTOR
FAIRBANKS, DOUGLAS JR.	575 PARK AVE.	NEW YORK	NY	10021	A	B	ACTOR - GUNGA DIN
FAIRCHILD, MORGAN	3480 BLAIR DR.	LOS ANGELES	CA	90068	U	U	ACTRESS - FALCON CREST
FALK, PETER	1004 N. ROXBURY DR.	BEVERLY HILLS	CA	90210	A	B	ACTOR/DIRECTOR - COLUMBO
FALKENBURG, JINX	10 SHELTER ROCK RD.	MANHASSET	NY	11030	U	U	ACTRESS/MODEL
FALWELL, REV. JERRY	3765 CANDLERS MOUNTAIN RD.	LYNCHBURG	VA	24502	A	B	EVANGELIST
FARACY, STEPHANIE	8765 LOOKOUT MOUNTAIN RD.	LOS ANGELES	CA	90046	U	U	ACTRESS
FARENTINO, JAMES	1340 LONDONDERRY PL.	LOS ANGELES	CA	90069	U	U	ACTOR - DYNASTY
FARGAS, ANTONIO	1930 CENTURY PARK W. #403	LOS ANGELES	CA	90067	U	U	ACTOR
FARGO, DONNA	P.O. BOX 15743	NASHVILLE	TN	37215	A	B+	SINGER
FARLEY, CHRIS	C/O BRILLSTEIN-GREY ENT., 9150 WILSHIRE BLVD. SUITE 350	BEVERLY HILLS	CA	90212	U	U	ACTOR - WAYNE'S WORLD - **AUTHOR'S CHOICE!** - SEE IF YOU'RE WORTHY!
FARNON, SHANNON	12743 MILBANK ST.	STUDIO CITY	CA	91604	B	B	ACTRESS
FARNSWORTH, RICHARD	C/O DIAMOND D RANCH, BOX 123	LINCOLN	NM	88338	A	B	ACTOR
FARR, FELICA	C/O JALEM PROD. INC., 141 S. EL CAMINO DR. #201	BEVERLY HILLS	CA	90212	A	F	ACTRESS - NO LONGER AUTOGRAPHS CARDS OR PHOTOS
FARR, JAMIE	53 RANCHERO	BELL CANYON	CA	91307	A	B	ACTOR/DIRECTOR - M*A*S*H
FARRAKHAN, LOUIS	734 W. 79TH ST.	CHICAGO	IL	60620	U	U	RELIGIOUS LEADER
FARRELL, MIKE	P.O. BOX 6010-826	SHERMAN OAKS	CA	91413	A	C	ACTOR/WRITER/DIRECTOR - M*A*S*H
FARRELL, SHARON	10637 BURBANK BLVD.	NORTH HOLLYWOOD	CA	91601	U	U	ACTRESS
FARRELL, SHEA	1930 CENTURY PARK W. #403	LOS ANGELES	CA	90067	U	U	ACTOR
FARROW, MIA	C/O WILLIAM MORRIS AGCY., 151 EL CAMINO DR.	BEVERLY HILLS	CA	90212	U	U	ACTRESS - ROSEMARY'S BABY - **AUTHOR'S CHOICE!**
FAUTS, DAN	P.O. BOX 20666	SAN DIEGO	CA	92120	U	U	FOOTBALL PLAYER
FAVRE, BRETT	C/O GREEN BAY PACKERS, 1265 LOMBARDI AVE.	GREEN BAY	WI	54304	U	U	FOOTBALL PLAYER - 1995 MVP - **AUTHOR'S CHOICE!**
FAWCETT, FARRAH	3130 ANTELO RD.	LOS ANGELES	CA	90024	U	U	ACTRESS/MODEL - CHARLIE'S ANGELS
FAYE, ALICE	49400 JFK TRAIL	PALM DESERT	CA	92260	A	C	ACTRESS/SINGER
FEARS, TOM	41470 WOODHAVEN DR. W.	PALM DESERT	CA	92260	A	B	FOOTBALL PLAYER
FEDOROV, SERGEI	C/O DETROIT RED WINGS, 600 CIVIC CTR. DR.	DETROIT	MI	48226	U	U	HOCKEY PLAYER
FEIFFER, JULES	325 W. END AVE.	NEW YORK	NY	10023	U	U	WRITER
FEINSTEIN, MICHAEL	2233 CHEREMOYA AVE.	LOS ANGELES	CA	90068	A	B	ACTOR

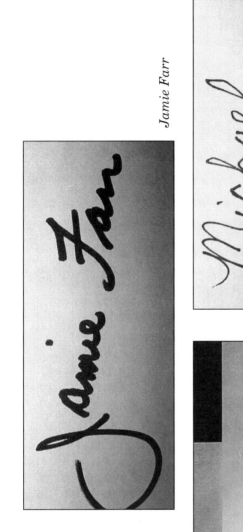

Jamie Farr

Michael Fishman

Michael
Fishman
="D.J." on
Roseanne

Betty Ford

Mrs. Gerald R. Ford

September 3, 1981

Dear Mr. Baker:

Thank you for your kind letter. I am
want to include my autograph in your coll

With warm best wishes,

Sincerely,

Betty Ford

Mark A. Baker
719 South Manlius Rd.
Fayetteville, New York 13066

December 4, 1980

Dear Mr. Baker:

Thank you for your kind letter. I am pleased
that you want to include my autograph in your
collection.

With warm best wishes,

Sincerely,

Betty Ford

Mr. Mark A. Baker
719 South Manlius Road
Fayetteville, New York 13066

Name	Address	City	State	Zip Code	Resp. Time	Resp. Qual.	Comments
FEINSTEIN, SEN. DIANNE	331 HART OFFICE BLDG.	WASHINGTON	DC	20510	A	B	POLITICIAN - WATCH FOR AUTOPEN!
FELD, FRITZ	12348 ROCHEDALE LN.	LOS ANGELES	CA	90049	U	U	ACTOR
FELDON, BARBARA	14 E. 74TH ST.	NEW YORK	NY	10021	A	B	ACTRESS/MODEL - GET SMART
FELDSHUH, TOVAH	322 CENTRAL PARK W. #118	NEW YORK	NY	10025	A	B	ACTOR - THE IDOLMAKER
FELDSTEIN, MARTIN	147 CLIFTON ST.	BELMONT	MA	02178	A	B	ECONOMIST
FELICIANO, JOSE	266 LYONS PLAIN RD.	WESTON	CT	06883	U	U	SINGER/GUITARIST - "CHICO AND THE MAN"
FELL, NORMAN	4335 MARINA CITY DR.	MARINA DEL REY	CA	90292	U	U	ACTOR - THREE'S COMPANY
FELLER, BOB	P.O. BOX 157	GATES MILLS	OH	44040	A	F	BASEBALL PLAYER - AFTER YEARS OF BEING A GREAT SIGNER, NOW CHARGES $20 FOR EACH SIGNATURE!
FELLOWS, EDITH	2016 1/2 N. VISTA DEL MAR	LOS ANGELES	CA	90068	C	B	ACTRESS
FELLOWS, MEGAN	121 N. SAN VICENTE BLVD.	BEVERLY HILLS	CA	90211	U	U	ACTRESS - ANNE OF GREEN GABLES
FELTS, NORMAN	2005 NARVEL FELTS AVE.	MALDEN	MO	63863	A	B	SINGER
FERGUSON, JAY	4465 STERN AVE.	SHERMAN OAKS	CA	91423	U	U	SINGER
FERGUSON, MAYNARD	P.O. BOX 716	OJAI	CA	93023	A	B+	TRUMPETER
FERRANTE & TEICHER	P.O. BOX 12403, NS STATION	ATLANTA	GA	30355	U	U	PIANO DUO
FERRARE, CRISTINA	1280 STONE CANYON	LOS ANGELES	CA	90077	U	U	ACTRESS/MODEL
FERRARO, GERALDINE	22 DEEPDENE RD.	FOREST HILLS	CA	11375	U	U	FORMER CONGRESSWOMAN/VICE PRESIDENTIAL CANDIDATE
FERRELL, CONCHATA	1347 N. SEWARD ST.	LOS ANGELES	CA	90028	U	U	ACTRESS
FERRER, MEL	6590 CAMINO CARRETA	CARPENTERIA	CA	93013	A	B	ACTOR - FALCON CREST
FERRER, MIGUEL	4334 KESTER AVE.	SHERMAN OAKS	CA	91403	U	U	ACTOR - TWIN PEAKS
FERRIGNO, LOU	621 - 17TH ST.	SANTA MONICA	CA	90402	U	U	ACTOR/BODYBUILDER - THE INCREDIBLE HULK
FIDRYCH, MARK	259 CRAWFORD	NORTHBOROUGH	MA	01532	A	B	BASEBALL PLAYER - "THE BIRD"
FIEDLER, JOHN	225 ADAMS ST. #10B	BROOKLYN	NY	11201	A	B	ACTOR
FIELD, CHELSEA	P.O. BOX 5617	BEVERLY HILLS	CA	90210	U	U	ACTRESS
FIELD, SALLY	C/O CREATIVE ARTISTS AGCY., 9830 WILSHIRE BLVD.	BEVERLY HILLS	CA	90212	A	F	ACTRESS - THE FLYING NUN - RESPONDS WITH FACSIMILE SIGNED PHOTO - AUTHOR'S CHOICE!
FIELDS, FREDDIE	1005 BENEDICT CANYON DR.	BEVERLY HILLS	CA	90210	U	U	FILM PRODUCER
FIELDS, KIM	23460 HATTERAS ST.	WOODLAND HILLS	CA	91367	U	U	ACTRESS - THE FACTS OF LIFE
FIENNES, RALPH	C/O CREATIVE ARTISTS AGCY., 9830 WILSHIRE BLVD.	BEVERLY HILLS	CA	90212	U	U	ACTOR - SCHINDLER'S LIST - AUTHOR'S CHOICE!
FIERSTEIN, HARVEY	1479 CARLA RIDGE DR.	BEVERLY HILLS	CA	90210	U	U	DRAMATIST/ACTOR - MRS. DOUBTFIRE
FINGERS, ROLLIE	4944 SMITH CANYON CT.	SAN DIEGO	CA	92126	U	U	MEMBER OF THE BASEBALL HALL OF FAME
FIORENTINO, LINDA	9560 WILSHIRE BLVD. #500	BEVERLY HILLS	CA	90212	U	U	ACTRESS - THE LAST SEDUCTION - AUTHOR'S CHOICE!
FIRESTONE, EDDIE	303 S. CRESCENT HEIGHTS	LOS ANGELES	CA	90048	A	D	ACTOR

173

Peggy Fleming

Rev. Jerry Falwell

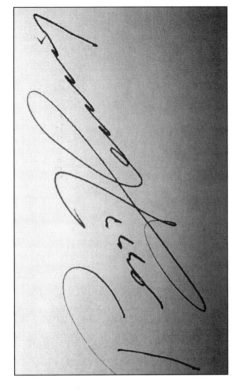

Thank you for your recent inquiry.

Regrettably, the "Candid Camera" office gets so many requests that it is simply not possible to honor each with a personal reply.

We hope you will understand, and by all means remember to smile.

ALLEN FUNT

An Allen Funt response

Gerald Ford

Name	Address	City	State	Zip Code	Resp. Time	Resp. Qual.	Comments
FISCHER, BOBBY	186 RT. 9W	NEW WINDSOR	NY	12550	U	U	CHESS MASTER
FISHBURNE, LAWRENCE	5200 LANKERSHIM BLVD. #260	NORTH HOLLYWOOD	CA	91601	B	F	ACTOR - NOTE STATING THAT HE CAN'T RESPOND TO EACH REQUEST! - AUTHOR'S CHOICE!
FISHER, CARRIE	C/O KAUFMAN EISENBERG, 1201 ALTA LOMA RD.	WEST HOLLYWOOD	CA	90069	U	U	ACTRESS - AUTHOR'S CHOICE!
FISHER, EDDIE	1000 N. POINT ST. #1802	SAN FRANCISCO	CA	94109	C	B	ACTOR/SINGER - THE EDDIE FISHER SHOW
FISHER, TERRY LOUISE	5314 PACIFIC AVE.	MARINA DEL REY	CA	90292	A	D	TELEVISION WRITER/PRODUCER
FISHMAN, MICHAEL	P.O. BOX 827	LOS ALAMITOS	CA	90720	A	B	ACTOR
FISK, CARLTON	16612 CATAWBA RD.	LOCKPORT	IL	60441	U	U	BASEBALL PLAYER
FITZGERALD, ELLA	908 N. WHITTIER DR.	BEVERLY HILLS	CA	90210	A	F	SINGER - RESPONDS WITH FACSIMILE SIGNED PHOTO!
FITZSIMMONS, COTTON	2910 N. CENTRAL	PHOENIX	AZ	85012	A	B	BASKETBALL COACH
FITZWATER, MARLIN	2001 SWAN TERR.	ALEXANDRIA	VA	22307	A	B	FORMER PRESIDENTIAL PRESS SECRETARY
FLACK, ROBERTA	1 W. 72ND ST.	NEW YORK	NY	10023	U	U	SINGER/SONGWRITER - "THE FIRST TIME EVER I SAW YOUR FACE"
FLAGG, FANNY	1520 WILLINA LN.	MONTECITO	CA	93108	U	U	ACTRESS
FLANAGAN, FIONNULA	13438 JAVA DR.	BEVERLY HILLS	CA	90210	U	U	ACTRESS
FLANNERY, SUSAN	480 PIMIENTO LN.	SANTA MONICA	CA	93108	U	U	ACTRESS
FLASH CADILLAC	P.O. BOX 6588	SAN ANTONIO	TX	78209	U	U	ROCK GROUP
FLEISHER, CHARLES	749 N. CRESCENT HEIGHTS BLVD.	LOS ANGELES	CA	90038	U	U	ACTOR
FLEISHER, RICHARD	169 S. ROCKINGHAM AVE.	LOS ANGELES	CA	90049	A	B	FILM DIRECTOR
FLEISS, HEIDI	505 S. BEVERLY DR. #508	BEVERLY HILLS	CA	90212	A	B	ALLEGED MADAM
FLEMING, PEGGY	16387 AZTEC RIDGE	LOS GATOS	CA	95030	A	B	ICE SKATER
FLEMING, RHONDA	2129 CENTURY WOODS WAY	LOS ANGELES	CA	90067	C	D	ACTRESS
FLETCHER, LOUISE	1520 CAMDEN AVE. #105	LOS ANGELES	CA	90025	A	B	ACTRESS - ONE FLEW OVER THE CUCKOO'S NEST
FLIPPIN, LUCY LEE	1753 CANFIELD AVE.	LOS ANGELES	CA	90035	U	U	ACTRESS
FLOCK OF SEAGULLS	526 NICOLLET MALL	MINNEAPOLIS	MN	55402	U	U	ROCK GROUP
FLOOD, CURT	4139 CLOVERDALE AVE.	LOS ANGELES	CA	90008	A	U	BASEBALL PLAYER - NO SIGNATURE BUT ASKS FOR DONATION - SAVE YOUR STAMPS!
FLOREN, MYRON	26 GEORGEFF RD.	ROLLING HILLS	CA	90274	A	B+	COMPOSER - OFTEN ADDS TRADING CARD
FLORES, TOM	11220 N.E. 53RD ST.	KIRKLAND	WA	98033	A	B	FOOTBALL EXECUTIVE
FLOYD, RAY	1 ERIEVIEW PLAZA #1300	CLEVELAND	OH	44114	A	B	GOLFER
FOGELBERG, DAN	MOUNTAIN BIRD RANCH, P.O. BOX 824	PAGOSA SPRINGS	CO	81147	U	U	SINGER/SONGWRITER
FOGLIO, KAJA	C/O WIZARDS OF THE COAST, INC., P.O. BOX 707	RENTON	WA	98057	U	U	ILLUSTRATOR - "MAGIC" CARDS

Myron Floran

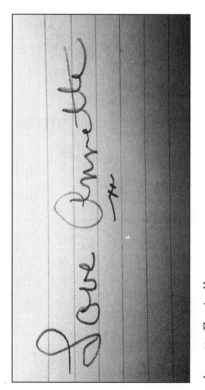

Annette Funicello

176

Name	Address	City	State	Zip Code	Resp. Time	Resp. Qual.	Comments
FOGLIO, PHIL	C/O WIZARDS OF THE COAST, INC., P.O. BOX 707	RENTON	WA	98057	U	U	ILLUSTRATOR - "MAGIC" CARDS
FONDA, BRIDGET	9560 WILSHIRE BLVD. #500	BEVERLY HILLS	CA	90212	U	U	ACTRESS - **AUTHOR'S CHOICE!**
FONDA, JANE	1050 TECHWOOD DR. N.W.	ATLANTA	GA	30318	A	B	ACTRESS/WRITER - ON GOLDEN POND - **AUTHOR'S CHOICE!**
FONDA, PETER	RR #318	LIVINGSTON	MT	59047	C	D	ACTOR/WRITER/DIRECTOR - EASY RIDER
FONDA, SHIRLEE	110 E. 57TH ST.	NEW YORK	NY	10022	C	D	MRS. HENRY FONDA
FONTAINE, JOAN	P.O. BOX 222600	CARMEL	CA	93922	A	C	ACTRESS - SUSPICION
FOOTE, HORTON	95 HORATIO ST. #332	NEW YORK	NY	10014	A	D	SCREENWRITER
FORAY, JUNE	22745 ERWIN ST.	WOODLAND HILLS	CA	91367	U	U	ACTRESS
FORD, CHARLOTTE	25 SUTTON PL.	NEW YORK	NY	10023	U	U	DAUGHTER OF HENRY FORD II
FORD, DOUG	100 AVE. OF THE CHAMPIONS	PALM BEACH GARDENS	FL	33418	A	B	GOLFER
FORD, EILEEN OTTE	344 E. 59TH ST.	NEW YORK	NY	10022	U	U	MODELING AGENT
FORD, FAITH	7920 SUNSET BLVD. #350	LOS ANGELES	CA	90046	A	D	ACTRESS/MODEL - MURPHY BROWN
FORD, GERALD R.	40365 SAN DUNE RD.	RANCHO MIRAGE	CA	92270	A	C	FORMER PRESIDENT OF THE UNITED STATES - RESPONSIVE TO FAN MAIL - **AUTHOR'S CHOICE!**
FORD, GLENN	911 OXFORD WAY	BEVERLY HILLS	CA	90210	U	U	ACTOR
FORD, HARRISON	P.O. BOX 49344	LOS ANGELES	CA	90049	U	U	ACTOR - INDIANA JONES - **AUTHOR'S CHOICE!** - NOT AN EASY SIGNATURE
FORD, JACK	C/O NBC, 30 ROCKEFELLER PLAZA	NEW YORK	NY	10112	U	U	BROADCAST JOURNALIST
FORD, MRS. BETTY	40365 SAN DUNE RD.	RANCHO MIRAGE	CA	92270	A	C	FORMER FIRST LADY/AUTHOR
FORD, RUTH	1 W. 72ND ST.	NEW YORK	NY	10023	A	B+	ACTRESS
FORD, WHITEY	38 SCHOOLHOUSE LN.	LAKE SUCCESS	NY	11020	U	U	MEMBER OF THE BASEBALL HALL OF FAME
FOREMAN, DEBORAH	1341 OCEAN AVE. #213	SANTA MONICA	CA	90401	U	U	ACTRESS
FOREMAN, GEORGE	4402 WALHAM COURT	KINGWOOD	TX	77345	B	B	BOXER - FORMER HEAVYWEIGHT CHAMPION - OLDEST EVER - **AUTHOR'S CHOICE!**
FORESTER SISTERS	P.O. BOX 1456	TRENTON	GA	30752	U	U	COUNTRY WESTERN GROUP
FORMAN, MILOS	HAMPSHIRE HOUSE, 150 CENTRAL PARK S.	NEW YORK	NY	10019	A	B	FILM DIRECTOR
FORREST, FREDERICK	11100 HORTENSE ST.	NORTH HOLLYWOOD	CA	91602	U	U	ACTOR
FORREST, HELEN	1870 CEMINITO DEL CIELO	GLENDALE	CA	91208	U	U	SINGER
FORREST, SALLY	1125 ANGELO DR.	BEVERLY HILLS	CA	90210	A	B	ACTRESS
FORREST, STEVE	1605 MICHAEL LN.	PACIFIC PALISADES	CA	90272	A	B	ACTOR
FORSLUND, CONSTANCE	853 - 7TH AVE. #9-A	NEW YORK	NY	10019	U	U	ACTRESS
FORSTER, BRIAN	16172 FLAMSTEAD DR.	HACIENDA HEIGHTS	CA	91745	U	U	ACTOR

177

Name	Address	City	State	Zip Code	Resp. Time	Resp. Qual.	Comments
FORSTER, ROBERT	8550 HOLLYWOOD DR. #402	LOS ANGELES	CA	90069	A	D	ACTOR - BANYON
FORSYTHE, HENDERSON	204 ELM ST.	TENAFLY	NJ	07670	A	C	ACTOR
FORSYTHE, ROSEMARY	1591 BENEDICT CANYON	BEVERLY HILLS	CA	90210	A	B	ACTRESS
FORTE, FABIAN	6671 SUNSET BLVD. #1502	LOS ANGELES	CA	90028	U	U	ACTOR/SINGER
FOSBURY, DICK	680 2ND AVE. N.	KETCHUM	ID	83440	U	U	TRACK/FIELD ATHLETE
FOSS, GEN. JOE	P.O. BOX 566	SCOTTSDALE	AZ	85252	A	D	HIGHLY DECORATED VETERAN - A REAL HERO - **AUTHOR'S CHOICE!**
FOSTER, JODIE	C/O ICM, 8942 WILSHIRE BLVD.	BEVERLY HILLS	CA	90211	U	U	ACTRESS - SILENCE OF THE LAMBS - **AUTHOR'S CHOICE!**
FOSTER, KIMBERLY	957 N. COLE AVE.	LOS ANGELES	CA	90038	U	U	ACTRESS
FOSTER, MEG	10866 WILSHIRE BLVD. #1100	LOS ANGELES	CA	90024	U	U	ACTRESS - CAGNEY & LACEY
FOUNTAIN, PETE	237 N. PETERS ST. # 400	NEW ORLEANS	LA	70130	A	A+	CLARINETIST - VERY RESPONSIVE TO FAN MAIL
FOUR ACES	12 MARSHALL ST. #8Q	IRVINGTON	NJ	07111	U	U	VOCAL GROUP
FOUR LADS	32500 CONCORD DR. #221	MADISON HEIGHTS	MI	49071	U	U	VOCAL GROUP
FOUR SEASONS, THE	P.O. BOX 262	CARTERET	NJ	07008	U	U	ROCK GROUP
FOWLER, GENE JR.	7261 OUTPOST COVE DR.	LOS ANGELES	CA	90068	A	A	FILM DIRECTOR
FOWLEY, DOUGLAS V.	38510 GLEN ABBEY LN.	MURIETTA	CA	92362	A	B	ACTOR - DOESN'T SIGN INDEX CARDS
FOX, MICHAEL J.	C/O CREATIVE ARTISTS AGCY., 9830 WILSHIRE BLVD.	BEVERLY HILLS	CA	90212	U	U	ACTOR - FAMILY TIES - **AUTHOR'S CHOICE!**
FOXWORTH, ROBERT	1230 BENEDICT CANYON DR.	BEVERLY HILLS	CA	90210	U	U	ACTOR - FALCON CREST
FOYT, A.J.	6415 TOLEDO	HOUSTON	TX	77008	A	D	AUTO RACER - ONE OF THE BEST - **AUTHOR'S CHOICE!**
FRAKES, JONATHAN	10100 SANTA MONICA BLVD. #700	LOS ANGELES	CA	90067	U	U	ACTOR - STAR TREK: THE NEXT GENERATION
FRAMPTON, PETER	2669 LARMAR RD.	LOS ANGELES	CA	90068	U	U	SINGER/GUITARIST
FRANCIOSA, TONY	567 TIGERTAIL RD.	LOS ANGELES	CA	90049	A	B	ACTOR - THE LONG, HOT SUMMER
FRANCIS, ANNE	P.O. BOX 5417	SANTA BARBARA	CA	93103	U	U	ACTRESS/CHILD MODEL
FRANCIS, CONNIE	7305 W. SAMPLE RD. #101	CORAL SPRINGS	FL	33065	C	B	SINGER/ACTRESS - WHERE THE BOYS ARE
FRANCIS, GENIE	7 W. 81ST ST. #7B	NEW YORK	NY	10024	U	U	ACTRESS - GENERAL HOSPITAL
FRANK, CHARLES	9744 WILSHIRE BLVD. #308	BEVERLY HILLS	CA	90212	U	U	ACTOR
FRANK, GARY	11401 AYRSHIRE RD.	LOS ANGELES	CA	90049	U	U	ACTOR
FRANK, JOANNA	1274 CAPRI DR.	PACIFIC PALISADES	CA	90272	U	U	ACTRESS
FRANK, REP. BARNIE	HOUSE RAYBURN BLDG. #2404	WASHINGTON	DC	20515	U	U	POLITICIAN
FRANKENHEIMER, JOHN	3114 ABINGTON DR.	BEVERLY HILLS	CA	90210	U	U	DIRECTOR/PRODUCER
FRANKLIN, ARETHA	P.O. BOX 12137	BIRMINGHAM	MI	48012	U	U	SINGER/SONGWRITER - "PINK CADILLAC" - **AUTHOR'S CHOICE!**
FRANKLIN, BONNIE	5750 WILSHIRE BLVD. #512	LOS ANGELES	CA	90036	A	A+	ACTRESS - ONE DAY AT A TIME

Name	Address	City	State	Zip Code	Resp. Time	Resp. Qual.	Comments
FRANKLIN, JOE	P.O. BOX 1	LYNBROOK	NY	11563	U	U	TELEVISION HOST
FRANN, MARY	261 N. ROBERTSON	BEVERLY HILLS	CA	90211	U	U	ACTRESS
FRANZ, ARTHUR	32960 PACIFIC COAST HWY	MALIBU	CA	90265	A	B	ACTOR
FRANZ, DENNIS	11805 BELLAGIO RD.	LOS ANGELES	CA	90049	U	U	ACTOR - *NYPD BLUE* - **AUTHOR'S CHOICE!**
FRASER, BRENDAN	151 EL CAMINO DR.	BEVERLY HILLS	CA	90212	U	U	ACTOR - *ENCINO MAN*
FRASER, DOUGLAS	800 E. JEFFERSON ST.	DETROIT	MI	48214	A	B	FORMER UNION LEADER
FRATIANNE, LINDA	1177 N. VISTA VESPERO	PALM SPRINGS	CA	92262	U	U	ICE SKATER
FRAZIER, DAN	C/O WIZARDS OF THE COAST, INC., P.O. BOX 707	RENTON	WA	98057	U	U	ILLUSTRATOR - "MAGIC" CARDS
FRAZIER, JOE	2917 N. BROAD ST.	PHILADELPHIA	PA	19132	A	B	MEMBER OF THE INTERNATIONAL BOXING HALL OF FAME
FRAZIER, WALT	675 FLAMINGO DR.	ATLANTA	GA	30311	U	U	MEMBER OF THE BASKETBALL HALL OF FAME - "CLYDE"
FREBERG, STAN	10450 WILSHIRE BLVD. APT. 1-A	LOS ANGELES	CA	90024	U	U	ACTOR/DIRECTOR
FREEMAN, AL JR.	10000 SANTA MONICA BLVD. #305	LOS ANGELES	CA	90067	U	U	ACTOR
FREEMAN, KATHLEEN	6247 ORION AVE.	VAN NUYS	CA	91411	C	B	ACTRESS
FREEMAN, MONA	608 N. ALPINE DR.	BEVERLY HILLS	CA	90210	U	U	ACTRESS
FREEMAN, MORGAN	C/O JEFF HUNTER, TRIAD ARTISTS, 888 7TH AVE. #1610	NEW YORK	NY	10036	U	U	ACTOR - **AUTHOR'S CHOICE!**
FRELICH, PHYLLIS	8485-E MELROSE PL.	LOS ANGELES	CA	90069	A	C	ACTRESS
FRENCH, LEIGH	1850 N. VISTA AVE.	LOS ANGELES	CA	90046	U	U	ACTOR
FRENCH, SUSAN	110 E. 9TH ST. #C-1005	LOS ANGELES	CA	90079	U	U	ACTRESS
FRIDELL, SQUIRE	7080 HOLLYWOOD BLVD. #704	LOS ANGELES	CA	90028	A	B	ACTOR
FRIEDKIN, WILLIAM	1363 ANGELO DR.	BEVERLY HILLS	CA	90210	U	U	FILM DIRECTOR
FRIEDMAN, MILTON	QUADRANGLE OFFICE, HOOVER INST. STANFORD UNIV.	PALO ALTO	CA	94305	A	D	ECONOMIST
FRIENDS	C/O SPELLING TELEVISION, 5700 WILSHIRE BLVD.	LOS ANGELES	CA	90030	U	U	TELEVISION SERIES
FRONTIERE, GEORGIA	2327 W. LINCOLN AVE.	ANAHEIM	CA	92801	U	U	FOOTBALL TEAM OWNER
FROST, DAVID	130 W. 57TH ST.	NEW YORK	NY	10019	U	U	TELEVISION HOST
FROST, LINDSAY	310 MADISON AVE. #232	NEW YORK	NY	10017	U	U	ACTRESS
FRYE, SOLEIL MOON	2713 N. KEYSTONE	BURBANK	CA	91504	U	U	ACTRESS
FUCHS, LEO	609 N. KILKEA DR.	LOS ANGELES	CA	90048	U	U	ACTOR
FUDGE, ALAN	355 S. REXFORD DR.	BEVERLY HILLS	CA	90212	U	U	ACTOR
FULL HOUSE	WARNER BROS. TELEVISION, 4000 WARNER BLVD.	BURBANK	CA	91522	U	U	TELEVISION SERIES

Name	Address	City	State	Zip Code	Resp. Time	Resp. Qual.	Comments
FULLER, LANCE	8831 SUNSET BLVD. #402	LOS ANGELES	CA	90069	U	U	ACTOR
FULLER, PENNY	12428 HESBY ST.	NORTH HOLLYWOOD	CA	91607	U	U	ACTRESS
FULLER, SAMUEL	7628 WOODROW WILSON DR.	LOS ANGELES	CA	90046	U	U	FILM WRITER/PRODUCER
FULTON, EILEEN	301 W. 57TH ST.	NEW YORK	NY	10019	C	B	ACTRESS
FULTON, WENDY	C/O PAUL KAHNER INC., 9300 WILSHIRE BLVD. #555	BEVERLY HILLS	CA	90212	U	U	ACTRESS
FUNICELLO, ANNETTE	16102 SANDY LN.	ENCINO	CA	91316	A	D	ACTRESS - *BEACH BLANKET BINGO* - SIGNS "LOVE ANNETTE"
FUNT, ALLEN	2359 NICHOLS CANYON	LOS ANGELES	CA	90068	A	F	TELEVISION HOST/DIRECTOR - SENDS REGRETS ON POSTCARD
FURLONG, EDWARD	P.O. BOX 853	LOS ANGELES	CA	90064	U	U	ACTOR
FURST, STEPHEN	3900 HUNTERCREST COURT	MOORPARK	CA	93021	U	U	ACTOR
G, KENNY	648 N. ROBERTSON BLVD.	LOS ANGELES	CA	90048	U	U	MUSICIAN
GABOR, ZSA ZSA	1001 BEL AIR RD.	LOS ANGELES	CA	90024	U	U	ACTRESS - **AUTHOR'S CHOICE!**
GABRIEL, JOHN	100 W. 57TH ST. #5-Q	NEW YORK	NY	10019	A	B	ACTOR
GAIL, MAX	29451 BLUEWATER	MALIBU	CA	90265	C	B	ACTOR - *BARNEY MILLER*
GALBRAITH, JOHN KENNETH	30 FRANCIS AVE.	CAMBRIDGE	MA	02138	A	C	ECONOMIST
GALELLA, RON	17 GLOVER AVE.	YONKERS	NY	10704	A	C	PHOTOJOURNALIST
GALLAGHER, HELEN	260 W. END AVE.	NEW YORK	NY	10023	U	U	ACTRESS
GALLAGHER, PETER	151 EL CAMINO DR.	BEVERLY HILLS	CA	90212	U	U	ACTOR - *SEX, LIES AND VIDEOTAPE*
GALLEGO, GINA	6550 MURIETTA AVE.	VAN NUYS	CA	91401	U	U	ACTRESS
GALLIGAN, ZACK	9000 SUNSET BLVD. #1200	LOS ANGELES	CA	90069	U	U	ACTOR
GALLISON, JOE	3760 GREEN VISTA DR.	ENCINO	CA	91436	U	U	ACTOR
GALLOWAY, DON	GALLOWAY & J. MILLER, 1800 CENTURY PARK E. #300	LOS ANGELES	CA	90067	U	U	ACTOR
GAM, RITA	180 W. 58TH ST. #8	NEW YORK	NY	10019	A	B	ACTRESS
GANZEL, TERESA	300 WILSHIRE BLVD. #410	BEVERLY HILLS	CA	90212	U	U	ACTRESS
GARAGIOLA, JOE	6221 E. HUNTRESS DR.	PARADISE VALLEY	AZ	85253	A	F	TELEVISION HOST/SPORTSCASTER - REQUESTS $10 EACH FOR B.A.T.
GARAS, KAZ	31276 BAILARD RD.	MALIBU	CA	90265	U	U	ACTOR/DIRECTOR
GARBER, TERRI	10100 SANTA MONICA BLVD. # 700	LOS ANGELES	CA	90067	U	U	ACTRESS
GARBER, VICTOR	40 W. 57TH ST.	NEW YORK	NY	10019	U	U	ACTOR
GARCIA, ANDY	4519 VARNA AVE.	SHERMAN OAKS	CA	91423	U	U	ACTOR - **AUTHOR'S CHOICE!**
GARDNER, RANDY	4640 GLENCOVE AVE. #6	MARINA DEL REY	CA	90291	U	U	ICE SKATER
GARFUNKEL, ART	9 E. 79TH ST.	NEW YORK	NY	10021	U	U	SINGER/SONGWRITER - SIMON & GARFUNKEL

180

Name	Address	City	State	Zip Code	Resp. Time	Resp. Qual.	Comments
GARLAND, BEVERLY	8014 BRIAR SUMMIT DR.	LOS ANGELES	CA	90046	A	A	ACTRESS - *MY THREE SONS*
GARN, JAKE	2000 EAGLE GATE TOWER	SALT LAKE CITY	UT	84111	A	D	FORMER SENATOR/ASTRONAUT - WATCH FOR AUTOPEN!
GARNER, JAMES	33 OAKMONT DR.	LOS ANGELES	CA	90049	A	B	ACTOR/DIRECTOR - **AUTHOR'S CHOICE!**
GAROFALO, JANEANE	C/O UNITED TALENT AGCY., 9560 WILSHIRE BLVD. SUITE 500	BEVERLY HILLS	CA	90212	U	U	ACTRESS - **AUTHOR'S CHOICE!**
GARRETT, BETTY	3231 OAKDELL RD.	STUDIO CITY	CA	91604	A	B	ACTRESS - *ALL IN THE FAMILY*
GARRISON, GREG	1655 HIDDEN VALLEY RD.	THOUSAND OAKS	CA	91361	U	U	DIRECTOR
GARRISON, ZINA	P.O. BOX 272305	HOUSTON	TX	77077	U	U	TENNIS PLAYER
GARTH, JENNIE	3500 W. OLIVE #1400	BURBANK	CA	91505	A	F	ACTRESS - *BEVERLY HILLS 90210* - SENDS FACSIMILE SIGNED POSTCARD - SAVE YOUR STAMPS!
GARVER, KATHY	170 WOODBRIDGE RD.	HILLSBOROUGH	CA	94010	A	B	ACTRESS
GARVEY, CYNDY	3516 MALIBU COUNTRY DR.	MALIBU	CA	90265	U	U	TELEVISION/RADIO PERSONALITY
GARVEY, STEVE	228 S. ANITA	LOS ANGELES	CA	90049	A	C+	BASEBALL PLAYER
GARY, LORRAINE	1158 TOWER DR.	BEVERLY HILLS	CA	90210	U	U	ACTRESS
GATES, BILL	C/O MICROSOFT, 1 MICROSOFT WAY	REDMOND	WA	98052	B	B	SOFTWARE GURU!
GATES, DARYL	756 PORTOLA TERR.	LOS ANGELES	CA	90042	A	B	FORMER POLICE CHIEF
GATES, LARRY	1015 GAYLEY AVE. #300	LOS ANGELES	CA	90024	U	U	ACTOR
GAULT, WILLIE	332 CENTER ST.	EL SEGUNDO	CA	90245	U	U	FOOTBALL PLAYER
GAUTIER, DICK	11333 MOORPARK ST. #59	NORTH HOLLYWOOD	CA	91602	U	U	ACTOR/WRITER
GAYLE, CRYSTAL	51 MUSIC SQUARE E.	NASHVILLE	TN	37203	A	C	SINGER
GAYLORD, MITCH	8485-E MELROSE PL.	LOS ANGELES	CA	90069	U	U	ACTOR/GYMNAST
GAYNES, GEORGE	3344 CAMPANIL DR.	SANTA BARBARA	CA	93109	U	U	ACTOR/DIRECTOR
GAYNOR, MITZI	610 N. ARDEN DR.	BEVERLY HILLS	CA	90210	A	F	ACTOR/DANCER - *ANYTHING GOES* - REQUESTS $5 FOR AUTOGRAPHED PHOTO
GAZZARA, BEN	1080 MADISON AVE.	NEW YORK	NY	10028	A	B	ACTOR - *INCHON*
GEARY, TONY	7010 PACIFIC VIEW DR.	LOS ANGELES	CA	90068	C	F	ACTOR - FACSIMILE SIGNED PHOTO
GEER, ELLEN	21418 W. ENTRADA RD.	TOPANGA	CA	90290	A	C	ACTRESS
GEFFEN, DAVID	9130 SUNSET BLVD.	LOS ANGELES	CA	90069	U	U	RECORD EXECUTIVE - **AUTHOR'S CHOICE!**
GEHMAN, MARTHA	2488 CHEREMOYA AVE.	LOS ANGELES	CA	90068	U	U	ACTRESS
GELBART, LARRY	807 N. ALPINE DR.	BEVERLY HILLS	CA	90210	U	U	WRITER/PRODUCER
GELDOF, SIR BOB	DAVINGTON PRIORY	FAVERSHAM KEN	ENG		U	U	SINGER - BOOMTOWN RATS
GENESSE, BRYAN	9000 SUNSET BLVD. #1200	LOS ANGELES	CA	90069	U	U	ACTOR
GENNARO, PETER	115 CENTRAL PARK W.	NEW YORK	NY	10024	A	B	CHOREOGRAPHER
GENTRY, RACE	2379 MOUNTAIN VIEW DR.	ESCONDIDO	CA	92116	U	U	ACTRESS

181

LOGO ENTERTAINMENT

November 9, 1995

Mark Allen Baker
P.O. Box 2492
Liverpool, NY 13089

Dear Mark,

Thank you so much for writing! I greatly appreciate your interest: your note lets me know that I am reaching people in a positive way. I hope you enjoy the enclosed, and many thanks again for your note and support.

Best wishes,

LOUIS GOSSETT, JR.

LG:kc (As dictated)
Enclosure

Louis Gossett, Jr.

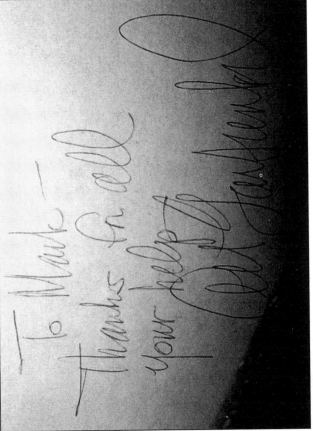

Art Garfunkel

Name	Address	City	State	Zip Code	Resp. Time	Resp. Qual.	Comments
GEORGE, LYNDA DAY	10310 RIVERSIDE DR. #104	TOLUCA LAKE	CA	91602	A	B+	ACTRESS
GEORGE, PHYLLIS	CAVE HILL, BOX 4308	LEXINGTON	KY	40503	C	B	TELEVISION PERSONALITY
GEORGE, SUSAN	520 WASHINGTON BLVD. # 187	MARINA DEL REY	CA	90292	U	U	ACTRESS
GEORGE, WALLY	14155 MAGNOLIA BLVD. # 127	SHERMAN OAKS	CA	91423	C	C	TELEVISION HOST
GERE, RICHARD	45 E. 9TH ST.	NEW YORK	NY	10003	C	B	ACTOR - **AUTHOR'S CHOICE!**
GERTZ, JAMI	8942 WILSHIRE BLVD.	BEVERLY HILLS	CA	90211	B	F	ACTRESS - *LESS THAN ZERO* - RESPONDS WITH FACSIMILE SIGNED PHOTO
GETTY, BATHAZAR	151 EL CAMINO DR.	BEVERLY HILLS	CA	90212	U	U	ACTOR - *WHERE THE DAY TAKES YOU*
GETTY, ESTELLE	7560 HOLLYWOOD BLVD. #207	LOS ANGELES	CA	90046	A	B	ACTRESS - *THE GOLDEN GIRLS*
GETTY, GORDON	2880 BROADWAY	SAN FRANCISCO	CA	94115	U	U	EXECUTIVE/COMPOSER
GETTY, MRS. J. PAUL	1535 N. BEVERLY DR.	BEVERLY HILLS	CA	90210	U	U	PHILANTHROPIST
GETZ, JOHN	402 - 21ST PL.	SANTA MONICA	CA	90402	U	U	ACTOR
GHOSTLEY, ALICE	3800 REKLAW DR.	NORTH HOLLYWOOD	CA	91604	A	B	ACTRESS - *BEWITCHED*
GIBB, BARRY	3088 S. MANN	LAS VEGAS	NV	89102	B	F	SINGER
GIBB, CYNTHIA	1139 S. HILL ST. #177	LOS ANGELES	CA	90015	U	U	ACTRESS
GIBB, MAURICE	1801 N. BAY RD.	MIAMI BEACH	FL	33139	B	F	SINGER/SONGWRITER
GIBB, ROBIN	1801 N. BAY RD.	MIAMI BEACH	FL	33139	B	F	SINGER/SONGWRITER
GIBBONS, LEEZA	5555 MELROSE AVE. #L	LOS ANGELES	CA	90038	U	U	TALK SHOW HOST - *ENTERTAINMENT TONIGHT*
GIBBS, GEORGIA	965 FIFTH AVE.	NEW YORK	NY	10021	U	U	SINGER
GIBBS, MARLA	2323 W. M.L. KING JR. BLVD.	LOS ANGELES	CA	90008	A	B	ACTRESS - *THE JEFFERSONS*
GIBBS, TERRI	110 - 30TH AVE.	NASHVILLE	TN	37203	U	U	SINGER/SONGWRITER
GIBSON, BOB	215 BELLEVIEW BLVD. S.	BELLEVIEW	NE	68005	U	U	MEMBER OF THE BASEBALL HALL OF FAME
GIBSON, CHARLES	1965 BROADWAY #500	NEW YORK	NY	10023	U	U	TELEVISION HOST - *GOOD MORNING AMERICA*
GIBSON, DON	P.O. BOX 50474	NASHVILLE	TN	37205	A	B	SINGER/SONGWRITER
GIBSON, HENRY	26740 LATIGO SHORE DR.	MALIBU	CA	90265	U	U	ACTOR - *LAUGH-IN*
GIBSON, MEL	2800 NIELSON WAY #1536	SANTA MONICA	CA	90405	U	U	ACTOR/WRITER/DIRECTOR - *BRAVEHEART* - **AUTHOR'S CHOICE!**
GIBSON-DARBEU, ALTHEA	275 PROSPECT ST. #768	EAST ORANGE	NJ	07017	U	U	TENNIS PLAYER
GIFFORD, FRANK	625 MADISON AVE. #1200	NEW YORK	NY	10022	U	U	SPORTSCASTER - *MONDAY NIGHT FOOTBALL*
GIFFORD, KATHY LEE	625 MADISON AVE. #1200	NEW YORK	NY	10022	U	U	TELEVISION HOST - *LIVE WITH REGIS & KATHY LEE* - **AUTHOR'S CHOICE!**
GIFTOS, ELAINE	10351 SANTA MONICA BLVD. #211	LOS ANGELES	CA	90025	U	U	ACTRESS
GILBERT, ELSIE	1016 N. ORANGE GROVE #4	LOS ANGELES	CA	90046	U	U	ACTRESS
GILBERT, HERSCHEL BURKE	2451 NICHOLS CANYON	LOS ANGELES	CA	90046	U	U	COMPOSER/CONDUCTOR

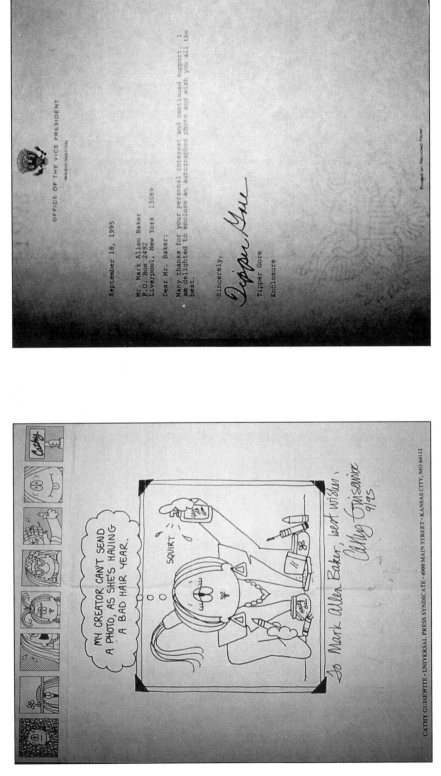

Cathy Guisewite

Tipper Gore

Name	Address	City	State	Zip Code	Resp. Time	Resp. Qual.	Comments
GILBERT, MELISSA	C/O WILLIAM MORRIS AGCY., 151 EL CAMINO DR.	BEVERLY HILLS	CA	90212	U	U	ACTRESS - *LITTLE HOUSE* ... **AUTHOR'S CHOICE!**
GILBERT, SARA	16254 HIGH VALLEY DR.	ENCINO	CA	91346	U	U	ACTRESS - *ROSEANNE*
GILL, JOHNNY	17539 CORINTHIAN DR.	ENCINO	CA	91316	U	U	SINGER/SONGWRITER
GILL, VINCE	2325 CRESTMOOR RD.	NASHVILLE	TN	37215	A	B	SINGER/SONGWRITER - **AUTHOR'S CHOICE!**
GILLEY, MICKEY	P.O. BOX 1242	PASADENA	TX	77501	A	C	SINGER/SONGWRITER
GILLIAM, TERRY	THE OLD HALL, S. GROVE HIGHGATE	LONDON	ENG	W6	U	U	ACTOR/WRITER/DIRECTOR - *MONTY PYTHON AND THE HOLY GRAIL*
GILLILAND, RICHARD	1990 WESTWOOD BLVD. #200	LOS ANGELES	CA	90025	A	A+	ACTOR
GILROY, FRANK	6 MAGNIN RD.	MONROE	NY	10950	U	U	DRAMATIST
GING, JACK	10000 SANTA MONICA BLVD. #305	LOS ANGELES	CA	90067	U	U	ACTOR
GINGRICH, REP. NEWT	HOUSE RAYBURN BLDG. #2438	WASHINGTON	DC	20515	U	U	POLITICIAN
GINSBERG, ALLEN	P.O. BOX 582, STUYVESANT STATION	NEW YORK	NY	10009	U	U	POET - A TOUGH SIGNATURE!
GINSBURG, RUTH BADER	1 - 1ST ST. N.E.	WASHINGTON	DC	20543	A	D	SUPREME COURT JUSTICES
GIRLS NEXT DOOR, THE	P.O. BOX 2977	GOODLETTSVILLE	TN	37077	A	B	COUNTRY WESTERN GROUP
GISH, ANNABETH	8942 WILSHIRE BLVD.	BEVERLY HILLS	CA	90211	U	U	ACTRESS
GIVENS, ROBIN	885 - 3RD AVE. #2900	NEW YORK	NY	10022	U	U	ACTRESS - *HEAD OF THE CLASS*
GLASER, PAUL MICHAEL	317 GEORGINA AVE.	SANTA MONICA	CA	90402	U	U	ACTOR/DIRECTOR - *STARSKY & HUTCH*
GLASS, PHILIP	231 - 2ND AVE.	NEW YORK	NY	10003	U	U	COMPOSER
GLASS, RON	2485 WILD OAK DR.	LOS ANGELES	CA	90068	C	B	ACTOR - *BARNEY MILLER*
GLEASON, PAUL	10100 SANTA MONICA BLVD. # 700	LOS ANGELES	CA	90067	U	U	ACTOR
GLENN, SCOTT	P.O. BOX 1018	KETCHUM	ID	83340	A	D	ACTOR - *THE RIGHT STUFF*
GLESS, SHARON	4709 TEESDALE AVE.	STUDIO CITY	CA	91604	U	U	ACTRESS - *CAGNEY AND LACEY*
GLOVER, CRISPIN	1811 N. WHITLEY #1400	LOS ANGELES	CA	90028	U	U	ACTOR - *BACK TO THE FUTURE*
GLOVER, DANNY	41 SUTTER ST. #1648	SAN FRANCISCO	CA	94104	B	B	ACTOR - *LETHAL WEAPON*
GLOVER, JOHN	2517 MICHELTORENA ST.	LOS ANGELES	CA	90039	A	B	ACTOR - *SHAMUS*
GOEN, BOB	21767 PLAINWOOD DR.	WOODLAND HILLS	CA	91364	U	U	TELEVISION PERFORMER
GOETZ, BERNHARD	55 W. 14TH ST.	NEW YORK	NY	10011	U	U	SUBWAY VIGILANTE
GOLD, TRACEY	12631 ADDISON ST.	NORTH HOLLYWOOD	CA	91607	U	U	ACTRESS - *GROWING PAINS*
GOLDBERG, LEONARD	235 LADERA DR.	BEVERLY HILLS	CA	90210	A	B	TELEVISION & FILM PRODUCER
GOLDBERG, WHOOPI	C/O CREATIVE ARTISTS AGCY., 9830 WILSHIRE BLVD.	BEVERLY HILLS	CA	90212	B	B	ACTRESS - *GHOST*, **AUTHOR'S CHOICE!**
GOLDBLUM, JEFF	8942 WILSHIRE BLVD.	BEVERLY HILLS	CA	90211	A	D	ACTOR - *JURASSIC PARK* - **AUTHOR'S CHOICE!** - PRINTS NAME
GOLDEN, WILLIAM LEE	RT. 2, SAUNDERSVILLE RD.	HENDERSONVILLE	TN	37075	U	U	SINGER/SONGWRITER

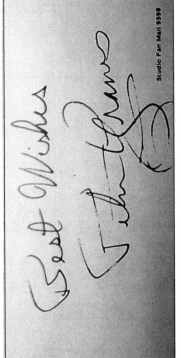

Peter Graves

Steve Garvey

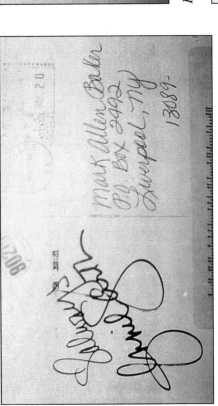

Jennie Garth (facsimile)

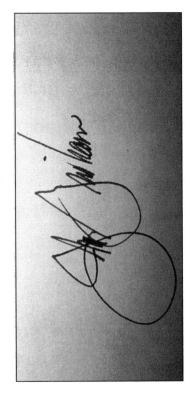

John Grisham

Name	Address	City	State	Zip Code	Resp. Time	Resp. Qual.	Comments
GOLDMAN, WILLIAM	50 E. 77TH ST. #30	NEW YORK	NY	10021	U	U	SCREENWRITER
GOLDSBORO, BOBBY	P.O. BOX 5250	OCALA	FL	32678	U	U	SINGER/SONGWRITER
GOLDTHWAIT, BOB	3950 FREDONIA DR.	LOS ANGELES	CA	90068	U	U	ACTOR/COMEDIAN - *POLICE ACADEMY*
GOLDWATER, BARRY	6250 HOGAHN	PARADISE VALLEY	AZ	85253	U	U	FORMER SENATOR
GOLDWYN, SAM JR.	10203 SANTA MONICA BLVD. # 500	LOS ANGELES	CA	90067	U	U	DIRECTOR/PRODUCER
GOLDWYN, TONY	9830 WILSHIRE BLVD.	BEVERLY HILLS	CA	90212	A	B	ACTOR - *GHOST*
GOLINO, VALERIE	8036 WOODROW WILSON DR.	LOS ANGELES	CA	90046	U	U	ACTRESS - *RAIN MAN*
GOLONKA, ARLENE	1835 PANDORA AVE. #3	LOS ANGELES	CA	90025	A	D	ACTRESS
GOLUB, RICHARD	42 E. 64TH ST.	NEW YORK	NY	10021	U	U	LAWYER
GONZALEZ-GONZALEZ PEDRO	4154 CHARLES AVE.	CULVER CITY	CA	90203	A	B+	ACTOR
GOODEVE, GRANT	21416 N.E. 68TH COURT	REDMOND	WA	98053	U	U	ACTOR - *EIGHT IS ENOUGH*
GOODFRIEND, LINDA	5700 ETIWANDA #150	TARZANA	CA	91365	U	U	ACTRESS
GOODING, CUBA JR.	10100 SANTA MONICA BLVD. #700	LOS ANGELES	CA	90067	U	U	ACTOR - *BOYZ N THE HOOD*
GOODMAN, DODY	10144 CULVER BLVD. #21	CULVER CITY	CA	90232	U	U	ACTRESS
GOODMAN, JOHN	5180 LOUISE AVE.	ENCINO	CA	91316	U	U	ACTOR - **AUTHOR'S CHOICE!**
GORDON, BARRY	3500 W. OLIVE #1400	BURBANK	CA	91505	U	U	ACTOR
GORDON, JEFF	C/O RON MILLER, PERFORMANCE PR PLUS, 529 N. COLLEGE ST.	CHARLOTTE	NC	28202	U	U	AUTO RACER - 1995 NASCAR WINSTON CUP CHAMPION
GORDON, IRVING	C/O ASCAP, 1 LINCOLN PLAZA	NEW YORK	NY	10023	U	U	SONGWRITER - "UNFORGETTABLE"
GORDY, BARRY	878 STRADELLA RD.	LOS ANGELES	CA	90077	U	U	RECORD EXECUTIVE
GORE, LESLEY	170 E. 77TH ST. #2-A	NEW YORK	NY	10162	A	B	ACTRESS/SINGER
GORE, MICHAEL	310 W. END AVE. #12C	NEW YORK	NY	10023	U	U	COMPOSER
GORE, TIPPER	ADMIRAL HOUSE, 34TH & MASSACHUSETTS	WASHINGTON	DC	20005	A	F	WIFE OF VICE PRESIDENT AL GORE - RESPONDS WITH AUTOPEN (FACSIMILE) SIGNED PHOTO
GORE, ALBERT JR.	ADMIRAL HOUSE, 34TH & MASSACHUSETTS	WASHINGTON	DC	20005	A	F	VICE PRESIDENT OF THE UNITED STATES - RESPONDS WITH AUTOPEN (FACSIMILE) SIGNED PHOTO
GORMAN, CLIFF	333 W. 57TH ST.	NEW YORK	NY	10019	A	B	ACTOR
GORME, EYDIE	820 GREENWAY DR.	BEVERLY HILLS	CA	90210	U	U	SINGER - STEVE & EYDIE
GORNEY, KAREN LYNN	853 - 7TH AVE. #7-C	NEW YORK	NY	10019	A	B+	ACTRESS
GOSDIN, VERN	151 TRAILS CIRCLE	NASHVILLE	TN	37214	U	U	SINGER/SONGWRITER
GOSSELAAR, MARK PAUL	20612 LUCERNE COURT	VALENCIA	CA	91355	U	U	ACTOR
GOSSETT, LOUIS JR.	P.O. BOX 6187	MALIBU	CA	90264	A	B	ACTOR/DIRECTOR - *AN OFFICER AND A GENTLEMAN* - HAS ALWAYS BEEN RESPONSIVE TO FAN MAIL!
GOULD, ELLIOTT	21250 CALIFA #201	WOODLAND HILLS	CA	91367	C	B	ACTOR - *BOB & CAROL & TED & ALICE*
GOULD, HAROLD	603 OCEAN AVE., 4 E.	SANTA MONICA	CA	90402	A	D	ACTOR

187

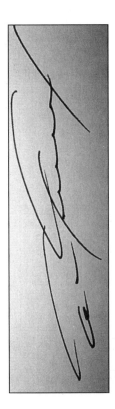

Crystal Gale

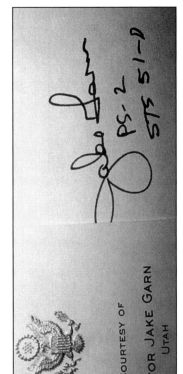

Jake Garn

Dan Gurney

James Garner

Estelle Getty

188

Name	Address	City	State	Zip Code	Resp. Time	Resp. Qual.	Comments
GOULD, JASON	446 N. ORLANDO AVE.	LOS ANGELES	CA	90048	U	U	FINANCIER
GOULD, MORTON	231 SHOREWARD DR.	GREAT NECK	NY	10201	U	U	COMPOSER/CONDUCTOR
GOULD, SANDRA	3219 OAKDELL LN.	STUDIO CITY	CA	91604	U	U	ACTRESS
GOULET, ROBERT	3110 MONTE ROSA	LAS VEGAS	NV	89120	A	B	SINGER/ESPN COMMERCIAL STAR
GOWDY, CURT	300 BOYLSTON ST. #506	BOSTON	MA	02116	C	B	SPORTSCASTER
GRAF, STEFFI	LUFTSCHIFFRING 8	D-6835 BRUHL	GER		U	U	TENNIS PLAYER
GRAFF, ILENE	11455 SUNSHINE TERR.	STUDIO CITY	CA	91604	C	D	ACTRESS
GRAHAM, KATHERINE	2920 "R" ST. N.W.	WASHINGTON	DC	20007	U	U	PUBLISHING EXECUTIVE
GRAHAM, OTTO	2241 BENEVA TERR.	SARASOTA	FL	33582	C	D	MEMBER OF FOOTBALL HALL OF FAME
GRAHAM, REV. BILLY	1300 HARMON PL.	MINNEAPOLIS	MN	55408	A	F	EVANGELIST - "TOO BUSY" - WAS GOOD SIGNER IN EARLIER YEARS
GRAHAM, RONNY	863 CASTAC PL.	PACIFIC PALISADES	CA	90272	U	U	TELEVISION WRITER
GRAHAN, NANCY	4910 AGNES AVE.	NORTH HOLLYWOOD	CA	91607	U	U	ACTRESS
GRAMMER, KELSEY	3266 CORNELL RD.	AGOURA HILLS	CA	91301	U	U	ACTOR - *FRASIER* - **AUTHOR'S CHOICE!**
GRANGER, DOROTHY	11903 W. PICO BLVD.	LOS ANGELES	CA	90064	U	U	ACTRESS
GRANGER, FARLEY	18 W. 72ND ST. #25D	NEW YORK	NY	10023	A	B	ACTOR - *STRANGERS ON A TRAIN*
GRANT, AMY	P.O. BOX 50701	NASHVILLE	TN	37205	U	U	SINGER - "BABY, BABY" - **AUTHOR'S CHOICE!**
GRANT, DR. TONY	610 S. ARDMORE AVE.	LOS ANGELES	CA	90005	U	U	RADIO PERSONALITY
GRANT, GOGI	10323 ALAMO AVE. # 202	LOS ANGELES	CA	90064	A	B	SINGER
GRANT, HUGH	C/O CREATIVE ARTISTS AGCY., 9830 WILSHIRE BLVD.	BEVERLY HILLS	CA	90212	U	U	ACTOR - *FOUR WEDDINGS AND A FUNERAL* - **AUTHOR'S CHOICE!**
GRANT, LEE	610 W. END AVE. #7B	NEW YORK	NY	10024	A	B	ACTRESS/DIRECTOR - *PEYTON PLACE*
GRANT, MRS. BARBARA	9966 BEVERLY GROVE DR.	BEVERLY HILLS	CA	90210	U	U	CARY GRANT'S WIDOW
GRATEFUL DEAD	BOX 1566, MAIN STATION	MONTCLAIR	NJ	07043	U	U	ROCK GROUP
GRAVES, PETER	660 E. CHANNEL RD.	SANTA MONICA	CA	90402	A	F	ACTOR - *MISSION IMPOSSIBLE* - RESPONDS WITH FACSIMILE SIGNED PHOTO - STUDIO FAN MAIL!
GRAVES, TERESA	3437 W. 78TH PL.	LOS ANGELES	CA	90043	U	U	ACTRESS
GRAY, BILLY	19612 GRANDVIEW DR.	TOPANGA	CA	90290	U	U	ACTOR
GRAY, COLLEEN	1432 N. KENWOOD ST.	BURBANK	CA	91505	A	A+	ACTRESS
GRAY, ERIN	10921 ALTA VIEW	STUDIO CITY	CA	91604	A	B	ACTRESS
GRAY, LINDA	C/O AGCY. FOR THE PERFORMING ARTS, 9000 SUNSET BLVD. SUITE 1200	LOS ANGELES	CA	90069	U	U	ACTRESS- *DALLAS*
GRAYSON, KATHRYN	2009 LA MESA DR.	SANTA MONICA	CA	90402	A	A+	ACTRESS/SINGER
GREEN, AL	P.O. BOX 456	MEMPHIS	TN	38053	U	U	SINGER/CLERGY
GREEN, KERRY	232 N. CANON DR. #201	BEVERLY HILLS	CA	90210	U	U	ACTRESS

189

Pedro Gonzalez-Gonzalez

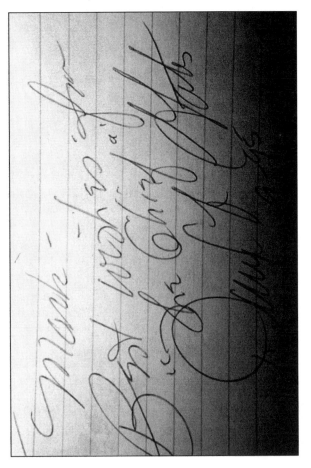

Daryl Gates

Name	Address	City	State	Zip Code	Resp. Time	Resp. Qual.	Comments
GREENE, ELLEN	151 S. EL CAMINO DR.	BEVERLY HILLS	CA	90212	U	U	ACTRESS/SINGER
GREENE, MICHELE	2281 HOLLY DR.	LOS ANGELES	CA	90068	U	U	ACTRESS
GREENE, SHECKY	1220 SHADOW LN.	LAS VEGAS	NV	89102	A	B	COMEDIAN
GREENLEE, DAVID	1811 N. WHITLEY #800	LOS ANGELES	CA	90028	U	U	ACTOR
GREENSPAN, ALAN	FEDERAL RESERVE, 21ST AND CONSTITUTION AVE. N.W.	WASHINGTON	DC	20551	U	U	ECONOMIST
GREENSPAN, BUD	33 E. 68TH ST.	NEW YORK	NY	10021	U	U	WRITER/PRODUCER
GREENWOOD, LEE	1311 ELM HILL PIKE	NASHVILLE	TN	37214	U	U	SINGER/SONGWRITER
GREER, (BETTY) JANE	966 MORAGA DR.	LOS ANGELES	CA	90049	C	B	ACTRESS
GREER, DABS	284 S. MADISON #102	PASADENA	CA	91101	A	B	ACTOR
GREGORY, DICK	P.O. BOX 3270	PLYMOUTH	MA	02361	A	B	ACTIVIST/COMEDIAN
GREGORY, JAMES	55 CATHEDRAL ROCK DR. #33	SEDONA	AZ	86336	A	B	ACTOR
GREGORY, MARY	1350 N. HIGHLAND AVE. #24	LOS ANGELES	CA	90028	A	B	ACTRESS
GREGORY, PAUL	P.O. BOX 38	PALM SPRINGS	CA	92262	A	B	FILM PRODUCER
GREISE, BOB	3250 MARY ST.	MIAMI	FL	33133	A	D	MEMBER OF FOOTBALL HALL OF FAME
GRETZKY, WAYNE	C/O NEW YORK RANGERS, MSG 4 PENNSYLVANIA PL.	NEW YORK	NY	10001	U	U	HOCKEY FRANCHISE PLAYER - "THE GREAT ONE" - **AUTHOR'S CHOICE!**
GREY, JENNIFER	500 S. SEPULVEDA BLVD. # 500	LOS ANGELES	CA	90049	U	U	ACTRESS - *DIRTY DANCING*
GREY, JOEL	7515 CLINTON ST.	LOS ANGELES	CA	90036	C	B	ACTOR/SINGER - *CABARET*
GREY, VIRGINIA	15101 MAGNOLIA BLVD. #54	SHERMAN OAKS	CA	91403	A	C	ACTRESS
GRIECO, RICHARD	15263 MULHOLLAND DR.	LOS ANGELES	CA	90077	U	U	ACTOR
GRIER, PAM	3790 S. ROSLYN WAY	DENVER	CO	80037	U	U	ACTRESS
GRIER, ROSEY	11656 MONTANA #301	LOS ANGELES	CA	90049	C	B	ACTOR/FOOTBALL PLAYER/CLERGY
GRIFFEY, JR., KEN	C/O SEATTLE MARINERS, P.O. BOX 4100	SEATTLE	WA	98104	U	U	BASEBALL PLAYER
GRIFFIN, MERV	9860 WILSHIRE BLVD.	BEVERLY HILLS	CA	90210	U	U	SINGER/PRODUCER/BUSINESSMAN
GRIFFITH, ANDY	P.O. BOX 1968	MANTEO	NC	27984	U	U	ACTOR - *THE ANDY GRIFFITH SHOW*
GRIFFITH, MELANIE	9555 HEATHER RD.	BEVERLY HILLS	CA	90210	U	U	ACTRESS - **AUTHOR'S CHOICE!**
GRIFFITH, NANCI	C/O MCA MUSIC ENT. GRP.,70 UNIVERSAL CITY PLAZA	UNIVERSAL CITY	CA	91608	U	U	SINGER - "FROM A DISTANCE" - **AUTHOR'S CHOICE!**
GRIFFITH, THOMAS IAN	5444 AGNES AVE.	NORTH HOLLYWOOD	CA	91607	U	U	ACTOR
GRIFFITH-JOYNER, FLORENCE	27758 SANTA MARGARITA #385	MISSION VIEJO	CA	92691	U	U	TRACK ATHLETE
GRIMES, TAMMY	10 E. 44TH ST. #700	NEW YORK	NY	10017	U	U	ACTRESS
GRISHAM, JOHN	C/O JAY GARON-BROOK ASSOC., 101 W. 55TH ST.	NEW YORK	NY	10019	B	B	AUTHOR - *THE FIRM* - **AUTHOR'S CHOICE!**
GRIZZARD, GEORGE	400 E. 54TH ST.	NEW YORK	NY	10022	A	C	ACTOR

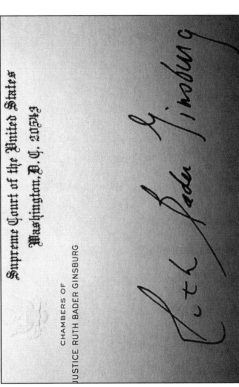

Ruth Bader Ginsburg

To Mark
Keep on pushing
Danny Glover

Danny Glover

Name	Address	City	State	Zip Code	Resp. Time	Resp. Qual.	Comments
GRODIN, CHARLES	C/O UNITED TALENT AGCY., 9560 WILSHIRE BLVD. SUITE 500	BEVERLY HILLS	CA	90212	U	U	ACTOR - *MIDNIGHT RUN* - **AUTHOR'S CHOICE!**
GROENING, MATT	C/O FOX BROADCASTING CO., 10201 W. PICO BLVD.	LOS ANGELES	CA	90035	A	F	CARTOONIST - SENDS UNAUTOGRAPHED SIMPSON COLLECTIBLES - **AUTHOR'S CHOICE!**
GROH, DAVID	8485-E MELROSE PL.	LOS ANGELES	CA	90069	U	U	ACTOR - *RHODA*
GROSS, MICHAEL	P.O. BOX 522	LA CANADA	CA	91012	B	F	ACTOR - *FAMILY TIES* - NO LONGER HONORS AUTOGRAPH REQUESTS - SAVE YOUR STAMPS!
GROZA, LOU	5287 PARKWAY DR.	BEREA	OH	44017	U	U	MEMBER OF FOOTBALL HALL OF FAME - $5 FEE
GRUBBS, GARY	9744 WILSHIRE BLVD. #308	BEVERLY HILLS	CA	90212	U	U	ACTOR
GUARDINO, HARRY	9738 ARBY DR.	BEVERLY HILLS	CA	90210	A	F	ACTOR - SENT EVERYTHING BACK UNSIGNED
GUBER, PETER	760 LAUSANNE RD.	LOS ANGELES	CA	90077	U	U	FILM PRODUCER
GUCCIONE, BOB	1965 BROADWAY	NEW YORK	NY	10023	U	U	MAGAZINE PUBLISHER - *PENTHOUSE*
GUEST, CHRISTOPHER	P.O. BOX 2358	RUNNING SPRINGS	CA	92382	U	U	ACTOR/WRITER - *THIS IS SPINAL TAP*
GUILBERT, ANN MORGAN	5750 WILSHIRE BLVD. #512	LOS ANGELES	CA	90036	U	U	ACTRESS
GUILLAUME, ROBERT	11963 CREST PL.	BEVERLY HILLS	CA	90210	A	B	ACTOR
GUINNESS, SIR ALEC	KETTLE BROOK MEADOWS	PETERSFIELD, HAMPSHIRE	ENG		U	U	ACTOR/DIRECTOR - *THE BRIDGE ON THE RIVER KWAI*
GUISEWITE, CATHY	4900 MAIN ST.	KANSAS CITY	MO	64112	A	C	CARTOONIST - *CATHY*
GULLIVER, DOROTHY	28792 LAJOS LN.	VALLEY CENTER	CA	92082	U	U	ACTRESS
GUMBEL, BRYANT	30 ROCKEFELLER PLAZA #1508	NEW YORK	NY	10020	C	B	TELEVISION HOST - *TODAY*
GUMBEL, GREG	347 W. 57TH ST.	NEW YORK	NY	10019	U	U	SPORTSCASTER
GUNN, MOSES	395 NUT PLAINS RD.	GUILFORD	CT	06430	A	B	ACTOR
GUNS N' ROSES	1830 S. ROBERTSON BLVD. #201	LOS ANGELES	CA	90035	U	U	ROCK GROUP - "WELCOME TO THE JUNGLE"
GURNEY, DAN	2334 S. BROADWAY	SANTA ANA	CA	92707	A	A	AUTO RACER - TOUGH TO IDENTIFY SIGNATURE
GUTHRIE, ARLO	THE FARM	WASHINGTON	MA	01223	B	F	SINGER/SONGWRITER - "ALICE'S RESTAURANT" - NO FREE AUTOGRAPHS HERE!
GUTTENBURG, STEVE	15237 SUNSET BLVD. # 48	PACIFIC PALISADES	CA	90272	C	F	ACTOR - *THREE MEN AND A BABY* - FACSIMILE SIGNED PHOTO
GUTTERIDGE, LUCY	2666 LA CUESTA DR.	LOS ANGELES	CA	90046	U	U	ACTRESS
GUY, JASMINE	21243 VENTURA BLVD. #101	WOODLAND HILLS	CA	91364	A	F	ACTRESS/SINGER - *A DIFFERENT WORLD* - RESPONDS WITH FACSIMILE SIGNED PHOTO
GWYNN, TONY	C/O SAN DIEGO PADRES, P.O. BOX 2000	SAN DIEGO	CA	92120	U	U	BASEBALL PLAYER - "HIT COLLECTOR"
GWYNNE, ANNE	4350 COLFAX	NORTH HOLLYWOOD	CA	91604	U	U	ACTRESS/FORMER MODEL
HAAKE, JAMES "GYPSY"	1256 N. FLORES	LOS ANGELES	CA	90069	U	U	ACTOR
HACK, SHELLEY	1208 GEORGINA	SANTA MONICA	CA	90402	U	U	ACTRESS/MODEL - *CHARLIE'S ANGELS*
HACKETT, BUDDY	800 N. WHITTIER DR.	BEVERLY HILLS	CA	90210	A	C	COMEDIAN/ACTOR - *THE LOVE BUG*

Name	Address	City	State	Zip Code	Resp. Time	Resp. Qual.	Comments
HACKFORD, TAYLOR	2003 LA BREA TERR.	LOS ANGELES	CA	90046	U	U	ACTOR
HACKMAN, GENE	118 S. BEVERLY DR.	BEVERLY HILLS	CA	90212	U	U	ACTOR - **AUTHOR'S CHOICE!**
HAGAN, MOLLY	10351 SANTA MONICA BLVD. # 211	LOS ANGELES	CA	90025	U	U	ACTRESS
HAGAR, SAMMY	P.O. BOX 667	MILL VALLEY	CA	94941	B	B	SINGER - "RED ROCKER"
HAGEN, UTA	27 WASHINGTON SQUARE N.	NEW YORK	NY	10011	A	A	ACTRESS
HAGGARD, MERLE	P.O. BOX 536	PALO CEDRO	CA	96073	A	B	SINGER
HAGMAN, LARRY	23730 MALIBU COLONY RD.	MALIBU	CA	90265	C	F	ACTOR/DIRECTOR - *DALLAS*
HAGUE, ALBERT	4346 REDWOOD AVE. #304A	MARINA DEL REY	CA	90292	A	D	ACTOR/COMPOSER
HAID, CHARLES	4376 FORMAN AVE.	NORTH HOLLYWOOD	CA	91602	U	U	ACTOR/PRODUCER - *HILL STREET BLUES*
HAINES, CONNIE	888 MANDALAY #C-315	CLEARWATER	FL	33515	A	C	SINGER
HAINES, RANDA	1033 GAYLEY AVE.	LOS ANGELES	CA	90024	U	U	TELEVISION DIRECTOR
HAIRSTON, JESTER	5047 VALLEY RIDGE AVE.	LOS ANGELES	CA	90024	A	B+	ACTOR
HAJE, KHRYSTYNE	P.O. BOX 8750	UNIVERSAL CITY	CA	91608	U	U	ACTRESS
HALBERSTAM, DAVID	C/O VILLARD PUBS., 27 W. 67TH ST.	NEW YORK	NY	10023	U	U	AUTHOR
HALE, BARBARA	P.O. BOX 1980	NORTH HOLLYWOOD	CA	91604	U	U	ACTRESS - *PERRY MASON*
HALE, MONTE	11732 MOORPARK #B	STUDIO CITY	CA	91604	A	D	ACTOR
HALEY, JACK JR.	1443 DEVLIN DR.	LOS ANGELES	CA	90069	U	U	WRITER/PRODUCER
HALEY, JACKIE EARLE	10000 RIVERSIDE DR. #6	TOLUCA LAKE	CA	91602	A	B	ACTOR - *SIXTEEN CANDLES*
HALL, ANTHONY MICHAEL	574 W. END AVE. #4	NEW YORK	NY	10024	U	U	ACTOR
HALL, ARSENIO	PARMOUNT PICTURES, 5555 MELROSE AVE.	LOS ANGELES	CA	90038	U	U	TALK SHOW HOST - **AUTHOR'S CHOICE!**
HALL, BRIDGET	FORD MODELING AGCY., 344 E. 59TH ST.	NEW YORK	NY	10022	U	U	SUPERMODEL
HALL, DARYL	130 W. 57TH ST. #2A	NEW YORK	NY	10019	U	U	SINGER - HALL & OATES
HALL, DIERDRE	215 STRADA CORTA RD.	LOS ANGELES	CA	90077	U	U	ACTRESS - *DAYS OF OUR LIVES*
HALL, FAWN	1319 BISHOP LN.	ALEXANDRIA	VA	22302	U	U	SECRETARY/MODEL - IRAN/CONTRA SCANDAL
HALL, GUS	235 W. 23RD ST.	NEW YORK	NY	10011	A	B	POLITICIAN
HALL, HUNTZ	12512 CHANDLER BLVD. #307	NORTH HOLLYWOOD	CA	91607	U	U	ACTOR
HALL, JERRY	304 W. 81ST ST.	NEW YORK	NY	10024	B	B+	MODEL - MRS. MICK JAGGER
HALL, LANI	31930 PACIFIC COAST HWY.	MALIBU	CA	90265	U	U	SINGER/SONGWRITER
HALL, MONTY	519 N. ARDEN DR.	BEVERLY HILLS	CA	90210	A	B	TELEVISION HOST - *LET'S MAKE A DEAL*
HALL, TOM T.	P.O. BOX 1246	FRANKLIN	TN	37065	A	D	SINGER/SONGWRITER
HALLAHAN, CHARLES	1975 W. SILVERLAKE DR.	LOS ANGELES	CA	90039	A	B	ACTOR
HALLICK, TOM	13900 TAHITI WAY #108	MARINA DEL REY	CA	90292	U	U	ACTOR
HALLSTROM, HOLLY	5750 WILSHIRE BLVD. #475-W	LOS ANGELES	CA	90036	A	F	MODEL - SENDS FACSIMILE SIGNED PHOTO!

194

Name	Address	City	State	Zip Code	Resp. Time	Resp. Qual.	Comments
HALSEY, BRETT	103 AVENUE RD. UNIT 702	TORONTO, ONT.	CAN	M5R 2G9	A	B	ACTOR
HAMEL, ALAN	433 S. BEVERLY DR.	BEVERLY HILLS	CA	90212	U	U	TELEVISION PERSONALITY
HAMEL, VERONICA	129 N. WOODBURN	LOS ANGELES	CA	90049	A	B	ACTRESS - HILL STREET BLUES
HAMILL, MARK	P.O. BOX 124	MALIBU	CA	90265	B	B-	ACTOR - STAR WARS
HAMILTON, CARRIE	2114 RIDGEMONT	LOS ANGELES	CA	90046	U	U	CAROL BURNETT'S DAUGHTER
HAMILTON, DONALD	984 ACEQUIA MADRE, P.O. BOX 1045	SANTA FE	NM	87501	A	B	AUTHOR
HAMILTON, GEORGE IV	P.O. BOX 1558	GAINESVILLE	FL	32602	U	U	SINGER
HAMILTON, KIM	1229 N. HORN AVE.	LOS ANGELES	CA	90069	U	U	ACTRESS
HAMILTON, LINDA	8955 NORMAN PL.	LOS ANGELES	CA	90069	U	U	ACTRESS - THE TERMINATOR
HAMILTON, SCOTT	1 ERIEVIEW PLAZA	CLEVELAND	OH	44114	A	U	ICE SKATER - HAVE RECEIVED BOTH AUTHENTIC & FACSIMILE SIGNED PHOTOGRAPHS
HAMLIN, HARRY	612 N. SEPULVEDA BLVD. #10	LOS ANGELES	CA	90049	U	U	ACTOR - L.A. LAW
HAMLISCH, MARVIN	970 PARK AVE. #65	NEW YORK	NY	10028	U	U	COMPOSER/PIANIST - "THE WAY WE WERE"
HAMMER	44896 VISTA DEL SOL	FREMONT	CA	94539	U	U	RAP SINGER - "U CAN'T TOUCH THIS" - AUTHOR'S CHOICE! - FORMER BAT BOY
HAMMOND, NICHOLAS	1930 CENTURY PARK W. #303	LOS ANGELES	CA	90067	U	U	ACTOR
HAMNER, EARL	11575 AMANDA DR.	STUDIO CITY	CA	91604	A	B	TELEVISION WRITER/PRODUCER - THE WALTONS
HAMPTON, LIONEL	20 W. 64TH ST. #28K	NEW YORK	NY	10023	B	D	MUSICIAN
HANCOCK, HERBIE	1250 N. DOHENY DR.	LOS ANGELES	CA	90069	A	B	PIANIST/COMPOSER - "ROCK IT"
HANG TIME	NBC-TV, 3000 W. ALAMEDA AVE.	BURBANK	CA	91523	U	U	TELEVISION SERIES - CAST: DANIELLA DEUTSCHER, CHAD GABRIEL, DAVID HANSON, MEGAN PARLEN
HANKS, TOM	C/O CREATIVE ARTISTS AGCY., 9830 WILSHIRE BLVD.	BEVERLY HILLS	CA	90212	U	U	ACTOR - PHILADELPHIA - AUTHOR'S CHOICE!
HANLEY, BRIDGET	16671 OAK VIEW DR.	ENCINO	CA	91316	U	U	ACTRESS
HANNAH, DARYL	C/O ICM, 8942 WILSHIRE BLVD.	BEVERLY HILLS	CA	90211	U	U	ACTRESS - SPLASH - AUTHOR'S CHOICE!
HARBACH, OTTO	876 PARK AVE. #7N	NEW YORK	NY	10021	U	U	LYRICIST
HARDAWAY, ANFERNEE	C/O ORLANDO MAGIC, 1 MAGIC PL.	ORLANDO	FL	32801	U	D	BASKETBALL PLAYER - "PENNY"
HARDIN, JERRY	3033 VISTA CREST DR.	LOS ANGELES	CA	90068	A	D	ACTOR
HARDING, TONYA	4632 S.E. OXBOW PKWY.	GRESHAM	OR	97080	U	U	FORMER FIGURE SKATER
HARDWICK, BILLY	1576 S. WHITE STATION	MEMPHIS	TN	38117	A	A	BOWLER - OFTEN ADDS TRADING CARD!
HARGIS, BILLY JAMES	ROSE OF SHARON FARM	NEOSHO	MO	64840	A	D	EVANGELIST
HARGITAY, MARISKA	9274 WARBLER WAY	LOS ANGELES	CA	90069	U	U	ACTRESS
HARGITAY, MICKEY	1255 N. SYCAMORE AVE.	LOS ANGELES	CA	90038	U	U	ACTOR
HARGROVE, DEAN	474 HALVERN DR.	LOS ANGELES	CA	90049	U	U	TELEVISION WRITER/PRODUCER
HARGROVE, MARION	401 MONICA AVE. #6	SANTA MONICA	CA	90403	U	U	TELEVISION WRITER

Merle Haggard

Buddy Hackett

Elroy "Crazy Legs" Hirsch

Lionel Hampton

196

Name	Address	City	State	Zip Code	Resp. Time	Resp. Qual.	Comments
HARMON, DEBBIE	13243 VALLEY HEART	SHERMAN OAKS	CA	91423	A	B	ACTRESS
HARMON, KELLY	13224 OLD OAK LN.	LOS ANGELES	CA	90049	U	U	ACTRESS
HARMON, MANNY	8350 SANTA MONICA BLVD.	LOS ANGELES	CA	90069	U	U	CONDUCTOR
HARMON, MARK	2236 ENCINITAS BLVD. #A	ENCINITAS	CA	92024	A	D	ACTOR - *ST. ELSEWHERE*
HAROUT, MAGDA	13452 VOSE ST.	VAN NUYS	CA	91405	A	B	ACTRESS
HARPER, JESSICA	3454 GLORIETTA PL.	SHERMAN OAKS	CA	91423	A	C	ACTRESS
HARPER, RON	3349 CAHUENGA BLVD. W. #2	LOS ANGELES	CA	90068	U	U	ACTOR
HARPER, VALERIE	616 N. MAPLE DR.	BEVERLY HILLS	CA	90210	C	C	ACTRESS - *RHODA*
HARRELSON, WOODY	9830 WILSHIRE BLVD.	BEVERLY HILLS	CA	90212	U	U	ACTOR - *CHEERS* - **AUTHOR'S CHOICE!**
HARRINGTON, CURTIS	6286 VINE WAY	LOS ANGELES	CA	90028	A	B	FILM DIRECTOR
HARRINGTON, PAT	730 MARZELLA AVE.	LOS ANGELES	CA	90049	U	U	ACTOR/WRITER - *ONE DAY AT A TIME*
HARRIS, BISHOP BARBARA	138 TREMONT ST.	BOSTON	MA	02111	A	C	CLERGY - 1ST FEMALE EPISCOPALIAN BISHOP
HARRIS, ED	1427 N. POINSETTIA PL. #303	LOS ANGELES	CA	90046	U	U	ACTOR - *THE RIGHT STUFF* - **AUTHOR'S CHOICE!**
HARRIS, EMMYLOU	P.O. BOX 159007	NASHVILLE	TN	37215	B	F	SINGER/SONGWRITER - SENDS FAN CLUB INFO ONLY - GOOD IN PERSON!
HARRIS, FRANCO	400 W. NORTH AVE.	OLD ALLEGHENY	PA	15212	A	F	FOOTBALL PLAYER - SENDS FACSIMILE SIGNED PHOTO!
HARRIS, JONATHAN	16830 MARMADUKE PL.	ENCINO	CA	91316	A	D	ACTOR
HARRIS, JULIE	132 BARN HILL RD.	WEST CHATHAM	MA	02669	C	A	ACTRESS - *KNOTS LANDING*
HARRIS, MEL	10390 SANTA MONICA BLVD. #300	LOS ANGELES	CA	90025	U	U	ACTRESS - *THIRTYSOMETHING*
HARRIS, MRS. JEAN	C/O GENERAL DELIVERY	MONROE	NH	03771	A	U	CONVICTED KILLER OF THE SCARSDALE DIET DOCTOR - MAY SEND POLITE NOTE!
HARRIS, NEIL PATRICK	14624 ROUND VALLEY DR.	SHERMAN OAKS	CA	91403	U	U	ACTOR - *DOOGIE HOWSER, M.D.*
HARRIS, RICHARD	31/32 SOHO SQUARE	LONDON	ENG	W1V 5DG	U	U	ACTOR - *A MAN CALLED HORSE*
HARRIS, SUSAN	11828 LA GRANGE #200	LOS ANGELES	CA	90025	A	D	TELEVISION PRODUCER
HARRISON, GEORGE	FRIAR PARK RD.	HENLEY-ON-THAMES	ENG		U	U	SINGER/SONGWRITER
HARRISON, LINDA	211 N. MAIN ST. #A	BERLIN	MD	21811	A	B+	ACTRESS
HARROLD, KATHRYN	151 EL CAMINO DR.	BEVERLY HILLS	CA	90212	U	U	ACTRESS
HARRY, DEBORAH	1350 AVE. OF THE AMERICAS	NEW YORK	NY	10019	U	U	SINGER - BLONDIE
HART, CECILIA	5750 WILSHIRE BLVD. #512	LOS ANGELES	CA	90036	U	U	ACTRESS
HART, DOROTHY	430 HAYWOOD RD.	ASHEVILLE	NC	28806	U	U	ACTRESS
HART, FREDDIE	505 CANTON PL.	MADISON	TN	37115	U	U	SINGER
HART, JOHN	35109 HWY. 79 #134	WARNER SPRINGS	CA	92086	A	C	ACTOR
HART, MARY	150 S. EL CAMINO DR. #303	BEVERLY HILLS	CA	90212	U	U	TELEVISION HOST - *ENTERTAINMENT TONIGHT*

Charlton Heston

Dear Mark

Every good wish to you —

L. Dolores Hart OSB

Nov. 1995

R. M. Dolores Hart, O.S.B.
PERPETUAL VOWS - July 11, 1970
CONSECRATION OF A VIRGIN - September 18, 1970
Regina Laudis Monastery, Bethlehem, Connecticut

R. M. Dolores Hart

Bob Hope

HIRSCHFELD 4/7/95

Al Hirschfield

Name	Address	City	State	Zip Code	Resp. Time	Resp. Qual.	Comments
HART, MOTHER (DOLORES)	REGINA LAUDIS CONVENT	BETHLEHEM	CT	06751	A	D	ACTRESS/NUN
HARTMAN BLACK, LISA	C/O HARTMAN BLACK ENT., 8489 N. 3RD ST., 2ND FL.	LOS ANGELES	CA	90048	A	B+	ACTRESS/MODEL - *KNOTS LANDING*
HARTMAN, PHIL	C/O WILLIAM MORRIS AGCY., 151 EL CAMINO DR.	BEVERLY HILLS	CA	90212	U	U	ACTOR/WRITER - *SATURDAY NIGHT LIVE* - **AUTHOR'S CHOICE!**
HARVEY, PAUL	1035 PARK AVE.	RIVER FOREST	IL	60305	A	B	RADIO PERSONALITY
HARVEY, RODNEY	9057A NEMO ST.	WEST HOLLYWOOD	CA	90069	U	U	ACTOR
HASENFUS, EUGENE	C/O GENERAL DELIVERY	MARINETTE	WI	54143	U	U	FORMER FLIGHT MASTER
HASKELL, PETER	19924 ACRE ST.	NORTHRIDGE	CA	91324	U	U	ACTOR
HASSELHOFF, DAVID	4310 SUTTON PL.	VAN NUYS	CA	91403	U	U	ACTOR/SINGER - *BAYWATCH* - **AUTHOR'S CHOICE!**
HASSETT, MARILYN	8485 BRIER DR.	LOS ANGELES	CA	90046	A	D	ACTRESS
HASSO, SIGNE	582 S. ORANGE GROVE AVE.	LOS ANGELES	CA	90036	U	U	ACTRESS
HATCH, RICHARD	1604 N. COURTNEY AVE.	LOS ANGELES	CA	90046	A	D	ACTOR
HATCHER, TERI	P.O. BOX 1101	SUNLAND	CA	91040	U	U	ACTRESS - *LOIS AND CLARK* - **AUTHOR'S CHOICE!**
HATFIELD, BOBBY	1824 PORT WHEELER DR.	NEWPORT BEACH	CA	92660	U	U	SINGER
HAUER, RUTGER	8091 SELMA AVE.	LOS ANGELES	CA	90046	U	U	ACTOR - *BLADE RUNNER*
HAVENS, RICHIE	123 W. 44TH ST. #11A	NEW YORK	NY	10036	A	B	SINGER/GUITARIST - PERFORMED AT BOTH WOODSTOCK FESTIVALS!
HAVER MAC MURRAY, JUNE	485 HALVERN DR.	LOS ANGELES	CA	90049	U	U	ACTRESS
HAVER, JUNE	405 OLD LONG RIDGE RD.	STAMFORD	CT	06903	A	B	ACTRESS
HAWKE, ETHAN	9830 WILSHIRE BLVD.	BEVERLY HILLS	CA	90212	A	B	ACTOR - NOTE FROM GRANDMOTHER WHO ANSWERS HIS MAIL - **AUTHOR'S CHOICE!**
HAWKING, STEPHEN	DAMTP U. CAMBRIDGE, SILVER ST.	CAMBRIDGE, ENGLAND	UK	CB3 9EW	U	U	AUTHOR - **AUTHOR'S CHOICE!**
HAWKINS, SOPHIE B.	C/O COLUMBIA RECORDS, 51 W. 52ND ST.	NEW YORK	NY	10019	U	U	SINGER
HAWN, GOLDIE	955 S. CARRILLO DR. #200	LOS ANGELES	CA	90048	U	U	ACTRESS - *PVT. BENJAMIN*
HAWORTH, JILL	300 E. 51ST ST.	NEW YORK	NY	10019	U	U	ACTRESS
HAYEK, JULIE	5645 BURNING TREE DR.	LA CANADA	CA	91011	B	B+	ACTRESS/MODEL
HAYES, BILL	4528 BECK AVE.	NORTH HOLLYWOOD	CA	91602	U	U	ACTOR
HAYES, ISAAC	1962 SPECTRUM CIRCLE #700	MARIETTA	GA	30067	U	U	SINGER/SONGWRITER
HAYES, PETER LIND	3538 PUEBLO WAY	LAS VEGAS	NV	89109	A	B	ACTOR/COMEDIAN
HAYES, SUSAN SEAFORTH	4528 BECK AVE.	NORTH HOLLYWOOD	CA	91602	U	U	ACTRESS
HAYSBERT, DENNIS	3624 CANYON CREST	ALTADENA	CA	91001	U	U	ACTOR
HAYWARD, BROOKE	305 MADISON AVE. #956	NEW YORK	NY	10165	A	C+	AUTHOR/ACTRESS
HAZE, JONATHAN	3636 WOODHILL CANYON	STUDIO CITY	CA	91604	U	U	ACTOR
HEADLEY, GLENNE	8942 WILSHIRE BLVD.	BEVERLY HILLS	CA	90211	U	U	ACTRESS - *DIRTY ROTTEN SCOUNDRELS*

199

Katharine Houghton Hepburn

x - 5 - 1995

Dear Markallen Baker -

Thank you for your nice note -

I'm sorry but Miss Hepburn does not
sign or send photographs - or other

items -

Sharon Powers

Sharon Powers
for Miss Hepburn

Sharon Powers for Katharine Hepburn

Celeste Holm
88 Central Park West
New York, NY 10023

Dear M. Baker —

Miss Holm will be very happy to grant your reque
if you will remit 50 cents for each autograph.
This contribution is donated to UNICEF.

Just so you know; Sincerely, *Barry Hoff*
Miss Holm has now
given UNICEF over $24,000.
by "selling" her autograph. Secretary to Miss Ho
And thank you for your request.

A Celeste Holm response

FIGHT
BACK!
WITH DAVID
HOROWITZ.

david horowitz

32 USA

MACKALLEN BAKER
P.O. BOX 2492
LIVERPOOL, N.Y. 13089-USA

David Horowitz

200

Name	Address	City	State	Zip Code	Resp. Time	Resp. Qual.	Comments
HEALY, MARY	3538 PUEBLO WAY	LAS VEGAS	NV	89109	A	B	ACTRESS
HEARD, JOHN	347 W. 84TH ST. #5	NEW YORK	NY	10024	U	U	ACTOR - HOME ALONE
HEARNS, TOMMY	19785 W. 12 MILE RD.	SOUTHFIELD	MI	48076	U	U	BOXER
HEARST, MRS. VICTORIA	865 COMSTOCK AVE. #168	LOS ANGELES	CA	90024	U	U	WIFE OF WILLIAM HEARST
HEARST, PATRICIA	110 - 5TH ST.	SAN FRANCISCO	CA	94103	U	U	AUTHOR
HECHT-HERSKOWITZ, GINA	5930 FOOTHILL DR.	LOS ANGELES	CA	90068	U	U	ACTRESS
HECKART, EILEEN	1223 FOXBORO DR.	NORWALK	CT	06851	A	C	ACTRESS
HEDISON, DAVID (AL)	9454 WILSHIRE BLVD. #405	BEVERLY HILLS	CA	90212	U	U	ACTOR
HEDREN, TIPPI	P.O. BOX 189	ACTON	CA	93510	B	F	ACTRESS - THE BIRDS - REQUESTS $25 DONATION FOR AUTOGRAPHED PHOTO OR COPY OF BOOK
HEE HAW	P.O. BOX 140400	NASHVILLE	TN	37214	U	U	COMEDY SHOW
HEFNER, CHRISTIE	10236 CHARING CROSS RD.	LOS ANGELES	CA	90024	A	D	MAGAZINE EDITOR - DAUGHTER OF HUGH HEFNER
HEFNER, HUGH	10236 CHARING CROSS RD.	LOS ANGELES	CA	90024	U	U	PUBLISHING EXECUTIVE - PLAYBOY
HEIDEN, BETH	3505 BLACKHAWK DR.	MADISON	WI	53704	A	B	SPEED SKATER
HEIDEN, ERIC	3505 BLACKHAWK DR.	MADISON	WI	53704	U	U	SPEED SKATER
HEISS, CAROL	809 LAFAYETTE DR.	AKRON	OH	44303	U	U	ACTRESS
HELD, CARL	1817 HILLCREST RD. #51	LOS ANGELES	CA	90068	A	B	ACTOR
HELGENBERGER, MARG	816 N. STANLEY	LOS ANGELES	CA	90046	U	U	ACTRESS
HELMOND, KATHERINE	2035 DAVIES WAY	LOS ANGELES	CA	90046	U	U	ACTRESS/DIRECTOR - WHO'S THE BOSS?
HELMSLEY, LEONA	PARK LANE HOTEL, 36 CENTRAL PARK S.	NEW YORK	NY	10019	U	U	REAL ESTATE EXECUTIVE
HEMINGWAY, MARIEL	P.O. BOX 2249	KETCHUM	ID	83340	U	U	ACTRESS - MANHATTAN
HEMPHILL, SHIRLEY	539 TRONA AVE.	WEST COVINA	CA	91790	U	U	ACTRESS
HEMSLEY, SHERMAN	15043 VALLEY HEART DR.	SHERMAN OAKS	CA	91403	A	C	ACTOR - THE JEFFERSONS - NICE IN PERSON
HENDERSON, FLORENCE	P.O. BOX 11295	MARINA DEL REY	CA	90295	A	A	SINGER/ACTRESS - THE BRADY BUNCH
HENDERSON, SKITCH	HUNT HILL FARM, RFD #3 UPLAND RD.	NEW MILFORD	CT	06776	A	B	COMPOSER/CONDUCTOR
HENDLER, LAURI	4034 STONE CANYON AVE.	SHERMAN OAKS	CA	91403	U	U	ACTRESS
HENLEY, DON	C/O GEFFEN RECORDS, 9130 SUNSET BLVD.	LOS ANGELES	CA	90069	U	U	SINGER - THE EAGLES - AUTHOR'S CHOICE!
HENNER, MARILU	2101 CASTILIAN	LOS ANGELES	CA	90068	U	U	ACTRESS - TAXI
HENNING, LINDA KAYE	11846 VENTURA BLVD. #100	STUDIO CITY	CA	91604	U	U	ACTRESS
HENRIKSEN, LANCE	9540 DALE AVE.	SUNLAND	CA	91040	U	U	ACTOR - ALIENS
HENRY, BUCK	760 N. LA CIENEGA BLVD.	LOS ANGELES	CA	90069	A	B	WRITER/PRODUCER - GET SMART
HENRY, GREGG	737 N. SEWARD ST. #1	LOS ANGELES	CA	90038	U	U	ACTOR
HENRY, JUSTIN	3 CLARK LN.	RYE	NY	10580	A	B	CHILD ACTOR - KRAMER VS. KRAMER

Greetings. I appreciate your interest and encouragement.

Very best wishes,

Ethan Hawke

****

Born: November 6, 1970, Austin, Texas.
Movies: *Explorers, Dead Poets Society, Dad, White Fang, Mystery Date, A Midnight Clear, Waterland, Rich in Love, Alive, Reality Bites,* and *Before Sunrise* (February 1995).

Note from Ethan Hawke's grandmother

THE JEFFERSONS

© 1983 EMBASSY TELEVISION

TAMKIN COLOR

EMBASSY TELEVISION

Sherman Hemsley (facsimile signatures from The Jeffersons)

Name	Address	City	State	Zip Code	Resp. Time	Resp. Qual.	Comments
HENSLEY, PAMELA	9526 DALEGROVE DR.	BEVERLY HILLS	CA	90210	A+	A+	ACTRESS - VERY RESPONSIVE TO FAN MAIL!
HEPBURN, KATHERINE	244 E. 49TH ST.	NEW YORK	NY	10017	A	F	ACTRESS - DON'T EVEN THINK ABOUT IT - **AUTHOR'S CHOICE!**
HERD, RICHARD	4610 WOOSTER AVE.	SHERMAN OAKS	CA	91423	A	B	ACTOR
HERRING, LYNN	3500 W. OLIVE #1400	BURBANK	CA	91505	U	U	ACTRESS
HERSHEY, BARBARA	9830 WILSHIRE BLVD.	BEVERLY HILLS	CA	90211	U	U	ACTRESS - BEACHES
HERVEY, IRENE	7432 SYLVIA AVE.	RESEDA	CA	91335	U	U	ACTRESS
HERVEY, JASON	1280 SUNSET PLAZA DR.	LOS ANGELES	CA	90069	U	U	ACTOR - THE WONDER YEARS
HESSEMAN, HOWARD	7146 LA PRESA	LOS ANGELES	CA	90068	C	B	ACTOR/DIRECTOR - WKRP IN CINCINNATI
HESTON, CHARLTON	2859 COLDWATER CANYON	BEVERLY HILLS	CA	90210	A	B	ACTOR/DIRECTOR - THE TEN COMMANDMENTS
HEWETT, CHRISTOPHER	1422 N. SWEETZER #110	LOS ANGELES	CA	90069	U	U	ACTOR/DIRECTOR
HEWITT, DON	555 W. 57TH ST.	NEW YORK	NY	10019	A	D	WRITER/PRODUCER - 60 MINUTES
HEWITT, MARTIN	8942 WILSHIRE BLVD.	BEVERLY HILLS	CA	90211	U	U	ACTOR
HEYERDAHL, THOR	HULEN MEADOWS	KETCHUM	ID	83340	U	U	ETHNOLOGIST/EXPLORER
HEYWOOD, ANNE	9966 LIEBE DR.	BEVERLY HILLS	CA	90210	U	U	ACTRESS
HICKEY, WILLIAM	69 W. 12TH ST.	NEW YORK	NY	10011	U	U	ACTOR
HICKMAN, DWAYNE	812 - 16TH ST. #1	SANTA MONICA	CA	91403	C	F	ACTOR - DOBIE GILLIS - SENDS PRICE LIST
HICKS, CATHERINE	121 N. SAN VICENTE BLVD.	BEVERLY HILLS	CA	90211	U	U	ACTRESS - PEGGY SUE GOT MARRIED
HICKS, DAN	P.O. BOX 5481	MILL VALLEY	CA	94942	A	C	SINGER/SONGWRITER
HIGGINS, JOEL	151 EL CAMINO DR.	BEVERLY HILLS	CA	90212	A	C	ACTOR
HIKEN, GERALD	910 MORENO AVE.	PALO ALTO	CA	94303	A	C	ACTOR
HILDEGARDE	230 E. 48TH ST.	NEW YORK	NY	10017	A	B	SINGER
HILL, ANITA	300 TIMBERDELL RD.	NORMAN	OK	73019	U	U	LAW PROFESSOR
HILL, ARTHUR	1515 CLUBVIEW DR.	LOS ANGELES	CA	90024	U	U	ACTOR - OWEN MARSHALL, COUNSELOR AT LAW
HILL, DANA	11763 CANTON PL.	STUDIO CITY	CA	91604	A	B	ACTRESS
HILL, STEVEN	18 JILL LN.	MONSEY	NY	10952	U	U	ACTOR
HILL, TERRENCE	P.O. BOX 818	STOCKBRIDGE	MA	01262	U	U	ACTOR
HILLER, ARTHUR	1218 BENEDICT CANYON	BEVERLY HILLS	CA	90210	A	C	FILM DIRECTOR
HILLERMAN, JOHN	7102 LA PRESA DR.	LOS ANGELES	CA	90068	U	U	ACTOR
HILTON, BARRON	28775 SEA RANCH WAY	MALIBU	CA	90265	U	U	HOTEL EXECUTIVE
HINCKLEY, JOHN JR.	ST. ELIZABETH'S HOSPITAL, 2700 MARTIN LUTHER KING AVE.	WASHINGTON	DC	20005	U	U	ATTEMPTED MURDERER OF RONALD REAGAN
HINDLE, ART	3500 W. OLIVE AVE. #1400	BURBANK	CA	91505	U	U	ACTOR
HINES, GREGORY	377 W. 11TH ST. PH 4-A	NEW YORK	NY	10014	U	U	ACTOR - WAITING TO EXHALE

Name	Address	City	State	Zip Code	Resp. Time	Resp. Qual.	Comments
HINES, MIMI	1605 S. 11TH ST.	LAS VEGAS	NV	89109	U	U	ACTRESS
HINTON, DARBY	1234 BEL AIR RD.	LOS ANGELES	CA	90024	U	U	ACTOR
HINTON, JAMES DAVID	2808 OAK POINT DR.	LOS ANGELES	CA	90068	U	U	ACTOR
HINTON, S.E.	8955 BEVERLY BLVD.	LOS ANGELES	CA	90048	U	U	SCREENWRITER
HIRSCH, ELROY	1440 MONROE ST.	MADISON	WI	53711	U	U	MEMBER FOOTBALL HALL OF FAME
HIRSCH, JUDD	P.O. BOX 25909	LOS ANGELES	CA	90025	U	U	ACTOR - *TAXI*
HIRSCHFIELD, AL	122 E. 95TH ST.	NEW YORK	NY	10028	A	C	CARICATURIST - **AUTHOR'S CHOICE!**
HO, DON	277 LEWERS	HONOLULU	HI	96814	A	F	SINGER/SONGWRITER - "TINY BUBBLES" - SENDS FACSIMILE SIGNED PHOTO
HOBART, ROSE	23388 MULHOLLAND DR.	WOODLAND HILLS	CA	91364	A	B	ACTRESS
HOCKNEY, DAVID	2907 MT. CALM AVE.	LOS ANGELES	CA	90046	A	B	ARTIST
HODGES SCHIESS, JOY	RFD #3, BOX 254	KATONAH	NY	10536	A	B	ACTRESS
HOFFMAN, ALICE	3 HURLBUT ST.	CAMBRIDGE	MA	02138	U	U	SCREENWRITER
HOFFMAN, DUSTIN	540 MADISON AVE. #2700	NEW YORK	NY	10022	U	U	ACTOR - *TOOTSIE* - **AUTHOR'S CHOICE!**
HOFFS, SUSANNA	9720 WILSHIRE BLVD. #400	BEVERLY HILLS	CA	90212	U	U	SINGER
HOGAN, BEN	2911 W. PAFFORD	FORT WORTH	TX	76110	A	D	GOLFER
HOGAN, HULK	4505 MORELLA AVE.	NORTH HOLLYWOOD	CA	91607	A	B	WRESTLER
HOGAN, PAUL	55 LAVENDER PL., MILSON'S POINT	SYDNEY	AUST	NSW 2060	U	U	ACTOR - *CROCODILE DUNDEE*
HOGAN, ROBERT	344 W. 89TH ST. #1B	NEW YORK	NY	10024	U	U	ACTOR
HOGESTYN, DRAKE	9255 SUNSET BLVD. #515	LOS ANGELES	CA	90069	U	U	ACTOR
HOLBROOK, HAL	618 S. LUCERNE BLVD.	LOS ANGELES	CA	90005	U	U	ACTOR - *ALL THE PRESIDENT'S MEN*
HOLDEN, REBECCA	1105 - 16TH AVE. S. #C	NASHVILLE	TN	37212	C	B	ACTRESS/SINGER - ADDS FAN CLUB INFO
HOLE, JONATHAN	5024 BALBOA BLVD.	ENCINO	CA	91316	A	D	ACTOR
HOLLIDAY, POLLY	888 - 7TH AVE. #2500	NEW YORK	NY	10106	U	U	ACTRESS
HOLLIMAN, EARL	4249 BELLINGHAM AVE.	STUDIO CITY	CA	91604	C	B+	ACTOR - *POLICE WOMAN*
HOLLY, LAUREN	C/O UNITED TALENT AGCY., 9560 WILSHIRE BLVD. SUITE 500	BEVERLY HILLS	CA	90212	U	U	ACTRESS - *PICKET FENCES* - **AUTHOR'S CHOICE!**
HOLM, CELESTE	88 CENTRAL PARK W.	NEW YORK	NY	10023	A	F	ACTRESS - *ALL ABOUT EVE* - ASKS FOR FIFTY CENT DONATION TO UNICEF
HOLMES, JENNIFER	P.O. BOX 6303	CARMEL	CA	93921	U	U	ACTRESS
HOLMES, LARRY	413 N.HAMPTON ST.	EASTON	PA	18042	A	D	FORMER HEAVYWEIGHT BOXING CHAMPION - MAY CHARGE $10
HOLT, CHARLENE	151 EL CAMINO DR.	BEVERLY HILLS	CA	90212	U	U	ACTRESS
HOLYFIELD, EVANDER	310 MADISON AVE. #804	NEW YORK	NY	10017	U	U	HEAVYWEIGHT BOXING CHAMPION

Name	Address	City	State	Zip Code	Resp. Time	Resp. Qual.	Comments
HOME COURT, THE	NBC-TV, 3000 W. ALAMEDA AVE.	BURBANK	CA	91523	U	U	TELEVISION SERIES - CAST: MEGHANN HALDEMAN, BRECKIN MEYER
HOME IMPROVEMENT	ABC-TV, 2040 AVE. OF THE STARS	LOS ANGELES	CA	90067	U	U	TELEVISION SERIES - CAST: ZACHERY TY BRYAN, TARAN NOAH SMITH, JONATHAN TAYLOR THOMAS
HOOKS, BEN	260 5TH AVE.	NEW YORK	NY	10001	U	U	ACTIVIST
HOOKS, BENJAMIN	260 FIFTH AVE.	NEW YORK	NY	10027	U	U	FORMER NAACP PRESIDENT
HOOKS, JAN	151 EL CAMINO DR.	BEVERLY HILLS	CA	90212	U	U	ACTRESS
HOOKS, KEVIN	15534 MORRISON ST.	SHERMAN OAKS	CA	91403	U	U	ACTOR/DIRECTOR
HOOKS, ROBERT	145 N. VALLEY ST.	BURBANK	CA	91505	U	U	ACTOR
HOOTIE & THE BLOWFISH	C/O ATLANTIC RECORDS, 75 ROCKEFELLER PLAZA	NEW YORK	NY	10019	U	U	MUSIC GROUP - "CRACKED REAR VIEW"
HOPE, BOB	10346 MOORPARK	NORTH HOLLYWOOD	CA	91602	A	B	ACTOR/COMEDIAN - *THE ROAD MOVIES SERIES*
HOPE, LESLIE	151 EL CAMINO DR.	BEVERLY HILLS	CA	90212	U	U	ACTRESS/SINGER
HOPKINS, ANTHONY	C/O ICM, 8942 WILSHIRE BLVD.	BEVERLY HILLS	CA	90211	U	U	ACTOR - *THE SILENCE OF THE LAMBS* - **AUTHOR'S CHOICE!**
HOPKINS, BO	6620 ETHEL AVE.	NORTH HOLLYWOOD	CA	91606	A	B	ACTOR
HOPKINS, LINDA	2055 N. IVAR PH	LOS ANGELES	CA	90068	U	U	SINGER
HOPPER, DENNIS	330 INDIANA	VENICE	CA	90291	U	U	ACTOR/DIRECTOR - *EASY RIDER*
HORNE, LENA	23 E. 74TH ST.	NEW YORK	NY	10021	U	U	SINGER
HORNE, MARILYN	165 W. 57TH ST.	NEW YORK	NY	10019	U	U	MEZZO-SOPRANO
HORNER, JAMES	C/O GORFAINE SCHWARTZ AGCY., 3301 BARHAM BLVD. SUITE 201	LOS ANGELES	CA	90068	U	U	COMPOSER - "FIELD OF DREAMS" - **AUTHOR'S CHOICE!**
HORNSBY, BRUCE	P.O. BOX 3545	WILLIAMSBURG	CA	23187	A	B	MUSICIAN - BRUCE HORNSBY & THE RANGE
HOROWITZ, DAVID	P.O. BOX 49915	LOS ANGELES	CA	90049	A	B	TELEVISION HOST
HORSLEY, LEE	1941 CUMMINGS DR.	LOS ANGELES	CA	90027	B	D	ACTOR
HORTON, PETER	345 N. MAPLE DR. #185	BEVERLY HILLS	CA	90210	U	U	ACTOR
HORTON, ROBERT	5317 ANADSOL AVE.	ENCINO	CA	91316	U	U	ACTOR
HOUGHTON, JAMES	8585 WALNUT DR	LOS ANGELES	CA	90046	U	U	ACTOR/WRITER
HOUGHTON, KATHARINE	134 STEELE RD.	WEST HARTFORD	CT	06119	U	U	ACTRESS
HOUSER, JERRY	3236 BRENDA ST.	LOS ANGELES	CA	90068	A	B	ACTOR
HOUSTON, CISSY	2160 N. CENTRAL RD.	FT. LEE	NJ	07024	A	B	SINGER
HOUSTON, THELMA	4296 MOUNT VERNON	LOS ANGELES	CA	90008	U	U	SINGER/ACTRESS - *TONY ORLANDO & DAWN*
HOUSTON, WHITNEY	2160 N. CENTRAL RD.	FT. LEE	NJ	07024	C	F	SINGER/ACTRESS - *WAITING TO EXHALE* - **AUTHOR'S CHOICE!** - ANSWERS WITH FAN CLUB INFO!
HOWARD, CLINT	4286 CLYBOURNE AVE.	BURBANK	CA	91505	A	C	ACTOR

Name	Address	City	State	Zip Code	Resp. Time	Resp. Qual.	Comments
HOWARD, JOHN	2311 GAINSBOROUGH AVE.	SANTA ROSA	CA	95405	U	U	ACTOR
HOWARD, KEN	59 E. 54TH ST.	NEW YORK	NY	10022	A	D	ACTOR - *THE WHITE SHADOW*
HOWARD, RANCE	4286 CLYBOURN AVE.	BURBANK	CA	91505	A	B	ACTOR/WRITER
HOWARD, RON	1875 CENTURY PARK E. #3600	LOS ANGELES	CA	90067	U	U	ACTOR/DIRECTOR - *APOLLO 13* - **AUTHOR'S CHOICE!**
HOWELL, C. THOMAS	3950 VANTAGE AVE.	STUDIO CITY	CA	91604	U	U	ACTOR
HOWLAND, BETH	8428-C MELROSE PL.	LOS ANGELES	CA	90069	U	U	ACTRESS
HUBLEY, WHIP	9000 SUNSET BLVD. #1200	LOS ANGELES	CA	90069	A	B	ACTOR
HUCKABEE, COOPER	1800 E. CERRITO PL. #34	LOS ANGELES	CA	90068	A	B	ACTOR
HUDDLESTON, DAVID	9200 SUNSET BLVD. #625	LOS ANGELES	CA	90069	U	U	ACTOR
HUDSON BROTHERS	151 EL CAMINO DR.	BEVERLY HILLS	CA	90212	U	U	VOCAL GROUP
HUDSON, BILL	7023 BIRDVIEW	MALIBU	CA	90265	U	U	SINGER/ACTOR
HUES CORPORATION	P.O. BOX 5295	SANTA MONICA	CA	90405	U	U	VOCAL GROUP
HUFF, BRENT	2203 RIDGEMONT DR.	TARZANA	CA	91356	A	B	ACTOR
HUFSEY, BILLY	19134 GAYLE PL.	NEW YORK	NY	10036	U	U	ACTOR
HUGH-KELLY, DANIEL	130 W. 42ND ST. #2400	NEW YORK	NY	10025	U	U	ACTOR
HUGHES, BARNARD	250 W. 94TH ST.	FLINTRIDGE	CA	91011	U	U	ACTRESS
HUGHES, FINOLA	4334 BEL AIR DR.	CHICAGO	IL	60611	U	U	JOURNALIST
HUGHES, IRENE	500 N. MICHIGAN AVE. #1029	LOS ANGELES	CA	90069	U	U	ACTRESS
HUGHES, KATHLEEN	8818 RISING GLEN PL.	LOS ANGELES	CA	90046	U	U	ACTOR - *AMADEUS*
HULCE, THOMAS	2305 STANLEY HILLS	ST. LOUIS	MO	63110	U	U	HOCKEY PLAYER - A TOUGH SIGNATURE!
HULL, BRETT	C/O ST. LOUIS BLUES, 5700 OAKLAND AVE.	WASHINGTON	DC	20036	U	U	JOURNALIST
HUME, BRIT	ABC NEWS, 1717 DESALLES ST.	STUDIO CITY	CA	91604	A	B	ACTRESS/MODEL
HUMES, MARY MARGARET	P.O. BOX 1168-714	BEVERLY HILLS	CA	90209	U	U	SINGER
HUMPERDINCK, ENGLEBERT	P.O. BOX 5734	BEVERLY HILLS	CA	90212	U	U	ACTRESS - *MAD ABOUT YOU* - **AUTHOR'S CHOICE!**
HUNT, HELEN	9830 WILSHIRE BLVD.	KANSAS CITY	MO	64129	U	U	FOOTBALL TEAM OWNER
HUNT, LAMAR	1 ARROWHEAD DR.	VAN NUYS	CA	91403	U	U	ACTRESS
HUNT, MARSHA	13131 MAGNOLIA BLVD.	SANTA MONICA	CA	90403	U	U	ACTRESS - *THE FIRM*
HUNTER, HOLLY	1223 WILSHIRE BLVD. #668	NEW YORK	NY	10014	U	U	ACTRESS
HUNTER, KIM	42 COMMERCE ST.	SANTA FE	NM	87501	U	U	ACTOR - *DAMN YANKEES*
HUNTER, TAB	P.O. BOX 1048, LA TIERRA	BEVERLY HILLS	CA	90210	A	B	FILM PRODUCER
HURD, GALE ANN	270 N. CANON DR. #1195	BEVERLY HILLS	CA	90212	U	U	ACTRESS/MODEL - *CHRISTABEL* - **AUTHOR'S CHOICE!**
HURLEY, ELIZABETH	C/O CREATIVE ARTISTS AGCY., 9830 WILSHIRE BLVD.	LONDON	ENG	WC1	U	U	ACTOR - *THE ELEPHANT MAN*
HURT, JOHN	BURRY PLACE, 22 PIED BULL COURT						

206

Name	Address	City	State	Zip Code	Resp. Time	Resp. Qual.	Comments
HURT, MARY BETH	1619 BROADWAY #900	NEW YORK	NY	10019	U	U	ACTRESS - *THE WORLD ACCORDING TO GARP*
HURT, WILLIAM	151 EL CAMINO DR.	BEVERLY HILLS	CA	90212	U	U	ACTOR - *BODY HEAT*
HUSKY, FERLIN	38 MUSIC SQUARE E.	NASHVILLE	TN	37203	U	U	SINGER/SONGWRITER
HUSSEY, OLIVIA	4872 TOPANGA CANYON BLVD. #301	WOODLAND HILLS	CA	91364	U	U	ACTRESS
HUSSEY, RUTH	3361 DON PABLO DR.	CARLSBAD	CA	92008	A	B	ACTRESS
HUSTON, ANGELICA	2771 HUTTON DR.	BEVERLY HILLS	CA	90210	A	B	ACTRESS - *PRIZZI'S HONOR*
HUTCHINS, WILL	3461 WAVERLY DR. #108	LOS ANGELES	CA	90027	A	B+	ACTOR
HUTTON, BETTY	HARRISON AVE.	NEWPORT	RI	02840	U	U	ACTRESS
HUTTON, DANNY	2437 HORSESHOE CANYON RD.	LOS ANGELES	CA	90046	C	D	SINGER/SONGWRITER - THREE DOG NIGHT
HUTTON, LAUREN	382 LAFAYETTE ST. #6	NEW YORK	NY	10003	A	A+	ACTRESS/MODEL/TALK SHOW HOST - *AMERICAN GIGOLO*
HUTTON, TIMOTHY	RR2, BOX 3318, CUSHMAN RD.	PATTERSON	NY	12563	U	U	ACTOR - *ORDINARY PEOPLE*
HUXLEY, LAURA	6233 MULHOLLAND DR.	LOS ANGELES	CA	90068	A	A	AUTHOR
HYDE-WHITE, ALEX	8271 MELROSE AVE. #110	LOS ANGELES	CA	90046	U	U	ACTOR
HYER, MARTHA	1216 LA RAMBLA	SANTA FE	NM	87501	A	A	ACTRESS
HYLANDS, SCOTT	128 31 MULHOLLAND DR.	BEVERLY HILLS	CA	90210	U	U	ACTOR
IACOCCA, LEE	30 SCENIC OAKS	BLOOMFIELD HILLS	MI	48304	A	D	AUTOMOBILE EXECUTIVE/AUTHOR
ICAHN, CARL	100 S. BEDFORD DR.	MT. KISCO	NY	10549	U	U	BUSINESS EXECUTIVE
ICE CUBE (O'SHEA JACKSON)	6809 VICTORIA AVE.	LOS ANGELES	CA	90043	U	U	RAP SINGER - "BOYZ N THE HOOD" - **AUTHOR'S CHOICE!**
ICE-T (TRACY MORROW)	2287 SUNSET PLAZA DR.	LOS ANGELES	CA	90069	U	U	RAP SINGER - "NEW JACK CITY" - **AUTHOR'S CHOICE!**
IDOL, BILLY	8209 MELROSE AVE.	LOS ANGELES	CA	90046	U	U	SINGER/SONGWRITER
IGLESIAS, JULIO	4770 BISCAYNE BLVD. #1420	MIAMI BEACH	FL	33137	U	U	SINGER
IKE, REV.	4140 BROADWAY	NEW YORK	NY	10004	U	U	EVANGELIST
IMAN	111 E. 22ND ST. #200	NEW YORK	NY	10010	U	U	MODEL/MRS. DAVID BOWIE
IMMATURE	C/O MCA RECORDS, 1755 BROADWAY	NEW YORK	NY	10019	U	U	MUSIC GROUP
INGELS, MARTY	701 N. OAKHURST DR.	BEVERLY HILLS	CA	90210	A	B	ACTOR/COMEDIAN - *THE PRUITTS OF SOUTHAMPTON*
INGRAM, JAMES	867 MUIRFIELD RD.	LOS ANGELES	CA	90005	U	U	SINGER
INNIS, ROY	800 RIVERSIDE DR. #6E	NEW YORK	NY	10032	A	B	CIVIL RIGHTS LEADER
IRELAND, KATHY	1900 AVE. OF THE STARS # 739	LOS ANGELES	CA	90069	A	F	MODEL
IRIS, DONNIE	807 DARLINGTON RD.	BEAVER FALLS	PA	15010	A	B	SINGER
IRONS, JEREMY	C/O CREATIVE ARTISTS AGCY., 9830 WILSHIRE BLVD.	BEVERLY HILLS	CA	90212	U	U	ACTOR - *DEAD RINGERS* - **AUTHOR'S CHOICE!**
IRONSIDE, MICHAEL	3500 W. OLIVE #1400	BURBANK	CA	91505	U	U	ACTOR

Julio Iglesias

Dear Friend,

I thank you from the bottom of my heart for thinking of me and taking the time to write. It is your love and support that keeps me going and your kindness that makes me continue to love what I do.

I love reading each of your letters and hearing all of your kind words. My crazy schedule keeps me from writing to each of you individually however, my heart is with each of you.

I am looking forward to seeing you at a concert very soon.

Best regards,

Julio Iglesias (B)

Thank you for writing! Best wishes and God bless you! Kathy Ireland

Kathy Ireland (facsimile)

INTERNATIONAL FAN CLUB

Thank you for requesting information on joining the JULIO IGLESIAS INTERNATIONAL FAN CLUB. We are excited that you would like to be a part of the club dedicated to supporting the most popular artist in the world.

As a Julio Fan Club member, you will receive:

- 8x10 Photo
- Keychain
- Membership Card
- Information Hotline
- Special Fan Club Mailings
- Exclusive Fan Club Opportunities
- Biography
- Newsletters

We look forward to having you as a member! Annual membership fee is $10(US) / $15 Outside the US (US FUNDS ONLY). Please print clearly.

Name:
Address:
City: State: Zip:
Day Phone: Evening Phone: Birthdate:

Julio Iglesias International Fan Club · 1177 Kane Concourse, Penthouse
Bay Harbor Islands, FL 33154
Please allow 6 weeks for delivery.

Julio Iglesias (A)

Name	Address	City	State	Zip Code	Resp. Time	Resp. Qual.	Comments
IRVIN, MICHAEL	C/O DALLAS COWBOYS, 1 COWBOYS PKWY.	IRVING	TX	75063	U	U	FOOTBALL PLAYER
IRVIN, MONTE	11 DOUGLAS CT. S.	HOMOSASSA	FL	32646	U	U	MEMBER OF THE BASEBALL HALL OF FAME
IRVING, AMY	11693 SAN VICENTE BLVD. #335	LOS ANGELES	CA	90049	U	U	ACTRESS - *YENTL*
IRVING, JOHN	C/O WILLIAM MORROW & CO., 105 MADISON AVE.	NEW YORK	NY	10016	U	U	AUTHOR - *THE WORLD ACCORDING TO GARP*
IRWIN, HALE	12444 POWERSCOURT DR. #284	ST. LOUIS	MO	63131	A	B	GOLFER
ISAACKSEN, PETER	4635 PLACIDIA AVE.	NORTH HOLLYWOOD	CA	91602	U	U	ACTOR
ISAAK, CHRIS	P.O. BOX 547	LARKSPUR	CA	94939	U	U	SINGER - **AUTHOR'S CHOICE!**
ISLEY BROTHERS	446 LIBERTY RD.	ENGLEWOOD	NJ	07631	U	U	R&B GROUP
ITO, JUDGE LANCE	CRIMINAL COURTS BLDG., 210 W. TEMPLE ST.	LOS ANGELES	CA	90012	U	U	JUDGE - PRESIDED OVER "PEOPLE VS. O. J. SIMPSON" - **AUTHOR'S CHOICE!**
ITO, ROBERT	4916 1/2 MC CONNELL AVE.	LOS ANGELES	CA	90066	U	U	ACTOR
IVANEK, ZELJKO	145 W. 45TH ST. #1204	NEW YORK	NY	10036	U	U	ACTOR
IVORY, JAMES	9830 WILSHIRE BLVD.	BEVERLY HILLS	CA	90212	U	U	DIRECTOR - *HOWARD'S END*
JACKEE (HARRY)	8649 METZ PL.	LOS ANGELES	CA	90069	C	B	ACTRESS - *227* - SIGNS "JACKEE" ONLY!
JACKSON, ALAN	C/O ARISTA RECORDS, 6 W. 57TH ST.	NEW YORK	NY	10019	U	U	SINGER - NEON RAINBOW - **AUTHOR'S CHOICE!**
JACKSON, ANNE	90 RIVERSIDE DR.	NEW YORK	NY	10024	A	D	ACTRESS
JACKSON, BO	100 OAK RIDGE DR.	BURR RIDGE	IL	60521	U	U	ATHLETE/ACTOR
JACKSON, FREDDIE	231 W. 58TH ST.	NEW YORK	NY	10019	U	U	SINGER
JACKSON, JANET	C/O VIRGIN RECORDS, 1790 BROADWAY	NEW YORK	NY	10019	U	U	SINGER - "THAT'S THE WAY LOVE GOES" - **AUTHOR'S CHOICE!**
JACKSON, JEREMY	BAYWATCH, C/O ALL AMERICAN DIST.,, 5433 BEETHOVEN ST.	LOS ANGELES	CA	90066	U	U	ACTOR - *BAYWATCH*
JACKSON, JESSE JR.	733 -15TH ST. N.W.	WASHINGTON	DC	20005	U	U	POLITICIAN/SON OF JESSE JACKSON
JACKSON, KATE	1628 MARLAY DR.	LOS ANGELES	CA	90069	U	U	ACTRESS - *CHARLIE'S ANGELS*
JACKSON, KEITH	ABC SPORTS, 47 W. 66TH ST.	NEW YORK	NY	10023	U	U	BROADCASTER
JACKSON, MARLON	4641 HAVENHURST AVE.	ENCINO	CA	91316	U	U	SINGER
JACKSON, MARY ANN	1242 ALESSANDRO DR.	NEWBURY PARK	CA	91320	A	B	ACTRESS - *OUR GANG*
JACKSON, MAYNARD	68 MITCHELL	ATLANTA	GA	30303	U	U	MAYOR OF ATLANTA
JACKSON, MICHAEL	NEVERLAND RANCH	LOS OLIVOS	CA	93441	F	F	SINGER/SONGWRITER - **AUTHOR'S CHOICE!**
	1420 MORAGA DR.	LOS ANGELES	CA	90049	U	U	TALK SHOW HOST
	4641 HAYVENHURST DR.	ENCINO	CA	91316	U	U	SINGER
	4641 HAYVENHURST DR.	ENCINO	CA	91316	U	U	SINGER
	325 ELDER AVE.	SEASIDE	CA	93955	F	F	MEMBER OF THE BASEBALL HALL OF FAME

209

1e	Address	City	State	Zip Code	Resp. Time	Resp. Qual.	Comments
JACKSON, REV. JESSE	400 "T" ST. N.W.	WASHINGTON	DC	20001	A	B+	MINISTER/POLITICIAN - **AUTHOR'S CHOICE!**
JACKSON, SAMUEL L.	C/O ICM, 8942 WILSHIRE BLVD.	BEVERLY HILLS	CA	90211	U	U	ACTOR - *PULP FICTION* - **AUTHOR'S CHOICE!**
JACKSON, SHERRY	4933 ENCINO AVE.	ENCINO	CA	91316	U	U	ACTRESS
JACKSON, STONEWALL	6007 CLOVERLAND DR.	BRENTWOOD	TN	37027	A	B	SINGER/SONGWRITER
JACKSON, STONEY	1602 N. FULLER AVE. #102	LOS ANGELES	CA	90046	U	U	ACTOR
JACKSON, TITO	15255 DEL GADO DR.	SHERMAN OAKS	CA	91403	U	U	SINGER
JACKSON, VICTORIA	8330 LOOKOUT MOUNTAIN	LOS ANGELES	CA	90046	U	U	ACTRESS - *SATURDAY NIGHT LIVE*
JACOBI, DEREK	22 CHELSHAM RD.	LONDON	ENG	SW4	U	U	ACTOR - *THE DAY OF THE JACKAL*
JACOBI, LOU	240 CENTRAL PARK S.	NEW YORK	NY	10019	A	B	ACTOR - *IRMA LA DOUCE*
JACOBS, JOHN E.	500 E. 60TH ST.	NEW YORK	NY	10001	U	U	ACTIVIST
JACOBS, LAWRENCE-HILTON	3804 EVANS #2	LOS ANGELES	CA	90027	U	U	ACTOR
JACOBY, BILLY	P.O. BOX 46324	LOS ANGELES	CA	90046	U	U	ACTOR
JACOBY, SCOTT	1006 N. EDINBURGH AVE.	LOS ANGELES	CA	90046	U	U	ACTOR
JAECKEL, RICHARD	475 AVONDALE AVE.	LOS ANGELES	CA	90049	U	U	ACTOR
JAGGER, BIANCA	530 PARK AVE. #18-D	NEW YORK	NY	10021	U	U	ACTRESS/MODEL
JAGGER, MICK	304 W.81ST ST.	NEW YORK	NY	10024	U	U	SINGER - THE ROLLING STONES
JAGLOM, HENRY	8235 MONTEEL RD.	LOS ANGELES	CA	90069	A	B	ACTOR
JAGR, JAROMIR	C/O PITTSBURGH PENGUINS, CIVIC ARENA	PITTSBURGH	PA	15219	C	C	HOCKEY PLAYER - **AUTHOR'S CHOICE!**
JAKES, JOHN	19 W. 44TH ST.	NEW YORK	NY	10036	A	D	AUTHOR
JAMES, CLIFTON	95 BUTTONWOOD DR.	DIX HILLS	NY	11746	A	B	ACTOR - *COOL HAND LUKE*
JAMES, DALTON	178 S. VICTORY BLVD. #208	BURBANK	CA	91502	U	U	ACTOR
JAMES, DENNIS	3581 CARIBETH DR.	ENCINO	CA	91316	A	B	TELEVISION PERSONALITY
JAMES, ETTA	4031 PANAMA COURT	PIEDMONT	CA	94611	A	B+	SINGER
JAMES, SONNY	818 -18TH AVE.	NASHVILLE	TN	37203	C	D	SINGER/SONGWRITER
JAMES-KUEHL, SHEILA	3201 PEARL ST.	SANTA MONICA	CA	90405	A	B	ACTRESS
JAN & DEAN	18932 GREGORY LN.	HUNTINGTON BEACH	CA	92648	A	B	VOCAL DUO
JANIS, CONRAD	300 N. SWALL DR. #251	BEVERLY HILLS	CA	90211	A	B	ACTOR - *MORK AND MINDY*
JANUARY, DON	P.O. BOX 109601	PALM BEACH GARDEN	FL	33410	A	B	GOLFER
JANUARY, LOIS	225 N. CRESCENT DR. #103	BEVERLY HILLS	CA	90210	A	B	ACTRESS
JARDINE, AL	P.O. BOX 36	BIG SUR	CA	93920	U	U	SINGER/MUSICIAN - THE BEACH BOYS
JARMAN, CLAUDE JR.	11 DOS ENCINAS	ORINDA	CA	94563	A	B	ACTOR
JARRE, MAURICE	27011 SEA VISTA DR.	MALIBU	CA	90265	U	U	COMPOSER
JARREAU, AL	16121 MORRISON	ENCINO	CA	91316	U	U	MUSICIAN - "MOONLIGHTING"
JARRELL, TOM	641 FIFTH AVE.	NEW YORK	NY	10022	U	U	NEWS CORRESPONDENT - *20/20*

210

Name	Address	City	State	Zip Code	Resp. Time	Resp. Qual.	Comments
JARVIS, GRAHAM	15351 VIA DE LAS OLAS	PACIFIC PALISADES	CA	90272	A	B	ACTOR
JARVIS, LUCY	171 W. 57TH ST.	NEW YORK	NY	10019	A	D	TELEVISION EXECUTIVE/PRODUCER
JASON, HARVEY	1280 SUNSET PLAZA DR.	LOS ANGELES	CA	90069	U	U	WRITER
JASTROW, TERRY	13201 OLD OAK LN.	LOS ANGELES	CA	90049	A	B	DIRECTOR/PRODUCER
JAY & THE AMERICANS	P.O. BOX 262	CARTARET	NJ	07008	U	U	ROCK GROUP
D. J. JAZZY JEFF & THE FRESH PRINCE	298 ELIZABETH ST. #100	NEW YORK	NY	10012	U	U	RAP GROUP
JEAN, GLORIA (SCHOONOVER)	20309 LEADWELL	WINNETKA	CA	91306	A	B	ACTRESS
JEFFREYS, ANNE	121 S. BENTLEY AVE.	LOS ANGELES	CA	90049	A	C	ACTRESS
JEFRIES, HERB	P.O. BOX C	RIVER EDGE	NJ	07601	U	U	SINGER
JEFRIES, LEONARD	CITY COLLEGE OF N.Y., 138TH AND CONVENT AVE. #4150	NEW YORK	NY	10031	U	U	ACTIVIST
JENKINS, CAROL HEISER	809 LAFAYETTE DR.	AKRON	OH	44303	A	B	SKATER
JENKINS, CAROL MAYO	606 N. LARCHMONT BLVD. #309	LOS ANGELES	CA	90004	U	U	ACTRESS
JENKINS, FERGUSON	P.O. BOX 1202	GUTHRIE	OK	73044	U	U	MEMBER OF THE BASEBALL HALL OF FAME
JENNINGS, PETER	77 W. 66TH ST.	NEW YORK	NY	10023	U	U	NEWS ANCHORMAN
JENS, SALOME	9400 READCREST DR.	BEVERLY HILLS	CA	90210	U	U	ACTRESS
JENSEN, MAREN	8828 WONDERLAND PARK AVE.	LOS ANGELES	CA	90046	U	U	ACTRESS
JERGENS LANGAN, ADELE	32108 VILLAGE 32	CAMARILLO	CA	93010	U	U	ACTRESS
JETER, MICHAEL	4571 N. FIGUEROA #20	LOS ANGELES	CA	90065	U	U	ACTOR - EVENING SHADE
JETT, JOAN	750 SHORE RD.	LONG BEACH	NY	11561	U	U	ROCK GROUP - "I LOVE ROCK & ROLL"
JEWISON, NORMAN	23752 MALIBU RD.	MALIBU	CA	90265	U	U	DIRECTOR/PRODUCER
JILLIAN, ANN	4241 WOODCLIFF RD.	SHERMAN OAKS	CA	91403	U	U	ACTRESS/SINGER - IT'S A LIVING
JIM & JESSE	P.O. BOX 27	GALLATIN	TN	37066	A	B	COUNTRY WESTERN GROUP
JOBIN, ANTONIO CARLOS	233 1/2 E. 48TH ST.	NEW YORK	NY	10017	U	U	GUITARIST/SONGWRITER
JOBS, STEVE	900 CHESAPEAKE DR.	REDWOOD CITY	CA	94063	U	U	COMPUTER EXECUTIVE
JOEL, BILLY	C/O QBQ ENT., 341 MADISON AVE., 14TH FL.	NEW YORK	NY	10017	U	U	SINGER - "PIANO MAN" - **AUTHOR'S CHOICE!** - NICE IN PERSON
JOHANSEN, DAVID	200 W. 58TH ST.	NEW YORK	NY	10019	U	U	ACTOR - SCROOGED
JOHN, ELTON	32 GALENDA RD.	LONDON	ENG	W6 0LT	U	U	SINGER/SONGWRITER
JOHNS, GLYNIS	121 N. SAN VICENTE BLVD.	BEVERLY HILLS	CA	90211	U	U	ACTRESS - GLYNIS
JOHNS, JASPER	225 E. HOUSTON ST.	NEW YORK	NY	10002	U	U	ARTIST
JOHNSON, ANNE-MARIE	2606 IVAN HILL TERR.	LOS ANGELES	CA	90024	U	U	ACTRESS
JOHNSON, ARTE	2725 BOTTLEBRUSH DR.	LOS ANGELES	CA	90077	A	D	ACTOR/COMEDIAN - LAUGH-IN
JOHNSON, DON	C/O ICM, 8942 WILSHIRE BLVD.	BEVERLY HILLS	CA	90211	U	U	ACTOR - MIAMI VICE - **AUTHOR'S CHOICE!**

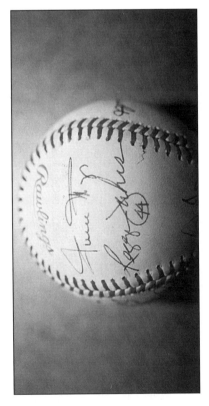

A Jan and Dean response

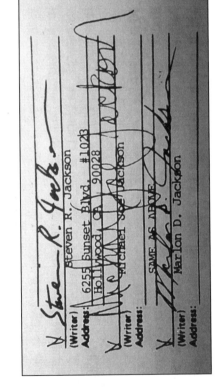

A Michael Jackson signed contract

Willie Mays / Reggie Jackson

Name	Address	City	State	Zip Code	Resp. Time	Resp. Qual.	Comments
JOHNSON, EARVIN "MAGIC"	13100 MULHOLLAND DR.	BEVERLY HILLS	CA	90210	A	D	BASKETBALL PLAYER
JOHNSON, GEORGANN	218 N. GLENROY PL.	LOS ANGELES	CA	90049	C	B	ACTRESS
JOHNSON, KEVIN	2910 N. CENTRAL AVE.	PHOENIX	AZ	85012	A	F	BASKETBALL PLAYER - DOESN'T SIGN "KJ" ANYMORE!
JOHNSON, LAMONT	601 PASEO MIRAMAR	PACIFIC PALISADES	CA	90272	C	C	PRODUCER
JOHNSON, LAURA	1917 WEEPAH	LOS ANGELES	CA	90046	U	U	ACTRESS
JOHNSON, LUCIE BAINES	13809 RESEARCH BLVD. #400	AUSTIN	TX	78750	U	U	DAUGHTER OF MR. & MRS. LYNDON B. JOHNSON
JOHNSON, LYNN-HOLLY	32402 BARKENTINE	LAGUNA NIGUEL	CA	92677	U	U	ACTRESS
JOHNSON, MICHELLE	10351 SANTA MONICA BLVD. #211	LOS ANGELES	CA	90025	U	U	ACTRESS
JOHNSON, MRS. LADY BIRD	LBJ RANCH STONEWALL	AUSTIN	TX	78701	A	F	FORMER FIRST LADY - NO LONGER SIGNS AUTOGRAPHS!
JOHNSON, RAFER	4217 WOODCLIFF RD.	SHERMAN OAKS	CA	91403	U	U	ATHLETE
JOHNSON, RUSSELL	6310 SAN VICENTE BLVD. #407	LOS ANGELES	CA	90048	A	D	ACTOR
JOHNSON, VAN	405 E. 54TH ST.	NEW YORK	NY	10022	U	U	ACTOR - THE CAINE MUTINY
JOHNSTON BAND, TOM	P.O. BOX 878	SONOMA	CA	95476	U	U	ROCK GROUP
JONES GIRLS, THE	P.O. BOX 6010, DEPT. 761	SHERMAN OAKS	CA	91413	U	U	VOCAL GROUP
JONES, CHRISTOPHER	7936 SANTA MONICA BLVD.	LOS ANGELES	CA	90046	U	U	ACTOR
JONES, CHUCK	P.O.BOX 2319	COSTA MESA	CA	92628	B	B	ANIMATED FILM PRODUCER
JONES, DAVY	P.O. BOX 400	BEAVERTOWN	PA	17813	U	U	SINGER/ACTOR
JONES, DEAN	5055 CASA DR.	TARZANA	CA	91356	A	D	ACTOR - THE SHAGGY D.A.
JONES, GEORGE	48 MUSIC SQUARE E. #300	NASHVILLE	TN	37203	A	B	SINGER/SONGWRITER
JONES, GRACE	P.O. BOX 82	GREAT NECK	NY	10014	U	U	ACTRESS/MODEL - A VIEW TO KILL
JONES, GRANDPA	P.O. BOX 57	MOUNTAIN VIEW	AR	72560	A	A	SINGER/GUITARIST
JONES, HENRY	502 - 9TH ST.	SANTA MONICA	CA	90402	A	B	ACTOR
JONES, JAMES EARL	P.O. BOX 55337	SHERMAN OAKS	CA	91413	B	F	ACTOR - SENDS FACSIMILE SIGNED PHOTO!
JONES, JANET	14135 BERESFORD DR.	BEVERLY HILLS	CA	90210	U	U	ACTRESS
JONES, JENNY	454 N. COLUMBUS DR.	CHICAGO	IL	60611	U	U	TALK SHOW HOST
JONES, JESUE	193 JORALEMON ST. #300	BROOKLYN	NY	11201	U	U	SINGER
JONES, L.Q.	2144 1/2 N. CAHUENGA BLVD.	LOS ANGELES	CA	90068	B	B+	ACTOR/DIRECTOR
JONES, MARCIA MAE	4541 HAZELTINE AVE. #4	SHERMAN OAKS	CA	91423	A	B	ACTRESS
JONES, PARNELLI	20550 EARL ST.	TORRANCE	CA	90503	A	D	AUTO RACER
JONES, QUINCY	C/O WILLIAM MORRIS AGCY., 151 EL CAMINO DR.	BEVERLY HILLS	CA	90212	U	U	PRODUCER/COMPOSER - **AUTHOR'S CHOICE!**
JONES, SHIRLEY	701 N. OAKHURST DR.	BEVERLY HILLS	CA	90210	B	B	ACTRESS - THE PARTRIDGE FAMILY
JONES, TOM	363 COPA DE ORO DR.	LOS ANGELES	CA	90077	A	B	SINGER - SIGNED PHOTO IN SILVER INK!

Jesse Jackson

JOHN JAKES

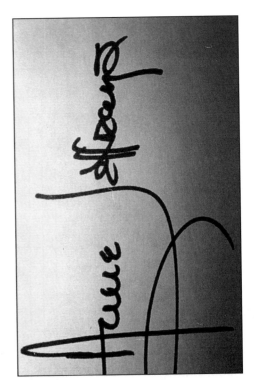

John Jakes

Anne Jeffreys

214

Name	Address	City	State	Zip Code	Resp. Time	Resp. Qual.	Comments
JONES, TOMMY LEE	P.O. BOX 966	SAN SABA	TX	76877	U	U	ACTOR - *THE FUGITIVE* - **AUTHOR'S CHOICE!** - A TOUGH SIGNATURE!
JONES-SIMON, JENNIFER	264 N. GLENROY AVE.	LOS ANGELES	CA	90077	U	U	ACTRESS - *THE SONG OF BERNADETTE*
JONG, ERICA	121 DAVIS HILLS RD.	WESTON	CT	06883	U	U	AUTHOR/POET
JORDAN, HAMILTON	333 MAIN AVE. W.	NASHVILLE	TN	37902	A	F	FORMER GOVERNMENT OFFICIAL - RETURNS ITEMS UNSIGNED
JORDAN, JAMES CARROLL	8333 LOOKOUT MOUNTAIN AVE.	LOS ANGELES	CA	90046	U	U	ACTOR
JORDAN, LEE ROY	2425 BURBANK	DALLAS	TX	75235	A	B	FOOTBALL PLAYER
JORDAN, MICHAEL	980 N. MICHIGAN AVE. #1600	CHICAGO	IL	60611	B	F	BASKETBALL PLAYER - HIS "AIRNESS" - RESPONDS WITH NICE NIKE PAMPHLET, BUT NO AUTOGRAPHS - **AUTHOR'S CHOICE!**
JORDAN, STANLEY	9000 SUNSET BLVD. #1200	LOS ANGELES	CA	90069	U	U	GUITARIST
JORDAN, VERNON E. JR.	1333 NEW HAMPSHIRE AVE. N.W. #400	WASHINGTON	DC	20036	A	B	POLITICIAN
JORDAN, WILL	435 W. 57TH ST. #10-F	NEW YORK	NY	10019	A	F	COMEDIAN - SENDS BACK ITEMS AND ASKS, "WHERE DID YOU GET MY ADDRESS?" - NO AUTOGRAPHS HERE!
JOSEPH, JACKIE	111 N. VALLEY	BURBANK	CA	91505	U	U	ACTRESS/WRITER
JOURDAN, LOUIS	1139 MAYBROOK	BEVERLY HILLS	CA	90210	U	U	ACTOR
JOVOVICH, MILLA	933 N. LA BREA AVE.	LOS ANGELES	CA	90038	U	U	MODEL/ACTRESS
JOYCE, ELAINE	724 N. ROXBURY DR.	BEVERLY HILLS	CA	90210	A	B	ACTRESS - INCLUDES FAN CLUB INFO!
JOYNER-KERSEE, JACKIE	20214 LEADWELL	CANOGA PARK	CA	91304	A	D	TRACK/FIELD ATHLETE
JUDD, NAOMI	P.O. BOX 17087	NASHVILLE	TN	37217	C	D	SINGER - MOTHER OF WYNONNA - THE JUDDS - WATCH FOR AUTOPENS!
JUDD, WYNONNA	P.O. BOX 17087	NASHVILLE	TN	37217	U	U	SINGER - THE JUDDS - **AUTHOR'S CHOICE!** - WATCH FOR AUTOPENS!
JUMP, GORDON	1631 HILLCREST	GLENDALE	CA	91202	U	U	ACTOR - *WKRP IN CINCINNATI*
JURGENSEN, SONNY	P.O. BOX 53	MT. VERNON	VA	22121	A	D	MEMBER OF THE FOOTBALL HALL OF FAME
JUSTICE, CHARLIE	P.O. BOX 819	CHERRYVILLE	NC	28021	A	D	VIOLINIST - INCLUDES NOTE THAT HE DOESN'T CHARGE FOR HIS AUTOGRAPH
JUSTICE, DAVID	C/O ATLANTA BRAVES, P.O. BOX 4064	ATLANTA	GA	30302	U	U	BASEBALL PLAYER
KAEL, PAULINE	2 BERKSHIRE HEIGHTS RD.	GREAT BARRINGTON	MA	02130	U	U	FILM CRITIC/AUTHOR
KAELIN, BRIAN "KATO"	360 ROCKINGHAM AVE.	BRENTWOOD	CA	94513	U	U	FAMOUS HOUSEGUEST
KAGEN, DAVID	6457 FIRMAMENT AVE.	VAN NUYS	CA	91406	U	U	ACTOR
KAHN, MADELINE	975 PARK AVE. #9A	NEW YORK	NY	10028	A	D	ACTRESS/SINGER - *BLAZING SADDLES*
KALB, MARVIN	79 JOHN F. KENNEDY ST.	CAMBRIDGE	MA	01238	A	F	JOURNALIST - DOES NOT HONOR REQUESTS - SAVE YOUR STAMPS!

Magic Johnson

The Judds (autopen samples)

216

Name	Address	City	State	Zip Code	Resp. Time	Resp. Qual.	Comments
KALEMBER, PATRICIA	P.O. BOX 5617	BEVERLY HILLS	CA	90210	U	U	ACTRESS
KALINE, AL	945 TIMBERLAKE DR.	BLOOMFIELD HILLS	MI	48013	U	U	MEMBER OF THE BASEBALL HALL OF FAME
KALLIANIDES, HELENA	12830 MULHOLLAND DR.	BEVERLY HILLS	CA	90210	U	U	ACTRESS/WRITER/DIRECTOR
KALMBACH, HERBERT	1056 SANTIAGO DR.	NEWPORT BEACH	CA	92660	A	D	WATERGATE CO-CONSPIRATOR
KAMEL, STANLEY	9300 WILSHIRE BLVD. #410	BEVERLY HILLS	CA	90210	U	U	ACTOR
KANALY, STEVEN	828 FOOTHILL LN.	OJAI	CA	93023	A	B+	ACTOR
KANE, BIG DADDY	151 EL CAMINO DR.	BEVERLY HILLS	CA	90212	U	U	RAP SINGER - "LONG LIVE THE KANE"
KANE, BOB	8455 FOUNTAIN AVE. #725	LOS ANGELES	CA	90069	U	U	CARTOONIST
KANE, CAROL	1416 N. HAVENHURST #1-C	LOS ANGELES	CA	90046	U	U	ACTRESS - TAXI
KANIN, FAY	653 OCEAN FRONT	SANTA MONICA	CA	90402	U	U	SCREENWRITER
KANIN, GARSON	210 CENTRAL PARK S.	NEW YORK	NY	10019	U	U	WRITER/PRODUCER
KANN, STAN	570 N. ROSSMORE AVE.	LOS ANGELES	CA	90004	A	B	ACTOR
KANTER, HAL	15941 WOODVALE RD.	ENCINO	CA	91316	A	D	WRITER/PRODUCER
KANTER, MICKEY	600 - 17TH ST. N.W.	WASHINGTON	DC	20506	U	U	U.S. TRADE REPRESENTATIVE
KAPLAN, GABRIEL	9551 HIDDEN VALLEY RD.	BEVERLY HILLS	CA	90210	U	U	COMEDIAN/ACTOR - WELCOME BACK, KOTTER
KAPLAN, MARVIN	7600 CLAYBECK AVE.	BURBANK	CA	91505	U	U	ACTOR
KARAN, DONNA	DONNA KARAN CO., 550 7TH AVE.	NEW YORK	NY	10018	U	U	FASHION DESIGNER - **AUTHOR'S CHOICE!**
KAREN, JAMES	4455 LOS FELIZ BLVD. #807	LOS ANGELES	CA	90027	A	B	ACTOR
KARENGA, MAULANA	AFRICAN AMERICAN STUDIES, 1250 BELLFLOWER BLVD.	LONG BEACH	CA	90840	U	U	ACTIVIST
KARLEN, JOHN	911 - 2ND ST. #16	SANTA MONICA	CA	90403	U	U	ACTOR
KAROLYI, BELA	17203 BAMWOOD	HOUSTON	TX	77090	A	B	GYMNAST COACH
KARRAS, ALEX	7943 WOODROW WILSON DR.	LOS ANGELES	CA	90046	U	U	FOOTBALL PLAYER/ACTOR - WEBSTER
KARSH, YOUSUF	CHATEAU LAURIER	OTTAWA, ONTARIO	CAN	K1N 8S7	A	D	PHOTOGRAPHER - **AUTHOR'S CHOICE!** - A LIVING LEGEND!
KASDAN, LAWRENCE	10345 W. OLYMPIC BLVD.	LOS ANGELES	CA	90064	U	U	DIRECTOR/PRODUCER
KASEM, CASEY	138 N. MAPLETON DR.	LOS ANGELES	CA	90077	B	B+	RADIO/TELEVISION PERSONALITY
KASEM, JEAN	138 N. MAPLETON DR.	LOS ANGELES	CA	90077	A	B	ACTRESS - CHEERS
KASSIR, JOHN	7474 HILLSIDE DR.	LOS ANGELES	CA	90046	U	U	COMEDIAN
KASSORLA, DR. IRENE	10231 CHARING CROSS RD.	LOS ANGELES	CA	90024	A	B	PSYCHOLOGIST/AUTHOR
KATT, WILLIAM	10000 SANTA MONICA BLVD. #305	LOS ANGELES	CA	90067	U	U	ACTOR - THE GREATEST AMERICAN HERO!
KATZENBERG, JEFF	C/O DREAMWORKS SKG, 100 UNIVERSAL CITY PLAZA	UNIVERSAL CITY	CA	91608	U	U	STUDIO EXECUTIVE - CO-OWNER OF "DIVE" WITH SPIELBERG - **AUTHOR'S CHOICE!**
KAUFMAN, WENDY	C/O SNAPPLE, INC., 175 N. CENTRAL AVE.	VALLEY STREAM	NY	11580	U	U	SPOKESPERSON FOR SNAPPLE!
KAVNER, JULIE	25154 MALIBU RD. #2	MALIBU	CA	90265	U	U	ACTRESS - RHODA, THE SIMPSONS

Ted Kennedy

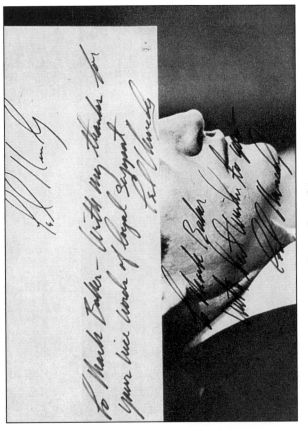

Ted Kennedy's signature throughout his career

Name	Address	City	State	Zip Code	Resp. Time	Resp. Qual.	Comments
KAY, DIANNE	1559 PALISADES DR.	PACIFIC PALISADES	CA	90272	U	U	ACTRESS
KAYE, CAREN	217-16TH ST.	SANTA MONICA	CA	90402	U	U	ACTRESS
KAYE, MELVINA	P.O. BOX 6085	BURBANK	CA	90510	A	B	SINGER
KAZAN, ELIA	174 E. 95TH ST.	NEW YORK	NY	10128	A	D	DIRECTOR/PRODUCER
KAZAN, LAINIE	9903 SANTA MONICA BLVD. #283	BEVERLY HILLS	CA	90212	U	U	SINGER/ACTRESS
KEACH, JAMES	P.O. BOX 548	AGOURA	CA	91376	U	U	ACTOR
KEACH, STACY JR.	27525 WINDING WAY	MALIBU	CA	90265	A	D	ACTOR - MIKE HAMMER
KEACH, STACY SR.	3969 LONGRIDGE AVE.	SHERMAN OAKS	CA	91423	A	C	ACTOR
KEAN, JANE	28128 W. PACIFIC COAST HWY.	MALIBU	CA	90265	U	U	ACTRESS
KEANE, JAMES	10206 CAMARILLO PL. #6	NORTH HOLLYWOOD	CA	91602	U	U	ACTOR
KEATING, CHARLES	#H32037, CA. MEN'S COLONY, P.O. BOX 8101	SAN LUIS OBISPO	CA	93409	U	U	CONVICTED OF S&L CRISIS!
KEATON, DIANE	2255 VERDE OAK DR.	LOS ANGELES	CA	90068	U	U	ACTRESS/DIRECTOR - FATHER OF THE BRIDE
KEATON, MICHAEL	10866 WILSHIRE BLVD. 10TH FL.	LOS ANGELES	CA	90024	U	U	ACTOR - BATMAN
KEEFER, DON	4146 ALLOT AVE.	SHERMAN OAKS	CA	91403	A	B	ACTOR
KEEGAN, ANDREW	P.O. BOX 1633	SUN VALLEY	CA	91352	U	U	ACTOR
KEEL, HOWARD	15353 LONGBOW DR.	SHERMAN OAKS	CA	91403	A	F	ACTOR/SINGER - DALLAS - SENDS A FLYER ONLY! WHAT? HELLO THERE, ANYBODY HOME?
KEESHAN, BOB (CAPT. KANGAROO)	40 W. 57TH ST. #1600	NEW YORK	NY	10019	U	U	CHILDREN'S TELEVISION SHOW HOST - **AUTHOR'S CHOICE!**
KEILLOR, GARRISON	300 CENTRAL PARK W.	NEW YORK	NY	10024	B	B	AUTHOR/RADIO PERSONALITY - PRAIRIE HOME COMPANION - **AUTHOR'S CHOICE!**
KEIM, BETTY LOU	10642 ARNEL PL.	CHATSWORTH	CA	91311	U	U	ACTRESS
KEITEL, HARVEY	110 HUDSON ST. #9A	NEW YORK	NY	10013	U	U	ACTOR - BAD LIEUTENANT - **AUTHOR'S CHOICE!**
KEITH, BRIAN	23449 MALIBU COLONY RD.	MALIBU	CA	90265	U	U	ACTOR - FAMILY AFFAIR
KEITH, DAVID	8221 SUNSET BLVD.	LOS ANGELES	CA	90069	U	U	ACTOR - AN OFFICER AND A GENTLEMAN
KELL, GEORGE	WDIV-TV, 550 W. LAFAYETTE	DETROIT	MI	48226	U	U	MEMBER OF THE BASEBALL HALL OF FAME
KELLER, MARY PAGE	151 EL CAMINO DR.	BEVERLY HILLS	CA	90212	U	U	ACTRESS
KELLERMAN, SALLY	7944 WOODROW WILSON DR.	LOS ANGELES	CA	90046	U	U	ACTRESS - M*A*S*H
KELLEY, KITTY	3929 HIGHWOOD COURT N.W.	WASHINGTON	DC	20007	U	U	AUTHOR/UNAUTHORIZED BIOGRAPHER
KELLEY, JIM	C/O BUFFALO BILLS, 1 BILLS DR.	ORCHARD PARK	NY	14127	C	F	FOOTBALL PLAYER - YOU SEND THEM AND JIM WILL STAMP THEM!
KELLY, PAULA	1801 AVE. OF STARS #1250	LOS ANGELES	CA	90067	U	U	ACTRESS/DANCER
KELLY, ROZ	5614 LEMP AVE.	NORTH HOLLYWOOD	CA	91601	U	U	ACTRESS
KEMMER, ED	11 RIVERSIDE DR. #17PE	NEW YORK	NY	10022	A	A	ACTOR

Andrea King

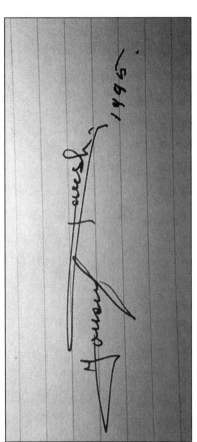

Madeline Kahn

Yousuf Karsh

220

Name	Address	City	State	Zip Code	Resp. Time	Resp. Qual.	Comments
KEMP, JACK	1776 "I" ST. N.W. #800	WASHINGTON	DC	20006	A	D	POLITICIAN/FORMER FOOTBALL PLAYER - WATCH FOR AUTOPEN SIGNATURES!
KENNEDY SCHLOSSEBERG, CAROLINE	888 PARK AVE.	NEW YORK	NY	10021	F	F	JFK'S DAUGHTER - UNRESPONSIVE TO FAN MAIL!
KENNEDY, ADAMS	P.O. BOX 679	KENT	CT	06757	A	D	SCREENWRITER
KENNEDY, ANTHONY	1 - 1ST ST. N.E.	WASHINGTON	DC	20543	U	U	SUPREME COURT JUSTICE
KENNEDY, BURT	13138 MAGNOLIA BLVD.	SHERMAN OAKS	CA	91423	U	U	FILM WRITER/DIRECTOR
KENNEDY, ETHEL	1147 CHAIN BRIDGE RD.	MCLEAN	VA	22101	U	U	WIDOW OF ROBERT KENNEDY
KENNEDY, GEORGE	10100 SANTA MONICA BLVD. #2500	LOS ANGELES	CA	90067	B	F	ACTOR - COOL HAND LUKE - ANOTHER STUDIO FAN MAIL VICTIM - SENDS OUT FACSIMILE SIGNED PHOTO!
KENNEDY, JOAN	SQUAW ISLAND	HYANNISPORT	MA	02647	A	B	TED KENNEDY'S EX-WIFE
KENNEDY, JOHN F. JR.	1041 FIFTH AVE.	NEW YORK	NY	10028	F	F	JFK'S SON, MAGAZINE PUBLISHER - GEORGE - AUTHOR'S CHOICE! - UNRESPONSIVE TO FAN MAIL!
KENNEDY, JOSEPH II	1210 LONGWORTH HOUSE BLDG.	WASHINGTON	DC	20510	A	C	POLITICIAN
KENNEDY, MIMI	151 EL CAMINO DR.	BEVERLY HILLS	CA	90212	U	U	ACTRESS
KENNEDY, ROBERT F. JR.	78 N. BROADWAY	WHITE PLAINS	NY	10603	A	B+	ROBERT KENNEDY'S SON
KENNEDY, SEN. EDWARD	315 RUSSELL OFFICE BLDG.	WASHINGTON	DC	20510	A	B	POLITICIAN - TRADITIONALLY VERY RESPONSIVE!
KENNEDY, TED JR.	636 CHAIN BRIDGE RD.	MCLEAN	VA	22101	U	U	SEN. TED KENNEDY'S SON
KENNEDY-OVERTON, JAYNE	230 SUNRIDGE ST.	PLAYA DEL REY	CA	90293	U	U	ACTRESS/MODEL
KEPLER, SHELL	3123 BELDEN DR.	LOS ANGELES	CA	90068	C	B	ACTRESS
KERNS, JOANNA	P.O. BOX 49216	LOS ANGELES	CA	90049	A	F	ACTRESS - GROWING PAINS - SENDS OUT FACSIMILE SIGNED PHOTO!
KERNS, SANDRA	620 RESOLANO DR.	PACIFIC PALISADES	CA	90272	U	U	ACTRESS
KERR, DEBORAH	LOS MONTERAS, E-29600 MARBELLA	MALAGA	SPA		U	U	ACTRESS - AN AFFAIR TO REMEMBER
KERR, JEAN	1 BEACH AVE.	LARCHMONT	NY	10538	U	U	DRAMATIST
KERRIGAN, LINDA	9812 W. OLYMPIC BLVD.	BEVERLY HILLS	CA	90212	A	B	ACTRESS/MODEL
KERRIGAN, NANCY	1101 WILSON BLVD. #1800	ARLINGTON	VA	22209	A	B	ICE SKATER
KERRY, SEN. JOHN	SENATE RUSSELL BLDG. #421	WASHINGTON	DC	20510	A	D	POLITICIAN
KERSEE , JACKIE JOYNER-	20214 LEADWELL	CANOGA PARK	CA	91304	U	U	ATHLETE
KETCHAM, HANK	P.O. BOX 800	PEBBLE BEACH	CA	93953	A	B+	CARTOONIST - TYPICALLY ADDS A SKETCH!
KEVORKIAN, DR. JACK	4870 LOCKHART ST.	W. BLOOMFIELD	MI	48323	F	F	PHYSICIAN - ASSISTED SUICIDE ADVOCATE
KEY, TED	1694 GLENHARDIE RD.	WAYNE	PA	19087	A	C	CARTOONIST
KEYES, EVELYN	999 N. DOHENY DR. #509	LOS ANGELES	CA	90069	A	B	ACTRESS
KEYLOUN, MARK	3500 W. OLIVE AVE. #1400	BURBANK	CA	91505	U	U	ACTOR

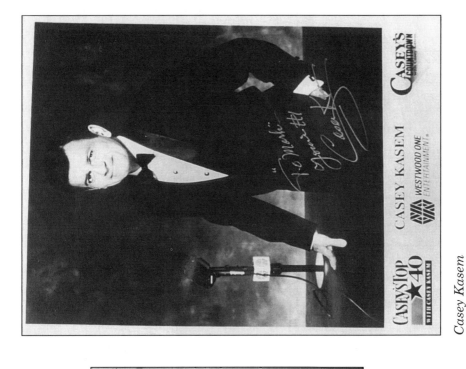

Casey Kasem

Stephen King does not send out autographed pictures (he feel that is for movie stars, not authors) and because of the tremendous increase in requests for autographs over the last couple of years, he has been forced to limit requests to books only.

The policy at this time is that Stephen will sign no more th two books per fan provided they are sent with a stamped retu mailer. Your book/s and mailer should be sent to: 49 Flori Avenue, Bangor, ME 04401-3005.

He also personalizes all books he signs, so be sure to inclu the name of the person you want the book/s inscribed to.

Sincerely,

Juliann Eugley
Assistant to Stephen King

A Stephen King response

Name	Address	City	State	Zip Code	Resp. Time	Resp. Qual.	Comments
KHAMBATTA, PERSIS	P.O. BOX 46539	LOS ANGELES	CA	90046	U	U	ACTRESS/MODEL
KHAN, CHAKA	P.O. BOX 16680	BEVERLY HILLS	CA	90209	A	D	SINGER - "RUFUS"
KHAN, PRINCESS YASMIN	146 CENTRAL PARK W.	NEW YORK	NY	10023	U	U	ROYALTY
KIAM, VICTOR II	60 MAIN ST.	BRIDGEPORT	CT	06602	A	B	EXECUTIVE - BUYS COMPANY IF HE LIKES THE PRODUCT!
KIBRICK, SIDNEY	711 N. OAKHURST DR.	BEVERLY HILLS	CA	90210	A	A	ACTOR
KIDD, BILLY	P.O. BOX 803291	SANTA CLARITA	CA	91380	U	U	SKIER
KIDMAN, NICOLE	12725-H VENTURA BLVD.	STUDIO CITY	CA	91604	U	U	ACTRESS - *BATMAN FOREVER* - **AUTHOR'S CHOICE!** - MARRIED TO TOM CRUISE!
KIEDIA, ANTHONY	WARNER BROTHERS RECORDING, 3300 WARNER BLVD.	BURBANK	CA	91505	U	U	SINGER - RED HOT CHILI PEPPERS - **AUTHOR'S CHOICE!**
KIEL, RICHARD	40356-T OAK PKWY.	OAKHURST	CA	93644	U	U	ACTOR - *THE SPY WHO LOVED ME*
KIFF, KALEENA	1800 N. VINE ST. #120	LOS ANGELES	CA	90028	A	C	ACTRESS
KILBURN, TERRY	OBERLAND UNIVERSITY, WALTON & SQUIRREL	ROCHESTER	MI	48063	U	U	ACTOR/TEACHER
KILEY, RICHARD	RYERSON RD.	WARWICK	NY	10990	A	B+	ACTOR
KILGORE, MERLE	P.O. BOX 850	PARIS	TN	38242	A	B	SINGER/SONGWRITER
KILLEBREW, HARMON	P.O. BOX 14550	SCOTTSDALE	AZ	85267	U	U	MEMBER OF THE BASEBALL HALL OF FAME
KILMER, VAL	P.O. BOX 362	TESUQUE	NM	87574	U	U	ACTOR - *BATMAN FOREVER* - **AUTHOR'S CHOICE!** - GOOD IN PERSON!
KILPATRICK, ERIC	6330 SIMPSON AVE. #3	NORTH HOLLYWOOD	CA	91606	U	U	ACTOR
KILPATRICK, JAMES L.	WHITE WALNUT HILL	WOODVILLE	VA	22749	U	U	JOURNALIST/COLUMNIST
KIMBALL, WARD	8910 ARDENDALE AVE.	SAN GABRIEL	CA	91775	C	D	ANIMATION DIRECTOR
KIMMEL, BRUCE	12230 OTSEGO ST.	NORTH HOLLYWOOD	CA	91607	U	U	WRITER/DIRECTOR
KINCAID, AARON	12307-C VENTURA BLVD.	NORTH HOLLYWOOD	CA	91601	U	U	ACTOR
KIND, ROSLYN	8871 BURTON WAY #303	LOS ANGELES	CA	90048	U	U	ACTRESS
KING CONLON, CAMMIE	511 CYPRESS ST. #2	FT. BRAGG	CA	95437	A	B	ACTRESS
KING, ALAN	888 - 7TH AVE., 38TH FL.	NEW YORK	NY	10106	U	U	COMEDIAN/ACTOR - *THE ANDERSON TAPES*
KING, ANDREA	1225 SUNSET PLAZA DR. #3	LOS ANGELES	CA	90069	A	A+	ACTRESS - VERY RESPONSIVE TO FAN MAIL!
KING, B.B.	P.O. BOX 4396	LAS VEGAS	NV	89107	C	D	SINGER/GUITARIST
KING, BEN E.	1301 PRINCETON RD.	TEANECK	NJ	07666	A	B+	SINGER/SONGWRITER - *THE DRIFTERS* - **AUTHOR'S CHOICE!**
KING, CORETTA SCOTT	234 SUNSET AVE. N.W.	ATLANTA	GA	30314	U	U	MRS. MARTIN LUTHER KING JR.
KING, DON	968 PINEHURST DR.	LAS VEGAS	NV	89109	C	D	FIGHT PROMOTER
KING, LARRY	111 MASSACHUSETTS AVE. N.W. SUITE #300	WASHINGTON	DC	20001	A	D	RADIO/TELEVISION INTERVIEWER - **AUTHOR'S CHOICE!** (MAYBE THIS WILL GET ME ON HIS SHOW!)

223

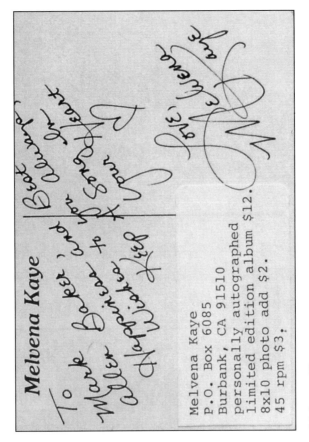

Melvena Kaye

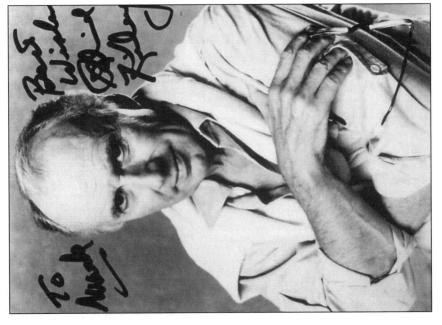

Richard Kiley

Name	Address	City	State	Zip Code	Resp. Time	Resp. Qual.	Comments
KING, PERRY	3647 WRIGHTWOOD DR.	STUDIO CITY	CA	91604	C	D	ACTOR - *RIPTIDE*
KING, REGINA	3814 DUNFORD LN.	INGLEWOOD	CA	90305	A	B	ACTRESS
KING, RODNEY	9100 WILSHIRE BLVD. #250-W	BEVERLY HILLS	CA	90212	U	U	BEATEN MOTORIST
KING, STEPHEN	47 W. BROADWAY	BANGOR	ME	04401	A	F	NOVELIST - *CUJO* - EVERY TIME I WRITE TO HIM HE HAS A DIFFERENT AUTOGRAPH POLICY - **AUTHOR'S CHOICE!**
KING, ZALMAN	1393 ROSE AVE.	VENICE	CA	90291	A	B	WRITER
KINGDOM, ROGER	322 MALL BLVD. #303	MONROEVILLE	PA	15146	U	U	TRACK ATHLETE
KINGSLEY, BEN	STRATFORD UPON AVON, NEW PENWORTH HOUSE	WARWICKSHIRE	ENG	OV3 7QX	U	U	ACTOR - *GANDHI*
KINGSMEN, THE	P.O. BOX 2622	ASHEVILLE	NC	28801	U	U	VOCAL GROUP
KINGSTON TRIO, THE	P.O. BOX 34397	SAN DIEGO	CA	92103	A	A	VOCAL TRIO- ALL THREE WILL SIGN FOR YOU!
KINMONT, KATHLEEN	641 MARIPOSA DR.	BURBANK	CA	91506	A	A+	ACTRESS - OUTSTANDING RESPONSE TO FAN MAIL!
KINSKI, NASTASSJA	11 W. 81ST ST.	NEW YORK	NY	10024	U	U	ACTRESS/MODEL - *TESS*
KIRBY, DURWARD	RT. 37, BOX 374	SHERMAN	CT	06784	U	U	SCREENWRITER
KIRK, PHYLLIS	321-M S. BEVERLY DR.	BEVERLY HILLS	CA	90212	U	U	ACTRESS
KIRKCONNELL, CLARE	515 S. IRVING BLVD.	LOS ANGELES	CA	90020	U	U	ACTRESS
KIRKLAND, LANE	815 - 16TH ST. N.W.	WASHINGTON	DC	20006	B	B	UNION EXECUTIVE
KIRKLAND, SALLY	1284 N. HAVENHURST #209	LOS ANGELES	CA	90046	U	U	ACTRESS - *ANNA*
KISS	6363 SUNSET BLVD. #417	LOS ANGELES	CA	90028	U	U	ROCK GROUP
KISSINGER, DR. HENRY	435 E. 52ND ST.	NEW YORK	NY	10022	U	U	FORMER SECRETARY OF STATE - A TOUGH SIGNATURE!
KITAEN, TAWNY	P.O. BOX 16693	BEVERLY HILLS	CA	90209	U	U	ACTRESS
KITT, EARTHA	1524 LABAIG AVE.	LOS ANGELES	CA	90028	U	U	SINGER/ACTRESS - *THE MARK OF THE HAWK*
KLAMMER, FRANZ	MOOSWALD 22	A-9712 FRIESACH	AUS		U	U	SKIER
KLEIN, CALVIN	205 W. 39TH ST.	NEW YORK	NY	10018	A	B	FASHION DESIGNER - **AUTHOR'S CHOICE!**
KLEMPERER, WERNER	44 W. 62ND ST., 10TH FL.	NEW YORK	NY	10023	C	D	ACTOR - *HOGAN'S HEROES*
KLINE, KEVIN	9830 WILSHIRE BLVD.	BEVERLY HILLS	CA	90212	U	U	ACTOR - *THE BIG CHILL*
KLINE, ROBERT	14322 MULHOLLAND DR.	LOS ANGELES	CA	90067	A	B	COMEDIAN
KLOUS, PATRICIA	18095 KAREN DR.	ENCINO	CA	91316	U	U	ACTRESS
KLUGMAN, JACK	22548 PACIFIC COAST HWY #8	MALIBU	CA	90265	C	C	ACTOR/WRITER - *THE ODD COUPLE*
KNIGHT, CHRISTOPHER	7738 CHANDELLE PL.	LOS ANGELES	CA	90046	U	U	ACTOR
KNIGHT, HOLLY	1299 OCEAN AVE. SUITE 316	SANTA MONICA	CA	90401	U	U	SINGER/SONGWRITER
KNIGHT, MICHAEL E.	10100 SANTA MONICA BLVD. #2500	LOS ANGELES	CA	90067	U	U	ACTOR - *ALL MY CHILDREN*
KNIGHT, SHIRLEY	2130 N. BEACHWOOD DR. #8	LOS ANGELES	CA	90068	U	U	ACTRESS - *THE DARK AT THE TOP OF THE STAIRS*

Kathleen Kinmont

DEAN KOONTZ

Although mail from readers has for some time averaged 10,000 letters annually, I was able until recently to answer everyone with at least a few handwritten lines. Volume is increasingly weekly, however, and I've finally had to admit that I'm overwhelmed. I'm also on an unusual number of book and screenplay deadlines. For a while, therefore, a personal response isn't going to be possible, unless I clone myself. Cloning myself would not be a good idea, of course, because any clone would turn out to be my evil twin, and the last thing I want is to find myself living in a Koontz novel!

For those of you seeking information for high school, college, and postgraduate papers that you're writing about my novels, please see the reference to THE DEAN KOONTZ COMPANION on page four of the enclosed flyer. It is currently the best source for background. In fact, it will tell you more about me than any sane person could want to know. Your library probably has it; your bookstore can order it for you; or it can be ordered directly from Berkley Books.

As for THE BOOK OF COUNTED SORROWS: I will collect all the poetry I've written for it and publish the volume in late 1996 or the spring of 1997. I'm amazed and delighted by your strong response to those verses.

As for the poem about Santa's bad-boy brother in MR. MURDER: After receiving thousands of requests to finish the poem and publish it as a gift book, I have decided to do so. Phil Parks, the artist who worked with me on ODDKINS, is creating twenty beautiful full-color illustrations, and we hope to have the book in stores for Christmas of 1996.

For other news, please see pages 4 and 5 of the enclosed flyer.

Though I'm no longer able to give a personal answer to everyone, I still read EVERY letter that I receive, and I enjoy your comments, pro or con. Your correspondence is often humorous, sometimes touching, and unfailingly interesting. It's gratifying that the people who read my books are so intelligent and perceptive.

And, yes, I loathed the movie version of HIDEAWAY and fought the studio for months in an attempt to get my name removed and the title changed. See page 4 of the enclosed flyer for movie news.

Now remember: Something's out there. It's really hungry. Try not to look like food!

Dean Koontz

Post Office Box 9529, Newport Beach, California 92658-9529

Dean Koontz

Name	Address	City	State	Zip Code	Resp. Time	Resp. Qual.	Comments
KNOTTS, DON	1854 S. BEVERLY GLEN #402	LOS ANGELES	CA	90025	U	U	ACTOR - *THE ANDY GRIFFITH SHOW*
KNOWLES, PATRIC	6243 RANDI AVE.	WOODLAND HILLS	CA	91367	U	U	ACTOR - *HOW GREEN WAS MY VALLEY*
KNOX, TERENCE	1440 S. SEPULVEDA BLVD. #200	LOS ANGELES	CA	90025	U	U	ACTOR
KNOX-HARMON, ELYSE	320 N. GUNSTON	LOS ANGELES	CA	90049	A	B	ACTRESS
KOCH, EDWARD I.	1290 AVE. OF THE AMERICAS, 30TH FL.	NEW YORK	NY	10104	A	B	FORMER MAYOR
KOENIG, WALTER	P.O. BOX 4395	NORTH HOLLYWOOD	CA	91607	U	U	ACTOR/WRITER - *STAR TREK*
KOHNER, SUSAN	710 MARK AVE. #14-E	NEW YORK	NY	10021	A	C	ACTRESS
KOMACK, JAMES	617 N. BEVERLY DR.	BEVERLY HILLS	CA	90210	A	B	ACTOR/WRITER/DIRECTOR
KONRAD, DOROTHY	10650 MISSOURI AVE. #2	LOS ANGELES	CA	90025	C	B	ACTRESS
KOOL MOE DEE	151 EL CAMINO DR.	BEVERLY HILLS	CA	90212	A	C	RAP SINGER
KOONTZ, DEAN R.	200 MADISON AVE.	NEW YORK	NY	10016	A	B+	WRITER
KOPEL, BERNIE	19413 OLIVOS	TARZANA	CA	91356	A	D	ACTOR/WRITER - *THE LOVE BOAT*
KOPPEL, TED	1717 DESALES N.W. #300	WASHINGTON	DC	20036	U	U	BROADCAST JOURNALIST - *NIGHTLINE* - **AUTHOR'S CHOICE!**
KORMAN, HARVEY	1136 STRADELLA	LOS ANGELES	CA	90077	U	U	ACTOR/DIRECTOR - *THE CAROL BURNETT SHOW*
KOSLECK, MARTIN	1026 N. LAUREL AVE.	LOS ANGELES	CA	90046	U	U	ACTOR
KOTTO, YAPHET	1930 CENTURY PARK W. #303	LOS ANGELES	CA	90067	U	U	ACTOR - *LIVE AND LET DIE*
KOUFAX, SANDY	2327 W. LINCOLN AVE.	ANAHEIM	CA	92801	U	U	MEMBER OF THE BASEBALL HALL OF FAME - VERY RECLUSIVE!
KOZAK, HARLEY JANE	8730 SUNSET BLVD. #480	LOS ANGELES	CA	90069	U	U	ACTOR
KRAGEN, KEN	240 BARODA	LOS ANGELES	CA	90077	A	D	TALENT AGENT
KRAMER, JACK	231 N. GLENROY PL.	LOS ANGELES	CA	90049	C	B	TENNIS PLAYER
KRAMER, STEPHANIE	8455 BEVERLY BLVD. #505	LOS ANGELES	CA	90048	U	U	ACTRESS/DIRECTOR
KRANTZ, JUDITH	166 GROVERTON PL.	LOS ANGELES	CA	90077	U	U	AUTHOR - *SCRUPLES*
KRAVITZ, LENNY	UPTOWN STATION, P.O. BOX 3340	HOBOKEN	NJ	07030	U	U	SINGER - "ARE YOU GONNA GO MY WAY?"
KREPPEL, PAUL	14300 KILLION ST.	VAN NUYS	CA	91401	U	U	ACTOR
KRESKIN	P.O. BOX 1383	WEST CALDWELL	NJ	07006	U	U	PSYCHIC
KRIEGER, ROBBIE	2548 HUTTON DR.	BEVERLY HILLS	CA	90210	B	D	MUSICIAN - THE DOORS
KRIGE, ALICE	10816 LINDBROOK DR.	LOS ANGELES	CA	90024	U	U	ACTRESS - *CHARIOTS OF FIRE*
KRIMMER, WORTHAM	1642 REDESDALE AVE.	LOS ANGELES	CA	90026	U	U	ACTOR
KRISTAL, SYLVIA	8955 NORMA PL.	LOS ANGELES	CA	90069	U	U	ACTRESS
KRISTOFFERSON, KRIS	P.O. BOX 2147	MALIBU	CA	90265	U	U	SINGER/ACTOR/WRITER - *AMERIKA*
KROFFT, MARTY	7710 WOODROW WILSON DR.	LOS ANGELES	CA	90046	U	U	PUPPETEER/PRODUCER
KROFFT, SID	7710 WOODROW WILSON DR.	LOS ANGELES	CA	90046	U	U	PUPPETEER/PRODUCER

Joanna Kerns

Kay Kuter

Name	Address	City	State	Zip Code	Resp. Time	Resp. Qual.	Comments
KROSS, KRIS	9380 S.W. 72ND ST. #B-220	MIAMI	FL	33173	U	U	R&B DUO
KRUGER, HARDY	P.O. BOX 726	CRESTLINE	CA	92325	U	U	ACTOR
KUBRICK, STANLEY	P.O. BOX 123	BOREHAMWOOD, HERTS.	ENG		U	U	FILM DIRECTOR - 2001: A SPACE ODYSSEY
KURALT, CHARLES	119 W. 57TH, PENTHOUSE 1600	NEW YORK	NY	10019	U	U	CORRESPONDENT
KURTZ, SWOOSIE	320 CENTRAL PARK W.	NEW YORK	NY	10025	A	F	ACTRESS - SISTERS - SENDS FACSIMILE SIGNED PHOTO!
KUTER, KAY	6207 SATSUMA AVE.	NORTH HOLLYWOOD	CA	91606	A	A+	ACTOR - VERY RESPONSIVE TO FAN MAIL!
KWAN, NANCY	4154 WOODMAN AVE.	SHERMAN OAKS	CA	91403	U	U	ACTRESS - THE WORLD OF SUZIE WONG
LA PLACA, ALISON	9000 SUNSET BLVD. #1200	LOS ANGELES	CA	90069	U	U	ACTRESS
LA PLANTE ASHER, LAURA	MOTION PICTURE COUNTRY HOME 2338 MULHOLLAND DR.	WOODLAND HILLS	CA	91364	A	B	ACTRESS
LA RUE, FLORENCE	4300 LOUIS AVE.	ENCINO	CA	91316	U	U	SINGER
LABELLE, PATTI (HOLT)	1212 GRENNOX RD.	WYNNEWOOD	PA	19096	C	D	SINGER/ACTRESS
LABORTEAUX, MATTHEW	1050 N. MAPLE	BURBANK	CA	91505	U	U	ACTOR
LADD, ALAN JR.	1010 N. CRESCENT DR.	BEVERLY HILLS	CA	90210	U	U	FILM EXECUTIVE
LADD, CHERYL	P.O. BOX 1329	SANTA YNEZ	CA	93460	A	A+	SINGER/ACTRESS - CHARLIE'S ANGELS - OUTSTANDING!
LADD, DAVID	9212 HAZEN DR.	BEVERLY HILLS	CA	90210	U	U	ACTOR
LADD, DIANE	P.O. BOX 17111	BEVERLY HILLS	CA	90209	U	U	ACTRESS - ALICE DOESN'T LIVE HERE ANYMORE
LADD, MARGARET	444 - 21ST. ST.	SANTA MONICA	CA	90402	A	B	ACTRESS
LAFFER, DR. ARTHUR	P.O. BOX 1167	RANCHO SANTA FE	CA	92067	A	B+	ECONOMIST
LAFFERTY, PERRY	335 S. BRISTOL	LOS ANGELES	CA	90049	U	U	TELEVISION EXECUTIVE
LAFLEUR, GUY	2313 ST. CATHERINE ST.	W. MONTREAL, QUE.	CAN	H3H 1N2	U	U	HOCKEY PLAYER
LAFONTAINE, PAT	C/O BUFFALO SABRES, MEMORIAL AUDITORIUM	BUFFALO	NY	14202	U	U	HOCKEY PLAYER
LAGERFELD, KARL	3 W. 57TH ST.	NEW YORK	NY	10019	U	U	FASHION DESIGNER - AUTHOR'S CHOICE!
LAHTI, CHRISTINE	927 BERKELEY ST.	SANTA MONICA	CA	90403	A	D	ACTRESS - SWING SHIFT
LAINE, FRANKIE	352 SAN GORGONIA ST.	SAN DIEGO	CA	92106	A	B	SINGER/ACTOR - ADDS FAN CLUB INFO!
LAIRD, MELVIN	1730 RHODE ISLAND AVE.	WASHINGTON	DC	20036	U	U	POLITICIAN
LAKE, RICKI	222 ST. PAUL PL.	BALTIMORE	MD	21202	A	B	ACTRESS/TALK SHOW HOST - HAIRSPRAY - AUTHOR'S CHOICE!
LAMARR, HEDY	568 ORANGE DR. #47	ALTAMONTE SPRINGS	FL	32701	U	U	ACTRESS - ECSTASY
LAMB, GIL	755 MADRID CIRCLE	PALM SPRINGS	CA	92262	U	U	ACTOR
LAMBERT, CHRISTOPHER	9560 WILSHIRE BLVD. #500	BEVERLY HILLS	CA	90212	U	U	ACTOR - THE LEGEND OF TARZAN
LAMBERT, JACK	222 HIGHLAND DR.	CARMEL	CA	93921	U	U	FOOTBALL PLAYER

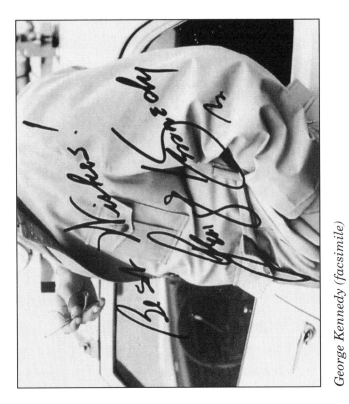

George Kennedy (facsimile)

Sidney Kibrick

Name	Address	City	State	Zip Code	Resp. Time	Resp. Qual.	Comments
LAMBERT, JERRY	P.O. BOX 25371	CHARLOTTE	NC	28212	U	U	SINGER
LAMBERT, L.W.	RT. #1	OLIN	NC	28868	U	U	COUNTRY WESTERN SINGER
LAMM, ROBERT	1113 SUTTON WAY	BEVERLY HILLS	CA	90210	U	U	MUSICIAN / SONGWRITER
LAMOTTA, JAKE	400 E. 57TH ST.	NEW YORK	NY	10022	F	F	BOXER - "RAGING BULL" - FORGET ABOUT IT! MONEY TALKS OR THE BULL WALKS!
LAMPARSKI, RICHARD	924-D GARDEN ST.	SANTA BARBARA	CA	93101	A	B	AUTHOR
LAMPLEY, JIM	3347 TARECO DR.	LOS ANGELES	CA	90068	U	U	SPORTSCASTER
LANDAU, MARTIN	7455 PALO VISTA DR.	LOS ANGELES	CA	90046	U	U	ACTOR - MISSION IMPOSSIBLE
LANDER, DAVID L.	7009 W. SENALDA DR.	LOS ANGELES	CA	90069	U	U	ACTOR / WRITER
LANDERS, ANN	435 N. MICHIGAN AVE.	CHICAGO	IL	60611	U	U	ADVICE COLUMNIST
LANDERS, AUDREY	3112 NICKA DR.	LOS ANGELES	CA	90077	U	U	SINGER / ACTRESS - DALLAS
LANDERS, JUDY	9849 DENBIGH	BEVERLY HILLS	CA	90210	A	B+	ACTRESS/MODEL
LANDESBURG, STEVE	355 N. GENESEE AVE.	LOS ANGELES	CA	90036	A	B+	ACTOR - BARNEY MILLER
LANDIS, JOHN	9369 LLOYDCREST DR.	BEVERLY HILLS	CA	90210	U	U	FILM WRITER/DIRECTOR - TWILIGHT ZONE: THE MOVIE
LANDO, JOE	5750 WILSHIRE BLVD. #512	LOS ANGELES	CA	90036	C	F	ACTOR - SENDS FACSIMILE SIGNED PHOTO!
LANDRIEU, MOON	4301 S. PRIEUR	NEW ORLEANS	LA	70125	A	B	FORMER MAYOR
LANDRY, TOM	8411 PRESTON RD. #720	DALLAS	TX	75225	A	D	MEMBER OF THE FOOTBALL HALL OF FAME
LANDSBURG, VALERIE	22745 CHAMERA LN.	TOPANGA	CA	90290	A	B	ACTRESS
LANDZAAT, ANDRE	7500 DEVISTA DR.	LOS ANGELES	CA	90046	U	U	ACTOR
LANE, ABBE	444 N. FARING RD.	LOS ANGELES	CA	90077	A	C	ACTRESS/SINGER - XAVIER COUGAT SHOW
LANE, CHARLES	321 GRETNA GREEN WAY	LOS ANGELES	CA	90049	U	U	ACTOR - SIDEWALK STORIES
LANE, CHRISTY	1225 APACHE LN.	MADISON	TN	37115	A	A	GOSPEL SINGER
LANE, DIANE	111 W. 40TH ST., 20TH FL.	NEW YORK	NY	10019	U	U	ACTRESS - RUMBLE FISH
LANE, DICK "NIGHT TRAIN"	18100 MEYER	DETROIT	MI	48235	A	C	MEMBER OF THE FOOTBALL HALL OF FAME
LANEUVILLE, ERIC	8383 WILSHIRE BLVD. #923	BEVERLY HILLS	CA	90211	A	A+	ACTOR - OUTSTANDING RESPONSE TO FAN MAIL!
LANG, K.D.	C/O SIRE RECORDS, 75 ROCKEFELLER PLAZA	NEW YORK	NY	10019	U	U	SINGER - "CRYING" - **AUTHOR'S CHOICE!**
LANG, KATHERINE KELLY	317 S. CARMELINA AVE.	LOS ANGELES	CA	90049	U	U	ACTRESS
LANG-MORGAN, JUNE	12756 KAHLENBERG LN.	NORTH HOLLYWOOD	CA	91607	A	B	ACTRESS
LANGDON, SUEANNE	14724 VENTURA BLVD. #401	SHERMAN OAKS	CA	91403	U	U	ACTRESS
LANGE, HOPE	803 BRAMBLE	LOS ANGELES	CA	90049	A	B	ACTRESS - THE GHOST AND MRS. MUIR
LANGE, JESSICA	9830 WILSHIRE BLVD.	BEVERLY HILLS	CA	90212	U	U	ACTRESS - TOOTSIE - **AUTHOR'S CHOICE!**
LANGE, TED	19305 REDWING ST.	TARZANA	CA	91355	U	U	ACTOR/WRITER/DIRECTOR - THE LOVE BOAT
LANGELLA, FRANK	21114 LIGHTHILL DR.	TOPANGA	CA	90290	U	U	ACTOR - DRACULA

Calvin Klein

Ben E. King

Name	Address	City	State	Zip Code	Resp. Time	Resp. Qual.	Comments
LANGENKAMP, HEATHER	10351 SANTA MONICA BLVD. #211	LOS ANGELES	CA	90025	U	U	ACTRESS
LANGER, BERNHARD	1120 S.W. 21ST. LN.	BOCA RATON	FL	33486	U	U	GOLFER
LANGFORD, FRANCES	P.O. BOX 96	JENSEN BEACH	FL	33457	U	U	SINGER
LANGSTON, MURRAY	RR #3, BOX 4630-31	TEHACHAPI	CA	93561	A	C	COMEDIAN/ACTOR - "THE UNKNOWN COMIC"
LANIN, LESTER	157 W. 57TH ST.	NEW YORK	NY	10019	U	U	BAND LEADER
LANKFORD, KIM	9000 SUNSET BLVD. #1200	LOS ANGELES	CA	90069	U	U	ACTRESS
LANSBURY, ANGELA	635 BONHILL RD.	LOS ANGELES	CA	90049	A	D	ACTRESS - *MURDER SHE WROTE* - **AUTHOR'S CHOICE!**
LANSING, ROBERT	10 E. 44TH ST. #700	NEW YORK	NY	10017	U	U	ACTOR / DIRECTOR - *THE MAN WHO NEVER WAS*
LANSING, SHERRY	1363 ANGELO DR.	BEVERLY HILLS	CA	90210	U	U	FILM EXECUTIVE
LARCH, JOHN	4506 VARNA AVE.	SHERMAN OAKS	CA	91403	U	U	ACTOR
LARDNER, RING JR.	55 CENTRAL PARK W.	NEW YORK	NY	10023	A	B	WRITER
LAROSA, JULIUS	67 SYCAMORE LN.	IRVINGTON	NY	10533	A	B	ACTOR/SINGER
LARROQUETTE, JOHN	C/O CREATIVE ARTISTS AGCY., 9830 WILSHIRE BLVD.	BEVERLY HILLS	CA	90212	U	U	ACTOR - *NIGHT COURT* - **AUTHOR'S CHOICE!**
LARSON, GARY	4900 MAIN ST. #900	KANSAS CITY	MO	62114	A	F	CARTOONIST - *TOO BUSY* - FORM LETTER! SAVE YOUR STAMPS!
LARSON, GLEN	351 DELFERN DR.	LOS ANGELES	CA	90024	U	U	TELEVISION WRITER/PRODUCER
LARSON, JACK	449 SKYWAY RD. N.	LOS ANGELES	CA	90049	A	D	ACTOR
LASORDA, TOMMY	1473 W. MAXZIM AVE.	FULLERTON	CA	92633	U	U	BASEBALL MANAGER
LASSER, LOUISE	200 E. 71ST ST. #20C	NEW YORK	NY	10021	A	B	ACTRESS/WRITER - *MARY HARTMAN, MARY HARTMAN*
LASSWELL, FRED	1111 N. WESTSHORE BLVD. #604	TAMPA	FL	33607	U	U	CARTOONIST
LATHAM, LOUISE	2125 PIEDRAS	SANTA BARBARA	CA	93108	A	B	ACTRESS
LATIFAH, QUEEN	C/O WILLIAM MORRIS AGCY.,151 EL CAMINO DR.	BEVERLY HILLS	CA	90212	C	F	RAP SINGER/ACTRESS - **AUTHOR'S CHOICE!**
LATTANZI, MATT	P.O. BOX 2710	MALIBU	CA	90265	B	D	ACTOR
LAUDER, ESTEE	767 FIFTH AVE.	NEW YORK	NY	10153	A	U	COSMETICS EXECUTIVE - SENDS COLOGNE SAMPLE, BUT NO AUTOGRAPH - WORTH A STAMP!
LAURANCE, MITCHELL	2250 MALCOLM AVE.	LOS ANGELES	CA	90064	U	U	ACTOR
LAUREN, RALPH	1107 - 5TH AVE.	NEW YORK	NY	10028	A	F	FASHION DESIGNER - "TOO BUSY TO REPLY" - MAIL YOUR POLO BACK!
LAURENTS, ARTHUR	P.O. BOX 582	QUOQUE	NY	11959	A	B	WRITER - ALWAYS NICE!
LAURER, MATT	NBC, 30 ROCKEFELLER PLAZA	NEW YORK	NY	10112	U	U	BROADCASTER
LAURIA, DAN	601 N. CHEROKEE AVE.	LOS ANGELES	CA	90004	A	B	ACTOR
LAURIE, PIPER	2210 WILSHIRE BLVD. #931	SANTA MONICA	CA	90403	U	U	ACTRESS - *CARRIE*

Spike Lee

Greg LeMond

Janet Leigh

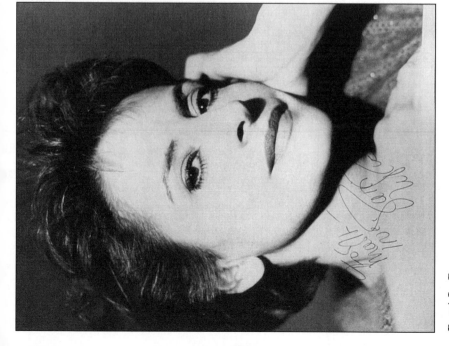

Patti LuPone

Eric Laneuville

Carl Lewis

Name	Address	City	State	Zip Code	Resp. Time	Resp. Qual.	Comments
LAVER, ROD	P.O. BOX 4798	HILTON HEAD	SC	29928	A	C	TENNIS PLAYER
LAVIN, LINDA	20781 BIG ROCK RD.	MALIBU	CA	90265	U	U	ACTRESS/DIRECTOR - ALICE
LAW, JOHN PHILLIP	1339 MILLER DR.	LOS ANGELES	CA	90069	A	A	ACTOR
LAWFORD, PATRICIA KENNEDY	1 SUTTON PL. S.	NEW YORK	NY	10021	A	D	WIDOW OF PETER LAWFORD
LAWRENCE, CAROL	12337 RIDGE CIRCLE	LOS ANGELES	CA	90049	A	B+	ACTRESS/SINGER - WEST SIDE STORY
LAWRENCE, JOEY	846 N. CAHUENGA BLVD.	LOS ANGELES	CA	90038	U	U	ACTOR - BLOSSOM
LAWRENCE, LINDA	4926 COMMONWEALTH	LOS ANGELES CANADA	CA	91011	U	U	ACTRESS
LAWRENCE, MARC	2200 N. VISTA GRANDE AVE.	PALM SPRINGS	CA	92262	U	U	ACTOR/DIRECTOR
LAWRENCE, MARTIN	6310 SAN VICENTE BLVD. #407	LOS ANGELES	CA	90048	U	U	ACTOR - MARTIN - AUTHOR'S CHOICE!
LAWRENCE, STEVE	820 GREENWAY DR.	BEVERLY HILLS	CA	90210	B	B	SINGER/WRITER
LAWRENCE-SHULTZ, VICKI	6000 LIDO AVE.	LONG BEACH	CA	90803	A	D	ACTRESS/SINGER - THE CAROL BURNETT SHOW
LAWS, HUBERT	1078 S. OGDEN DR.	LOS ANGELES	CA	90019	U	U	FLUTIST
LAZAR, IRVING PAUL	1840 CARLA RIDGE DR.	BEVERLY HILLS	CA	90210	U	U	TALENT AGENT
LAZENBY, GEORGE	1127 - 21ST ST.	SANTA MONICA	CA	90403	U	U	ACTOR
LE CARRE, JOHN	TREGIFFIAN, ST. BURYAN	PENZANCE, CORNWALL	ENG		U	U	WRITER
LE MAT, PAUL	1100 N. ALTA LOMA #805	LOS ANGELES	CA	90069	A	B	ACTOR - AMERICAN GRAFFITI
LE ROY, GLORIA	3500 W. OLIVE #1400	BURBANK	CA	91505	U	U	ACTRESS
LEACH, ROBIN	875 THIRD AVE. #1800	NEW YORK	NY	10022	B	B	TELEVISION PERSONALITY - LIFESTYLES OF THE RICH AND FAMOUS
LEAR, NORMAN	1999 AVE. OF THE STARS #500	LOS ANGELES	CA	90067	A	B	TELEVISION WRITER/PRODUCER - ALL IN THE FAMILY
LEARNED, MICHAEL	850 - 7TH AVE. #1003	NEW YORK	NY	10019	A	B	ACTRESS - THE WALTONS
LEARY, BRIANNE	9229 SUNSET BLVD. #607	LOS ANGELES	CA	90069	U	U	ACTRESS
LEBEAUF, SABRINA	133 ST. NICHOLS AVE.	ENGLEWOOD	NJ	07632	C	B	ACTRESS
LEBROCK, KELLY	2282 MANDEVILLE CANYON	LOS ANGELES	CA	90049	B	F	ACTRESS/MODEL - SENDS FACSIMILE SIGNED PHOTO!
LED ZEPPELIN	57-A GR. TICHFIELD ST.	LONDON	ENG	W1 7FL	U	U	ROCK GROUP - "STAIRWAY TO HEAVEN"
LEDERER, FRANCIS	23134 SHERMAN WAY	CANOGA PARK	CA	91307	U	U	ACTOR/DIRECTOR
LEDOUX, CHRIS	4205 HILLSBORO RD. #208	NASHVILLE	TN	37215	U	U	SINGER/SONGWRITER
LEE, ANNA	1240 N. DOHENY DR.	LOS ANGELES	CA	90069	A	D	ACTRESS - SIGNS VERY LIGHT!
LEE, BRENDA	2175 CARSON ST.	NASHVILLE	TN	37210	A	B	SINGER
LEE, DOROTHY	434 SANTA DOMINGA	SOLANA BEACH	CA	92075	A	B	ACTRESS
LEE, DR. SAMMY	16537 HARBOUR LN.	HUNTINGTON BEACH	CA	92649	A	B	PHYSICIAN / ATHLETE
LEE, HYAPATIA	15127 CALIFA ST.	VAN NUYS	CA	91411	A	C	ACTRESS/MODEL
LEE, MICHELLE	830 BIRCHWOOD	LOS ANGELES	CA	90024	U	U	ACTRESS - KNOTS LANDING

Jerry Lewis

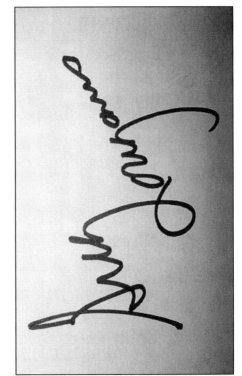

Greg Louganis

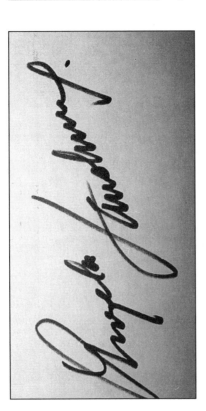

Angela Lansbury

Rod Laver

Reginald Lane

Joe Lando

Ketty Lester

Christopher Lloyd (facsimile)

Name	Address	City	State	Zip Code	Resp. Time	Resp. Qual.	Comments
LEE, PAMELA	8730 SUNSET BLVD., #220	LOS ANGELES	CA	90069	U	U	ACTRESS - *BAYWATCH* - **AUTHOR'S CHOICE!**
LEE, PEGGY	11404 BELLAGIO RD.	LOS ANGELES	CA	90024	U	U	SINGER/ACTRESS - *THE JAZZ SINGER*
LEE, RUTA	2623 LAUREL CANYON RD.	LOS ANGELES	CA	90046	C	A	ACTRESS
LEE, SHERYL	331 N. MARTEL	LOS ANGELES	CA	90036	U	U	ACTRESS
LEE, SPIKE	40 ACRES & A MULE FILM WORKS, 124 DE KALB AVE. #2	BROOKLYN	NY	11217	A	B	ACTOR/FILM DIRECTOR - *DO THE RIGHT THING* - **AUTHOR'S CHOICE!**
LEEDS, PETER	626 N. SCREENLAND DR.	BURBANK	CA	91505	U	U	ACTOR
LEFEBVRE, JIM	1060 W. ADDISON ST.	CHICAGO	IL	60613	U	U	ACTOR
LEHRER, JIM	P.O. BOX 2626	WASHINGTON	DC	20013	U	U	BROADCAST JOURNALIST
LEIBMAN, RON	10530 STRATHMORE DR.	LOS ANGELES	CA	90024	A	B	ACTOR/WRITER
LEIBOVITZ, ANNIE	55 VANDAM ST.	NEW YORK	NY	10013	A	B	PHOTOGRAPHER - **AUTHOR'S CHOICE!**
LEIGH, JANET	1625 SUMMITRIDGE DR.	BEVERLY HILLS	CA	90210	A	A+	ACTRESS - *PSYCHO* - OUTSTANDING!
LEIGH, JENNIFER JASON	335 N. MAPLE DR. #254	BEVERLY HILLS	CA	90210	U	U	ACTRESS - *THE BEST LITTLE GIRL ...* - **AUTHOR'S CHOICE!**
LEIGHTON, LAURA	924 WESTWOOD BLVD., 9TH FL.	LOS ANGELES	CA	90024	U	U	ACTRESS - *MELROSE PLACE* - **AUTHOR'S CHOICE!**
LEITCH, DONOVAN	8528 WALNUT DR.	LOS ANGELES	CA	90046	U	U	ACTOR
LEMBECK, MICHAEL	13530 ERWIN ST.	VAN NUYS	CA	91401	U	U	ACTOR
LEMIEUX, MARIO	C/O PITTSBURGH PENGUINS, CIVIC ARENA	PITTSBURGH	PA	15219	U	U	HOCKEY PLAYER - "SUPER MARIO" - NICE IN PERSON!
LEMMON, JACK	141 S. EL CAMINO DR. #201	BEVERLY HILLS	CA	90212	B	B	ACTOR/DIRECTOR - *SOME LIKE IT HOT* - **AUTHOR'S CHOICE!**
LEMOND, GREG	1101 WILSON BLVD. #1800	WASHINGTON	DC	22209	A	B	BICYCLIST - MAY INCLUDE AUTOGRAPHED TRADING CARD - **AUTHOR'S CHOICE!**
LENARD, MARK	6767 FOREST LAWN DR. #115	LOS ANGELES	CA	90068	U	U	ACTOR
LENDL, IVAN	60 ARCH ST.	GREENWICH	CT	06830	A	B	TENNIS PLAYER
LENNON SISTERS	1984 ST. HGWY. 165	BRANSON	MO	65616	A	C	SINGING GROUP
LENNON, JANET	14234 DICKENS ST. #1	SHERMAN OAKS	CA	91423	U	U	SINGER
LENNON, JULIAN	12721 MULHOLLAND DR.	BEVERLY HILLS	CA	90210	U	U	SINGER/COMPOSER - SON OF JOHN LENNON
LENNON, SEAN	1 W. 72ND ST.	NEW YORK	NY	10023	U	U	SON OF JOHN LENNON
LENNOX, ANNIE	28 ALEXANDER ST.	LONDON	ENG	W2	U	U	SINGER - EURYTHMICS
LENO, JAY	P.O. BOX 7885	BURBANK	CA	91510	A	F	TALK SHOW HOST/COMEDIAN - *THE TONIGHT SHOW* - SENDS OUT FACSIMILE SIGNED PHOTO, JUST LIKE CARSON! - **AUTHOR'S CHOICE!**
LENZ, KAY	5930 MANOLA WAY	LOS ANGELES	CA	90068	U	U	ACTRESS
LENZ, RICK	12955 CALVERT ST.	VAN NUYS	CA	91401	U	U	ACTOR
LEONARD, ELMORE	2192 YARMOUTH RD.	BLOOMFIELD VILLAGE	MI	48301	A	B	AUTHOR/SCREENWRITER

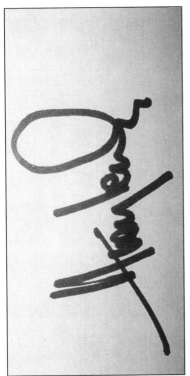

Huey Lewis

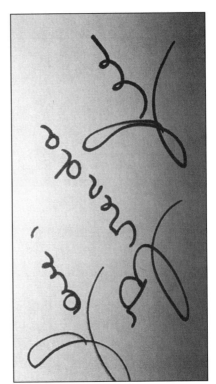

Brenda Lee

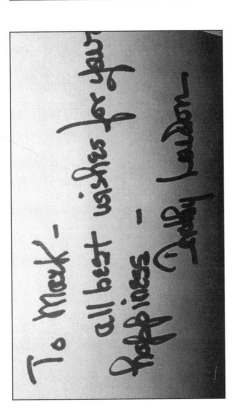

Dorothy Loudon

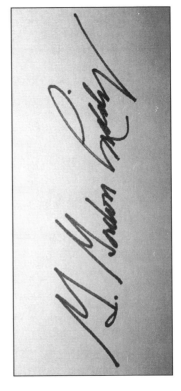

G. Gordon Liddy

Name	Address	City	State	Zip Code	Resp. Time	Resp. Qual.	Comments
LEONARD, LU	12245 CHANDLER BLVD.	NORTH HOLLYWOOD	CA	91607	A	B	ACTRESS
LEONARD, SHELDON	1141 LOMA VISTA	BEVERLY HILLS	CA	90210	A	B	ACTOR/DIRECTOR - *IT'S A WONDERFUL LIFE*
LEONARD, SUGAR RAY	13916 KING GEORGE WAY	UPPER MARLBORO	MD	20772	U	U	BOXER
LEONI, TEA	3500 W. OLIVE #1400	BURBANK	CA	91505	U	U	ACTRESS
LERNER, MICHAEL	8347 SUNSET VIEW	LOS ANGELES	CA	90069	U	U	ACTRESS - *BARTON FINK*
LESLIE CALDWELL, JOAN	2228 N. CATILINA AVE.	LOS ANGELES	CA	90027	A	B-	ACTRESS
LESLIE, ALEEN	1700 LEXINGTON RD.	BEVERLY HILLS	CA	90210	A	C	WRITER
LESTER, BETHEL	393 W. END AVE. #11C	NEW YORK	NY	10024	A	D	ACTRESS/WRITER
LESTER, KETTY	5931 COMEY AVE.	LOS ANGELES	CA	90034	B	A	ACTRESS
LESTER, TERRY	6427 LA PUNTA DR.	LOS ANGELES	CA	90068	U	U	ACTOR
LETTERMAN, DAVID	1697 BROADWAY	NEW YORK	NY	10019	F	F	TALK SHOW HOST - *LATE NIGHT WITH DAVID LETTERMAN* - SAVE YOUR STAMPS AND MAIL TO CONAN!
LEWIS, AL	P.O. BOX 277	NEW YORK	NY	10044	A	D	ACTOR - *THE MUNSTERS*
LEWIS, CARL	1801 OCEAN PARK BLVD. #112	SANTA MONICA	CA	90405	A	B	TRACK ATHLETE/SINGER (?) - "CARL" ONLY!
LEWIS, DAWNN	9229 SUNSET BLVD. #607	LOS ANGELES	CA	90069	U	U	ACTRESS
LEWIS, GEOFFREY	19756 COLLIER	WOODLAND HILLS	CA	91364	U	U	ACTOR
LEWIS, HUEY	P.O. BOX 819	MILL VALLEY	CA	94942	A	D	SINGER - HUEY LEWIS AND THE NEWS
LEWIS, JERRY	1701 WALDMAN AVE.	LAS VEGAS	NV	89102	A	C	COMEDIAN/ACTOR - *THE NUTTY PROFESSOR*
LEWIS, JERRY LEE	P.O. BOX 3864	MEMPHIS	TN	38173	U	U	SINGER/COMPOSER - "GREAT BALLS OF FIRE" - A $25 FEE!
LEWIS, JULIETTE	151 EL CAMINO DR.	BEVERLY HILLS	CA	90212	U	U	ACTRESS - *CAPE FEAR* - **AUTHOR'S CHOICE!**
LEWIS, SHARI	603 N. ALTA DR.	BEVERLY HILLS	CA	90210	A	C	VENTRILOQUIST - "LAMB CHOP" - GREAT WITH KIDS!
LIBERTINI, RICHARD	2313 MC KINLEY AVE.	VENICE	CA	90291	A	C	ACTOR
LICHENSTEIN, ROY	P.O. BOX 1369	SOUTHAMPTON	NY	11968	U	U	ARTIST
LIDDY, G. GORDON	9112 RIVERSIDE DR.	FT. WASHINGTON	MD	20744	A	D	FORMER GOVERNMENT OFFICIAL/RADIO PERSONALITY - *THE G. GORDON LIDDY SHOW*
LIGHT, JUDITH	8942 WILSHIRE BLVD.	BEVERLY HILLS	CA	90211	A	A+	ACTRESS - *WHO'S THE BOSS?*
LIGON, TOM	227 WAVERLY PL.	NEW YORK	NY	10014	U	U	ACTOR
LIMAN, ARTHUR L.	1285 AVE. OF THE AMERICAS	NEW YORK	NY	10019	A	C	MUSICIAN
LIMBAUGH, RUSH	342 MADISON AVE. #920	NEW YORK	NY	10173	A	F	RADIO PERSONALITY - SAVE YOUR STAMPS! - SENDS TIE CATALOG AND FACSIMILE SIGNED PHOTO!
LINDBERGH, ANN MORROW	P.O. BOX 98	ST. JOHNSBURY	VT	05819	F	F	AVIATRIX/AUTHOR
LINDEN, HAL	151 EL CAMINO DR.	BEVERLY HILLS	CA	90212	U	U	ACTOR/DIRECTOR - *BARNEY MILLER*
LINDEN, KATE	9111 WONDERLAND	LOS ANGELES	CA	90046	U	U	ACTRESS

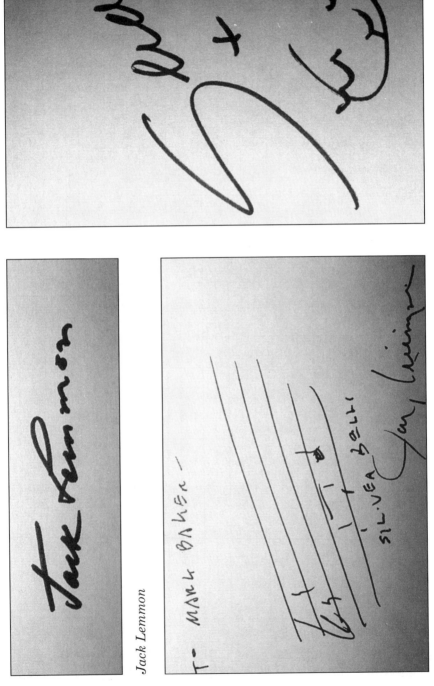

Shari Lewis

Jack Lemmon

Jay Livingston

Name	Address	City	State	Zip Code	Resp. Time	Resp. Qual.	Comments
LINDFORS, VIVICA	172 E. 95TH ST.	NEW YORK	NY	10028	U	U	ACTRESS
LINDROS, ERIC	C/O PHILADELPHIA FLYERS, THE SPECTRUM, PATTISON PL.	PHILADELPHIA	PA	19148	B	F	HOCKEY PLAYER - RESPONDS WITH FACSIMILE SIGNED POSTCARD!
LINDSEY, MORT	6970 FERNHILL DR.	MALIBU	CA	90265	U	U	COMPOSER/CONDUCTOR
LINDSTROM, PIA	30 ROCKEFELLER PLAZA, 7TH FL.	NEW YORK	NY	10020	U	B	FILM CRITIC
LINKLETTER, ART	1100 BEL AIR RD.	LOS ANGELES	CA	90024	A	B	TELEVISION PERSONALITY - PEOPLE ARE FUNNY
LINKLETTER, JACK	765 BAKER ST.	COSTA MESA	CA	92626	U	U	TELEVISION PERSONALITY
LINN, TERI ANN	4267 MARINA CITY DR. #312	MARINA DEL REY	CA	90292	A	B	ACTRESS
LINN-BAKER, MARK	2625 - 16TH ST. #2	SANTA MONICA	CA	90405	U	U	ACTOR - PERFECT STRANGERS
LINVILLE, JOANNE	3148 FRYMAN RD.	STUDIO CITY	CA	91604	U	U	ACTRESS
LINVILLE, LARRY	18261 SAN FERNANDO MISSION BLVD.	NORTHRIDGE	CA	91326	U	U	ACTOR - M*A*S*H
LIPTON, PEGGY	15250 VENTURA BLVD. #900	SHERMAN OAKS	CA	91403	U	U	ACTRESS - THE MOD SQUAD
LIPTON, ROBERT	9300 WILSHIRE BLVD. #410	BEVERLY HILLS	CA	90212	U	U	ACTOR
LISA LISA	747 - 10TH AVE.	NEW YORK	NY	10019	U	U	R&B GROUP
LITHGOW, JOHN	1319 WARNALL AVE.	LOS ANGELES	CA	90024	A	A+	ACTOR - THE WORLD ACCORDING TO GARP - OUTSTANDING! - AUTHOR'S CHOICE!
LITTLE RICHARD	HYATT SUNSET HOTEL, 8401 SUNSET BLVD.	LOS ANGELES	CA	90069	U	U	SINGER/SONGWRITER
LITTLE RIVER BAND	87-91 PALMERSTIN CRES., ALBERT PARK	MELBOURNE, VIC.	AUS	3206	U	U	ROCK GROUP
LITTLE, BIG TINY	W. 3985 TAFT DR.	SPOKANE	WA	98208	U	U	SINGER/SONGWRITER
LITTLE, TAWNY	5515 MELROSE AVE.	LOS ANGELES	CA	90038	A	B	TELEVISION HOST
LITTLER, GENE	P.O. BOX 1919	RANCHO SANTA FE	CA	92067	A	B	GOLFER
LIVENGOOD, VICTORIA ANN	C/O BARRETT MGMT., 1776 BROADWAY #1610	NEW YORK	NY	10019	A	A+	OPERA SINGER - OUTSTANDING!
LIVINGSTON, JAY	C/O ASCAP, 1 LINCOLN PLAZA	NEW YORK	NY	10023	A	B	COMPOSER/LYRICIST!
LIVINGSTON, STANLEY	P.O. BOX 1785	STUDIO CITY	CA	91604	A	B	ACTOR
LL COOL J	298 ELIZABETH ST.	NEW YORK	NY	10012	U	U	RAP SINGER
LLEWELYN, DOUG	8075 W. THIRD ST. #303	LOS ANGELES	CA	90048	U	U	ACTOR - THE PEOPLE'S COURT
LLOYD, CHRISTOPHER	P.O. BOX 491264	LOS ANGELES	CA	90049	C	F	ACTOR - BACK TO THE FUTURE - SENDS FACSIMILE SIGNED PHOTO!
LLOYD, EMILY	151 EL CAMINO DR.	BEVERLY HILLS	CA	90212	U	U	ACTRESS
LLOYD, NORMAN	1813 OLD RANCH RD.	LOS ANGELES	CA	90049	A	B	ACTOR/DIRECTOR
LOCKE, SONDRA	P.O. BOX 69865	LOS ANGELES	CA	90069	U	U	ACTRESS - THE GAUNTLET
LOCKERMAN, BRAD	10351 SANTA MONICA BLVD. #211	LOS ANGELES	CA	90025	U	U	ACTOR
LOCKHART, ANNE	28245 DRIVER AVE.	AGOURA HILLS	CA	91301	U	U	ACTRESS

Trini Lopez

To Mark,
All my love Patti LaBelle

Patti LaBelle

246

Name	Address	City	State	Zip Code	Resp. Time	Resp. Qual.	Comments
LOCKHART, JUNE	404 SAN VICENTE BLVD. #208	SANTA MONICA	CA	90402	C	F	ACTRESS - LOST IN SPACE - $12 PER PHOTO
LOCKHART, KEITH	C/O BOSTON SYMPHONY ORCH., SYMPHONY HALL	BOSTON	MA	02115	U	U	ORCHESTRA LEADER - "BSO" - **AUTHOR'S CHOICE!**
LOCKLEAR, HEATHER	4970 SUMMIT VIEW DR.	WESTLAKE VILLAGE	CA	91362	U	U	ACTRESS/MODEL - MELROSE PLACE - **AUTHOR'S CHOICE!**
LOCKWOOD, GARY	3083 1/2 RAMBLA PACIFICA	MALIBU	CA	90265	U	U	ACTOR - 2001: A SPACE ODYSSEY
LOGAN, ROBERT	10637 BURBANK BLVD.	NORTH HOLLYWOOD	CA	91601	U	U	ACTOR
LOGGINS, KENNY	775 SANDPOINT RD.	CARPINTERIA	CA	93013	U	U	SINGER/SONGWRITER
LOLLOBRIGIDA, GINA	VIA APPINO ANTICA 223	ROME	ITA		U	U	ACTRESS - CIRCUS
LONDON, JULIE	16074 ROYAL OAKS	ENCINO	CA	91436	U	U	ACTRESS/SINGER
LONG, HOWIE	26 STRAWBERRY LN.	ROLLING HILLS	CA	90274	U	U	FOOTBALL PLAYER/ACTOR
LONG, SHELLEY	15237 SUNSET BLVD.	PACIFIC PALISADES	CA	90272	U	U	ACTRESS - CHEERS
LONGO, TONY	24 WESTWIND ST.	MARINA DEL REY	CA	90292	U	U	ACTOR
LOPEZ, AL	3601 BEACH DR.	TAMPA	FL	33609	U	U	MEMBER OF THE BASEBALL HALL OF FAME
LOPEZ, NANCY	1 ERIEVIEW PLAZA #1300	CLEVELAND	OH	44114	A	D	GOLFER
LOPEZ, TRINI	1139 ABRIGO RD.	PALM SPRINGS	CA	92762	A	A+	SINGER/ACTRESS
LOPRIENO, JOHN	924 WESTWOOD BLVD. #900	LOS ANGELES	CA	90024	U	U	ACTOR
LORANT, STEFAN	215 W. MOUNTAIN RD.	LENOX	MA	01240	A	D	PHOTOJOURNALIST/AUTHOR
LORD, JACK	4999 KAHALA AVE.	HONOLULU	HI	96816	A	U	ACTOR - HAWAII FIVE-O
LORD, MARJORIE	1110 MAYTOR PL.	BEVERLY HILLS	CA	90210	U	U	ACTRESS
LORDS, TRACI	3349 CAHUENGA BLVD. W. #2-B	LOS ANGELES	CA	90068	U	U	ACTRESS - MELROSE PLACE
LOREN, SOPHIA	1151 HIDDEN VALLEY RD.	THOUSAND OAKS	CA	91360	U	U	ACTRESS - TWO WOMEN
LORING, GLORIA	4125 PAWA AVE.	LOS ANGELES	CA	90027	A	B	ACTRESS
LORING, LISA	51 W. 52ND ST.	NEW YORK	NY	10019	U	U	ACTRESS
LORING, LYNN	506 N. CAMDEN DR.	BEVERLY HILLS	CA	90210	U	U	ACTRESS/TELEVISION PRODUCER
LORING, JOAN	345 E. 68TH ST.	NEW YORK	NY	10021	A	D	ACTRESS
LOUDON, DOROTHY	101 CENTRAL PARK W.	NEW YORK	NY	10023	A	B	ACTRESS
LOUGANIS, GREG	P.O. BOX 4068	MALIBU	CA	90265	A	B	DIVER - AN INSPIRATION - **AUTHOR'S CHOICE!**
LOUGHLIN, LORI	9279 SIERRA MAR DR.	LOS ANGELES	CA	90069	U	U	ACTRESS
LOUIS-DREYFUS, JULIA	9150 WILSHIRE BLVD. #205	BEVERLY HILLS	CA	90212	A	F	ACTRESS - SEINFELD - SENDS OUT FACSIMILE SIGNED PHOTO - **AUTHOR'S CHOICE!**
LOUISE, TINA	310 E. 46TH ST. #18T	NEW YORK	NY	10017	A	D	ACTRESS - GILLIGAN'S ISLAND
LOVE, COURTNEY	C/O WILLIAM MORRIS AGCY., 151 EL CAMINO DR.	BEVERLY HILLS	CA	90212	U	U	SINGER - HOLE - **AUTHOR'S CHOICE!**
LOVE, PETER	5955 TUJUNGA AVE.	NORTH HOLLYWOOD	CA	91601	U	U	ACTOR

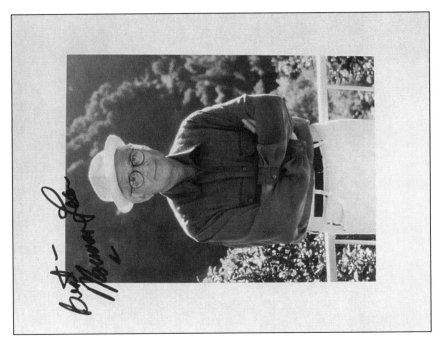

Norman Lear

"CHAMPAGNE WISHES & CAVIAR DREAMS"™

Robin Leach

Name	Address	City	State	Zip Code	Resp. Time	Resp. Qual.	Comments
LOVELACE, LINDA	120 ENTERPRISE	SECAUCUS	NJ	07094	U	U	ACTRESS
LOVELESS, PATTY	42 MUSIC SQUARE W. #111	NASHVILLE	TN	37203	U	U	SINGER
LOVELL, JAMES	5725 E. RIVER RD.	CHICAGO	IL	60611	A	F	ASTRONAUT - AUTOGRAPHS FOR $10 EACH - "HOUSTON, WE HAVE A PROBLEM."
LOVETT, LYLE	C/O ICM, 8942 WILSHIRE BLVD.	BEVERLY HILLS	CA	90211	U	U	SINGER - **AUTHOR'S CHOICE!** - GOTTA LOVETT!
LOVITZ, JON	C/O CREATIVE ARTISTS AGCY., 9830 WILSHIRE BLVD.	BEVERLY HILLS	CA	90212	U	U	ACTOR - SATURDAY NIGHT LIVE - **AUTHOR'S CHOICE!**
LOWE, CHAD	151 EL CAMINO DR.	BEVERLY HILLS	CA	90212	U	U	ACTOR - LIFE GOES ON
LOWE, ROB	270 N. CANON DR. #1072	BEVERLY HILLS	CA	90212	U	U	ACTOR - **AUTHOR'S CHOICE!**
LOWELL, CAREY	8942 WILSHIRE BLVD.	BEVERLY HILLS	CA	90211	U	U	MODEL/ACTRESS
LU PONE, PATTI	130 W. 42ND ST. #2400	NEW YORK	NY	10036	A	B	ACTRESS - LIFE GOES ON
LUCAS, GEORGE	P.O. BOX 2009	SAN RAFAEL	CA	94912	A	F	WRITER/PRODUCER/DIRECTOR - STAR WARS - SENDS OUT FACSIMILE SIGNED PHOTO! SAVE YOUR STAMPS!
LUCCI, SUSAN	P.O. BOX 621	QUOGUE	NY	11959	C	F	SOAP OPERA ACTRESS - SENDS OUT FACSIMILE SIGNED PHOTO!
LUCHENBILL, GLORIA	415 S. SHIRLEY PL.	BEVERLY HILLS	CA	90212	U	U	ACTRESS
LUCKING, WILLIAM	10100 SANTA MONICA BLVD. #700	LOS ANGELES	CA	90067	U	U	ACTOR
LUCKMAN, SID	5303 ST. CHARLES RD.	BELLWOOD	IL	60104	A	B	FORMER FOOTBALL PLAYER
LUDLUM, ROBERT	C/O HENRY MORRISON INC., P.O. BOX 235	BEDFORD HILLS	NY	10507	U	U	AUTHOR - THE INHERITANCE
LUFT, LORNA	2501 ZORADA DR.	LOS ANGELES	CA	90046	U	U	ACTRESS
LUISI, JAMES	14315 RIVERSIDE DR.	SHERMAN OAKS	CA	91423	A	D	ACTOR
LUMBLY, CARL	924 WESTWOOD BLVD. #900	LOS ANGELES	CA	90024	U	U	ACTOR
LUMET, SIDNEY	1380 LEXINGTON AVE.	NEW YORK	NY	10028	U	U	FILM WRITER/DIRECTOR
LUNA, BARBARA	18026 RODARTE WAY	ENCINO	CA	91316	U	U	ACTRESS
LUND HIGGINS, LUCILLE	3424 SHORE HEIGHTS DR.	MALIBU	CA	90265	A	B	ACTRESS
LUND, DEANNA	1948 BENECIA AVE.	LOS ANGELES	CA	90025	A	D	ACTRESS - SENDS OUT CHEAP COLOR COPY NEWSLETTER!
LUNDEN, JOAN	C/O GOOD MORNING AMERICA, ABC, 77 W. 66TH ST.	NEW YORK	NY	10023	U	U	TELEVISION HOST - **AUTHOR'S CHOICE!**
LUNDQUIST, STEVE	3448 SOUTHBAY DR.	JONESBORO	GA	30236	U	U	SWIMMER
LUPUS, PETER	11375 DONA LISA DR.	STUDIO CITY	CA	91604	A	C+	ACTOR - MISSION IMPOSSIBLE
LUTCHER, NELLIE	1524 LA BAIG AVE.	LOS ANGELES	CA	90028	U	U	PIANIST/VOCALIST
LUZ, FRANK	606 N. LARCHMONT BLVD. #309	LOS ANGELES	CA	90004	A	B	ACTOR
LYDON, JIMMY	1317 LOS ARBOLES AVE. N.W.	ALBUQUERQUE	NM	87107	U	U	ACTOR
LYLES, A.C.	2115 LINDA FLORA	LOS ANGELES	CA	90024	A	B	WRITER/PRODUCER

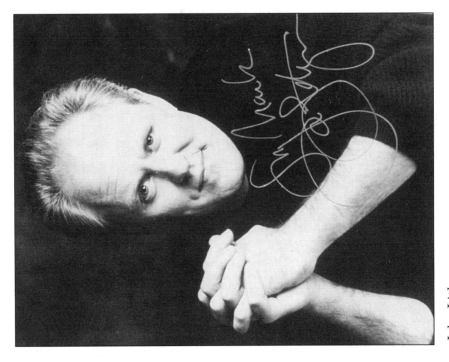

John Lithgow

A Susan Lucci stock response

Name	Address	City	State	Zip Code	Resp. Time	Resp. Qual.	Comments
LYMAN, DOROTHY	1930 CENTURY PARK W. #403	LOS ANGELES	CA	90067	U	U	ACTRESS
LYNCH, DAVID	P.O. BOX 93624	LOS ANGELES	CA	90093	U	U	TELEVISION WRITER
LYNCH, KELLY	804 WOODACRES RD.	SANTA MONICA	CA	90402	U	U	ACTRESS
LYNLEY, CAROL	P.O. BOX 2190	MALIBU	CA	90265	U	U	ACTRESS
LYNN, BETTY	10424 TENNESSEE AVE.	LOS ANGELES	CA	90064	U	U	ACTRESS
LYNN, FRED	24 HAYKEY WAY	BOSTON	MA	02115	A	D	FUTURE MEMBER OF BASEBALL HALL OF FAME!
LYNN, JEFFREY	11600 ACAMA ST.	STUDIO CITY	CA	91604	A	D	ACTOR
LYNN, LORETTA	MCA RECORDS, 70 UNIVERSAL PL.	UNIVERSAL CITY	CA	91608	C	C	MEMBER OF COUNTRY MUSIC HALL OF FAME! - AUTHOR'S CHOICE!
LYNNE, JEFF	2621 DEEP CANYON DR.	BEVERLY HILLS	CA	90210	U	U	MUSICIAN/COMPOSER
LYON, SUE	1244 N. HAVENHURST DR.	LOS ANGELES	CA	90046	U	U	ACTRESS
MA, YO-YO	40 W. 57TH ST.	NEW YORK	NY	10019	A	D	CELLO VIRTUOSO
MAC ARTHUR, JAMES	P.O. BOX 230	CRESTED BUTTE	CO	81224	U	U	ACTOR - HAWAII FIVE-O
MAC ARTHUR, MRS. JEAN	WALDORF TOWERS, 100 E. 50TH ST.	NEW YORK	NY	10022	A	D	WIDOW OF GEN. DOUGLAS MAC ARTHUR
MAC CORKINDALE, SIMON	520 WASHINGTON BLVD. #187	MARINA DEL REY	CA	90292	U	U	ACTOR - FALCON CREST
MAC DONALD, DR. JEFFREY	FEDERAL CORRECTIONAL INSTITUTE	BASTROP	TX	78602	A	F	CONVICTED OF KILLING HIS FAMILY - REFUSED LETTER!
MAC DOWELL, ANDIE	8942 WILSHIRE BLVD.	BEVERLY HILLS	CA	90211	U	U	ACTRESS - GREEN CARD - AUTHOR'S CHOICE!
MAC GRAW, ALI	10345 W. OLYMPIC BLVD. #200	LOS ANGELES	CA	90064	A	B	ACTRESS/MODEL - LOVE STORY - POSSIBLE AUTOPEN!
MAC GREGOR, JEFF	151 EL CAMINO DR.	BEVERLY HILLS	CA	90212	U	U	TELEVISION PERSONALITY
MAC KENZIE, GISELE	11014 BLIX ST.	NORTH HOLLYWOOD	CA	91604	A	B	ACTRESS
MAC KENZIE, PATCH	3500 W. OLIVE AVE. #1400	BURBANK	CA	91505	U	U	ACTRESS
MAC LACHLAN, JANET	1919 N. TAFT AVE.	LOS ANGELES	CA	90068	U	U	ACTRESS
MAC LACHLAN, KYLE	1033 GAYLEY AVE. #208	LOS ANGELES	CA	90024	U	U	ACTOR - TWIN PEAKS - AUTHOR'S CHOICE!
MAC LAINE, SHIRLEY	25200 OLD MALIBU RD.	MALIBU	CA	90265	U	U	ACTRESS - TERMS OF ENDEARMENT - AUTHOR'S CHOICE!
MAC LEOD, GAVIN	11641 CURRY AVE.	GRANADA HILLS	CA	91344	A	B+	ACTOR - THE LOVE BOAT
MAC PHERSON, ELLE	40 E. 61ST ST.	NEW YORK	NY	10021	C	B	SUPERMODEL - AUTHOR'S CHOICE!
MAC RAE, MEREDITH	4430 HAVENHURST AVE.	ENCINO	CA	91436	U	U	ACTRESS
MACCHIO, RALPH	451 DEERPARK AVE.	DIX HILLS	NY	11746	U	U	ACTOR - THE KARATE KID
MACHADO, MARIO	5750 BRIARCLIFF RD.	LOS ANGELES	CA	90068	A	A+	ACTOR - VERY RESPONSIVE TO FAN MAIL!
MACHT, STEPHEN	248 S. RODEO DR.	BEVERLY HILLS	CA	90212	U	U	ACTOR
MACK, SEN. CONNIE	SENATE HART BLDG. #517	WASHINGTON	DC	20510	A	D	POLITICIAN
MACNEE, PATRICK	39 GUILDFORD PARK RD.	SURREY	ENG	GUZ 5NA	U	U	ACTOR - THE AVENGERS

Ivan Lendl

Cheryl Ladd

Name	Address	City	State	Zip Code	Resp. Time	Resp. Qual.	Comments
MACNEIL, ROBERT	356 W. 58TH ST.	NEW YORK	NY	10019	U	U	NEWS CORRESPONDENT - *THE MACNEIL/LEHRER REPORT*
MACREA, SHEILA	301 N. CANON DR. #305	BEVERLY HILLS	CA	90210	A	B	SINGER/ACTRESS
MACY, BILL	10130 ANGELO CIRCLE	BEVERLY HILLS	CA	90210	A	A	ACTOR
MADDEN, JOHN	1 W. 72ND ST.	NEW YORK	NY	10023	A	D	SPORTSCASTER - FOUNDER OF ALL-MADDEN TEAM!
MADDOCKS, ANSON	C/O WIZARDS OF THE COAST, INC., P.O. BOX 707	RENTON	WA	98057	U	U	ILLUSTRATOR - "MAGIC" CARDS
MADDOX, LESTER	3155 JOHNSON FERRY RD. N.E.	MARIETTA	GA	30062	A	B	FORMER GOVERNOR
MADDUX, GREG	C/O ATLANTA BRAVES, P.O. BOX 4064	ATLANTA	GA	30302	U	U	BASEBALL PLAYER - COLLECTS "CY YOUNG AWARDS"!
MADIGAN, AMY	662 N. VAN NESS AVE. #305	LOS ANGELES	CA	90004	U	U	ACTRESS - *FIELD OF DREAMS*
MADONNA	8000 BEVERLY DR.	LOS ANGELES	CA	90048	C	F	SINGER/ACTRESS - **AUTHOR'S CHOICE!** - A VERY TOUGH SIGNATURE!
MAFFETT, DEBRA SUE	2969 PASSMORE DR.	LOS ANGELES	CA	90068	U	U	ACTRESS/MODEL
MAGGART, BRANDON	9200 SUNSET BLVD. #710	LOS ANGELES	CA	90069	U	U	ACTOR
MAGNUSON, ANN	1317 MALTMAN AVE.	LOS ANGELES	CA	90026	U	U	PERFORMANCE ARTIST - "ANYTHING BUT LOVE"
MAGRUDER, JEB STUART	720 W. MONUMENT ST.	COLORADO SPRINGS	CO	80901	U	U	FORMER GOVERNMENT OFFICIAL
MAHAFFEY, JOHN	3100 RICHMOND AVE. #500	HOUSTON	TX	77098	U	U	GOLFER
MAHAFFEY, VALERIE	121 N. SAN VICENTE BLVD.	BEVERLY HILLS	CA	90211	U	U	ACTRESS
MAHARIS, GEORGE	13150 MULHOLLAND DR.	BEVERLY HILLS	CA	90210	A	B	ACTOR
MAHONEY, CARDINAL ROGER	1531 W. 9TH ST.	LOS ANGELES	CA	90012	A	D	CLERGY
MAHRE, PHIL	WHITE PASS DR.	NACHES	WA	98937	A	B	SKIER
MAHRE, STEVE	2408 N. 52ND AVE.	YAKIMA	WA	98908	A	B	SKIER
MAILER, NORMAN	142 COLUMBIA HEIGHTS	BROOKLYN	NY	11201	C	D	AUTHOR
MAJAL, TAJ	1671 APPIAN WAY	SANTA MONICA	CA	90401	B	B+	SINGER/SONGWRITER
MAJORS, LEE	411 ISLE OF CAPRI DR.	FT. LAUDERDALE	FL	33301	U	U	ACTOR - *THE SIX MILLION DOLLAR MAN*
MAKEM, TOMMY	2 LONGMEADOW RD.	DOVER	NH	03820	A	B	SINGER
MAKEPEACE, CHRIS	BOX 1095, STATION Q	TORONTO, ONTARIO	CAN	M4T 2P2	U	U	ACTOR - *MY BODYGUARD*
MALDEN, KARL	1845 MANDEVILLE CANYON	LOS ANGELES	CA	90049	A	C	ACTOR - *STREETS OF SAN FRANCISCO*
MALKOVICH, JOHN	346 S. LUCERNE BLVD.	LOS ANGELES	CA	90020	U	U	ACTOR - *DANGEROUS LIAISONS* - **AUTHOR'S CHOICE!**
MALLORY, CAROLE	2300 - 5TH AVE.	NEW YORK	NY	10037	U	U	MODEL/ACTRESS/AUTHOR
MALMUTY, BRUCE	9981 ROBIN DR.	BEVERLY HILLS	CA	90210	U	U	SCREENWRITER/DIRECTOR
MALONE, KARL	C/O UTAH JAZZ, 5 TRIAD CTR.	SALT LAKE CITY	UT	84180	U	U	BASKETBALL PLAYER
MALTIN, LEONARD	10424 WHIPPLE ST.	TOLUCA LAKE	CA	91602	U	U	FILM CRITIC/AUTHOR - *ENTERTAINMENT TONIGHT*

Ricki Lake

A Dorothy Lamour (deceased) marketing flyer

Name	Address	City	State	Zip Code	Resp. Time	Resp. Qual.	Comments
MAMET, DAVID	P.O. BOX 381589	CAMBRIDGE	MA	02238	U	U	WRITER/DIRECTOR - *GLENGARRY GLEN ROSS* - **AUTHOR'S CHOICE!**
MANATT, CHARLES T.	4814 WOODWAY LN. N.W.	WASHINGTON	DC	20016	U	U	POLITICIAN
MANCHESTER, MELISSA	15822 HIGH KNOLL RD.	ENCINO	CA	91436	A	F	SINGER/SONGWRITER - SENDS FAN CLUB INFO ONLY!
MANCHESTER, WILLIAM	P.O. BOX 329 WESLEYAN STATION	MIDDLETOWN	CT	06457	U	U	AUTHOR
MANDEL, BABALOO	5121 VAN ALDEN	TARZANA	CA	91356	U	U	SCREENWRITER
MANDEL, JOHNNY	28946 CLIFFSIDE DR.	MALIBU	CA	90265	U	U	COMPOSER/CONDUCTOR
MANDEL, LORING	555 W. 57TH ST. #1230	NEW YORK	NY	10019	U	U	SCREENWRITER
MANDELA, NELSON	ORLANDO WEST, SOWETO	JOHANNESBURG	S.AFR		U	U	PRESIDENT OF SOUTH AFRICA - **AUTHOR'S CHOICE!**
MANDEN, ROBERT	10351 SANTA MONICA BLVD. #211	LOS ANGELES	CA	90025	U	U	ACTOR
MANDRELL, BARBARA	P.O. BOX 800	HENDERSONVILLE	TN	37075	A	F	SINGER/SONGWRITER - THE MANDRELL SISTERS - SENDS FAN CLUB INFO ONLY!
MANDRELL, ERLINE	P.O. BOX 800	HENDERSONVILLE	TN	37075	U	U	ACTRESS/DRUMMER - THE MANDRELL SISTERS
MANDRELL, LOUISE	OLD HICKORY LAKE	HENDERSONVILLE	TN	37075	A	B+	SINGER/MUSICIAN - THE MANDRELL SISTERS
MANDYLOR, COSTAS	C/O WILLIAM MORRIS AGCY., 151 EL CAMINO DR.	BEVERLY HILLS	CA	90212	U	U	ACTOR
MANETI, LARRY	4615 WINNETKA	WOODLAND HILLS	CA	91364	U	U	ACTOR - *MAGNUM P.I.*
MANGIONE, CHUCK	1850 WINTON RD. S.	ROCHESTER	NY	14618	C	B+	JAZZ MUSICIAN
MANHATTAN TRANSFER	3575 CAHUENGA BLVD. W. #450	LOS ANGELES	CA	90068	U	U	VOCAL GROUP
MANILOW, BARRY	5443 BEETHOVEN ST.	LOS ANGELES	CA	90066	A	F	SINGER/COMPOSER - SENDS REJECTION NOTICE!
MANKIEWICZ, TOM	1609 MAGNETIC TERR.	LOS ANGELES	CA	90069	A	B	WRITER/PRODUCER
MANN, ABBY	1240 LA COLLINA DR.	BEVERLY HILLS	CA	90210	U	U	WRITER/PRODUCER
MANN, DELBERT	401 S. BURNSIDE AVE. SUITE #11D	LOS ANGELES	CA	90036	A	D	DIRECTOR/PRODUCER
MANN, JOHNNY	C/O JOHNNY MANN MANAGEMENT, 78516 GORHAM LN.	INDIO	CA	92203	A	B	COMPOSER/CONDUCTOR
MANN, MICHAEL	13746 SUNSET BLVD.	PACIFIC PALISADES	CA	90272	U	U	WRITER/PRODUCER
MANNERS, DAVID	3010 FOOTHILL RD.	SANTA BARBARA	CA	93105	A	D	ACTOR
MANNERS, DOROTHY	744 N. DOHENY DR.	LOS ANGELES	CA	90069	U	U	ACTRESS
MANNERS, MISS	1651 HARVARD ST. N.W.	WASHINGTON	DC	20009	U	U	ETIQUETTE EXPERT
MANNING, IRENE	3165 LA MESA DR.	SANTA CLARA	CA	94070	U	U	ACTRESS/SINGER/AUTHOR
MANOFF, DINAH	21244 VENTURA BLVD. #101	WOODLAND HILLS	CA	91364	U	U	ACTRESS - *EMPTY NEST*
MANSON, CHARLES	CORCORAN PRISON, 1002 DAIRY AVE.	CORCORAN	CA	93212	U	U	CONVICTED MURDERER/HIPPIE CULT LEADER
MANTEGNA, JOE	1500 BROADWAY #2001	NEW YORK	NY	10036	U	U	ACTOR - *THE GODFATHER, PT. II*
MANTLEY, JOHN	4121 LONDRIDGE AVE.	SHERMAN OAKS	CA	91423	A	B	SCREENWRITER

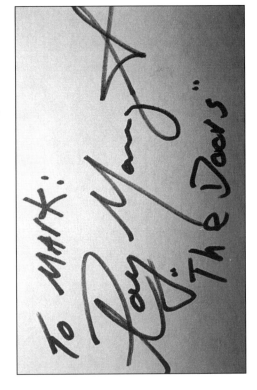

Elle Macpherson

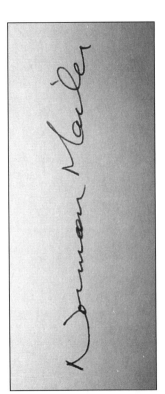

Norman Mailer

Ray Manzarek

256

Name	Address	City	State	Zip Code	Resp. Time	Resp. Qual.	Comments
MANULIS, MARTIN	242 COPA DE ORO RD.	LOS ANGELES	CA	90077	U	U	TELEVISION PRODUCER
MANZA, RALPH	550 HYDEIA AVE.	LEUCADIA	CA	92024	U	U	ACTOR
MANZAREK, RAY	232 S. RODEO DR.	BEVERLY HILLS	CA	90212	A	D	KEYBOARDIST - THE DOORS
MAPLES, MARLA (MRS. TRUMP)	150 W. 51ST ST. #802	NEW YORK	NY	10019	U	U	ACTRESS
MARA HUGGINS, ADELA	1928 MANDEVILLE CANYON	LOS ANGELES	CA	90049	U	U	DANCER/ACTRESS
MARCEAU, MARCEL	21 RUE JEAN MERMOZ	F-75008 PARIS		FRANCE	U	U	MIME - OFTEN RESPONDS WHEN IN THIS COUNTRY - **AUTHOR'S CHOICE!**
MARCELINO, MARIO	1418 N. HIGHLAND AVE. #102	LOS ANGELES	CA	90028	U	U	ACTOR/WRITER
MARCELLINO, MUZZY	14633 ROUND VALLEY DR.	SHERMAN OAKS	CA	91403	A	B	COMPOSER
MARCHAND, NANCY	250 W. 89TH ST.	NEW YORK	NY	10024	A	B	ACTRESS - *LOU GRANT*
MARCOVICCI, ANDREA	8273 W. NORTON AVE.	LOS ANGELES	CA	90046	A	B	ACTRESS/SINGER - *TRAPPER JOHN M.D.*
MARGARET SMITH, ANN-	P.O. BOX 57593	SHERMAN OAKS	CA	91403	U	U	ACTRESS
MARGOLIN, STUART	9401 WILSHIRE BLVD. #700	BEVERLY HILLS	CA	90212	U	U	ACTOR/DIRECTOR
MARGOLYES, MIRIAM	121 N. SAN VICENTE BLVD.	BEVERLY HILLS	CA	90211	A	D	ACTRESS
MARGULIES, STAN	16965 STRAWBERRY DR.	ENCINO	CA	91316	U	U	TELEVISION PRODUCER
MARICHAL, JUAN	9458 N.W. 54 DORAL CIRCLE LN.	MIAMI	FL	33128	U	U	MEMBER OF THE BASEBALL HALL OF FAME
MARIE, TEENA	1000 LAGUNA RD.	PASADENA	CA	91105	U	U	ACTRESS
MARIN, RICHARD	32020 PACIFIC COAST HWY	MALIBU	CA	90265	U	U	ACTOR/COMEDIAN - *CHEECH AND CHONG*
MARINARO, ED	1466 N. DOHENY DR.	LOS ANGELES	CA	90069	U	U	FOOTBALL PLAYER/ACTOR - *HILL ST. BLUES*
MARINO, DAN	2269 N.W. 199TH ST.	MIAMI	FL	33056	A	F	FOOTBALL PLAYER - RESPONDS WITH FACSIMILE SIGNED PHOTO - RIDES IN THE EQUIPMENT TRUCK AFTER GAME!
MARK, MARKY	888 - 7TH AVE. #2900	NEW YORK	NY	10019	U	U	RAP SINGER
MARKHAN, MONTE	P.O. BOX 607	MALIBU	CA	90265	A	B	ACTOR
MARLEY, ZIGGY	JACK'S HILL	KINGSTON	JAM		A	D	REGGAE SINGER
MARLOWE, JEAN	32 EXETER RD.	LONDON	ENG	NW2	U	U	ACTRESS
MARLOWE, SCOTT	1427 - 3RD ST. #205	SANTA MONICA	CA	90401	U	U	ACTOR
MARSALIS, BRANFORD	C/O THE TONIGHT SHOW, 330 BOB HOPE DR.	BURBANK	CA	91523	U	U	SAXOPHONIST
MARSALIS, WYNTON	3 LINCOLN CTR. #2911	NEW YORK	NY	10023	A	B	TRUMPETER - MULTIPLE GRAMMY WINNER - **AUTHOR'S CHOICE!**
MARSH, LINDA	4041 ALTA MESA	STUDIO CITY	CA	91604	A	D	ACTRESS
MARSH, MARIAN	P.O. BOX 1	PALM DESERT	CA	92260	U	U	ACTRESS
MARSHALL, E.G.	RFD #2, OREGON RD.	MT. KISCO	NY	10549	U	U	ACTOR - *TWELVE ANGRY MEN*

Tim Matheson

Ali MacGraw

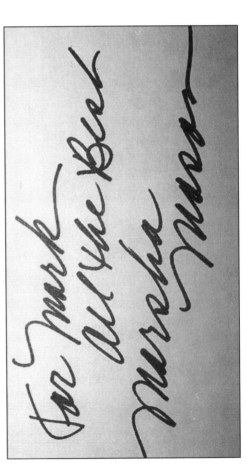

Marsha Mason

Name	Address	City	State	Zip Code	Resp. Time	Resp. Qual.	Comments
MARSHALL, GARY	10459 SARAH ST.	TOLUCA LAKE	CA	91602	U	U	WRITER/PRODUCER - HAPPY DAYS
MARSHALL, JAMES	30710 MONTE LADO DR.	MALIBU	CA	90265	A	B	AUTHOR
MARSHALL, PENNY	7150 LA PRESA DR.	LOS ANGELES	CA	90068	U	U	ACTRESS/ DIRECTOR - A LEAGUE OF THEIR OWN - AUTHOR'S CHOICE!
MARSHALL, PETER	16714 OAKVIEW DR.	ENCINO	CA	91316	A	B	ACTOR/TELEVISION HOST - THE HOLLYWOOD SQUARES
MARSHALL, TRUDY	1852 MARCHEETA PL.	LOS ANGELES	CA	90069	A	B	ACTRESS
MARSHALL, WILLIAM	11351 DRONFIELD AVE.	PACOIMA	CA	91331	A	C+	ACTOR
MARTH, FRANK	8538 EASTWOOD RD.	LOS ANGELES	CA	90069	U	U	SINGER/ACTOR
MARTIN, BARNEY	12838 MILBANK ST.	STUDIO CITY	CA	91604	U	U	ACTOR
MARTIN, DICK	11030 CHALON RD.	LOS ANGELES	CA	90077	U	U	ACTOR/WRITER/COMEDIAN - LAUGH-IN
MARTIN, MILLICENT	P.O. BOX 101	REDDING	CT	06875	B	B	SINGER/ACTRESS
MARTIN, NAN	33604 PACIFIC COAST HWY.	MALIBU	CA	90265	A	B	ACTRESS
MARTIN, STEVE	P.O. BOX 929	BEVERLY HILLS	CA	90213	A	B	ACTOR/COMEDIAN - AUTHOR'S CHOICE!
MARTIN, TONY	10724 WILSHIRE BLVD. #1406	LOS ANGELES	CA	90024	U	U	ACTOR/SINGER
MARTINEZ, A.	6835 WILD LIFE RD.	MALIBU	CA	90265	U	U	ACTOR
MARTINO, AL	927 N. REXFORD DR.	BEVERLY HILLS	CA	90210	A	A-	SINGER
MARX, MRS. HARPO	37631 PALM VIEW RD.	RANCHO MIRAGE	CA	92270	A	B+	WIDOW OF HARPO MARX
MARX, RICHARD	15250 VENTURA BLVD. #900	SHERMAN OAKS	CA	91403	C	D	MUSICIAN - FAN CLUB INFO ADDED
MASAK, RON	5440 SHIRLEY AVE.	TARZANA	CA	91356	A	A+	ACTOR
MASHBURN, JAMAL	C/O DALLAS MAVERICKS, 777 SPORTS DR.	DALLAS	TX	75207	U	U	BASKETBALL PLAYER
MASON, JACKIE	30 PARK AVE.	NEW YORK	NY	10016	U	U	COMEDIAN - CHICKEN SOUP
MASON, MARLYN	8242 HILLSIDE AVE.	LOS ANGELES	CA	90069	U	U	ACTRESS/SINGER
MASON, MARSHA	C/O COLLETT & LEVY, 10100 SANTA MONICA BLVD. #400	LOS ANGELES	CA	90067	A	B+	ACTRESS - THE GOODBYE GIRL - WILL SEND PHOTO IF YOU SEND LARGE S.A.S.E. - VERY RESPONSIVE TO HER FANS!
MASON, TOM	853 - 7TH AVE. #9A	NEW YORK	NY	10019	U	U	ACTOR
MASSEN, OSA	10501 WILSHIRE BLVD. #704	LOS ANGELES	CA	90024	U	U	ACTRESS
MASTERSON, MARY STUART	40 W. 57TH ST.	NEW YORK	NY	10067	U	U	ACTRESS - FRIED GREEN TOMATOES
MASUR, RICHARD	121 N. SAN VICENTE BLVD.	BEVERLY HILLS	CA	90211	U	U	ACTOR/WRITER - ONE DAY AT A TIME
MATHERS, JERRY	23965 VIA ARANDA	VALENCIA	CA	91355	U	U	ACTOR - LEAVE IT TO BEAVER
MATHESON, TIM	830 RIVER ROCK RD.	SANTA BARBARA	CA	93108	A	B	ACTOR - ANIMAL HOUSE
MATHEWS, EDDIE	13744 RECUERDO DR.	DEL MAR	CA	92014	U	U	MEMBER OF THE BASEBALL HALL OF FAME
MATHIAS, BOB	7469 E. PINE AVE.	FRESNO	CA	93727	U	U	ACTOR/ATHLETE
MATHIS, JOHNNY	3500 W. OLIVE AVE. #750	BURBANK	CA	91505	U	U	SINGER

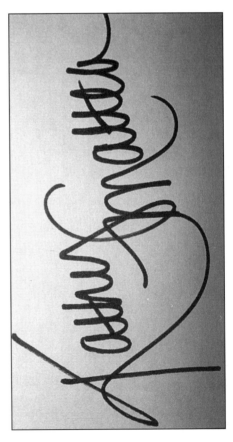

Johnny Mathis

Bob Mathias

Kathy Mattea

Name	Address	City	State	Zip Code	Resp. Time	Resp. Qual.	Comments
MATHIS, SAMANTHA	P.O. BOX 480137	LOS ANGELES	CA	90048	U	U	ORCHESTRA LEADER
MATHISON, MELISSA	655 MAC CULLOCH DR.	LOS ANGELES	CA	90049	U	U	SCREENWRITER
MATLIN, MARLEE	12304 SANTA MONICA BLVD. #119	LOS ANGELES	CA	90025	U	U	ACTRESS - *CHILDREN OF A LESSER GOD* - **AUTHOR'S CHOICE!**
MATTEA, KATHY	P.O. BOX 158482	NASHVILLE	TN	37215	A	B	SINGER - ALSO SENDS FAN CLUB INFO!
MATTHAU, WALTER	1999 AVE. OF THE STARS #2100	LOS ANGELES	CA	90067	C	B	ACTOR - *GRUMPY OLD MEN*
MATTHEWS, KERWIN	67-A BUENA VISTA TERR.	SAN FRANCISCO	CA	94117	A	B	ACTOR
MATTINGLY, THOMAS	MARTIN MARIETTA CORPORATION, SPACE SYSTEMS DIVISION, P.O. BOX 85990	SAN DIEGO	CA	92186	U	U	FORMER ASTRONAUT
MATTSON, ROBIN	917 MANNING AVE.	LOS ANGELES	CA	90024	A	A+	ACTRESS - VERY RESPONSIVE TO FAN MAIL!
MATURE, VICTOR	P.O. BOX 706	RANCHO SANTA FE	CA	92067	A	D	ACTOR - *SAMSON AND DELILAH*
MAUCH, BOBBY	23427 CANZONET ST.	WOODLAND HILLS	CA	91364	U	U	ACTOR
MAULE, BRAD	4136 DIXIE CANYON	SHERMAN OAKS	CA	91423	U	U	ACTOR
MAVEN, MAX	1746 N. ORANGE DR. #1106	LOS ANGELES	CA	90046	U	U	MIND READER
MAX, PETER	118 RIVERSIDE DR.	NEW YORK	NY	10024	U	U	ARTIST/DESIGNER
MAXWELL, FRANK	447 SAN VICENTE BLVD. #301	SANTA MONICA	CA	90401	U	U	ACTOR
MAY, ELAINE	2017 CALIFORNIA AVE.	SANTA MONICA	CA	90403	U	U	ACTRESS/WRITER/DIRECTOR
MAYNE, FERDINAND	100 S. DOHENY DR.	LOS ANGELES	CA	90048	U	U	ACTOR
MAYNOR, ASA	P.O. BOX 1641	BEVERLY HILLS	CA	90213	A	D	ACTRESS/PRODUCER
MAYO, VIRGINIA	109 E. AVE. DE LOS ARBOLES	THOUSAND OAKS	CA	91360	A	D	ACTRESS
MAYRON, MELANIE	210 W. 70TH ST. #1503	NEW YORK	NY	10023	B	B	ACTRESS/WRITER
MAYS, WILLIE	51 MT. VERNON LN.	ATHERTON	CA	94025	U	U	MEMBER OF THE BASEBALL HALL OF FAME
MAZEROSKI, BILL	RR6, BOX 130	GREENSBURG	PA	15601	U	U	BASEBALL PLAYER
MC ARDLE, ANDREA	713 DISATON ST.	PHILADELPHIA	PA	19111	C	B	ACTRESS- INCLUDES FAN CLUB INFO
MC ARTHUR, ALEX	10435 WHEATLAND AVE.	SUNLAND	CA	91040	U	U	ACTOR
MC BAIN, DIANE	27533 CHERRY CREEK DR.	VALENCIA	CA	91355	U	U	ACTOR
MC BROOM, AMANDA	22903 MARIANO	WOODLAND HILLS	CA	91364	U	U	SINGER/SONGWRITER
MC CAIN, FRANCES LEE	8075 W. 3RD ST. #303	LOS ANGELES	CA	90048	U	U	ACTRESS
MC CALL, MITZI	3635 WRIGHTWOOD DR.	STUDIO CITY	CA	91604	A	B	ACTRESS
MC CALLA, IRISH	920 OAK TERR.	PRESCOTT	AZ	86301	A	F	ACTRESS - SENDS PRICE LIST: $5 - CARD, $10 - PHOTO
MC CALLISTER, LON	P.O. BOX 6030	STATELINE	NV	89449	C	B	ACTOR
MC CALLUM, DAVID	91 THE GROVE	LONDON	ENG	N13 5JS	U	U	ACTOR - *THE GREAT ESCAPE*
MC CANN, CHUCK	2941 BRIAR KNOLL DR.	LOS ANGELES	CA	90046	U	U	ACTOR/COMEDIAN
MC CARREN, FRED	9200 SUNSET BLVD. #710	LOS ANGELES	CA	90069	U	U	ACTOR

Liza Minneli

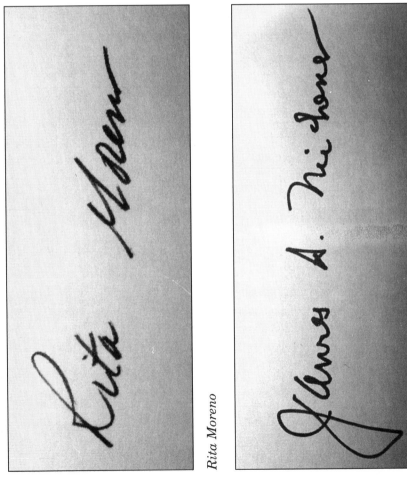

Rita Moreno

James Michener

Name	Address	City	State	Zip Code	Resp. Time	Resp. Qual.	Comments
MC CARRON, CHRIS	3328 CLARENDON DR. #216	BEVERLY HILLS	CA	90210	U	U	JOCKEY
MC CARTHY, ANDREW	4708 VESPER AVE.	SHERMAN OAKS	CA	91403	U	U	ACTOR - *LESS THAN ZERO*
MC CARTHY, EUGENE	P.O. BOX 22	WOODVILLE	VA	22749	A	B	FORMER SENATOR
MC CARTHY, KEVIN	14854 SUTTON ST.	SHERMAN OAKS	CA	91403	C	C	ACTOR - *INVASION OF THE BODY SNATCHERS*
MC CARTHY, LIN	233 N. SWALL dR.	BEVERLY HILLS	CA	90210	U	U	ACTOR
MC CARTNEY, PAUL	WATERFALL ESTATE, PEAMARSH, ST. LEONARD -ON-THE SEA	SUSSEX, ENGLAD	UK		U	U	COMPOSER - "THE BEATLES" - **AUTHOR'S CHOICE!**
MC CARVER, TIM	1518 YOUNGFORD RD.	GLADWYNNE	PA	19035	A	D	BASEBALL PLAYER/SPORTSCASTER
MC CASHIN, CONSTANCE	2037 DESFORD DR.	BEVERLY HILLS	CA	90210	U	U	ACTRESS
MC CAY, PEGGY	8811 WONDERLAND AVE.	LOS ANGELES	CA	90046	A	C	ACTRESS
MC CKEN, DON	2933 - 28TH ST. N.W.	WASHINGTON	DC	20006	A	B	NEWS CORRESPONDENT
MC CLANAHAN, RUE	16601 WOODVALE RD.	ENCINO	CA	91436	A	B	ACTRESS
MC CLOSKY, PETE	2200 GENGO RD.	PALO ALTO	CA	94304	U	U	FORMER CONGRESSMAN
MC CLURE, MARC	1420 BEAUDRY BLVD.	GLENDALE	CA	91208	U	U	ACTOR
MC CONNELL, JUDITH	3300 BENNETT DR.	LOS ANGELES	CA	90068	U	U	ACTRESS
MC COO-DAVIS, MARILYN	P.O. BOX 7905	BEVERLY HILLS	CA	90212	U	U	SINGER - THE FIFTH DIMENSION
MC COOK, JOHN	4154 COLBATH AVE.	SHERMAN OAKS	CA	91423	U	U	ACTOR/WRITER/DIRECTOR
MC CORD, KENT	1738 N. ORANGE GROVE	LOS ANGELES	CA	90046	U	U	ACTOR - *ADAM 12*
MC CORMICK, MAUREEN	C/O WILLIAM MORRIS AGCY., 151 EL CAMINO DR.	BEVERLY HILLS	CA	90212	A	A+	ACTRESS - VERY RESPONSIVE TO FAN MAIL!
MC CORMICK, PAT	P.O. BOX 250	SEAL BEACH	CA	90740	A	B	SWIMMER
MC COVEY, WILLIE	P.O. BOX 620342	WOODSIDE	CA	94062	U	U	MEMBER OF THE BASEBALL HALL OF FAME
MC COY, CHARLIE	P.O. BOX 158558	NASHVILLE	TN	37215	U	U	SINGER/GUITARIST
MC CREA, JODY	RT. #1, BOX 575	CAMARILLO	CA	93010	U	U	ACTOR
MC CULLOUGH, SHANNA	7920 ALABAMA AVE.	CANOGA PARK	CA	91304	U	U	ACTRESS
MC DANIEL, MEL	191 DICKERSON BAY RD.	GALLATIN	TN	37066	U	U	SINGER
MC DERMOTT, DYLAN	2700 NEILSON WAY #1133	SANTA MONICA	CA	90405	U	U	ACTOR
MC DIVITT, JAMES	P.O. BOX 3105	ANAHEIM	CA	92803	U	U	ASTRONAUT
MC DONALD GREEN, GRACE	6115 LINCOLN DR.	MINNEAPOLIS	MN	55436	U	U	SINGER/DANCER
MC DONALD, "COUNTRY" JOE	P.O. BOX 7158	BERKELEY	CA	94707	U	U	SINGER - COUNTRY JOE & THE FISH
MC DONALD, CHRISTOPHER	8033 SUNSET BLVD. #4011	LOS ANGELES	CA	90046	U	U	ACTOR
MC DONNELL, MARY	C/O WILLIAM MORRIS AGCY., 151 EL CAMINO DR.	BEVERLY HILLS	CA	90212	A	B	ACTRESS - *DANCES WITH WOLVES*
MC DONOUGH, MARY	6858 CANTELOPE AVE.	VAN NUYS	CA	91405	U	U	ACTRESS
MC DORMAND, FRANCES	333 W. END AVE. #12C	NEW YORK	NY	10023	U	U	ACTRESS - *MISSISSIPPI BURNING*

Hello and good Luck
To
MARK! (Baker)
from
Burgess Meredith

Burgess Meredith

Ronnie Milsap

Ricardo Montalbon

264

Name	Address	City	State	Zip Code	Resp. Time	Resp. Qual.	Comments
MC DOWALL, MALCOLM	76 OXFORD ST.	LONDON	ENG	W1R 1RB	U	U	ACTOR - A CLOCKWORK ORANGE
MC DOWALL, RODDY	3110 BROOKDALE RD.	STUDIO CITY	CA	91604	A	B	ACTOR - PLANET OF THE APES
MC DOWELL, RONNIE	P.O. BOX 53	PORTLAND	TN	37148	U	U	SINGER
MC ENROE, JOHN	23712 MALIBU COLONY RD.	MALIBU	CA	90265	U	U	TENNIS PLAYER
MC ENTIRE, REBA	511 FAIRGROUND COURT	NASHVILLE	TN	37204	A	B	SINGER - AUTHOR'S CHOICE!
MC EWEN, MARK	C/O CBS-TV, 524 W. 57TH ST.	NEW YORK	NY	10019	U	U	WEATHERMAN
MC FADDEN, GATES	1999 AVE. OF THE STARS #2850	LOS ANGELES	CA	90067	A	F	ACTOR - SENDS FACSIMILE SIGNED PHOTO & LETTER!
MC FARLANE, ROBERT C.	3414 PROSPECT ST. N.W.	WASHINGTON	DC	20007	A	D	POLITICIAN
MC FERRIN, BOBBY	P.O. BOX 460189	SAN FRANCISCO	CA	94146	C	B	SINGER - "DON'T WORRY, BE HAPPY"
MC GAVIN, DARREN	P.O. BOX 2939	BEVERLY HILLS	CA	90213	U	U	ACTOR - THE NIGHT STALKER
MC GEE, VONETTA	9744 WILSHIRE BLVD. #308	BEVERLY HILLS	CA	90212	U	U	ACTRESS
MC GILLIS, KELLY	303 WHITEHEAD ST.	KEY WEST	FL	33040	U	U	ACTRESS - WITNESS
MC GINLEY, TED	4000 WARNER BLVD. #133-202	BURBANK	CA	91533	U	U	ACTOR
MC GINNIN, HOWARD	151 EL CAMINO DR.	BEVERLY HILLS	CA	90212	U	U	ACTOR/SINGER
MC GOOHAN, PATRICK	16808 BOLLINGER DR.	PACIFIC PALISADES	CA	90272	U	U	ACTOR/WRITER/PRODUCER
MC GOVERN, ELIZABETH	17319 MAGNOLIA BLVD.	ENCINO	CA	91316	U	U	ACTRESS - RAGTIME
MC GOVERN, GEORGE	P.O. BOX 5591	WASHINGTON	DC	20016	B	B	FORMER SENATOR
MC GOVERN, MAUREEN	163 AMSTERDAM AVE. BOX 174	NEW YORK	NY	10023	A	B	SINGER - "THE MORNING AFTER"
MC GUIRE SISTERS	100 RANCHO CIRCLE	LAS VEGAS	NV	89119	U	U	VOCAL GROUP
MC GUIRE, DOROTHY	121 COPLEY PL	BEVERLY HILLS	CA	90210	A	B	ACTRESS
MC GUIRE, PHYLLIS	100 RANCHO CIRCLE	LAS VEGAS	NV	89119	B	B	SINGER
MC KAY, GARDNER	445 KAWAILOA RD. #10	KAILUA	HI	96734	U	U	ACTOR
MC KAY, JIM	47 W. 66TH ST.	NEW YORK	NY	10023	A	B	SPORTSCASTER - ABC'S WIDE WORLD OF SPORTS
MC KAY, JOHN	1 BUCCANEER RD.	TAMPA	FL	33607	A	D	FOOTBALL COACH
MC KEE, TODD	32362 LAKE PLEASANT DR.	WESTLAKE VILLAGE	CA	91361	U	U	ACTOR
MC KELLAR, DANICA	4151 PROSPECT AVE.	HOLLYWOOD	CA	90027	U	U	ACTRESS - THE WONDER YEARS
MC KEON, DOUG	818 - 6TH ST. #202	SANTA MONICA	CA	90403	B	B	ACTOR
MC KEON, NANCY	P.O. BOX 6778	BURBANK	CA	91510	U	U	ACTRESS - THE FACTS OF LIFE
MC KINNEY, TAMARA	4935 PARKERS MILL RD.	LEXINGTON	KY	40502	U	U	SKIER
MC KUEN, ROD	1155 ANGELO DR.	BEVERLY HILLS	CA	90210	U	U	SINGER/POET
MC LAGLEN, ANDREW	P.O. BOX 1056	FRIDAY HARBOR	WA	98250	A	A+	FILM DIRECTOR - VERY RESPONSIVE TO FAN MAIL!
MC LAUGHLIN, JOHN	1211 CONNECTICUT AVE N.W.	WASHINGTON	DC	20036	U	U	NEWS CORRESPONDENT

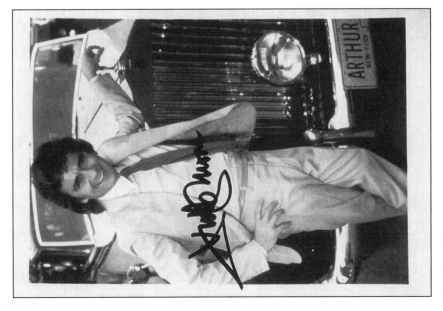

Dudley Moore

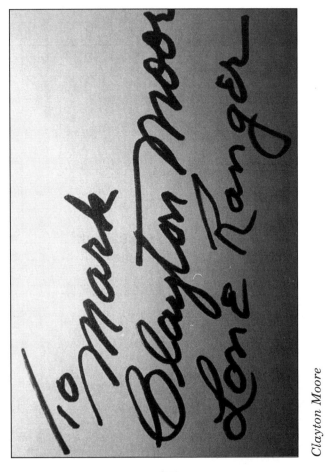

Clayton Moore

Name	Address	City	State	Zip Code	Resp. Time	Resp. Qual.	Comments
MC LEAN, DON	P.O. BOX 102	CASTINE	ME	04421	U	U	SINGER/SONGWRITER
MC LEOD, CATHERINE	4146 ALLOTT AVE.	VAN NUYS	CA	91423	A	D	ACTRESS
MC LERIE, ALLYN ANN	3344 CAMPANIL DR.	SANTA BARBARA	CA	93109	U	U	ACTRESS
MC LISH, RACHEL	120 S. EL CAMINO DR. #116	BEVERLY HILLS	CA	90212	U	U	ACTRESS
MC MAHON, ED	12000 CREST COURT	BEVERLY HILLS	CA	90210	A	B	TALK SHOW SIDEKICK - *THE TONIGHT SHOW*
MC MULLEN, JIM	515 MT. HOLYOKE AVE.	PACIFIC PALISADES	CA	90272	A	A	ACTOR
MC MURTRY, LARRY	P.O. BOX 552	ARCHER CITY	TX	76351	U	U	SCREENWRITER
MC NALLY, STEPHEN	624 N. HILLCREST RD.	BEVERLY HILLS	CA	90210	U	U	ACTOR
MC NAMARA, JULIANNE	3500 W. OLIVE AVE. #1400	BURBANK	CA	91505	U	U	ACTRESS
MC NAMARA, ROBERT	2412 TRACY PL. N.W.	WASHINGTON	DC	20008	A	C	BANKER/FORMER GOVERNMENT OFFICIAL
MC NEILL, ROBERT DUNCAN	121 N. SAN VICENTE BLVD.	BEVERLY HILLS	CA	90211	U	U	ACTOR
MC NICHOL, KRISTY	15060 VENTURA BLVD. #350	SHERMAN OAKS	CA	91403	U	U	ACTRESS - *EMPTY NEST*
MC QUEEN, CHAD	8306 WILSHIRE BLVD. #438	BEVERLY HILLS	CA	90211	U	U	ACTOR
MC QUEEN, NIELE	2323 BOWMONT DR.	BEVERLY HILLS	CA	90210	U	U	ACTRESS
MC RANEY, GERALD	329 N. WETHERLY DR. #101	BEVERLY HILLS	CA	90211	B	F	ACTOR/DIRECTOR - *MAJOR DAD* - ALWAYS SENDS FACSIMILE SIGNED PHOTO!
MC REYNOLDS, JIM & JESSE	P.O. BOX 304	GALLATIN	TN	37066	A	C	SINGER/GUITARIST
MC VIE, CHRISTINE	8306 WILSHIRE BLVD. #1008	BEVERLY HILLS	CA	90211	U	U	SINGER/SONGWRITER
MCGRIFF, FRED	C/O ATLANTA BRAVES, P.O. BOX 4064	ATLANTA	GA	30302	U	U	BASEBALL PLAYER
MEADE, JULIA	1010 FIFTH AVE.	NEW YORK	NY	10021	A	C	ACTRESS
MEADOWS, JAYNE	16185 WOODVALE	ENCINO	CA	91316	U	U	ACTRESS
MEAGHER, MARY T.	4100 ORMOND DR.	LOUISVILLE	KY	40207	A	A	SWIMMER
MEARA, ANNE	1999 AVE. OF THE STARS #2850	LOS ANGELES	CA	90067	A	B	ACTRESS/COMEDIAN - *THE OUT-OF-TOWNERS*
MEATLOAF	BOX68, STOCKPORT	CHESHIRE	ENG	SK3 0JY	U	U	SINGER/COMPOSER - **AUTHOR'S CHOICE!**
MEDINA, PATRICIA	10590 WILSHIRE BLVD. #1202	LOS ANGELES	CA	90024	C	B	ACTRESS
MEDLEY, BILL	RCA RECORDS, 1133 SIXTH AVE.	NEW YORK	NY	10019	U	U	MUSICIAN - THE RIGHTEOUS BROTHERS
MEDVED, MICHAEL	1224 ASHLAND AVE.	SANTA MONICA	CA	90405	A	B	WRITER/FILM CRITIC
MEECHAM, EVAN	4510 W. GLENDALE AVE.	GLENDALE	AZ	85301	U	U	FORMER GOVERNOR
MEEHAN, THOMAS	BROOK HOUSE, OBTUSE RD.	NEWTOWN	CT	06470	U	U	SCREENWRITER
MEESE, EDWIN	1075 SPRINGHILL RD.	MC LEAN	VA	22102	U	U	POLITICIAN
MELLENCAMP, JOHN	RT 1, BOX 361	NASHVILLE	IN	47448	U	U	SINGER/SONGWRITER
MELNICK, DANIEL	1123 SUNSET HILLS DR.	LOS ANGELES	CA	90069	A	F	FILM PRODUCER - DECLINES AUTOGRAPH REQUESTS!
MELROSE PLACE	C/O FOX BROADCASTING CO., 10201 W. PICO BLVD.	LOS ANGELES	CA	90035	U	U	TELEVISION SERIES

Esther Muir

in

A Day at the Races [4]

with

the many Brothers for m

Esther Muir

Name	Address	City	State	Zip Code	Resp. Time	Resp. Qual.	Comments
MELTON, SID	5347 CEDROS AVE.	VAN NUYS	CA	91411	U	U	ACTOR
MELVIN, ALLEN	271 N. BOWLING GREEN WAY	LOS ANGELES	CA	90049	A	B+	ACTOR
MELVIN, HAROLD	P.O. BOX 82	GREAT NECK	NY	11021	U	U	SINGER/SONGWRITER
MENENDEZ, LYLE & ERIC	L.A. CNTY. JAIL, 441 BOUCHET ST.	LOS ANGELES	CA	90012	U	U	PATRICIDE DEFENDANTS
MENGES, JEFF A.	C/O WIZARDS OF THE COAST, INC., P.O. BOX 707	RENTON	WA	98057	U	U	ILLUSTRATOR - "MAGIC" CARDS
MENZIES, HEATHER	P.O. BOX 5973-1006	SHERMAN OAKS	CA	91403	U	U	ACTRESS
MERCER, MARIAN	121 N. SAN VICENTE	BEVERLY HILLS	CA	90211	A	B	ACTRESS
MERCHANT, NATALIE	C/O ELEKTRA ENT., 75 ROCKEFELLER PLAZA	NEW YORK	NY	10019	U	U	SINGER - 10,000 MANIACS - **AUTHOR'S CHOICE!**
MEREDITH, BURGESS	25 MALIBU COLONY RD.	MALIBU	CA	90265	A	C	ACTOR/WRITER/DIRECTOR - *BATMAN* - **AUTHOR'S CHOICE!**
MEREDITH, DON	P.O. BOX 597	SANTA FE	NM	87504	U	U	FOOTBALL PLAYER
MERIWETHER, LEE ANN	P.O. BOX 260402	ENCINO	CA	91316	U	U	ACTRESS
MERLIN, JAN	9016 WONDERLAND AVE.	LOS ANGELES	CA	90046	A	B	ACTOR/DIRECTOR
MERRILL, DINA	435 E. 52ND ST.	NEW YORK	NY	10022	U	U	ACTRESS
MERRILL, ROBERT	79 OXFORD DR.	NEW ROCHELLE	NY	10801	B	D	BARITONE
MERRITT, TERESA	192-06 100TH RD.	ST. ALBANS	NY	11412	U	U	ACTRESS
MESSICK, DALE	64 E. CONCORD ST.	ORLANDO	FL	32801	U	U	CARTOONIST
MESSICK, DON	P.O. BOX 5426	SANTA BARBARA	CA	93150	A	B	ACTOR
METCALF, LAURIE	11845 KLING ST.	NORTH HOLLYWOOD	CA	91607	U	U	ACTRESS
METCALFE, BURT	11800 BROOKDALE LN.	STUDIO CITY	CA	91604	U	U	TELEVISION WRITER/PRODUCER
METHENY, PAT	175 BRIGHTON AVE.	BOSTON	MA	02134	U	U	JAZZ MUSICIAN
METRANO, ART	1330 N. DOHENY DR.	LOS ANGELES	CA	90069	A	B+	ACTOR
MEYER, NICHOLAS	2109 STANLEY HILLS DR.	LOS ANGELES	CA	90046	U	U	WRITER/PRODUCER
MEYER, RUSS	3121 ARROWHEAD DR.	LOS ANGELES	CA	90068	A	B	FILM WRITER/PRODUCER
MEYERS, ARI	301 N. CANON DR. #203	BEVERLY HILLS	CA	90210	B	B	ACTRESS - *KATE AND ALLIE*
MICHAEL, GEORGE	2222 MT. CALVARY RD.	SANTA BARBARA	CA	93105	U	U	SINGER/COMPOSER
MICHAELS, AL	C/O ABC SPORTS, 524 W. 57TH ST.	NEW YORK	NY	10019	U	U	SPORTS ANNOUNCER
MICHAELS, LORNE	88 CENTRAL PARK W.	NEW YORK	NY	10023	U	U	TELEVISION WRITER/PRODUCER - *SATURDAY NIGHT LIVE* - **AUTHOR'S CHOICE!**
MICHAELS, MARILYN	185 W. END AVE.	NEW YORK	NY	10023	A	B	COMEDIENNE - TYPICALLY ADDS DRAWINGS!
MICHAELSON, KARI	1717 N. HIGHLAND AVE. #414	LOS ANGELES	CA	90028	U	U	NEWS CORRESPONDENT
MICHELL, KEITH	130 W. 57TH ST. #10-A	NEW YORK	NY	10019	U	U	ACTOR
MICHENER, JAMES	4650 - 54TH AVE.	ST. PETERSBURG	FL	33711	A	C	AUTHOR - *TEXAS* - **AUTHOR'S CHOICE!**

269

Name	Address	City	State	Zip Code	Resp. Time	Resp. Qual.	Comments
MIDLER, BETTE	820 N. SAN VICENTE BLVD. #690	LOS ANGELES	CA	90069	U	U	SINGER/ACTRESS - *THE ROSE*
MIGHTY MORPHIN POWER RANGERS	C/O FOX BROADCASTING CO., 10201 W. PICO BLVD.	LOS ANGELES	CA	90035	U	U	FREEDOM FIGHTERS
MILANO, ALYSSA	151 EL CAMINO DR.	BEVERLY HILLS	CA	90212	U	U	ACTRESS - *WHO'S THE BOSS?*
MILES, JOANNA	2062 N. VINE ST.	LOS ANGELES	CA	90028	U	U	ACTRESS
MILES, SARAH	6A DANBURY ST.	LONDON	ENG	N1 8JJ	U	U	ACTRESS/SINGER - *RYAN'S DAUGHTER*
MILES, SYLVIA	240 CENTRAL PARK S.	NEW YORK	NY	10019	A	B	ACTRESS - *MIDNIGHT COWBOY*
MILES, VERA	P.O. BOX 1704	BIG BEAR LAKE	CA	92315	A	D	ACTRESS - *PSYCHO*
MILFORD, JOHN	334 S. BENTLEY AVE.	LOS ANGELES	CA	90049	U	U	ACTOR
MILKEN, MICHAEL	4543 TARA DR.	ENCINO	CA	91436	U	U	STOCKBROKER
MILLER, ANN	618 N. ALTA DR.	BEVERLY HILLS	CA	90210	A	A+	ACTRESS/DANCER - *ON THE TOWN* - VERY RESPONSIVE TO FAN MAIL!
MILLER, ARTHUR	BOX 320, RR#1, TOPHET RD.	ROXBURY	CT	06783	C	D	AUTHOR/DRAMATIST - *DEATH OF A SALESMAN* - **AUTHOR'S CHOICE!**
MILLER, CHERYL	6767 FOREST LAWN DR. #115	LOS ANGELES	CA	90068	U	U	SPORTS ANALYST
MILLER, JASON	10000 SANTA MONICA BLVD. #305	LOS ANGELES	CA	90067	U	U	ACTOR/WRITER/DIRECTOR
MILLER, JEREMY	6057 RHODES AVE.	NORTH HOLLYWOOD	CA	91606	U	U	ACTOR
MILLER, JODY	RT#3	BLANCHARD	OK	73010	A	B+	SINGER
MILLER, JOHNNY	P.O. BOX 2260	NAPA	CA	94558	A	B	GOLFER
MILLER, LARRY	9000 SUNSET BLVD. #1200	LOS ANGELES	CA	90069	U	U	WRITER
MILLER, MITCH	345 W. 58TH ST.	NEW YORK	NY	10019	A	B	MUSICIAN/COMPOSER
MILLER, PATSY RUTH	425 SIERRA MADRE N.	PALM DESERT	CA	92260	U	U	ACTRESS
MILLER, RAND & ROBYN	C/O BRODERBUND SOFTWARE, INC.,500 REDWOOD BLVD.	NOVATO	CA	94948	U	U	CREATORS OF "MYST" - **AUTHOR'S CHOICE!** - "A GREAT INJUSTICE HAS BEEN DONE ... AND I"
MILLER, SHANNON	715 S. KELLEY AVE.	EDMOND	OK	73034	A	A	GYMNAST
MILLER, SIDNEY	2724 BOTTLEBRUSH DR.	LOS ANGELES	CA	90077	A	B	ACTOR/DIRECTOR
MILLS, ALLEY	444 CAROL CANAL	VENICE	CA	90291	U	U	ACTRESS
MILLS, DONNA	2660 BENEDICT CANYON	BEVERLY HILLS	CA	90210	U	U	ACTRESS/MODEL - *KNOT'S LANDING*
MILLS, HAYLEY	81 HIGH ST.	HAMPTON, MIDDLESEX	ENG		U	U	ACTRESS - *THE PARENT TRAP*
MILLS, JULIET	2890 HIDDEN VALLEY LN.	SANTA BARBARA	CA	93108	U	U	ACTRESS - *NANNY AND THE PROFESSOR*
MILO, APRILE ELIZABETH	METROPOLITAN OPERA ASSOC. INC., LINCOLN CENTER	NEW YORK	NY	10023	A	A+	OPERA SINGER - OUTSTANDING RESPONSE TO HER FAN MAIL!
MILSAP, RONNIE	12 MUSIC CIRCLE SQUARE S.	NASHVILLE	TN	37203	A	B+	SINGER/SONGWRITER
MIMIEUX, YVETTE	500 PERUGIA WAY	LOS ANGELES	CA	90077	U	U	ACTRESS/WRITER - *THE BLACK HOLE*
MINER, JAN	P.O. BOX 293	SOUTHBURY	CT	06488	A	B	ACTRESS

270

Name	Address	City	State	Zip Code	Resp. Time	Resp. Qual.	Comments
MINNELLI, LIZA	150 E. 69TH ST. #21-G	NEW YORK	NY	10021	U	U	ACTRESS/SINGER - *CABARET*
MIRISCH, WALTER	647 WARNER AVE.	LOS ANGELES	CA	90024	A	D	FILM EXECUTIVE/PRODUCER
MISSING PERSONS	11935 LAUREL HILLS RD.	STUDIO CITY	CA	91604	U	U	ROCK GROUP
MITCHELL, DON	1930 S. MARVIN	LOS ANGELES	CA	90016	U	U	ACTOR
MITCHELL, JAMES	330 W. 72ND ST. #12C	NEW YORK	NY	10023	A	B	ACTOR
MITCHELL, JONI	10960 WILSHIRE BLVD. #938	LOS ANGELES	CA	90024	U	U	SINGER/SONGWRITER
MITCHELL, SCOEY	664 W. BROADWAY #A	GLENDALE	CA	91204	U	U	COMEDIAN
MITCHUM, JIM	8942 WILSHIRE BLVD.	BEVERLY HILLS	CA	90211	U	U	ACTOR - *THUNDER ROAD*
MITCHUM, ROBERT	860 SAN YSIDRO RD.	SANTA BARBARA	CA	93108	C	F	ACTOR - *CAPE FEAR* - USES STUDIO FAN MAIL SERVICE TO SEND OUT FACSIMILE SIGNED PHOTO!
MIYORI, KIM	121 N. SAN VICENTE BLVD.	BEVERLY HILLS	CA	90211	U	U	ACTRESS
MODEAN, JAYNE	10000 SANTA MONICA BLVD. #305	LOS ANGELES	CA	90025	A	B	ACTRESS
MODINE, MATTHEW	9696 CULVER BLVD. #203	CULVER CITY	CA	90232	A	A	ACTOR - *VISION QUEST*
MOE, TOMMY	U.S. OLYMPIC COM., 1750 E. BOULDER ST.	COLORADO SPRINGS	CO	80909	U	U	SKIER
MOLINARO, AL	P.O. BOX 9218	GLENDALE	CA	91226	U	U	ACTOR
MOLL, RICHARD	1119 AMALFI DR.	PACIFIC PALISADES	CA	90272	U	U	ACTOR - *NIGHT COURT*
MONASH, PAUL	912 ALTO CEDRO DR.	BEVERLY HILLS	CA	90210	U	U	WRITER/PRODUCER
MONDALE, WALTER	2200 - 1ST BANK PL. E.	MINNEAPOLIS	MN	55402	C	D	FORMER VICE PRESIDENT
MONEY, EDDIE	P.O. BOX 1994	SAN FRANCISCO	CA	94101	A	A+	SINGER - SENT AUTOGRAPHED PHOTO AND INCLUDED LATEST CD SINGLE - AWESOME!
MONKEES	P.O. BOX 1461, RADIO CITY STATION	NEW YORK	NY	10101	U	U	ROCK GROUP - BEST TO TRY IN PERSON - POSSIBLY AT MEMORABILIA SHOW!
MONROE, EARL	113 W. 88TH ST.	NEW YORK	NY	10025	U	U	MEMBER OF THE BASKETBALL HALL OF FAME
MONTAGUE, ASHLEY	321 CHERRY HILL RD.	PRINCETON	NJ	08540	U	U	MODEL
MONTALBAN, RICARDO	1423 ORIOLE DR.	LOS ANGELES	CA	90069	C	B	ACTOR/DIRECTOR - *FANTASY ISLAND*
MONTANA, JOE	C/O NBC SPORTS, 30 ROCKEFELLER PLAZA	NEW YORK	NY	10112	U	U	FUTURE FOOTBALL HALL OF FAME MEMBER - **AUTHOR'S CHOICE!**
MONTANA, MONTE	10326 MONTANA LN.	AGUA DULCE	CA	91350	A	D+	ACTOR
MONTGOMERY, GEORGE	137 S. REEVES DR. #406	BEVERLY HILLS	CA	90212	A	D	ACTOR - *THE TEXAS RANGER*
MONTGOMERY, JULIA	10100 SANTA MONICA BLVD. #2500	LOS ANGELES	CA	90067	U	U	ACTRESS
MOOMAW, DONN	3124 CORDA DR.	LOS ANGELES	CA	90049	A	B	CLERGY
MOON, REV. SUN MYUNG	4 W. 43RD ST.	NEW YORK	NY	10010	U	U	CULT LEADER
MOORE, ALVY	8546 AMESTOV AVE.	NORTHRIDGE	CA	91324	A	B+	ACTOR
MOORE, CLAYTON	4720 PARKOLIVO	CALABASAS	CA	91302	A	B	ACTOR - *THE LONE RANGER*
MOORE, CONSTANCE	10450 WILSHIRE BLVD. #1-B	LOS ANGELES	CA	90024	U	U	ACTRESS

Name	Address	City	State	Zip Code	Resp. Time	Resp. Qual.	Comments
MOORE, DEMI	1453 - 3RD ST. #420	SANTA MONICA	CA	90401	U	U	ACTRESS - *GHOST* - **AUTHOR'S CHOICE!**
MOORE, DICKIE	165 W. 46TH ST. #907	NEW YORK	NY	10036	A	D	ACTOR
MOORE, DUDLEY	73 MARKET ST.	VENICE	CA	90291	A	F	ACTOR/WRITER/PIANIST - *ARTHUR* - STILL SENDING OUT FACSIMILE SIGNED PHOTO FROM *ARTHUR!*
MOORE, JUANITA	3802-L DUNSFORD LN.	INGLEWOOD	CA	90305	A	B	ACTRESS
MOORE, MARY TYLER	927 FIFTH AVE.	NEW YORK	NY	10021	C	F	ACTRESS - *THE MARY TYLER MOORE SHOW* - SENDS OUT FACSIMILE SIGNED PHOTO!
MOORE, MELBA	7004 KENNEDY BLVD. e #325D	GUTTENBERG	NJ	07093	U	U	SINGER
MOORE, TERRY	833 OCEAN AVE. #104	SANTA MONICA	CA	90403	U	U	ACTRESS
MORA, JIM	6928 SAINTS DR.	METAIRIE	LA	70003	A	B	FOOTBALL COACH
MORALES, ESAI	1147 S. WOOSTER ST.	LOS ANGELES	CA	90035	U	U	ACTOR
MORAN, PEGGY	3101 VILLAGE #3	CAMARILLO	CA	93010	A	B	ACTRESS
MORANIS, RICK	90 RIVERSIDE DR. #14-E	NEW YORK	NY	10024	U	U	ACTOR - *HONEY, I SHRUNK THE KIDS*
MORDENTE, TONY	4541 COMBER	ENCINO	CA	91316	A	D	FILM DIRECTOR
MORENO, RITA	1620 AMALFI DR.	PACIFIC PALISADES	CA	90272	A	B	ACTRESS - *WEST SIDE STORY*
MORGAN WEINTRAUB, JANE	27740 PACIFIC COAST HWY.	MALIBU	CA	90265	U	U	ACTRESS
MORGAN, DEDDIE	9000 SUNSET BLVD. #1200	LOS ANGELES	CA	90069	U	U	ACTRESS
MORGAN, HARRY	13172 BOCA DE CANON LN.	LOS ANGELES	CA	90049	U	U	ACTOR/DIRECTOR - *M*A*S*H*
MORGAN, JAYE P.	30835 MAINMAST DR.	AGOURA	CA	91301	U	U	ACTRESS
MORGAN, LORRIE	1209 - 16TH AVE. S.	NASHVILLE	TN	37212	U	U	SINGER
MORGANTHAU, ROBERT M.	1085 PARK AVE.	NEW YORK	NY	10028	U	U	LAWYER
MORIARTY, MICHAEL	200 W. 58TH ST. #3B	NEW YORK	NY	10019	A	B	ACTOR - *LAW AND ORDER*
MORISON, PATRICIA	400 S. HAUSER BLVD.	LOS ANGELES	CA	90036	C	B	ACTRESS/SINGER
MORITA, NORIYUKI "PAT"	P.O. BOX 491278	LOS ANGELES	CA	90049	U	U	ACTOR/COMEDIAN - *THE KARATE KID*
MORLEY, KAREN	75320 BEN AVE. #3	NORTH HOLLYWOOD	CA	91607	U	U	ACTRESS
MORRIS, PHIL	704 STRAND	MANHATTAN BEACH	CA	90266	U	U	ACTOR
MORRISON, TONI	C/O ICM, 8942 WILSHIRE BLVD.	BEVERLY HILLS	CA	90211	U	U	AUTHOR - *BELOVED* - **AUTHOR'S CHOICE!**
MORRISON, VAN	12304 SANTA MONICA BLVD. #300	LOS ANGELES	CA	90025	F	F	SINGER/SONGWRITER - *BROWN EYED GIRL* - **AUTHOR'S CHOICE!** - TYPICALLY UNRESPONSIVE TO FAN MAIL!
MORROW, JEFF	4828-B BALBOA AVE.	ENCINO	CA	91316	U	U	ACTOR
MORROW, KAREN	9400 READCREST DR.	BEVERLY HILLS	CA	90210	U	U	ACTRESS
MORROW, ROB	C/O WILLIAM MORRIS AGCY., 151 EL CAMINO DR.	BEVERLY HILLS	CA	90212	U	U	ACTOR - *NORTHERN EXPOSURE* - **AUTHOR'S CHOICE!**
MORSE, ROBERT	13830 DAVANA TERR.	SHERMAN OAKS	CA	91403	A	B	ACTOR - OFTEN ADDS HAPPY FACE TO SIGNATURE!

Name	Address	City	State	Zip Code	Resp. Time	Resp. Qual.	Comments
MORTON, GARY	40241 CLUBVIEW DR.	RANCHO MIRAGE	CA	92270	A	C	COMEDIAN
MORTON, HOWARD	12311 CANTURA ST.	STUDIO CITY	CA	91604	A	B	ACTOR
MORTON, JOE	606 N. LARCHMONT BLVD. #309	LOS ANGELES	CA	90004	U	U	ACTOR - TERMINATOR 2: JUDGEMENT DAY
MOSCHITTA, JOHN JR.	8033 SUNSET BLVD. #41	LOS ANGELES	CA	90046	A	C	ACTOR
MOSELEY, ROGER E.	3756 PRESTWICK DR.	LOS ANGELES	CA	90027	U	U	ACTOR
MOSES, BILLY	405 SYCAMORE RD.	SANTA MONICA	CA	90402	U	U	ACTOR
MOSS, RONN	7800 BEVERLY BLVD. #3371	LOS ANGELES	CA	90036	C	B+	ACTOR
MOST, DONNY	6301 LANGHALL COURT	AGOURA HILLS	CA	91301	U	U	ACTOR - HAPPY DAYS
MOTHERSBAUGH, MARK	2164 SUNSET PLAZA DR.	LOS ANGELES	CA	90046	U	U	WRITER
MOTT, STEWART	515 MADISON AVE.	NEW YORK	NY	10022	A	F	PHILANTHROPIST - DOESN'T SIGN AUTOGRAPHS ANYMORE!
MOVITA	2766 MOTOR AVE.	LOS ANGELES	CA	90064	A	B	ACTRESS
MOYERS, BILL	524 W. 57TH ST.	NEW YORK	NY	10019	U	U	NEWS CORRESPONDENT - BILL MOYERS' JOURNAL
MR. MISTER	P.O. BOX 69343	LOS ANGELES	CA	90069	U	U	ROCK GROUP
MR. T	395 GREEN BAY RD.	LAKE FORREST	IL	60045	U	U	ACTOR - "PITY, THE FOOL" - THE A-TEAM
MTV NETWORKS	1515 BROADWAY	NEW YORK	NY	10019	U	U	TELEVISION NETWORK
MUDD, ROGER	7167 OLD DOMINION DR.	MC LEAN	VA	22101	A	D	NEWS CORRESPONDENT
MUIR, ESTHER	587-D HERITAGE HILLS DR.	SOMER	NY	10589	A	A	ACTRESS - VERY NICE AND RESPONSIVE TO HER FANS!
MULDAUR, DIANA	259 QUADRO VECCHIO DR.	PACIFIC PALISADES	CA	90272	U	U	ACTRESS - STAR TREK: VOYAGER
MULDAUR, MARIA	P.O. BOX 5535	MILL VALLEY	CA	94942	U	U	SINGER/SONGWRITER
MULGREW, KATE	11938 FOXBORO DR.	LOS ANGELES	CA	90049	U	U	ACTRESS - RYAN'S HOPE
MULHARE, EDWARD	6045 SUNNYSLOPE AVE.	VAN NUYS	CA	91401	B	D	ACTOR - KNIGHT RIDER
MULL, MARTIN	338 CHADBOURNE AVE.	LOS ANGELES	CA	90049	B	B	ACTOR/COMEDIAN/WRITER - MARY HARTMAN, MARY HARTMAN
MULLIGAN, RICHARD	145 S. BEACHWOOD DR.	LOS ANGELES	CA	90004	A	F	ACTOR - EMPTY NEST - SENDS OUT FACSIMILE SIGNED CAST PHOTO!
MULLOY, GARDNER	1 FISHER ISLAND DR.	FISHER ISLAND	FL	33109	A	B	TENNIS PLAYER
MULRONEY, DERMOT	439 N. GOWER	LOS ANGELES	CA	90004	U	U	ACTOR
MUMY, BILLY	8383 WILSHIRE BLVD. #954	BEVERLY HILLS	CA	90211	U	U	ACTOR - LOST IN SPACE
MURDOCH, RUPERT	210 SOUTH ST.	NEW YORK	NY	10002	A	B	PUBLISHER
MURDOCK, GEORGE	5733 SUNFIELD AVE.	LAKEWOOD	CA	90712	U	U	ACTOR
MURPHY, BEN	3601 VISTA PACIFICA #17	MALIBU	CA	90265	U	B+	ACTOR
MURPHY, DALE	P.O. BOX 4064	ATLANTA	GA	30302	B	C	FORMER BASEBALL PLAYER
MURPHY, EDDIE	2727 BENEDICT CANYON DR.	BEVERLY HILLS	CA	90210	A	C	ACTOR/COMEDIAN - **AUTHOR'S CHOICE!**

Name	Address	City	State	Zip Code	Resp. Time	Resp. Qual.	Comments
MURPHY, MICHAEL	P.O. BOX FFF	TAOS	NM	87571	A	B	ACTOR
MURPHY, ROSEMARY	220 E. 73RD ST.	NEW YORK	NY	10021	A	A+	ACTRESS - VERY RESPONSIVE TO FAN MAIL!
MURRAY, BILL	RFD 1, BOX 573	PALISADES	NY	10964	U	U	ACTOR - CATCH HIM AT A CELEBRITY PRO-AM GOLF TOURNAMENT - **AUTHOR'S CHOICE!**
MURRAY, EDDIE	C/O BALTIMORE ORIOLES, 333 W. CAMDEN ST.	BALTIMORE	MD	21201	U	U	BASEBALL PLAYER
MURRAY, JAN	1157 CALLE VISTA	BEVERLY HILLS	CA	93108	A	B	ACTOR/COMEDIAN
MURRAY, KATHERINE	2877 KALAKAUA AVE.	HONOLULU	HI	96815	A	F	DANCE INSTRUCTOR - NO LONGER HONORING AUTOGRAPH REQUESTS!
MURTAGH, KATE	15146 MOORPARK ST.	SHERMAN OAKS	CA	91403	U	U	ACTRESS
MUSANTE, TONY	20TH CENTURY ARTISTS, 15315 MAGNOLIA BLVD. SUITE #429	SHERMAN OAKS	CA	91403	A	A+	ACTOR/WRITER - VERY RESPONSIVE TO FAN MAIL!
MUSBURGER, BRENT	51 W. 52ND ST.	NEW YORK	NY	10019	U	U	SPORTSCASTER
MUSIAL, STAN	85 TRENT DR.	LADUE	MO	63124	U	U	MEMBER OF THE BASEBALL HALL OF FAME
MUSIC, LORENZO	1717 N. HIGHLAND AVE. #414	LOS ANGELES	CA	90028	U	U	WRITER - *RHODA*
MUTCHIE, MARJORIE ANN	1169 MARY CIRCLE	LA VERNE	CA	91750	U	U	ACTRESS
MYERS, DEE DEE	1600 PENNSYLVANIA AVE.	WASHINGTON	DC	20500	A	D	FORMER PRESS SECRETARY
MYERS, MIKE	C/O UNITED TALENT AGCY, 9560 WILSHIRE BLVD. SUITE 500	BEVERLY HILLS	CA	90212	U	U	ACTOR - *WAYNE'S WORLD* - **AUTHOR'S CHOICE!** - SEE IF YOU'RE WORTHY!
MYERSON, BESS	3 E. 71ST ST.	NEW YORK	NY	10021	U	U	COLUMNIST
NABER, JOHN	P.O. BOX 50107	PASADENA	CA	91105	C	D	SWIMMER
NABORS, JIM	215 KALAMANU	HONOLULU	HI	96816	A	D	SINGER/ACTOR - *GOMER PYLE*
NADER, GEORGE	52 S. IWA PL.	LA HAINA	CA	96761	A	D	ACTOR
NADER, MICHAEL	7565 JALMIA WAY	LOS ANGELES	CA	90046	U	U	ACTOR
NADER, RALPH	P.O. BOX 19367	WASHINGTON	DC	20036	U	U	CONSUMER ADVOCATE - *UNSAFE AT ANY SPEED*
NAJIMY, KATHY	40 W. 57TH ST.	NEW YORK	NY	10019	U	U	ACTRESS - *SISTER ACT*
NAMATH, JOE	300 E. 51ST ST. #11-A	NEW YORK	NY	10022	U	U	FOOTBALL PLAYER
NARZ, JACK	1905 BEVERLY PL.	BEVERLY HILLS	CA	90210	U	U	TELEVISION HOST
NASH, GRAHAM	584 N. LARCHMONT BLVD.	HOLLYWOOD	CA	90004	U	U	SINGER/SONGWRITER
NASTASE, ILIE	15 E. 69TH ST.	NEW YORK	NY	10021	U	U	TENNIS PLAYER
NAUD, MELINDA	12330 VIEWCREST RD.	STUDIO CITY	CA	91604	U	U	ACTRESS
NAUGHTON, DAVID	3500 W. OLIVE #1400	BURBANK	CA	91505	C	D	ACTOR/SINGER - *AN AMERICAN WEREWOLF IN LONDON*
NAUGHTON, JAMES	8942 WILSHIRE BLVD.	BEVERLY HILLS	CA	90211	C	B	ACTOR - *THE GOOD MOTHER*
NAVRATILOVA, MARTINA	133 - 1ST ST. N.E.	ST. PETERSBURG	FL	33701	U	U	TENNIS PLAYER

274

Name	Address	City	State	Zip Code	Resp. Time	Resp. Qual.	Comments
NEAL, PATRICIA	P.O. BOX 1043	EDGARTOWN	MA	02539	A	B+	ACTRESS - HUD - SIGNS IN DIFFERENT COLOR INKS!
NEAME, RONALD	2317 KIMRIDGE DR.	BEVERLY HILLS	CA	90210	A	B	FILM DIRECTOR
NEAR, HOLLY	1222 PRESERVATION PKWY.	OAKLAND	CA	94612	A	D	SINGER
NEEDHAM, CONNIE	19721 CASTLEBAR DR.	ROWLAND HEIGHTS	CA	91748	U	U	ACTRESS
NEEDHAM, HAL	2220 AVE. OF THE STARS #302	LOS ANGELES	CA	90067	A	B	WRITER/PRODUCER
NEEDHAM, TRACEY	9229 SUNSET BLVD. #311	LOS ANGELES	CA	90069	U	U	ACTRESS
NEESON, LIAM	9830 WILSHIRE BLVD.	BEVERLY HILLS	CA	90212	A	B	ACTOR - SCHINDLER'S LIST - AUTHOR'S CHOICE!
NEGRON, TAYLOR	9000 SUNSET BLVD. #1200	LOS ANGELES	CA	90069	U	U	ACTOR
NEILL, NOEL	331 SAGE LN.	SANTA MONICA	CA	90402	A	D	ACTRESS - SUPERMAN - NICE IN PERSON!
NEILL, SAM	76 OXFORD ST.	LONDON	ENG	W1R 1RB	U	U	ACTOR - JURASSIC PARK
NEIMAN, LE ROY	1 W. 67TH ST.	NEW YORK	NY	10023	A	D	ARTIST - SPORTS
NELKIN, STACEY	2770 HUTTON DR.	BEVERLY HILLS	CA	90210	U	U	ACTRESS
NELLIGAN, KATE	PRINCE OF WALES THEATRE, COVENTRY STREET	LONDON	ENG	W1	U	U	ACTRESS - THE PRINCE OF TIDES
NELSON, BARRY	134 W. 58TH ST.	NEW YORK	NY	10019	A	C	ACTOR
NELSON, BYRON	FAIRWAY RANCH, RT.2	ROANOKE	TX	76262	A	C	GOLFER
NELSON, DAVID	4179 VALLEY MEADOW RD.	ENCINO	CA	91316	U	U	ACTOR/DIRECTOR - THE ADV. OF OZZIE & HARRIET
NELSON, ED	124 OLD PECAN GROVE	WAVELAND	MS	39576	A	B	ACTOR
NELSON, FRANK	8906 EVANVIEW DR.	LOS ANGELES	CA	90069	U	U	ACTOR
NELSON, HARRIET HILLIARD	4179 VALLEY MEADOW	ENCINO	CA	91316	U	U	ACTRESS/SINGER
NELSON, JOHN ALLEN	9000 SUNSET BLVD. #1200	LOS ANGELES	CA	90069	U	U	ACTOR
NELSON, TRACY	405 SYCAMORE RD.	SANTA MONICA	CA	90402	U	U	ACTRESS - FATHER DOWLING MYSTERIES
NELSON, WILLIE	MARK ROTHBAUM & ASSOC., P.O. BOX 2689	DANBURY	CT	06813	U	U	SINGER - "MAMAS, DON'T LET YOUR BABIES... COWBOYS" - AUTHOR'S CHOICE!
NESMITH, MICHAEL	11858 LE GRANGE AVE.	LOS ANGELES	CA	90025	U	U	SINGER/PRODUCER - THE MONKEES
NETTLETON, LOIS	11762-G MOORPARK ST.	STUDIO CITY	CA	91604	U	U	ACTRESS
NEUWIRTH, BEBE	212-1/2 S. POINSETTIA PL.	LOS ANGELES	CA	90036	U	U	ACTRESS - CHEERS
NEVILLE, AARON	P.O. BOX 750187	NEW ORLEANS	LA	70184	U	U	SINGER - AUTHOR'S CHOICE!
NEWCOME, JOHN	P.O. BOX 469	NEW BRAUNFELS	TX	78130	U	U	TENNIS PLAYER
NEWHART, BOB	420 AMAPOLA LN.	LOS ANGELES	CA	90077	A	D	ACTOR/COMEDIAN - THE BOB NEWHART SHOW
NEWHOUSER, HAL	2584 MARCY CT.	BLOOMFIELD HILLS	MI	48013	U	U	MEMBER OF THE BASEBALL HALL OF FAME
NEWLAND, JOHN	1727 NICHOLS CANYON	LOS ANGELES	CA	90046	A	C	ACTOR
NEWMAN, BARRY	425 N. OAKHURST DR.	BEVERLY HILLS	CA	90210	U	U	ACTOR
NEWMAN, LARAINE	10480 ASHTON AVE.	LOS ANGELES	CA	90024	U	U	ACTRESS - SATURDAY NIGHT LIVE

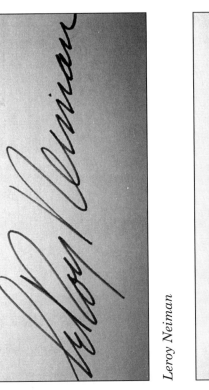

Leroy Neiman

Byron Nelson

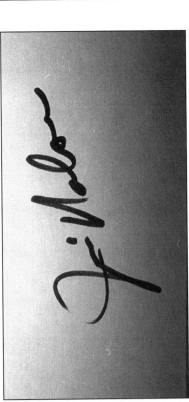

Jim Nabors

Liam Neeson

Name	Address	City	State	Zip Code	Resp. Time	Resp. Qual.	Comments
NEWMAN, PAUL	1120 - 5TH AVE. #1-C	NEW YORK	NY	10128	C	F	ACTOR/AUTO RACER - *THE STING* - SENDS FACSIMILE SIGNED PHOTOGRAPH - **AUTHOR'S CHOICE!** - TOUGH!
NEWMAN, PHYLLIS	529 W. 42ND ST. #7	NEW YORK	NY	10036	U	U	ACTRESS
NEWMAN, RANDY	470 - 26TH ST.	SANTA MONICA	CA	90402	A	B	SINGER/SONGWRITER
NEWMAR, JULIE	204 S. CARMELINA AVE.	LOS ANGELES	CA	90049	U	U	ACTRESS/MODEL
NEWSON, TOMMY	19315 WELLS DR.	TARZANA	CA	91356	U	U	CONDUCTOR
NEWTON, JUICE	P.O. BOX 2993323	LEWISVILLE	TX	75029	A	F	SINGER - "ANGEL OF THE MORNING" - SENDS PRICE LIST - $3 FOR AUTOGRAPHED PHOTO
NEWTON, WAYNE	6629 S. PECOS	LAS VEGAS	NV	89120	U	U	SINGER/ACTOR - "DANKE SHOEN" - **AUTHOR'S CHOICE!**
NEWTON-JOHN, OLIVIA	P.O. BOX 2710	MALIBU	CA	90265	C	D	SINGER/ACTRESS - *GREASE*
NEY, RICHARD	800 S. SAN RAFAEL AVE.	PASADENA	CA	91105	U	U	ACTOR
NICASTRO, MICHELLE	10351 SANTA MONICA BLVD. #211	LOS ANGELES	CA	90025	U	U	ACTRESS
NICHOLAS, DENISE	9169 SUNSET BLVD.	LOS ANGELES	CA	90069	B	B	ACTRESS/SINGER
NICHOLAS, FAYARD	23388 MULHOLLAND DR. #5	WOODLAND HILLS	CA	91364	A	B	DANCER
NICHOLAS, THOMAS IAN	C/O 20TH CENTURY FOX FAN MAIL, BLDG. 89, P.O. BOX 900	BEVERLY HILLS	CA	90213	U	U	ACTOR
NICHOLS, MICHELE	23281 LEONORA DR.	WOODLAND HILLS	CA	91367	U	U	ACTRESS
NICHOLS, MIKE	15 E. 69TH ST.	NEW YORK	NY	10021	U	U	FILM WRITER/DIRECTOR
NICHOLS, STEPHEN	6287 VIEW WAY	LOS ANGELES	CA	90068	U	U	ACTOR
NICHOLSON, JACK	15760 VENTURA BLVD. SUITE 1730	ENCINO	CA	91426	C	B	ACTOR - *BATMAN* - **AUTHOR'S CHOICE!** - CATCH HIM AT HOME LAKERS GAMES!
NICKLAUS, JACK	11760 U.S. HIGHWAY 1 #6	NORTH PALM BEACH	FL	33408	C	B	GOLFER
NICKS, STEVIE	P.O. BOX 6907	ALHAMBRA	CA	91802	U	U	SINGER/SONGWRITER - FLEETWOOD MAC
NICKSON SOUL, JULIA	2232 MORENO DR.	LOS ANGELES	CA	90039	U	U	ACTRESS
NICOL, ALEX	1496 SAN LEANDRO PARK	SANTA BARBARA	CA	93108	A	B	ACTOR
NIELSEN, BRIGITTE	P.O. BOX 57593	SHERMAN OAKS	CA	91403	U	U	ACTRESS - *RED SONJA*
NIELSEN, LESLIE	15760 VENTURA BLVD. #1730	ENCINO	CA	91436	U	U	ACTOR - *NAKED GUN* - **AUTHOR'S CHOICE!**
NIMOY, LEONARD	P.O. BOX 5617	BEVERLY HILLS	CA	90210	A	F	ACTOR/WRITER/DIRECTOR - *STAR TREK* - SENDS OUT FACSIMILE SIGNED PHOTO!
NIPAR, YVETTE	9300 WILSHIRE BLVD. #410	BEVERLY HILLS	CA	90212	U	U	ACTRESS
NIXON, AGNES	774 CONESTOGA RD.	ROSEMONT	PA	19010	A	D	WRITER/PRODUCER
NOBLE, CHELSEA	8730 SUNSET BLVD. #220 - W	LOS ANGELES	CA	90069	U	U	ACTRESS
NOBLE, JAMES	80 BYWATER LN.	BLACK ROCK	CT	06605	A	B	ACTOR
NOGUCHI, DR. THOMAS	1110 AVOCA AVE.	PASADENA	CA	91105	U	U	CORONER

Leonard Nimoy (facsimile)

Denise Nicholas

Denise Nicholas

Name	Address	City	State	Zip Code	Resp. Time	Resp. Qual.	Comments
NOLAN, JEANETTE	RR #1	TROY	MT	59935	U	U	ACTRESS
NOLAN, KATHLEEN	360 E. 55TH ST.	NEW YORK	NY	10022	U	U	ACTRESS
NOLAN, TOM	1334 N. ONTARIO ST.	BURBANK	CA	91505	U	U	WRITER
NOLL, CHUCK	300 STADIUM CIRCLE	PITTSBURGH	PA	15212	A	C	FORMER FOOTBALL COACH
NOLTE, NICK	6174 BONSALL DR.	MALIBU	CA	90265	U	U	ACTOR - 48 HOURS
NOONE, KATHLEEN	12747 RIVERSIDE DR. #208	VALLEY VILLAGE	CA	91607	U	U	ACTRESS
NOONE, PETER	9265 ROBIN LN.	LOS ANGELES	CA	90069	U	U	SINGER - HERMAN'S HERMITS
NORCROSS, CLAYTON	951 GALLOWAY ST.	PACIFIC PALISADES	CA	90272	U	U	ACTOR
NORIEGA, GEN. MANUEL	#28699-079, 15801 S.W. 137 AVE.	MIAMI	FL	33177	B	D	FORMER LEADER OF PANAMA
NORMAN, GREG	P.O. BOX 1189	HOBE SOUND	FL	33475	U	U	GOLFER
NORMAN, MAIDE	455 E. CHARLESTON RD. #132-B	PALO ALTO	CA	94306	A	B	ACTRESS
NORRIS, CHRISTOPHER	3812 WESLIN AVE.	SHERMAN OAKS	CA	91423	U	U	ACTOR
NORRIS, CHUCK	P.O. BOX 872	NAVOSOTA	TX	77868	C	B	ACTOR - GOOD GUYS WEAR BLACK
NORTH, JAY	6259 COLDWATER CANYON #33	NORTH HOLLYWOOD	CA	91606	U	U	ACTOR
NORTH, OLIVER	RR #1, BOX 560	BLUEMONT	VA	22012	U	U	FORMER LT. COL. - IRAN-CONTRA AFFAIR
NORTH, SHEREE	1467 PALISADES DR.	PACIFIC PALISADES	CA	90272	A	A	ACTRESS
NORTHRUP, WAYNE	21919 W. CANON DR.	TOPANGA	CA	90290	U	U	ACTOR
NORTON, KEN	16 S. PECK DR.	LAGUNA NIGUEL	CA	92677	U	U	BOXER/ACTOR
NORTON-TAYLOR, JUDY	6767 FOREST LAWN DR. #115	LOS ANGELES	CA	90068	B	B	ACTRESS/MODEL
NORVILLE, DEBORAH	829 PARK AVE. #10-A	NEW YORK	NY	10021	U	U	RADIO/TELEVISION HOST
NOVACK, WILLIAM	3 ASHTON	NEWTON	MA	02149	U	U	AUTHOR
NOVAK, ROBERT	1750 PENNSYLVANIA AVE. N.W. #1312	WASHINGTON	DC	20006	U	U	NEWS JOURNALIST / COLUMNIST
NOVELLO, DON	P.O. BOX 245	FAIRFAX	CA	94930	A	B	ACTOR/WRITER/COMEDIAN - "FATHER GUIDO SARDUCCI"
NUGENT, TED	8000 ECKERT	CONCORD	MI	49237	U	U	SINGER/GUITARIST
NUYEN, FRANCE	1930 CENTURY PARK W. #303	LOS ANGELES	CA	90067	U	U	ACTRESS
NYE, CARRIE	200 W. 57TH ST. #900	NEW YORK	NY	10019	U	U	ACTRESS
NYE, LOUIS	1241 CORSICA DR.	PACIFIC PALISADES	CA	90272	A	B	ACTOR/COMEDIAN
NYRO, LAURA	P.O. BOX 186	SHOREHAM	NY	11786	U	U	SINGER/SONGWRITER
O'BRIAN, HUGH	10880 WILSHIRE BLVD. #1500	LOS ANGELES	CA	90024	A	F	ACTOR - REQUESTS $25 DONATION FOR AUTOGRAPHED PHOTO! - **AUTHOR'S CHOICE!**
O'BRIEN, CONAN	C/O NBC, 30 ROCKEFELLER PLAZA	NEW YORK	NY	10112	C	B	TALK SHOW HOST
O'BRIEN, MARGARET	1250 LA PERESA DR.	THOUSAND OAKS	CA	91362	A	F	ACTRESS - SENDS PRICE LIST: $5 - CARD, $20 - PHOTO
O'CONNOR, CARROLL	30826 BROAD BEACH RD.	MALIBU	CA	90265	A	B	ACTOR/WRITER/DIRECTOR - ALL IN THE FAMILY

Hideo Nomo signature, write to him c/o Los Angeles Dodgers

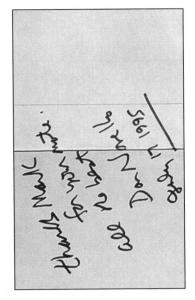

Chuck Norris

To Mark Allen
All The Best
Bob Newhart

Bob Newhart

Thanks Mark
Best wishes to
all Don Novello
11/17 1995

Don Novello

Name	Address	City	State	Zip Code	Resp. Time	Resp. Qual.	Comments
O'CONNOR, DONALD	P.O. BOX 4524	NORTH HOLLYWOOD	CA	91607	U	U	ACTOR/DIRECTOR - SINGIN' IN THE RAIN
O'CONNOR, SANDRA DAY	1 - 1ST ST. N.E.	WASHINGTON	DC	20543	A	D	SUPREME COURT JUSTICE
O'CONNOR, TIM	10000 SANTA MONICA BLVD. #305	LOS ANGELES	CA	90067	A	B	ACTOR
O'DAY, ANITA	RD1, BOX 91	TANNERSVILLE	PA	18372	A	B	ENTERTAINER/SINGER
O'DAY, MOLLY	P.O. BOX 2123	AVILA BEACH	CA	93424	A	B	ACTRESS
O'DELL, TONY	417 GRIFFITH PARK DR.	BURBANK	CA	91506	U	U	ACTOR
O'DONNELL, CHRIS	C/O CREATIVE ARTISTS AGCY., 9560 WILSHIRE BLVD. #900	BEVERLY HILLS	CA	90212	U	U	ACTOR - BATMAN FOREVER - **AUTHOR'S CHOICE!**
O'DONNELL, ROSIE	C/O ICM, 8942 WILSHIRE BLVD.	BEVERLY HILLS	CA	90211	U	U	ACTRESS - **AUTHOR'S CHOICE!**
O'DRISCOLL APPLETON, MARTHA	22 INDIAN CREEK VILLAGE	MIAMI BEACH	FL	33154	A	B	ACTRESS
O'HARA, JENNY	50 W. 13TH ST.	NEW YORK	NY	10011	U	U	ACTRESS
O'HARA, MAUREEN	P.O. BOX 1400, CHRISTIANSTED 00820	ST. CROIX	VI		A	D	ACTRESS - HOW GREEN WAS MY VALLEY
O'KEEFFE, MILES	P.O. BOX 216	MALIBU	CA	90265	A	D	ACTOR
O'LEARY, MICHAEL	8075 W. 3RD ST. #303	LOS ANGELES	CA	90048	A	C	ACTRESS
O'LOUGHLIN, GERALD	P.O. BOX 832	ARLETA	CA	91331	A	B	ACTOR/DIRECTOR
O'NEAL, GRIFFIN	21368 PACIFIC COAST HWY.	MALIBU	CA	90265	U	U	SCREENWRITER
O'NEAL, RYAN	21368 PACIFIC COAST HWY.	MALIBU	CA	90265	U	U	ACTOR - LOVE STORY
O'NEAL, SHAQUILLE	C/O LOS ANGELES LAKERS, 3900 MANCHESTER BLVD., P.O. BOX 10	NGLEWOOD	CA	90306	U	U	BASKETBALL PLAYER - DON'T EVEN THINK ABOUT IT! - SAVE YOUR STAMPS!
O'NEAL, TATUM	211 CENTRAL PARK W.	NEW YORK	NY	10024	A	B+	ACTRESS - PAPER MOON
O'NEIL, DICK	230 S. LASKY DR.	BEVERLY HILLS	CA	90212	A	B	ACTOR
O'NEIL, JENNIFER	32356 MULHOLLAND HWY.	MALIBU	CA	90265	U	U	ACTRESS/MODEL
O'NEILL, ED	2607 GRAND CANAL	VENICE	CA	90291	U	U	ACTOR - MARRIED ... WITH CHILDREN
O'ROUKE, P.J.	THE ATLANTIC MONTHLY, 8 ARLINGTON ST.	BOSTON	MA	02116	U	U	EDITOR
O'SHEA, MILO	40 W. 72ND ST. #17-A	NEW YORK	NY	10023	A	B	ACTOR - THE VERDICT
O'SULLIVAN, MAUREEN	1839 UNION ST.	SCHENECTADY	NY	12309	U	U	ACTRESS - HANNAH AND HER SISTERS
O'TOOLE, ANNETTE	360 MORTON ST.	ASHLAND	OR	97520	U	U	ACTRESS - SUPERMAN III
O'TOOLE, PETER	98 HEATH ST.	LONDON	ENG	NW3	U	U	ACTOR - LAWRENCE OF ARABIA
OAK RIDGE BOYS	329 ROCKLAND RD.	HENDERSONVILLE	TN	37075	A	B	COUNTRY WESTERN GROUP
OATES, ADAM	C/O BOSTON BRUINS, 150 CAUSEWAY ST.	BOSTON	MA	02114	U	U	HOCKEY PLAYER!
OATES, JOHN	130 W. 57TH ST. #12B	NEW YORK	NY	10019	U	U	SINGER/SONGWRITER - HALL & OATES
OERTER, AL	5485 AVENIEDA PESCADERA	FT. MEYERS	FL	33931	U	U	EXECUTIVE/DISCUS THROWER

281

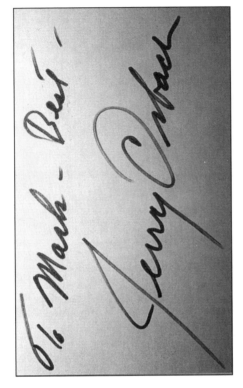

The Oak Ridge Boys

Jerry Orbach

Buck Owens

Carroll O'Connor

Name	Address	City	State	Zip Code	Resp. Time	Resp. Qual.	Comments
OLAJUWON, HAKEEM	C/O HOUSTON ROCKETS, 10 GREENWAY RIVER PLAZA E., P.O. BOX 272349	HOUSTON	TX	77277	U	U	BASKETBALL PLAYER! - "THE DREAM"
OLANDT, KEN	3500 W. OLIVE #1400	BURBANK	CA	91505	A	B	ACTOR
OLDENBURG, CLAUS	556 BROOM ST.	NEW YORK	NY	10013	U	U	ARTIST
OLDHAM, GARY	76 OXFORD ST.	LONDON	ENG	W1R 1RB	U	U	ACTOR - *BRAM STOKER'S DRACULA*
OLEFSON, KEN	6720 HILLPARK DR. #301	LOS ANGELES	CA	90068	A	D	ACTOR
OLIN, KEN	11840 CHAPPARAL ST.	LOS ANGELES	CA	90049	U	U	ACTOR - *THIRTYSOMETHING*
OLIN, LENA	8942 WILSHIRE BLVD.	BEVERLY HILLS	CA	90211	U	U	ACTRESS - *HAVANA*
OLIVER, DAVID	2567 N. BEACHWOOD DR.	LOS ANGELES	CA	90068	U	U	ACTOR
OLMOS, EDWARD JAMES	18034 VENTURA BLVD. #228	ENCINO	CA	91316	C	B	ACTOR - *MIAMI VICE* - WAITED 3-1/2 YEARS FOR A REPLY!
OLSEN, ASHLEY	1450 BELFAST DR.	LOS ANGELES	CA	90069	U	U	ACTRESS - *FULL HOUSE* - **AUTHOR'S CHOICE!**
OLSEN, MARY KATE	1450 BELFAST DR.	LOS ANGELES	CA	90069	U	U	ACTRESS - *FULL HOUSE* - **AUTHOR'S CHOICE!**
OLSEN, NANCY	945 N. ALPINE DR.	BEVERLY HILLS	CA	90210	U	U	ACTRESS
OLSON, JAMES	250 W. 57TH ST. #2223	NEW YORK	NY	10019	A	C	ACTOR
OMARR, SYDNEY	201 OCEAN AVE. #1706-B	SANTA MONICA	CA	90402	U	U	ASTROLOGER/WRITER
ONO, YOKO (LENNON)	1 W. 72ND ST.	NEW YORK	NY	10023	U	U	SINGER/SONGWRITER
ONTKEAN, MICHAEL	7120 GRASSWOOD	MALIBU	CA	90265	U	U	ACTOR - *TWIN PEAKS*
OPATASHU, DAVID	4161 DIXIE CANYON AVE.	SHERMAN OAKS	CA	91423	U	U	ACTOR/WRITER
ORBACH, JERRY	1930 CENTURY PARK W. #403	LOS ANGELES	CA	90067	A	C	ACTOR - *LAW AND ORDER*
ORLANDO, TONY	151 EL CAMINO DR.	BEVERLY HILLS	CA	90212	U	U	SINGER - "TIE A YELLOW RIBBON"
ORLOV, YURI	CORNELL UNIVERSITY, NEWMAN LAB	ITHACA	NY	14853	A	D	SCIENTIST
ORMOND, JULIA	C/O CREATIVE ARTISTS AGCY., 9830 WILSHIRE BLVD.	BEVERLY HILLS	CA	90212	U	U	ACTRESS - *LEGENDS OF THE FALL* - **AUTHOR'S CHOICE!**
ORR, BOBBY	1800 W. MADISON ST.	CHICAGO	IL	60612	U	U	HOCKEY PLAYER
OSBOURNE, OZZY	C/O WILLIAM MORRIS AGCY., 151 EL CAMINO DR.	BEVERLY HILLS	CA	90212	U	U	SINGER - BLACK SABBATH - **AUTHOR'S CHOICE!**
OSLIN, K.T.	1103 - 16TH AVE.	NASHVILLE	TN	37212	U	U	SINGER
OSMOND, CLIFF	630 BIENVENIDA	PACIFIC PALISADES	CA	90272	U	U	SCREENWRITER
OSMOND, KEN	9863 WORNOM AVE.	SUNLAND	CA	91040	A	D	ACTOR
OSMOND, MARIE	P.O. BOX 150245	NASHVILLE	TN	37215	U	U	SINGER/ACTRESS - *THE DONNY & MARIE SHOW*
OSMONDS, THE	P.O. BOX 7122	BRANSON	MO	65616	U	U	VOCAL GROUP
OSTERHAGE, JEFF	210-D N. CORDOVA	BURBANK	CA	91505	U	U	ACTOR
OSTERWALD, BIBI	341 CARROL PARK W.	LONG BEACH	CA	90815	C	B	ACTRESS

Name	Address	City	State	Zip Code	Resp. Time	Resp. Qual.	Comments
OVERALL, PARK	4904 SANCOLA AVE.	NORTH HOLLYWOOD	CA	91602	C	B+	ACTRESS
OVERSTREET, PAUL	P.O. BOX 2977	HENDERSONVILLE	TN	37077	C	D	SINGER
OVITZ, MICHAEL	WALT DISNEY STUDIOS, 500 S. BUENA VISTA ST.	BURBANK	CA	91521	U	U	PRESIDENT OF WALT DISNEY CO. - **AUTHOR'S CHOICE!**
OWEN, RANDY	RT #4	FT. PAYNE	AL	35967	U	U	GUITARIST/SINGER - ALABAMA
OWENS, BUCK	3223 SILLECT AVE.	BAKERSFIELD	CA	93308	A	D	SINGER/SONGWRITER
OWENS, GARY	17856 VIA VALLARTA	ENCINO	CA	91316	A	B	RADIO/TELEVISION PERSONALITY
OWENS, GEOFFREY	19 W. 44TH ST. #1500	NEW YORK	NY	10036	U	U	NEWSPAPER EDITOR
OXENBERG, CATHERINE	1800 CENTURY PARK E. #600	LOS ANGELES	CA	90067	U	U	ACTRESS/MODEL - *DYNASTY*
OZ, FRANK	117 E. 69TH ST.	NEW YORK	NY	10024	C	B	PUPPETEER - *THE MUPPET SHOW*
PAAR, JACK	9 CHATEAU RIDGE DR.	GREENWICH	CT	06830	A	F	FORMER TELEVISION HOST - STAMPS ITEMS WITH FACSIMILE SIGNATURE!
PACE, JUDY	4139 CLOVERDALE	LOS ANGELES	CA	94941	U	U	ACTRESS
PACINO, AL	350 PARK AVE. #900	NEW YORK	NY	10022	A	C	ACTOR - *THE GODFATHER* - **AUTHOR'S CHOICE!**
PACKARD, DAVID	1501 PAGE MILL RD.	PALO ALTO	CA	94304	A	D	BUSINESS EXECUTIVE
PACKARD, VANCE	MILL RD.	NEW CANAAN	CT	06840	U	U	AUTHOR
PACULA, JOANNA	P.O. BOX 5617	BEVERLY HILLS	CA	90210	U	U	ACTRESS - *GORKY PARK*
PAGE, ANITA	929 RUTLAND AVE.	LOS ANGELES	CA	90042	U	U	ACTRESS
PAGE, LAWANDA	1056 W. 84TH ST.	LOS ANGELES	CA	90044	U	U	ACTRESS
PAGE, PATTI	1412 SAN LUCUS COURT	SOLANA BEACH	CA	92075	A	B+	SINGER - ALSO SENDS CHRISTMAS MAPLE PRODUCTS BROCHURE
PAGET, DEBRA	411 KARI COURT	HOUSTON	TX	77024	B	B	ACTRESS
PAIGE, JANIS	1700 RISING GLEN RD.	LOS ANGELES	CA	90069	U	U	ACTRESS
PAKULA, ALAN	330 W. 58TH ST. #5-H	NEW YORK	NY	10019	U	U	WRITER/PRODUCER
PALANCE, HOLLY	2753 ROSCOMARE	LOS ANGELES	CA	90077	U	U	ACTRESS
PALANCE, JACK	15301 VENTURA BLVD. #345	SHERMAN OAKS	CA	91403	U	U	ACTOR - *CITY SLICKERS*
PALMER, ARNOLD	P.O. BOX 52	YOUNGTOWN	PA	15696	A	D	GOLFER
PALMER, BETSY	4040 FARMDALE	STUDIO CITY	CA	91604	A	B	ACTRESS - *I'VE GOT A SECRET*
PALMER, GREGG	5726 GRAVES AVE.	ENCINO	CA	91316	A	B+	ACTOR
PALMER, JIM	BOX 145	BROOKLANDVILLE	MD	21022	U	U	MEMBER OF THE BASEBALL HALL OF FAME - VERY NICE IN PERSON!
PALMER, PETER	1930 CENTURY PARK W. #403	LOS ANGELES	CA	90067	U	U	ACTOR
PALMER, SCOTT	4455 SALTILLO ST.	WOODLAND HILLS	CA	91364	U	U	ACTOR
PALMINTERI, CHAZZ	C/O CREATIVE ARTISTS AGCY., 9830 WILSHIRE BLVD.	BEVERLY HILLS	CA	90212	U	U	ACTOR - *A BRONX TALE* - **AUTHOR'S CHOICE!**

Name	Address	City	State	Zip Code	Resp. Time	Resp. Qual.	Comments
PANETTA, LEON	OFFICE OF MGMT & BUDGET	WASHINGTON	DC	20503	A	C	GOVERNMENT OFFICIAL
PANG, MAY	1619 THIRD AVE. #9D	NEW YORK	NY	10128	A	C	JOHN LENNON'S MISTRESS
PANTALIANO, JOE	2313-30TH ST.	SANTA MONICA	CA	90405	U	U	ACTOR
PARE, MICHAEL	2804 PACIFIC AVE.	VENICE	CA	90291	U	U	ACTOR - *EDDIE & THE CRUISERS*
PARENT, GAIL	2001 MANDEVILLE CANYON	LOS ANGELES	CA	90024	U	U	SCREENWRITER
PARKER, COREY	10431 SCENARIO LN.	LOS ANGELES	CA	90077	U	U	ACTOR
PARKER, ELEANOR	2195 LA PAZ WAY	PALM SPRINGS	CA	92262	A	B	ACTRESS
PARKER, FESS	P.O. BOX 908	LOS OLIVOS	CA	93441	U	U	ACTOR - *DANIEL BOONE*
PARKER, JAMESON	1604 N. VISTA AVE.	LOS ANGELES	CA	90046	U	U	ACTOR - *SIMON & SIMON*
PARKER, LARA	1441 BONNELL	TOPANGA	CA	90290	U	U	ACTRESS
PARKER, SARAH JESSICA	P.O. BOX 611	ENGLEWOOD	NJ	07631	U	U	ACTRESS - **AUTHOR'S CHOICE!**
PARKER, WILLARD	74580 FAIRWAY DR.	INDIAN WELLS	CA	92260	U	U	ACTOR
PARKER-DILLMAN, SUZY	770 HOT SPRINGS RD.	SANTA BARBARA	CA	93103	A	B	ACTRESS
PARKS, ANDREW	1830 GRACE AVE.	LOS ANGELES	CA	90028	C	B	ACTOR
PARKS, MICHAEL	9000 SUNSET BLVD. #1200	LOS ANGELES	CA	90069	U	U	ACTOR
PARKS, ROSA	305 FEDERAL BLDG., 231 W. LAFAYETTE ST.	DETROIT	MI	48226	U	U	ACTIVIST
PARKS, VAN DYKE	837 MELROSE HILL COURT	LOS ANGELES	CA	90036	A	C	SONGWRITER
PARRISH, JULIE	P.O. BOX 247	SANTA MONICA	CA	90406	C	B	ACTRESS - SENDS FLYER WITH PICTURE OF HERSELF WITH ELVIS!
PARROS, PETER	7651 CAMELLIA AVE.	NORTH HOLLYWOOD	CA	91605	U	U	ACTOR
PARSONS, ESTELLE	505 W. END AVE.	NEW YORK	NY	10024	A	D	ACTRESS - *ROSEANNE*
PARSONS, NANCY	121 N SAN VICENTE BLVD.	BEVERLY HILLS	NY	90211	U	U	ACTRESS
PARTON, DOLLY	RT #1, CROCKETT RD.	BRENTWOOD	TN	37027	B	B	SINGER/ACTRESS - "9 TO 5" - **AUTHOR'S CHOICE!**
PARTON, STELLA	P.O. BOX 120295	NASHVILLE	TN	37212	U	U	SINGER
PARTY OF FIVE	C/O FOX BROADCASTING CO., 10201 W. PICO BLVD.	LOS ANGELES	CA	90035	U	U	TELEVISION SERIES - CAST: NEVE CAMPBELL, LACEY CHABERT, MATTHEW FOX, MICHAEL GOORJIAN, SCOTT GRIMES, LOVE HEWITT, AND SCOTT WOLF!
PASDAR, ADRIAN	4250 WILSHIRE BLVD.	LOS ANGELES	CA	90010	U	U	ACTOR
PASTORELLI, ROBERT	2751 HOLLY RIDGE DR.	LOS ANGELES	CA	90068	A	B	ACTOR
PATAKI, GEORGE	STATE OF NEW YORK, EXECUTIVE CHAMBER	ALBANY	NY	12224	U	U	GOVERNOR
PATINKIN, MANDY	200 W. 90TH ST.	NEW YORK	NY	10024	U	U	ACTRESS - *YENTL*
PATRIC, JASON	335 N. MAPLE DR. #250	BEVERLY HILLS	CA	90210	U	U	ACTRESS
PATRICK, ROBERT	9560 WILSHIRE #500	BEVERLY HILLS	CA	90211	U	U	ACTOR - *TERMINATOR 2: JUDGMENT DAY*

285

Arnold Palmer

Patti Page

Name	Address	City	State	Zip Code	Resp. Time	Resp. Qual.	Comments
PATTERSON, FLOYD	P.O. BOX 336	NEW PLATZ	NY	12561	F	F	MEMBER OF THE INTERNATIONAL BOXING HALL OF FAME
PATTERSON, LORNA	10100 SANTA MONICA BLVD. #2500	LOS ANGELES	CA	90067	U	U	ACTRESS - *PRIVATE BENJAMIN*
PATTERSON, NEVA	2498 MANEVILLE CANYON RD.	LOS ANGELES	CA	90049	U	U	ACTRESS
PAUL, DON MICHAEL	3104 WALNUT AVE.	MANHATTAN BEACH	CA	90266	U	U	ACTOR
PAUL, LES	78 DEERHAVEN RD.	MAHWAH	NJ	07610	A	B	GUITARIST
PAUL, RICHARD	3614 WILLOWCREST AVE.	STUDIO CITY	CA	91604	A	B	ACTOR
PAULEY, JANE	271 CENTRAL PARK W. #10-E	NEW YORK	NY	10024	U	U	TELEVISION HOST - *DATELINE NBC* - **AUTHOR'S CHOICE!**
PAVAROTTI, LUCIANO	941 VIA GIARDINI	41040 SALICETA	IT		U	U	TENOR - **AUTHOR'S CHOICE!**
PAVIA, RIA	2110 CALIFORNIA AVE.	SANTA MONICA	CA	90403	B	B+	ACTRESS
PAXTON, BILL	C/O WILLIAM MORRIS AGCY., 151 EL CAMINO DR.	BEVERLY HILLS	CA	90212	U	U	ACTOR
PAYNE, FREDA	10160 CIELO DR.	BEVERLY HILLS	CA	90210	C	B	SINGER
PAYTON, WALTER	1251 E. GOLF RD.	SCHAUMBURG	IL	60195	U	U	EX-FOOTBALL PLAYER/AUTO RACE TEAM OWNER - **AUTHOR'S CHOICE!** - CATCH HIM AT AN INDYCAR RACE!
PAZ, OCTAVIO	LEONARDO DE VINCI 17	MEXICO 19 DF	MX		U	U	POET/DIPLOMAT
PAZIENZA, VINNIE	64 WATERMAN AVE.	CRANSTON	RI	02910	A	B-	BOXER
PEAKER, E.J.	4935 DENSMORE AVE.	ENCINO	CA	91436	C	B	ACTRESS
PEARSON, DURK	P.O. BOX 1067	HOLLYWOOD	FL	33022	U	U	SCIENTIST/AUTHOR
PEASE, PATSY	13538 VALLEY HEART DR.	SHERMAN OAKS	CA	91403	U	U	ACTRESS
PECK, GREGORY	P.O. BOX 837	BEVERLY HILLS	CA	90213	U	U	ACTOR - *TO KILL A MOCKINGBIRD*
PELE (PEROLA NEUGRA)	75 ROCKERFELLER PLAZA	NEW YORK	NY	10019	U	U	SOCCER PLAYER
PELIKAN, LISA	P.O. BOX 57333	SHERMAN OAKS	CA	91406	C	B	ACTRESS
PELL, SEN. CLAIBORNE	335 RUSSELL BLDG.	WASHINGTON	DC	20510	U	U	POLITICIAN
PELUCE, MEENO	2713 N. KEYSTONE	BURBANK	CA	91504	U	U	ACTOR
PENDERGRASS, TEDDY	1505 FLAT ROCK RD.	NARBERTH	PA	19072	A	B	SINGER/SONGWRITER - SENDS AUTOGRAPHED TRADING CARDS!
PENDLETON, AUSTIN	155 E. 76TH ST.	NEW YORK	NY	10021	C	B	ACTOR - *WHAT'S UP DOC*
PENGHLIS, THAO	7187 MACAPA DR.	LOS ANGELES	CA	90068	U	U	ACTOR
PENHALIGON, SUSAN	109 JERMYN ST.	LONDON SW1	ENG		U	U	ACTRESS
PENN & TELLER	P.O. BOX 1196	NEW YORK	NY	10185	U	U	MAGICIANS
PENN, CHRISTOPHER	6728 ZUMIREZ DR.	MALIBU	CA	90265	A	B	ACTOR
PENN, IRVING	PENN STUDIOS, BOX 934, FDR STATION	NEW YORK	NY	10150	U	U	PHOTOGRAPHER

287

Lisa Pelikan

Leon Panetta

Name	Address	City	State	Zip Code	Resp. Time	Resp. Qual.	Comments
PENN, LEO	6728 ZUMIREZ DR.	MALIBU	CA	90265	A	D	FILMWRITER/DIRECTOR
PENN, SEAN	C/O WILLIAM MORRIS AGCY., 151 EL CAMINO DR.	BEVERLY HILLS	CA	90212	U	U	ACTOR - *DEAD MAN WALKING* - **AUTHOR'S CHOICE!**
PENNER, JONATHAN	10351 SANTA MONICA BLVD. #211	LOS ANGELES	CA	90025	U	U	ACTOR
PENNINGTON, ANN	701 N. OAKHURST DR.	BEVERLY HILLS	CA	90210	U	U	ACTRESS/MODEL
PENNINGTON, JANICE	10644 LECONTE AVE.	LOS ANGELES	CA	90024	U	U	MODEL/ACTRESS
PENNY, JOE	10453 SARAH	NORTH HOLLYWOOD	CA	91602	U	U	ACTOR - *JAKE & THE FATMAN*
PENSKE, ROGER	366 PENSKE PLAZA	READING	PA	19603	A	D	AUTO RACING EXECUTIVE
PEP, WILLIE	166 BUNCE RD.	WETHERSFIELD	CT	06109	A	A+	MEMBER OF THE INTERNATIONAL BOXING HALL OF FAME!
PEPA	C/O NEXT PLATEAU RECORDS, 1650 BROADWAY, ROOM 1103	NEW YORK	NY	10019	U	U	SINGER - SALT-N-PEPA - **AUTHOR'S CHOICE!**
PEPPARD, GEORGE	P.O. BOX 1643	BEVERLY HILLS	CA	90213	U	U	ACTOR/DIRECTOR
PEREZ, ROSIE	1135 KENISTON AVE.	LOS ANGELES	CA	90019	U	U	ACTRESS - *DO THE RIGHT THING* - **AUTHOR'S CHOICE!**
PERKINS, CARL	459 COUNTRY CLUB LN.	JACKSON	TN	38301	A	B	SINGER/SONGWRITER - *BLUE SUEDE SHOES*
PERKINS, ELIZABETH	500 S. SEPULVEDA BLVD. #500	LOS ANGELES	CA	90049	U	U	ACTRESS - *BIG*
PERKINS, MILLIE	2511 CANYON DR.	LOS ANGELES	CA	90068	U	U	ACTRESS
PERLMAN, ITZHAK	40 W. 57TH ST.	NEW YORK	NY	10019	B	B	VIOLINIST
PERLMAN, RHEA	31020 BROAD BEACH RD.	MALIBU	CA	90265	U	U	ACTRESS - *CHEERS*
PERLMAN, RON	345 N. MAPLE DR. #183	BEVERLY HILLS	CA	90210	U	U	ACTOR - *BEAUTY & THE BEAST*
PEROT, H. ROSS	1700 LAKESIDE SQUARE	DALLAS	TX	75251	C	D	BUSINESSMAN/SELF-MADE BILLIONAIRE
PERREAU, GIGI	268 N. BOWLING GREEN WAY	LOS ANGELES	CA	90049	A	D	ACTRESS
PERRINO, VALERIE	14411 RIVERSIDE DR.	SHERMAN OAKS	CA	914236	A	D	ACTRESS/MODEL - *LENNY*
PERRY, BARBARA	6926 LA PRESA DR.	LOS ANGELES	CA	90068	A	D+	ACTRESS
PERRY, FELTON	540 S. ST ANDREWS PL.	LOS ANGELES	CA	90020	A	D	ACTOR
PERRY, GAYLORD	320 E. JEFFERIES ST.	GAFFNEY	SC	29342	U	U	MEMBER OF THE BASEBALL HALL OF FAME - SENDS PRICE LIST!
PERRY, JEFF	8458 RIDPATH AVE.	LOS ANGELES	CA	90046	B	B	ACTOR
PERRY, JOHN BENNETT	606 N LARCHMONT BLVD. #309	LOS ANGELES	CA	90004	U	U	ACTOR
PERRY, LUKE	C/O BEVERLY HILLS 90210, FOX BROADCASTING CO., 10201 W. PICO BLVD.	LOS ANGELES	CA	90035	A	F	ACTOR - SENDS OUT FACSIMILE SIGNED POSTCARD!
PERRY, WILLIAM (REFRIGERATOR)	250 N. WASHINGTON RD.	LAKE FOREST	IL	60045	U	U	FOOTBALL PLAYER
PERSOFF, NEHEMIA	5847 TAMPA AVE.	TARZANA	CA	91356	A	C	ACTOR
PESCI, JOE	149 HARRISON ST.	BLOOMFIELD	NJ	07003	A	B	ACTOR - *RAGING BULL* - **AUTHOR'S CHOICE!**

"COMPUTER ERROR!" ON MAILING ADDRESSES IN A JULIE PARRISH NEWS ITEM IN JAILHOUSE ROCKER NEWS #16! -- SEE CORRECTED VERSION BELOW.

Look For Elvis' Co-Star
JULIE PARRISH in TV Series BEVERLY HILLS 90210!

In an episode to be aired on January 10th, 1996, **Julie Parrish** will be playing "Joan Diamond", a new character who was engaged to "Nat", who owns the diner/night club "The Peach Pit"/"After Dark".

Julie played "Joanna" in Elvis' film *"Paradise Hawaiian Style"*. She hasn't been very supportive of Jailhouse Rockers of California, has been a guest speaker at a monthly meeting, and also attended Elvis World – Beverly Hills' as a guest celebrity.

Now, it's our turn to help this loving and caring lady. Please send Julie "fan mail" at any or all of the following addresses. Tell her in your own words that you enjoy the new "Joan Diamond" character, and how nice it is to see her on 90210!, you hope to see her on more episodes! (and, whatever else you'd like to say).

Your Local TV Station:
JULIE PARRISH
C/O BEVERLY HILLS 90210
(Send to your local FOX TV station)

Show:
JULIE PARRISH
C/O BEVERLY HILLS 90210
15001 CALVERT STREET
VAN NUYS   CA   91401

Network:
JULIE PARRISH
C/O BEVERLY HILLS 90210
FOX TELEVISION
SPELLING TELEVISION, INC.
5700 WILSHIRE BOULEVARD
LOS ANGELES   CA   90036

REMEMBER! – PLEASE WAIT UNTIL THE
EPISODE IS AIRED ON JANUARY 10TH.
JULIE THANKS YOU VERY VERY MUCH!

had suffered domestic violence; I wanted a chance to help others.)

It's GREAT to be acting again too! It felt wonderful being on "BEVERLY HILLS 90210" as Joan Diamond!

I really hope to hear from some of you as your letters will help me a lot with keeping the part. I'd love to hear from you anyway, because I know you're ELVIS fans too!
God bless you, Julie

Letter From Julie Parrish:
December 19, 1995

Dear Jailhouse Rockers members,

I want to thank you very much for all of your kind support over the years.

After playing "Maggie Brady" on the CBS soap "Capitol" for 4 ½ years, I went back to school and became a counselor. I now work as a staff counselor at a shelter for battered women and their children. (I chose this career after my sister

Julie Parrish flyer

TAMKIN COLOR

Mark A. Baker
P.O. Box 2492
Liverpool, N.Y.
13089

A Luke Perry facsimile signed postcard response

290

Name	Address	City	State	Zip Code	Resp. Time	Resp. Qual.	Comments
PESCOW, DONNA	2179 W. 21ST ST.	LOS ANGELES	CA	90018	U	U	ACTRESS - *SATURDAY NIGHT FEVER*
PETER, PAUL & MARY	27 W. 67TH ST.	NEW YORK	NY	10023	U	U	VOCAL TRIO
PETERS, BERNADETTE	323 W. 80TH ST.	NEW YORK	NY	10024	U	U	ACTRESS - *PENNIES FROM HEAVEN*
PETERS, BROCK	1420 RISING GLEN RD.	LOS ANGELES	CA	90069	A	C	ACTOR/WRITER/DIRECTOR - *TO KILL A MOCKINGBIRD*
PETERS, JEAN	507 N. PALM DR.	BEVERLY HILLS	CA	90210	U	U	ACTRESS
PETERS, JON	9 BEVERLY PARK	BEVERLY HILLS	CA	90210	U	U	FILM PRODUCER
PETERS, ROBERTA	64 GARDEN RD.	SCARSDALE	NY	10583	A	B	SINGER
PETERSEN, PAT	1634 VETERAN AVE.	LOS ANGELES	CA	90025	U	U	ACTOR
PETERSEN, WILLIAM	8942 WILSHIRE BLVD.	BEVERLY HILLS	CA	90211	U	U	ACTOR - *TO LIVE & DIE IN L.A.*
PETERSON, AMANDA	11350 VENTURA BLVD. #206	STUDIO CITY	CA	91604	U	U	ACTRESS
PETERSON, PAUL	14530 DENKER AVE.	GARDENA	CA	90247	A	D	ACTOR
PETRI, SEN. THOMAS E	HOUSE RAYBURN BLDG. #2262	WASHINGTON	DC	20515	U	U	POLITICIAN
PETTIT, DAN	1808 CARLEN DR.	PLACENTIA	CA	92670	U	U	BASEBALL PLAYER
PETTIT, JOANNA	10100 SANTA MONICA BLVD. #700	LOS ANGELES	CA	90067	U	U	ACTRESS
PETTY, KYLE	830 LEXINGTON RD.	HIGH POINT	NC	27262	C	B	RACE CAR DRIVER - BEST AFTER SEASON!
PETTY, RICHARD	RT #3, BOX 631	RANDLEMAN	NC	27317	A	D	AUTO RACER - "KING RICHARD" - **AUTHOR'S CHOICE!**
PETTY, TOM	8730 SUNSET BLVD., 6TH FL.	LOS ANGELES	CA	90069	U	U	SINGER - "FREE FALLIN" - **AUTHOR'S CHOICE!**
PEYSER, PENNY	22039 ALIZONDO DR.	WOODLAND HILLS	CA	91364	U	U	ACTRESS
PFEIFFER, MICHELLE	C/O ICM, 8942 WILSHIRE BLVD.	BEVERLY HILLS	CA	90211	F	F	ACTRESS - *THE FABULOUS BAKER BOYS* - **AUTHOR'S CHOICE!**
PHAIR, LIZ	C/O ICM, 8942 WILSHIRE BLVD.	BEVERLY HILLS	CA	90211	U	U	SINGER/SONGWRITER - "EXILE IN GUYVILLE" - **AUTHOR'S CHOICE!**
PHILBIN, REGIS	955 PARK AVE.	NEW YORK	NY	10028	A	D	TELEVISION HOST - *LIVE WITH REGIS & KATHIE LEE*
PHILLIPS, CHYNNA	938 - 2ND ST. #302	SANTA MONICA	CA	90403	C	B+	SINGER
PHILLIPS, JOSEPH CA	8730 SUNSET BLVD. #480	LOS ANGELES	CA	90069	U	U	ACTOR
PHILLIPS, JULIA	2534 BENEDICT CANYON	BEVERLY HILLS	CA	90210	U	U	FILM PRODUCER/DIRECTOR
PHILLIPS, LOU DIAMOND	11766 WILSHIRE BLVD. #1470	LOS ANGELES	CA	90025	A	F	ACTOR - *LA BAMBA* - SENDS FACSIMILE SIGNED PHOTO!
PIAZZA, MIKE	C/O LOS ANGELES DODGERS, 1000 ELYSIAN PARK AVE.	LOS ANGELES	CA	90012	U	U	BASEBALL PLAYER
PICERNI, PAUL	19119 WELLS DR.	TARZANA	CA	91356	A	B	ACTOR
PICKLES, CHRISTINA	137 S. WESTGATE AVE.	LOS ANGELES	CA	90049	U	U	ACTRESS
PICKLES, VIVIAN	91 REGENT ST.	LONDON	ENG	W1R 8RU	U	U	ACTRESS
PIERCE, CHARLES	4445 CARTWRIGHT AVE. #309	NORTH HOLLYWOOD	CA	91602	A	B+	IMPERSONATOR

291

Tom Poston

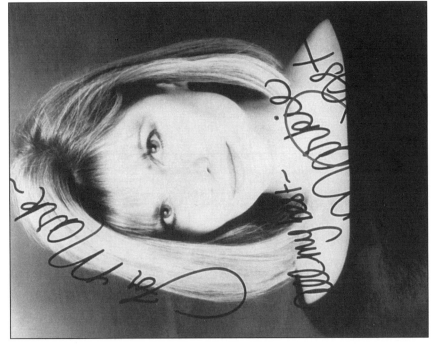

Markie Post

Name	Address	City	State	Zip Code	Resp. Time	Resp. Qual.	Comments
PIERCE, DAVID HYDE	J. MICHAEL BLOOM, 9255 SUNSET BLVD. SUITE 710	LOS ANGELES	CA	90069	U	U	ACTOR - *FRASIER* - **AUTHOR'S CHOICE!**
PIERPOINT, ERIC	10929 MORRISON ST. #14	NORTH HOLLYWOOD	CA	91601	A	B	ACTOR
PIERSALL, JIMMY	1105 OAKVIEW DR.	WHEATON	IL	60187	U	U	BASEBALL PLAYER
PIGOTT-SMITH, TIM	235-241 REGENT ST.	LONDON	ENG	W1R-4PH	U	U	ACTOR
PINCHOT, BRONSON	9200 SUNSET BLVD. #428	LOS ANGELES	CA	90069	U	U	ACTOR - *PERFECT STRANGERS*
PINSENT, GORDON	180 BLOOR ST. W.	TORONTO, ONTARIO	CAN	M5S 2V6	U	U	ACTOR/WRITER
PIRNER, DAVE	COLUMBIA RECORDS, 51 W. 52ND ST.	NEW YORK	NY	10019	U	U	SINGER/SONGWRITER - SOUL ASYLUM - **AUTHOR'S CHOICE!**
PISIER, MARIE-FRANCE	3, QUAI MALAQUAIS	75006 PARIS	FRA		U	U	ACTRESS
PITCHFORD, DEAN	1701 QUEENS RD.	LOS ANGELES	CA	90069	A	D	PRODUCER - *FOOTLOOSE*
PITNEY, GENE	8901 6 MILE RD.	CALEDONIA	WI	53108	U	U	SINGER
PITT, BRAD	C/O CREATIVE ARTISTS AGCY., 9830 WILSHIRE BLVD.	BEVERLY HILLS	CA	90212	U	U	ACTOR - *LEGENDS OF THE FALL* - **AUTHOR'S CHOICE!**
PLACE, MARY KAY	2739 MOTOR AVE.	LOS ANGELES	CA	90064	U	U	ACTRESS/WRITER - *THE BIG CHILL*
PLANT, SCOTT	151 EL CAMINO DR.	BEVERLY HILLS	CA	90212	U	U	ACTOR
PLESHETTE, JOHN	2643 CRESTON DR.	LOS ANGELES	CA	90068	U	U	ACTOR/WRITER - *KNOTS LANDING*
PLESHETTE, SUZANNE	P.O. BOX 1492	BEVERLY HILLS	CA	90213	U	U	ACTRESS - *THE BOB NEWHART SHOW*
PLIMPTON, GEORGE	541 E. 72ND ST.	NEW YORK	NY	10021	U	U	AUTHOR - *FIREWORKS*
PLIMPTON, MARTHA	40 W. 57TH ST.	NEW YORK	NY	10019	U	U	MODEL/ACTRESS
PLUMB, EVE	280 S BEVERLY DR. #400	BEVERLY HILLS	CA	90212	U	U	ACTRESS - *THE BRADY BUNCH*
PLUMMER, AMANDA	49 WAMPUM HILL RD.	WESTON	CT	06883	U	U	ACTRESS - *THE FISHER KING*
PLUMMER, CHRISTOPHER	49 WAMPUM HILL RD.	WESTON	CT	06883	U	U	ACTOR - *THE SOUND OF MUSIC*
PLUMMER, GLENN	924 WESTWOOD BLVD. #900	LOS ANGELES	CA	90024	U	U	ACTOR
PLUNKETT, JIM	51 KILROY WAY	ATHERTON	CA	94025	U	U	FOOTBALL PLAYER
PODEWELL, CATHY	17328 S. CREST DR.	LOS ANGELES	CA	90035	A	B	ACTRESS
POINDEXTER, BUSTER	200 W. 58TH ST.	NEW YORK	NY	10019	U	U	SINGER
POINTER SISTERS	151 EL CAMINO DR.	BEVERLY HILLS	CA	90212	U	U	VOCAL TRIO
POINTER, ANITA	12060 CREST COURT	BEVERLY HILLS	CA	90210	U	U	SINGER
POITIER, SIDNEY	1007 COVE WAY	BEVERLY HILLS	CA	90210	A	F	ACTOR/WRITER/PRODUCER - SENDS FACSIMILE SIGNED PHOTO!
POLANSKI, ROMAN	43 AVE. MONTAIGNE	PARIS	FRA	75008	U	U	ACTOR/WRITER/DIRECTOR - *ROSEMARY'S BABY*
POLLACK, SYDNEY	13525 LUCCA DR.	PACIFIC PALISADES	CA	90272	U	U	WRITER/PRODUCER - *THE WAY WE WERE*
POLLAK, CHERYL	10390 SANTA MONICA BLVD. #300	LOS ANGELES	CA	90025	U	U	MODEL

293

Kelly Preston

Stephanie Powers

Name	Address	City	State	Zip Code	Resp. Time	Resp. Qual.	Comments
POLLARD, MICHAEL J	520 S. BURNSIDE AVE. #12-A	LOS ANGELES	CA	90036	U	U	ACTOR
POOLE, MARK	C/O WIZARDS OF THE COAST, INC., BOX 707	RENTON	WA	98057	B	B	ILLUSTRATOR - "MAGIC" CARDS
POP, IGGY	449 S BEVERLY DR. #102	BEVERLY HILLS	CA	90212	U	U	SINGER
PORIZKOVA, PAULINA	331 NEWBURY ST.	BOSTON	MA	02115	A	D	SUPERMODEL
PORTER, JEAN	3945 WESTFALL DR.	ENCINO	CA	91436	A	D	ACTRESS
PORTER, MARINA OSWALD	RT#1, ROCKWELL COUNTY	HEATH	TX	75087	U	U	WIDOW OF LEE HARVEY OSWALD
POSNER, VLADIMIR	1125-16TH ST. N.W.	WASHINGTON	DC	20036	U	U	RUSSIAN SPOKESMAN
POST, MARKIE	10153 -1/2 RIVERSIDE DR. #333	TOLUCA LAKE	CA	91602	A	A+	ACTRESS - *NIGHT COURT*
POSTON, TOM	2930 DEEP CANYON DR.	BEVERLY HILLS	CA	90210	A	A+	ACTOR
POTTER, CAROL	151 EL CAMINO DR.	BEVERLY HILLS	CA	90210	U	U	ACTRESS - *BEVERLY HILLS 90210*
POTTS, ANNIE	C/O ERWIN STOFF, 7920 SUNSET BLVD. #350	LOS ANGELES	CA	90046	U	U	ACTRESS - *DESIGNING WOMEN*
POTTS, CLIFF	21423 HIGHVALLEY TERR.	TOPANGA	CA	90290	B	C	ACTOR
POUNDER, CCH	121 N. SAN VICENTE BLVD.	BEVERLY HILLS	CA	90211	B	C	ACTOR
POUNDSTONE PAULA	1223 BROADWAY SUITE #162	SANTA MONICA	CA	90404	B	B	COMEDIENNE/TELEVISION SHOW HOST
POVICH, MAURY	250 W. 57TH ST. #26-W	NEW YORK	NY	10019	B	B+	NEWSCASTER - *A CURRENT AFFAIR*
POWELL, GEN. COLIN L.	310 S. HENRY ST.	ALEXANDRIA	VA	22314	U	U	MILITARY LEADER - CATCH HIM ON A BOOK TOUR - TOUGH SIGNATURE!
POWELL, JANE	230 W. 55TH ST. #14-B	NEW YORK	NY	10019	U	U	ACTRESS
POWERS, MALA	10543 VALLEY SPRING LN.	NORTH HOLLYWOOD	CA	91602	A	A+	ACTRESS
POWERS, STEFANIE	P.O. BOX 67981	LOS ANGELES	CA	90067	A	F	ACTRESS - *HART TO HART* - SENDS FACSIMILE SIGNED PHOTO!
POWTER, SUSAN	RPR & ASSOC., 5952 ROYAL LN. SUITE 264	DALLAS	TX	75230	U	U	WEIGHT-LOSS EXPERT! - **AUTHOR'S CHOICE!**
PRANGE, LAURIE	1519 SARGENT PL.	LOS ANGELES	CA	90026	U	U	ACTRESS
PRATHER, JOAN	31647 SEA LEVEL DR.	MALIBU	CA	90265	U	U	ACTRESS
PRATT, JUDSON	8745 OAK PARK AVE.	NORTHRIDGE	CA	91325	U	U	ACTOR
PREMICE, JOSEPHINE	755 W. END AVE.	NEW YORK	NY	10023	U	U	ACTRESS/SINGER/DANCER
PRENTISS, PAULA	719 N. FOOTHILL RD.	BEVERLY HILLS	CA	90120	A	B	ACTRESS - *WHAT'S NEW PUSSYCAT?*
PRESLE, MICHELINE	6 RUE ANTOINE DUBOIS	PARIS	FRA	75006	U	U	ACTRESS
PRESLEY, LISA-MARIE	1167 SUMMIT DR.	BEVERLY HILLS	CA	90210	U	U	ACTRESS - FORMER MRS. MICHAEL JACKSON - **AUTHOR'S CHOICE!**
PRESLEY, PRISCILLA	1167 SUMMIT DR.	BEVERLY HILLS	CA	90210	U	U	ACTRESS/MODEL - *DALLAS* - **AUTHOR'S CHOICE!**
PRESLEY, VESTER	3764 ELVIS PRESLEY BLVD.	MEMPHIS	TN	38116	A	F	SENDS CATALOGS - MAY AUTOGRAPH A COOKBOOK IN THE CATALOG!

Denver Pyle

Name	Address	City	State	Zip Code	Resp. Time	Resp. Qual.	Comments
PRESSMAN, LAWRENCE	15033 ENCANTO DR.	SHERMAN OAKS	CA	91403	U	U	ACTOR
PRESTON, BILLY	4271 GARTHWAITE AVE.	LOS ANGELES	CA	90008	U	U	SINGER
PRESTON, KELLY	12522 MOORPARK ST. #109	STUDIO CITY	CA	91604	U	U	ACTRESS - *52 PICKUP*
PREVIN, ANDRE	8 SHERWOOD LN.	BEDFORD HILLS	NY	10507	U	U	COMPOSER/CONDUCTOR
PREVINE, FRANCOISE	5 RUE BRENZIN	PARIS	FRA	75015	U	U	ACTOR
PRICE, MARC	8444 MAGNOLIA DR.	LOS ANGELES	CA	90046	B	B	ACTOR
PRICE, RAY	P.O. BOX 1986	MT. PLEASANT	TX	75230	U	U	SINGER
PRIDDY, NANCY	329 N. WETHERLY DR. #101	BEVERLY HILLS	CA	90211	U	U	ACTRESS
PRIDE, CHARLIE	3198 ROYAL LN. #204	DALLAS	TX	75229	A	B	SINGER
PRIEST, PAT	P.O. BOX 1298	HATLEY	ID	83333	C	B	ACTRESS - $5 PER PHOTO
PRIESTLEY, JASON	1033 GAYLEY AVE. #208	LOS ANGELES	CA	90024	U	U	ACTOR - *BEVERLY HILLS 90210* - SENDS FACSIMILE SIGNED PHOTO!
PRIMUS, BARRY	2735 CRESTON DR.	LOS ANGELES	CA	90068	A	D	ACTOR/DIRECTOR
PRINCE, CLAYTON	877 RED BARN LN.	HUNTINGDON VALLEY	PA	19006	A	B	ACTOR
PRINCE, JONATHAN	10340 CALVIN AVE.	LOS ANGELES	CA	90025	U	U	ACTOR
PRINCE, WILLIAM	750 N. KINGS RD.	LOS ANGELES	CA	90069	U	U	ACTOR
PRINE, ANDREW	3364 LONGRIDGE AVE.	SHERMAN OAKS	CA	91403	U	U	ACTOR
PRINGLE, JOAN	3500 W. OLIVE #1400	BURBANK	CA	91505	U	U	ACTRESS
PROPHET, RONNIE	1227 SAXON DR.	NASHVILLE	TN	37215	A	D	SINGER/SONGWRITER
PROVINE DAY, DOROTHY	8832 FERNCLIFF N.E.	BAINBRIDGE ISLAND	WA	98110	U	U	ACTRESS
PRUDHOMME, PAUL	P.O. BOX 770034	NEW ORLEANS	LA	70177	U	U	CHEF
PRUETT, JEANNE	1300 DIVISION ST. #103	NASHVILLE	TN	37203	A	B	SINGER
PRYCE, JONATHAN	233 PARK AVE S. - 10TH FL.	NEW YORK	NY	10003	U	U	ACTOR - *MISS SAIGON*
PRYOR, RAIN	730 CLYBOURN AVE.	BURBANK	CA	91505	U	U	ACTRESS/MUSICIAN
PRYOR, RICHARD	16030 VENTURA BLVD. #380	ENCINO	CA	91436	B	B	ACTOR/COMEDIAN - *STIR CRAZY*
PUCK, WOLFGANG	805 N. SIERRA DR.	BEVERLY HILLS	CA	91765	A	D	CHEF/RESTAURATEUR
PUCKETT, KIRBY	C/O MINNESOTA TWINS, 501 CHICAGO AVE. S.	MINNEAPOLIS	MN	55415	U	U	RETIRED BASEBALL PLAYER
PUENTE, TITO	15 GREGG COURT	TAPPAN	NY	10983	A	D	JAZZ MUSICIAN
PUETT, TOMMY	23441 GOLDEN SPRINGS #199	DIAMOND BAR	CA	91765	U	U	ACTOR
PULITZER, ROXANNE	363 COCOANUT ROW	PALM BEACH	FL	33480	U	U	EX-WIFE OF PETER PULITZER
PULLIAM, KESHIA KNIGHT	P.O. BOX 866	TEANECK	NJ	07666	U	U	ACTRESS
PUNSLEY, BERNARD (DR.)	1415 GRANVIA ALTEMEIA	RANCHO PALOS VERDES	CA	90274	U	U	ACTOR
PURCELL, LEE	1317 N. SAN FERNANDO RD. #167	BURBANK	CA	91504	U	U	ACTRESS

Name	Address	City	State	Zip Code	Resp. Time	Resp. Qual.	Comments
PURCELL, SARAH	6524 EXPLANADE ST.	PLAYA DEL REY	CA	90293	U	U	ACTRESS - REAL PEOPLE
PURL LINDA	10417 RAVENWOOD COURT	LOS ANGELES	CA	90077	U	U	ACTRESS
PUTCH, JOHN	5750 WILSHIRE BLVD. #512	LOS ANGELES	CA	90036	A	B	ACTOR
PUZO, MARIO	866 MANON LN.	BAY SHORE	NY	11706	U	U	AUTHOR/SCREENWRITER
PYKE, DENVER	10614 WHIPPLE ST.	NORTH HOLLYWOOD	CA	91602	A	A+	ACTOR/WRITER/DIRECTOR
THE PLATTERS	P.O. BOX 39	LAS VEGAS	NV	89101	U	U	VOCAL GROUP
QADDAFI, COLONEL MUAMMAR EL	OFFICE OF THE PRESIDENT	TRIPOLI		LIBYA	U	U	PRESIDENT OF LIBYA
QUAID, DENNIS	8942 WILSHIRE BLVD.	BEVERLY HILLS	CA	90211	U	U	ACTOR - AUTHOR'S CHOICE!
QUAID, RANDY	P.O. BOX 17372	BEVERLY HILLS	CA	90209	B	F	ACTOR - BEST KNOWN FOR THE LAST PICTURE SHOW
QUARLES, NORMA	1 CNN CENTER, P.O. BOX 30348	ATLANTA	GA	30348	U	U	BROADCAST JOURNALIST
QUAYLE, DAN	11711 N. PENNSYLVANIA ST. #100	CARMEL	IN	46032	A	C	EX-VICE PRESIDENT OF U.S.
QUESTEL, MAE	27 E. 65TH ST.	NEW YORK	NY	10021	U	U	ACTRESS
QUIGLEY, JOAN	1055 CALIFORNIA ST. #14	SAN FRANCISCO	CA	94108	U	U	ASTROLOGER
QUIGLEY, LINNEA	12710 BLYTHE ST.	NORTH HOLLYWOOD	CA	91605	U	U	ACTRESS/MODEL
QUINN, ADRIAN	9830 WILSHIRE BLVD.	BEVERLY HILLS	CA	90212	U	U	ACTOR
QUINN, AILEEN	170 W. END AVE. #3K	NEW YORK	NY	10023	U	U	ACTRESS
QUINN, ANTHONY	60 E. END AVE.	NEW YORK	NY	10028	B	D	ACTOR/DIRECTOR - ZORBA THE GREEK
QUINN, FRANCESCO	1230 N. HORN AVE. #730	LOS ANGELES	CA	90069	B	C	ACTOR
QUINN, GLENN	1999 AVE. OF THE STARS #2850	LOS ANGELES	CA	90067	U	U	ACTOR
QUINN, SALLY	3014 "N" ST. N.W.	WASHINGTON	DC	20007	A	D	JOURNALIST
R.E.M.	P.O. BOX 8032	ATHENS	GA	30603	C	U	ROCK & ROLL GROUP - SENDS FLYER SAYING THAT TIME DOESN'T PERMIT!
RABBITT, EDDIE	P.O. BOX 35286	CLEVELAND	OH	44135	C	D	SINGER - "I LOVE A RAINY NIGHT"
RADZIWELL, LEE	9255 SUNSET BLVD. #901	LOS ANGELES	CA	90069	U	U	SOCIETY LEADER
RAE, CHARLOTTE	P.O. BOX 49991	LOS ANGELES	CA	90049	U	U	ACTRESS
RAFFIN, DEBORAH	2630 EDEN PL.	BEVERLY HILLS	CA	90210	U	U	ACTRESS - ONCE IS NOT ENOUGH
RAFKO, DAYE LANI RAE	4932 FRARY LN.	MONROE	MI	48161	A	A+	FORMER MISS AMERICA
RAFSHOON, GERALD	3028 "Q" ST. N.W.	WASHINGTON	DC	20006	U	U	FORMER PRESIDENTIAL AIDE
RAGIN, JOHN S	5706 BRIARCLIFF RD.	LOS ANGELES	CA	90068	A	B	ACTOR
RAHAL, BOBBY	934A CRESCENT BLVD.	GLEN ELLYN	IL	60137	U	U	RACE CAR DRIVER
RAILSBACK, STEVE	P.O. BOX 1308	LOS ANGELES	CA	90078	U	U	ACTOR
RAINEY, FORD	3821 CARBON CANYON	MALIBU	CA	90265	A	B+	ACTOR - SIGNED BOTH SIDES OF INDEX CARDS!
RAITT, BONNIE	P.O. BOX 626	LOS ANGELES	CA	90078	A	B	SINGER - AUTHOR'S CHOICE!

Name	Address	City	State	Zip Code	Resp. Time	Resp. Qual.	Comments
RAITT, JOHN	1164 NAPOLI DR.	PACIFIC PALISADES	CA	90272	C	A	ACTOR
RALPH, SHERYL LEE	938 S. LONGWOOD	LOS ANGELES	CA	90019	U	U	ACTRESS - *THE DISTINGUISHED GENTLEMAN*
RALSTON, VERA HRUBA	4121 CRECIENTA DR.	SANTA BARBARA	CA	93110	A	C	ACTRESS
RAMSEY, LOGAN	12932 KILLION ST.	VAN NUYS	CA	91401	A	C	ACTRESS
RANDALL, TONY	ONE W. 81ST ST. #6-D	NEW YORK	NY	10024	A	A	ACTOR/DIRECTOR - *THE ODD COUPLE* - A FIRST CLASS GENTLEMAN!
RANDAZZO, TEDDY	5254 OAK ISLAND RD.	ORLANDO	FL	32809	U	U	SINGER
RANDOLPH, BOOTS	209 PRINTERS ALLEY	NASHVILLE	TN	37201	A	B	SAXOPHONIST
RANDOLPH, JOHN	1850 N. WHITLEY PL.	LOS ANGELES	CA	90028	C	B	ACTOR
RANDOLPH, JOYCE	295 CENTRAL PARK W.	NEW YORK	NY	10024	A	B+	ACTRESS - *THE HONEYMOONERS*
RAPHAEL, SALLY JESSY	510 W. 57TH ST. #200	NEW YORK	NY	10019	A	B	TELEVISION SHOW HOST
RASCHE, DAVID	1166 FISKE ST.	PACIFIC PALISADES	CA	90272	U	U	ACTOR - *SLEDGE HAMMER*
RASHAD, AHMAD	30 ROCKEFELLER PLAZA #1411	NEW YORK	NY	10020	C	F	FOOTBALL PLAYER/SPORTSCASTER - FACSIMILE SIGNED PHOTO
RASHAD, PHYLICIA	130 W. 42ND ST. #1804	NEW YORK	NY	10036	U	U	ACTRESS - *THE COSBY SHOW*
RATHER, DAN	524 W. 57TH ST.	NEW YORK	NY	10019	F	F	NEWSCASTER - **AUTHOR'S CHOICE!**
RAUSCHENBERG, ROBERT	C/O LEO CASTELLI GALLERY, 420 W. BROADWAY	NEW YORK	NY	10012	U	U	ARTIST
RAVEN, EDDY	P.O. BOX 1402	HENDERSONVILLE	TN	37075	U	U	SINGER/SONGWRITER
RAWLS, LOU	109 FREMONT PL.	LOS ANGELES	CA	90005	U	U	SINGER
RAYE, MARGUERITE	1329 N. VISTA #106	LOS ANGELES	CA	90046	A	B	ACTRESS
RAYMOND, GENE	250 TRINO WAY	PACIFIC PALISADES	CA	90272	A	D	ACTOR
RAYMOND, GUY	550 ERSKINE DR.	PACIFIC PALISADES	CA	90272	C	D	ACTOR
RAYMOND, PAULA	P.O. BOX 86	BEVERLY HILLS	CA	90213	C	B	ACTRESS
REA, STEPHEN	76 OXFORD ST.	LONDON	ENG	W1N 0AX	U	U	ACTOR
REAGAN, JR. RON	1283 DEVON AVE.	LOS ANGELES	CA	90024	U	U	TELEVISION HOST/DANCER/EX-PRESIDENT'S SON
REAGAN, MAUREEN	10317 DUNLEER	LOS ANGELES	CA	90064	U	U	EX-PRESIDENT'S DAUGHTER
REAGAN, MICHAEL	4740 ALLOTT AVE.	SHERMAN OAKS	CA	91403	U	U	EX-PRESIDENT'S SON
REAGAN, NANCY	668 ST. CLOUD RD.	LOS ANGELES	CA	90077	C	F	EX-FIRST LADY - SENDS FACSIMILE SIGNED PHOTO!
REAGAN, RONALD	668 ST. CLOUD RD.	LOS ANGELES	CA	90077	C	F	ACTOR/EX-PRESIDENT - SENDS FACSIMILE SIGNED PHOTO - **AUTHOR'S CHOICE!**
REASON, REX	20105 RHAPSODY RD.	WALNUT	CA	91789	B	B	ACTOR - *THE ISLAND EARTH*
REASON, RHODES	409 WINCHESTER AVE.	GLENDALE	CA	91201	U	U	ACTOR
RECKELL, PETER	8033 SUNSET BLVD. #4016	LOS ANGELES	CA	90046	U	U	ACTOR

Randy Quaid

Dan Quayle

Francesco Quinn

Name	Address	City	State	Zip Code	Resp. Time	Resp. Qual.	Comments
RED HOT CHILI PEPPERS	11116 AQUA VISTA #39	NORTH HOLLYWOOD	CA	91602	U	U	MUSIC GROUP
REDBONE, LEON	179 AAUESTONG RD.	NEW HOPE	PA	18938	U	U	SINGER/GUITARIST
REDDY, HELEN	820 STANFORD	SANTA MONICA	CA	90403	A	B	SINGER - *THE HELEN REDDY SHOW*
REDDY, JULI	115 N. CAROLWOOD DR.	LOS ANGELES	CA	90077	U	U	ACTRESS
REDFIELD, JAMES	C/O WARNER BOOKS, 666 FIFTH AVE.	NEW YORK	NY	10103	U	U	AUTHOR - *CELESTINE PROPHECY: AN ADVENTURE*
REDFORD, ROBERT	1101-E MONTANA AVE.	SANTA MONICA	CA	90403	B	U	ACTOR/DIRECTOR - **AUTHOR'S CHOICE!** - ALWAYS A TOUGH SIGNATURE! WATCH OUT FOR GHOST SIGNERS!
REDGRAVE, LYNN	21342 COLINA DR.	TOPANGA	CA	90290	A	B	ACTRESS - *HOUSE CALLS*
REDMOND, MARGE	420 MADISON AVE. #1400	NEW YORK	NY	10017	U	U	ACTRESS
REED, LOU	38 E. 68TH ST.	NEW YORK	NY	10021	U	U	MUSICIAN - "SWEET JANE"
REED, MARGARET	524 W. 57TH ST. #5330	NEW YORK	NY	10019	U	U	ACTRESS
REED, PAMELA	1875 CENTURY PARK E. #1300	LOS ANGELES	CA	90067	A	C	ACTRESS
REED, PHILIP	969 BEL AIR RD.	LOS ANGELES	CA	90077	U	U	ACTOR
REED, REX	ONE W. 72ND ST. #86	NEW YORK	NY	10023	A	B	FILM CRITIC
REED-HALL, ALAINA	10636 RATHBURN	NORTHRIDGE	CA	91326	U	U	ACTRESS
REESE, "PEE WEE"	3211 BEALS BRANCH RD.	LOUISVILLE	KY	40206	U	U	MEMBER OF THE BASEBALL HALL OF FAME
REESE, DELLA	P.O. BOX 2812	BEVERLY HILLS	CA	90210	A	A+	SINGER/ACTRESS
REEVE, CHRISTOPHER	RR #2	BEDFORD	CA	10506	U	U	ACTOR - *SUPERMAN* - AN INSPIRATION - **AUTHOR'S CHOICE!**
REEVES, DAN	C/O GIANTS STADIUM	EAST RUTHERFORD	NJ	07073	A	B	FOOTBALL COACH
REEVES, DEL	2804 OPRYLAND DR.	NASHVILLE	TN	37214	A	B	SINGER
REEVES, KEANU	7920 SUNSET BLVD. #350	LOS ANGELES	CA	90046	U	U	ACTOR - *SPEED* - **AUTHOR'S CHOICE!**
REEVES, MARTHA	168 ORCHID DR.	PEARL RIVER	NY	10965	A	F	SINGER - SENDS FAN CLUB FLYER - $5 FOR AUTOGRAPH!
REEVES, STEVE	P.O. BOX 807	VALLEY CENTER	CA	92082	A	F	ACTOR/BODYBUILDER - IT WILL COST YOU SOME MONEY FOR AN AUTOGRAPH FROM "HERCULES"!
REGALBUTO, JOE	724-24TH ST.	SANTA MONICA	CA	90402	U	U	ACTOR - *MURPHY BROWN*
REGEHR, DUNCAN	2501 MAIN ST.	SANTA MONICA	CA	90405	U	U	ACTOR
REGINE	502 PARK AVE.	NEW YORK	NY	10022	U	U	SINGER
REHNQUIST, WILLIAM	ONE 1ST ST. N.E.	WASHINGTON	DC	20543	A	U	SUPREME COURT CHIEF JUSTICE - WATCH FOR AUTOPEN!
REID, DAPHNE MAXWELL	11342 DONA LISA DR.	STUDIO CITY	CA	91604	C	A+	ACTRESS
REID, J.R.	2 FIRST UNION CENTER #2600	CHARLOTTE	NC	28282	U	U	BASKETBALL PLAYER
REILLY, CHARLES NELSON	2341 GLOAMING WAY	BEVERLY HILLS	CA	90210	A	B	ACTOR

301

Della Reese

Ronald Reagan (facsimile)

Nancy Reagan (facsimile)

Name	Address	City	State	Zip Code	Resp. Time	Resp. Qual.	Comments
REILLY, JOHN	602 N. LAS PALMAS AVE.	LOS ANGELES	CA	90004	U	U	ACTOR
REILLY, TOM	8200 WILSHIRE BLVD. #218	BEVERLY HILLS	CA	90211	U	U	ACTOR
REINER, CARL	714 N. RODEO DR.	BEVERLY HILLS	CA	90210	A	D	ACTOR/DIRECTOR - THE DICK VAN DYKE SHOW
REINER, ROB	225 CHADBOURNE AVE.	LOS ANGELES	CA	90049	A	C	ACTOR/DIRECTOR - ALL IN THE FAMILY
REINHOLD, JUDGE	1341 OCEAN AVE. #113	SANTA MONICA	CA	90401	A	A+	ACTOR - BEVERLY HILLS COP
REISER, PAUL	C/O UNITED TALENT AGCY., 9560 WILSHIRE BLVD. SUITE 500	BEVERLY HILLS	CA	90212	U	U	ACTOR - MAD ABOUT YOU - AUTHOR'S CHOICE!
REMSEN, BERT	5722 MAMMOTH AVE.	VAN NUYS	CA	91401	U	U	ACTOR
RENAUD, LINE	1417 N. SPAULDING AVE.	LOS ANGELES	CA	90046	U	U	ACTRESS
RENAY, LIZ	3708 SAN ANGELO AVE.	LAS VEGAS	NV	89102	A	B	BURLESQUE
RENFRO, BRAD	C/O UNITED TALENT AGCY., 9560 WILSHIRE BLVD.	BEVERLY HILLS	CA	90212	U	U	ACTOR
RENO, JANET	DEPT. OF JUSTICE, 10TH & CONSTITUTION	WASHINGTON	DC	20530	U	U	U.S. ATTORNEY GENERAL
RESTON, JAMES	1804 KALLORAMA SQUARE N.W.	WASHINGTON	DC	20008	A	B	COLUMNIST
RETTON, MARY LOU	1815 VIA EL PRADO #209	REDONDO BEACH	CA	90277	C	B	GYMNAST/ACTRESS
REUBENS, PAUL	P.O. BOX 29373	LOS ANGELES	CA	90029	U	U	ACTOR - "PEE WEE HERMAN"
REVILL, CLIVE	15029 ENCANTO DR.	SHERMAN OAKS	CA	91403	U	U	ACTOR
REY, FERNANDO	ORENSE 62	MADRID	SPA	20	U	U	ACTOR
REYES, JR., ERNIE	110351 SANTA MONICA BLVD. #211	LOS ANGELES	CA	90025	U	U	ACTOR
REYNOLDS, BURT	1001 INDIANTOWN RD.	JUPITER	FL	33458	U	U	ACTOR/DIRECTOR - SMOKEY AND THE BANDIT - AUTHOR'S CHOICE!
REYNOLDS, DEBBIE	6514 LANKERSHIM BLVD.	NORTH HOLLYWOOD	CA	91606	A	C	ACTRESS - SINGING IN THE RAIN
REYNOLDS, GENE	2034 CASTILLIAN DR.	LOS ANGELES	CA	90068	A	D	ACTOR/DIRECTOR
REYNOLDS, JAMES	1925 HAMSCOM DR.	SOUTH PASADENA	CA	91109	U	U	ACTOR
REYNOLDS-HAFFEN, MARJORIE	3 CATALINA COURT	MANHATTAN BEACH	CA	90266	C	D	ACTRESS - THE LIFE OF RILEY
REZNOR, TRENT	NOTHING RECORDS, 2337 W. 11TH ST. SUITE 7	CLEVELAND	OH	44113	U	U	SINGER - NINE INCH NAILS - AUTHOR'S CHOICE!
RHETT, ALICIA	50 TRADD ST.	CHARLESTON	SC	29401	U	U	ACTRESS
RHOADES, BARBARA	12366 RIDGE CIRCLE	LOS ANGELES	CA	90049	U	U	ACTRESS
RHODES (BROWN) BETTY	9719 HEATHER RD.	BEVERLY HILLS	CA	90210	U	U	ACTRESS
RHODES, CYNTHIA	15250 VENTURA BLVD. #900	SHERMAN OAKS	CA	91403	U	U	ACTRESS/DANCER
RHODES, DONNELLY	9744 WILSHIRE BLVD. #308	BEVERLY HILLS	CA	90212	U	U	ACTOR
RHUE, MADLYN	148 S. MAPLE DR. #D	BEVERLY HILLS	CA	90212	U	U	ACTRESS
RIBEIO, ALFONSO	19122 HALSTED ST.	NORTHRIDGE	CA	91324	U	U	ACTOR - FRESH PRINCE OF BEL AIR
RIBICOFF, ABRAHAM	425 PARK AVE.	NEW YORK	NY	10022	C	D	EX-GOVERNOR

303

Wayne Rogers

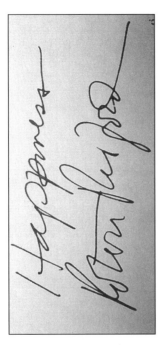

Robert Redford

Al Roker

Name	Address	City	State	Zip Code	Resp. Time	Resp. Qual.	Comments
RICE, ANNE	C/O ALFRED A. KNOPF, 201 E. 50TH ST.	NEW YORK	NY	10022	U	U	AUTHOR - *INTERVIEW WITH THE VAMPIRE* - **AUTHOR'S CHOICE!**
RICE, BOBBY G	505 CANTON PASS	MADISON	TN	37115	A	B	SINGER
RICE, DONNA	P.O. BOX 773	GREAT FALLS	VA	22066	U	U	ACTRESS/MODEL
RICE, JERRY	4949 CENTENNIAL BLVD.	SANTA CLARA	CA	95054	U	U	FOOTBALL PLAYER
RICE, JIM	RR#8	ANDERSON	SC	29621	U	U	EX-BASEBALL PLAYER
RICE, TIM	500 S. BUENA VISTA ST.	BURBANK	CA	91521	U	U	LYRICIST
RICH, ADAM	21848 VANTAGE	CHATSWORTH	CA	91311	U	U	ACTOR - *EIGHT IS ENOUGH*
RICH, CHRISTOPHER	15760 VENTURA BLVD. #1730	ENCINO	CA	91436	U	U	ACTOR
RICHARD, CLIFF	PORTSMOUTH RD., BOX 46A ESHER	SURREY	ENG	KT10 9AA	U	U	SINGER/ACTOR
RICHARD, MAURICE	10950 PELOQUIN	MONTREAL	CAN	PQH2C2 KB	U	U	HOCKEY PLAYER
RICHARDS, ANN GOV.	P.O. BOX 12428	AUSTIN	TX	78711	U	U	GOVERNOR
RICHARDS, BEAH	1842 S. SYCAMORE AVE.	LOS ANGELES	CA	90019	B	B	ACTRESS
RICHARDS, EVAN	10351 SANTA MONICA BLVD. #211	LOS ANGELES	CA	90025	U	U	ACTOR
RICHARDS, KEITH	"REDLANDS" WEST WHITTERING	NEAR CHICESTER SUSSEX	ENG		U	U	MUSICIAN - ROLLING STONES
RICHARDS, MICHAEL	C/O ICM, 8942 WILSHIRE BLVD.	BEVERLY HILLS	CA	90211	U	U	ACTOR - *SEINFELD*
RICHARDSON, BILL REP (MN)	RAYBURN HOUSE OFFICE BLDG. #234	WASHINGTON	DC	20515	U	U	POLITICIAN
RICHARDSON, ELLIOT	1100 CREST LN.	MCLEAN	VA	22101	U	U	DIPLOMAT
RICHARDSON, IAN	131 LAVENDAR SWEEP	LONDON	ENG	SW 11	U	U	ACTOR
RICHARDSON, MIRANDA	195 DEVONSHIRE RD. FOREST HILL	LONDON	ENG	SE 23	U	U	ACTRESS - *THE CRYING GAME*
RICHARDSON, NATASHA	180 W. 58TH ST.	NEW YORK	NY	10019	U	U	ACTRESS/V. REDGRAVE'S DAUGHTER - **AUTHOR'S CHOICE!**
RICHARDSON, PATRICIA	253 - 26TH ST. #A-312	SANTA MONICA	CA	90402	U	U	ACTRESS
RICHIE, LIONEL	5750 WILSHIRE BLVD. #590	LOS ANGELES	CA	90036	A	D	SINGER/SONGWRITER - THE COMMODORES
RICHMAN, PETER MARK	5114 DEL MORENO DR.	WOODLAND HILLS	CA	91364	A	C	ACTOR
RICHTER, JASON JAMES	C/O THE GERSH AGCY., P.O. BOX 5617	BEVERLY HILLS	CA	90212	U	U	ACTOR
RICKLES, DON	925 N. ALPINE DR.	BEVERLY HILLS	CA	90210	A	B	COMEDIAN/ACTOR - *THE DON RICKLES SHOW*
RICKMAN, ALAN	162 - 170 WARDOUR ST.	LONDON	ENG	W1V3AT	U	U	ACTOR - *DIE HARD*
RIDE, SALLY DR.	9500 GILLMAN DR. MS0221	LA JOLLA	CA	92093	A	F	ASTRONAUT - REQUESTS $10 FOR SIGNATURE - **AUTHOR'S CHOICE!**
RIEFENSTAHL, LENI	TENGSTRASSE 20	8000 MUNICH 40	GER		B	B	FILM DIRECTOR
RIFKIN, RON	5604 HOLLY OAK	LOS ANGELES	CA	90068	A	B	ACTOR
RIGBY ,CATHY MCCOY	100 E. WILSHIRE #200	FULLERTON	CA	92632	A	B	GYMNAST

Marion Ross

Billy Joe Royal

Name	Address	City	State	Zip Code	Resp. Time	Resp. Qual.	Comments
RIGG, DIANA	2-4 NOEL ST.	LONDON	ENG	W1V 3RB	U	U	ACTRESS - *THE AVENGERS*
RIGHTEOUS BROTHERS	9841 HOT SPRINGS DR.	HUNTINGTON BEACH	CA	92646	U	U	VOCAL GROUP
RIKER-HALSEY, ROBIN	1089 N. OXFORD AVE.	LOS ANGELES	CA	90029	U	U	ACTRESS
RIKLIS, MESHULAM	23720 MALIBU COLONY RD.	MALIBU	CA	90265	U	U	FILM PRODUCER
RINGWALD, MOLLY	12038 HARTSOOK	NORTH HOLLYWOOD	CA	91607	U	U	ACTRESS - *SIXTEEN CANDLES*
RIORDAN, MAYOR RICHARD	200 N. SPRING ST.	LOS ANGELES	CA	90012	A	B	MAYOR OF LOS ANGELES
RIPKEN, CAL JR.	C/O BALTIMORE ORIOLES, 33 W. CAMDEN ST.	BALTIMORE	MD	21201	U	U	BASEBALL PLAYER - "IRON MAN" - **AUTHOR'S CHOICE!**
RIPPEY, RODNEY ALLEN	1800 N. VINE ST. #120	LOS ANGELES	CA	90028	U	U	ACTOR
RIST, ROBBY	P.O. BOX 867	WOODLAND HILLS	CA	91365	U	U	ACTOR
RITCHIE, CLINT	10000 RIVERSIDE DR. #6	TOLUCA LAKE	CA	91602	U	U	ACTOR
RITENOUR, LEE	P.O. BOX 6774	MALIBU	CA	90265	A	B	GUITARIST
RITTER, JOHN	151 EL CAMINO DR.	BEVERLY HILLS	CA	90212	U	U	ACTOR - *THREE'S COMPANY*
RITTER, TEX (MRS.)	14151 VALLEY VISTA	SHERMAN OAKS	CA	91423	U	U	TEX RITTER'S WIDOW
RIVERA, CHITA	1350 AVE. OF THE AMERICAS	NEW YORK	NY	10019	U	U	ACTRESS/SINGER/DANCER
RIVERA, GERALDO	555 W. 57TH ST. #1100	NEW YORK	NY	10019	A	F	TELEVISION HOST/AUTHOR - NO AUTOGRAPH, SENT MISSING PERSONS LETTER? WHAT?
RIVERO, JORGE	SALVADOR NOVO 71	CUYOACAN 21 DF	MEX		U	U	ACTOR
RIVERS, JOAN	524 W. 57TH ST.	NEW YORK	NY	10019	U	U	COMEDIENNE/TELEVISION HOST - *CAN WE TALK?* - **AUTHOR'S CHOICE!**
RIZZUTO, PHIL	912 WESTMINSTER AVE.	HILLSIDE	NJ	07205	A	A	MEMBER OF THE BASEBALL HALL OF FAME!
ROARKD, ADAM	4520 AIDA PL.	WOODLAND HILLS	CA	91364	U	U	ACTOR
ROBARDS, JASON	10 E. 44TH ST. #500	NEW YORK	NY	10017	A	C	ACTOR - *INHERIT THE WIND*
ROBBIE, SEYMOUR	9980 LIEBE DR.	BEVERLY HILLS	CA	90210	U	U	TELEVISION DIRECTOR
ROBBINS, BRIAN	7743 WOODROW WILSON BLVD.	LOS ANGELES	CA	90046	U	U	ACTOR
ROBBINS, HAROLD	905 N. BEVERLY DR.	BEVERLY HILLS	CA	90210	A	C	NOVELIST
ROBBINS, JEROME	117 E. 81ST ST.	NEW YORK	NY	10028	A	F	CHOREOGRAPHER - "DOESN'T HAVE TIME"
ROBBINS, MARY (MRS.)	713 - 18TH AVE. S.	NASHVILLE	TN	37203	A	C	MARTY ROBBINS'S WIDOW
ROBBINS, TIM	40 W. 57TH ST.	NEW YORK	NY	10019	U	U	ACTOR/DIRECTOR - *DEAD MAN WALKING* - **AUTHOR'S CHOICE!**
ROBERTS, BEVERLY	30912 ARIANA LN.	LAGUNA NIGUEL	CA	92677	C	A	ACTRESS
ROBERTS, COKIE	1717 DESALES ST. N.W.	WASHINGTON	DC	20036	B	B+	NEWS CORRESPONDENT - **AUTHOR'S CHOICE!** - A FIRST CLASS LADY!
ROBERTS, DORIS	6225 QUEBEC DR.	LOS ANGELES	CA	90068	C	B	ACTRESS/DIRECTOR

Name	Address	City	State	Zip Code	Resp. Time	Resp. Qual.	Comments
ROBERTS, JAKE "THE SNAKE"	P.O. BOX 3859	STAMFORD	CT	06905	U	U	WRESTLER
ROBERTS, JULIA	C/O E. GOLDSMITH, 8942 WILSHIRE BLVD.	BEVERLY HILLS	CA	90211	U	U	ACTRESS - *PRETTY WOMAN* - **AUTHOR'S CHOICE!**
ROBERTS, ORAL	7777 LEWIS ST.	TULSA	OK	74130	U	U	EVANGELIST
ROBERTS, PAT REP (KS)	HOUSE LONGWORTH BLDG. #1125	WASHINGTON	DC	20515	U	U	POLITICIAN
ROBERTS, PERNELL	20395 SEABORAD RD.	MALIBU	CA	90265	U	U	ACTOR
ROBERTS, ROBIN	504 TERRACE HILL DR.	TEMPLE TERRACE	FL	33617	U	U	MEMBER OF THE BASEBALL HALL OF FAME
ROBERTS, TONY	970 PARK AVE. #8-N	NEW YORK	NY	10028	C	B	ACTOR - *PLAY IT AGAIN SAM*
ROBERTSON, CLIFF	325 DUNMERE DR.	LA JOLLA	CA	92037	U	U	ACTOR/WRITER/DIRECTOR
ROBERTSON, DALE	15301 VENTURA BLVD. #345	SHERMAN OAKS	CA	91403	U	U	ACTOR
ROBERTSON, OSCAR	P.O. BOX 179	SPRINGFIELD	MA	01101	U	U	FORMER BASKETBALL PLAYER
ROBERTSON, PAT	100 CENTERVILLE TURNPIKE	VIRGINIA BEACH	VA	23463	A	F	EVANGELIST - SENDS UNSIGNED PHOTO!
ROBINSON, BROOKS	36 S. CHARLES ST. #2000	BALTIMORE	MD	21201	U	U	MEMBER OF BASEBALL HALL OF FAME
ROBINSON, CHARLES KNOX	10637 BURBANK BLVD.	NORTH HOLLYWOOD	CA	91601	U	U	ACTOR
ROBINSON, CHRIS	9300 WILSHIRE BLVD. #410	BEVERLY HILLS	CA	90212	U	U	ACTOR/DIRECTOR
ROBINSON, DAVID	C/O SAN ANTONIO SPURS, 100 MONTANA ST.	SAN ANTONIO	TX	78203	U	U	BASKETBALL PLAYER
ROBINSON, FRANK	15557 AQUA VERDE DR.	LOS ANGELES	CA	90077	U	U	MEMBER OF THE BASEBALL HALL OF FAME
ROBINSON, JAY	13757 MILBANK AVE.	SHERMAN OAKS	CA	91403	U	U	ACTOR - *THE ROBE*
ROBINSON, RANDALL	545 - 8TH ST. S.E. #200	WASHINGTON	DC	20003	U	U	ACTIVIST
ROBINSON, SMOKEY	17085 RANCHO ST.	ENCINO	CA	91316	U	U	SINGER/SONGWRITER
ROBUSTELLI, ANDY	74 WEDGEMERE RD.	STAMFORD	CT	06901	A	B	MEMBER OF THE FOOTBALL HALL OF FAME!
ROCCO, ALEX	1755 OCEAN OAKS RD.	CARPINTERIA	CA	93013	A	B	ACTOR
ROCKEFELLER, DAVID JR.	30 ROCKEFELLER PLAZA #5600	NEW YORK	NY	10112	B	F	BUSINESSMAN - "COMPANY POLICY PROHIBITS FULFILLING REQUESTS" - WHAT?
ROCKEFELLER, MRS. NELSON	812 FIFTH AVE.	NEW YORK	NY	10024	U	U	WIDOW OF NELSON ROCKEFELLER
ROCKEFELLER, SHARON	2121 PARK RD. N.W.	WASHINGTON	DC	20010	A	C	WIFE OF JOHN D. ROCKEFELLER
ROCKWELL, ROBERT	650 TOYOPA DR.	PACIFIC PALISADES	CA	90272	A	B	ACTOR
RODD, MARCIA	11738 MOORPARK ST. #C	STUDIO CITY	CA	91604	A	B	ACTRESS
RODMAN, DENNIS	C/O CHICAGO BULLS, 980 N. MICHIGAN AVE. SUITE 1600	CHICAGO	IL	60611	U	U	BASKETBALL PLAYER - "HAIR" RODMAN!
RODRIGUEZ, CHI CHI	1720 MERRIMAN RD., P.O. BOX 5118	AKRON	OH	44334	A	F	GOLFER - SENDS FACSIMILE SIGNED REPRODUCTION!
RODRIGUEZ, JOHNNY	P.O. BOX 120725	NASHVILLE	TN	37212	U	U	SINGER/SONGWRITER
ROE, TOMMY	P.O. BOX 26037	MINNEAPOLIS	MN	55426	A	B	SINGER/SONGWRITER
ROGER, CHARLES "BUDDY"	1147 PICKFAIR WAY	BEVERLY HILLS	CA	90210	U	U	ACTOR

308

Name	Address	City	State	Zip Code	Resp. Time	Resp. Qual.	Comments
ROGERS, KENNY	RT. 1, BOX 100	COLBERT	GA	30628	U	U	SINGER/SONGWRITER - "THE GAMBLER"
ROGERS, MIMI	9830 WILSHIRE BLVD.	BEVERLY HILLS	CA	90212	C	D	ACTRESS - SOMEONE TO WATCH OVER ME
ROGERS, MR. (FRED)	4802 - 5TH AVE.	PITTSBURGH	PA	15213	A	A	CHILDREN'S TELEVISION SHOW HOST - A FIRST CLASS GENTLEMAN! - AUTHOR'S CHOICE!
ROGERS, ROY	15650 SENECA RD.	VICTORVILLE	CA	92392	A	F	ACTOR/SINGER/GUITARIST - SAVE YOUR STAMPS!
ROGERS, SUZANNE	11266 CANTON DR.	STUDIO CITY	CA	91604	U	U	ACTRESS
ROGERS, TRISTAN	8550 HOLLYWAY DR. #301	LOS ANGELES	CA	90069	U	U	ACTOR
ROGGIN, FRED	11828 LA GRANGE AVE.	LOS ANGELES	CA	90025	A	A+	ACTOR/WRITER/DIRECTOR - M*A*S*H
ROKER, AL	3000 W. ALAMEDA AVE.	BURBANK	CA	91523	U	U	TELEVISION HOST
ROLLE, ESTHER	C/O NBC, 30 ROCKEFELLER PLAZA	NEW YORK	NY	10112	A	A+	TELEVISION WEATHERMAN
ROLLING STONES	P.O. BOX 8986	LOS ANGELES	CA	90008	B	B	ACTRESS - DRIVING MISS DAISY
ROLLINS, HOWARD E. JR.	1776 BROADWAY #507	NEW YORK	NY	10019	U	U	ROCK GROUP - GOOD IN PERSON!
ROLLINS, SONNY	123 W. 85TH ST. #4-F	NEW YORK	NY	10024	A	D	ACTOR - IN THE HEAT OF THE NIGHT
ROMAN, LULU	RT. 9-G	GERMANTOWN	NY	12526	A	D	SAXOPHONIST
ROMAN, RUTH	P.O. BOX 140400	NASHVILLE	TN	37214	A	B	ACTRESS
ROMANUS, RICHARD	1225 CLIFF DR.	LAGUNA BEACH	CA	92651	U	U	ACTRESS - THE LONG, HOT SUMMER
ROMERO, GEORGE	1840 CAMINO PALMERO	LOS ANGELES	CA	90046	C	B	ACTOR
ROMERO, NED	3364 LAKE RD. N.	SANIBEL	FL	33957	U	U	FILMMAKER/SCREENWRITER
RONSTADT, LINDA	9255 SUNSET BLVD. #515	LOS ANGELES	CA	90069	A	D	ACTOR
ROONEY, ANDY	644 N. DOHENY	LOS ANGELES	CA	90069	U	U	SINGER - "PIRATES OF PENZANCE"
ROONEY, MICKEY	254 ROWAYTON AVE.	ROWAYTON	CT	06853	U	U	WRITER/BROADCAST JOURNALIST - 60 MINUTES
ROSE MARIE	1400 REDSAIL CIRCLE	WESTLAKE VILLAGE	CA	91361	A	B	ACTOR - NATIONAL VELVET
ROSE, AXL	6916 CHISHOLM AVE.	VAN NUYS	CA	91406	U	U	ACTRESS/SINGER - THE DICK VAN DYKE SHOW
ROSE, CHARLIE	C/O GEFFEN RECORDS, 9130 SUNSET BLVD.	LOS ANGELES	CA	90069	U	U	SINGER - GUNS N' ROSES - UNPREDICTABLE IN PERSON OR IN ANY SITUATION - AUTHOR'S CHOICE!
	136 STATE CAPITOL BLDG., 356 W. 58TH ST., 15TH FL.	NEW YORK	NY	10019	U	U	TALK SHOW HOST
ROSE, JAMIE	335 N. MAPLE DR. #250	BEVERLY HILLS	CA	90210	U	U	ACTRESS
ROSE, MURRAY	3305 CARSE DR.	LOS ANGELES	CA	90028	U	U	SWIMMER
ROSE, SHERRI	1758 LAUREL CANYON BLVD.	LOS ANGELES	CA	90046	U	U	ACTRESS
ROSEANNE	C/O WILLIAM MORRIS AGCY., 151 EL CAMINO BLVD.	BEVERLY HILLS	CA	90212	A	F	ACTRESS - ROSEANNE - SENDS FACSIMILE SIGNED PHOTO! AUTHOR'S CHOICE! GOOD LUCK!
ROSENZWEIG, BARNEY	308 N. SYCAMORE #502	LOS ANGELES	CA	90036	U	U	TELEVISION WRITER/PRODUCER
ROSS, DIANA	P.O. BOX 11059, GLENVILLE STATION	GREENWICH	CT	06831	U	U	SINGER/ACTRESS - "LADY SINGS THE BLUES"
ROSS, KATHERINE	33050 PACIFIC COAST HWY.	MALIBU	CA	90265	U	U	ACTRESS - THE GRADUATE

Name	Address	City	State	Zip Code	Resp. Time	Resp. Qual.	Comments
ROSS, MARION	14159 RIVERSIDE DR. #101	SHERMAN OAKS	CA	91423	A	B	ACTRESS - *HAPPY DAYS*
ROSS, STAN	1410 N. GARDNER	LOS ANGELES	CA	90046	U	U	ACTOR
ROSSELLINI, ISABELLA	881 - 7TH AVE. #1110	NEW YORK	NY	10019	U	U	ACTRESS/MODEL - *BLUE VELVET*
ROSSEN, CAROL	1119 - 23RD ST. #8	SANTA MONICA	CA	90403	U	U	ACTRESS
ROSTOW, WALT	1 WILDWIND POINT	AUSTIN	TX	78746	A	B	ECONOMIST
ROSTROPOVICH, MISTISLAV	NATIONAL SYMPHONY ORCHESTRA, KENNEDY CENTER	WASHINGTON	DC	20566	U	U	COMPOSER/CELLIST
ROTH, DAVID LEE	9016 WILSHIRE BLVD. #346	BEVERLY HILLS	CA	90211	U	U	SINGER/SONGWRITER - "JUST A GIGOLO"
ROTHROCK, CYNTHIA	4201 VANOWEN PL.	BURBANK	CA	91505	C	D	MARTIAL ARTS STAR
ROWE, MISTY	880 GREENLEAF CANYON	TOPANGA	CA	90290	U	U	ACTRESS
ROWLAND, BETTY	125 N. BARRINGTON AVE. #103	LOS ANGELES	CA	90049	U	U	BURLESQUE
ROWLANDS, GENA	7917 WOODROW WILSON DR.	LOS ANGELES	CA	90046	A	C	ACTRESS - *GLORIA*
ROY, PATRICK	C/O COLORADO AVALANCHE, MCNICHOLS SPORTS ARENA, 1635 CLAY ST.	DENVER	CO	80204	C	B	HOCKEY GOALIE
ROYAL, BILLY JOE	48 MUSIC SQUARE E.	NASHVILLE	TN	37203	C	B	SINGER/SONGWRITER
ROYKO, MIKE	435 N. MICHIGAN AVE.	CHICAGO	IL	60611	U	U	COLUMNIST
ROZELLE, PETE	P.O. BOX 9686	RANCHO SANTA FE	CA	92067	U	U	FORMER FOOTBALL COMMISSIONER
RUBINSTEIN, ZELDA	8730 SUNSET BLVD. #220-W	LOS ANGELES	CA	90069	U	U	ACTRESS
RUDDY, AL	1601 CLEARVIEW DR.	BEVERLY HILLS	CA	90210	A	C	FILM WRITER/PRODUCER
RUDNER, RITA	2934 BEVERLY GLEN CIRCLE #389	LOS ANGELES	CA	90077	U	U	COMEDIENNE
RUEHL, MERCEDES	129 MAC DOUGAL ST.	NEW YORK	NY	10012	U	U	ACTRESS - *LOST IN YONKERS*
RULE, JANICE	105 W. 72ND ST. #12B	NEW YORK	NY	10023	U	U	ACTRESS
RUN D.M.C.	296 ELIZABETH ST.	NEW YORK	NY	10012	U	U	RAP GROUP
RUNYON, JENNIFER	7309 W. 82ND ST.	LOS ANGELES	CA	90045	U	U	ACTRESS
RUSH, BARBARA	1709 TROPICAL AVE.	BEVERLY HILLS	CA	90210	A	B	ACTRESS
RUSH, CHRISTOPHER	C/O WIZARDS OF THE COAST, INC., P.O. BOX 707	RENTON	WA	98057	U	U	ILLUSTRATOR - "MAGIC" CARDS
RUSH, JENNIFER	145 CENTRAL PARK W.	NEW YORK	NY	10023	U	U	SINGER
RUSHTON, JARED	104 LEMON GROVE	IRVINE	CA	92720	U	U	ACTOR
RUSSELL, BILL	P.O. BOX 58	MERCER ISLAND	WA	98040	U	U	MEMBER OF BASKETBALL HALL OF FAME - A TOUGH SIGNATURE, REAL TOUGH!
RUSSELL, BING	229 E. GAINSBOROUGH RD.	THOUSAND OAKS	CA	91360	U	U	ACTOR
RUSSELL, BRENDA	9000 SUNSET BLVD. #1200	LOS ANGELES	CA	90069	U	U	SINGER
RUSSELL, HAROLD	34 OLD TOWN RD.	HYANNIS	MA	02601	U	U	GOVERNMENT OFFICIAL
RUSSELL, JANE	2934 TORITO RD.	SANTA BARBARA	CA	93108	U	U	ACTRESS - *GENTLEMEN PREFER BLONDES*

Name	Address	City	State	Zip Code	Resp. Time	Resp. Qual.	Comments
RUSSELL, JOHNNY	P.O. BOX DRAWER 37	HENDERSONVILLE	TN	37075	C	B	SINGER/SONGWRITER
RUSSELL, KIMBERLY	11617 LAURELWOOD	STUDIO CITY	CA	91604	U	U	ACTRESS
RUSSELL, KURT	1900 AVE. OF THE STARS #1240	LOS ANGELES	CA	90067	U	U	ACTOR - *TOMBSTONE*
RUSSELL, MARK	2800 WISCONSIN AVE. #810	WASHINGTON	DC	20007	U	U	SATIRIST/COMEDIAN
RUSSELL, NIPSEY	353 W. 57TH ST.	NEW YORK	NY	10019	U	U	COMEDIAN/WRITER/DIRECTOR - *CAR 54, WHERE ARE YOU?*
RUSSELL, THERESA	9454 LLOYD CREST DR.	BEVERLY HILLS	CA	90210	U	U	ACTRESS - *BLACK WIDOW*
RUTHERFORD, ANN	826 GREENWAY DR.	BEVERLY HILLS	CA	90210	C	B	ACTRESS
RUTHERFORD, JOHNNY	4919 BLACK OAK LN.	FORT WORTH	TX	76114	B	D	AUTO RACER
RYAN, FRANK	4204 WOODLAND	BURBANK	CA	91505	C	B	ACTOR
RYAN, MEG	11718 BARRINGTON COURT #508	LOS ANGELES	CA	90049	U	U	ACTRESS - *WHEN HARRY MET SALLY* - **AUTHOR'S CHOICE!**
RYAN, MITCHELL	30355 MULHOLLAND DR.	CORNELL	CA	91301	U	U	ACTOR
RYAN, NOLAN	P.O. BOX 670	ALVIN	TX	77512	A	D	BASEBALL PLAYER - WATCH FOR AUTOPEN!
RYAN, PEGGY	1821 E. OAKLEY BLVD.	LAS VEGAS	NV	89104	C	B	ACTRESS
RYDELL, BOBBY	917 BRYN MAWR AVE.	NARBERTH	PA	19072	A	B	SINGER
RYDELL, CHRISTOPHER	911 N. SWEETZER #C	LOS ANGELES	CA	90069	U	U	ACTOR
RYDELL, MARK	1 TOPSAIL	MARINA DEL REY	CA	90292	C	D	ACTOR/DIRECTOR
RYDER, WINONA	1636 N. BEVERLY DR.	BEVERLY HILLS	CA	90210	U	U	ACTRESS - *LITTLE WOMEN* - **AUTHOR'S CHOICE!**
RYERSON, ANN	935 GAYLEY AVE.	LOS ANGELES	CA	90024	U	U	ACTRESS
RYUN, JIM	RT. 3, BOX 62-B	LAWRENCE	KS	66044	A	F	TRACK ATHLETE - SENDS PRICE LIST!
SABATINI, GABRIELA	133 - 1ST ST. N.E.	ST. PETERSBERG	FL	33701	U	U	TENNIS PLAYER
SACCHI, ROBERT	232 S. WINDSOR BLVD.	LOS ANGELES	CA	90004	U	U	ACTOR
SADE	1-3 MORTIMER ST.	LONDON	ENG	W1	U	U	SINGER/SONGWRITER
SAFER, MORLEY	51 W. 52ND ST.	NEW YORK	NY	10019	U	U	BROADCAST JOURNALIST - *60 MINUTES*
SAFIRE, WILLIAM	6200 ELMWOOD RD.	CHEVY CHASE	MD	20815	U	U	COLUMNIST
SAGAL, JEAN	10351 SANTA MONICA BLVD. #211	LOS ANGELES	CA	90025	U	U	ACTRESS
SAGAL, KATEY	7095 HOLLYWOOD BLVD. #792	LOS ANGELES	CA	90028	U	U	ACTRESS - *MARRIED … WITH CHILDREN*
SAGAL, LIZ	10351 SANTA MONICA BLVD. #211	LOS ANGELES	CA	90025	U	U	ACTRESS
SAGAN, DR. CARL E.	CORNELL UNIV. SPACE/SCIENCE BLDG.	ITHACA	NY	14853	A	U	ASTRONOMER/WRITER - COULDN'T SIGN DUE TO HEALTH
SAGER, CAROLE BAYER	280 N. CAROLWOOD DR.	LOS ANGELES	CA	90077	A	B	SINGER/SONGWRITER
SAHL, MORT	2325 SAN YSIDRO DR.	BEVERLY HILLS	CA	90210	U	U	COMEDIAN/WRITER
SAINT JAMES, SUSAN	9830 WILSHIRE BLVD.	BEVERLY HILLS	CA	90212	U	U	ACTRESS - *KATE & ALLIE*
SAINT , EVA MARIE	10590 WILSHIRE BLVD. #408	LOS ANGELES	CA	90024	A	D	ACTRESS - *ON THE WATERFRONT*

Name	Address	City	State	Zip Code	Resp. Time	Resp. Qual.	Comments
SAINTE-MARIE, BUFFY	RR #1, BOX 368	KAPAA, KAUAI	HI	96746	U	U	SINGER/SONGWRITER
SAJAK, PAT	3400 RIVERSIDE DR.	BURBANK	CA	91505	U	U	TELEVISION HOST - *WHEEL OF FORTUNE*
SALDANA, TERESA	10637 BURBANK BLVD.	NORTH HOLLYWOOD	CA	91601	U	U	ACTRESS - *THE COMMISH*
SALENGER, MEREDITH	12700 VENTURA BLVD. #100	STUDIO CITY	CA	91604	U	U	ACTRESS
SALES, SOUPY	245 E. 35TH ST.	NEW YORK	NY	10016	U	U	ACTOR/COMEDIAN - *THE SOUPY SALES SHOW*
SALINGER, J.D.	RR #3, BOX 176	CORNISH FLAT	NH	03746	U	F	AUTHOR - *CATCHER IN THE RYE* - IMPOSSIBLE!
SALINGER, MATT	21604 PASEO SERRA	MALIBU	CA	90265	U	U	ACTOR
SALINGER, PIERRE	1850 "M" ST. N.W. #900	WASHINGTON	DC	20036	A	B	NEWS CORRESPONDENT
SALT	C/O NEXT PLATEAU RECORDS, 1650 BROADWAY, ROOM 1103	NEW YORK	NY	10019	U	U	SINGER - SALT-N-PEPA - **AUTHOR'S CHOICE!**
SALTER, HANS J.	3658 WOODHILL CANYON PL.	STUDIO CITY	CA	91604	U	U	COMPOSER/CONDUCTOR
SAM THE SHAM	3667 TETWILER AVE.	MEMPHIS	TN	38122	A	B	VOCAL GROUP
SAMMS, EMMA	335 N. MAPLE DR. #360	BEVERLY HILLS	CA	90210	U	U	ACTRESS - *DYNASTY*
SAMUELS, RON	120 S. EL CAMINO DR. #116	BEVERLY HILLS	CA	90212	U	U	TALENT AGENT
SAN GIACOMO, LAURA	335 N. MAPLE DR. #254	BEVERLY HILLS	CA	90210	U	U	ACTRESS - *SEX, LIES AND VIDEOTAPE*
SAN JUAN, OLGA	4845 WILLOWCREST AVE.	STUDIO CITY	CA	91604	U	U	DANCER/COMEDIENNE
SAND, PAUL	10100 SANTA MONICA BLVD. #2500	LOS ANGELES	CA	90067	U	U	ACTOR
SANDERS, BARRY	C/O DETROIT LIONS, P.O. BOX 4200	PONTIAC	MI	48057	U	U	FOOTBALL PLAYER
SANDERS, DEION	C/O DALLAS COWBOYS, 1 COWBOY PKWY.	IRVING	TX	75063	U	U	"NEON DEION" - ATHLETE, ACTOR, OR "BOTH"
SANDERS, DOUG	8828 SANDRINGHAM	HOUSTON	TX	77024	B	D	GOLFER
SANDERS, SUMMER	730 SUNRISE AVE.	ROSEVILLE	CA	95661	B	B	SWIMMER
SANDERSON, WILLIAM	8271 MELROSE AVE. #110	LOS ANGELES	CA	90046	U	U	ACTOR
SANDLER, ADAM	C/O CREATIVE ARTISTS AGCY., 9830 WILSHIRE BLVD.	BEVERLY HILLS	CA	90212	U	U	ACTOR - **AUTHOR'S CHOICE!**
SANDRICH, JAY	610 N. MAPLE DR.	BEVERLY HILLS	CA	90210	U	U	ACTOR/DIRECTOR
SANDS, TOMMY	11833 GILMORE ST. #17	NORTH HOLLYWOOD	CA	91606	U	U	ACTOR/SINGER
SANDY, BABY	6846 HAYWOOD	TUJUNGA	CA	91042	U	U	ACTRESS
SANTANA	P.O. BOX 881630	SAN FRANCISCO	CA	94188	U	U	ROCK GROUP
SANTONI, PENNY	1918 N. EDGEMONT ST.	LOS ANGELES	CA	90027	U	U	ACTRESS
SANTONI, RENI	247 S. BEVERLY DR. #102	BEVERLY HILLS	CA	90212	U	U	ACTOR
SARA, MIA	130 W. 42ND ST. #1804	NEW YORK	NY	10036	U	U	ACTRESS
SARANDON, CHRIS	107 GLASCO TURNPIKE	WOODSTOCK	NY	12498	U	U	ACTOR - *DOG DAY AFTERNOON*
SARANDON, SUSAN	C/O CINDY BERGER, PMK, 1776 BROADWAY, 8TH FL.	NEW YORK	NY	10019	U	U	ACTRESS - *DEAD MAN WALKING* - **AUTHOR'S CHOICE!**
SARAZEN, GENE	EMERALD BEACH, P.O. BOX 677	MARCO	FL	33937	A	B	GOLFER

Name	Address	City	State	Zip Code	Resp. Time	Resp. Qual.	Comments
SARDI, VINCENT JR.	234 W. 44TH ST.	NEW YORK	NY	10036	U	U	RESTAURATEUR
SARRAZIN, MICHAEL	9920 BEVERLY GROVE	BEVERLY HILLS	CA	90210	U	U	ACTOR
SASSOON, VIDAL	1163 CALLE VISTA	BEVERLY HILLS	CA	90210	A	C	HAIR STYLIST
SAVAGE, ANN	8218-B DE LONGPRE AVE.	LOS ANGELES	CA	90069	C	D	ACTRESS
SAVAGE, FRED	9830 WILSHIRE BLVD.	BEVERLY HILLS	CA	90212	C	F	ACTOR - *THE WONDER YEARS* - SENDS FACSIMILE SIGNED CARD
SAVAGE, TRACIE	6212 BANNER AVE.	LOS ANGELES	CA	90038	U	U	ACTRESS
SAVED BY THE BELL	NBC-TV, 3000 W. ALAMEDA AVE.	BURBANK	CA	91523	U	U	TELEVISION SERIES
SAVIDGE, JENNIFER	2705 GLENDOWER AVE.	LOS ANGELES	CA	90027	U	U	ACTRESS
SAWA, DEVON	C/O KAZARIAN, SPENCER & ASSOC., INC., 11365 VENTURA BLVD., SUITE 100	STUDIO CITY	CA	91604	U	U	ACTOR
SAWYER, DIANE	1965 BROADWAY #400	NEW YORK	NY	10023	A	B	BROADCAST JOURNALIST - *60 MINUTES* - **AUTHOR'S CHOICE!**
SAXON, JOHN	2432 BANYAN DR.	LOS ANGELES	CA	90049	U	U	ACTOR/WRITER
SAYERS, GALE	624 BUCH RD.	NORTHBROOK	IL	60062	U	U	FOOTBALL PLAYER
SCALIA, ANTONIN	1 - 1ST ST. N.E.	WASHINGTON	DC	20543	U	U	SUPREME COURT JUSTICE
SCALIA, JACK	P.O. BOX 215	NEW CANTON	VA	23123	U	U	ACTOR - *WOLF*
SCARWID, DIANA	P.O. BOX 3614	SAVANNAH	GA	31404	U	U	ACTRESS
SCAVULLO, FRANCESCO	216 E. 63RD ST.	NEW YORK	NY	10021	A	B	PHOTOGRAPHER
SCHAAL, WENDY	C/O GAGE GROUP, 9255 SUNSET BLVD. #515	LOS ANGELES	CA	90069	A	B+	ACTRESS
SCHAEFFER, GEORGE	1040 WOODLAND DR.	BEVERLY HILLS	CA	90210	A	C	TELEVISION PRODUCER/DIRECTOR
SCHALLERT, WILLIAM	14920 RAMOS PL.	PACIFIC PALISADES	CA	90272	U	U	ACTOR
SCHEIDER, ROY	1775 BROADWAY #609	NEW YORK	NY	10019	U	U	ACTOR - *JAWS*
SCHELL, MAXIMILIAN	P.O. BOX 7426	BEVERLY HILLS	CA	90212	U	U	ACTOR - *JUDGMENT AT NUREMBURG*
SCHELL, RONNIE	4024 SAPPHIRE DR.	ENCINO	CA	91316	U	U	COMEDIAN/ACTOR
SCHEMBECHLER, BO	1000 S. STATE ST.	ANN ARBOR	MI	48109	A	B	FORMER FOOTBALL/BASEBALL COACH
SCHERRER, PAUL	9000 SUNSET BLVD. #1200	LOS ANGELES	CA	90069	U	U	ACTOR
SCHIAVELLI, VINCENT	450 N. ROSSMORE AVE. #206	LOS ANGELES	CA	90004	A	B	ACTOR
SCHIEFFER, BOB	2020 "M" ST. N.W.	WASHINGTON	DC	20036	A	B+	BROADCAST JOURNALIST
SCHIFFER, CLAUDIA	5 UNION SQUARE W. #500	NEW YORK	NY	10003	C	A	SUPERMODEL - **AUTHOR'S CHOICE!**
SCHIFRIN, LALO	710 N. HILLCREST RD.	BEVERLY HILLS	CA	90210	C	C	COMPOSER/CONDUCTOR
SCHILLING, WILLIAM	626 N. VALLEY ST.	BURBANK	CA	91505	A	C	ACTOR
SCHIRRA, WALTER	P.O. BOX 73	RANCHO SANTA FE	CA	92067	U	U	ASTRONAUT
SCHLAFLY, PHYLLIS	68 FAIRMONT	ALTON	IL	62002	A	C	AUTHOR/POLITICIAN

Vito Scotti

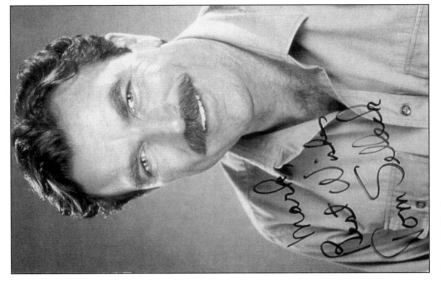

Tom Selleck

Name	Address	City	State	Zip Code	Resp. Time	Resp. Qual.	Comments
SCHLATTER, CHARLIE	13501 CONTOUR DR.	SHERMAN OAKS	CA	91423	U	U	ACTOR
SCHLATTER, GEORGE	400 ROBERT LN.	BEVERLY HILLS	CA	90210	A	D	WRITER/PRODUCER
SCHLESINGER, ARTHUR JR.	33 W. 42ND ST.	NEW YORK	NY	10036	A	B	HISTORIAN/AUTHOR
SCHLOSSBERG, EDWIN	641 AVE. OF THE AMERICAS	NEW YORK	NY	10011	U	U	ARTIST
SCHMELING, MAX	2114 HOLLENSTEDT	NORDHEIDE	GER		U	U	BOXER
SCHNEIDER, JOHN	12031 VENTURA BLVD. #1	STUDIO CITY	CA	91604	U	U	ACTOR/WRITER/SINGER - THE DUKES OF HAZZARD
SCHNETZER, STEPHEN	448 W. 44TH ST.	NEW YORK	NY	10036	U	U	ACTOR
SCHOCK, GINA	P.O. BOX 4398	NORTH HOLLYWOOD	CA	91617	U	U	DRUMMER/SINGER
SCHOELLKOPF, CAROLYN HUNT	100 CRESCENT #1700	DALLAS	TX	75201	U	U	BUSINESSWOMAN
SCHOENDIENST, RED	331 LADUE WOODS CT.	CREVE COUER	MO	63141	U	U	MEMBER OF THE BASEBALL HALL OF FAME
SCHORR, DANIEL	3113 WOODLEY RD.	WASHINGTON	DC	20008	A	B	BROADCAST JOURNALIST
SCHOTT, MARGE	100 RIVERFRONT STADIUM	CINCINNATI	OH	45202	A	D	BASEBALL TEAM OWNER - MAY ADD DOG PRINT
SCHRAMM, TEX	9355 SUNNYBROOK	DALLAS	TX	75220	C	B	FOOTBALL TEAM EXECUTIVE
SCHREIBER, AVERY	6612 RANCHITO	VAN NUYS	CA	91405	A	B	ACTOR/COMEDIAN
SCHROEDER, BARBET	1478 N. KINGS RD.	LOS ANGELES	CA	90069	U	U	FILM DIRECTOR
SCHUBB, MARK	9744 WILSHIRE BLVD. #308	BEVERLY HILLS	CA	90212	U	U	ACTOR
SCHUCK, JOHN	702 CALIFORNIA COURT	VENICE	CA	90291	U	U	ACTOR
SCHULBERG, BUDD	P.O. BOX 707, BROOKSIDE	WESTHAMPTON BEACH	NY	11978	U	U	TELEVISION WRITER
SCHULLER, DR. ROBERT	464 S. ESPLANADE	ORANGE	CA	92669	A	B+	EVANGELIST
SCHULZ, CHARLES	1 SNOOPY PL.	SANTA ROSA	CA	95401	A	F	CARTOONIST - PEANUTS - NO LONGER SIGNS AUTOGRAPHS
SCHUUR, DIANE	9000 SUNSET BLVD. #1200	LOS ANGELES	CA	90069	A	D	SINGER
SCHWAB, CHARLES	101 MONTGOMERY ST.	SAN FRANCISCO	CA	94104	U	U	SECURITIES ANALYST
SCHWARZENEGGER, ARNOLD	P.O. BOX 1234	SANTA MONICA	CA	90406	C	B	ACTOR - THE TERMINATOR - **AUTHOR'S CHOICE!**
SCHWARZKOPF, GEN. NORMAN	400 N. ASHLEY DR. #3050	TAMPA	FL	33602	U	U	MILITARY LEADER - A VERY TOUGH SIGNATURE!
SCIALFA, PATTI	11 GIMBEL PL.	OCEAN	NJ	07712	U	U	SINGER - BRUCE SPRINGSTEEN & THE E STREET BAND
SCIORRA, ANNABELLA	1033 GAYLEY AVE. #208	LOS ANGELES	CA	90024	U	U	ACTRESS - THE HAND THAT ROCKS THE CRADLE
SCOGGINS, TRACY	1131 ALTA LOMA RD. #515	LOS ANGELES	CA	90069	U	U	ACTRESS/MODEL
SCOLARI, PETER	1104 FOOTHILL BLVD.	OJAI	CA	93023	U	U	ACTOR - NEWHART
SCORSESE, MARTIN	445 PARK AVE. #700	NEW YORK	NY	10022	U	U	FILM WRITER/PRODUCER - **AUTHOR'S CHOICE!**
SCOTT, BYRON	31815 CAMINO CAPISTRANO #C	SAN JUAN CAPISTRANO	CA	92675	U	U	BASKETBALL PLAYER
SCOTT, CAMPBELL	3211 RETREAT COURT	MALIBU	CA	90265	U	U	ACTOR
SCOTT, DR. GENE	1615 GLENDALE AVE.	GLENDALE	CA	91205	U	U	TELEVISION HOST/TEACHER

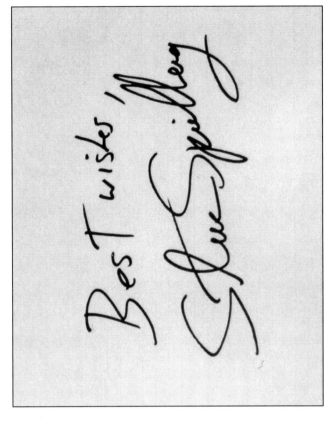

Steven Spielberg (facsimile)

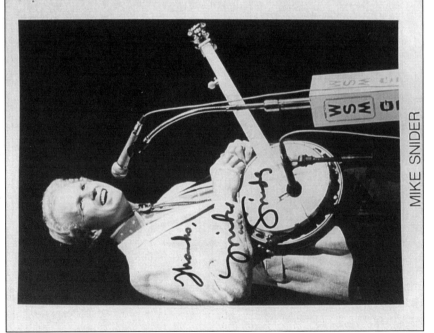

Mike Snider

Name	Address	City	State	Zip Code	Resp. Time	Resp. Qual.	Comments
SCOTT, FRED	1716 E. RAMON RD. #42	PALM SPRINGS	CA	92264	U	U	ACTOR
SCOTT, GEORGE C.	3211 RETREAT COURT	MALIBU	CA	90265	U	U	ACTOR/DIRECTOR - *PATTON*
SCOTT, JACQUELINE	12456 VENTURA BLVD. #1	STUDIO CITY	CA	91604	U	U	ACTRESS
SCOTT, JUDSON	10000 SANTA MONICA BLVD. #305	LOS ANGELES	CA	90067	A	B	ACTOR
SCOTT, LIZABETH	P.O. BOX 69405	LOS ANGELES	CA	90069	U	U	ACTRESS
SCOTT, MARTHA	14054 CHANDLER BLVD.	VAN NUYS	CA	91401	A	C+	ACTRESS
SCOTT, WILLARD	30 ROCKEFELLER PLAZA #304	NEW YORK	NY	10012	C	A+	TELEVISION WEATHERMAN - *TODAY*
SCOTTI, VITO	5456 VAN ALDEN AVE.	TARZANA	CA	91356	A	A+	ACTOR
SCOTTO, RENATO	61 W. 62ND ST. #6F	NEW YORK	NY	10023	U	U	SOPRANO
SCROWCROFT, GEN. BRENT	350 PARK AVE. #2600	NEW YORK	NY	10022	U	U	FORMER MILITARY LEADER/POLITICIAN
SCRUGGS, EARL	P.O. BOX 66	MADISON	TN	37115	A	D	BANJOIST/SONGWRITER
SCULLY, VIN	1555 CAPRI DR.	PACIFIC PALISADES	CA	90272	A	D	SPORTSCASTER
SEAGAL, STEVEN	2282 MANDEVILLE CANYON	LOS ANGELES	CA	90049	U	U	ACTOR - *ABOVE THE LAW* - **AUTHOR'S CHOICE!**
SEALE, BOBBY	302 W. CHELTON AVE.	PHILADELPHIA	PA	19144	U	U	ACTIVIST/AUTHOR - CO-FOUNDER OF THE BLACK PANTHERS
SEALS, DAN	P.O. BOX 1770	HENDERSONVILLE	TN	37077	U	U	SINGER/SONGWRITER
SEARCHERS, THE	P.O. BOX 262	CARTARET	NJ	07008	U	U	VOCAL GROUP
SEAVORG, GLENN T.	1 CYCLOTRON RD.	BERKELEY	CA	94720	A	B	CHEMIST
SEBASTIAN, JOHN	12744 WEDDINGTON	NORTH HOLLYWOOD	CA	91607	U	U	SINGER/SONGWRITER - THE LOVIN' SPOONFUL
SECADA, JON	291 W. 41ST ST.	HIALEAH	FL	33012	A	A+	SINGER
SECOR, KYLE	538 N. MANSFIELD AVE.	LOS ANGELES	CA	90036	U	U	ACTOR
SECORD, GEN. RICHARD	1 PENNSYLVANIA PLAZA #2400	NEW YORK	NY	10119	U	U	MILITARY LEADER
SEDAKA, NEIL	8787 SHOREHAM DR.	LOS ANGELES	CA	90069	A	B	SINGER/SONGWRITER - "LAUGHTER IN THE RAIN"
SEDGWICK, KYRA	1724 N. VISTA	LOS ANGELES	CA	90046	U	U	ACTRESS
SEGER, MICHAEL	P.O. BOX 1592	LEXINGTON	VA	24450	U	U	MUSICIAN
SEGER, PETE	P.O. BOX 431, DUCHESS JUNCTION	BEACON	NY	12508	A	D	SINGER/SONGWRITER - FOUNDED THE WEAVERS
SEGAL, GEORGE	810 HOLMBY AVE.	LOS ANGELES	CA	90024	U	U	ACTOR - *LOOK WHO'S TALKING*
SEGER, BOB	567 PURDY	BIRMINGHAM	MI	48009	U	U	SINGER - BOB SEGER & THE SILVER BULLET BAND
SEGURA, PANCHO	LA COSTA HOTEL & SPAS, COSTA DEL MAR RD.	CARLSBAD	CA	92008	U	U	TENNIS PLAYER
SEINFELD, JERRY	147 EL CAMINO DR. #205	BEVERLY HILLS	CA	90212	B	F	COMEDIAN/ACTOR - *SEINFELD* - SENDS FACSIMILE SIGNED PHOTO - **AUTHOR'S CHOICE!**
SELBY, DAVID	15152 ENCANTO DR.	SHERMAN OAKS	CA	91403	U	U	ACTOR
SELES, MONICA	5500 - 34TH ST. W.	BRADENTON	FL	34210	U	U	TENNIS PLAYER
SELLECA, CONNIE	14755 VENTURA BLVD. #355	SHERMAN OAKS	CA	91403	C	B	ACTRESS - *HOTEL* - MRS. JOHN TESH

P. J. Soles

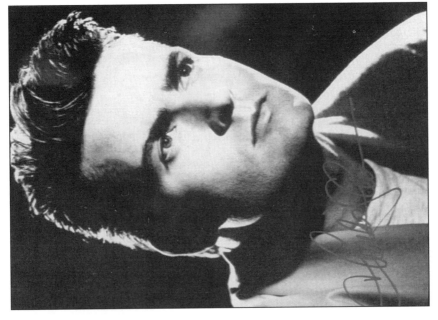

Charlie Sheen (facsimile)

318

Name	Address	City	State	Zip Code	Resp. Time	Resp. Qual.	Comments
SELLECK, TOM	331 SAGE LN.	SANTA MONICA	CA	90402	B	B	ACTOR - *MAGNUM, P.I.* - ALWAYS RESPONSIVE - **AUTHOR'S CHOICE!**
SELZER, MILTON	575 SAN JUAN ST.	SANTA PAULA	CA	93060	U	U	ACTOR
SERNA, PEPE	2321 HILL DR.	LOS ANGELES	CA	90041	A	B	ACTOR
SESAME STREET	ONE LINCOLN PLAZA	NEW YORK	NY	10022	U	U	CHILDREN'S TELEVISION SHOW
SEVEN, JOHNNY	11213 MC LENNAN AVE.	GRANADA HILLS	CA	91344	A	D	ACTOR/DIRECTOR - ADDS PHOTO LIST AND PRICES
SEYMOUR, JANE	P.O. BOX 548	AGOURA	CA	91376	C	F	ACTRESS/MODEL - *DR. QUINN, MEDICINE WOMAN* - SENDS FACSIMILE SIGNED PHOTO - **AUTHOR'S CHOICE!**
SHABAZZ, BETTY	MEDGAR EVERS COLLEGE, 1659 BEDFORD AVE.	BROOKLYN	NY	11225	U	U	ACTIVIST
SHACKELFORD, TED	12305 VALLEY HEART DR.	STUDIO CITY	CA	91604	U	U	ACTOR - *KNOTS LANDING*
SHAFFER, PAUL	1697 BROADWAY	NEW YORK	NY	10019	A	B	KEYBOARDIST - *LATE NIGHT WITH DAVID LETTERMAN* - **AUTHOR'S CHOICE!**
SHALALA, SEC. DONNA	200 INDEPENDENCE AVE. S.W.	WASHINGTON	DC	20201	U	U	SECRETARY OF HEALTH & HUMAN SERVICES
SHALIT, GENE	225 E. 79TH ST.	NEW YORK	NY	10021	U	U	FILM CRITIC - *TODAY*
SHANDLING, GARRY	C/O CREATIVE ARTISTS AGCY., 9830 WILSHIRE BLVD.	BEVERLY HILLS	CA	90212	U	U	ACTOR - *THE LARRY SANDERS SHOW*
SHANICE	8455 FOUNTAIN AVE. # 530	LOS ANGELES	CA	90069	U	U	SINGER
SHAPIRO, ESTHER	617 N. ALTA DR.	BEVERLY HILLS	CA	90210	U	U	SOAP OPERA TELEVISION WRITER/PRODUCER
SHAPIRO, RICHARD	617 N. ALTA DR.	BEVERLY HILLS	CA	90210	U	U	SOAP OPERA TELEVISION WRITER/PRODUCER
SHAPIRO, ROBERT	2121 AVE. OF THE STARS, 19TH FL.	LOS ANGELES	CA	90067	U	U	ATTORNEY - MEMBER OF O. J. SIMPSON "DREAM TEAM" - **AUTHOR'S CHOICE!**
SHARIF, OMAR	18 RUE TROYAN	PARIS	FRA	F-75017	U	U	ACTOR - *DR. ZHIVAGO*
SHARMA, BARBARA	145 S. FAIRFAX AVE. #310	LOS ANGELES	CA	90036	U	U	ACTRESS
SHARPTON, AL	NATIONAL ACTION NETWORK, 1133 BEDFORD AVE.	BROOKLYN	NY	11216	U	U	ACTIVIST
SHATNER, WILLIAM	3674 BERRY AVE.	STUDIO CITY	CA	91604	U	U	ACTOR - *STAR TREK* - **AUTHOR'S CHOICE!**
SHAUGHNESSY, CHARLES	1817 ASHLAND AVE.	SANTA MONICA	CA	90405	U	U	ACTOR - *THE NANNY*
SHAVELSON, MEL	11947 SUNSHINE TERR.	NORTH HOLLYWOOD	CA	91604	A	B	WRITER/PRODUCER
SHAVER, HELEN	P.O. BOX 5617	BEVERLY HILLS	CA	90210	C	A+	ACTRESS - *THE AMITYVILLE HORROR*
SHAW, ARTIE	2127 W. PALOS COURT	NEWBURY PARK	CA	91320	U	U	BAND LEADER
SHAW, BERNARD	111 MASSACHUSETTS N.W.	WASHINGTON	DC	20001	A	B	NEWS CORRESPONDENT
SHAW, TOMMY	134 W. 88TH ST. #1	NEW YORK	NY	10024	U	U	SINGER/SONGWRITER - STYX
SHEA, GEORGE BEVERLY	1300 HARMON PL.	MINNEAPOLIS	MN	55403	U	U	SINGER
SHEA, JOHN	955 S. CARRILLO DR. #300	LOS ANGELES	CA	90048	U	U	ACTOR - *LOIS & CLARK*

319

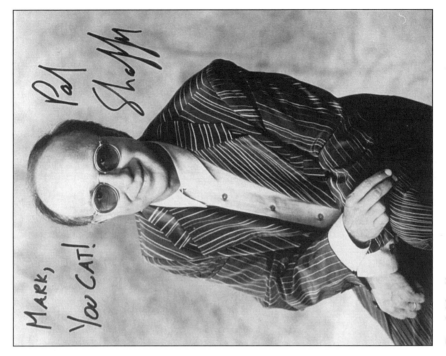

Mark,
You CAT!

Pal Shaffer

Paul Shaffer

To Mark Ellen Baker-Alsop
Cordially – Isaac Stern 1995

Isaac Stern

Name	Address	City	State	Zip Code	Resp. Time	Resp. Qual.	Comments
SHEAR, RHONDA	2049 CENTURY PARK E. #2550	LOS ANGELES	CA	90067	A	D	ACTRESS/MODEL
SHEARER, HARRY	119 OCEAN PARK BLVD.	SANTA MONICA	CA	90405	U	U	TELEVISION WRITER/DIRECTOR - *THIS IS SPINAL TAP*
SHEEHAN, DOUG	4019 - 137 GOLDFINCH ST.	SAN DIEGO	CA	92103	U	U	ACTOR
SHEEHY, GAIL	300 E. 57TH ST. #18-D	NEW YORK	NY	10022	U	U	AUTHOR/JOURNALIST
SHEEKMAN, GLORIA STUART	884 S. BUNDY DR.	LOS ANGELES	CA	90049	C	B	ACTRESS
SHEEN, CHARLIE	335 N. MAPLE DR. #360	BEVERLY HILLS	CA	90210	A	F	ACTOR - *MAJOR LEAGUE* - SENDS FACSIMILE SIGNED PHOTO - **AUTHOR'S CHOICE!**
SHEEN, MARTIN	6916 DUNE DR.	MALIBU	CA	90265	A	C	ACTOR/TELEVISION DIRECTOR - *APOCALYPSE NOW*
SHEFFIELD, JOHNNY	834 FIRST AVE.	CHULA VISTA	CA	92011	A	D	ACTOR
SHELDON, DEBORAH	1690 COLDWATER CANYON	BEVERLY HILLS	CA	90210	U	U	ACTRESS
SHELDON, REID	1524 LABAIG AVE.	LOS ANGELES	CA	90028	U	U	ACTRESS
SHELDON, SIDNEY	10250 SUNSET BLVD.	LOS ANGELES	CA	90077	A	B	WRITER - *THE OTHER SIDE OF MIDNIGHT* - **AUTHOR'S CHOICE!**
SHELL, ART	30816 RUE DE LA PIERRE	RANCHO PALOS VERDES	CA	90274	U	U	FOOTBALL PLAYER & COACH
SHELLEY, CAROLE	333 W. 56TH ST.	NEW YORK	NY	10019	U	U	ACTRESS - *THE ELEPHANT MAN*
SHEPHERD, CYBILL	16037 ROYAL OAK RD.	ENCINO	CA	91436	A	F	ACTRESS/MODEL - *MOONLIGHTING* - SENDS FACSIMILE SIGNED POSTCARD - USES STUDIO FAN MAIL SERVICE - SAVE YOUR STAMPS!
SHEPHERD, SAM	240 W. 44TH ST.	NEW YORK	NY	10036	U	U	ACTOR/DIRECTOR - *THE RIGHT STUFF*
SHEPPARD, T.G.	916 S. BYRNE #2	TOLEDO	OH	43609	U	U	SINGER
SHERIDAN, JAMEY	8942 WILSHIRE BLVD.	BEVERLY HILLS	CA	90211	U	U	ACTOR
SHERIDAN, NICOLETTE	8942 WILSHIRE BLVD.	BEVERLY HILLS	CA	90211	U	U	ACTRESS - *THE SURE THING*
SHERMAN, RICHARD	808 N. CRESCENT DR.	BEVERLY HILLS	CA	90210	U	U	COMPOSER/LYRICIST
SHERMAN, ROBERT	1817 SUNSET PLAZA DR.	LOS ANGELES	CA	90069	A	B	ACTOR/SINGER
SHERWOOD, MADELINE	32 LEROY ST.	NEW YORK	NY	10014	C	B	ACTRESS
SHERWOOD, ROBERTA	14154 MAGNOLIA BLVD. #126	SHERMAN OAKS	CA	91423	U	U	SINGER/ACTRESS
SHIELDS, BROOKE	P.O. BOX B	HAWORTH	NJ	07641	C	F	ACTRESS/MODEL - *PRETTY BABY* - **AUTHOR'S CHOICE!**
SHIMKUS, JOANNA	9255 DOHENY RD.	WEST HOLLYWOOD	CA	90069	U	U	ACTRESS
SHIRE, TALIA	16633 VENTURA BLVD. #1450	ENCINO	CA	91436	U	U	ACTRESS - *ROCKY I-V*
SHOEMAKER, BILL	2545 FAIRFIELD PL.	SAN MARINO	CA	91108	U	U	JOCKEY
SHORE, PAULY	1375 N. DOHENY DR.	LOS ANGELES	CA	90069	U	U	ACTOR
SHORR, LONNIE	141 S. EL CAMINO DR. #205	BEVERLY HILLS	CA	90212	U	U	COMEDIAN
SHORT, BOBBY	444 E. 57TH ST. #9E	NEW YORK	NY	10022	C	D	PIANIST/SINGER
SHORT, MARTIN	15907 ALCIMA AVE.	PACIFIC PALISADES	CA	90272	U	U	ACTOR - *FATHER OF THE BRIDE*
SHORTER, FRANK	787 LINCOLN PL.	BOULDER	CO	80302	C	D	TRACK ATHLETE

Carrie Snodgrass

Summer Sanders

Name	Address	City	State	Zip Code	Resp. Time	Resp. Qual.	Comments
SHORTRIDGE, STEVE	1707 CLEARVIEW DR.	BEVERLY HILLS	CA	90210	U	U	ACTOR
SHOW, GRANT	937 S. TREMAINE	LOS ANGELES	CA	90019	U	U	ACTOR - **AUTHOR'S CHOICE!**
SHOWALTER, MAX	5 GILBERT HILL RD.	CHESTER	CT	06412	C	B+	ACTOR - *IT'S A SMALL WORLD*
SHRINER, KIN	4664 S. WILLIS AVE.	SHERMAN OAKS	CA	91403	U	U	ACTOR
SHRINER, WIL	5313 QUAKERTOWN AVE.	WOODLAND HILLS	CA	91364	U	U	ACTOR/WRITER/COMEDIAN
SHRIVER, EUNICE KENNEDY	1350 NEW YORK AVE. N.W.	WASHINGTON	DC	20005	U	U	FORMER PRESIDENT'S SISTER
SHRIVER, MARIA (SCHWARZENEGGER)	3110 MAIN ST. #300	SANTA MONICA	CA	90405	C	C	BROADCAST JOURNALIST - *FIRST PERSON WITH MARIA SHRIVER*
SHRIVER, R. SARGENT	1350 NEW YORK AVE. N.W.	WASHINGTON	DC	20005	C	D	POLITICIAN
SHUE, ANDREW	9560 WILSHIRE BLVD. #500	BEVERLY HILLS	CA	90212	U	U	ACTOR - *MELROSE PLACE* - **AUTHOR'S CHOICE!**
SHUE, ELISABETH	P.O. BOX 464	SOUTH ORANGE	NJ	07079	A	A	ACTRESS - *LEAVING LAS VEGAS*
SHULER, DOUGLAS	C/O WIZARDS OF THE COAST, INC., BOX 707	RENTON	WA	98057	U	U	ILLUSTRATOR - "MAGIC" CARDS
SHULL, RICHARD B.	16 GRAMERCY PARK	NEW YORK	NY	10003	U	U	ACTOR
SHULTZ, GEORGE P.	776 DOLORES ST.	STANFORD	CA	94305	A	B	FORMER GOVERNMENT OFFICIAL
SIDEY, HUGH	1050 CONNECTICUT AVE.	WASHINGTON	DC	20036	C	C+	COLUMNIST
SIDNEY, SYLVIA	9744 WILSHIRE BLVD. #308	BEVERLY HILLS	CA	90212	U	U	ACTRESS
SIEBERG, CHARLES	15301 VENTURA BLVD. #345	SHERMAN OAKS	CA	91403	U	U	ACTOR/DIRECTOR
SIEGFRIED & ROY	1639 N. VALLEY DR.	LAS VEGAS	NV	89109	U	U	CIRCUS ACT
SIERRA, GREGORY	10000 SANTA MONICA BLVD. #305	LOS ANGELES	CA	90067	C	B	ACTOR
SIGOLOFF, SANFORD	320 CLIFFWOOD AVE.	LOS ANGELES	CA	90049	U	U	BUSINESSMAN
SIKES, CYNTHIA	250 DELFERN DR.	LOS ANGELES	CA	90077	A	B	ACTRESS
SILLIPHANT, STIRLING	P.O. BOX 351119	LOS ANGELES	CA	90035	U	U	FILM WRITER/PRODUCER
SILLS, BEVERLY	211 CENTRAL PARK W. #4F	NEW YORK	NY	10024	A	A	OPERA SOPRANO
SILVA, HENRY	5226 BECKFORD	TARZANA	CA	91356	U	U	ACTOR
SILVERMAN, FRED	12400 WILSHIRE BLVD. #920	LOS ANGELES	CA	90025	U	U	TELEVISION EXECUTIVE/PRODUCER
SILVERMAN, JONATHAN	854 BIRCHWOOD DR.	LOS ANGELES	CA	90024	B	B	ACTOR - *BRIGHTON BEACH MEMOIRS*
SILVERSTEIN, SHEL	C/O HARPER COLLINS PULBISHING GROUP, 10 E. 53RD ST.	NEW YORK	NY	10022	U	U	AUTHOR - *A LIGHT IN THE ATTIC*
SILVERSTONE, ALICIA	C/O PREMIER ARTISTS AGCY., 8899 BEVERLY BLVD., SUITE 102	LOS ANGELES	CA	90048	U	U	MUSIC VIDEO STAR - **AUTHOR'S CHOICE!**
SIMMONS, JEAN	636 ADELAIDE WAY	SANTA MONICA	CA	90402	C	D	ACTRESS - *THE THORN BIRDS*
SIMMONS, RICHARD	P.O. BOX 5403	BEVERLY HILLS	CA	90209	A	D	HEALTH GURU
SIMMS, LARRY	P.O. BOX 85	GRAY RIVER	WA	98621	U	U	ACTOR
SIMON, CARLY	135 CENTRAL PARK W.	NEW YORK	NY	10023	C	F	SINGER/SONGWRITER - FACSIMILE SIGNED PHOTO

Hugh Sidey

Kevin Spacey

Name	Address	City	State	Zip Code	Resp. Time	Resp. Qual.	Comments
SIMON, NEIL	10745 CHALON RD.	LOS ANGELES	CA	90077	A	B	PLAYWRIGHT - *CHAPTER TWO* - **AUTHOR'S CHOICE!**
SIMON, PAUL	1619 BROADWAY, SUITE 500	NEW YORK	NY	10019	U	U	COMPOSER - "GRACELAND" - **AUTHOR'S CHOICE!**
SIMON, WILLIAM	330 SOUTH ST.	MORRISTOWN	NJ	07960	A	B	FORMER SECRETARY OF THE TREASURY
SIMONE, NINA	7250 FRANKLIN AVE. #115	LOS ANGELES	CA	90046	U	U	SINGER/PIANIST - "THE CRYING GAME"
SIMPSON, O.J.	360 ROCKINGHAM AVE.	LOS ANGELES	CA	90049	U	U	MEMBER OF THE FOOTBALL HALL OF FAME - **AUTHOR'S CHOICE!**
SINATRA, FRANK	70-558 FRANK SINATRA DR.	RANCHO MIRAGE	CA	92270	U	U	SINGER/ACTOR - "MY WAY" - MEMBER OF RAT PACK - **AUTHOR'S CHOICE!**
SINATRA, FRANK JR.	2211 FLORIAN PL.	BEVERLY HILLS	CA	90210	U	U	SINGER
SINATRA, MRS. NANCY	720 N. CRESCENT DR.	BEVERLY HILLS	CA	90210	U	U	EX-WIFE OF FRANK SINATRA
SINATRA, NANCY JR.	P.O. BOX 69453	LOS ANGELES	CA	90069	U	U	SINGER/ACTRESS
SINATRA, TINA	9461 LLOYDCREST DR.	BEVERLY HILLS	CA	90210	U	U	SINGER
SINBAD (DAVID ADKINS)	9514 OAKRIDGE PL.	CHATSWORTH	CA	91311	U	U	COMEDIAN/ACTOR
SINGER, LORI	9830 WILSHIRE BLVD.	BEVERLY HILLS	CA	90212	U	U	ACTRESS - *FOOTLOOSE*
SINGER, MARC	11218 CANTON DR.	STUDIO CITY	CA	91604	U	U	ACTOR
SINGLETON, JOHN	4223 DON CARLOS DR.	LOS ANGELES	CA	90008	U	U	DIRECTOR - *BOYZ N THE HOOD*
SINGLETON, MARGIE	P.O. BOX 567	HENDERSONVILLE	TN	37077	U	U	SINGER/GUITARIST
SINGLETON, PENNY	13419 RIVERSIDE DR. #C	SHERMAN OAKS	CA	91423	U	U	ACTRESS
SIOMAK, CURT	OLD S.FORK RANCH, 43422 S. FORK DR.	THREE RIVERS	CA	93271	U	U	WRITER/PRODUCER
SIRTIS, MARINA	2436 CRESTON WAY	LOS ANGELES	CA	90068	U	U	ACTRESS
SISKEL, GENE	1301 N. ASTOR	CHICAGO	IL	60610	U	U	FILM CRITIC - *SISKEL & EBERT AT THE MOVIES*
SISTER SLEDGE	151 EL CAMINO DR.	BEVERLY HILLS	CA	90212	U	U	VOCAL GROUP
SISTER, SISTER	WB NETWORK, 3701 OAK ST.	BURBANK	CA	91505	U	U	TELEVISION SERIES - CAST: TIA & TAMERA MOWRY
SKAGGS, RICKY	380 FOREST RETREAT	HENDERSONVILLE	TN	37075	U	U	SINGER/GUITARIST
SKELTON, RED	37801 THOMPSON RD.	RANCHO MIRAGE	CA	92270	A	F	ACTOR/COMEDIAN - *THE RED SKELTON SHOW* - SENDS REGRETS
SKERRITT, TOM	335 N. MAPLE DR. #360	BEVERLY HILLS	CA	90210	A	B	ACTOR - *PICKET FENCES*
SKYE, IONE	8794 LOOKOUT MOUNTAIN AVE.	LOS ANGELES	CA	90046	U	U	ACTRESS - *SAY ANYTHING*
SLASH	C/O GEFFEN RECORDS, 9130 SUNSET BLVD.	LOS ANGELES	CA	90069	U	U	GUITARIST - GUNS N' ROSES - **AUTHOR'S CHOICE!**
SLATE, HENRY	6310 SAN VICENTE BLVD. #407	LOS ANGELES	CA	90048	U	U	ACTOR
SLATER, CHRISTIAN	9830 WILSHIRE BLVD.	BEVERLY HILLS	CA	90212	U	U	ACTOR - *ROBIN HOOD: PRINCE OF THIEVES* - **AUTHOR'S CHOICE!**
SLATER, HELEN	151 S. EL CAMINO DR.	BEVERLY HILLS	CA	90212	U	U	ACTRESS - *SUPERGIRL*

Cybill Shepherd (facsimile)

Jacklyn Smith (facsimile)

Elizabeth Shue

326

Name	Address	City	State	Zip Code	Resp. Time	Resp. Qual.	Comments
SLATER, RYAN	C/O AMAZING PANDA ADVENTURE, WB STUDIOS, 4000 WARNER BLVD.	BURBANK	CA	91522	U	U	ACTOR
SLATTERY, RICHARD X.	P.O. BOX 2410	AVALON	CA	90704	U	U	ACTOR
SLATZER, ROBERT F.	3033 HOLLYCREST DR. #2	LOS ANGELES	CA	90068	A	C	WRITER/PRODUCER
SLAUGHTER, DR. FRANK	P.O. BOX 14, ORTEGA STATION	JACKSONVILLE	FL	32210	C	D	AUTHOR/SURGEON
SLAUGHTER, ENOS	959 LAWSON CHAPEL CHURCH RD.	ROXBORO	NC	27573	A	C	MEMBER OF THE BASEBALL HALL OF FAME
SLEDGE, PERCY	5524 CLARESHOLM ST.	GAUTIER	MS	39553	U	U	SINGER
SLICK, GRACE	18 ESCALON DR.	MILL VALLEY	CA	94941	A	B	SINGER/SONGWRITER - JEFFERSON AIRPLANE
SLIWA, CURTIS	628 W. 28TH ST.	NEW YORK	NY	10001	C	D	FOUNDER OF THE GUARDIAN ANGELS
SMART, JEAN	151 EL CAMINO DR.	BEVERLY HILLS	CA	90212	U	U	ACTRESS - *DESIGNING WOMEN*
SMITH, ALLISON	9000 SUNSET BLVD. #1200	LOS ANGELES	CA	90069	U	U	ACTRESS
SMITH, ANNA NICOLE	C/O ELITE MODELING MGMT CORP., 111 E. 22ND ST., 2ND FL.	NEW YORK	NY	10010	U	U	SUPERMODEL
SMITH, BUBBA	5178 SUNLIGHT PL.	LOS ANGELES	CA	90016	U	U	ACTOR/FOOTBALL PLAYER
SMITH, BUFFALO BOB	500 OVERLOOK DR.	FLAT ROCK	NC	28731	U	U	ACTOR - *HOWDY DOODY* - SIGNS AT MEMORABILIA SHOWS
SMITH, CHARLIE MARTIN	31515 GERMAINE LN.	WESTLAKE VILLAGE	CA	91361	U	U	ACTOR - *AMERICAN GRAFFITI*
SMITH, COTTER	14755 VENTURA BLVD. #1-904	SHERMAN OAKS	CA	91403	U	U	ACTOR
SMITH, EMMITT	C/O DALLAS COWBOYS, 1 COWBOY PKWY.	IRVING	TX	75063	U	U	FOOTBALL PLAYER
SMITH, HARRY	524 W. 57TH ST.	NEW YORK	NY	10019	A	B	TELEVISION HOST
SMITH, ILAN MITCHELL	104-60 QUEENS BLVD. #10-C	FOX HILLS	NY	11375	U	U	ACTOR
SMITH, JACLYN	P.O. BOX 57413	SHERMAN OAKS	CA	91403	C	F	ACTRESS - *CHARLIE'S ANGELS* - RESPONDS WITH FACSIMILE SIGNED PHOTO
SMITH, KATHY	117 S. LAXTON DR.	LOS ANGELES	CA	90049	A	B	ACTRESS
SMITH, LEWIS	8271 MELROSE AVE. #110	LOS ANGELES	CA	90046	U	U	ACTOR
SMITH, LIZ	160 E. 38TH ST.	NEW YORK	NY	10016	A	B	GOSSIP COLUMNIST
SMITH, MARTHA	9690 HEATHER RD.	BEVERLY HILLS	CA	90210	U	U	ACTRESS/MODEL
SMITH, ROGER	2707 BENEDICT CANYON	BEVERLY HILLS	CA	90210	U	U	ACTOR/WRITER
SMITH, SHAWNEE	5200 LANKERSHIM BLVD. #260	NORTH HOLLYWOOD	CA	91601	U	U	ACTRESS
SMITH, WENDY	2925 TUNA CANYON RD.	TOPANGA	CA	90290	U	U	ACTRESS
SMITH, WILL	298 ELIZABETH ST. #100	NEW YORK	NY	10012	U	U	ACTOR - **AUTHOR'S CHOICE!**
SMITH, WILLIAM	2552 LAUREL CANYON	LOS ANGELES	CA	90046	U	U	ACTOR
SMITH, WILLIAM KENNEDY	500 5TH AVE. #4700	NEW YORK	NY	10110	U	U	SENATOR TED KENNEDY'S NEPHEW
SMITHERS, WILLIAM	11664 LAURELCREST DR.	STUDIO CITY	CA	91604	U	U	ACTOR
SMITROVICH, BILL	5052 RUBIO AVE.	ENCINO	CA	91436	A	B	ACTOR

James Stewart

Jerry Seinfeld (facsimile)

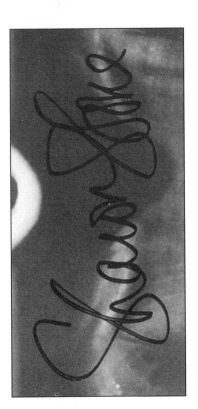

Sharon Stone (possible ghost signature)

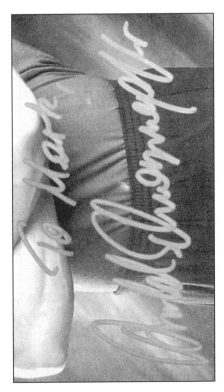

Arnold Schwarzenegger

Name	Address	City	State	Zip Code	Resp. Time	Resp. Qual.	Comments
SMITS, JIMMY	110 S. WESTGATE AVE.	LOS ANGELES	CA	90049	U	U	ACTOR - *L.A. LAW*
SMOTHERS, DICK	8489 W. THIRD ST. #1020	LOS ANGELES	CA	90048	U	U	ACTOR/COMEDIAN
SMOTHERS, TOM	1976 WARM SPRINGS RD.	KENWOOD	CA	95452	U	U	COMEDIAN/ACTOR
SNEAD, SAM	P.O. BOX 777	HOT SPRINGS	VA	24445	A	C	GOLFER
SNIDER, DUKE	3037 LAKEMONT DR.	FALLBROOK	CA	92028	U	U	MEMBER OF THE BASEBALL HALL OF FAME
SNIDER, MIKE	P.O. BOX 140710	NASHVILLE	TN	37214	A	C	BLUEGRASS MUSICIAN
SNIPES, WESLEY	335 N. MAPLE DR. #250	BEVERLY HILLS	CA	90210	U	U	ACTOR - **AUTHOR'S CHOICE!**
SNODDY, BRIAN	C/O WIZARDS OF THE COAST, INC., BOX 707	RENTON	WA	98057	U	U	ILLUSTRATOR - "MAGIC" CARDS
SNODGRASS, CARRIE	3025 SURRY ST.	LOS ANGELES	CA	90027	A	A+	ACTRESS - *DIARY OF A MAD HOUSEWIFE*
SNOOP DOGGY DOGG	C/O ICM, 8942 WILSHIRE BLVD.	BEVERLY HILLS	CA	90211	U	U	RAP ARTIST - **AUTHOR'S CHOICE!**
SNOW, HANK	P.O. BOX 1084	NASHVILLE	TN	37202	U	U	SINGER/SONGWRITER
SNYDER, TOM	1225 BEVERLY ESTATES DR.	BEVERLY HILLS	CA	90210	U	U	TALK SHOW HOST - **AUTHOR'S CHOICE!**
SOBEL, BARRY	9000 SUNSET BLVD. #1200	LOS ANGELES	CA	90069	U	U	COMEDIAN
SOLES, P.J.	P.O. BOX 2351	CAREFREE	AZ	85377	B	A	ACTRESS
SOMERS, SUZANNE	433 S. BEVERLY DR.	BEVERLY HILLS	CA	90212	U	U	ACTRESS/SINGER - *THREE'S COMPANY*
SOMMARS, JULIE	9744 WILSHIRE BLVD. #308	BEVERLY HILLS	CA	90212	U	U	ACTRESS
SOMMER, ELKE	540 N. BEVERLY GLEN	LOS ANGELES	CA	90024	B	B	ACTRESS - *A SHOT IN THE DARK*
SONDHEIM, STEPHEN	246 E. 49TH ST.	NEW YORK	NY	10017	U	U	COMPOSER/LYRICIST - **AUTHOR'S CHOICE!**
SOREL, LOUISE	10808 LINDBROOK DR.	LOS ANGELES	CA	90024	C	B	ACTRESS - *DAYS OF OUR LIVES*
SORENSON, TED	1285 AVE. OF THE AMERICAS	NEW YORK	NY	10019	A	B	FORMER GOVERNMENT OFFICIAL
SORKIN, ARLEEN	3226 N. KNOLL DR.	LOS ANGELES	CA	90068	U	U	WRITER/PRODUCER
SOTHERN, ANN	P.O. BOX 2285	KETCHUM	ID	83340	U	U	ACTRESS
SOTO, TALISA	9057A NEMO ST.	LOS ANGELES	CA	90069	U	U	ACTRESS/MODEL
SOUL, DAVID	2232 MORENO DR.	LOS ANGELES	CA	90039	U	U	ACTOR/SINGER/DIRECTOR - *STARSKY & HUTCH*
SOUTER, DAVID	1 -1ST ST. N.E.	WASHINGTON	DC	20543	A	D	SUPREME COURT JUSTICE
SOUTHERN, J.D.	8263 HOLLYWOOD BLVD.	LOS ANGELES	CA	90069	U	U	SINGER/SONGWRITER
SOUTHERN BELLES	11150 W. OLYMPIC BLVD. #1100	LOS ANGELES	CA	90064	U	U	WRESTLING TEAM
SOUTHERN, TERRY	RFD	EAST CANAAN	CT	06020	U	U	TELEVISION WRITER
SPACEK, SISSY	RT. 22, #640	COBHAM	VA	22929	U	U	ACTRESS - *COAL MINER'S DAUGHTER*
SPACEY, KEVIN	200 E. 58TH ST. #7H	NEW YORK	NY	10022	C	B+	ACTOR - *SEX, LIES & VIDEOTAPE*
SPADER, JAMES	8942 WILSHIRE BLVD.	BEVERLY HILLS	CA	90211	U	U	ACTOR - *SEX, LIES & VIDEOTAPE*
SPAHN, WARREN	RR2	HARTSHORNE	OK	74547	U	U	MEMBER OF THE BASEBALL HALL OF FAME
SPARY, CAMILLA	957 N. COLE AVE.	LOS ANGELES	CA	90038	U	U	ACTRESS

329

Jane Seymour (facsimile)

Name	Address	City	State	Zip Code	Resp. Time	Resp. Qual.	Comments
SPEARS, BILLY JOE	2804 OPRYLAND DR.	NASHVILLE	TN	37214	A	B	SINGER
SPECTOR, PHIL	1210 S. ARROYO BLVD.	PASADENA	CA	91101	A	B	RECORD PRODUCER
SPECTOR, RONNIE	7 MAPLECREST DR.	DANBURY	CT	06810	U	U	SINGER - THE RONETTES
SPELLING, AARON	594 N. MAPLETON DR.	LOS ANGELES	CA	90077	U	U	TELEVISION PRODUCER
SPELLING, TORI	594 N. MAPLETON DR.	LOS ANGELES	CA	90077	C	F	ACTRESS - *BEVERLY HILLS 90210* - **AUTHOR'S CHOICE!**
SPERBER, WENDY JO	15760 VENTURA BLVD. #1730	ENCINO	CA	91436	U	U	ACTRESS
SPHEERIS, PENELOPE	8301 KIRKWOOD DR.	LOS ANGELES	CA	90068	U	U	DIRECTOR/PRODUCER
SPIELBERG, DAVID	3531 BENTLEY AVE.	LOS ANGELES	CA	90034	U	U	ACTOR
SPIELBERG, STEVEN	P.O. BOX 6190	MALIBU	CA	90264	A	F	DIRECTOR/PRODUCER - *JURASSIC PARK* - **AUTHOR'S CHOICE!** - RESPONDS WITH FACSIMILE SIGNED PHOTO
SPILLANE, MICKEY	C/O GENERAL DELIVERY	MARRELLS INLET	SC	22117	C	A	WRITER - THE MIKE HAMMER DETECTIVE STORIES
SPILLMAN, SANDY	1353 ALVARADO TERR.	LOS ANGELES	CA	90017	U	U	ACTOR
SPINKS, MICHAEL	250 W. 57TH ST.	NEW YORK	NY	10107	C	F	MEMBER OF THE INTERNATIONAL BOXING HALL OF FAME - RESPONDS WITH FACSIMILE SIGNED PHOTO
SPINNERS	65 W. 55TH ST. #6C	NEW YORK	NY	10019	U	U	VOCAL GROUP
SPOCK, DR. BENJAMIN	P.O. BOX 1890	ST. THOMAS	VI	00803	C	D	PHYSICIAN - *COMMON SENSE BOOK OF BABY CARE*
SPOUND, MICHAEL	10351 SANTA MONICA BLVD. #211	LOS ANGELES	CA	90025	U	U	ACTOR
SPRADLIN, J.D.	P.O. BOX 5617	BEVERLY HILLS	CA	90210	U	U	ACTOR/DIRECTOR
SPRINGER, JERRY	MULTIMEDIA ENT., 45 ROCKEFELLER PLAZA, 35TH FL.	NEW YORK	NY	10111	U	U	TALK SHOW HOST
SPRINGFIELD, RICK	9200 SUNSET BLVD. PH-15	LOS ANGELES	CA	90069	U	U	SINGER/ACTOR - *GENERAL HOSPITAL*
SPRINGSTEEN, BRUCE	1224 BENEDICT CANYON	BEVERLY HILLS	CA	90210	U	U	SINGER/GUITARIST - **AUTHOR'S CHOICE!** - NICE IN PERSON
SQUIER, BILLY	145 CENTRAL PARK W.	NEW YORK	NY	10023	B	D	SINGER/GUITARIST
ST. CYR, LILI	624 N. PLYMOUTH BLVD. #7	LOS ANGELES	CA	90004	U	U	ENTERTAINER
ST. JOHN, JILL	8271 MELROSE AVE. #110	LOS ANGELES	CA	90046	U	U	ACTRESS
ST. LAURENT, YVES	15 COLUMBUS CIRCLE	NEW YORK	NY	10023	U	U	FASHION DESIGNER
STACK, ROBERT	321 ST. PIERRE RD.	LOS ANGELES	CA	90077	A	C	ACTOR - *THE UNTOUCHABLES*
STACY, JAMES	478 SEVERN AVE.	TAMPA	FL	33606	U	U	ACTOR
STAFFORD, JIM	P.O. BOX 6366	BRANSON	MO	65616	A	C	SINGER - "SPIDERS AND SNAKES"
STAFFORD, JO	2339 CENTURY HILL	LOS ANGELES	CA	90067	A	D	SINGER
STAFFORD, NANCY	13080 MINDANAO WAY #69	MARINA DEL REY	CA	90292	U	U	ACTRESS
STAFFORD, TOM	4200 PERIMETER CENTER DR. #101	OKLAHOMA CITY	OK	73112	U	U	ASTRONAUT/BUSINESSMAN

Name	Address	City	State	Zip Code	Resp. Time	Resp. Qual.	Comments
STAHL, LESLIE	524 W. 57TH ST.	NEW YORK	NY	10019	U	U	JOURNALIST
STALEY, JOAN	24516-B WINDSOR DR.	VALENCIA	CA	91355	U	U	ACTRESS
STALLONE, FRANK	10668 EASTBORNE #206	LOS ANGELES	CA	90025	A	B	ACTOR
STALLONE, SASHA	9 BEVERLY PARK	BEVERLY HILLS	CA	90210	U	U	FORMER WIFE OF SYLVESTER STALLONE
STALLONE, SYLVESTER	8800 SUNSET BLVD. #214	LOS ANGELES	CA	90069	U	U	ACTOR - *ROCKY* - **AUTHOR'S CHOICE!**
STAMPLEY, JOE	2137 ZERCHER RD.	SAN ANTONIO	TX	78209	U	U	SINGER
STANFILL, DENNIS	908 OAK GROVE AVE.	SAN MARINO	CA	91108	U	U	BUSINESSMAN
STANG, ARNOLD	P.O. BOX 786	NEW CANAAN	CT	06840	A	B	ACTOR
STANLEY, KIM	3640 MONON ST. APT. 111	LOS ANGELES	CA	90027	A	D	ACTRESS
STANS, MAURICE	211 S. ORANGE GROVE	PASADENA	CA	91105	U	U	GOVERNMENT OFFICIAL
STANSFIELD, LISA	43 HILLCREST RD.	ROCKDALE	ENG		U	U	SINGER - *ALL AROUND THE WORLD*
STANTON, HARRY DEAN	14527 MULHOLLAND DR.	LOS ANGELES	CA	90077	U	U	ACTOR - *PARIS, TEXAS*
STAPLETON, JEAN	635 PERUGIA WAY	LOS ANGELES	CA	90024	U	U	ACTRESS - *ALL IN THE FAMILY*
STAPLETON, MAUREEN	1 BOLTON DR.	LENOX	MA	01240	U	U	ACTRESS - *AIRPORT*
STARGELLL, WILLIE	1616 SHIPYARD BLVD. #278	WILMINGTON	NC	28412	U	U	MEMBER OF THE BASEBALL HALL OF FAME
STARK, RAY	232 S. MAPLETON DR.	LOS ANGELES	CA	90077	A	D	TELEVISION PRODUCER
STARR, KAY	223 ASHDALE AVE.	LOS ANGELES	CA	90024	U	U	SINGER
STARR, RINGO	2029 CENTURY PARK E. #1690	LOS ANGELES	CA	90067	U	U	SINGER/DRUMMER - THE BEATLES
STARSHIP (JEFFERSON AIRPLANE)	2400 FULTON ST.	SAN FRANCISCO	CA	94118	U	U	ROCK GROUP - SEND TO INDIVIDUALLY - GOOD IN PERSON
STATLER BROTHERS	P.O. BOX 2703	STAUNTON	VA	24401	C	B	VOCAL GROUP - RESPONSIVE TO FANS
STAUBACH, ROGER	6750 LBJ FREEWAY	DALLAS	TX	75109	C	D	FOOTBALL PLAYER
STEEL, AMY	331 N. MARTEL AVE.	LOS ANGELES	CA	90036	U	U	ACTRESS
STEEL, DANIELLE	330 BOB HOPE DR.	BURBANK	CA	90212	B	C	NOVELIST - DOES NOT SIGN CARDS - RESPONDS WITH LETTER - **AUTHOR'S CHOICE!**
STEELE, BARBARA	442 S. BEDFORD DR.	BEVERLY HILLS	CA	90212	U	U	ACTRESS
STEIGER, ROD	6324 ZUMIREZ DR.	MALIBU	CA	90265	A	B	ACTOR - *IN THE HEAT OF THE NIGHT*
STEIN, BEN	7251 PACIFIC VIEW DR.	LOS ANGELES	CA	90068	U	U	WRITER
STEINBERG, DAVID	16121 HIGH VALLEY PL.	ENCINO	CA	91436	U	U	COMEDIAN/WRITER/ACTOR - *PATERNITY*
STEINBRENNER, GEORGE	RIVER AVE. & E. 16TH ST.	NEW YORK	NY	10045	U	U	BASEBALL EXECUTIVE
STEINEM, GLORIA	118 E. 73RD ST.	NEW YORK	NY	10021	A	B+	AUTHOR/FEMINIST
STEPHANOPOULOS, GEORGE	1600 PENNSYLVANIA AVE.	WASHINGTON	DC	20500	U	U	WHITE HOUSE OFFICIAL
STERLING, JAN	245 WOODLAWN AVE. #H-6	CHULA VISTA	CA	91910	U	U	ACTRESS
STERLING, PHILIP	4114 BENEDICT CANYON	SHERMAN OAKS	CA	91423	U	U	ACTOR

332

Name	Address	City	State	Zip Code	Resp. Time	Resp. Qual.	Comments
STERLING, ROBERT	121 S. BENTLEY AVE.	LOS ANGELES	CA	90049	A	D	ACTOR
STERLING, TISHA	P.O. BOX 788	KETCHUM	ID	83340	U	U	ACTRESS
STERN, DANIEL	P.O. BOX 6788	MALIBU	CA	90264	C	B	ACTOR - *CITY SLICKERS*
STERN, HOWARD	10 E. 44TH ST. #400	NEW YORK	NY	10017	A	B	RADIO HOST - SHOCK JOCK - **AUTHOR'S CHOICE!**
STERN, ISAAC	211 CENTRAL PARK W.	NEW YORK	NY	10024	A	B	VIOLINIST
STERNHAGEN, FRANCES	152 SUTTON MANOR RD.	NEW ROCHELLE	NY	10805	A	B	ACTRESS - *DRIVING MISS DAISY*
STEVENS, ANDREW	10351 SANTA MONICA BLVD. # 211	LOS ANGELES	CA	90025	U	U	ACTOR - *DALLAS*
STEVENS, APRIL	19530 SUPERIOR ST.	NORTHRIDGE	CA	91324	U	U	SINGER
STEVENS, BRINKE	8033 SUNSET BLVD. #556	LOS ANGELES	CA	90046	A	B	ACTRESS/MODEL
STEVENS, CONNIE	8721 SUNSET BLVD. PH-1	LOS ANGELES	CA	90069	A	A+	ACTRESS/SINGER - *HAWAIIAN EYE* - EVEN SENDS COLOGNE SAMPLES - AWESOME!
STEVENS, FISHER	151 EL CAMINO DR.	BEVERLY HILLS	CA	90212	U	U	ACTOR - *SHORT CIRCUIT*
STEVENS, GEORGE JR.	JOHN F. KENNEDY CENTER	WASHINGTON	DC	20566	U	U	DIRECTOR/PRODUCER
STEVENS, MORGAN	14348 ROBLAR PL.	SHERMAN OAKS	CA	91423	U	U	ACTOR
STEVENS, RAY	1708 GRAND AVE.	NASHVILLE	TN	37212	A	D	SINGER/SONGWRITER - "ANDY WILLIAMS PRESENTS RAY STEVENS"
STEVENS, RISE	930 FIFTH AVE.	NEW YORK	NY	10021	A	B	MEZZO-SOPRANO
STEVENS, SHADOW	2570 BENEDICT CANYON	BEVERLY HILLS	CA	90210	U	U	RADIO/TELEVISION PERSONALITY
STEVENS, STELLA	2180 COLDWATER CANYON	BEVERLY HILLS	CA	90210	A	C+	ACTRESS - *SANTA BARBARA*
STEVENS, WARREN	14155 MAGNOLIA BLVD. #44	SHERMAN OAKS	CA	91403	C	C	ACTOR
STEWART, ALANA	12824 EVANSTON ST.	LOS ANGELES	CA	90049	A	B+	ACTRESS/TALK SHOW HOST
STEWART, JAMES	P.O. BOX 90	BEVERLY HILLS	CA	90213	A	B	ACTOR/DIRECTOR - *IT'S A WONDERFUL LIFE* - **AUTHOR'S CHOICE!**
STEWART, MARTHA	MARTHA STEWART LIVING, 20 W. 43RD ST.	NEW YORK	NY	10036	U	U	LIFESTYLE CONSULTANT!
STEWART, PATRICK	8942 WILSHIRE BLVD.	BEVERLY HILLS	CA	90211	U	U	ACTOR - **AUTHOR'S CHOICE!**
STEWART, PAYNE	2390 N. ORANGE AVE. #2600	ORLANDO	FL	32801	C	F	GOLFER , CLASSY DRESSER! - "TOO BUSY"!
STEWART, PEGGY	11139 HORTENSE ST.	NORTH HOLLYWOOD	CA	91602	C	B	ACTRESS
STEWART, ROD	C/O WARNER BROTHERS RECORDS, 3300 WARNER BLVD.	BURBANK	CA	91510	C	B	SINGER
STICKNEY, DOROTHY	13 E. 94TH ST.	NEW YORK	NY	10023	U	U	ACTRESS
STILLER, DAVID OGDEN	3827 RHONDA VISTA	LOS ANGELES	CA	90027	U	U	ACTOR/DIRECTOR - *M*A*S*H* - A VERY TOUGH SIGNATURE!
STILLER, BEN	C/O CREATIVE ARTISTS AGCY., 9830 WILSHIRE BLVD.	BEVERLY HILLS	CA	90212	U	U	ACTOR - *REALITY BITES* - **AUTHOR'S CHOICE!**
STILLS, STEPHEN	191 N. PHELPS AVE.	WINTER PARK	FL	32789	U	U	SINGER - CROSBY, NASH, STILLS & YOUNG

Name	Address	City	State	Zip Code	Resp. Time	Resp. Qual.	Comments
STINE, R.L.	C/O SCHOLASTIC INC., 555 BROADWAY	NEW YORK	NY	10012	U	U	AUTHOR - *GOOSEBUMPS* - **AUTHOR'S CHOICE!**
STING	THE BUGLE HOUSE, 21A NOEL ST.	LONDON, ENGLAND	UK		U	U	SINGER/SONGWRITER - THE POLICE - **AUTHOR'S CHOICE!**
STIPE, MICHAEL	C/O WARNER BROS. REC., 3300 WARNER BLVD.	BURBANK	CA	91505	U	U	SINGER - R.E.M. - A TOUGH SIGNATURE - **AUTHOR'S CHOICE!**
STOCK, BARBARA	3500 W. OLIVE AVE. #920	BURBANK	CA	91505	U	U	ACTRESS
STOCKDALE, ADM. JAMES	HOOVER INSTITUTION	STANFORD	CA	94305	B	C	ONE OF ROSS PEROT'S V.P. CANDIDATES
STOCKWELL, DEAN	P.O. BOX 6248	MALIBU	CA	90264	U	U	ACTOR - *QUANTUM LEAP*
STOCKWELL, GUY	4924 CAHUENGA BLVD.	NORTH HOLLYWOOD	CA	91601	U	U	ACTOR
STODDARD, BRANDON	241 N. GLENROY AVE.	LOS ANGELES	CA	90049	U	U	FILM/TELEVISION EXECUTIVE
STONE, CHRISTOPHER	23035 CUMORAH CREST DR.	WOODLAND HILLS	CA	91364	U	U	ACTOR/WRITER
STONE, CLIFFIE	P.O. BOX 2033	CANYON COUNTRY	CA	91386	U	U	MUSICIAN
STONE, OLIVER	201 SANTA MONICA BLVD. #601	SANTA MONICA	CA	90401	A	D	FILM WRITER/DIRECTOR - *NIXON* - **AUTHOR'S CHOICE!**
STONE, ROB	3725 LAUREL CANYON BLVD.	STUDIO CITY	CA	91604	U	U	ACTOR
STONE, SHARON	P.O. BOX 7304	NORTH HOLLYWOOD	CA	91603	C	B	ACTRESS/MODEL - **AUTHOR'S CHOICE!**
STONES, DWIGHT	12841 NEWPORT AVE.	TUSTIN	CA	92680	U	U	TRACK & FIELD ATHLETE
STORCH, LARRY	330 W. END AVE. #17-F	NEW YORK	NY	10023	C	B	ACTOR
STORM, GALE	308 N. SYCAMORE AVE. #104	LOS ANGELES	CA	90036	A	B	ACTRESS/SINGER - *MY LITTLE MARGIE*
STOSSEL, JOHN	211 CENTRAL PARK W. #15K	NEW YORK	NY	10024	U	U	BROADCAST JOURNALIST
STRAIGHT, BEATRICE	30 NORFORD RD.	SOUTHFIELD	MA	01259	U	U	ACTRESS
STRAIT, GEORGE	1000 - 18TH AVE. S.	NASHVILLE	TN	37212	B	B	SINGER/SONGWRITER
STRAITHAIRN, DAVID	9200 SUNSET BLVD. #625	LOS ANGELES	CA	90069	A	D	ACTOR
STRAM, HANK	194 BELLE TERRE BLVD.	COVINGTON	LA	70483	A	F	FOOTBALL COACH - STAMPS ITEMS WITH FACSIMILE SIGNATURE
STRAND, ROBIN	4118 ELMER	NORTH HOLLYWOOD	CA	91607	A	B	ACTOR
STRASBERG, SUSAN	135 CENTRAL PARK W.	NEW YORK	NY	10023	U	U	ACTRESS
STRASSMAN, MARCIA	520 - 18TH ST.	SANTA MONICA	CA	90402	U	U	ACTRESS - *WELCOME BACK, KOTTER*
STRATTON, GIL	4227-B COLFAX AVE. #B	STUDIO CITY	CA	91604	U	U	SPORTSCASTER
STRAUB, PETER	53 W. 85TH ST.	NEW YORK	NY	10026	A	B	AUTHOR
STRAUSS, PETER	609 N. PALM DR.	BEVERLY HILLS	CA	90210	U	U	ACTOR - *THE JERICHO MILE*
STRAUSS, ROBERT	1333 NEW HAMPSHIRE AVE. N.W. #1400	WASHINGTON	DC	20005	U	U	POLITICIAN
STREEP, MERYL	9830 WILSHIRE BLVD.	BEVERLY HILLS	CA	90212	U	U	ACTRESS - *BRIDGES OF MADISON COUNTY* - **AUTHOR'S CHOICE!**
STREET, PEEKABOO	C/O U.S. OLYMPIC COM., 1750 E. BOULDER ST.	COLORADO SPRINGS	CO	80909	U	U	SKIER

Name	Address	City	State	Zip Code	Resp. Time	Resp. Qual.	Comments
STREISAND, BARBRA	521 5TH AVE., 17TH FL.	NEW YORK	NY	10075	C	F	SINGER/ACTRESS/DIRECTOR - *YENTL* - SENDS OUT FACSIMILE SIGNED PHOTO - A VERY TOUGH SIGNATURE - **AUTHOR'S CHOICE!**
STRICKLAND, AMZIE	1329 N. OGDEN DR.	LOS ANGELES	CA	90046	C	B	ACTRESS
STRICKLAND, GAIL	14732 ORACLE PL.	PACIFIC PALISADES	CA	90272	U	U	ACTRESS
STRICKLYN, RAY	852 N. GENESEE AVE.	LOS ANGELES	CA	90046	A	B	ACTOR
STROUD, DON	17020 SUNSET BLVD. #20	PACIFIC PALISADES	CA	90272	U	U	ACTOR
STRUTHERS, SALLY	15301 VENTURA BLVD. #345	SHERMAN OAKS	CA	91403	A	D	ACTRESS - *ALL IN THE FAMILY* - INCLUDES SAVE THE CHILDREN FLYER
STUART, MAXINE	9744 WILSHIRE BLVD. #308	BEVERLY HILLS	CA	90212	U	U	ACTRESS
STUART, ROY	4948 RADFORD AVE.	NORTH HOLLYWOOD	CA	91602	A	B	ACTOR
STYRON, WILLIAM	12 RUCUM RD.	ROXBURY	CT	06783	A	B	AUTHOR
SUES, ALAN	9014 DORRINGTON AVE.	LOS ANGELES	CA	90048	C	B	ACTOR
SUGARMAN, BURT	150 S. EL CAMINO DR. #303	BEVERLY HILLS	CA	90212	U	U	ROCK PRODUCER
SULLIVAN, BARRY JR.	14687 ROUND VALLEY DR.	SHERMAN OAKS	CA	91403	U	U	ACTOR
SULLIVAN, DANNY	93 KERCHEVAL AVE. #3	GROSSE POINT FARMS	MI	48236	A	B	AUTO RACER - ALSO INCLUDES FAN CLUB INFO
SULLIVAN, SUSAN	8642 ALLENWOOD RD.	LOS ANGELES	CA	90046	C	D	ACTRESS - *FALCON CREST*
SULLIVAN, TOM	1504 VIA CASTILLA	PALOS VERDES	CA	90274	U	U	SINGER/SONGWRITER - "IF YOU COULD SEE WHAT I HEAR"
SULZBERGER, ARTHUR OCHS	229 W. 43RD ST.	NEW YORK	NY	10036	U	U	NEWSPAPER PUBLISHER
SUMAC, YMA	1524 LA BAIG AVE.	LOS ANGELES	CA	90028	U	U	SINGER
SUMMER, CREE	131 S. ORANGE DR.	LOS ANGELES	CA	90036	U	U	ACTRESS
SUMMER, DONNA	18165 ECCLES	NORTHRIDGE	CA	91324	U	U	SINGER - "LOVE TO LOVE YOU BABY"
SUMMERALL, PAT	C/O FOX BROADCASTING CO., 205 E. 67TH ST.	NEW YORK	NY	10021	U	U	BROADCASTER
SUNUNU, JOHN	24 SAMOSET DR.	SALEM	NH	03079	C	B	FORMER GOVERNOR
SURE, AL B	636 WARREN ST.	BROOKLYN	NY	11217	U	U	SINGER
SUROVY, NICOLAS	8942 WILSHIRE BLVD.	BEVERLY HILLS	CA	90211	U	U	ACTOR
SUSMAN, TODD	10340 KEOKUK AVE.	CHATSWORTH	CA	91311	U	U	ACTOR
SUTHERLAND, DONALD	760 N. LA CIENEGA BLVD. # 300	LOS ANGELES	CA	90069	U	U	ACTOR - *ORDINARY PEOPLE*
SUTHERLAND, KIEFER	1033 GAYLEY AVE. #208	LOS ANGELES	CA	90024	B	D	ACTOR - *FLATLINERS*
SWAGGART, JIMMY	P.O. BOX 2550	BATON ROUGE	LA	70821	U	U	EVANGELIST
SWAIM, CASKEY	1605 N. CAHUENGA BLVD. #202	LOS ANGELES	CA	90028	U	U	ACTOR
SWANN, LYNN	5750 WILSHIRE BLVD. #475W	LOS ANGELES	CA	90036	A	D	FOOTBALL PLAYER
SWAYZE, DON	247 S. BEVERLY DR. #102	BEVERLY HILLS	CA	90212	A	D	ACTOR

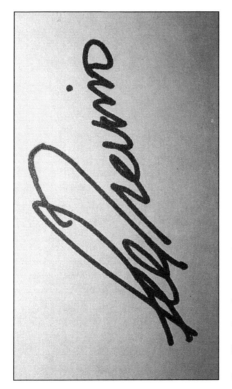

Lee Trevino (autopen)

Daniel J. Travanti

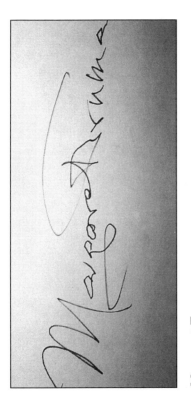

Margaret Truman

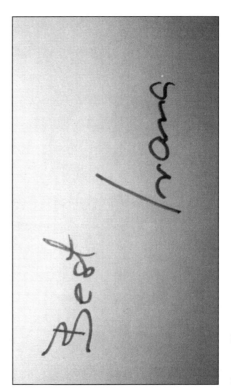

Ivana Trump

Name	Address	City	State	Zip Code	Resp. Time	Resp. Qual.	Comments
SWAYZE, PATRICK	1033 GAYLEY AVE. #8	LOS ANGELES	CA	90024	U	U	ACTOR - *GHOST*
SWEENEY, D.B.	9560 WILSHIRE BLVD. #500	BEVERLY HILLS	CA	90212	U	U	ACTOR - *THE CUTTING EDGE*
SWEET VALLEY HIGH	SABAN ENT., 4000 W. ALAMEDA BLVD.	BURBANK	CA	91505	U	U	TELEVISION SERIES
SWENSON, INGA	3475 CABRILLO	LOS ANGELES	CA	90066	U	U	ACTRESS - *BENSON*
SWERLING, JO JR.	25745 VISTA VERDE DR.	CALABASAS	CA	91302	U	U	WRITER/PRODUCER
SWIT, LORETTA	6363 WILSHIRE BLVD. #600	LOS ANGELES	CA	90048	C	B	ACTRESS - *M*A*S*H*
SYKES, TOM	P.O. BOX 29543	ATLANTA	GA	30359	U	U	SINGER
2 LIVE CREW	8400 N.E. 2ND AVE.	MIAMI	FL	33138	U	U	RAP GROUP
T, MR. (LAWRENCE TERO)	395 GREEN BAY RD.	LAKE FOREST	IL	60045	U	U	ACTOR - *THE A-TEAM* - NICE IN PERSON!
TABORI, KRISTOFFER	172 E. 95TH ST.	NEW YORK	NY	10028	U	U	ACTOR
TAKA, MIIKO	14560 ROUND VALLEY DR.	SHERMAN OAKS	CA	91403	U	U	ACTRESS
TAKE SIX	4404 SUMATRA DR.	NASHVILLE	TN	37218	U	U	VOCAL GROUP
TAKE THAT	C/O ARISTA RECORDS, 6 W. 57TH ST.	NEW YORK	NY	10022	U	U	MUSIC GROUP
TALBOT, NITA	3420 MERRIMAC RD.	LOS ANGELES	CA	90049	A	B	ACTRESS
TALESE, GAY	154 E. ATLANTIC BLVD.	OCEAN CITY	NJ	08226	A	B	WRITER
TALLCHIEF, MARIA	2739 ELSTON AVE.	CHICAGO	IL	60747	U	U	BALLERINA
TAMBOR, JEFFREY	5526 CALHOUN AVE.	VAN NUYS	CA	91401	U	U	ACTOR - *HILL STREET BLUES*
TANNER, ROSCOE	1109 GNOME TRAIL	LOOKOUT MOUNTAIN	TN	37350	U	U	TENNIS PLAYER
TARANTINO, QUENTIN	C/O WILLIAM MORRIS AGCY., 151 EL CAMINO DR.	BEVERLY HILLS	CA	90212	U	U	ACTOR/DIRECTOR - *PULP FICTION* - **AUTHOR'S CHOICE!**
TARKINGTON, FRAN	3345 PEACHTREE RD. N.E.	ATLANTA	GA	30326	A	F	FOOTBALL PLAYER - SENDS PRICE LIST, ITEMS RANGE FROM $15 - $350
TARTIKOFF, BRANDON	1479 LINDACREST DR.	BEVERLY HILLS	CA	90210	U	U	TELEVISION EXECUTIVE
TAUPIN, BERNIE	1422 DEVLIN DR.	LOS ANGELES	CA	90069	U	U	LYRICIST
TAYLOR, BUCK	2899 AGOURA RD. #275	WESTLAKE VILLAGE	CA	91361	U	U	ACTOR
TAYLOR, CLARICE	380 ELKWOOD TERR.	ENGLEWOOD	NJ	07631	U	U	ACTRESS
TAYLOR, DON	1111 SAN VICENTE BLVD.	SANTA MONICA	CA	90402	A	B	FILM DIRECTOR
TAYLOR, ELIZABETH	700 NIMES RD.	LOS ANGELES	CA	90077	A	F	ACTRESS - *NATIONAL VELVET* - RESPONDS WITH FACSIMILE SIGNED PHOTO - **AUTHOR'S CHOICE!**
TAYLOR, HOLLAND	1355 N. LAUREL AVE. #7	LOS ANGELES	CA	90046	A	B	ACTRESS
TAYLOR, JAMES	644 N. DOHENY DR.	LOS ANGELES	CA	90069	U	U	SINGER
TAYLOR, JOSH	422 S. CALIFORNIA	BURBANK	CA	91505	U	U	ACTOR
TAYLOR, MELDRICK	2917 N. 4TH ST.	PHILADELPHIA	PA	19132	U	U	BOXER
TAYLOR, MESHACH	369 E. CALAVERAS ST.	ALTADENA	CA	91001	U	U	ACTOR - *DESIGNING WOMEN*

John Thompson

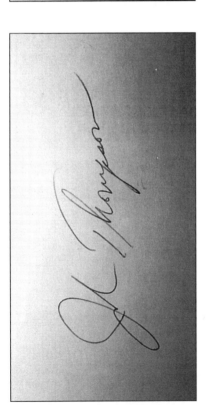

Cheryl Tiegs

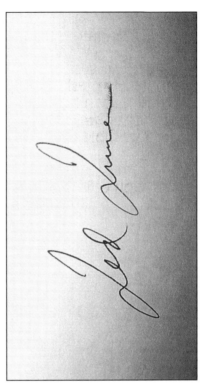

Ted Turner

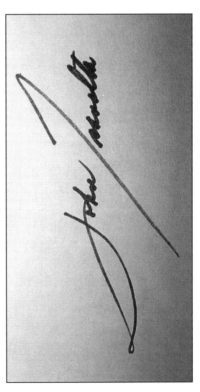

John Travolta

Name	Address	City	State	Zip Code	Resp. Time	Resp. Qual.	Comments
TAYLOR, PAUL	PAUL TAYLOR DANCE CO., 552 BROADWAY	NEW YORK	NY	10012	U	U	DANCER
TAYLOR, REGINA	151 EL CAMINO DR.	BEVERLY HILLS	CA	90212	U	U	ACTRESS
TAYLOR, RENEE	613 N. ARDEN DR.	BEVERLY HILLS	CA	90210	U	U	ACTRESS/WRITER
TAYLOR, RIP	1133 N. CLARK ST.	LOS ANGELES	CA	90069	A	A+	ACTOR
TAYLOR, ROD	2375 BOWMONT DR.	BEVERLY HILLS	CA	90210	A	D	ACTOR - THE TIME MACHINE
TAYLOR, SUSAN L.	C/O ESSENCE MAGAZINE, 1500 BROADWAY	NEW YORK	NY	10036	U	U	EDITOR/AUTHOR - AUTHOR'S CHOICE!
TEDIN, MARK	C/O WIZARD OF THE COAST, INC., P.O. BOX 707	RENTON	WA	98057	U	U	ILLUSTRATOR - "MAGIC" CARDS
TELLER, DR. EDWARD U.	RADIATION LAB, P.O. BOX 808	LIVERMORE	CA	94550	A	D	PHYSICIST/AUTHOR
TEMPLE-BLACK, SHIRLEY	115 LAKEVIEW DR.	WOODSIDE	CA	94062	A	D	ACTRESS/AMBASSADOR - THE GOOD SHIP LOLLIPOP
TEMPLETON, CHRISTOPHER	11333 MOORPARK ST.	NORTH HOLLYWOOD	CA	91602	U	U	ACTOR
TENNILLE, TONI	3612 LAKE VIEW RD.	CARSON CITY	NV	89703	C	D	SINGER
TENUTA, JUDY	332 E. EUCLID AVE.	OAK PARK	IL	60302	U	U	COMEDIENNE
TERKEL, STUDS	850 W. CASTLEWOOD	CHICAGO	IL	60640	A	B	NOVELIST
TESH, JOHN	C/O ET, 5555 MELROSE AVE.	HOLLYWOOD	CA	90038	A	B	TELEVISION HOST/MUSICIAN - AUTHOR'S CHOICE!
THARP, TWYLA	PMK, 1776 BROADWAY	NEW YORK	NY	10019	U	U	DANCER
THAXER, PHYLLIS	716 RIOMAR DR.	VERO BEACH	FL	32960	A	C	ACTRESS
THAYER, BRYNN	956 KAGAWA ST.	PACIFIC PALISADES	CA	90272	U	U	ACTRESS
THE BABY-SITTERS CLUB	C/O SONY PICTURES ENT., INC., 10202 W. WASHINGTON BLVD.	CULVER CITY	CA	90232	U	U	TELEVISION SERIES - CAST: RACHAEL LEIGH COOK, SCHUYLER FISK, AUSTIN O'BRIEN, CHRISTIAN OLIVER
THEISS, BROOKE	9744 WILSHIRE BLVD. #308	BEVERLY HILLS	CA	90212	U	U	ACTRESS
THICKE, ALAN	10153-1/2 RIVERSIDE DR. #119	TOLUCA LAKE	CA	91602	A	D	ACTOR/HOST/SINGER - GROWING PAINS
THIESS, URSULA (SCHACKER)	1940 BEL AIR RD.	LOS ANGELES	CA	90077	A	A+	ACTRESS
THINNES, ROY	8016 WILLOW GLEN RD.	LOS ANGELES	CA	90046	C	F	ACTOR - SENDS FACSIMILE SIGNED PHOTOGRAPH
THOMAS, B. J.	P.O. BOX 120003	ARLINGTON	TX	76012	U	U	SINGER/SONGWRITER
THOMAS, BETTY	P.O. BOX 1130	STUDIO CITY	CA	91604	C	D	ACTRESS - HILL STREET BLUES
THOMAS, CLARENCE	1 - 1ST ST. N.E.	WASHINGTON	DC	20543	A	B	SUPREME COURT JUSTICE
THOMAS, DEBI	22 E. 71ST ST.	NEW YORK	NY	10021	U	U	ICE SKATER
THOMAS, FRANK	C/O CHICAGO WHITE SOX, 333 W. 35TH ST.	CHICAGO	IL	60616	U	U	BASEBALL PLAYER - "THE BIG HURT" - AUTHOR'S CHOICE!
THOMAS, FRANKIE	13939 RIVERSIDE DR.	SHERMAN OAKS	CA	91423	U	U	ACTOR
THOMAS, HEATHER	1433 SAN VICENTE BLVD.	SANTA MONICA	CA	90402	C	F	ACTRESS/MODEL - FACSIMILE SIGNED PHOTO
THOMAS, HELEN	2501 CALVERT ST. N.W.	WASHINGTON	DC	20008	U	U	NEWS CORRESPONDENT

Randy Travis

Clarence Thomas

David Toma

Travis Tritt

Name	Address	City	State	Zip Code	Resp. Time	Resp. Qual.	Comments
THOMAS, JAY	10351 SANTA MONICA BLVD. #211	LOS ANGELES	CA	90025	U	U	ACTOR - *MURPHY BROWN*
THOMAS, JONATHAN TAYLOR	18711 TIFFENI DR. SUITE 17-203	TWAIN HARTE	CA	95383	U	U	ACTOR - *HOME IMPROVEMENT*
THOMAS, KURT	8431 N. 75TH ST.	SCOTTSDALE	AZ	85258	U	U	ACTOR/ATHLETE
THOMAS, MARLO	420 E. 54TH ST. #22-F	NEW YORK	NY	10022	C	F	ACTRESS/WRITER - *THAT GIRL* - FACSIMILE SIGNED PHOTO
THOMAS, PHILIP MICHAEL	12615 W. DIXIE HWY.	NORTH MIAMI	FL	33161	U	U	ACTOR - *MIAMI VICE*
THOMAS, RICHARD	C/O WIZARD OF THE COAST, INC., P.O. BOX 707	RENTON	WA	98057	U	U	ILLUSTRATOR - "MAGIC" CARDS
THOMAS, THURMAN	C/O BUFFALO BILLS, 1 BILLS DR.	ORCHARD PARK	NY	14127	U	U	FOOTBALL PLAYER
THOMAS-SCOTT, MELODY	20620 KINGSBORO WAY	WOODLAND HILLS	CA	91364	U	U	ACTRESS
THOMASON, HARRY	9220 SUNSET BLVD. #11	LOS ANGELES	CA	90069	U	U	FILM PRODUCER
THOMERSON, TIM	2440 LONG JACK RD.	ENCINITAS	CA	92024	U	U	ACTOR/COMEDIAN
THOMOPOULOS, TONY	1280 STONE CANYON	LOS ANGELES	CA	90077	U	U	FILM EXECUTIVE
THOMPSON, EMMA	56 KING'S RD.	KINGTON-UPON-THAMES	ENG	KT2 5HF	U	U	ACTRESS - **AUTHOR'S CHOICE!**
THOMPSON, ERNEST	RT.1, BOX 324B	ASHLAND	NH	03217	U	U	SCREENWRITER
THOMPSON, HANK	5 RUSHING CREEK COURT	ROANOKE	TX	76262	A	C	SINGER/SONGWRITER
THOMPSON, JOHN	GEORGETOWN UNIV. BASKETBALL	WASHINGTON	DC	20057	A	D	BASKETBALL COACH
THOMPSON, LEA	P.O. BOX 490	LOS ANGELES	CA	90046	U	U	ACTRESS - *BACK TO THE FUTURE*
THOMPSON, SADA	2515 ASTRAL DR.	SOUTHBURY	CT	06488	A	B	ACTRESS - *FAMILY*
THOMSON, GORDON	10100 SANTA MONICA BLVD. #2500	LOS ANGELES	CA	90046	U	U	ACTOR
THORNE-SMITH, COURTNEY	11805 MAYFIELD AVE. #306	LOS ANGELES	CA	90067	U	U	ACTRESS - *MELROSE PLACE*
THRONE, MALACHI	9057-A NEMO ST.	WEST HOLLYWOOD	CA	90049	C	B	ACTOR
THURMAN, UMA	444 E. 82ND ST.	NEW YORK	NY	10228	U	U	ACTRESS - *PULP FICTION* - **AUTHOR'S CHOICE!**
THYSSEN, GRETA	5574 KNOLLWOOD DR.	COLUMBUS	OH	43227	A	B	ACTRESS
TIBBETS, PAUL W.	9219 FLICKER WAY	LOS ANGELES	CA	90069	U	U	AVIATOR
TIEGS, CHERYL	3349 CAHUENGA BLVD. W. #1	LOS ANGELES	CA	90068	A	B	MODEL - "THE WAY TO NATURAL BEAUTY"
TIERNEY, LAWRENCE	2165 E. LEMON HEIGHT DR.	SANTA ANA	CA	92705	U	U	ACTOR
TIFFANY	15 W. 67TH ST.	NEW YORK	NY	10023	U	U	SINGER
TIFFIN, PAMELA	P.O. BOX 1626	BRANSON	MO	65616	A	B+	ACTRESS/MODEL
TILLIS, MEL	4 MUSIC SQUARE E.	NASHVILLE	TN	37203	A	C	SINGER
TILLMAN, FLOYD	17530 VENTURA BLVD. #108	ENCINO	CA	91316	U	U	SINGER
TILLOTSON, JOHNNY	9000 SUNSET BLVD. #1200	LOS ANGELES	CA	90069	U	U	SINGER
TILLY, JENNIFER	321 S. BEVERLY DR. #M	BEVERLY HILLS	CA	90212	U	U	ACTRESS
TILLY, MEG			CA		U	U	ACTRESS - *THE BIG CHILL*

Edward Teller

Mel Tillis

Name	Address	City	State	Zip Code	Resp. Time	Resp. Qual.	Comments
TILTON, CHARLENE	22050 GALVEZ ST.	WOODLAND HILLS	CA	91364	U	U	ACTRESS - *DALLAS*
TILTON, MARTHA	760 LAUSANNE RD.	LOS ANGELES	CA	90077	U	U	SINGER/ACTRESS
TINKER, GRANT	531 BARNABY RD.	LOS ANGELES	CA	90077	U	U	TELEVISION EXECUTIVE
TIPITT, WAYNE	8730 SUNSET BLVD. #220W	LOS ANGELES	CA	90069	A	B	ACTOR
TIPPIN, AARON	P.O. BOX 121709	NASHVILLE	TN	37212	U	U	SINGER
TLC	C/O ARISTA RECORDS, 6 W. 57TH ST.	NEW YORK	NY	10019	U	U	MUSIC GROUP
TOBEY, KENNETH	14155 MAGNOLIA BLVD.	SHERMAN OAKS	CA	91403	A	D	ACTOR
TODD, BEVERLY	4888 VALLEY RIDGE	LOS ANGELES	CA	90043	A	B	ACTRESS
TODD, HALLIE	10100 SANTA MONICA BLVD. #700	LOS ANGELES	CA	90067	U	U	ACTRESS
TOKYO ROSE (IVA TOGURI)	851 W. BELMONT AVE.	CHICAGO	IL	60611	U	U	WW II ENEMY BROADCASTER
TOLAND, JOHN	1 LONG RIDGE RD.	DANBURY	CT	06810	A	B	AUTHOR
TOLSKY, SUSAN	10815 ACAMA ST.	NORTH HOLLYWOOD	CA	91602	U	U	ACTRESS
TOMA, DAVID	P.O. BOX 854	CLARK	NJ	07066	A	B	WRITER
TOMEI, MARISA	1724 N. VISTA ST.	LOS ANGELES	CA	90046	U	U	ACTRESS - **AUTHOR'S CHOICE!**
TOMLIN, LILY	P.O. BOX 27700	LOS ANGELES	CA	90027	U	U	ACTRESS/WRITER/COMEDIAN - *LAUGH-IN*
TOMPKINS, ANGEL	9105 MORNING GLOW WAY	SUN VALLEY	CA	91532	A	D	ACTRESS
TONE LOC	C/O EAST WEST RECORDS, 75 ROCKEFELLER PLAZA	NEW YORK	NY	10019	U	U	RAPPER/ACTOR
TOOMEY, BILL	1750 E. BOULDER ST.	COLORADO SPRINGS	CO	80909	U	U	TRACK ATHLETE
TORME, MEL	1734 COLDWATER CANYON	BEVERLY HILLS	CA	90210	U	U	SINGER/ACTOR/WRITER
TORN, RIP	130 W. 42ND ST. #2400	NEW YORK	NY	10036	U	U	ACTOR/DIRECTOR - *BLIND AMBITION*
TORRENCE, GWEN	3606 SPRING POINT	DECATUR	GA	30034	A	B	TRACK/FIELD ATHLETE - ALSO INCLUDED AUTOGRAPHED TRADING CARD
TOTTER, AUDREY	1945 GLENDON AVE. #301	LOS ANGELES	CA	90025	C	B	ACTRESS
TOURE, KWAME	C/O RANDOM HOUSE, 201 E. 50TH ST.	NEW YORK	NY	10022	U	U	ACTIVIST
TOWERS, CONSTANCE	10651 CHALON RD.	LOS ANGELES	CA	90077	C	B	ACTRESS
TOWNE, ROBERT	1417 SAN REMO DR.	PACIFIC PALISADES	CA	90272	U	U	FILM WRITER/DIRECTOR
TOWNES, HARRY	805 RANDOLPH AVE. S.E.	HUNTSVILLE	AL	35801	C	C	ACTOR
TOWNSEND, BARBARA	1930 CENTURY PARK W. #303	LOS ANGELES	CA	90067	U	U	ACTRESS
TOWNSEND, CLAIRE	2424 LAUREL PASS	LOS ANGELES	CA	90046	U	U	ACTRESS
TOWNSEND, COLLEEN	508 SEWARD SQUARE S.E.	WASHINGTON	DC	20003	U	U	ACTRESS
TRACY, ARTHUR	350 W. 57TH ST.	NEW YORK	NY	10019	U	U	ACTOR
TRAMPS, THE	P.O. BOX 82	GREAT NECK	NY	10021	U	U	R&B GROUP
TRAVALANA, FRED	P.O. BOX 260171	ENCINO	CA	91426	C	B	ACTOR/WRITER/COMEDIAN

Mr. T

Name	Address	City	State	Zip Code	Resp. Time	Resp. Qual.	Comments
TRAVANTI, DANIEL J.	14205 SUNSET BLVD.	PACIFIC PALISADES	CA	90272	A	D	ACTOR - *HILL STREET BLUES*
TRAVIS, NANCY	9869 PORTOLA DR.	BEVERLY HILLS	CA	90210	C	B	ACTRESS
TRAVIS, RANDY	P.O. BOX 12712	NASHVILLE	TN	37212	A	C	SINGER/SONGWRITER
TRAVOLTA, JOEY	4975 CHIMINEAS AVE.	TARZANA	CA	91356	U	U	ACTOR
TRAVOLTA, JOHN	12522 MOORPARK ST. #109	STUDIO CITY	CA	91604	A	D	ACTOR/SINGER - *PULP FICTION* - **AUTHOR'S CHOICE!**
TREAS, TERRI	9000 SUNSET BLVD. #1200	LOS ANGELES	CA	90069	U	U	ACTRESS
TREBEK, ALEX	7966 MULHOLLAND DR.	LOS ANGELES	CA	90046	A	B+	GAME SHOW HOST - *JEOPARDY*
TREMAYNE, LES	901 S. BARRINGTON AVE.	LOS ANGELES	CA	90049	U	U	ACTOR
TREVINO, LEE	5757 ALPHA RD. #620	DALLAS	TX	75240	A	F	GOLFER - RESPONDS WITH AUTOPENED ITEMS!
TREVOR, CLAIRE	HOTEL PIERRE, 2 E. 61ST ST.	NEW YORK	NY	10022	U	U	ACTRESS - *KEY LARGO*
TRIPPLEHORN, JEANNE	C/O CREATIVE ARTISTS AGCY., 9830 WILSHIRE BLVD.	BEVERLY HILLS	CA	90212	U	U	ACTRESS - *BASIC INSTINCT* - **AUTHOR'S CHOICE!**
TRITT, TRAVIS	1112 N. SHERBOURNE DR.	LOS ANGELES	CA	90069	C	D	SINGER
TROUPE BOBBY	16074 ROYAL OAKS	ENCINO	CA	91436	C	B	ACTOR/COMEDIAN/SINGER
TROUPE, TOM	8829 ASHCROFT AVE.	LOS ANGELES	CA	90048	U	U	ACTOR
TRUDEAU, GARRY	4900 MAIN ST.	KANSAS CITY	MO	64112	U	U	CARTOONIST - *DOONESBURY*
TRUEX, MRS. ERNEST	3263 VIA ALTAMURA	FALLBROOK	CA	92028	A	C	WIDOW OF ERNEST TRUEX
TRUMAN, MARGARET (DANIEL)	830 PARK AVE.	NEW YORK	NY	10028	A	C	AUTHOR
TRUMBULL, DOUGLAS	13335 MAXELLA	VENICE	CA	90291	U	U	WRITER/PRODUCER
TRUMP, DONALD	721 FIFTH AVE.	NEW YORK	NY	10022	A	B+	REAL ESTATE DEVELOPER - "THE DONALD" - ALWAYS FIRST CLASS - **AUTHOR'S CHOICE!**
TRUMP, IVANA	725 FIFTH AVE.	NEW YORK	NY	10022	A	C+	AUTHOR/FORMER WIFE OF DONALD TRUMP
TSONGAS, PAUL	1 POST OFFICE SQUARE	BOSTON	MA	02109	A	D	FORMER SENATOR
TSU, IRENE	2760 HUTTON DR.	BEVERLY HILLS	CA	90210	U	U	ACTRESS
TUBB, BARRY	121 N. SAN VICENTE BLVD.	BEVERLY HILLS	CA	90211	U	U	ACTOR
TUCKER, DREW	C/O WIZARD OF THE COAST, INC., P.O. BOX 707	RENTON	WA	98057	U	U	ILLUSTRATOR - "MAGIC" CARDS
TUCKER, MICHAEL	2183 MANDEVILLE CANYON	LOS ANGELES	CA	90049	U	U	ACTOR - *L.A. LAW*
TUCKER, TANYA	5200 MARYLAND WAY	BRENTWOOD	TN	37027	C	D	SINGER - "DELTA DAWN" - ADDS FAN CLUB INFO
TULL, JETHRO	2 WANSDOWN PL.	LONDON	ENG	SW6	U	U	ROCK GROUP
TUNE, TOMMY	50 E. 89TH ST.	NEW YORK	NY	10128	U	U	DANCER/DIRECTOR
TUNNEY, JOHN	1819 OCEAN AVE.	SANTA MONICA	CA	90401	A	B+	FORMER SENATOR
TURGEON, PIERRE	C/O NY ISLANDERS, NASSAU COLISEUM	UNIONDALE	NY	11553	B	C	HOCKEY PLAYER
TURKEL, ANN	9877 BEVERLY GROVE	BEVERLY HILLS	CA	90210	U	U	ACTRESS
TURLINGTON, CHRISTY	C/O FORD MODELS, INC., 334 E. 59TH ST.	NEW YORK	NY	10022	U	U	SUPERMODEL - **AUTHOR'S CHOICE!**

Warm Regards

Liv Ullmann

Bobby Unser

Johnny Unitas

Leon Uris

Bob Uecker

Name	Address	City	State	Zip Code	Resp. Time	Resp. Qual.	Comments
TURMAN, GLYNN	9000 SUNSET BLVD. #1200	LOS ANGELES	CA	90069	U	U	ACTOR
TURNER, DEBBYE	1325 BOARDWALK	ATLANTIC CITY	NJ	08401	A	B	MISS AMERICA 1990
TURNER, JANINE	9830 WILSHIRE BLVD.	BEVERLY HILLS	CA	90212	U	U	ACTRESS - *NORTHERN EXPOSURE*
TURNER, KATHLEEN	163 AMSTERDAM AVE. #210	NEW YORK	NY	10023	C	C	ACTRESS - *THE JEWEL OF THE NILE* - **AUTHOR'S CHOICE!**
TURNER, TED	1050 TECHWOOD DR.	ATLANTA	GA	30318	A	D	TELEVISION AND SPORTS EXECUTIVE - **AUTHOR'S CHOICE!**
TURNER, TINA	MAARWEG 149, D-(W) 5000	COLOGNE 41	GER		A	F	SINGER - SENDS FAN CLUB INFO ONLY - **AUTHOR'S CHOICE!**
TUTU, BISHOP DESMOND	BOX 31190	JOHANNESBURG	S. AFRICA		U	U	ACTIVIST - **AUTHOR'S CHOICE!**
TWEED, SHANNON	3650 BENEDICT CANYON	BEVERLY HILLS	CA	90210	U	U	ACTRESS/MODEL
TYLER, ANNE	222 TUNBRIDGE RD.	BALTIMORE	MD	21212	U	U	AUTHOR
TYLER, BEVERLY	14585 GERONIMO TRAIL	RENO	NV	89551	A	B	ACTRESS
TYLER, STEVEN	C/O GEFFEN RECORDS, 9130 SUNSET BLVD.	LOS ANGELES	CA	90069	U	U	SINGER - AEROSMITH - **AUTHOR'S CHOICE!** - NICE IN PERSON
TYLER, WILLIE	9955 BALBOA BLVD.	NORTHRIDGE	CA	91325	U	U	VENTRILOQUIST
TYSON, CICELY	315 W. 70TH ST.	NEW YORK	NY	10023	U	U	ACTRESS - *THE AUTOBIOGRAPHY OF MISS JANE PITTMAN*
TYSON, MIKE	C/O DON KING PROD., 32 E. 69TH ST.	NEW YORK	NY	10021	U	U	BOXER - A TOUGH SIGNATURE - **AUTHOR'S CHOICE!**
TYSON, RICHARD	11500 W. OLYMPIC DR. #400	LOS ANGELES	CA	90064	U	U	ACTOR
U2	4 WINDMILL LN.	DUBLIN 4, IRELAND			U	U	MUSIC GROUP
UBERROTH, PETER	184 EMERALD BAY	LAGUNA BEACH	CA	92651	U	U	FORMER BASEBALL EXECUTIVE
UDALL, MORRIS K.	142 CALLE CHAPARITA	TUCSON	AZ	85716	U	U	GOVERNMENT OFFICIAL
UECKER, BOB	C/O MILWAUKEE COUNTY STADIUM	MILWAUKEE	WI	53214	A	D	ACTOR/BASEBALL ANNOUNCER - MR. BELVEDERE
UGGAMS, LESLIE	9255 SUNSET BLVD. #404	LOS ANGELES	CA	90069	A	B	SINGER/ACTRESS - *ROOTS*
UHLIG, ANNELIESE	1519 ESCALONA DR.	SANTA CRUZ	CA	95060	A	B	ACTRESS
ULENE, DR. ART	10810 VIA VERONA	LOS ANGELES	CA	90024	A	C	TELEVISION MEDICAL REPORTER
ULLMAN, LIV	15 W. 81ST ST.	NEW YORK	NY	10024	A	A+	ACTRESS - *PERSONA*
ULLMAN, TRACEY	13555 D'ESTE DR.	PACIFIC PALISADES	CA	90272	U	U	ACTRESS/SINGER
UNDERWOOD, BLAIR	5682 HOLLY OAKS DR.	LOS ANGELES	CA	90069	U	U	ACTOR - *L.A. LAW* - **AUTHOR'S CHOICE!**
UNDERWOOD, JAY	9000 SUNSET BLVD. #1200	LOS ANGELES	CA	90069	U	U	ACTOR
UNITAS, JOHNNY	5607 PATTERSON RD.	BALDWIN	MD	21013	A	C	FOOTBALL PLAYER
UNSER, AL	7625 CENTRAL N.W.	ALBUQUERQUE	NM	87105	A	C	AUTO RACER
UNSER, AL JR.	73243 CALLE DE DEBORAH N.W.	ALBUQUERQUE	NM	87104	A	C	AUTO RACER

347

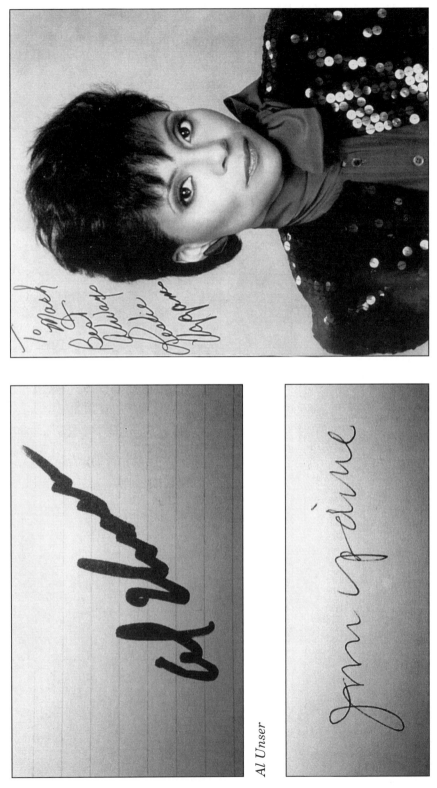

Leslie Uggams

Al Unser

John Updike

Name	Address	City	State	Zip Code	Resp. Time	Resp. Qual.	Comments
UNSER, BOBBY	7700 CENTRAL S.W.	ALBUQUERQUE	NM	87105	A	C	AUTO RACER
UPDIKE, JOHN	675 HALE ST.	BEVERLY FARM	MA	01915	A	D	AUTHOR - *RABBIT, RUN* - **AUTHOR'S CHOICE!**
URICH, ROBERT	P.O. BOX 5973-1006	SHERMAN OAKS	CA	91403	U	U	ACTOR/WRITER - *SPENCER FOR HIRE*
URIS, LEON	P.O. BOX 1559	ASPEN	CO	81611	A	C	AUTHOR
VACCARO, BRENDA	14423 DICKENS #3	SHERMAN OAKS	CA	91403	A	B	ACTRESS - *MIDNIGHT COWBOY*
VADIM, ROGER	2419 BEVERLY AVE.	SANTA MONICA	CA	90406	U	U	DIRECTOR
VALE, JERRY	621 N. PALM DR.	BEVERLY HILLS	CA	90210	A	B	SINGER - "INNAMORATA!"
VALEN, NANCY	10000 SANTA MONICA BLVD. SUITE #305	LOS ANGELES	CA	90067	C	B	ACTRESS
VALENTI, JACK	1600 EYE ST. N.W.	WASHINGTON	DC	20006	U	U	FILM DIRECTOR
VALENTINE, KAREN	P.O. BOX 1410	WASHINGTON DEPOT	CT	06793	U	U	ACTRESS
VALENTINO	2 E. 70TH ST.	NEW YORK	NY	10021	U	U	SINGER
VAN ARK, JOAN	10950 ALTA VIEW DR.	STUDIO CITY	CA	91604	U	U	ACTRESS - *KNOTS LANDING*
VAN BUREN, ABIGAIL	P.O. BOX 69440	LOS ANGELES	CA	90069	A	D	COLUMNIST
VAN DAMME, JEAN-CLAUDE	P.O. BOX 4149	CHATSWORTH	CA	91313	C	F	ACTOR - **AUTHOR'S CHOICE!**
VAN DEVERE, TRISH	3211 RETREAT CIRCLE	MALIBU	CA	90265	U	U	ACTRESS - *THE DAY OF THE DOLPHIN*
VAN DOREN, MAMIE	428 - 31ST ST.	NEWPORT BEACH	CA	92663	A	D	ACTRESS/SINGER - "AIN'T MISBEHAVIN'"
VAN DYKE, BARRY	27800 BLYTHDALE RD.	AGOURA	CA	91301	A	C	ACTOR
VAN DYKE, DICK	23215 MARIPOSA DE ORO	MALIBU	CA	90265	B	B	ACTOR
VAN DYKE, JERRY	1717 N. HOLLYWOOD AVE. #414	LOS ANGELES	CA	90028	U	U	ACTOR - *COACH*
VAN FLEET, JO	54 RIVERSIDE DR.	NEW YORK	NY	10024	U	U	ACTRESS
VAN HALEN	10100 SANTA MONICA BLVD. SUITE #2460	LOS ANGELES	CA	90067	C	B	ROCK & ROLL GROUP
VAN HALEN, ALEX	12024 SUMMIT CIRCLE	BEVERLY HILLS	CA	90210	U	U	MUSICIAN
VAN HALEN, EDDIE	31736 BROAD BEACH RD.	MALIBU	CA	90265	U	U	GUITARIST/SONGWRITER - **AUTHOR'S CHOICE!**
VAN PATTEN, DICK	13920 MAGNOLIA BLVD.	SHERMAN OAKS	CA	91423	A	A	ACTOR - *EIGHT IS ENOUGH*
VAN PATTEN, JAMES	14411 RIVERSIDE DR. #15	SHERMAN OAKS	CA	91423	U	U	ACTOR
VAN PATTEN, JOYCE	1321 N. HAYWORTH #C	SHERMAN OAKS	CA	91423	A	B	ACTOR
VAN PATTEN, NELS	14411 RIVERSIDE DR. #18	SHERMAN OAKS	CA	91423	U	U	ACTOR
VAN PATTEN, TIM	400 S. BEVERLY DR. #216	BEVERLY HILLS	CA	90212	U	U	ACTOR
VAN PATTEN, VINCENT	13926 MAGNOLIA BLVD.	SHERMAN OAKS	CA	91423	U	U	ACTOR
VAN PEEBLES, MARIO	11 TUXEDO	GLENRIDGE	NJ	07028	U	U	ACTOR/WRITER/DIRECTOR - *POSSE*
VAN PEEBLES, MELVIN	353 W. 56TH ST. #10-F	NEW YORK	NY	10019	U	U	ACTOR/WRITER/DIRECTOR
VAN SHELTON, RICKY	40 MUSIC SQUARE E.	NASHVILLE	TN	37203	C	B	SINGER
VAN VALKENBURGH, DEBORAH	2025 STANLEY HILLS DR.	LOS ANGELES	CA	90046	U	U	ACTRESS
VAN VOOREN, MONIQUE	165 E. 66TH ST.	NEW YORK	NY	10021	A	B	ACTRESS/SINGER

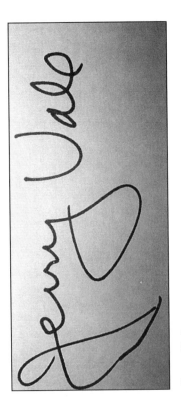

Diane Von Furstenberg

Jerry Vale

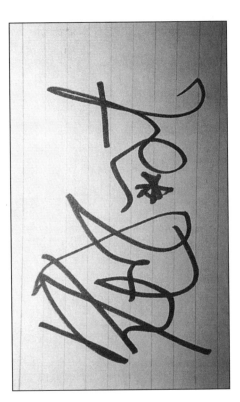

Dick Van Patten

Kurt Vonnegut

Name	Address	City	State	Zip Code	Resp. Time	Resp. Qual.	Comments
VAN ZANDT, STEVE	322 W. 57TH ST.	NEW YORK	NY	10019	U	U	SINGER/GUITARIST
VANCE, CYRUS	425 LEXINGTON AVE.	NEW YORK	NY	10017	C	D	GOVERNMENT OFFICIAL
VANDIS, TITOS	1930 CENTURY PARK E. #303	LOS ANGELES	CA	90067	U	U	ACTOR
VANDROSS, LUTHER	C/O ICM, 8942 WILSHIRE BLVD.	BEVERLY HILLS	CA	90211	U	U	SINGER - "HERE AND NOW" - **AUTHOR'S CHOICE!**
VANILLA ICE	1290 AVE. OF THE AMERICAS #4200	NEW YORK	NY	10104	U	U	RAP SINGER
VANITY (DENISE MATTHEWS)	151 S. EL CAMINO DR.	BEVERLY HILLS	CA	90212	U	U	SINGER/ACTRESS
VARNEY, STUART	C/O CNN, ONE CNN CTR., BOX 105366	ATLANTA	GA	30348	U	U	NEWSCASTER
VAUGHN, MO	C/O BOSTON RED SOX, 4 YAWKEY WAY	BOSTON	MA	02215	U	U	BASEBALL PLAYER - NICE IN PERSON
VAUGHN, ROBERT	162 OLD W. MOUNTAIN RD.	RIDGEFIELD	CT	06877	U	U	ACTOR/DIRECTOR - U.N.C.L.E.
VEDDER, EDDIE	C/O EPIC RECORDS, 550 MADISON AVE.	NEW YORK	NY	10022	U	U	SINGER - PEARL JAM - **AUTHOR'S CHOICE!**
VEE (VELLINE), BOBBY	P.O. BOX 41	SAULK RAPIDS	MN	56379	A	D	SINGER/SONGWRITER
VEL JOHNSON, REGINALD	8637 ALLENWOOD DR.	LOS ANGELES	CA	90046	U	U	ACTOR - FAMILY MATTERS
VELASQUEZ, JORGE	770 ALLERTON AVE.	BRONX	NY	10467	U	U	HORSE RACER
VELEZ, EDDIE	5439 ELLENVALE AVE.	WOODLAND HILLS	CA	91367	U	U	ACTOR - EXTREMITIES
VENTURI, KEN	P.O. BOX 5118	AKRON	OH	44334	A	B	GOLFER
VENUTA, BENAY	50 E. 79TH ST.	NEW YORK	NY	10021	U	U	ACTRESS
VERDUGO, ELENA	P.O. BOX 2048	CHULA VISTA	CA	92012	A	B	ACTRESS
VERMEIL, DICK	77 W. 66TH ST.	NEW YORK	NY	10023	A	D	SPORTSCASTER
VERNON, JOHN	15125 MULHOLLAND DR.	LOS ANGELES	CA	90077	A	B	ACTOR
VERNON, KATE	1999 AVE. OF THE STARS #2850	LOS ANGELES	CA	90067	U	U	ACTRESS
VERSACE, GIANNI	GIANNI VERSACE BOUTIQUE, 816 MADISON AVE.	NEW YORK	NY	10021	U	U	FASHION DESIGNER - **AUTHOR'S CHOICE!**
VICKERS, YVETTE	P.O. BOX 664	PINON HILLS	CA	92372	C	B	ACTRESS
VICTOR, JAMES	1944 N. WHITLEY AVE. #306	LOS ANGELES	CA	90036	C	B+	ACTOR
VIDAL, GORE	1201 ALTA LOMA RD.	LOS ANGELES	CA	90069	U	U	WRITER - LINCOLN: A NOVEL
VILLARD, TOM	9150 WILSHIRE BLVD. #205	BEVERLY HILLS	CA	90212	U	U	ACTOR
VINCENT, VIRGINIA	1001 HAMMOND ST.	LOS ANGELES	CA	90069	U	U	ACTOR
VINES, ELLSWORTH	P.O. BOX 821	LA QUINTA	CA	92253	U	U	TENNIS & GOLF PLAYER
VINSON, HELEN	2213 CAROL WOODS	CHAPEL HILL	NC	27514	U	U	ACTRESS
VINTON, BOBBY	P.O. BOX 6010	BRANSON	MO	65616	U	U	SINGER
VISCULO, SAL	6491 IVARENE AVE.	LOS ANGELES	CA	90068	U	U	ACTOR
VITALE, DICK	C/O ESPN, ESPN PLAZA	BRISTOL	CT	06010	U	U	SPORTSCASTER - SEND YOUR S.A.S.E. TO THIS P.T.P ER!
VOIGHT, JON	13340 GALEWOOD DR.	SHERMAN OAKS	CA	91423	U	U	ACTOR - MIDNIGHT COWBOY

351

Brenda Vaccaro

Dear Mark Allen Baker –
Thank you for your charming
note and kind words –
With All Good Wishes
and Best regards –
Abigail Van Buren
("Dear Abby")

Abigal Van Buren

Name	Address	City	State	Zip Code	Resp. Time	Resp. Qual.	Comments
VOLZ, NEDRA	615 TULARE WAY	UPLAND	CA	91786	A	A	ACTRESS
VON DOHLEN, LENNY	2271 BETTY LN.	BEVERLY HILLS	CA	90210	U	U	ACTOR
VON FURSTENBERG, DIANE	745 FIFTH AVE.	NEW YORK	NY	10151	A	B	FASHION DESIGNER
VON SUSTRON, GRETA	C/O CNN, ONE CNN CTR., BOX 105366	ATLANTA	GA	30348	U	U	NEWSCASTER/LAWYER
VONNEGUT JR., KURT	P.O. BOX 27	SAGAPONACK	NY	11962	A	D	AUTHOR - SLAUGHTERHOUSE 5 - AUTHOR'S CHOICE!
WADE, ADAM	118 E. 25TH ST. #600	NEW YORK	NY	10010	C	A+	ACTOR/SINGER
WADE, RUSSELL	47-287 W. ELDORADO DR.	INDIAN WELLS	CA	92260	A	B+	ACTOR
WADKINS, LANNY	P.O. BOX 673	RICHMOND	VA	23206	A	C	GOLFER
WAGGONER, LYLE	4450 BALBOA AVE.	ENCINO	CA	91316	A	B	ACTOR - WONDER WOMAN
WAGNER, CHUCK	50 BALSAM AVE.	TORONTO, ONTARIO	CAN	M4E 3B4	U	U	ACTOR
WAGNER, JANE	P.O. BOX 27700	LOS ANGELES	CA	90027	A	C	WRITER/PRODUCER
WAGNER, LINDSAY	P.O. BOX 188	PACIFIC PALISADES	CA	90272	C	F	ACTRESS - THE BIONIC WOMAN
WAGONER, PORTER	P.O. BOX 290785	NASHVILLE	TN	37229	A	C	SINGER/SONGWRITER
WAIN, BEA	9955 DURANT DR.	BEVERLY HILLS	CA	90212	A	C	SINGER
WAITS, TOM	P.O. BOX 498	VALLEY FORD	CA	94972	U	U	SINGER/SONGWRITER
WALCOTT, GREGORY	22246 SATICOY ST.	CANOGA PARK	CA	91306	A	A+	ACTOR
WALD, JEFF	227 TOYOPA DR.	PACIFIC PALISADES	CA	90272	U	U	TALENT AGENT
WALDEN, ROBERT	1450 ARROYO VIEW DR.	PASADENA	CA	91103	U	U	ACTOR
WALDO, JANET	15725 ROYAL OAK RD.	ENCINO	CA	91316	A	B	ACTRESS
WALKEN, CHRISTOPHER	142 CEDAR RD.	WILTON	CT	06897	U	U	ACTOR
WALKER, BREE	3347 TARECO DR.	LOS ANGELES	CA	90068	A	D	NEWSCASTER
WALKER, DOAK	P.O. BOX TT	STEAMBOAT SPRINGS	CO	80477	A	D	MEMBER OF FOOTBALL HALL OF FAME
WALKER, JUNIOR	141 DUNBAR AVE.	FORDS	NJ	08863	U	U	SAXOPHONIST
WALKER, KIM	151 EL CAMINO DR.	BEVERLY HILLS	CA	90210	U	U	ACTRESS
WALKER, MORT	61 STUDIO COURT	STAMFORD	CT	06903	A	D	CARTOONIST - BEETLE BAILEY
WALKER, NICHOLAS	6925 TUNA CANYON RD.	TOPANGA	CA	90290	U	U	ACTOR
WALKER, POLLY	924 WESTWOOD BLVD. #900	LOS ANGELES	CA	90024	U	U	ACTRESS
WALKER, ROBERT JR.	20828 PACIFIC COAST HWY.	MALIBU	CA	90265	U	U	ACTOR
WALLACE STONE, DEE	9000 SUNSET BLVD. #1200	LOS ANGELES	CA	90069	U	U	ACTRESS
WALLACE, CHRIS	1717 DESALES ST.	WASHINGTON	DC	20036	U	U	BROADCAST JOURNALIST
WALLACE, GEORGE	P.O. BOX 4419	MONTGOMERY	AL	36104	A	A+	FORMER GOVERNOR
WALLACE, MARCIA	1312 S. GENESEE AVE.	LOS ANGELES	CA	90019	A	B	ACTRESS
WALLACE, MARJORIE	901 BUNDY DR.	LOS ANGELES	CA	90049	U	U	JOURNALIST
WALLACE, MIKE	CBS NEWS, 524 W. 57TH ST.	NEW YORK	NY	10019	U	U	BROADCAST JOURNALIST - 60 MINUTES

353

Pamela Hensley Vincent

Dick Van Dyke

Eli Wallach

Robin Williams

Jim Wright

AUTOGRAPHS OF HOYT WILHELM

$5.00 per piece to be autographed
Balls or Bats $7.50 each

Special edition photos $10.00 each.
All funds are to help purchase
Equipment for Chance Collins,
an 8 year old with cerebral palsy.

Make checks payable to:

Chance Collins Fund

A Hoyt Wilhelm response

Denzel Washington (facsimile)

Name	Address	City	State	Zip Code	Resp. Time	Resp. Qual.	Comments
WALLACE, RUSTY	C/O TOM ROBERTS, P.O. BOX 890	GUNTERSVILLE	AL	35976	U	U	AUTO RACER
WALLACH, ELI	90 RIVERSIDE DR.	NEW YORK	NY	10024	A	B	ACTOR - *THE GOOD, THE BAD AND THE UGLY*
WALLENDAS, THE GREAT	138 FROG HOLLOW RD.	CHURCHVILLE	PA	18966	C	B	HIGH WIRE ACT
WALLER, ROBERT JAMES	C/O CREATIVE ARTISTS AGCY., 9830 WILSHIRE BLVD.	BEVERLY HILLS	CA	90212	U	U	AUTHOR - *THE BRIDGES OF MADISON COUNTY -* **AUTHOR'S CHOICE!**
WALLIS, SHANI	15460 VISTA HAVEN	SHERMAN OAKS	CA	91402	U	U	SINGER
WALMSLEY, JON	13810 MAGNOLIA BLVD.	SHERMAN OAKS	CA	91403	U	U	ACTOR
WALSH, BILL	STANFORD UNIVERSITY FOOTBALL	STANFORD	CA	94305	U	U	FOOTBALL COACH
WALSH, JOHN	5151 WISCONSIN AVE.	WASHINGTON	DC	20016	A	B	ACTOR
WALSH, M. EMMET	4173 MOTOR AVE.	CULVER CITY	CA	90232	A	B+	ACTOR - *BLOOD SIMPLE*
WALSTON, RAY	423 S. REXFORD DR. #205	BEVERLY HILLS	CA	90212	A	B	ACTOR - *MY FAVORITE MARTIAN*
WALTER, JESSICA	10530 STRATHMORE DR.	LOS ANGELES	CA	90024	A	B	ACTRESS - *PLAY MISTY FOR ME*
WALTER, TRACEY	257 N. REXFORD DR.	BEVERLY HILLS	CA	90210	A	B	ACTOR - *BATMAN*
WALTERS, BARBARA	33 W. 60TH ST.	NEW YORK	NY	10021	U	U	NEWS JOURNALIST
WALTERS, JAMIE	C/O ATLANTIC RECORDS, 75 ROCKEFELLER PLAZA	NEW YORK	NY	10019	U	U	SINGER
WALTERS, LAURIE	13428 MAXELLA #224	MARINA DEL REY	CA	90292	U	U	ACTRESS
WALTERS, SUSAN	151 EL CAMINO DR.	BEVERLY HILLS	CA	90212	U	U	ACTRESS
WALTON, JESS	4702 ETHEL AVE.	SHERMAN OAKS	CA	91423	U	U	ACTRESS
WALTRIP, DARRELL	P.O. BOX 855	FRANKLIN	TN	37065	A	B	RACE CAR DRIVER
WANAMAKER, SAM	354 N. CROFT AVE.	LOS ANGELES	CA	90048	U	U	ACTOR/DIRECTOR
WAPNER, JOSEPH A.	16616 PARK LANE PL.	LOS ANGELES	CA	90049	A	B	TELEVISION JUDGE
WARD, GEOFFREY	1 W. 85TH ST.	NEW YORK	NY	10024	U	U	AUTHOR
WARD, MEGAN	1999 AVE. OF THE STARS #2850	LOS ANGELES	CA	90067	U	U	ACTRESS
WARD, RACHEL	11620 WILSHIRE BLVD. #1000	LOS ANGELES	CA	90025	U	U	ACTRESS - *AGAINST ALL ODDS*
WARD, SKIP	P.O. BOX 755	BEVERLY HILLS	CA	90213	U	U	ACTOR
WARDEN, JACK	23604 MALIBU COLONY DR.	MALIBU	CA	90265	U	U	ACTOR - *CRAZY LIKE A FOX*
WARE, CLYDE	1252 N. LAUREL AVE.	LOS ANGELES	CA	90046	A	D	WRITER/PRODUCER
WARE, HERTA	P.O. BOX 151	TOPANGA	CA	90290	U	U	ACTRESS
WARFIELD, MARSHA	P.O. BOX 691713	LOS ANGELES	CA	90069	U	U	ACTRESS/COMEDIENNE - *NIGHT COURT*
WARGA, WAYNE	15320 KINGSWOOD LN.	SHERMAN OAKS	CA	91403	U	U	TELEVISION WRITER
WARINER, STEVE	P.O. BOX 1209	NASHVILLE	TN	37135	A	D	ACTOR
WARLOCK, BILLY	9200 SUNSET BLVD. #625	LOS ANGELES	CA	90069	U	U	ACTOR
WARMERDAM, CORNELIUS	3976 N. 1ST ST.	FRESNO	CA	93726	C	D	TRACK ATHLETE

Simon Wiesenthal

358

Name	Address	City	State	Zip Code	Resp. Time	Resp. Qual.	Comments
WARNER, MALCOLM-JAMAL	P.O. BOX 69646	LOS ANGELES	CA	90069	C	D	ACTOR - THE COSBY SHOW
WARREN, JENNIFER	1675 OLD OAK RD.	LOS ANGELES	CA	90049	A	B	ACTRESS
WARREN, LESLEY ANN	8942 WILSHIRE BLVD.	BEVERLY HILLS	CA	90212	C	B	ACTRESS - MISSION IMPOSSIBLE
WARREN, MICHAEL	189 GREENFIELD	LOS ANGELES	CA	90049	U	U	ACTOR
WARRICK, RUTH	903 PARK AVE.	NEW YORK	NY	10021	U	U	ACTRESS - ALL MY CHILDREN
WARWICK, DIONNE	806 N. ELM DR.	BEVERLY HILLS	CA	90210	A	B	SINGER/THE PSYCHIC HOT LINE
WASHINGTON, DENZEL	4701 SANCOLA	TOLUCA LAKE	CA	91602	A	F	ACTOR - RESPONDS WITH FACSIMILE SIGNED PHOTO - AUTHOR'S CHOICE!
WASHINGTON, GROVER JR.	C/O ZANE MGMT., BROAD AND WALNUT ST.	PHILADELPHIA	PA	19102	A	D	MUSICIAN
WASS, TED	7667 SEATTLE PL.	LOS ANGELES	CA	90046	U	U	ACTOR
WASSERMAN, LEW	911 N. FOOTHILL RD.	BEVERLY HILLS	CA	90210	U	U	FILM EXECUTIVE
WASSERSTEIN, WENDY	C/O VINTAGE BOOKS, 201 E. 50TH ST.	NEW YORK	NY	10022	U	U	PLAYWRIGHT - THE HEIDI CHRONICLES - AUTHOR'S CHOICE!
WASSON, CRAIG	P.O. BOX 735	MCCALL	ID	83638	A	F	ACTOR - SENDS NO AUTOGRAPH, BUT INCLUDES HIS VERSION OF THE LIFE OF JESUS
WATERMAN, ROBERT	C/O HARPER, 10 E. 53RD ST.	NEW YORK	NY	10022	U	U	AUTHOR - IN SEARCH OF EXCELLENCE
WATERS, JOHN	10 W. HIGHFIELD RD.	BALTIMORE	MD	21218	U	U	DIRECTOR/WRITER - HAIRSPRAY
WATERS, LOU	C/O CNN, ONE CNN CENTER, P.O. BOX 105366	ATLANTA	GA	30348	U	U	NEWSCASTER
WATERSON, SAM	RR BOX 232	WEST CORNWELL	CT	06796	U	U	ACTOR - THE KILLING FIELDS
WATSON, TOM	1901 W. 47TH PL. #200	WESTWOOD	KS	66205	A	B	GOLFER
WAYANS, KEENAN IVORY	16405 MULHOLLAND DR.	LOS ANGELES	CA	90049	U	U	ACTOR - IN LIVING COLOR
WAYANS, KIM	1742 GRANVILLE AVE. #2	LOS ANGELES	CA	90025	U	U	ACTRESS
WAYANS, MARLON	16405 MULHOLLAND	LOS ANGELES	CA	90049	U	U	ACTOR
WAYNE, FREDD	117 STRAND ST.	SANTA MONICA	CA	90405	A	B	ACTOR/WRITER
WAYNE, MICHAEL	10425 KLING ST.	N. HOLLYWOOD	CA	91602	U	U	FILM EXECUTIVE
WAYNE, PATRICK	10502 WHIPPLE ST.	N. HOLLYWOOD	CA	91602	U	U	ACTOR - MCCLINTOCK!
WAYNE, PILAR	30821 S. COAST HWY., TRLR. 9	LAGUNA BEACH	CA	92651	U	U	WIDOW OF JOHN WAYNE
WEATHERLY, SHAWN	838 S. BARRINGTON AVE. #304	LOS ANGELES	CA	90049	U	U	ACTRESS/MODEL
WEATHERS, CARL	10960 WILSHIRE BLVD. #826	LOS ANGELES	CA	90024	U	U	ACTOR - ROCKY
WEATHERWAX, BOB	16133 SOLEDAD CANYON RD.	CANYON COUNTRY	CA	91351	U	U	ANIMAL TRAINER
WEAVER, DENNIS	13867 COUNTY RD. 1	RIDGEWAY	CO	81432	C	B	ACTOR - MCCLOUD
WEAVER, FRITZ	161 W. 75TH ST.	NEW YORK	NY	10023	U	U	ACTOR - MARATHON MAN
WEAVER, MARJORIE	13038 SAN VICENTE BLVD.	LOS ANGELES	CA	90049	U	U	ACTRESS

Lyle Waggoner

Billy Wilder

Billy Williams

January 1996

Caspar W. Weinberger

Caspar W. Weinberger

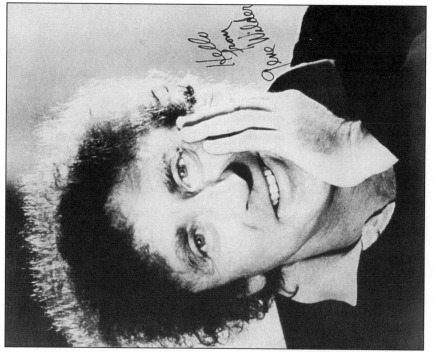

Gene Wilder (facsimile)

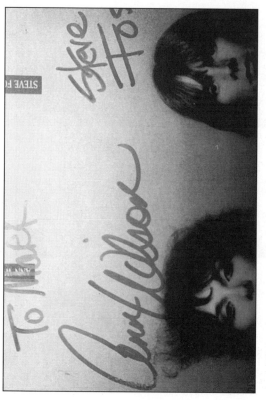

Ann Wilson of Heart, like most musicians, may respond when mail is forwarded from her record company.

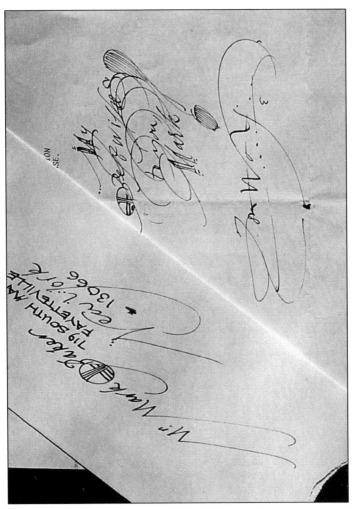

Tom Wolfe

Name	Address	City	State	Zip Code	Resp. Time	Resp. Qual.	Comments
WEAVER, SIGOURNEY	200 W. 57TH ST. #1306	NEW YORK	NY	10019	U	U	ACTRESS - *AUTHOR'S CHOICE!*
WEBB, JIMMY	1560 N. LAUREL AVE. #109	LOS ANGELES	CA	90046	U	U	SINGER/COMPOSER
WEBB, LUCY	1360 N. CRESCENT HTS. #3-B	LOS ANGELES	CA	90046	U	U	ACTRESS/COMEDIENNE
WEBBER, ANDREW LLOYD	TRUMP TOWER, 725 FIFTH AVE.	NEW YORK	NY	10022	C	F	COMPOSER - *AUTHOR'S CHOICE!* - "SIMPLY DOES NOT SIGN AUTOGRAPHS"
WEBER, AMY	C/O WIZARDS OF THE COAST, INC., P.O. BOX 707	RENTON	WA	98057	U	U	ILLUSTRATOR - "MAGIC" CARDS
WEBER, STEVEN	2805 LACUESTA DR.	LOS ANGELES	CA	90046	U	U	ACTOR
WEED, GENE	10405 OKLAHOMA AVE.	CHATSWORTH	CA	91311	U	U	WRITER/PRODUCER
WEINBERGER, CASPER	60 FIFTH AVE.	NEW YORK	NY	10011	A	D	FORMER GOVERNMENT OFFICIAL
WEINTRAUB, CARL	10390 SANTA MONICA BLVD. #300	LOS ANGELES	CA	90025	U	U	ACTOR
WEINTRAUB, JERRY	27740 PACIFIC COAST HWY.	MALIBU	CA	90265	A	B	FILM PRODUCER
WEIR, PETER	POST OFFICE	PALM BEACH 2108	AUSTRALIA		U	U	FILM DIRECTOR
WEISKOPF, TOM	5412 E. MORRISON LN.	PARADISE VALLEY	AZ	85253	A	B	GOLFER
WEISS, MICHAEL T.	151 S. EL CAMINO DR.	BEVERLY HILLS	CA	90212	U	U	ACTOR
WEISSER, MORGAN	1030 SUPERBA AVE.	VENICE	CA	90291	U	U	ACTOR
WEISSER, NORBERT	1030 SUPERBA AVE.	VENICE	CA	90291	U	U	ACTOR
WEITZ, BRUCE	18223 SUGARMAN ST.	TARZANA	CA	91356	U	U	ACTOR - *HILL STREET BLUES*
WELCH, RAQUEL	540 EVELYN PL.	BEVERLY HILLS	CA	90210	A	D	ACTRESS/SINGER/WRITER - *ONE MILLION YEARS, B.C.*
WELCH, TAHNEE	134 DUANE ST. #400	NEW YORK	NY	10013	U	U	ACTRESS
WELD, TUESDAY	P.O. BOX 367	VALLEY STREAM	NY	11589	A	F	ACTRESS - *LOOKING FOR MR. GOODBAR* - REFUSED LETTER
WELDON, ANN	11555 DONA TERESA DR.	STUDIO CITY	CA	91604	U	U	ACTRESS
WELLER, MARY LOUISE	1416 N. HAVENHURST DR. #11	LOS ANGELES	CA	90046	U	U	ACTRESS
WELLER, PETER	37 RIVERSIDE DR.	NEW YORK	NY	10021	U	U	ACTOR - *ROBO COP*
WELLER, ROBB	4249 BECK AVE.	STUDIO CITY	CA	91604	U	U	TELEVISION HOST
WELLMAN, WILLIAM JR.	410 N. BARRINGTON AVE.	LOS ANGELES	CA	90049	U	U	ACTOR
WELLS, DAWN	P.O. BOX 291817	LOS ANGELES	CA	90029	A	B+	ACTRESS - ALSO INCLUDES COOK BOOK FLYER!
WELLS, KITTY	240 OLD HICKORY BLVD.	MADISON	TN	35115	A	B	SINGER
WELTY, EUDORA	1119 PINEHURST ST.	JACKSON	MS	39202	A	B	AUTHOR - *AUTHOR'S CHOICE!*
WENCES, SENOR	204 W. 55TH ST. #701A	NEW YORK	NY	10019	A	B	VENTRILOQUIST
WENDELIN, RUDOLPH	4516-7TH AVE. N.	ARLINGTON	VA	22203	C	B	ILLUSTRATOR - SMOKEY THE BEAR
WENDT, GEORGE	3856 VANTAGE AVE.	STUDIO CITY	CA	91604	U	U	ACTOR - *CHEERS*

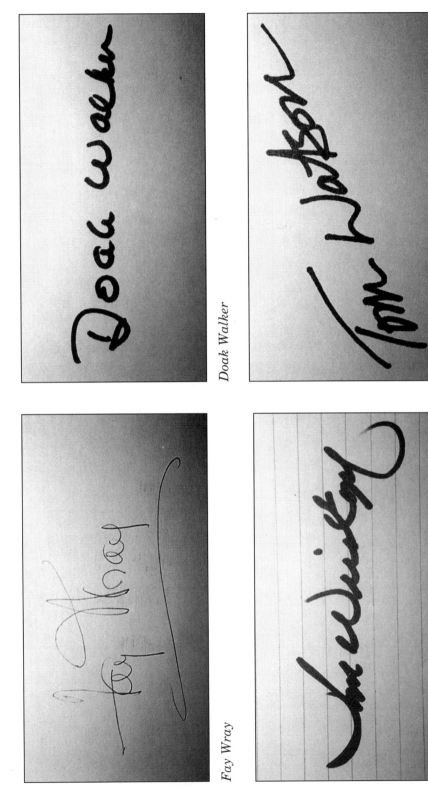

Doak Walker

Tom Watson

Fay Wray

Tom Weiskopf

364

Name	Address	City	State	Zip Code	Resp. Time	Resp. Qual.	Comments
WESSON, DICK	150 E. OLIVE AVE. #111	BURBANK	CA	91502	U	U	ACTOR/WRITER
WEST, ADAM	P.O. BOX 3446	KETCHUM	ID	83340	A	B	ACTOR
WEST, JERRY	P.O. BOX 10	INGLEWOOD	CA	90306	U	U	MEMBER OF THE BASKETBALL HALL OF FAME
WEST, RED	10637 BURBANK BLVD.	HOLLYWOOD	CA	91601	U	U	ACTOR/AUTHOR
WEST, SHELLY	P.O. BOX 2977	HENDERSONVILLE	CA	37077	U	U	SINGER
WESTHEIMER, DR. RUTH	900 W. 190TH ST.	NEW YORK	NY	10040	A	B	SEX THERAPIST - "ASK DR. RUTH"
WESTMORELAND, GEN. WILLIAM	107 1/2 TRADD ST., P.O. BOX 1059	CHARLESTON	SC	29401	A	D	MILITARY LEADER
WESTMORELAND, JAMES	8019 1/2 W. NORTON AVE.	LOS ANGELES	CA	90046	A	B	ACTOR
WETTIG, PATRICIA	11840 CHAPARAL ST.	LOS ANGELES	CA	90049	U	U	ACTRESS
WHALEY, FRANK	151 EL CAMINO	BEVERLY HILLS	CA	90212	U	U	ACTOR - *THE DOORS*
WHALEY-KILMER, JOANNE	P.O. BOX 362	TESUQUE	NM	87574	U	U	ACTRESS - *WILLOW*
WHEATON, WIL	P.O. BOX 12567	LA CRESCENTA	CA	91214	U	U	ACTOR
WHELCHEL, LISA	11906 SHOSHONE AVE.	GRANADA HILLS	CA	91344	U	U	ACTRESS - *THE FACTS OF LIFE*
WHITAKER, FOREST	10345 W. OLYMPIC BLVD. #200	LOS ANGELES	CA	90064-2524	U	U	ACTOR - *THE CRYING GAME*
WHITCOMB, IAN	P.O. BOX 451	ALTADENA	CA	91001	A	A+	SINGER/ACTOR/PRODUCER
WHITE, JESSE	1944 GLENDON AVE. #304	LOS ANGELES	CA	90025	C	D	ACTOR
WHITE, REGGIE	C/O GREEN BAY PACKERS, 1265 LOMBARDI AVE.	GREEN BAY	WI	54304	U	U	FOOTBALL PLAYER
WHITE, SHARON	380 FOREST RETREAT	HENDERSONVILLE	TN	37075	C	B	SINGER/GUITARIST
WHITE, VANNA	3400 RIVERSIDE DR.	BURBANK	CA	91505	A	A+	TELEVISION PERSONALITY/MODEL - *WHEEL OF FORTUNE*
WHITES, THE	P.O. BOX 2158	HENDERSONVILLE	TN	37075	A	B	COUNTRY WESTERN GROUP
WHITFIELD, LYNN	8942 WILSHIRE BLVD.	BEVERLY HILLS	CA	90211	U	U	ACTRESS
WHITING, BARBARA	1085 WADDINGTON ST.	BIRMINGHAM	MI	48009	A	B+	ACTRESS
WHITING, MARGARET	41 W. 58TH ST. #5A	NEW YORK	NY	10019	A	C	SINGER
WHITMAN, SLIM	1300 DIVISION ST. #103	NASHVILLE	TN	37203	U	U	SINGER
WHITMAN, STUART	749 SAN YSIDRO RD.	SANTA BARBARA	CA	93108	C	C	ACTOR
WHITMORE, JAMES	4990 PUESTA DEL SOL	MALIBU	CA	90265	A	D	ACTOR - *WILL ROGERS, USA*
WHITMORE, JAMES JR.	1284 LA BREA DR.	THOUSAND OAKS	CA	91362	U	U	ACTOR
WHITNEY, PHYLLIS	310 MADISON AVE. #607	NEW YORK	NY	10017	A	D	ACTRESS
WHITTINGHILL, DICK	11310 VALLEY SPRING LN.	TOLUCA LAKE	CA	91602	A	D	RADIO PERSONALITY
WHITTON, MARGARET	151 EL CAMINO DR.	BEVERLY HILLS	CA	90212	U	U	ACTRESS
WIDMARK, RICHARD	999 W. POTRERO RD.	THOUSAND OAKS	CA	91360	U	U	ACTOR

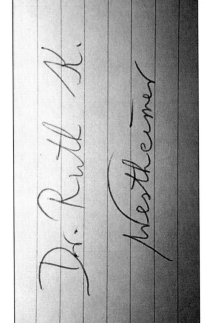

Dr. Ruth Westheimer

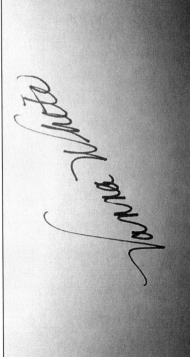

Vanna White

Rudolph Wendelin

Paul Williams

Name	Address	City	State	Zip Code	Resp. Time	Resp. Qual.	Comments
WIESEL, ELIE	40 BOSTON UNIVERISTY, 745 COMMONWEALTH AVE.	BOSTON	MA	02115	A	D	AUTHOR/JOURNALIST
WIEST, DIANNE	127 W. 79TH ST.	NEW YORK	NY	10024	A	D	ACTRESS - HANNAH AND HER SISTERS
WILCOX, LARRY	10 APPALOOSA LN., BELL CANYON	CANOGA PARK	CA	91304	U	U	ACTOR/DIRECTOR - CHIPS
WILCOX, SHANNON	105 S. MEDIO	LOS ANGELES	CA	90049	A	A+	ACTRESS
WILDER, BILLY	10375 WILSHIRE BLVD.	LOS ANGELES	CA	90024	A	D	WRITER/PRODUCER
WILDER, JAMES	9560 WILSHIRE BLVD. #500	BEVERLY HILLS	CA	90212	U	U	ACTOR
WILDING, MICHAEL JR.	8428-C MELROSE PL.	LOS ANGELES	CA	90069	U	U	ACTOR
WILHELM, HOYT	3102 N. HIMES AVE.	TAMPA	FL	33607	A	F	MEMBER OF THE BASEBALL HALL OF FAME - ASKS FOR DONATION
WILKES, DONNA	3802 N. EARL AVE.	ROSEMEAD	CA	91770	U	U	ACTRESS
WILKES, JAMAAL	7846 W. 81ST ST.	PLAYA DEL REY	CA	90291	A	B	FORMER BASKETBALL PLAYER
WILKINSON, JUNE	3653 FAIRESTA ST.	LA CRESCENTA	CA	91214	A	D	ACTRESS/MODEL - INCLUDES PHOTO FLYER, $6 PER B&W PHOTO
WILL, GEORGE	1150 - 15TH ST. N.W.	WASHINGTON	DC	20071	C	F	COLUMNIST/WRITER - STAFF RESPONDS - NO AUTOGRAPH
WILLETTE, JOANN	8091 SELMA AVE.	LOS ANGELES	CA	90046	U	U	ACTRESS
WILLIAMS & REE	P.O. BOX 163	HENDERSONVILLE	TN	37077	U	U	VOCAL DUO
WILLIAMS, ANDY	60 POINTE YALE DR.	BRANSON	MO	65616	A	D	SINGER/ACTOR - "WHERE DO I BEGIN?"
WILLIAMS, BARRY	3646 REINA COURT	CALABASAS	CA	91302	A	D	ACTOR - THE BRADY BUNCH
WILLIAMS, BILLY	586 PRINCE EDWARD	GLEN ELLYN	IL	60137	A	D	MEMBER OF THE BASEBALL HALL OF FAME
WILLIAMS, BRUCE	P.O. BOX 547	ELFERS	FL	34680	A	B	RADIO PERSONALITY
WILLIAMS, CINDY	7023 BIRDVIEW AVE.	MALIBU	CA	90265	U	U	ACTRESS - LAVERNE & SHIRLEY
WILLIAMS, CLARENCE III	9057A NEMO ST.	LOS ANGELES	CA	90069	U	U	ACTOR - THE MOD SQUAD
WILLIAMS, DARNELL	1930 CENTURY PK. W. #403	LOS ANGELES	CA	90067	U	U	ACTOR
WILLIAMS, DON	1103-16TH AVE. S.	NASHVILLE	TN	37203	U	U	SINGER/SONGWRITER
WILLIAMS, EDY	1638 BLUE JAY WAY	LOS ANGELES	CA	90069	U	U	ACTRESS/MODEL
WILLIAMS, ESTHER	9377 READCREST DR.	BEVERLY HILLS	CA	90210	A	D	ACTRESS - BATHING BEAUTY
WILLIAMS, HANK JR.	P.O. BOX 850	PARIS	TN	38242	A	C	SINGER/GUITARIST - TEXAS WOMEN
WILLIAMS, JOBETH	3529 BEVERLY GLEN BLVD.	SHERMAN OAKS	CA	91423	U	U	ACTRESS - THE BIG CHILL
WILLIAMS, JOE	3337 KNOLLWOOD COURT	LAS VEGAS	NV	89121	A	C	SINGER
WILLIAMS, JOHN	C/O MICHAEL GORGAINE, GORFAINE/ SCHWARTZ, 3301 BARHAM BLVD. SUITE 201	LOS ANGELES	CA	90068	U	U	COMPOSER
WILLIAMS, MASON	P.O. BOX 25	OAKBRIDGE	OR	97463	A	C	SINGER/SONGWRITER

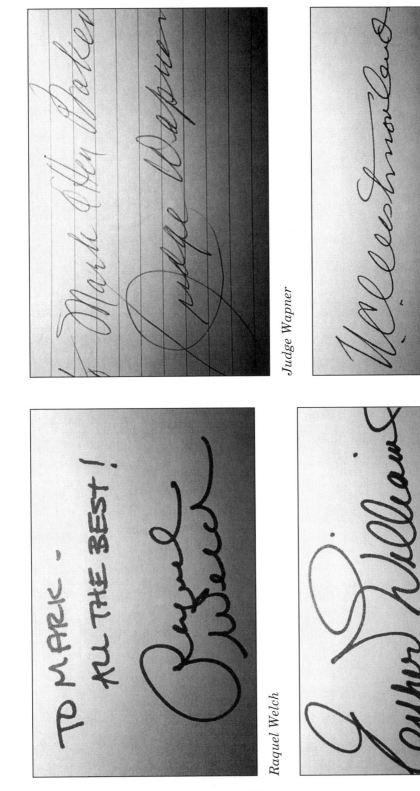

Judge Wapner

Gen. William Westmoreland

Raquel Welch

Esther Williams

Name	Address	City	State	Zip Code	Resp. Time	Resp. Qual.	Comments
WILLIAMS, MONTEL	1350 AVE. OF THE AMERICAS	NEW YORK	NY	10019	A	B	TELEVISION HOST
WILLIAMS, PAUL	645 SAND POINT RD.	CARPINTERIA	CA	93013	A	B	SINGER/SONGWRITER
WILLIAMS, ROBIN	1100 WALL RD.	NAPA	CA	94558	C	B	ACTOR/COMEDIAN/WRITER - GREAT RESPONSE TO CHILDREN - AUTHOR'S CHOICE!
WILLIAMS, ROGER	16150 CLEAR VALLEY PL.	ENCINO	CA	91436	B	C	PIANIST
WILLIAMS, STEPHANIE	1269 S. ORANGE #1	LOS ANGELES	CA	90019	U	U	ACTRESS
WILLIAMS, TED	P.O. BOX 1629	HERNANDO	FL	32642	U	U	MEMBER OF THE BASEBALL HALL OF FAME
WILLIAMS, TREAT	215 W. 78TH ST. #10-A	NEW YORK	NY	10024	U	U	ACTOR - PRINCE OF THE CITY
WILLIAMS, VAN	1630 OCEAN PARK BLVD.	SANTA MONICA	CA	90405	U	U	ACTOR
WILLIAMS, VANESSA	50 OLD FARM RD.	CHAPPAQUA	NY	10514	A	F	SINGER/ACTRESS - RESPONDS WITH FACSIMILE SIGNED PHOTO
WILLIAMS, WAYNE	CLASSIFICATION & DIAGNOSTIC CENTER	JACKSON	GA	30233	U	U	CHILD KILLER
WILLIS, BRUCE	1453 THIRD ST. #420	SANTA MONICA	CA	90401	B	F	ACTOR/SINGER - RESPONDS WITH FACSIMILE SIGNED CARD - STUDIO FAN MAIL - AUTHOR'S CHOICE!
WILSON PHILLIPS	1290 AVE. OF THE AMERICAS #4200	NEW YORK	NY	10104	U	U	ROCK & ROLL GROUP
WILSON, AUGUST	C/O PAUL WEISS, 1285 AVE. OF THE AMERICAS	NEW YORK	NY	10019	U	U	PLAYWRIGHT - THE PIANO LESSON
WILSON, CARL	8860 EVAN VIEW DR.	LOS ANGELES	CA	90069	U	U	SINGER/SONGWRITER
WILSON, CARNIE	13601 VENTURA BLVD. #286	SHERMAN OAKS	CA	91423	U	U	ACTRESS
WILSON, FLIP	21970 PACIFIC COAST HWY.	MALIBU	CA	90265	C	C	COMEDIAN/ACTOR/WRITER - THE FLIP WILSON SHOW
WILSON, GOV. PETE (CA)	STATE CAPITOL	SACRAMENTO	CA	95814	A	B	GOVERNOR
WILSON, JEANNIE	10358 - A RIVERSIDE DR.	N. HOLLYWOOD	CA	91602	U	U	ACTRESS
WILSON, NANCY	5455 WILSHIRE BLVD. #1606	LOS ANGELES	CA	90036	U	U	SINGER/ACTRESS
WIMMER, BRIAN	641 SWARTHMORE AVE.	PACIFIC PALISADES	CA	90272	U	U	ACTOR
WINCHELL, PAUL	32262 OAKSHORE DR.	WESTLAKE VILLAGE	CA	61361	U	U	ACTOR - VENTRILOQUIST
WINDOM, WILLIAM	6535 LANGDEN	VAN NUYS	CA	91406	A	B	ACTOR - MURDER SHE WROTE
WINDSOR, MARIE	9501 CHEROKEE LN.	BEVERLY HILLS	CA	90210	A	B	ACTRESS
WINFIELD, DAVE	11809 GWYNNE LN.	LOS ANGELES	CA	90077	U	U	BASEBALL PLAYER
WINFIELD, PAUL	5693 HOLLY OAK DR.	LOS ANGELES	CA	90068	U	U	ACTOR - SOUNDER
WINFREY, OPRAH	P.O. BOX 909715	CHICAGO	IL	60690	B	B	TELEVISION HOST/ACTRESS - WATCH FOR AUTOPEN! - AUTHOR'S CHOICE!
WINGER, DEBRA	P.O. BOX 9078	VAN NUYS	CA	91409	U	U	ACTRESS - AUTHOR'S CHOICE!
WINGREEN, JASON	4224 TEESDALE AVE.	N. HOLLYWOOD	CA	91604	A	B	ACTOR
WINNINGHAM, MARE	P.O. BOX 19	BECKWOURTH	CA	96219	A	B	ACTRESS - ST. ELMO'S FIRE

John Wooden

Elie Wiesel

Mort Walker

George Wallace

370

Name	Address	City	State	Zip Code	Resp. Time	Resp. Qual.	Comments
WINSLOW, MICHAEL	8730 SUNSET BLVD. #600	LOS ANGELES	CA	90069	U	U	ACTOR/COMEDIAN
WINTERS, JONATHAN	4310 ARCOLA AVE.	TOLUCA LAKE	CA	91602	C	C	COMEDIAN/ACTOR - *THE JONATHAN WINTERS SHOW*
WINTERS, SHELLEY	15 W. 72ND ST. #215	NEW YORK	NY	10024	B	B	ACTRESS - *THE POSEIDON ADVENTURE*
WIRTH, BILLY	8730 SUNSET BLVD. #220W	LOS ANGELES	CA	90069	U	U	ACTOR
WISE, ROBERT	2222 AVE. OF THE STARS #2303	LOS ANGELES	CA	90067	A	B	DIRECTOR/PRODUCER
WITHERS, BILL	2600 BENEDICT CANYON	BEVERLY HILLS	CA	90210	U	U	SINGER/SONGWRITER
WITHERS, JANE	4249 STERN AVE.	SHERMAN OAKS	CA	91423	U	U	ACTRESS
WITT, PAUL JUNGER	1438 N. GOWER ST.	LOS ANGELES	CA	90028	U	U	TELEVISION PRODUCER
WIXTED, KEVIN	10100 SANTA MONICA BLVD. SUITE #700	LOS ANGELES	CA	90067	U	U	ACTOR
WIZARD MR. (DON HERBERT)	P.O. BOX 83	CANOGA PARK	CA	91305	B	B	TELEVISION PERSONALITY
WOLFE, TOM	21 E. 79TH ST.	NEW YORK	NY	10021	A	D	AUTHOR - GREAT PENMANSHIP! - **AUTHOR'S CHOICE!**
WONDER, STEVIE	4616 MAGNOLIA BLVD.	BURBANK	CA	91505	U	U	MUSICIAN - **AUTHOR'S CHOICE!**
WOOD, ELIJAH	760 N. LA CIENEGA BLVD. #200	LOS ANGELES	CA	90069	A	F	ACTOR - RESPONDS WITH FACSIMILE SIGNED PHOTO - **AUTHOR'S CHOICE!**
WOOD, JUDITH	1300 1/2 N. SYCAMORE AVE.	LOS ANGELES	CA	90028	U	U	ACTRESS
WOOD, LANE	4129 WOODMAN AVE.	SHERMAN OAKS	CA	91423	U	U	ACTRESS
WOODARD, ALFRED	8942 WILSHIRE BLVD.	BEVERLY HILLS	CA	90211	U	U	ACTOR - *CROSS CREEK* - **AUTHOR'S CHOICE!**
WOODEN, JOHN	17711 MARGATE ST. #102	ENCINO	CA	91316	A	B+	BASKETBALL COACH - **AUTHOR'S CHOICE!**
WOODHEAD, CYNTHIA	P.O. BOX 1193	RIVERSIDE	CA	92501	U	U	SWIMMER
WOODRUFF, JUDY	P.O. BOX 2626	WASHINGTON	DC	20013	U	U	BROADCAST JOURNALIST
WOODS, DONALD	690 N. CAMINO REAL	PALM SPRINGS	CA	92262	A	C	ACTOR
WOODS, JAMES	1612 GILCREST DR.	BEVERLY HILLS	CA	90210	A	D	ACTOR/DIRECTOR
WOODS, ROBERT S.	227 CENTRAL PARK W. #5-A	NEW YORK	NY	10024	U	U	ACTOR
WOODWARD, BOB	1150 - 15TH ST. N.W.	WASHINGTON	DC	20005	A	D	NEWS CORRESPONDENT
WOODWARD, JOANNE	1120 FIFTH AVE. #1-C	NEW YORK	NY	10022	A	B	ACTRESS/DIRECTOR - *THE THREE FACES OF EVE* - MRS. PAUL NEWMAN
WOOLERY, CHUCK	620 N. LINDEN DR.	BEVERLY HILLS	CA	90210	U	U	TELEVISION HOST
WOOLEY, SHEB	RT. 3, BOX 231, SUNSET ISLAND TRAIL	GALLATIN	TN	37066	A	D	SINGER
WOPAT, TOM	12245 MORRISON ST.	N. HOLLYWOOD	CA	91607	U	U	ACTOR/DIRECTOR
WORLEY, JOANNE	4714 ARCOLA	TOLUCA LAKE	CA	91602	U	U	ACTRESS - *LAUGH-IN*
WORTY, IRENE	333 W. 56TH ST.	NEW YORK	NY	10018	U	U	ACTRESS
WOUK, HERMAN	3255 "N" ST. N.W.	WASHINGTON	DC	20007	U	U	AUTHOR
WOZNIAK, STEVE	475 ALBERTO WAY	LOS GATOS	CA	95030	U	U	COMPUTER BUILDER
WRAY, FAY	2160 CENTURY PARK E. #1901	LOS ANGELES	CA	90067	A	D	ACTRESS

Barry Williams

Grover Washington, Jr.

Stuart Whitman

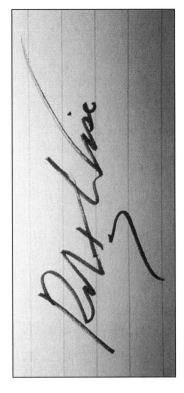

Robert Wise

Name	Address	City	State	Zip Code	Resp. Time	Resp. Qual.	Comments
WREN, CLARE	5750 WILSHIRE BLVD. #512	LOS ANGELES	CA	90036	U	U	ACTRESS
WRIGHT, COBINA JR.	1326 DOVE MEADOW RD.	SOLVANG	CA	93463	A	D	ACTRESS
WRIGHT, JENNY	245 W. 104TH ST.	NEW YORK	NY	10025	A	D	ACTRESS
WRIGHT, JIM	9A10 LANHAM FEDERAL BLDG., 819 TAYLOR ST.	FORT WORTH	TX	76102	U	U	FORMER HOUSE SPEAKER
WRIGHT, MAX	15760 VENTURA BLVD. #1730	ENCINO	CA	91436	U	U	ACTOR - ALF
WRIGHT, STEVEN	9000 SUNSET BLVD. #1200	LOS ANGELES	CA	90069	U	U	COMEDIAN
WRIGHT, TERESA	949 ROWAYTON WOOD DR.	NORWALK	CT	06854	U	U	ACTRESS
WRIGLEY, WILLIAM	410 N. MICHIGAN AVE.	CHICAGO	IL	60611	C	F	BASEBALL EXECUTIVE
WUHL, ROBERT	10590 HOLMAN AVE.	LOS ANGELES	CA	90024	U	U	COMEDIAN/ACTOR/WRITER - BULL DURHAM
WYATT, JANE	651 SIENA WAY	LOS ANGELES	CA	90024	B	D	ACTRESS - FATHER KNOWS BEST
WYATT, SHANNON	8949 FALLING CREEK CT.	ANNANDALE	VA	22003	U	U	ACTRESS
WYATT, SHARON	24549 PARK GRANDE	CALABASAS	CA	91302	U	U	ACTRESS
WYETH, ANDREW	C/O GENERAL DELIVERY	CHADDS FORD	PA	19317	F	F	ARTIST - AUTHOR'S CHOICE! - I HAVE WRITTEN HIM FOR DECADES AND NEVER RECEIVED A RESPONSE.
WYETH, JAMIE	C/O FRANK E. FOWLER, P.O. BOX 247	LOOKOUT MT.	TN	37350	U	U	ARTIST - SON OF ANDREW WYETH
WYLER, GRETCHEN	15215 WEDDINGTON ST.	VAN NUYS	CA	91411	A	C	ACTRESS
WYMAN, JANE	P.O. BOX 540148	ORLANDO	FL	32854	U	U	ACTRESS - FALCON CREST
WYNER, GEORGE	3450 LAURIE PL.	STUDIO CITY	CA	91604	A	B	ACTOR
WYNETTE, TAMMY	1222 - 16TH AVE.	NASHVILLE	TN	37203	U	U	SINGER/ACTRESS - STAND BY YOUR MAN
WYNN, EARLY	P.O. BOX 218	NOKOMIS	FL	34274	U	U	MEMBER OF THE BASEBALL HALL OF FAME
XUXA	7800 BEVERLY BLVD. #202	LOS ANGELES	CA	90036	U	U	ACTRESS
YABLANS, FRANK	2270 BOWMONT DR.	BEVERLY HILLS	CA	90210	U	U	FILM WRITER/PRODUCER
YAGHER, JEFF	10100 SANTA MONICA BLVD. #2500	LOS ANGELES	CA	90067	U	U	ACTOR
YANCEY, EMILY	247 S. BEVERLY DR. #102	BEVERLY HILLS	CA	90212	U	U	ACTRESS
YANKOVIC, WEIRD AL	8842 HOLLYWOOD BLVD.	LOS ANGELES	CA	90069	U	U	SINGER/SONGWRITER - "LIKE A SURGEON"
YANNI	8002 WILLOW GLEN	LOS ANGELES	CA	90046	A	U	NEW AGE MUSICIAN - SOMETIMES NO AUTOGRAPHS, JUST NEWSLETTER! - AUTHOR'S CHOICE!
YARBOROUGH, CALE	9617 DIXIE RIVER RD.	CHARLOTTE	NC	28270	A	B	RACE CAR DRIVER
YARD, MOLLIE	1000 - 16TH ST. N.W.	WASHINGTON	DC	20036	U	U	FEMINIST LEADER
YARLETT, CLAIRE	9300 WILSHIRE BLVD. #410	BEVERLY HILLS	CA	90212	U	U	ACTRESS
YASBECK, AMY	606 N. LARCHMONT BLVD. #309	LOS ANGELES	CA	90004	U	U	ACTRESS
YATES, PETER	334 CAROLINE AVE.	CULVER CITY	CA	90230	U	U	FILM DIRECTOR
YEAGER, GEN. CHUCK	P.O. BOX 128	CEDAR RIDGE	CA	95924	A	B	MILITARY TEST PILOT - AUTHOR'S CHOICE!
YEARWOOD, TRISHA	38 MUSIC SQUARE E. #300	NASHVILLE	TN	37203	A	B	SINGER

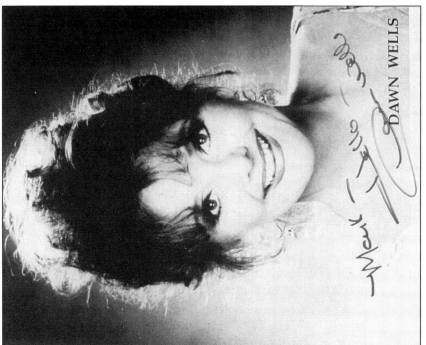

Dawn Wells

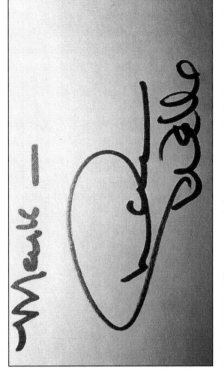

Dawn Wells, like some celebrities, may include signed cards with a photograph

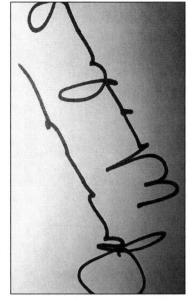

Joanne Woodward

Name	Address	City	State	Zip Code	Resp. Time	Resp. Qual.	Comments
YELLOWJACKETS	9220 SUNSET BLVD. #320	LOS ANGELES	CA	90069	U	U	JAZZ GROUP
YOAKUM, DWIGHT	6363 SUNSET BLVD. #800	LOS ANGELES	CA	90028	C	F	SINGER/GUITARIST
YORDAN, PHILIP	4894 MT. ELBRUS DR.	SAN DIEGO	CA	92117	A	C	SCREENWRITER
YORK, FRANCINE	14333 ADDISON ST. #315	SHERMAN OAKS	CA	91423	A	B	ACTRESS
YORK, MICHAEL	9100 CORDELL DR.	LOS ANGELES	CA	90069	A	B	ACTOR - *LOGAN'S RUN* - ILLEGIBLE SIGNATURE
YORKIN, BUD	250 DELFERN DR.	LOS ANGELES	CA	90077	A	B	WRITER/PRODUCER
YORTY, MAYOR SAM	12979 BLAIRWOOD DR.	STUDIO CITY	CA	91604	A	C	EX-MAYOR
YOUNG M.C.	8730 SUNSET BLVD. #600	LOS ANGELES	CA	90069	U	U	RAP SINGER
YOUNG, ANDREW	1088 VELTRIE CIRCLE S.W.	ATLANTA	GA	30311	C	F	EX-MAYOR - "TOO BUSY"
YOUNG, CHRIS T.	954 N. HAYWORTH	LOS ANGELES	CA	90046	U	U	ACTOR
YOUNG, DEAN	235 E. 45TH ST.	NEW YORK	NY	10017	B	D	CARTOONIST
YOUNG, FARON	P.O. BOX 526	OLD HICKORY	TN	37138	A	C	SINGER/SONGWRITER
YOUNG, LORETTA	1705 AMBASSADOR DR.	BEVERLY HILLS	CA	90210	A	F	ACTRESS - *THE FARMER'S DAUGHTER* - DOESN'T SIGN ANYMORE
YOUNG, NEIL	C/O GEFFEN RECORDS, 9126 SUNSET BLVD.	WEST HOLLYWOOD	CA	90069	U	U	SINGER - "HEART OF GOLD"
YOUNG, RICHARD	1275 WESTWOOD BLVD.	LOS ANGELES	CA	90024	U	U	ACTOR
YOUNG, ROBERT	31589 SADDLETREE DR.	WESTLAKE VILLAGE	CA	91261	U	U	ACTOR - *MARCUS WELBY M.D.*
YOUNG, SEAN	P.O. BOX 20547	SEDONA	AZ	86341	C	B	ACTRESS - *NO WAY OUT*
YOUNG, STEVE	C/O SAN FRANCISCO 49ERS, 4949 CENTENNIAL BLVD.	SANTA CLARA	CA	95054	B	D	FOOTBALL PLAYER
YOUNG,WILLIAM ALLEN	1213 W. 122ND ST.	LOS ANGELES	CA	90044	U	U	ACTOR
YOUNGFELLOW, BARRIE	10927 MISSOURI AVE.	LOS ANGELES	CA	90025	U	U	ACTRESS
YOUNGMAN, HENNY	77 W. 55TH ST.	NEW YORK	NY	10019	A	B	COMEDIAN - *TAKE MY WIFE ... PLEASE!*
YULIN, HARRIS	1630 CRESCENT PL.	VENICE	CA	90291	U	U	ACTOR
ZABKA, WILLIAM	345 N. MAPLE DR. #183	BEVERLY HILLS	CA	90210	U	U	ACTOR/SINGER
ZABRISKIE, GRACE	1800 S. ROBERTSON BLVD. #426	LOS ANGELES	CA	90035	U	U	ACTRESS
ZACCARO, JOHN	22 DEEPDENE RD.	FOREST HILLS	NY	11375	U	U	BUSINESSMAN
ZADORA, PIA	8 BEVERLY PK.	BEVERLY HILLS	CA	90120	C	B	ACTRESS/SINGER -*NAKED GUN 33 1/3*
ZAHN, PAULA	524 W. 57TH ST.	NEW YORK	NY	10019	U	U	TELEVISION HOST - *CBS THIS MORNING*
ZAL, ROXANNE	1450 BELFAST DR.	LOS ANGELES	CA	90069	U	U	ACTRESS - *SOMETHING ABOUT AMELIA*
ZANE, BILLY	450 N. ROSSMORE AVE. #1001	LOS ANGELES	CA	90004	U	U	ACTOR
ZANUCK, RICHARD	202 N. CANON DR.	BEVERLY HILLS	CA	90210	A	D	FILM PRODUCER
ZAPATA, CARMEN	6107 ETHEL AVE.	VAN NUYS	CA	91405	A	B	ACTRESS
ZAPPA, DWEEZIL	7885 WOODROW WILSON DR.	LOS ANGELES	CA	90046	U	U	SINGER
ZEMAN, JACKLYN	12186 LAUREL TERR.	STUDIO CITY	CA	91604	A	B+	ACTRESS

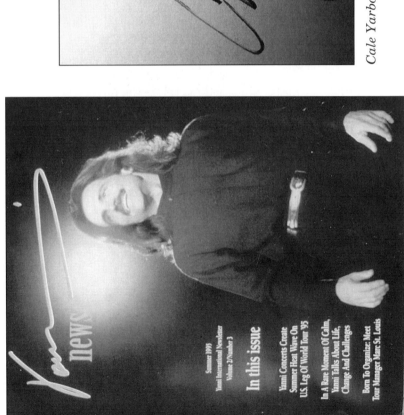

Cale Yarborough

Yanni newsletter, a probable response to your auto-graph request

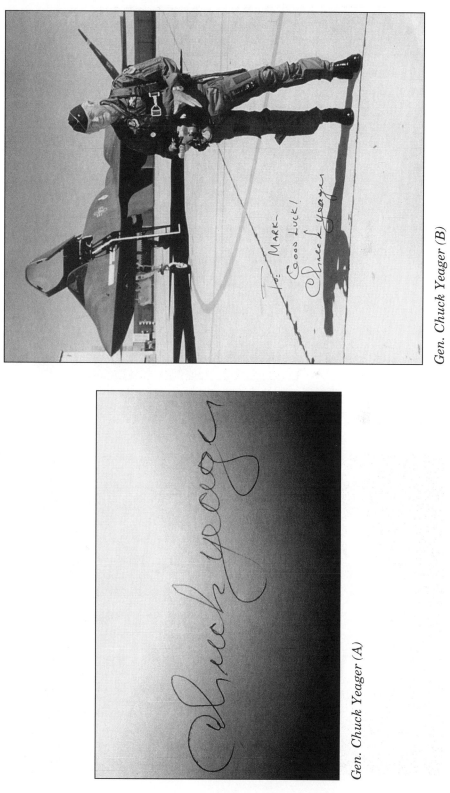

Gen. Chuck Yeager (B)

Gen. Chuck Yeager (A)

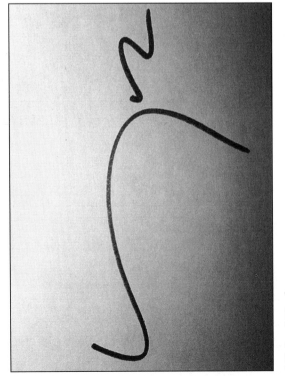

Henny Youngman

Michael York

Name	Address	City	State	Zip Code	Resp. Time	Resp. Qual.	Comments
ZEMECKIS, ROBERT	C/O CREATIVE ARTISTS AGCY., 9830 WILSHIRE BLVD.	BEVERLY HILLS	CA	90212	U	U	DIRECTOR - *FORREST GUMP* - **AUTHOR'S CHOICE!**
ZIMBALIST, EFREM JR.	4750 ENCINO AVE.	ENCINO	CA	91316	A	B	ACTOR
ZIMBALIST, STEPHANIE	16255 VENTURA BLVD. #1011	ENCINO	CA	91436	U	U	ACTRESS - *REMINGTON STEELE*
ZIMMER, KIM	25561 ALMENDRA DR.	SANTA CLARITA	CA	91355	A	D	ACTRESS
ZMESKAL, KIM	17203 BAMWOOD	HOUSTON	TX	77090	U	U	GYMNAST
ZUNIGA, DAPHNE	P.O. BOX 1249	WHITE RIVER JUNCTION	VT	05001	A	F	ACTRESS - *MELROSE PLACE* - RESPONDS WITH FACSIMILE SIGNED PHOTO - MAIL SERVICE
ZZ TOP	P.O. BOX 19744	HOUSTON	TX	77024	U	U	MUSIC GROUP

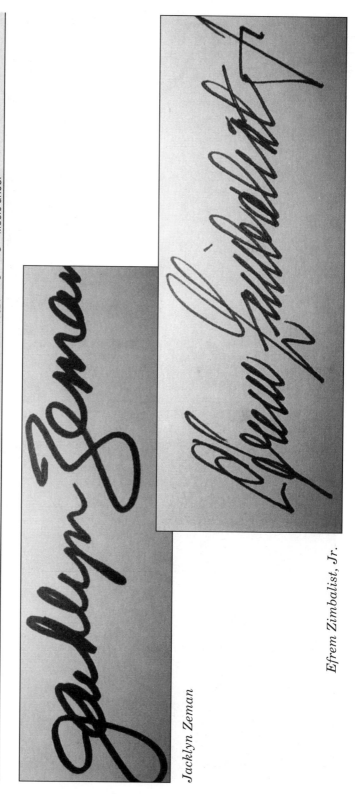

Jacklyn Zeman

Efrem Zimbalist, Jr.

Daphne Zuniga (facsimile)

Pia Zadora

Section III

Assorted Directories

Professional Sports Directory

Card Companies

Action Packed, 924 Avenue J. East, Grand Prairie, TX 75050, (214) 601-7000.

Bowman, see Topps.

Cardz Distribution, 2505 N. Highway 360, 7th Floor, Grand Prairie, TX 75050, (817) 640-1000.

Classic Inc., 1951 Old Cuthbert Road, Cherry Hill, NJ 08034, (609) 354-9000.

Collector's Edge, 2485 W. 2nd Ave. #14, Denver, CO 80223, (303) 727-9300.

Finish Line Collectibles, 615 Highway A1A North, Suite 105, Ponte Vedra Beach, FL 32082, (904) 285-6227.

Fleer Corp., Executive Plaza, Suite 300, 1120 Route 73, Mt. Laurel, NJ 08054, (609) 231-6200.

Leaf/Donruss, 500 N. Field Dr., Lake Forest, IL 60045, (708) 735-7772.

Maxx Racing, P.O. Box 13530, Charlotte, NC 28270, (704) 531-7447.

Megacards Inc., 5650 Wattsburg Road, Erie, PA 16509, (515) 472-4159.

Metallic Images 1502 N. Riverside Drive, Wilmington, NC 28405, (919) 251-1110.

NBA Hoops, see Fleer.

Pacific Trading Cards, 18424 Hwy. 99, Lynwood, WA 98037, (800) 551-2002.

Pinnacle Brands Inc. (Score), 924 Avenue J East, Grand Prairie, TX 75050, (214) 601-7000.

Playoff , see Cardz Distribution.

Press Pass, 14800 Quorum Drive, Suite 420, Dallas, TX 75240, (214) 385-3403.

Price International (Parkhurst), 135 W. Beaver Creek Road, Richmond Hill, Ontario, Canada L4B2C6, (905) 707-1962.

Signature Rookies, P.O. Box 12, Fleetville, PA 18420, (717) 945-7753.

SkyBox International, see Fleer.

Topps Co. Inc., One Whitehall Street, New York, NY 10004-2109, (212) 376-1589.

Upper Deck, 5909 Sea Otter Place, Carlsbad, CA 92008, (619) 929-6500.

Major League Baseball

350 Park Ave., New York, NY 10022, (212) 339-7800.

American League

350 Park Ave., New York, NY 10022, (212) 339-7600.

Baltimore Orioles, 333 W. Camden St., Baltimore, MD 21201.

Boston Red Sox, Fenway Park, 24 Yawkey Way, Boston, MA 02215.

California Angels, P.O. Box 2000, Anaheim, CA 92803.

Chicago White Sox, 333 W. 35th Street, Chicago, IL 60616.

Cleveland Indians, 2401 Ontario St., Cleveland, OH 44114-40003.

Detroit Tigers, 2121 Trumbull Ave., Detroit, MI 48216.

Kansas City Royals, P.O. Box 419969, Kansas City, MO 64141.

Milwaukee Brewers, Milwaukee County Stadium, Milwaukee, WI 53214.

Minnesota Twins, 501 Chicago Ave. South, Minneapolis, MN 55415.

New York Yankees, Yankee Stadium, Bronx, NY 10451.

Oakland Athletics, Oakland Coliseum, Oakland, CA 94621.

Seattle Mariners, P.O. Box 4100, Seattle, WA 98104.

Texas Rangers, P.O. Box 1111, Arlington, TX 76010.

Toronto Blue Jays, The SkyDome, 300 Bremner Blvd., Suite 3200, Toronto, Ontario, Canada M5V 3B3.

National League

350 Park Ave., New York, NY 10022, (212) 339-7700.

Atlanta Braves, P.O. Box 4064, Atlanta, GA 30302.

Chicago Cubs, 1060 W. Addison St., Chicago, IL 60613.

Cincinnati Reds, 100 Riverfront Stadium, Cincinnati, OH 45202.

Colorado Rockies, 1700 Broadway, Suite 2100, Denver, CO 80290.

Florida Marlins, 2267 NW 199th Street, Opa Locka, FL 33056-2600.

Houston Astros, P.O. Box 288, Houston, Texas 77001-0288.

Los Angeles Dodgers, 100 Elsian Park Ave., Los Angeles, CA 90012.

Montreal Expos, P.O. Box 500, Station M, Montreal, Quebec, Canada, HIV 3P2.

New York Mets, Shea Stadium, Flushing, NY 11368.

Philadelphia Phillies, P.O. Box 7575, Philadelphia, PA 19101.

Pittsburgh Pirates, Three Rivers Stadium, Pittsburgh, PA 15212.

San Diego Padres, P.O. Box 2000, San Diego, CA 92120.

San Francisco Giants, Candlestick Park, San Francisco, CA 94124.

St. Louis Cardinals, 250 Stadium Plaza, St. Louis, MO 63102.

Basketball

National Basketball Association, Olympic Tower, 645 Fifth Ave., New York. NY 10022, (212) 826-7000.

Atlanta Hawks, One CNN Center, Suite 405, Atlanta, GA 30303.

Boston Celtics, 151 Merrimac St., Boston, MA 02114.

Charlotte Hornets, Hive Drive, Charlotte, NC 28217.

Chicago Bulls, United Center, 1901 W. Madison St., Chicago, IL 60612.

Cleveland Cavaliers, P.O. Box 5000, Richfield, OH 44286-5000.

Dallas Mavericks, Reunion Arena, 777 Sports St., Dallas, TX 75207.

Denver Nuggets, 1635 Clay Street, Denver, CO 80204.

Detroit Pistons, Palace of Auburn Hills, Two Championship Drive, Auburn Hills, MI 48057.

Golden State Warriors, Oakland Coliseum Arena, Nimitz Freeway & Hegenberger Road, Oakland, CA 94621.

Houston Rockets, P.O. Box 272349, Houston, TX 77277.

Indiana Pacers, 300 E. Market St. Indianapolis, IN 46204.

Los Angeles Clippers, Los Angeles Sports Arena, 3939 S. Figueroa, Los Angeles, CA 90037.

Los Angeles Lakers, P.O. Box 10, Inglewood, CA 90306.

Miami Heat, Miami Arena, Miami, FL 33136-4102.

Milwaukee Bucks, 1001 North Fourth St., Milwaukee, WI 53203-1312.

Minnesota Timberwolves, 600 First Ave. North, Minneapolis, MN 55403.

New Jersey Nets, Brendan Byrne Arena, East Rutherford, NJ 07073.

New York Knicks, Two Pennsylvania Plaza, New York, NY 10001.

Orlando Magic, P.O. Box 76, Orlando, FL 32802.

Philadelphia 76ers, Veterans Stadium, P.O. Box 25040, Philadelphia, PA 19147.

Phoenix Suns. P.O. Box 1369, Phoenix, AZ 85001.

Portland Trailblazers, 700 NE Multnomah St., Suite 600, Portland, OR 97232.

Sacramento Kings, One Sports Parkway, Sacramento, CA 95834.

San Antonio Spurs, 600 E. Market, Suite 102, San Antonio, TX 78205.

Seattle Supersonics, Box C-9000911, Seattle, WA 98109-9711.

Toronto Raptors, 20 Bay St., Suite 1702, Toronto, Ontario, Canada M5J2N8.

Utah Jazz, 5 Triad Center, 5th Floor, Salt Lake City, UT 84108.

Vancouver Grizzlies, General Motors Place, 802 Griffiths Way, Vancouver, B.C. Canada V6B6G1.

Washington Bullets, U.S. Air Arena, One Harry Truman Drive, Landover, MD 20785.

Football

National Football League, 410 Park Ave., New York, NY 10022, (212) 758-1500.

American Conference

Buffalo Bills, One Bills Drive, Orchard Park, NY 14127.

Cincinnati Bengals, 200 Riverfront Stadium, Cincinnati, OH 45202.

Cleveland Browns, Cleveland Stadium, Cleveland, OH 44114.

Denver Broncos, 13655 E. Dove Valley Parkway, Englewood, CO 80112.

Houston Oilers, 6910 Fannin St., Houston, TX 77030.

Indianapolis Colts, 70001 W. 56th St., Indianapolis, IN 46224-0100.

Jacksonville Jaguars, 1 Stadium Place, Jacksonville, FL 32202

Kansas City Chiefs, One Arrowhead Drive, Kansas City, MO 64129.

Miami Dolphins, Joe Robbie Stadium, 2269 NW 199th St., Miami, FL 33056.

New England Patriots, Foxboro Stadium, Route 1, Foxboro, MA 02035.

New York Jets, 1000 Fulton Ave., Hempstead, NY 11550.

Oakland Raiders, Oakland-Alameda County Coliseum, Oakland, CA 94621

Pittsburgh Steelers, Three Rivers Stadium, 300 Stadium Circle, Pittsburgh, PA 15212.

San Diego Chargers. Jack Murphy Stadium, 9449 Friars Road, San Diego, CA 92108.

Seattle Seahawks, 11220 N.E. 53rd St., Kirkland, WA 98033.

National Conference

Atlanta Falcons, Suwanee Road at I-85, Suwanee, GA 30174.

Carolina Panthers, 227 W. Trade St., Suite #1600, Charlotte, NC 28202

Chicago Bears, Halas Hall, 250 N. Washington Road, Lake Forest, IL 60045.

Dallas Cowboys, Cowboys Center, 1 Cowboys Parkway, Irving, TX 75063-4727.

Detroit Lions, 1200 Featherstone Road, Pontiac, MI 48057.

Green Bay Packers, 1265 Lombardi Ave., Green Bay, WI 54304.

Minnesota Vikings, 9520 Viking Drive, Eden Prairie, MN 55344.

New Orleans Saints, 1500 Poydras St., New Orleans, LA 70003.

New York Giants, Giants Stadium, E. Rutherford, NJ 07073.

Philadelphia Eagles, Broad St. & Pattison Ave., Philadelphia, PA 19148.

Phoenix Cardinals, 8701 S. Hardy, Tempe, AZ 85285.

San Francisco 49ers, 4949 Centennial Blvd., Santa Clara, CA 95054-1229.

St. Louis Rams, 100 N. Broadway, St. Louis, MO 63102.

Tampa Bay Buccaneers, One Buccaneer Pl., Tampa, FL 33507.

Washington Redskins, P.O. Box 17247, Dulles International Airport, Washington, DC 20041.

Hockey

National Hockey League, 75 International Blvd., Suite 300, Rexdale, Ontario, Canada M9W 6L9, (416) 798-0809.

Boston Bruins, Fleet Center, Boston, MA 02114.

Buffalo Sabres, Memorial Auditorium, Buffalo, N.Y. 14202.

Calgary Flames, Saddledome, P.O. Box 1540, Station "M", Calgary, Alberta, Canada T2P 3B9.

Chicago Blackhawks, United Center, 1901 W. Madison St., Chicago, IL 60612.

Colorado Avalanche, McNichols Sports Arena, 1635 Clay St., Denver, CO 80204.

Dallas Stars, 901 Main St., Suite 2301, Dallas, TX 75202

Detroit Red Wings, Joe Louis Sports Arena, 600 Civic Center Drive, Detroit, MI 48226.

Edmonton Oilers, Northlands Coliseum, Edmonton, Alberta, Canada, T5B 4M9.

Florida Panthers, 100 N. 3rd Ave., 10th Floor, Ft. Lauderdale, FL 33301

Hartford Whalers, 274 Trumbell Dr., Hartford, CT 06013.

Los Angeles Kings, P.O. Box 17013, Inglewood, CA 90308.

Mighty Ducks of Anaheim, c/o Disney Sports Ent. Inc., 1313 S. Harbor Blvd., Anaheim, CA 92803

Montreal Canadiens, Montreal Forum, 2313 St. Catherine St. West, Montreal, Quebec, Canada H3H 1N2.

New Jersey Devils, Byrne Meadowlands Arena, P.O. Box 504, East Rutherford, NJ 07073.

New York Islanders, Nassau Veterans Memorial Coliseum, Uniondale, NY 11533.

New York Rangers, Madison Square Gardens, 4 Pennsylvania Plaza, New York, NY 10001.

Ottawa Senators, 301 Moodie Drive, Suite 411, Neapean, Ontario, K2H 9C4.

Philadelphia Flyers, The Spectrum, Pattison Place, Philadelphia, PA 19148.

Pittsburgh Penguins, Civic Arena, Pittsburgh, PA 15219.

San Jose Sharks, 10 Alamaden Blvd., Suite 600, San Jose, CA 95113-2233.

St. Louis Blues, St. Louis Arena, 5700 Oakland Ave., St. Louis, MO 63110.

Tampa Bay Lightning, Mack Center, 501 East Kennedy Blvd., Tampa, FL 33602.

Toronto Maple Leafs, Maple Leaf Gardens, 60 Carlton St., Toronto, Ontario, Canada M5B 1L1.

Vancouver Canucks, Pacific Coliseum, 100 North Renfew Street, Vancouver, B.C., Canada V5K 3N7.

Washington Capitals, U.S. Air Arena, Landover, MD 20785.

Winnipeg Jets, Winnipeg Arena, 15-1430 Maroons Road, Winnipeg, Manitoba, Canada R3G 0L5.

College Sports Directory

F = football coach

B = basketball coach

Atlantic Coast Conference

Clemson University
  Clemson, SC 29633
  F: Tommy West
  B: Rick Barnes

Duke University
  Durham, NC 27708
  F: Fred Goldsmith
  B: Mike Krzyzewski

Florida State University
  P.O. Box 2195
  Tallahassee, FL 32316
  F: Bobby Bowden
  B: Pat Kennedy

Georgia Tech
  150 Bobby Dodd Way
  Atlanta, GA 30332
  F: George O'Leary
  B: Bobby Cremins

University of Maryland
  P.O. Box 295
  College Park, MD 20741
  F: vacant
  B: Gary Williams

North Carolina State University
  P.O. Box 8501
  Raleigh, NC 27514
  F: Mike O'Cain
  B: Herb Sendek

University of North Carolina
  P.O. Box 2126
  Chapel Hill, NC 27514
  F: Mack Brown
  B: Dean Smith

University of Virginia
  P.O. Box 3785
  Charlottesville, VA 22903
  F: George Welsh
  B: Jeff Jones

Wake Forest University
  P.O. Box 7426
  Winston-Salem, NC 27109
  F: Jim Caldwell
  B: Dave Odom

Big East Conference

Boston College
  Chestnut Hill, MA 02167
  F: vacant
  B: Jim O'Brien

University of Connecticut
  2095 Hillside Rd.
  Storrs, CT 06269
  F: Skip Holtz
  B: Jim Calhoun

Georgetown University
  McDonough Arena, Box 571124
  Washington, DC 20057
  F: Robert Benson
  B: John Thompson

University of Miami
  One Hurricane Drive
  Coral Gables, FL 33146
  F: Butch Davis
  B: Leonard Hamilton

University of Notre Dame
Notre Dame, IN 46556
F: Bob Davie
B: John MacLeod

University of Pittsburgh
Dept. of Athletics, P.O. Box 7436
Pittsburgh, PA 15213
F: Johnny Majors
B: Ralph Willard

Providence College
River Ave.
Providence, RI 02918
F: N/A
B: Pete Gillen

Rutgers University
P.O. Box 1149
Piscataway, NJ 08855
F: Doug Graber
B: Bob Wenzel

St. John's University
8000 Utopia Parkway
Jamaica, NY 11439
F: Bob Ricca
B: Fran Fraschilla

Seton Hall University
400 S. Orange Ave.
S. Orange, NJ 07079
F: N/A
B: George Blaney

Syracuse University
Manley Field House
Syracuse, NY 13244
F: Paul Pasqualoni
B: Jim Boeheim

Temple University
McGonigie Hall
Philadelphia, PA 19122
F: Ron Dickerson
B: John Chaney

Villanova University
800 Lancaster Ave.
Villanova, PA 19085
F: Andy Tailey
B: Steve Lappas

Virginia Tech
Jamerson Athletic Center
Blacksburg, VA 24061
F: Frank Beamer
B: Bill Foster

West Virginia University
P.O. Box 0877
Morgantown, WV 26507
F: Don Nehlen
B: Gale Catlett

Big Ten Conference

University of Illinois
1817 S. Neil Street, Suite 201
Champaign, IL 61820
F: Lou Tepper
B: Lon Kruger

Indiana University
17th St. and Fee Lane/Assembly Hall
Bloomington, IN 47405
F: Cam Cameron
B: Bob Knight

University of Iowa
205 Carver-Hawkeye Arena
Iowa City, IA 52242
F: Hayden Fry
B: Tom Davis

Michigan State University
East Lansing, MI 48824
F: Nick Saban
B: Tom Izzo

University of Michigan
1000 S. State St.
Ann Arbor, MI 48109
F: Lloyd Carr
B: Steve Fisher

University of Minnesota
516 15th Ave. SE
Minneapolis, MN 55455
F: Jim Wacker
B: Clem Haskins

Northwestern University
    1501 Central St.
    Evanston, IL 60208
    F: Gary Barnett
    B: Ricky Byrdsong

Ohio State University
    410 Woody Hayes Dr., Room 124
    Columbus, OH 43210
    F: John Cooper
    B: Randy Ayers

Penn State University
    Recreation Building
    University Park, PA 16802
    F: Joe Paterno
    B: Jerry Dunn

Purdue University
    Mackey Arena, Room 15
    West Lafayette, IN 47907
    F: Jim Colleto
    B: Gene Keady

University of Wisconsin
    1440 Monroe St.
    Madison, WI 53711
    F: Barry Alvarez
    B: Dick Bennett

Big Twelve Conference

Baylor University
    150 Bear Run
    Waco, TX 76711
    F: Chuck Reedy
    B: Darrel Johnson

University of Colorado
    Campus Box 357
    Boulder, CO 80309
    F: Rick Neuheisel
    B: Ricardo Patten

Iowa State University
    1802 S. Fourth
    Olsen Annex
    Ames, IA 50011
    F: Dan McCarney
    B: Tim Floyd

Kansas State University
    Manhattan, KS 66502
    F: Bill Snyder
    B: Tom Asbury

University of Kansas
    Allen Field House, Room 104
    Lawrence, KS 66045
    F: Glen Mason
    B: Roy Williams

University of Missouri
    P.O. Box 677
    Columbia, MO 65205
    F: Larry Smith
    B: Norm Stewart

University of Nebraska
    116 S. Stadium
    Lincoln, NE 68588
    F: Tom Osborne
    B: Danny Nee

Oklahoma State University
    202 Gallagher-Iba Arena
    Stillwater, OK 74078
    F: Bob Simmons
    B: Eddie Sutton

University of Oklahoma
    180 W. Brooks, Room 235
    Norman, OK 73019
    F: John Blake
    B: Kelvin Sampson

Texas A&M University
    John Koldus Bldg.
    College Station, TX 77843
    F: R.C. Slocum
    B: Tony Barone

Texas Tech University
    P.O. Box 43021
    Lubbock, TX 79409
    F: Spike Dykes
    B: James Dickey

University of Texas
    P.O. Box 7399
    Austin, TX 78713
    F: John Mackovic
    B: Tom Penders

Big West Conference*

California State University-Fullerton
800 N. State College Blvd.
P.O. Box 34080
Fullerton, CA 92634
F: N/A
B: Bob Hawking

Fresno State University
5305 N. Campus Dr., Room 153
Fresno, CA 92634
F: Jim Sweeney
B: Jerry Tarkanian

Long Beach State University
1250 Bellflower Blvd.
Long Beach, CA 90840
F: N/A
B: Wayne Morgan

University of Nevada at Las Vegas
4505 Maryland Parkway
Las Vegas, NV 89154
F: Jeff Horton
B: Bill Bayno

New Mexico State University
Box 30001, Dept. 3145
Las Cruces, NM 88003
F: Jim Hess
B: Neil McCarthy

University of the Pacific
3601 Pacific Ave.
Stockton, CA 95211
F: N/A
B: Bob Thomason

San Jose State University
One Washington Square
San Jose, CA 95192
F: John Ralston
B: Stan Morrison

Utah State University
Logan, UT 84322
F: John L. Smith
B: Larry Eustachy

* Division restructured

Conference USA

University of Alabama-Birmingham
UAB Arena, 617 13th St. S.
Birmingham, AL 35294
F: Watson Brown
B: Murry Bartow

University of Cincinnati
Cincinnati, OH 45221
F: Rick Minter
B: Bob Huggins

DePaul University
1011 West Belden Ave.
Chicago, IL 60614
F: N/A
B: Joey Meyer

University of Houston
3100 Cullen Blvd.
Houston, TX 77004
F: Kim Helton
B: Alvin Brooks

University of Louisville
Louisville, KY 40292
F: Ron Cooper
B: Denny Crum

Marquette University
P.O. Box 1881
Milwaukee, WI 53201
F: N/A
B: Mike Deane

University of Memphis
Memphis, TN 38152
F: Rip Scherer
B: Larry Finch

University of North Carolina - Charlotte
9201 Univ. City Blvd., Belk
Gymnasium
Charlotte, NC 28223
F: N/A
B: Melvin Watkins

Saint Louis University
3672 West Pine Blvd.
St. Louis, MO 63108
F: N/A
B: Charlie Spoonhour

University of South Florida
4202 E. Fowler Ave., PED 214
Tampa, FL 33620
F: N/A
B: Seth Greenberg

University of Southern Mississippi
P.O. Box 5161
Hattiesburg, MS 39406
F: Jeff Bower
B: James Green

Tulane University
James Wilson Jr., Ctr. for Inter.
Athletics
New Orleans, LA
F: Eugene Teevens
B: Perry Clark

Ivy League

Brown University
Hope Street
Providence, RI 02912
F: Mark Whipple
B: Franklin Dobbs

Columbia University
Dodge Physical Fitness Center
New York, NY 10027
F: Ray Tellier
B: Armond Hill

Cornell University
Teagle Hall, Campus Rd.
Ithaca, NY 14853
F: Jim Hofher
B: Scott Thompson

Dartmouth University
6083 Alumni Gym.
Hanover, NH 03755
F: John Lyons
B: David Faucher

Harvard University
60 John F. Kennedy St.
Cambridge, MA 02138
F: Tim Murphy
B: Frank Sullivan

University of Pennsylvania
Weightman Hall N., 235 S. 33rd St.
Philadelphia, PA 19104
F: Al Bagnoli
B: Fran Dunphy

Princeton University
P.O. Box 71, Jadwin Gym
Princeton, NJ 08544
F: Steve Tosches
B: Bill Carmody

Yale University
Box 208216
New Haven, CT 06520
F: vacant
B: Dick Kuchen

Mid-American Conference

Ball State University
2000 University Ave.
Muncie, IN 47306
F: Bill Lynch
B: Ray MCallum

Bowling Green University
Bowling Green, OH 43403
F: Gary Blackney
B: Jim Larranga

Central Michigan University
Rose Center
Mount Pleasant, MI 48859
F: Dick Flynn
B: Leonard Drake

Eastern Michigan University
Bowen Fieldhouse
Ypsilanti, MI 48197
F: Rick Rasnick
B: Ben Braun

Kent State University
Kent, OH 44242
F: Jim Corrigall
B: Gary Watters

Miami University
Millett Hall
Oxford, OH 45056
F: Randy Walker
B: Charlie Coles

Ohio University
P.O. Box 689, Convocation Center
Athens, OH 45701
F: Jim Grobe
B: Larry Hunter

University of Toledo
2801 W. Bancroft St.
Toledo, OH 43606
F: Gary Pinkel
B: Larry Gipson

Western Michigan University
Kalamazoo, MI 49008
F: Al Molde
B: Bob Donewald

Pacific 10 Conference

Arizona State University
Tempe, AZ 85287
F: Bruce Snyder
B: Bill Frieder

University of Arizona
229 McHale Center
Tucson, AZ 85721
F: Jim Tomey
B: Lute Olson

University of California
Berkeley, CA 94720
F: Steve Mariucci
B: vacant

University of California at Los Angeles
P.O. Box 24044
Los Angeles, CA 90024
F: Terry Donahue
B: Jim Harrick

Oregon State University
Gill Coliseum
Corvallis, OR 97331
F: vacant
B: Eddie Payne

University of Oregon
Len Casanova Ath. Ctr.,
2727 L. Harris Pkwy.
Eugene, OR 97401
F: Mike Bellotti
B: Jerry Green

University of Southern California
Los Angeles, CA 90089
F: John Robinson
B: Henry Bibby

Stanford University
Stanford, CA 94305
F: Tyrone Willingham
B: Mike Montgomery

Washington State University
107 Bohler Gym
Pullman, WA 99164
F: Mike Price
B: Kevin Eastman

University of Washington
UW Media Rel., Graves Bldg., Box
354070
Seattle, WA 98195
F: Jim Lambright
B: Bob Bender

Southeastern Conference

University of Alabama
P.O. Box 870323, Paul Bryant Dr.
Tuscaloosa, AL 35487
F: Gene Stallings
B: David Hobbs

University of Arkansas
Boyles Athletic Center
Fayetteville, AR 72701
F: Danny Ford
B: Nolan Richardson

Auburn University
P.O. Box 351
Auburn, AL 36831
F: Terry Bowden
B: Cliff Ellis

University of Florida
P.O. Box 14485
Gainesville, FL 32604
F: Steve Spurrier
B: Billy Donavan

University of Georgia
P.O. Box 1472
Athens, GA 30603
F: Ray Goff
B: Tubby Smith

University of Kentucky
Memorial Coliseum
Lexington, KY 40506
F: Bill Curry
B: Rick Pitino

Louisiana State University
P.O. Box 25095
Baton Rouge, LA 70894
F: Gerry DiNardo
B: Dale Brown

Mississippi State University
P.O. Drawer 5308
Mississippi St., MS 39762
F: Jackie Sherrill
B: Richard Williams

University of Mississippi
P.O. Box 217
University, MS 38677
F: Tommy Tuberville
B: Robert Evans

University of South Carolina
Rex Enright Athletic Ctr., 1300
Rosewood Dr.
Columbia, SC 29208
F: Brad Scott
B: Eddie Fogler

University of Tennessee
P.O. Box 15016
Knoxville, TN 37901
F: Phillip Fulmer
B: Kevin O'Neil

Vanderbilt University
P.O. Box 120158
Nashville, TN 37212
F: Rod Dowhower
B: Jan Van Breda Kolff

Western Athletic Conference*

Air Force
USAF Academy, CO 80840
F: Fisher DeBerry
B: Reggie Minton

Brigham Young University
30 Smith Field House
Provo, UT 84602
F: LaVell Edwards
B: Roger Reid

Colorado State University
Moby Arena
Fort Collins, CO 80523
F: Sonny Lubick
B: Stew Morrill

University of Hawaii
1335 Lower Campus Rd.
Honolulu, HI 96822
F: Bob Wagner
B: Riley Wallace

University of New Mexico
1414 University S.E.
Albuquerque, NM 87131
F: Dennis Franchione
B: Dave Bliss

Rice University
6100 Main, MS548
Houston, TX 77005
F: Ken Hatfield
B: Willis Wilson

San Diego State University
San Diego, CA 92182
F: Ted Tollner
B: Fred Trenkle

Southern Methodist University
SMU Box 216
Dallas, TX 75275
F: vacant
B: Mike Dement

Texas Christian University
P.O. Box 32924
Fort Worth, TX 76129
F: Pat Sullivan
B: Billy Tubbs

* Division restructured

University of Texas at El Paso
201 Baltimore
El Paso, TX 79902
F: Charlie Bailey
B: Don Haskins

University of Tulsa
600 S. College
Tulsa, OK 74104
F: Dave Rader
B: Steve Robinson

University of Utah
Huntsman Center
Salt Lake City, UT 84112
F: Ron McBride
B: Rick Majerus

University of Wyoming
P.O. Box 3414
Laramie, WY 82071
F: Joe Tiller
B: Joby Wright

Soap Opera Directory

Before he ever drove *Miss Daisy*, Morgan Freeman was a soap star. Believe it or not, Freeman played an architect named Roy Bingham on *Another World*. Freeman is just one of the many actors who started in soap and ended up in cinema: below is a list of some others.

Celebrities Who Started on Daytime TV

Christopher Reeve
Jasmine Bleeth
Ricky Paull Goldin
Cynthia Gibb
Jack Wagner

Janine Turner
Lisa Rinna
David Hasselhoff
Lauren Holly
Patrick Muldoon

Harley Jane Kozak
Kathleen Turner
Marcia Cross

How to get in touch with your favorite soap star? Refer to the list below.

Soap Opera Show Addresses

ALL MY CHILDREN
ABC-TV
77 W. 66th St.
New York, NY 10023

ANOTHER WORLD
NBC-TV
30 Rockefeller Plaza
New York, NY 10112

AS THE WORLD TURNS
CBS-TV
51 W. 52nd St.
New York, NY 10019

BOLD & BEAUTIFUL
CBS-TV
7800 Beverly Blvd.
Los Angeles, CA 90036

DAYS OF OUR LIVES
NBC-TV
3000 W. Alameda Ave.
Burbank, CA 91523

GENERAL HOSPITAL
ABC-TV
4151 Prospect Ave.
Hollywood, CA 90027

GUIDING LIGHT
CBS-TV
51 W. 52nd St.
New York, NY 10019

ONE LIFE TO LIVE
ABC-TV
77 W. 66th St.
New York, NY 10023

THE CITY
ABC-TV
77 W. 66th St.
New York, NY 10023

YOUNG & RESTLESS
CBS-TV
7800 Beverly Blvd.
Los Angeles, CA 90036

Because the names of soap opera characters are often more memorable than that of the actor or actress who played them, we have included both in our Soap Opera Directory.

Soap Opera Directory

*= Original Cast

ALL MY CHILDREN

ACTOR	CHARACTER
BURSELL, MIKE *	Martin, Bobby
DAWSON, MARK *	Bryant, Ted
deVEGH, DIANA *	Tyler, Anne
DUMONT, PAUL *	Tyler, Lincoln
FICKET, MARY *	Brent, Ruth
FRANKLIN, HUGH *	Tyler, Dr. Charles
GORNEY, KAREN *	Martin, Tara
HAYNES, HILDA *	Sloan, Lois
HEFLIN, FRANCES *	Kane, Mona
KEITH, LARRY *	Kane, Nick
LUCCI, SUSAN *	Kane, Erica
MacDONNELL, RAY *	Martin, Dr. Joe
PRINZ, ROSEMARY *	Tyler, Amy
STAUFFER, JACK *	Tyler, Chuck
THOMAS, CHRISTINE *	Martin, Kate
WINES, CHRISTOPHER *	Martin, Jeff
ALEXANDER, KEVIN	Chandler, Jr., Adam
BARR, JULIA	English, Brooke
BLAKE, TERESA	Marsh, Gloria
BRUNO, CHRIS	Delaney, Michael
CALLAHAN, JOHN	Grey, Edmund
CANARY, DAVID	Chandler, Adam/ Stewart
CHRISTIAN, WILLIAM	Frye, Derek
COBB, KEITH HAMILTON	Keefer, Noah
COLLINS, PHOEBE	Dillon, Amanda
CONSUELOS, MARK	Santos, Mateo
DAVILA, RAUL	Santos, Hector
EDMONDS, LOUIS	Wallingford, Langley
FITZPATRICK, JAMES A.	Riley, Pierce
GARDNER, CATHERINE	Santos, Rosa
GASKILL, BRIAN	Warner, Bobby
HAWTHORNE, KIMBERLEY	Keefer, Belinda
HERLIE, EILEEN	Fargate, Myrtle
HULTEEN, CHERYL	Winifred
KIBERD, JAMES	Dillon, Trevor
KNIGHT, MICHAEL E.	Martin, Tad
LAFORTUNE, FELICITY	Dillon, Laurel
LARSON, JILL	Cortlandt, Opal
LARUE, EVA	Grey, Mariad
LAWFORD, CHRISTOPHER	Brent, Charlie
MARQUETTE, SEAN	Martin, Jaime

ACTOR	CHARACTER
MATTSON, ROBIN	Green, Janet
McCLAIN, CADY	Martin, Dixie
McDERMOTT, SHANE	Chandler, Scott
MEARA, ANNE	Moody, Peggy
MICHAELS, TOMMY J.	Dillon, Tommy
MITCHELL, JAMES	Cortlandt, Palmer
NADER, MICHAEL	Marek, Dimitri
NELSON, NAN-LYN	Roxburry- Barnes, Vivianne
NEVIN, ROSA	Davidson, Cecily
PENNY, SYDNEY	Santos, Julia
PEPE	Dillon, Harold
RIPA, KELLY	Vaughn, Hayley
ROMAN, LAUREN	Kirk, Laura
SABATINO, MICHAEL	Kinder, Dr. Jonathan
SANTIAGO, SOCORRO	Santos, Isabella
TAYLOR, KELLI	Roxburry-Cannon, Taylor
TEJEIRO, DARLENE	Santos, Anita
THIGPEN, LYNN	Keefer, Grace
TRACHTENBERG, MICHELLE	Montgomery, Lily
WALKER, MARCY	Colby, Liza
WARNER, T.C.	Brent, Kelsey
WARRICK, RUTH	Wallingford, Phoebe
WILLY, WALT	Montgomery, Jackson

ANOTHER WORLD

ALLEN, VERA *	Matthews, Grandma
BEAL, JOHN *	Matthews, Jim
CHAPMAN, LIZA *	Matthews, Janet
COURTNEY, JACQUELINE *	Matthews, Alice
CUNNINGHAM, SARAH *	Matthews, Liz
DWYER, VIRGINIA *	Matthews, Mary
GALLISON, JOE *	Matthews, Bill
PRINCE, WILLIAM *	Baxter, Ken
PRYOR, NICHOLAS *	Baxter, Tom
ROUX, CAROL *	Palmer, Missy
TRENT, JOEY *	Matthews, Russ
TRUSTMAN, SUSAN *	Matthews, Pat
BARBARA, JOE	Carlino, Joe
BARRETT, ALICE	Winthrop, Frankie Frame
BERJER, BARBARA	Connel, Bridget
BOLGER, JOHN	McNamara, Gabe
BROWN, KALE	Hudson, Michael
BUCHANAN, JENSEN	Hudson, Victoria
CARLSON, AMY	Watts, Josie
CHRISTOPHER, ROBIN	Devon, Lorna
CRANE, MATT	Cory, Matthew

ACTOR	CHARACTER
DANO, LINDA	Gallant, Felicia
EPLIN, TOM	McKinnon, Jake
FORSYTH, DAVID	Hudson, John
GIBBS, TIMOTHY	Sinclair, Gary
HOLBROOK, ANNA	Hudson, Sharlene Frame
HURD, MICHELLE	Kramer, Dana
KEATING, CHARLES	Hutchins, Carl
LUCIANO, JUDI EVANS	McKinnon, Paulina Cory
McCLATCHY, KEVIN	Terry, Nick
McCOUCH, GRAYSON	Winthrop, Morgan
NIELSEN, STINA	Evans, Dr. Courtney
PINTER, MARK	Harrison, Grant
SALEM, DAHLIA	Carlino, Sofia
SCHNETZER, STEPHEN	Winthrop, Cass
SERRANO, DIEGO	Rivera, Thomas
STUART, ANNA	Cory, Donna Love
VERNOFF, KAILI	Michaels, Laurie
WYNDHAM, VICTORIA	Cory, Rachel

AS THE WORLD TURNS

ALFORD, BOBBY *	Hughes, Bobby
BURR, ANN *	Lowell, Claire
DAMON, LES *	Lowell, Jr., Jim
DREW, WENDY *	Lowell, Ellen
JOHNSTONE, WILLIAM *	Lowell, James
McLAUGHLIN, DON *	Hughes, Chris
ORTEGA, SANTOS *	Hughes, Grandpa
WARRICK, RUTH *	Hughes, Edith
ALEXANDER, BROOKE	Markham, Samantha
BREWSTER, JORDANA	Graves, Nikki
BRYGGMAN, LARRY	Dixon, John
BYRNE, MARTHA	Grimaldi, Lily
CHRISTIAN, SHAWN	Kasnoff, Mike
DAUER, JOHN	Wheeler, Jeremy
DOLAN, ELLEN	Hughes, Margo
FRAZER, DAN	McCloskey, Dan
FULTON, EILEEN	Mitchell, Lisa
HASTINGS, DON	Hughes, Bob
HAYS, KATHRYN	Hughes, Kim
HENDRICKSON, BEN	Munson, Hal
HOLMES, SCOTT	Hughes, Tom
HUBBARD, ELIZABETH	Walsh, Lucinda
MASTERS, MARIE	McDermott, Susan
MENIGHAN, KELLEY	Stewart, Emily
PERRY, YVONNE	Cabot, Rosanna
PINTER, COLLEEN ZENK	Ryan, Barbara

ACTOR	CHARACTER
RINEHART, JOANNA	Griffin, Jessica
SEGANTI, PAOLO	Grimaldi, Damian
SEIFERT, CHRISTIAN	Hughes, Christopher
TAYLOR, ALLYSON RICE	Stricklyn, Connor
TOVATT, PATRICK	Stricklyn, Cal
WAGNER, HELEN	McCloskey, Nancy
WALTERS, ALEXANDER	Mark
WERT, DOUG	Eldridge, Scott
WEST, MAURA	Tenney, Carly
WIDDOES, KATHLEEN	Snyder, Emma
WIGGIN, TOM	Anderson, Kirk
WILLIAMS, ASHLEY	Andropolous, Danielle

THE BOLD AND THE BEAUTIFUL

BALDWIN, JUDITH *	Logan, Beth
FLANNERY, SUSAN *	Forrester, Stephanie
GENESSE, BRYAN *	Carner, Rocco
JOHNSON, JOANNA *	Spencer, Caroline
KOSLOW, LAUREN *	Lynley, Margo
LANG, KATHERINE KELLY *	Logan, Brooke
LINN, TERI ANN *	Forrester, Kristen
McCOOK, JOHN *	Forrester, Eric
MITCHUM, CARRIE *	Logan, Donna
MOSS, RONN *	Forrester, Ridge
NORCROSS, CLAYTON *	Forrester, Thorne
SHORTRIDGE, STEPHEN *	Reed, Dave
SLOAN, NANCY *	Logan, Katie
STORM, JIM *	Spencer, William
WAYNE, ETHAN *	Logan, Storm
BAKER, SCOTT THOMPSON	Davis, Conner
BREGMAN, TRACEY E.	Fenmore, Lauren
BROWN, KIMBERLIN	Carter, Sheila
BUCHANAN, IAN	Warwick, James
CONLEY, DARLENE	Spectra, Sally
CRAMPTON, BARBARA	Forrester, Maggie
EAKES, ROBIN	Forrester, Macy
FOX, MICHAEL	Feinstein, Saul
GOMEZ, RITA	Maria
HANES, KEN	Guthrie, Mike
HARRISON, SCHAE	Darla
HARTMAN, STEVEN	Forrester, Jr., Eric
JASMER, BRENT	Donovan, Sly
LaRON, KEN	Anderson, Keith
NEAL, DYLAN	Shaw, Dylan
PRICE, LINDSAY	Lai, Michael
SABIHY, KYLE	Garrison, C.J.

ACTOR	CHARACTER
SHRINER, KIN	Carey, Brian
TODD, RUSSELL	Birn, Jerry
TRACHTA, JEFF	Forrester, Thorne
TYLO, HUNTER	Forrester, Taylor
VOORHIES, LARK	Malone, Jasmine
WARD, MAITLAND	Forrester, Jessica

DAYS OF OUR LIVES

COLLA, DICK *	Merritt, Tony
DOUGHERTY, CARLA *	Olson, Julie
DOUGLAS, BURT *	Fisk, Jim
HUSTON, PAT *	Olson, Addie
KNAPP, ROBERT *	Olson, Ben
MARK, FLIP *	Olson, Steve
McKLEAN, DICK *	Merritt, Craig
REID, FRANCES *	Horton, Alice
STEVENSON, ROBERT J.*	Detective
ALFONSO, KRISTIAN	Brady, Hope
ANISTON, JOHN	Kiriakis, Victor
BAUER, JAMIE LYN	Horton, Laura
BOYD, TANYA	Celeste
BROOKS, JASON	Blake, Peter
CAMERON, STEPHANIE	Blake, Jennifer Deveraux
CLARK, CHRISTIE	Brady, Carrie
CLARKE, JOHN	Horton, Mickey
CRITCHLOW, ROARK	Horton, Mike
DATILLO, BRYAN R.	Roberts, Lucas
DAVIDSON, EILEEN	Blake, Kristen
G'VERA, IVAN	Marais, Ivan
HALL, DEIDRE	Evans, Marlena
HOGESTYN, DRAKE	Black, John
JONES, RENEE	Carver, Lexie
LEWIS, THYME	Carver, Jonah
MASCOLO, JOSEPH	DiMera, Stefano
McCAY, PEGGY	Brady, Caroline
MCDANIEL, KRISTI	Sarah
O'DONNELL, COLIN	Brady, Shawn- Douglas
PARKER, FRANK	Brady, Shawn
PARRISH, MIRIAM	Caldwell, Jamie
PECK, AUSTIN	Reed, Austin
RECKELL, PETER	Brady, Bo
REYNOLDS, JAMES	Carver, Abe
ROGERS, SUZANNE	Horton, Maggie
SOREL, LOUISE	Alamain, Vivian
SWEENEY, ALISON	Brady, Sami
TOWNSEND, TAMMY	Reardon, Wendy
VALLEY, MARK	Deveraux, Jack

ACTOR	CHARACTER

GENERAL HOSPITAL

BERNADINO, JOHN *	Hardy, Dr. Steve
BROWN, TOM *	Weeks, Al
CLARKE, ROBERT *	Lansing, Roy
CRAIG, CAROLYN *	Allyson, Cynthia
CURTIS, CRAIG *	Weeks, Eddie
HAMILTON, NEIL *	Mercer, Phillip
HAYES, ALLISON *	Longworth, Priscilla
KINGSTON, LENORE *	Weeks, Mrs.
MANZA, RALPH *	Costello, Mike
McLAUGHLIN, EMILY *	Brewer, Jessie
POWERS, HUNT *	Martin, Dr. Ken
STEVENS, K.T. *	Mercer, Peggy
THINNES, ROY *	Brewer, Dr. Phil
AMES, RACHEL	Hardy, Audrey
ASHENAFI, SENAIT	Ward, Keesha
ASHFORD, MATTHEW	Hardy, Tom
BELL, FELECIA	Hardy, Simone
BENARD, MAURICE	Corinthos, Sonny
BROWN, SUSAN	Baldwin, Gail
BURTON, STEVE	Quartermaine, Jason
CHARLESON, LESLIE	Quartermaine, Monica
CONNOLLY, NORMA	Anderson, Ruby
DAMON, STUART	Quartermaine, Alan
ELLINGTON, ZACHARY	Hardy, Jr., Tom
EVANS, MARY BETH	Bell, Katherine
FRANCIS, GENIE	Spencer, Laura
GEARY, ANTHONY	Spencer, Luke
HALE, RON	Corbin, Mike
HANSEN, PETER	Baldwin, Lee
HERRING, LYNN	Coe, Lucy
INGLE, JOHN	Quartermaine, Edward
JACKSON, JONATHAN	Spencer, Lucky
KEPLER, SHELL	Vining, Amy
KURTH, WALLACE	Ashton, Ned
LEE, ANNA	Quatermaine, Lila
LINDSTROM, JON	Collins, Kevin
MARCIL, VANESSA	Barrett, Brenda
MARTIN, RICKY	Morez, Miguel
MAULE, BRAD	Jones, Tony
McCULLOUGH, KIMBERLY	Scorpio, Robin
MELGAR, LILLY	Rivera, Lily
PHILLIPS, JOSEPH C.	Ward, Justus
RICHARDS, ROBYN	Jones, Maxie
SACANE, JAY	Jones, Lucas
SOFER, RENA	Ashton, Lois Cerullo

ACTOR	CHARACTER
TAMBLYN, AMBER	Bowen, Emily
WAGNER, KRISTINA	Jones, Felicia
YORK, JOHN J.	Scorpio, Mac
ZEMAN, JACKLYN	Jones, Bobbie

GUIDING LIGHT

ALLISON, JONE *	Banning, Meta
BAUER, CHARITA *	Bauer, Bert
DOUGLAS, SUSAN *	Grant, Kathy
GOETZ, THEO *	Bauer, Papa
LIPTON, JAMES *	Grant, Dr. Richard
NELSON, HERB *	Roberts, Joe
SUDROW, LYLE *	Bauer, Bill
YOURMAN, ALICE *	Grant, Laura
BEATTY, FRANK	Crane, Marian
BEATTY, FRANK	Lawrence, Brent
BROWN, KIMBERLY J.	Lewis, Marah
BROWN, LISA	Chamberlain, Nola Reardon
BUDIG, REBECCA	Bauer, Michelle
BUFFINTON, BRYAM	Lewis, Bill
BURKE, GREGORY	Reade, Ben
COOPER, BRETT	Lewis, Shayne
COX, AMY	Blume, Abagail
CROMELIN, CAREY	Hite, Wanda
CURRY, RUSSELL	Grant, David
DEAS, JUSTIN	Cooper, Buzz
DICOPOULOS, FRANK	Cooper, Frank
DUSAY, MARJ	Spaulding, Alexandra
EWING, GEOFFREY	Williams, Griffin
FONTENO, DAVID WOLOS-	Grant, Charles
GARRETT, MAUREEN	Lindsey, Holly
HAMMER, CHARLES JAY	Reade, Fletcher
HEARST, RICK	Spaulding, Alan-Michael
HILLARD, MARSHALL	Jessup, Hart
HYADEN, MELISSA	Reardon, Bridget
IRIZARRY, VINCENT	Spaulding, Nick McHenry
KEIFER, ELIZABETH	Marler, C. Blake Thorpe
KINKEAD, MAEVE	Chamberlain, Vanessa
MAMBO, KEVIN	Williams, Marcus
MARSHALL, AMELIA	Grant, Gilly
McKINNEY, KURT	Reardon, Matt
MONIZ, WENDY	Chamberlain, Dinah
NEWMAN, ROBERT	Lewis, Josh
PALEY, PETRONIA	Grant, Vivian
PETERSON, MARY	Cleary, Nell
POSER, TOBY	Spaulding, Amanda

ACTOR	CHARACTER
RAINES, RON	Spaulding, Alan
ROGERS, GIL	Shaye, Hawk
ROSZELL, JENNIFER	Cooper, Eleni
SATRA, SONIA	Cooper, Lucy
SIMON, PETER	Bauer, Ed
SLOAN, TINA	Raines, Lillian
TROOBNICK, EUGENE	Kouperakis, Stavros
VERDORN, Jerry	Marler, Ross
WATROS, CYNTHIA	Lewis, Annie
WILLIAMS, VINCE	Speakes, Hampton
ZASLOW, MICHAEL	Thorpe, Roger
ZIMMER, KIM	Lewis, Reva Shayne
ZUCKER, ALYSIA	Cooper, Marina

LOVING/THE CITY

ADDY, WESLEY *	Alden, Cabot
ASHE, JENNIFER *	Slater, Lily
BLAIR, PAMELA *	Bristow, Rita Mae
CRANSTON, BRYAN *	Donovan, Douglas
CUNNINGHAM, JOHN *	Slater, Garth
DABNEY, AUGUSTA *	Alden, Isabelle
DAVIES, PETER *	Vochek, Father Jim
EUBANKS, SHANNON *	Forbes, Ann Alden
KALEMBER, PATRICIA *	Vocheck, Merrill
KEANE, TERI *	Donovan, Rose
KIBERD, JAMES *	Donovan, Mike
LIGON, TOM *	Bristow, Billy
MARCANTEL, CHRIS *	Alden, Curtis
McINTYRE, MARILYN *	Donovan, Noreen
SHEARIN, JOHN *	Forbes, Roger
STEPHEN, PERRY *	Forbes, Jack
TAYLOR, LAUREN-MARIE *	Donovan, Stacey
WALTERS, SUSAN *	Forbes, Lorna
WILLIAMS, ANN *	Slater, June
ALLEN, JONI	Zoey
ANTHONY, PHILIP	Castro, Bernardo
BALLARD, ALIMI	Hubbard, Frankie
BORN, ROSCOE	Rivers, Nick
BROWN, PHILLIP	Huston, Buck
CHANG, CARLOTTA	C., Azure
DYE, MELISSA	Molly
FAIRCHILD, MORGAN	Chase, Lauren
HICKLAND, CATHERINE	Wilder, Tess
KING, T.W.	Roberts, Danny
LoCICERO, LISA	Browne, Jocelyn
MANTOOTH, RANDOLPH	Masters, Alex

ACTOR	CHARACTER
MORGAN, DEBBIE	Hubbard, Angie
PAGE, CORRIE	Wilkins, Richard
PALERMO, GEORGE	Solito, Tony
WILLIAMS, DARNELL	Foster, Jacob
WRIGHT, LAURA SISK	Bowman, Ally

ONE LIFE TO LIVE

BELAK, DORIS *	Wolek, Anna
DeANDA, PETER *	Trainor, Dr. Price
FLACKS, NIKI *	Martin, Karen
GALLISON, JOE *	Edwards, Tom
GRAVES, ERNEST *	Lord, Victor
HOLLY, ELLEN *	Lord, Carla
MILLER, ALLAN *	Siegel, Dave
PATTERSON, LEE *	Riley, Joe
VAN DEVERE, TRISH *	Lord, Meredith
BONARRIGO, LAURA	Carpenter, Cassie
CAREY, PHILLIP	Buchanan, Asa
CHAPPELL, CRYSTAL	Carpenter, Mary
DE PAIVA, JAMES	Holden, Max
DOUGLAS, CHRISTOPHER	Moody, Dylan
ELLIOTT, PATRICIA	Buchanan, Renee
FILLION,NATHAN	Buchanan, Joey
HASKELL, SUSAN	Saybrooke, Marty
KAYE, THORSTEN	Thornhart, Patrick
KRIMMER, WORTHAM	Carpenter, Andrew
LAVAN, RENE	Perez, Javier
LOPRIENO, JOHN	Roberts, Cord
MADERA, YORLIN	Vega, Cristian
MAUCERI, PATRICIA	Vega, Carlotta
MORROW, MARI	Gannon, Rachel
NOYES, TYLER	Roberts, C.J.
PANETTIERE, HAYDEN	Roberts, Sarah
PRATT, WENDEE	Harrison, Andy
PURDEE, NATHAN	Gannon, Hank
REYES, KAMAR DE LOS	Vega, Antonio
RITCHIE, CLINT	Buchanan, Clint
SLEZAK, ERIKA	Carpenter, Victoria Buchanan
SMITH, HILLARY B.	Buchanan, Nora Gannon
STICKNEY, TIMOTHY D.	Gannon, R.J.
STORM, MICHAEL	Wolek, Larry
STRASSER, ROBIN	Lord, Dorian
TESREAU, KRISTA	Roberts, Tina
TOGNONI, GINA	Cramer, Kelly
TORPEY, ERIN	Buchanan, Jessica
WALKER, TONJA	Buchanan, Alex Olanov

ACTOR	CHARACTER
WATKINS, TUC	Vickers, David
WESLEY, KASSIE	Manning, Blair
WILLIAMS, STEPHANIE E.	Gannon, Sheila
WOODS, ROBERT S.	Buchanan, Bo

THE YOUNG AND THE RESTLESS

CLARY, ROBERT *	Roulland, Pierre
COLBERT, ROBERT *	Brooks, Stuart
CRAWFORD, LEE *	McGuire, Sally
DICKSON, BRENDA *	Foster, Jill
ESPY, WILLIAM GRAY *	Foster, Snapper
GREEN, DOROTHY *	Brooks, Jennifer
HALLICK, TOM *	Eliot, Brad
HOUGHTON, JAMES *	Foster, Greg
LYNDE, JANICE *	Brooks, Leslie
McCARTHY, JULIANNA *	Foster, Liz
PETERS, PAMELA *	Brooks, Peggy
STEWART, TRISH *	Brooks, Chris
ACUNA, WANDA	Monroe, Keesha
ARNING, TINA	Green, Sasha
BARTON, DIANA	Mason, Mari Jo
BELL, LAURALEE	Blair, Christine
BERGMAN, PETER	Abbott, Jack
BIRN, LAURA BRYAN	Bassett, Lynne
BRAEDEN, ERIC	Newman, Victor
CASE, SHARON	Newman, Sharon
CAST, TRICIA	McNeil, Nina
CASTELLANOS, JOHN	Silva, John
CHAMPION, CHRISTINE	Paulsen, Jeri
CIBRIAN, EDDIE	Clark, Matt
COOPER, JEANNE	Sterling, Katherine Chancellor
DAMIAN, MICHAEL	Romalotti, Danny
DAVIDSON, DOUG	Williams, Paul
DIAMONT, DON	Carlton, Brad
DOUGLAS, JERRY	Abbott, John
EVANS, MICHAEL	Austin, Douglas
FARRELL, SHARON	Webster, Flo
FOX, VIVICA A.	Stephanie
HENSEL, KAREN	Collins, Doris
LINDER, KATE	Valentine, Esther
LINZ, ALEX	Chancellor III, Phillip
MAITLAND, BETH	Connelly, Traci
MICHAELS, FREEMAN	Belson, Drake
MOON, PHILIP	Volien, Keemo
MOORE, SHEMAR	Winters, Malcolm
MORRIS, JULIANNE	Wilson, Amy

ACTOR	CHARACTER
MORROW, JOSHUA	Newman, Nick
PECK, J. EDDIE	Howard, Cole
PENA, ANTHONY	Rodriguez, Miguel
REES, MARIANNE	Volien, Mai
REEVES, SCOTT	McNeil, Ryan
ROWELL, VICTORIA	Winters, Drucilla
SCOTT, MELODY THOMAS	Abbott, Nikki
ST. JOHN, KRISTOFF	Winters, Neil
STAFFORD, MICHELLE	Romalotti, Phyllis
SUNG, ELIZABETH	Abbott, Luan
TEMPLETON, CHRISTOPHER	Evans, Carol Robbins-
TOM, HEATHER	Howard, Victoria
WALTON, JESS	Abbott, Jill
WEAVER, PATTY	Raddison, Gina Roma
WHITE, ADAM LAZARRE	Hastings, Nathan
WILLIAMS, TONYA LEE	Hastings, Olivia
WINTERSOLE, WILLIAM	Sherman, Mitchell
WRANGLER, GREG	Connelley, Steve

Celebrity Hotspots in United States and Europe

A common question from most celebrity autograph seekers is, "Where do I go if I want to obtain an in-person celebrity signature?" Luckily, human beings are creatures of habit. Without guaranteeing anything I offer the following list of "hotspot" restaurants and clubs, which are either owned by stars or are known celebrity spots for in-person autographs. Remember, what's "hot" today is often "cold" tomorrow.

I apologize in advance if your favorite celebrity spot is not included. You might want to begin your search at an obvious place, such as any of the Hard Rock Cafes or Planet Hollywoods. From these franchises you can move on to the places listed below, where you're more likely to rub elbows with a celebrity or two.

Please also remember that restaurants & clubs often change names or owners, and even go out of business.

"21" Club
21 W. 52 nd St.
New York, NY 10019
Adolf Wagner Apfelweinwirtschaft
Schweizer Str. 71
D-60594 Frankfurt/Main
Germany

Alice's
1043 Westwood Blvd.
Los Angeles, CA 90024

Amsterdamn Billiard Club
344 Amsterdam Ave.
New York, NY 10024

Andre's of Beverly Hills
8635 Wilshire Blvd.
Beverly Hills, CA 90211

Anthony's
22235 Pacific Coast Highway
Malibu, CA 90265
Owners: Charlie Sheen, Emilio Estevez

Arena
6655 Wilshire Blvd.
Beverly Hills, CA 90038

Art Morton's of Chicago
The Steakhouse
435 S. La Cienega Blvd.
Los Angeles, CA 90035

Art's Delicatessen & Restaurant
12224 Ventura Blvd.
Studio City, CA 91604

Atlas
Innere Wiener Str. 2
D-81667 Munchen
Germany
Owner: Iris Berban

Atlas Bar & Grill
3760 Wilshire Blvd.
Los Angeles, CA 90010

Au Bar
41 E. 58th St.
New York, NY 10022

Babylon
616 N. Robertson Blvd.
W. Hollywood, CA 90069
Good place to catch younger stars

Bar "Les Bains"
7 rue Bourg l'Abbe
F-75003 Paris, France
A must-stop while in the city

Bar One
9229 Sunset Blvd.
Los Angeles, CA 90069
Bring your autograph supplies

Barney's Beanery
8447 Santa Monica
Los Angeles, CA 90069
Worth a stop

Bistro
246 N. Canon Drive
Beverly Hills, CA 90210

Bistro Garden
176 N. Canon Drive
Beverly Hills, CA 90210

Blue Shell
Luxemburger Str. 22
D-50674 Koln
Germany

Bobo's Restaurant
1700 N. Indian Ave.
Palm Springs, CA 92262
Owner: Sonny Bono

Border Grill
1445 4th Street
Santa Monica, CA 90401

Bowlmor Lanes
110 University Place
New York, NY 10003

Brasserie Bunuel
Am Markplatz 9
D-82031 Grunwald
Germany
Owner: Peter Fricke

Cafe Carlyle
35 E. 76th St.
New York, NY 10021

Cafe des Artists
1 W. 67th St.
New York, NY 10023

Cafe Luxembourg
200 W. 70th St.
New York, NY 10023

Cafe Swingers
8020 Beverly Blvd.
Los Angeles, CA 90048
Good place to catch younger stars

Cafe Tabac
232 E. 9th St.
New York, NY 10003
Worth a quick stop

Cafe Wiener Platz
Innere Wiener Str. 48
D-81667 Munchen
Germany
Owner: Iris Berban

California Pizza Kitchen
121 N. La Cienega Blvd.
Los Angeles, CA 90048
Another must-stop: keep your eyes
open

Campanile
624 S. La Brea Ave.
Los Angeles, CA 90036

Canter's Fairfax
419 N. Fairfax Ave.
Los Angeles, CA 90036

Carnegie Deli
854 7th Ave.
New York, NY 10019
From Woody Allen to Bill Cosby

Carroll O'Connor's
369 N. Bedford Dr.
Beverly Hills, CA 90210
Good for older lesser-known
celebrities

Chart House
18412 W. Pacific Coast Highway
Malibu, CA 90265

Chaya Brasserie
8741 Alden Drive
Los Angeles, CA 90048
Good for older celebrities

Chianti
7383 Melrose Ave.
Los Angeles, CA 90069

China Club
2130 Broadway
New York, NY 10023
A good stop for both film & rock stars

Chinois
2709 Main Street
Santa Monica, CA 90405

Club USA
218 W. 47 th St.
New York, NY 10036
Good mix of celebrities

Columbia Bar & Grill
1448 Gower St.
Hollywood, CA 90028
Worth stopping by

Columbus
201 Columbus Ave.
New York, NY 10023
Owner: Mikhail Baryshnikov
A great stop

Copacabana
617 W. 57th St.
New York, NY 10019

Da Claudio
Zum Jungen Str. 10
D-60320 Frankfurt/Main
Germany

Dan Tana's
9071 Santa Monica Blvd.
Los Angeles, CA 900069

Demon Dogs
944 Fullerton
Chicago, IL 60614

Disco "Bash"
655 Washington Ave.
Miami Beach, FL 33139
Owner: Sean Penn

Ditka's Restaurant
223 W. Ontario
Chicago, IL 60610

Dive
Shopping Center Century City
10250 Santa Monica Blvd. #194
Los Angeles, CA 90067
Spielberg's big splash

Dolly Parton's Dockside Plantation
377 Keahole St.
Honolulu, HI 96825
Owner: Dolly Parton

Eat
1064 Madison Ave.
New York, NY 10028

Eclipse
8800 Melrose Ave.
W. Hollywood, CA 90069
Owner: Whoopi Goldberg

Ed Debevic's
134 N. La Cienega Blvd.
Beverly Hills, CA 90211

El Coyote
7312 Beverly Blvd.
Los Angeles, CA 90036
Great to find newer rock band
members

Elaine's
1703 2nd Ave.
New York, NY 10128
Well known for stars

Elio's
1621 2nd Ave.
New York, NY 10028
A must-stop with a good reputation

Fabs
80755 Highway 111
Indio, CA 92201
Owner: William Devane

Farmer
1416 4th Street
Santa Monica, CA 90401

Figaro
9010 Melrose Ave.
Los Angeles, CA 90069

Galdstone's 4 Fish
17300 Pacific Coast Highway
Malibu, CA 90265

Georgia
7250 Melrose Ave.
Los Angeles, CA 90046
Stop, look and listen!

Glitter Bar
39 Coventry St.
London W1 England
Owner: Gary Glitter

Good Fellas
Theresienstr. 54
D-80333 Munchen
Germany
Owner: Charly Mohammad Huber

Granita
23725 Malibu Rd.
Malibu, CA 90265
Owner: Charles Bronson

Greenblatt's
8017 Sunset Blvd.
Los Angeles, CA 90046

Hamburger Hamlet
122 S. Beverly Dr.
Beverly Hills, CA 90210
Not as good as Hollywood Hamlet

Hamburger Hamlet
6914 Hollywood Blvd.
Hollywood, CA 90028
Great actress access here

Hanin's Pinte
Walter-Kolb-Str.
D-60594 Frankfurt/Main
Germany

Harry's Bar & American Grill
2020 Avenue of the Stars
Los Angeles, CA 90067

Hogs Breath Inn
Carlos Street
Carmel, CA 90265
Owner: Clint Eastwood

House of Blues
8430 Sunset Blvd.
Los Angeles, CA 90069
Owner: Dan Aykroyd, Aerosmith

Ivy
113 N. Robertson Blvd.
W. Hollywood, CA 90048
I.C.M. drop-in spot

Ivy at the Shore
1541 Ocean Blvd.
Santa Monica, CA 90401
Funky: from George Michael to Fawn
Hall

Jerry's Famous Deli
12655 Ventura Blvd.
Studio City, CA 91608
Great for *90210* and *Melrose* casts

Jimmy's
201 S. Moreno Dr.
Beverly Hills, CA 90210
Creative Artists Agency stars

Joe Allen
326 W. 46th St.
New York, NY 10036
A good place for Broadway stars

Johnny Rockets
7507 Melrose Ave.
Los Angeles, CA 90046
From Andrew Shue to Jason Patric

Kaffee Giesing
Bergstr. 5
D-81539 Munchen
Germany
Owner: Konstantin Wecker

King's Road Cafe
8361 Beverly Blvd.
Los Angeles, CA 90046

La Buca
Koniginstr. 34
D-80802 Munchen
Germany

La Cirque
58 E. 65 th St.
New York, NY 10021

La Grenouille
3 E. 52nd St.
New York, NY 10022
A good place for designer autographs

La Masia
9077 Santa Monica Blvd.
W. Hollywood, CA 90069

La Reserve
4 W. 49 th St.
New York, NY 10020

La Tante Claire
68 Royal Hospital Rd.
London SW3 4HP, England

La Vita
Magnusstr. 3
D-50662 Koln
Germany

Larios on the Beach
820 Ocean Drive
Miami Beach, FL 33139
Owner: Gloria Estefan

Laura Belle
120 W. 43rd St.
New York, NY 10036

Lawrey's the Prime Rib
100 N. La Cienega Blvd.
Beverly Hills, CA 90211

Le Dome
8720 Sunset Blvd.
Los Angeles, CA 90069
A must-stop: usually young celebrity
crowd

Leaf & Bean Coffeeshop
23 W. Main St.
Bozeman, VT
Owner: Glenn Close

Licour & Deli
8344 Melrose Ave.
Los Angeles, CA 90069

Louise's Trattoria
7505 Melrose Ave.
Los Angeles, CA 90046
From Nicholas Cage to Jason Priestly

Lutece
249 E. 50 th St.
New York, NY 10021

Ma Maison
8555 Beverly Blvd.
Los Angeles, CA 90069

Macaronni
Hahnenstr. 16
D-50667 Koln
Germany

Madam Wu's Garden
2201 Wilshire Blvd.
Santa Monica, CA 90403

Maple Drive
345 N. Maple Drive
Beverly Hills, CA 90210
Owner: Dudley Moore

Matteo's
2323 Westwood Blvd.
Los Angeles, CA 90024

Michael's Pub
211 E. 55th St.
New York, NY 10022
Another Woody Allen sighting here

Mickey Mantle's Restaurant & Sports
Bar
42 Central Park S.
New York, NY 10019

Mortimer's
1057 Lexington Ave.
New York, NY 10021
A diplomat crowd

Morton's
8764 Melrose Ave.
Los Angeles, CA 90069

Moustache Cafe
8155 Melrose Ave.
Los Angeles, CA 90046

Mullholland Drive Cafe
1059 Third Ave.
New York, NY 10021
Owner: Patrick Swayze

Musso & Frank Grill
6667 Hollywood Blvd.
Hollywood, CA 90028

Nate-N-Al Delicatessen & Restaurant
414 N. Beverly Drive
Beverly Hills, CA 90210

Nibbler's
8383 Wilshire Blvd.
Beverly Hills, CA 90211

Nicky Blair's
8730 Sunset Blvd.
Los Angeles, CA 90069
From Keanu Reeves to Johnny Depp

O'Neals
49 W. 64th St.
New York, NY 10023
A reported Madonna sighting

Olives on the Vine
38 N. Water St.
Edgartown, MA 02539
Owner: Michael J. Fox

Orso
322 W. 46 th St.
New York, NY 10036
Worth a quick stop

Pacific Dining Car
1310 W. 6th St.
Los Angeles, CA 90017

Pano Vino
8265 Beverly Blvd.
Los Angeles, CA 90046
Worth a quick stop

Paramount Bar
  Paramount Hotel
  235 W. 46th St.
  New York, NY 10036
  Owner: Matt Dillon

Patrick's Roadhouse
  106 Entrada Drive
  Santa Monica, CA 90402
  Established Hollywood stars only

Patsy's
  236 W. 56th St.
  New York, NY 10019

Peppermint Lounge
  Hohenstaufenring 23
  D-50674 Koln
  Germany

Polo Lounge, Beverly Hills Hotel
  9641 Sunset Blvd.
  Beverly Hills, CA 90210

Prego Restaurant
  362 N. Camden Dr.
  Beverly Hills, CA 90210
  Hey, you never know!

Punch
  11 W. 60 th St.
  New York, NY 10023
  A young celebrity crowd

Rex Ristorante
  617 S. Olive
  Los Angeles, CA 90014

Ristorante del Club '92
  Sradella Nava 8
  Santa Maria a Mugagno
  Italy
  Owner: Luciano Pavarotti

Rolling Thunder Coffee Bar
  2909 W. Olive Ave.
  Burbank, CA 91505
  Owner: Lorenzo Lamas

Roxbury
  8225 Sunset Blvd.
  Los Angeles, CA 90046
  Established stars

Roxy
  leopoldstr. 48
  D-80802 Munchen
  Germany
  Owner: Iris Berban

Roxy Nightclub
  8225 Sunset Blvd.
  Los Angeles, CA 90046
  A great night spot

Russian Tea Room
  150 W. 57 th St.
  New York, NY 10019
  Older celebrity crowd

Sam's Cafe
  1406 Third Ave.
  New York, NY 10021
  Owner: Mariel Hemingway

San Lorenzo
  22 Beauchamp Place
  London SW 3 England
  Lady Diana reportedly sighted here

Sarabeth's Kitchen
  423 Amsterdam Ave.
  New York, NY 10024

Sardi's234 W. 44th St.
  New York, NY 10036
  Good spot for theater stars

Schatzi
  3110 Main Street
  Santa Monica, CA 90405
  Owner: Arnold Schwarzenegger
  A must-stop

Serendipity 3
  225 E. 60th St.
  New York, NY 10022
  A good spot for younger celebrities

Sign of the Dove
  1110 3rd Ave.
  New York, NY 10021

Society Billiards
  101 E. 21st St.
  New York, NY 10022

Spago
  1114 Horn Ave.
  W. Hollywood, CA 90069
  Good reputation

Sportsmen's Lodge
12833 Ventura Blvd.
Studio City, CA 91604

Sticky Fingers Cafe
Troy Court, Phillimore Gardens
Kensington, London W8 England
Owner: Bill Wyman

Sunset Social Club
8210 Sunset Blvd.
Los Angeles, CA 90046
A worthwhile stop for younger
celebrities

Tatou Club
233 N. Beverly Dr.
Beverly Hills, CA 90210
Good for various celebrities

Temple Bar
332 Lafayette St.
New York, NY 10012

The Fashion Cafe
45 Rockefeller Plaza, 51st Fl.
New York, NY 10020
Owners: Campbell, Schiffer &
MacPherson

The Ginger Man
51 W. 64th St.
New York, NY 10023
Reported Madonna sighting

The Grill
9560 Dayton Way
Beverly Hills, CA 90210
The biggest stars: Wm. Morris
hangout

The Lobby Lounge
The Regent Beverly Wilshire Hotel
9500 Wilshire Blvd.
Beverly Hills, CA 90212
From Streisand to Pfeiffer

The Mandarette
8386 Beverly Blvd.
Los Angeles, CA 90048
From Drew Barrymore to Jennie Garth

The Old Spaghetti Factory
5939 W. Sunset Blvd.
Hollywood, CA 90028

The Palm Restaurant
9001 Santa Monica Blvd.
Los Angeles, CA 90069

The Peninsula
The Belvedere Restaurant, Peninsula
Hotel
9882 S. Santa Monica Blvd.
Beverly Hills, CA 90212
Catch as catch can

The Players
9513 Santa Monica Blvd.
W. Hollywood, CA 90069

The Restaurant
500 N. La Salle St.
Chicago, IL 60610
Owner: Michael Jordan

The Tower at Century Plaza
"The Living Room"
2025 Avenue of the Stars
Los Angeles, CA 90067

The Viper Room
8852 Sunset Blvd.
Los Angeles, CA 90069
Owner: Johnny Depp

The Whiskey
8901 Sunset Blvd.
W. Hollywood, CA 90069
Reputation, reputation, reputation!

The Windows Lounge
The Four Seasons Hotel
300 S. Doheny St.
Los Angeles, CA 90048

Thunder Roadhouse
8371 Main Street
West Hollywood, CA 90069
Owners: Dennis Hopper and Peter
Fonda

Tiramesu
500 Ocean Drive
Miami Beach, FL 33139
Owner: Don Johnson

Trader Vic's
The Beverly Hilton
9876 Wilshire Blvd.
Beverly Hills, CA 90210
Reputation, reputation, reputation

Trancas
30765 W. Pacific Coast Hwy.
Malibu, CA 90265

Trattoria dell' Arte
900 7th Ave.
New York, NY 10019

Tribeca
375 Greenwich St.
New York, NY 10013
Owners: R. DeNiro, Sean Penn & Bill Murray

Tristan "Edifico Cabitania"
Puerto Portals
Portals Nous
Palma de Mallorca, Spain
Good spot

Twin Palms
101 W. Green St.
Pasadena, CA 91105
Owner: Kevin Costner

Two Eleven
211 W. Broadway
New York, NY 10013
Worth a quick stop

Victoria Station
"Universal Studios"
3850 Lankershim Blvd.
Universal City, CA 91608

Webster Hall
125 E. 11th St.
New York, NY 10003

Yamashiro
1999 N. Sycamore Ave.
Los Angeles, CA

Zacher Bar
Methfasselstr. 4
D-10965 Berlin
Germany
Owner: Rolf Zacher

Selected Bibliography, Source Notes and Recommended Reading

Baker, Mark A. *Sports Collectors Digest Baseball Autograph Handbook*. Iola, WI: Krause Publications, 1990.

Baker, Mark A. *Sports Collectors Digest Baseball Autograph Handbook*. 2nd ed. Iola, WI: Krause Publications, 1991.

Baker, Mark A. *Sports Collectors Digest Team Baseballs*. Iola, WI: Krause Publications, 1992.

Baker, Mark A. *Sports Collectors Digest All Sport Autograph Guide*. Iola, WI: Krause Publications, 1995.

Baker, Mark A. *Auto Racing Memorabilia and Price Guide*. Iola, WI: Krause Publications, 1996.

Benjamin, Mary A. *Autographs: A Key to Collecting*. New York: R. R. Bowker, 1946. Revised edition, 1963.

Berkeley, Edmund, Herbert Klinghofer, and Kenneth Rendell, eds. *Autographs and Manuscripts: A Collector's Manual*. New York: Charles Scribner's Sons, 1978.

Bowden, Glen. *Collectible Fountain Pens*. Glenview, IL: Glen Bowden Communications.

Carvalho, David N. *Forty Centuries of Ink, or a Chronological Narrative Concerning Ink and Its Background*. New York: Banks Law Publishing Co., 1904.

The Celebrity Directory. Ann Arbor, MI: Axiom Information Resources Inc.

Clapp, Anne F. *Curatorial Care of Works of Art on Paper*. Oberlin: Intermuseum Conservation Association, 1973.

Crayton, Tabatha. *The African-American Address Book*. New York: The Berkley Publishing Group, 1995.

Doloff, Francis W., and Roy L. Perkinson. *How to Care for Works of Art on Paper*. Boston, MA: Museum of Fine Arts, 1971.

Gunderson, Ted L. with Roger McGovern. *How to Locate Anyone Anywhere, Without Leaving Home*. New York: The Penguin Group, 1991.

Harrison, Wilson R. *Suspect Documents: Their Scientific Examination*. London: Sweet and Maxwell, 1958.

Kathpalia, Yash Pal. *Conservation and Restoration of Archive Materials*. Paris: UNESCO, 1973.

Lawerence, Cliff. *Official P.F.C. Pen Guide*. Dunedin, FL.

Levine, Michael. *How To Reach Anyone Who Is Anyone, The Address Book*. New York: The Berkley Publishing Group, 1995.

Nickell, Joe. *Pen, Ink, & Evidence*. Lexington, KY: The University Press of Kentucky, 1990.

People Weekly. *1996 People Entertainment Almanac*. New York: Little, Brown and Company, 1995.

Saferstein, Richard, ed. *Forensic Science Handbook*. Englewood Cliffs, NJ: Prentice-Hall, Inc., 1982.

Saferstein, Richard. *Criminalistics: An Introduction to Forensic Science*. Englewood Cliffs, NJ: Prentice-Hall, Inc., 1987.

Sanders, George, Helen Sanders, and Ralph Roberts. *The Price Guide to Autographs*. 2nd ed. Radnor, PA: Wallace-Homestead Book Co., 1991.

Smalling, R. J. "Jack." *The Sports Baseball Address List No.8*. Cleveland, OH: Edgewater Book Co.

Sports Illustrated. *1996 Sports Almanac*. New York: Little, Brown and Company, 1996.

Periodicals

Autograph Times. 1125 W. Baseline Rd. #2-153, Mesa, AZ 85210

Daytime TV. The Sterling/Macfadden Partnership, 233 Park Ave. S., New York, NY 10003

Entertainment Weekly. c/o Time Inc., 1675 Broadway, New York, NY 10019

People Weekly. Time & Life Bldg., Rockefeller Ctr., New York, NY 10020

Sports Collectors Digest. Krause Publications, 700 E. State Street, Iola, WI 54990

The Autograph Collector's Magazine. P.O. Box 55328, Stockton, CA 95205

The Autograph Review. 305 Carlton Rd., Syracuse, NY 13207

Additional Source Material and Notes

Section I

Chapter 4

Sharpie is a registered trademark of the Sanford Corporation of Bellwood, IL.

Nation's Business. "Mighty Battle of the Pens," November 1946.

Additional source material available in *Forensic Science International.*

Additional source material provided by Parker and PaperMate, a division of the Gillette Company.

Chapter 5

Autographed single-signature baseballs quoted from advertisements in the March 18, 1994 issue of *Sports Collectors Digest.*

Section II

The accuracy of the celebrity addresses included in this section cannot be guaranteed. The dynamic nature of this book prohibits it from being totally accurate. The information on the type of item received may also vary, as it is based only on an impersonal form letter. Additionally, responses of any nature are no guarantee of an item's authenticity. Responses may be secretarial, autopens, stamped signatures, or even photographic reproductions of an original. A majority of the quality ratings are based only on the material received during the fall and winter of 1995. As such, work schedules, illnesses, travel or similar circumstances may have impacted a rating. Please note that these ratings may vary dramatically over time. If you feel a celebrity was overlooked or improperly identified or rated, please don't hesitate to contact me for further information.

Section III

The accuracy of the celebrity addresses included in this section cannot be guaranteed, as explained above.

Both restaurants and clubs are dynamic and vary in their longevity and ability to attract celebrities. Because of this, no guarantees are associated with any of the businesses represented on this list. They are included in this section to provide guidance, should you attempt a celebrity autograph hunt in person.

*Note: To help me keep my database current, please send me any additions, updates and forwarding addresses c/o Krause Publications.